ARMAMENTS AND THE COMING OF WAR

ARMAMENTS AND THE COMING OF WAR

Europe, 1904–1914

DAVID STEVENSON

CLARENDON PRESS · OXFORD

1996

Oxford University Press, Walton Street, Oxford OX2 6DP

Oxford New York
Athens Auckland Bangkok Bombay
Calcutta Cape Town Dar es Salaam Delhi
Florence Hong Kong Istanbul Karachi
Kuala Lumpur Madras Madrid Melbourne
Mexico City Nairobi Paris Singapore
Taipei Tokyo Toronto
and associated companies in
Berlin Ibadan

Oxford is a trade mark of Oxford University Press

Published in the United States
by Oxford University Press Inc., New York

British Library Cataloguing in Publication Data
Data available

Library of Congress Cataloging in Publication Data
Stevenson, D. (David), 1954–
Armaments and the coming of war:
Europe, 1904–1914/David Stevenson.
p. cm.
Includes bibliographical references
1. World War, 1914–1918—Causes.
2. Europe—Politics and government—1871–1918.
3. Military weapons. I. Title.
D511.S815 1996 940.3'112—dc20 95-40415
ISBN 0-19-820208-3

1 3 5 7 9 10 8 6 4 2

Typeset by Hope Services (Abingdon) Ltd.
Printed in Great Britain
on acid-free paper by
Bookcraft Ltd., Midsomer Norton, Avon

Preface

This book is a history of the politics of armaments in Europe before 1914. By analysing competition in military preparedness, it seeks to remedy a salient weakness in our understanding of the origins of the First World War. It is an international history, concerned with interstate relations as well as with national decision-making. The diplomacy of these fateful years has long been treated at both levels; defence policy rarely so. Although what follows is primarily an essay in historical interpretation, it is also offered as a case study of the general relationship between armaments and international conflict.

Over the past eight years the difficulties of researching and of writing such a history have been made abundantly clear to me. The task would have been impossible without help from very many quarters, which it is a great pleasure here to acknowledge. I have been outstandingly well served by the staff of the libraries and archives where I have worked, which, in addition to those listed in the bibliography include particularly the British Library, the British Library of Political and Economic Science, and the Institute of Historical Research. At the risk of being invidious I should like to record my special thanks to the Vienna Kriegsarchiv, the Krupp Archive in Essen, the divisions of the Bundesarchiv in Koblenz and Freiburg, and the Service historique de l'armée de terre in Paris. The Bodleian Library and Jane Bonham-Carter allowed me to quote from the Asquith papers, and the Photograph Archive of the Imperial War Museum permitted me to reproduce the jacket illustration. The London School of Economics and Political Science gave me two periods of sabbatical leave, and I am extremely grateful to my colleagues and students in the Department of International History. The Nuffield Foundation and the Deutscher Akademische Austauschdienst have given generous financial support, as has the LSE Staff Research Fund. Tony Morris has been an unfailingly helpful and enthusiastic publisher; and Karen Partridge has word-processed a forbidding manuscript with exemplary care and efficiency. I am indebted to Anna Illingworth, Michael Belson, and Jane Robson of Oxford University Press, and to Ann Hall for compiling the index. Kind hospitality was provided by Dr Martin Weinzierl and the Bridge family in Vienna, Dr Jürgen Förster in Freiburg, Jean-Claude and Nicole Montant in Paris, and David and Judy Watson in Edinburgh. For specialized guidance I am indebted to Jack Snyder (strategic theory); Roy Bridge, Lothar Höbelt, and Scott Lackey (Austria); Wolfgang Mommsen and Stig Förster (Germany); Peter Gatrell (Russia); John Gooch (Italy); Bill Philpott (Belgium); André Sidorowicz (Britain); and John Hobson (on the statistics)—to mention only some of the most prominent among many. I was grateful for the opportunity to discuss with David Herrmann, then of Yale University, his forthcoming study of the evolution of the European military balance. Roy Bridge, Peter Gatrell, John Hobson, Hew Strachan, and Williamson Murray read portions (in the last case all) of the draft, and saved me from numerous errors and infelicities. I owe a great debt to my family and friends, and most of all to my beloved wife Sue, not only for her perspicacious comments on the typescript but also for her exceptional generosity and patience as it inched towards completion. It has taken an unconscionably long time, but I hope that the book will be some recompense. For the failings that remain in it, I take full responsibility.

D.S.

London School of Economics & Political Science

Contents

List of Figures

List of Tables

Abbreviations

AA	Auswärtiges Amt (German Foreign Ministry)
AGRB	Archives Générales du Royaume, Brussels
AMAE	Archives du Ministère des affaires Etrangères, Paris
AN	Archives nationales, Paris
ASC	Archivio di Stato centrale, Rome
BA	Bundesarchiv, Koblenz
BA-MA	Bundesarchiv—Militärarchiv, Freiburg im Breisgau
BD	*British Documents on the Origins of the War, 1898–1914*, ed. G. P. Gooch and H. V. Temperley (11 vols., London, 1926–38).
BDFA	*British Documents on Foreign Affairs: Reports and Papers from the Foreign Office Confidential Print*, ed. K. Bourne and D. Cameron Watt: series I.A. Russia, 1859–1914, ed. D. C. B. Lieven and I. F. *Europe, 1848–1914*, ed. J. F. V. Keiger and D. Stevenson (Frederick, Md., 1983 and 1987–91).
BEF	British Expeditionary Force
BLO	Bodleian Library, Oxford
BN	Bibliothèque nationale, Paris
BSA	Birmingham Small Arms Company
CAB	Cabinet
CAS	Chief of Admiralty Staff
CCAC	Churchill College Archive Centre, Cambridge
CEMA	Chef de l'état-major de l'armée
CGS	Chief of General Staff
CGT	Confédération générale du travail
CID	Committee of Imperial Defence
CNS	Chief of Naval Staff
CSDN	Conseil supérieur de la défense nationale
CSG	Conseil supérieur de la guerre
DDF	Commission de publication des documents relatifs aux origines de la guerre de 1914, *Documents diplomatiques français, 1871–1914* (41 vols., Paris, 1929–59).
DDK	*Die deutschen Dokumente zum Kriegsausbruch, 1914*, ed. M. Montgelas and W. Schücking (3rd edn., 3 vols., Berlin, 1926).
DMO	Director of Military Operations
DWMF	Deutsche Waffen- und Munitions Fabriken
DWV	Deutscher Wehrverein
EMA	Etat-major de l'armée
FAW	Finanzarchiv, Vienna
FO	Foreign Office
GGS	Grosser Generalstab (Prussian Great General Staff)
GMR	Gemeinsamer Ministerrat (Austro-Hungarian Joint Council of Ministers)
GP	*Die Grosse Politik der Europäischen Kabinette*

GSM	Geheimes Staatsarchiv, Munich
Gstb	Generalstab (General Staff)
HHStA	Haus-, Hof-, und Staatsarchiv, Vienna
HS	Haupstaatsarchiv, Stuttgart
HSMA	Hauptstaatsarchiv, Stuttgart—Militärarchiv
IB	*Die Internationalen Beziehungen im Zeitalter des Imperialismus: Dokumente aus den Archiven der Zarischen und der Provisorischen Regierung, 1878–1917*, ed. E. Hoetzsch (Series I, vol. v, German edn., Berlin, 1934).
INDMB	Indépendance, Neutralité, Défense militaire de la Belgique (MAEB)
IWM	Imperial War Museum
KAE	Krupp Archive, Essen
KAM	Bayerische Hauptstaatsarchiv, Munich—Militärchiv
KAW	Kriegsarchiv, Vienna
MAEB	Ministère des affaires étrangères, Brussels
MFF	Ministère des finances, Paris
MGFA	Militärgeschichtliches Forschungsamt, Freiburg im Breisgau
NLS	National Library of Scotland, Edinburgh
ÖUA	*Österreich-Ungarns Aussenpolitik von der Bosnischen Krise 1908 bis zum Kriegsausbruch 1914*, ed. L. Bittner and H. Übersberger (9 vols., Vienna, 1930).
PAAA	Politisches Archiv des Auswärtigen Amtes, Bonn
PRO	Public Record Office, Kew
Rklei	Akten der Reichskanzlei (BA)
SFIO	Socialist Party (France)
SGO	Council of State Defence (Russia)
SHA	Service historique de l'armée, Paris
SHM	Service historique de la marine, Paris
SPD	Social Democratic Party (Germany)
VA	Vickers Archive, Cambridge

Introduction

> The enormous growth of armaments in Europe, the sense of insecurity and fear caused by them—it was these that made war inevitable. This, it seems to me, is the truest reading of history, and the lesson that the present should be learning from the past in the interests of future peace, the warning to be handed on to those who come after us. This is the real and final account of the origins of the Great War.
>
> (Sir Edward Grey[1])

The first test of Sir Edward Grey's assessment must be statistical. Like other such tests, it is problematic. In the early twentieth century all the major Powers, including Russia after 1906, had relatively open political systems, in which War and Navy Ministry budgets were public knowledge and were scrutinized in Parliament. For practical purposes their currencies were fixed in value in relation to each other and to gold. Inflation was low. Comparisons are hampered, however, by differing accounting practices, sometimes intentionally misleading, and by problems of definition. Spending totals for each country make no allowance for international variations in purchasing power, and bear no constant relation to the size of forces in being (as measured in infantry divisions or squadrons of battleships). As well as armaments items, such as turrets and shells, they include routine categories, such as fodder and wages. Even so, they bring out the orders of magnitude and the overriding trends, and are the best point of departure.

Table 1 summarizes total military and naval spending by the six European Great Powers between 1900 and 1913;[2] Table 2 and Figure 1 represent

---

[1] E. Grey, *Twenty-Five Years, 1892–1916* (2 vols., London, 1925), i. 90.

[2] In preparing the statistical material in the Introduction I have been enormously assisted by Dr John M. Hobson, and have drawn on the data in his article, 'The Military-Extraction Gap and the Wary Titan: The Fiscal Sociology of British Defence Policy, 1870–1913', *Journal of European Economic History*, 22 (1993), 461–506. Among the problems of definition are those of how to treat extraordinary as opposed to ordinary (i.e. recurrent) expenditure, and whether to include categories such as pensions and strategic railways built by transport ministries. Table 1 is based on ibid. 501–2 (app. 1), and the sources cited there. For Britain see B. R. Mitchell and P. Deane, *Abstract of British Historical Statistics* (Cambridge, 1962), 398, but note that I have moved their annual expenditure figures back by one year. This is because (e.g.) the British fiscal year ending 31 Mar. 1914 overlaps more closely with the French or Russian calendar year 1913 than with the calendar year 1914. For France, see L. Fontvielle, 'Évolution et croissance de l'État français de 1815 à 1969', *Économies et sociétés*, 13 (1976), 2122–4, table 133; for Italy, G. Rochat and G. Massobrio, *Breve storia dell'esercito italiano dal 1861 al 1943* (Turin, 1978), 68; for Russia, P. A. Khromov, *Ekonomicheskoe razvitie Rossii v XIX i XX vekakh (1800–1917)* (Moscow, 1950), 524–9. For Austria-Hungary, A. Wandruszka and P. Urbanitsch (eds.), *Die Habsburgermonarchie, 1848–1914* (Vienna, 1987), 591, for 1900–12, but I have given figures for the Monarchy as a whole, whereas Hobson gives them for the Austrian portion. For 1913 ibid. i. 574 gives figures for the common army and navy but not for the *Landwehr*

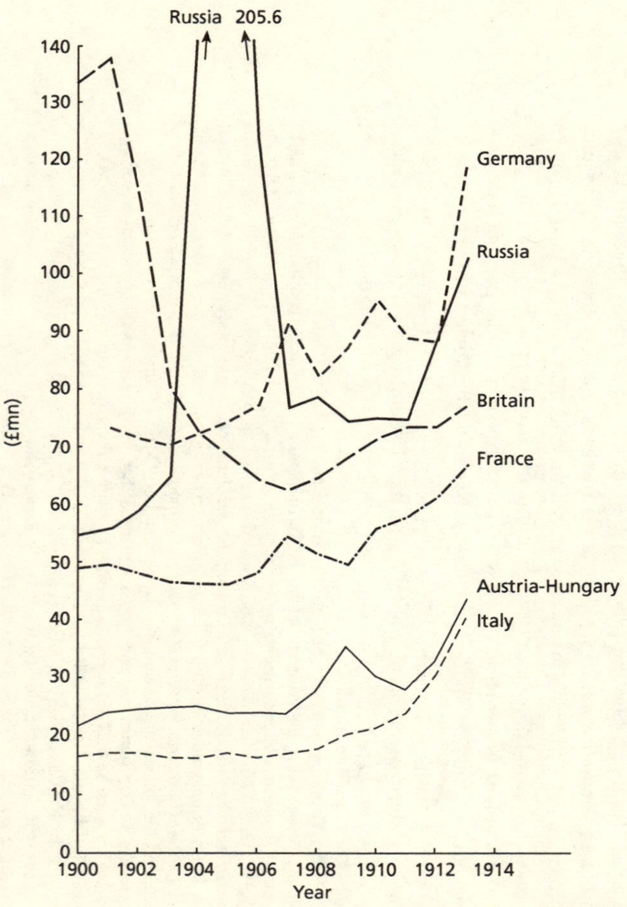

Table 1. *Defence expenditure of the European Powers, 1900–1913 in current prices* (mn of each currency)

	Britain (£)	France (fr)	Russia (rbl)	Austria–Hungary (kr)	Germany (mk)	Italy (li)
1900	121.0	1,114	420.1	410.3	—	356.0
1901	123.3	1,126	427.7	439.3	1,162.9	372.3
1902	100.6	1,080	443.6	455.4	1,122.8	373.3
1903	72.2	1,042	464.9	464.0	1,105.7	361.6
1904	66.0	1,033	1,162.2	478.3	1,152.2	362.1
1905	62.2	1,030	1,632.1	481.1	1,233.5	377.4
1906	59.2	1,087	1,032.9	488.4	1,358.2	374.3
1907	58.5	1,245	679.1	507.2	1,631.1	404.9
1908	59.0	1,194	673.8	597.9	1,463.7	422.4
1909	63.0	1,147	647.9	759.6	1,593.6	467.4
1910	67.8	1,301	650.4	681.9	1,771.3	498.5
1911	70.5	1,412	671.3	657.8	1,707.5	577.3
1912	72.5	1,493	814.8	780.9	1,781.3	754.7
1913	77.2	1,630	961.6	1,030.9	2,406.4	999.7

Notes: British and German figures are for the years ending 31 Mar. 1914; the Italian for those ending 30 June 1913; figures for Austria-Hungary, France, and Italy are for calendar years.

Sources: See Introduction, n.2

Fig. 1. Defence expenditure of the European Powers, 1900–1913
Sources: See Introduction, n. 2 and n. 3.

expenditure in constant prices.[3] Germany and Russia stand out as the armaments giants; Austria-Hungary and Italy as also-rans. Although distorted by Britain's war in South Africa (1899–1902), Russia's in Manchuria (1904–5), and Italy's in Libya (from 1911), the tables demonstrate the acceleration in peacetime expenditure. Italy and Britain moved upwards from 1907 and 1908; Russia from 1911. France jumped in 1906–7 and 1911, Germany in 1905–7, and Austria-Hungary in 1908–9. In 1912–14 there was a near-universal steep increase. Total expenditure by the six Powers in money terms rose between 1908 and 1913 by some 50 per cent, which may be compared with the Stockholm International Peace Research Institute's estimates of world military spending growth in Table 3.[4] American defence spending was equivalent to Britain's by 1914, but had grown much more slowly than did European spending in the pre-war quinquennium; Japan was comparable to Austria-Hungary, and after it defeated Russia in 1904–5 its spending remained stable.[5] Europe was the powerhouse of global armaments growth. The increase was less dramatic than the trebling of military budgets in the 1930s or their 100 per cent increase in eight years during the early Cold War, but when set against the doubling of the big six European budgets between 1872 and 1908[6] and the stagnation in the first five years of the new century, the eve of war stands out for its synchronized, rapid, and accelerating expansion.

Table 4 tabulates defence spending as a percentage of net national product.[7]

and *Honvéd* (these latter are discussed in Ch. 1). I have used 1912 figures for these two components of expenditure, thus somewhat understating the total. For Germany I have used P.-C. Witt, *Die Finanzpolitik des deutschen Reiches von 1903 bis 1913* (Lübeck, 1970), 380–1, rather than S. Andic and J. Veverka, 'The Growth of Government Expenditure in Germany since the Unification', *Finanz Archiv*, 23/2 (1964), 169–278. However, Witt's figures overstate German defence expenditure in comparison with the series for the other Powers used here, mainly because they include debt service on military loans and outlays on strategic railways. Expenditure on strategic railways, 1887–1909, averaged 12 million marks annually (Wermuth to Bethmann Hollweg, 30 Nov. 1909, BA Rklei R.43F/107): the appropriate deduction to be made is probably a little under 10%. See the discussion in Hobson, 'Military-Extraction Gap', n. 42. N. Ferguson, 'Public Finance and National Security: The Domestic Origins of the First World War Revisited', *Past and Present*, 142 (1994), 141–68 gives on p. 152 a sense of the discrepancies in the available estimates.

[3] For conversions into constant prices, I have used (for Britain, France, Germany, and Italy), the consumer price indices in B. R. Mitchell, *International Historical Statistics: Europe, 1750–1988* (Basingstoke, 1992), 84; for Austria, that in V. Mühlpeck *et al.*, 'Index der Verbraucherpreise, 1800–1914', in *Geschichte und Ergebnisse der Zentralen Amtlichen Statistik in Österreich, 1829–1979: Beiträge zur Österreichischen Statistik. Heft 550* (Vienna, 1979), 678; for Russia, the aggregate price deflator for defence in P. R. Gregory, *Russian National Income, 1885–1913* (Cambridge, 1982), table F3, pp. 254–5. Wholesale price indices would have been preferable, but I have not been able to locate them for all the European Powers. For currency conversions I have used R. L. Bidwell, *Currency Conversion Tables: A Hundred Years of Change* (London, 1970). £1 = 25.221 lire = 20.429 marks = 9.45 roubles = 25.22 francs = 24.02 crowns (Austria-Hungary). The reader should be aware that using statistics such as these to compare the military strengths and defence efforts of the Powers is extremely problematic. See the discussion in Hobson, 'Military-Extraction Gap', 466 ff.

[4] Taken from M. Thee (ed.), *Arms and Disarmament: SIPRI Findings* (Oxford, 1986), 18.

[5] Hobson, 'Military-Extraction Gap', 464–5, table 1.   [6] Ibid.

[7] Taken from ibid. 478–9, table 3, but using the Fontvieille figures for France and Witt's for Germany, as explained in n. 2. The British figures are adjusted to allow for my realignment of the Mitchell and Deane statistics. The Austrian series is for the Austrian half of the Habsburg Monarchy, as Net National Product figures are not available for the Hungarian half. I have followed Hobson's estimates of the proportion of defence expenditure falling on the Austrian half of the Monarchy, though use a higher estimate for 1913.

Table 2. *Defence expenditure of the European Powers, 1900–1913* (£mn, constant prices)

	Britain	France	Russia	Austria–Hungary	Germany	Italy
1900	133.0	48.5	54.2	21.2	—	16.0
1901	137.0	49.0	55.2	23.4	72.9	16.8
1902	111.8	47.1	58.6	24.1	70.5	16.8
1903	79.3	45.9	63.8	24.2	69.4	15.9
1904	71.7	45.5	150.0	24.5	71.4	15.8
1905	67.6	45.4	205.6	23.4	73.6	16.4
1906	63.7	47.4	122.8	23.4	76.4	16.0
1907	61.6	53.6	75.6	23.4	90.7	16.4
1908	63.4	50.9	77.5	27.4	81.4	17.3
1909	67.0	48.9	73.7	34.5	86.7	19.7
1910	70.6	54.9	74.0	29.8	94.2	20.5
1911	72.6	57.1	74.0	27.5	88.0	23.1
1912	72.5	60.4	88.0	32.3	87.2	29.9
1913	75.7	65.9	101.8	42.4	117.8	39.6

Sources: See Introduction, n.2 and n.3.

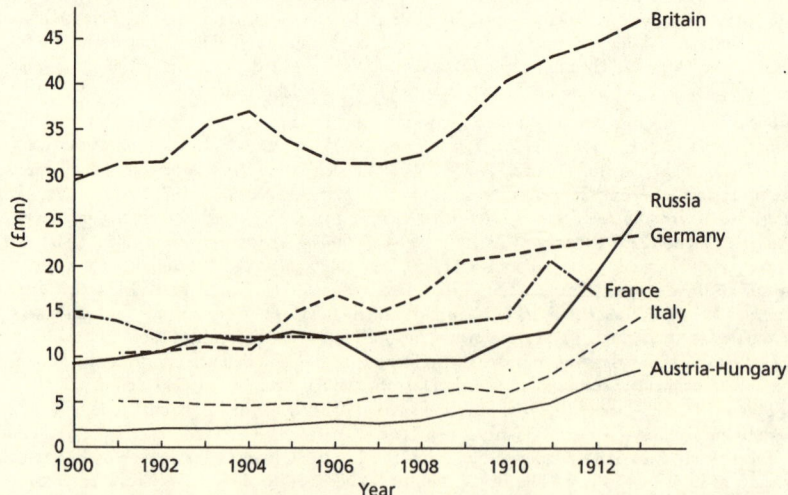

Fig. 2. Naval expenditure of the European Powers, 1900–1913
Sources: See Introduction, n. 9.

Table 3. *World defence expenditure, 1908–1985*
($bn, 1980 prices)

Year	Expenditure
1908	19
1913	30
1933	41
1938	127
1948	133
1953	290
1972	433
1985	663

Source: See Introduction, n.4

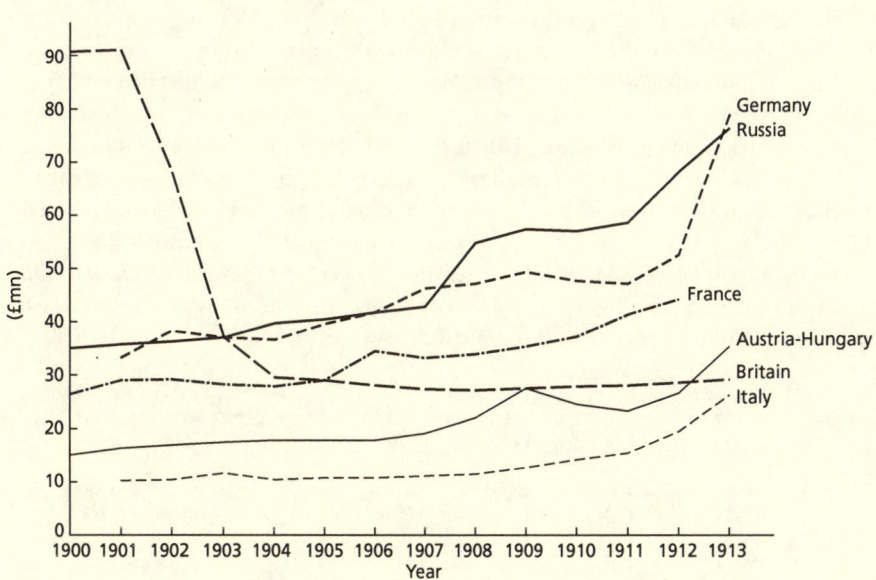

Fig. 3. Army expenditure of the European Powers, 1900–1913
Sources: See Introduction, n. 11.

Table 4. *Real defence burden (defence expenditure/net national product), 1900–1913* (%)

	Britain	France	Russia	'Austria'	Germany	Italy
1900	6.9	4.4	4.0	2.7	—	3.1
1901	7.1	4.6	3.9	2.7	4.1	3.2
1902	5.8	4.5	3.7	2.7	3.9	3.3
1903	4.2	4.1	4.1	2.8	3.6	2.9
1904	3.9	4.0	9.2	2.8	3.6	3.0
1905	3.5	3.9	13.8	2.5	3.6	2.9
1906	3.1	3.9	8.7	2.3	3.8	2.7
1907	2.9	4.2	5.4	2.2	4.2	2.7
1908	3.1	4.1	4.7	2.4	3.8	2.8
1909	3.3	3.8	4.3	3.0	4.0	2.9
1910	3.4	4.1	4.0	2.6	4.2	3.0
1911	3.4	4.1	4.3	2.4	3.9	3.3
1912	3.3	4.0	4.5	2.6	3.8	4.0
1913	3.4	4.3	5.1	3.5	4.9	5.1

Sources: See Introduction, n. 7.

This measure is now accepted as the best economic indicator of the defence 'burden', and it suggests the political priority accorded to the armed forces. It was not available to contemporaries, who used per capita figures such as those in Table 5.[8] The latter shows Britain in the lead, followed by France and Germany: but these were the countries with the highest per capita income. Russia, despite its enormous absolute spending, joins Italy at the bottom. Table 4, in contrast, shows Russia and arguably France as more highly militarized than Germany, and Britain and Italy assuming comparable burdens to those of the biggest three Continental Powers only when at war. Relative to the 1930s or 1950s even the 1912–13 percentages are low, although higher than those characteristic at the turn of the century. They were borne, however, by much poorer societies than those of our own day, in which military and naval budgets normally accounted for the majority of central government spending and therefore of taxation requirements. Nor should we forget the impact, in a world of shorter life expectancies, of the 'blood tax' of conscription that took young men from their homes and loved ones for up to four formative years.

Table 5. *Per capita defence expenditure in sterling equivalent, 1900–1913* (£ annual averages)

	Britain	France	Russia	'Austria'	Germany	Italy
1900–4	2.33	0.91	0.45	0.47	0.96	0.44
1905–9	1.38	1.15	0.66	0.56	1.15	0.48
1910–13	1.59	1.63	0.49	0.72	1.43	0.80
1900–12	1.76	1.19	0.53	0.55	1.16	0.52

Sources: See Introduction, n. 8.

[8] Based on Hobson, 'Military-Extraction Gap', 466, table 2, but using Fontvielle figures for France and Witt figures for Germany.

Table 6. *Naval expenditure of the European Powers, 1900–1913* (£mn, current prices)

	Britain	France	Russia	Austria-Hungary	Germany	Italy
1900	29.5	14.9	9.4	1.9	—	—
1901	31.0	13.7	9.8	1.9	10.2	5.0
1902	31.2	11.9	10.6	2.1	10.6	4.9
1903	35.5	12.1	12.1	2.1	11.0	4.7
1904	36.8	11.7	11.9	2.3	10.7	4.7
1905	33.3	12.6	12.3	2.7	12.0	4.9
1906	31.4	12.2	12.3	2.9	12.7	4.8
1907	31.1	12.6	9.3	2.6	14.9	5.8
1908	32.2	13.2	9.9	3.1	17.0	5.9
1909	35.8	13.9	9.8	4.2	20.6	6.6
1910	40.4	14.5	11.9	4.2	21.3	6.3
1911	42.9	20.7	12.8	5.0	22.1	8.2
1912	44.4	17.1	18.6	7.1	22.7	11.2
1913	48.8	—	25.9	8.7	23.5	14.4

Sources: See Introduction, n. 9.

From here on it is necessary to disaggregate. Table 6 and Figure 2, showing naval spending, demonstrate Britain's maintenance of its advantage over Germany, and Anglo-German dominance over everybody else, at least during the climax of the North Sea naval race in 1907–11.[9] By the end of the period the duopoly was weakening, Germany (though not Britain) slackening off as the other Powers intensified their efforts and as Russia, especially, moved startlingly ahead. Table 7, drawn from a contemporary French estimate of construction budgets, highlights the trends. All the Powers were increasing naval building, but the Anglo-German competition was losing impetus at the moment when the rise in general armaments expenditure was steepest.[10] Table 8 and Figure 3, conversely, show how the soldiers took the lead.[11] On land Russia was the largest spender, followed by Germany, with France a poor third. Britain had a small but expensive army, whose cost held steady after the 1907–9 Haldane reforms. The budgets of the five Continental Powers, however, close to stasis at the turn of

[9] Hobson does not give separate figures for naval and army spending. See n. 2 above. For Table 6 and Fig. 2. I have used Mitchell and Deane for Britain, Rochat for Italy, Khromov for Russia, Wandruszka (ed.), for Austria-Hungary, and Witt for Germany. Fontvielle does not give separate army and navy figures, and for France I have therefore used the *Annuaire statistique*, xxxiii (Paris, 1914), 140F, 267; and xxxii (Paris, 1913), 287. (The figures given there for 1913 and 1914 are estimates rather than expenditure: this and a change in statistical procedures may account for the apparent fall in army expenditure in 1913.)

[10] *Situation des marines étrangères au 1er janvier 1914* (Ministère de la Marine, Paris, 1914), 260. Original figures in French francs. I have included this table as an example of a contemporary comparative estimate, but it should be treated with caution. F. Crouzet, 'Recherches sur la production d'armements en France (1815–1913)', *Revue historique*, 509 (1974), 83–4, suggests a higher figure for the French naval construction budget, especially in 1913.

[11] See n. 9 for sources. I have added military pensions to Witt's figures for Germany; I have not included the costs to Russia of the war with Japan, although they do appear in Table 1. The costs of the South African and Libyan Wars are included, however, in the British and Italian figures. Russian figures include the extraordinary expenditures listed in Khromov, *Razvitie*, 528–9.

Introduction

Table 7. *Naval construction budgets of the European Powers, 1900–1913*
(£mn, current prices)

	Britain	France	Russia	Austria-Hungary	Germany	Italy
1900	11.2	4.6	3.1	0.6	3.2	1.5
1901	11.1	4.5	3.1	0.8	5.3	1.2
1902	10.7	4.6	2.6	0.9	5.5	0.9
1903	13.9	4.8	3.3	1.0	5.3	1.2
1904	14.1	4.7	4.1	1.1	5.1	1.4
1905	12.1	4.8	4.1	2.6	5.3	1.0
1906	11.1	4.9	4.3	1.2	5.8	1.7
1907	10.6	4.4	2.6	1.2	6.6	2.1
1908	9.4	4.8	2.2	0.8	9.0	2.4
1909	11.2	4.6	1.4	0.8	11.5	2.2
1910	16.7	5.3	1.8	1.8	12.7	2.2
1911	18.9	6.7	3.2	3.1	13.1	3.5
1912	17.3	6.2	6.2	3.6	12.2	4.3
1913	17.1	7.0	11.1	4.4	11.4	—

Source: See Introduction, n. 10.

Table 8. *Army expenditure of the European Powers, 1900–1913* (£mn, current prices)

	Britain	France	Russia	Austria-Hungary	Germany	Italy
1900	91.5	26.8	35.1	15.2	—	—
1901	92.3	29.0	35.4	16.4	33.2	9.8
1902	69.4	29.2	36.3	16.9	38.0	10.0
1903	36.7	28.1	37.1	17.2	37.6	11.3
1904	29.2	28.0	39.4	17.6	36.6	9.7
1905	28.9	28.5	40.0	17.4	39.7	10.1
1906	27.8	34.2	41.5	17.4	41.5	10.1
1907	27.1	32.7	42.9	18.5	46.0	10.3
1908	26.8	33.3	54.4	21.1	47.0	10.9
1909	27.2	34.7	57.0	27.4	49.0	12.0
1910	27.4	36.4	56.6	24.2	47.3	13.5
1911	27.6	40.5	58.1	22.4	46.9	14.7
1912	28.1	43.4	67.6	25.4	52.1	18.7
1913	28.3	—	75.8	34.4	78.3	25.3

Sources: See Introduction, n. 11.

the century, were rocketing by 1912–14, to the accompaniment of a succession of major military bills. Italy's budget expanded from 1907, although its military progress within Europe was hobbled by the Libyan War; France increased its spending in the Moroccan crisis of 1905–6 and more continuously from 1909; Austria-Hungary in the Balkan crises of 1908–9 and 1912–13. As for the two pace-setters, Russia had an established lead over Germany, and widened it in 1909 and 1911–12; German outlays grew in 1905–7, and fastest of all the Powers in 1912–13. Before 1909–10, there was approximate equilibrium, albeit disturbed by crises in Morocco and the Balkans and by the expense of re-equipping the field artillery. Thereafter the tide was rising, France and Russia leading but closely followed by their enemies.

Intensifying army spending by the Continental Powers dominated European armaments on the eve of war. In contrast, half a decade earlier the most dynamic and dangerous armaments competition had been the Anglo-German naval race. A second rivalry, between Austria-Hungary and Italy, was both naval and land-focused. Yet, ostensibly, Austria-Hungary and Italy were partners, with each other and with Germany, in the Triple Alliance of 1882. Britain had ententes, or informal special relationships, with France after 1904 and Russia after 1907, but no binding ties. Both Rome and London were semi-detached, and at this stage the fields of force in armaments politics bore little relation to diplomatic alignments. By 1913, however, the central military antagonism polarized the two big blocs: the Austro-German alliance of 1879 and the Franco-Russian of 1891–4. Such an antagonism was more likely to presage a general war, especially as it was accompanied by a subsidiary rivalry between Austria-Hungary and its Balkan neighbours. Serbian defence expenditure rose by half in 1907–13; Romanian by still more. Until the drastic increase in German army spending in 1913, moreover, both the Continental and the Balkan military balances had been moving inexorably against the two Central Powers, and in 1914 seemed likely to move further against them in the years ahead.

To speak of a single 'arms race' before the First World War obscures the issue. The phenomenon was multiple. But the July 1914 crisis began as a Balkan confrontation between Austria-Hungary and Serbia, and exploded into a Continental showdown between the two alliances, in which Britain and Italy tried vainly to mediate. The origins and repercussion of the inter-bloc land arms race therefore have the greatest bearing on the outbreak of war and will form the leitmotiv of this study. In common with the usage of Grey and other writers of the time, however, the term employed here will normally be not 'arms race' but 'armaments'. The sporting metaphor was in currency before 1914,[12] and is a convenient shorthand, but misleading. The contestants in an arms race may know neither the location of the finishing tape (the timing of the outbreak of war) nor even if there is a tape at all. It is anyway difficult to define or generalize about a phenomenon of which there have been few major historical instances, although Hedley Bull's characterization—'intense competition between Powers or groups of Powers, each trying to achieve an advantage in military power by increasing the quantity or improving the quality of its armaments or armed forces'[13]—will do. Arms racing is a state of mind, of deliberate emulation on both sides. It is

[12] e.g. Admiral Tirpitz to Prince Henry of Prussia, 28 Jan. 1907, in V. R. Berghahn and W. Deist (eds.), *Rüstung im Zeichen der Wilhelminischen Weltpolitik: Grundlegende Dokumente, 1890–1914* (Düsseldorf, 1988), 323.

[13] H. Bull, *The Control of the Arms Race: Disarmament and Arms Control in the Missile Age* (London, 1961), 4.

difficult to distinguish it as something exceptional, marked out from a more normal concern to maintain national strength at the appropriate standard. The contrast sometimes drawn between 'qualitative' (or technological) and 'quantitative' competition is more suggestive than definite. Rather, there is a spectrum, between Bull's 'intense competition' at one end and at the other a routine upgrading of armed forces with reference to some autonomous measure of requirements rather than to the capacities of potential enemies.[14]

If 'racing' is a treacherous concept, so is that of 'armaments', which in its Edwardian English usage, like that of its Continental synonyms (*Rüstungen*, *armements*), might embrace organization, manpower, and deployments, and was identified less exclusively with weaponry than it has become since. Competition in armaments meant competition in war preparedness (*Kriegsbereitschaft*) rather than simply accumulating hardware.[15] Preparedness might be long term and qualitative, achieved by introducing high-technology innovations with extended lead times, such as heavy artillery and capital ships. It might be medium term, pursued through redrafted mobilization plans, army laws to increase call-up ratios and intensify reservist training, or special credits to increase stocks of existing weapons rather than to devise new ones. Finally, it might be short term, expressed in crisis decisions to strengthen frontier garrisons, place units on alert, or stockpile munitions. July 1914 marked the convergence of all these strands: an underlying growth in political tension and a movement in the military balance linked to enhanced long- and medium-term preparedness, and a chain of diplomatic crises in which measures to increase short-term readiness were increasingly prominent.

The crucial question is that of how the different strands interacted. Diplomatic crises can accentuate armaments rivalries; but the same rivalries make crises harder to settle, and a statistical correlation has been detected between arms races and crises that end in war.[16] Governments may build up armaments not only to prepare for or insure against hostilities, but also to add

[14] For general discussions of arms racing, S. P. Huntington, 'Arms Races: Prerequisites and Results', in R. J. Art and K. N. Waltz (eds.), *The Use of Force: International Politics and Foreign Policy* (Lanham, Md., 1983), 439–77; C. S. Gray, 'The Arms Race Phenomenon', *World Politics*, 24 (1971), 39–79; B. Buzan, *An Introduction to Strategic Studies: Military Technology and International Relations* (Basingstoke, 1987).

[15] In 1905–13 only 5.12% of French War Ministry expenditure was on artillery, hand arms, and munitions; although 37.49% of French Marine Ministry spending was on 'armaments' including warships (Crouzet, 'Recherches', 69). Expenditure on weapons and ammunition never exceeded 15% of the Russian War Ministry budget in the decade before 1914; though to this should be added between 5 and 12% on fortification. Construction, armament, and repair of warships rose from 43 to 62% of the naval budget in 1908–13. P. Gatrell, *Government, Industry, and Rearmament in Russia, 1900–1914: The Last Argument of Tsarism* (Cambridge, 1994), 141. Of 987 million marks of expenditure associated with the German army law of 1913, 210 million was for fortification and 71 million for artillery. KAE W.A. VII f. 1104, 'Zur Denkschrift: die Firma Krupp im Weltkriege', B.V.12.e, p. 2. The contrast between land and sea, and the relatively small share for hardware in army budgets, emerge clearly.

[16] M. D. Wallace, 'Arms Races and Escalation: Some New Evidence', *Journal of Conflict Resolution*, 23 (1979), 3–16; 'Armaments and Escalation: Two Conflicting Hypotheses', *International Studies Quarterly*, 26 (1982), 37–56.

force to their diplomacy. Since the Cuban confrontation of 1962 a literature has grown up on the art of 'managing' international crises.[17] As defining features of such crises it includes a threat (usually unexpected) to vital or important interests, a perception of heightened danger of war, and a limited response time. Its premiss is that in most crises the protagonists at the outset may be ready for brinkmanship but do not wish to fight, and that if war results it is because of developments during the crisis rather than pre-existing sources of antagonism.[18] It is a premiss that is questionable for 1914 itself, but will hold for the earlier pre-war trials of strength. The goal of 'management' is to attain the maximum of one's objectives without fighting, and co-ordinating military preparedness with diplomacy is vital for success. Once the military leaders perceive that war is closer, they may demand a higher level of readiness; but to concede it may be misinterpreted by the adversary government as showing belligerent intent. On the other hand, while a lower level of readiness may give reassurance and win time for measured decision-making, it may also be ineffective as a means of pressure and invite aggression.[19] Crisis management, like arms racing, is bound up with the 'security dilemma' in international politics: one state's efforts to increase its sense of security are liable to diminish the sense of security felt by its neighbours, with the consequence of greater danger for all concerned. Absolute security for one Power means absolute insecurity for all the others.[20] Historians examined the July 1914 mobilization measures from this perspective long before the crisis became a *locus classicus* for strategic analysts, but the preceding Moroccan and Balkan crises—or 'periods of political tension', to use the jargon of the time—have in comparison been neglected. This book will argue from an analysis of these conflicts that European statesmen understood both the risk of unintended escalation and the possibility that heightening military readiness could help them get their way. Armed diplomacy became habitual, although it would be too simple to see a relentless escalatory spiral into hostilities.

Theorists of long- and medium-term preparedness, in contrast to short-term crisis measures, have developed three main interpretations of armaments competition: the 'action–reaction', 'domestic structure', and 'technological imperative' models.[21] They are not mutually exclusive, and their appropriateness varies from case to case. The first corresponds to the common sense picture: country A expands its armaments in response to a prior expansion by country B, and may do so by more, thus starting a process of leapfrogging. According to this view,

[17] I have used O. R. Holsti, *Crisis–Escalation–War* (London, 1972), P. Williams, *Crisis Management: Confrontation and Diplomacy in the Nuclear Age* (London, 1972), R. N. Lebow, *Between Peace and War: The Nature of International Crisis* (Baltimore, 1981), A. L. George (ed.), *Avoiding War: Problems of Crisis Management* (Boulder, Col., 1991).

[18] Lebow, *Peace and War*, 334.

[19] A. L. George, 'Crisis Management: The Interaction of Political and Military Considerations', *Survival*, 26 (1984), 223–34.

[20] R. Jervis, 'Co-operation under the Security Dilemma', *World Politics*, 30 (1978), 167–214. H. A. Kissinger, *A World Restored: Metternich, Castlereagh, and the Problems of Peace, 1812–1822* (London, 1957), 2.

[21] Buzan, *Strategic Studies*, 74.

arms races are endemic to a system based on sovereign states in which no overriding authority exists to guarantee national safety. Attempts to formulate mathematical models of arms races have taken the theory as their starting-point.[22] The obvious objections to it are that it is descriptive rather than explanatory, and fails to account for country B's opening move. Country B may be a Power dissatisfied with the *status quo*, and seeking a means of pressure to change it. If this is so, however, the arms race arises from prior territorial, economic, or ideological conflict, although once it starts it can contribute to tension in its own right. Implicit in the theory is the assumption that Powers expand their armaments because they feel a need to challenge the international *status quo* or uphold it against competitors. Internal pressures in the societies concerned are of minor significance.

In the second model, in contrast, armaments are seen as being expanded primarily to meet domestic exigencies, the actions of other states being irrelevant, except as scarecrows for propagandist rationalization. The exigencies may be those of a 'military–industrial complex' of business and armed-service lobbyists, or the authorities may expand armaments as a diversionary strategy against domestic opposition. The theory helps explain how interest groups may perpetuate arms races, and perhaps why Powers start them in the absence of an external threat. It fails to explain how armaments lobbyists prevail over opposing groups, who wish to cut expenditure and taxes and to reduce conscription. Moreover, in pre-1914 Europe countries that were extremely varied in their domestic politics expanded their armaments more or less simultaneously. The improbability of this happening by coincidence shifts the burden of explanation back into the international domain.

The third interpretation sees technological change as an explanatory variable independent both of international and domestic developments. Autonomous advances in science and technology generate successive opportunities to modernize and 'improve' armaments, which governments neglect at their peril. Before 1914 much weapons development was by private companies, and linked to advances in the civilian economy. Even so, most military research, even in the private sector, was officially commissioned or sponsored, and new technology became politically significant only if backed by naval and military petitioners or if foreign governments might use it to gain an edge. No more than the other two interpretations can this one serve alone, and it better explains the long-term qualitative improvements in weaponry than the medium- or short-term measures that most exacerbated international conflict. It does point up, however, the importance of the prevailing forms of military technology. Some weapons bring the security dilemma into play much more powerfully than do others. If frontier and coastal fortresses, for example, give adequate protection against invasion, they will deter attack much less provocatively than would fleets of tanks or

---

[22] L. F. Richardson, *Arms and Insecurity: A Mathematical Study of the Causes and Origins of War* (London, 1960) is the starting-point for the quantitative literature: Richardson's ch. 7 examines the pre-1914 arms race.

battleships.[23] Although on both land and sea before 1914 technology was evolving so as to favour the defender, governments and their military advisers still assumed that a first attack might win a decisive advantage. This assumption intensified their anxieties about the military balance and their fears of pre-emption in a crisis.[24]

All three theoretical approaches to arms races have something to offer; none suffices in isolation. The task is simplified if we remember what we are trying to explain. As the twentieth century opened, the land arms race between the Continental blocs was in suspension or slow motion, and primarily qualitative. The peacetime strengths of the Continental armies were static or declining. The competition that developed in 1912–14, in contrast, was primarily quantitative, both in manpower and in *matériel*, and was meant to maximize war readiness. The technological imperative model is of questionable applicability here, and the domestic structure model is inadequate in that, until as late as 1909–10, the internal pressures within the Continental Powers to restrain the growth of armies outweighed those for expansion. We are left with the action–reaction model, but this fails to explain how a competitive escalation was triggered in the first place. This study will argue that internal pressures and technological change both contributed, but that the international crises of the pre-war decade, long emphasized in diplomatic accounts of the origins of the war, were the essential destabilizing factor. They came unpredictably, in quick succession, and were thought to show the need for permanently higher levels of preparedness. The short-term measures taken during the crises, and the long- and medium-term ones taken between them, were aspects of a single process of enhancing readiness. This process must be studied at three levels: pressures for qualitative change generated by technological innovation and by the military and industry; the quantitative increase in land military preparedness after about 1910 and more particularly after 1912, coinciding with a ground swell of international tension; and the crisis measures that culminated in the mobilizations of 1914.[25]

There remains the question of whether the land arms race inevitably led to war. This seems doubtful, especially if we locate it in the sequence of modern, or technological, arms races that began with the industrialization of weapons manufacture in the 1840s. Franco-British naval rivalry between 1840 and 1866 had been followed by a Franco-Prussian land race in 1866–70; a further Franco-German land race, drawing in Austria-Hungary and Russia, from 1874 to 1893; a British naval race with France and Russia in 1884–1904; and then the Anglo-German naval race that gathered momentum from 1902 to 1912 and the Austro-Italian one of 1904–11. There had been a cyclical movement between peripheral and central arms races, which completed another transition in 1911–12. But thus

[23] M. W. Hoag, 'On Stability in Deterrent Races', *World Politics*, 13 (1961), 505–27.

[24] S. van Evera, 'The Cult of the Offensive and the Origins of the First World War', *International Security*, 9 (1984), 58–107; J. Snyder, 'Civil–Military Relations and the Cult of the Offensive, 1914 and 1984', ibid. 108–46.

[25] The idea of preparedness is discussed in T. C. Schelling, 'War Without Pain, and Other Models', *World Politics*, 15 (1963), 465–87.

far only the race of 1866–70 had ended in war, rather than accommodation, exhaustion, or the diversion of resources to a different race elsewhere. Arms races had contributed to tension but had not usually led to bloodshed, and not all wars had been preceded by armaments competition. In theory, armaments may even, by strengthening mutual deterrence, reduce the danger of hostilities, although this is less likely to occur in a conventional than in a nuclear context.[26] The fearful climax to the 1912–14 race suggests, however, that in this instance armaments did indeed inhibit crisis management and helped to bury the long European peace. This race differed from its predecessors in a manner that compels investigation. It is with the galvanizing impact of technology that our investigation starts.

[26] On these points, Huntington, 'Arms Races'; P. M. Kennedy, 'Arms Races and the Causes of War, 1850–1945', in his *Strategy and Diplomacy, 1870–1945* (London, 1984), 163–77; J. A. Vasquez, ' "The Steps to War": Towards a Scientific Explanation of Correlates of War Findings', *World Politics*, 40 (1987), 108–45.

I

Arms and the Men

1. Unbinding Prometheus

For a century and a half before the 1840s land and naval armaments had scarcely changed. But from that time on, the industrialization of weapons manufacture transformed the power to produce and to destroy. It took almost twenty years to re-equip the Prussian infantry with the first standard-issue rifle: subsequent replacements, even in much larger armies, needed only four.[1] The wars and economic boom of the mid-nineteenth century ushered in a revolution in technology and organization that set the mould in which twentieth-century armies still operated. The impetus behind this revolution came from the mechanization of transport and communications and from the transformation of the arms themselves.

Prussia's use of railways in the wars of 1866 and 1870 had seized the European imagination. Forty years on, more powerful locomotives, automatic wagon brakes and couplings, and new signalling devices were further accelerating the passage of military trains. The French estimated that modifications to their railway system in 1912–13 knocked a day off mobilization time;[2] the Russians, conversely, were handicapped by wood-burning engines and outdated signalling and braking.[3] None the less, the railway was a mature technology. It was by building more lines, and by double- and quadruple-tracking existing ones, that the Germans in the Eifel and the Russians in Poland used rail to tilt the balance in the pre-war years. At sea, by contrast, there was continuing innovation in ship design. Steam propulsion, steel hulls, and screw propellers in the middle decades of the nineteenth century were followed in the 1880s by the triple expansion engine, which allowed navies to steam further without refuelling and to dispense with sail altogether, at the price of dependence on coaling stations. After 1898 the reciprocating engine began to give way to the turbine, while diesel and electric motors made possible the modern submarine. Oil burning in place of coal for surface ships was not far down the line.[4]

In the generation after Waterloo the standard army weapons had been

---

[1] W. H. McNeill, *The Pursuit of Power: Technology, Armed Force and Society since A.D. 1000* (Oxford, 1983), 236.

[2] EMA 3rd Bureau, 'Plan XVII: Bases du Plan', 2 May 1913, SHA, 1.N. 11.

[3] Lt.-Col. Janin to Col. Vignal, 10 June 1911, SHA 7.N. 1485.

[4] J. T. Sumida, 'The Royal Navy and Technological Change, 1815–1945', in R. Haycock and K. Neilson (eds.), *Men, Machines, and War* (Waterloo, Ontario, 1988), 75–91. K. Lautenschläger, 'Technology and the Evolution of Naval Warfare', *International Security*, 8 (1983), 3–51.

muzzle-loading smoothbore muskets, and cannon firing solid round shot or shrapnel with a black powder charge. They were individually produced by arti-sanal methods, mostly in state arsenals. Once the American producers of the Connecticut valley had pioneered small-arms manufacture by means of machine tools turning out interchangeable parts, their equipment was brought to Britain by Enfield Arsenal in the Crimean emergency of 1854 and by the newly created Birmingham Small Arms Company in 1861; and to Austria by Joseph Werndl's Steyr Waffenfabrik.[5] Rifled barrels and cylindrical bullets came in in the 1850s; breech loading in the following decade. The mass-produced breech-loading rifle, unlike the musket, could be aimed from a prone or crouched position, and fired more accurately, further, and faster. For the parallel revolution in artillery, the precondition was cheap, quality-controlled steel. This the Bessemer converter and the Siemens-Martin open-hearth process provided, but they required capi-tal and expertise that *laissez-faire* governments were loath to commit. Hence the military were pushed into collaboration with private manufacturers at the expense of the state armaments monopolies. The Austrian army, whose field guns came from the Arsenal in Vienna, remained loyal to steel-bronze down to 1914, but elsewhere the triumph of Krupp steel rifled breech-loaders over the French in 1870 settled the issue.[6] At sea, rifled breech-loaders firing cylindrical projectiles became general in the 1880s, forcing navies to protect their ships of the line with armour-plate and thereby creating another critical sector of depen-dence on private suppliers.[7] No sooner had this cycle of innovation been com-pleted, however, than in the last two decades of the nineteenth century a new cluster of changes modified naval warfare even more profoundly, and had far-reaching repercussions on land.

This time the explosives were the starting-point. Black powder (a mixture of sulphur, saltpetre, and charcoal) required skilled hand-mixing, rather than sci-ence to produce; it was dangerous to handle and ruined by damp; and when fired it gave off clouds of smoke and fouled the guns. Alfred Nobel's dynamite, based on nitroglycerine, was the first marketable chemical explosive, but too powerful to be of military use as a propellant. Only in the 1880s were ballistite, cordite, and the French *poudre B* developed for rifles. They offered near smokeless det-onations, concealing the soldier's position, and enabled much greater range and velocity of fire, as well as providing high explosive charges for shells.[8]

The new explosives saved gun-carrying warships when they seemed threat-ened with obsolescence by the self-propelled torpedo, introduced in 1868 and launched from small and cheap boats. A new generation of heavy guns, using

[5] E. Ames and N. Rosenberg, 'The Enfield Arsenal in Theory and History', *Economic Journal*, 78 (1968), 827–42. D. M. Ward, *The Other Battle* (York, 1946), 13. H. Doppler, *75 Jahre Steyr-Werke* (Vienna, 1939), 19.

[6] D. Showalter, 'Prussia, Technology, and War: Artillery from 1815 to 1914', in Haycock and Neilson (eds.), *Men, Machines*, 113–51.

[7] A. Grant, *Steel and Ships: The History of John Brown's* (London, 1956), 20.

[8] W. J. Reader, *Imperial Chemical Industries: A History*, i (London, 1970), discusses the history of explosives.

cordite and telescopic sights, permitted action at 6,000–7,000 instead of 2,000 yards. Quick-firing guns, whose barrels returned automatically into position after recoil, were fast and accurate enough to hit incoming torpedo vessels. Greater protection against the new heavy guns came with advances in armour plate, H. A. Harvey patenting his 'cemented' nickel steel in 1891 and the Krupp firm its nickel-chrome armour five years later. Twice as effective for a given thickness as iron and steel compound plate, Krupp steel could shield a battleship's upper hull and ordnance without dangerously increasing topweight, enabling battles to be fought away from coastal waters and out on the high seas.[9]

On land, small arms and artillery were similarly modified. Expenditure mounted as armies re-equipped with the repeating (magazine) rifle, using smokeless powder. The German Mauser dated from 1884; the French Lebel from 1886; the Austrian Mannlicher from 1885; the British Lee-Enfield from 1891. Once again, private manufacturers such as Steyr and BSA were drawn in to assist production.[10] The magazine rifle could fire several rounds without reloading, but it did not fire continuously for as long as the trigger was pressed. The 1884 Maxim machine gun, however, was a true automatic weapon, using the recoil from each bullet to insert and detonate a fresh cartridge up to 600 times a minute. This was an awesome engine of slaughter, although Continental armies ordered few of them until after the turn of the century.[11]

The use of high explosives by siege guns made brick fortifications obsolete, and revolutionized fortress design. Rotating cupolas, reinforced concrete, and armour plate were complemented by machine guns, wireless, and searchlights, obliging yet further recourse to private industry.[12] High explosive used in field artillery, however, intensified the recoil that forced the gunner to stand clear from the weapon on firing and to reposition it before the next round. The Armstrong quick-firing naval gun used a hydraulic cylinder to absorb the recoil and reposition the barrel automatically, but the extra weight of the device seemed to invalidate it as an army weapon. The German *Feldkanone* 96 used a trail spade, a hinged arm on the gun carriage that could be dug into the ground; but it was immediately outclassed by the French 75 mm of 1897. The 75 mm had a 'long recoil' hydraulic cylinder and a piston fixed parallel to the barrel, a shield to protect the guncrew, a cartridge combining charge and ignition that could be loaded in one movement, and a breech mechanism that could eject the spent round with a flick of the wrist. It could fire up to twenty rounds a minute; its predecessor four to six. It gave France the advantage against Germany for a decade. Re-equipment with quick-firers dominated army weapons budgets for

[9] Lautenschläger, 'Naval Warfare', 12–14. A. D. Stacey, 'An Historical Survey of the Manufacture of Naval Armour by Vickers Sons & Co. and their Successors, 1888–1936', VA #1153. I. V. Hogg, *A History of Artillery* (London, 1974), 117–24.

[10] H. Strachowsky, 'Die Waffen-Industrie in Österreich', in *Die Grossindustrie Österreichs* (Vienna, 1898), 142–3. Ward, *Battle*, 20.

[11] J. Ellis, *The Social History of the Machine Gun* (London, 1975), ch. 2.

[12] *Encyclopaedia Britannica*, 11th edn. (29 vols., London, 1910–11), x, 'Fortification and Siegecraft', 696–707. Q. Hughes, *Military Architecture* (London, 1974).

years ahead, and their principles were soon extended to howitzers and heavy artillery. The question of divisional heavy artillery, in which France and Austria-Hungary were marking time, was a focus of concern on the eve of 1914.[13] If to quick-firers are added machine guns, wireless, telephones, field kitchens, and aircraft and dirigibles, the decade after 1900 saw the greatest changes in army weaponry since Bismarck's wars.

2. The Armaments Geography of Europe

The mid-nineteenth century revolution in weapons technology had opened Pandora's Box. Development became continuous, and in 1900 it was gathering pace. In a competitive environment governments felt compelled to imitate, and in this sense they were victims of armaments innovation, although they were also its willing accomplices. Powered flight, wireless, and even high explosive were developed initially for civilian purposes, and for adaptation to military ones they needed War Ministries to provide finance. The Maxim gun was developed at private initiative, but the quick-firing naval gun, designed by Armstrongs to meet British Admiralty specifications, or the 75 mm, produced in the French state arsenal at Puteaux, were command technologies.[14]

A novel feature of the pre-war world, however, was a global network of private armaments companies. The market leaders were at least as innovative as the state sector, and had larger productive capacity. Governments needed them; but the companies needed governments. The investments required for weapons manufacture were huge. Steel armour needed 8,000-ton presses and planing machines with a stroke of 38 feet; heavy guns were prepared on 90-foot lathes, and their mountings with 30-foot circular saws.[15] By 1914 Krupp had a workforce of 81,000 and their central works at Essen was Germany's greatest industrial plant, using as much electricity each year as the whole of Berlin and containing enough railway track to link Frankfurt to Munich.[16] The specialized labour and equipment, at least for heavy weapons, had little alternative use, but it depended for orders on export markets in the world's turbulent fringes, and on unpredictable official purchases. In these circumstances the arms firms took on characteristics for which radical critics have assailed them ever since. They were condemned for bribing officers and civil servants and for taking them into their employ; for suborning parliamentarians and the press; for forming 'rings' to throttle competition; for blocking disarmament and subsidizing militarist leagues; for fabricating panics and scares; and for selling to potential enemies. Perhaps they too were victims (as well as beneficiaries) of a system tolerated and

---

[13] Showalter, 'Prussia', 140–2. Hogg, *Artillery*, 94–100. J. Doise and M. Vaïsse, *Diplomatie et outil militaire* (Paris, 1987), 102–8. The importance of divisional artillery is stressed by Professor Hew Strachan.

[14] Ibid. 102. McNeill, *Pursuit*, 279.

[15] R. C. B. Trebilcock, *The Vickers Brothers: Armaments and Enterprise, 1854–1914* (London, 1977), 8.

[16] B. Menne, *Krupp: Or the Lords of Essen* (London, 1937), 303.

encouraged by governments, but their behaviour threatened stability and peace.[17]

The validity of these criticisms varied from Power to Power, and an excursion is required here into armaments geography. Britain, France, and Germany had the most powerful arms firms, although even they retained a large state sector. Austria-Hungary and the United States could meet their own needs, but exported little. Russia, Italy, Belgium, Sweden, and Japan also had significant private manufacturers, although they needed to import some items. In Latin America, the Mediterranean, the Balkans, Near East, and China, there were state arsenals and shipyards, but private producers were few and feeble and all sophisticated army and navy equipment had to come from abroad. The focus here will be on the state versus private balance in the first three of these four circles, and on the influence of the private sector on armaments policy. Germany is the obvious place to start.

* * *

The Prussian army cooked its bread, tinned its meat, and tailored its uniforms; it made rifles, machine guns, and cannon in half a dozen arsenals, foremost among them Spandau. In the last pre-war years, however, half or fewer of its equipment orders went to its own establishments. It would turn to private industry in war or crisis, or to assist if a weapon was being completely replaced.[18] Explosives came from Nobel and the other members of the Anglo-German cartel known as the General Pooling Arrangement; optical instruments from Zeiss of Jena; small arms from the Deutsche Waffen- und Munitions Fabriken (DWMF), founded by Ludwig Loewe and centred in Berlin, which was linked in a cartel with the Mauser rifle plant at Oberndorf in the Neckar valley. The cartel manufactured Maxim guns, under licence from Vickers, and the M1904 infantry rifle; it was also a big exporter.[19] Artillery and shells came from Heinrich Ehrhardt's Rheinische Metallwaren- und Maschinenfabrik (Rheinmetall), located outside Düsseldorf, but above all from the Friedrich Krupp Aktiengesellschaft, which was by far the army's largest private supplier.[20] The navy had shipyards at Danzig, Kiel, and Wilhelmshaven but, as it expanded, the share of warship orders going to the private sector rose from 50 per cent in 1889–98 to 78 per cent in 1906–13.[21] Initially, four private yards could build capital ships: the Krupp-owned Germaniawerft at Kiel, Blohm and Voss of Hamburg, Stettiner

---

[17] P. Noel-Baker, *The Private Manufacture of Armaments* (London, 1936), i, for the classic indictment.

[18] Reichsarchiv, *Der Weltkrieg, 1914–1918. Kriegsrüstung und Kriegswirtschaft* (Berlin, 1930), i. 389–94. Testimony of Maj.-Gen. Wandel in Reichstag Budget Commission, 17 Feb. 1911, KAM Mkr. 5584. M. Epkenhans, 'The German Armament Industry and Economic Development, 1870–1914', European Univ. Institute Colloquium Paper 303/91 Col. 15 (Florence, 1991). I am indebted to Dr Peter Gatrell for showing me this paper.

[19] Wenninger to Bavarian War Ministry, 10 Jan. 1914, KAM Mkr. 5444 (pamphlet on DWMF). *Eine Werksgeschichte: Fünfzig Jahre Mauser, 1896–1946* (Cologne, 1949). Reichsarchiv, *Weltkrieg*, i. 387.

[20] Ibid. 384.

[21] Proceedings of Reichstag Commission on arms procurement, 14/15 Nov. 1913, HSMA M 1/6.

Fig. 4. Europe in 1914

Vulcan, and Schichau. Two weaker firms received orders after 1904.[22] In a cartel with the Dillengen Hüttenwerke of the Saar, Krupp turned out all the navy's armour-plate, and it was its sole supplier of heavy guns.[23]

In addition to its dominance of the private manufacture of armaments, Krupp had a special relationship with the Hohenzollern dynasty and a salient role in German politics. The relationship dated back to Alfred Krupp, the moody, obsessional architect of the company's fortunes as a cannon producer.[24] His son, Friedrich Alfred, who committed suicide in 1902, was friendly with Wilhelm II and perhaps a kindred spirit. The Emperor visited him at the Villa Hügel, the Krupp family seat, bestowed distinctions on him, and delivered an overblown oration at his graveside.[25] He helped arrange the marriage of Friedrich Alfred's daughter to the Prussian diplomat Gustav von Bohlen und Halbach, who became chairman in 1909, and permitted Gustav to take 'Krupp' into his family name.[26] Although the firm became a joint-stock company in 1903, all but four of the 160,000 shares remained in family hands; its annual reports gave only perfunctory information and it was sheltered from commercial exigencies.[27] This allowed it, for example, to co-operate with the General Staff in the secret development over four years at the firm's expense of the *M-Gerät*, a 42-ton mortar that was unleashed against the Belgian fortresses in 1914.[28] In 1903 the company's supervisory board included the Prussian Railway Minister, the former head of the Equipment Department in the Navy Office, and Wilhelm's court banker.[29] Alfred Hugenberg, who became Managing Director under Gustav, came from the Prussian Finance Ministry.[30] The Krupp directors owned several major newspapers, subsidized conservative political parties and pressure groups, and were leaders of the Ruhr business community.

The firm thus seemed outstandingly well placed to help determine armaments policy, and apparently formed a solid front with the public authorities. Wilhelm and his retinue graced the pompous centenary celebrations at Essen in 1912. In the 'Krupp scandal' of the following year the Socialist deputy, Karl Liebknecht, disclosed evidence that the head of the company's office in Berlin, Lieutenant

[22] M. Epkenhans, 'Grossindustrie und Schlachtflottenbau, 1897–1914', *Militärgeschichtliche Mitteilungen*, 43/1 (1988), 87, and cf. the same author's *Die Wilhelminische Flottenrüstung, 1908–1914: Weltmachtstreben, industrieller Fortschritt, soziale Integration* (Munich, 1991).

[23] R. Owen, 'Military–Industrial Relations: Krupp and the Imperial Navy Office', in R. J. Evans (ed.), *Society and Politics in Imperial Germany* (London, 1978), 75–6. 'Kriegsdenkschrift: Die Firma Krupp im Weltkrieg und in der Nachkriegszeit, 1914–1925', 6, KAE W.A. VII f. 1070.

[24] W. Manchester, *The Arms of Krupp, 1587–1968* (London, 1968) for a general history. See the discussion by H. Pogge von Strandmann, 'Der Kaiser und die Industriellen. Vom Primat der Rüstung', in J. C. G. Röhl (ed.), *Der Ort Kaiser Wilhelms II in der deutschen Geschichte* (Munich, 1991).

[25] Menne, *Krupp*, 165. W. Boelcke (ed.), *Krupp und die Hohenzollern: Aus der Korrespondenz der Familie Krupp, 1850–1916* (Berlin, 1956), 65–7, 101.

[26] Manchester, *Krupp*, 286–7.

[27] Ibid. 279. For Tirpitz's and Wilhelm's opposition to Krupp becoming a limited company, Epkenhans, 'Grossindustrie', 72.

[28] 'Kriegsdenkschrift', 12, cf. n. 23 above.

[29] Boelcke, *Krupp*, 66, 109. Menne, *Krupp*, 265. Board minutes in KAE W.A. 41/2–184, 185.

[30] Menne, *Krupp*, 251.

Brandt, had bribed War Ministry officials in exchange for secret information about competitors. The War Minister, Josias von Heeringen, resigned over the allegations, but not before asking Liebknecht in the Reichstag to 'suspend judgment . . . as regards the firm', because of the length of the army's connection with it.

It is not the case that I favour private industry. But we are dependent on it. In critical times we must have great masses of material immediately ready. This cannot be secured in a State factory. On the other hand we cannot give the private firms enough orders to keep them solvent in peacetime. Hence they are dependent on private orders.[31]

The Ministry's case was similar to that presented by the Chief Engineer of the DWMF to a Reichstag commission on arms procurement set up after the Brandt affair: private industry provided indispensable reserve capacity that could pay its way in peacetime only by exporting and would be too expensive for the state to sustain. In addition, it was the leading source of innovation. If Germany did not meet the foreign demand for armaments, others would do so.[32] The Krupp directors expanded on this rationale: a nationalized concern, they contended, would have less success in export markets, because of foreign reluctance to depend directly on the German Government. Nor would it be cushioned by the civilian production lines that permitted Krupp to keep plant and workers active when military demand was slack. The company's export sales allowed it to gather information about its rivals and about foreign governments' technical specifications, as well as forcing it to keep up a quality and dynamism impossible for a state enterprise.[33] When war broke out in 1914, Krupp lost its markets abroad but doubled its home artillery output, for which purpose manganese and nickel had been expensively stockpiled.[34]

Yet in general, Krupp was less profitable than purely civilian steel and metalworking firms, and its special relationship with the state authorities probably impeded it from maximizing its rate of return.[35] This already makes problematic who manipulated whom. The limits to Krupp's influence are further demonstrated by the history of the warship-building programme initiated by the Navy Laws of 1898 and 1900, from which it appeared the firm might benefit handsomely. Its export sales, traditionally centred on artillery, fell from 85 per cent to under half its output between 1890–1 and 1914 as French and British competitors successfully challenged it. In 1890, however, the navy invited Krupp to move into armour-plate production. The firm established the cartel with Dillingen, patented nickel-chrome steel, and in 1896 purchased the Germania shipyard, thus making itself an integrated or complete-cycle armaments concern,

---

[31] Noel-Baker, *Armaments*, i. 62, 66.
[32] Document submitted to the Reichstag commission, 8/10 Jan. 1914, HSMA M 1/6.
[33] Memoranda by Ehrensberger and Hugenberg, Mar. and Apr. 1914, KAE W.A. IV. 1957.
[34] W. Berdrow, 'Die Firma Krupp im Weltkrieg und in der Nachkriegszeit, 1914–1919', 11–13, 20–1. KAE FAH. IV. E10.
[35] Epkenhans, 'Grossindustrie', 80–1. Hugenberg memorandum, Apr. 1914, KAE W.A. IV. 1957.

able to deliver all types of land and naval weapon.[36] Before the 1898 navy bill
was introduced, Wilhelm advised Alfred von Tirpitz, the new Navy Secretary,
to work up an agitation behind it and to contact Friedrich Alfred. The latter
nominated Victor Schweinburg, the editor of one of his newspapers, and a press
campaign followed. When the German Navy League was founded in April 1898,
as a pressure group ostensibly independent of government, Schweinburg became
secretary and Friedrich Alfred joined its executive committee. When Wilhelm
and Tirpitz urged the latter to expand his armour and naval gun capacity, he
replied reassuringly.[37]

It should be underlined that Krupp began producing armour plate and backed
the Navy League in response to state initiatives; and that although there was a
mutual interest in co-operation the partnership was often strained. Tirpitz told
the Reichstag Budget Commission in 1910 that no other navy got ordnance of
such quality as did Germany from Krupp, and that German armour plate was
probably the cheapest in the world.[38] To keep parliamentary support and avoid
provoking the British, however, he needed a gradual and cheap expansion whose
pace he could control. He distrusted the Navy League enthusiasts and was able
to remove Schweinburg; when Schweinburg went Krupp did also, withdrawing
his subsidy from the body. Tirpitz also clashed with Krupp over the price of
armour-plate and guns, trying unsuccessfully to bring rival German and
American firms into the market, and feeding damaging information to Krupp's
press and parliamentary critics. The price of armour-plate was forced down from
2,500 to 1,550 marks per tonne between 1897–8 and 1913–14, although this still
left Krupp with a very substantial gross profit.[39] On naval guns its rate of return
was probably much lower, Wilhelm himself in 1905 appealing to the company's
sense of patriotism and asking it to lower its estimates.[40] Gustav considered
Tirpitz to be thoroughly untrustworthy; yet attempts to make Wilhelm intervene
against him had little success.[41] Between 1904 and 1911, moreover, the company
completely re-equipped its Essen works to enhance its capacity as a naval supplier.[42] But from 1912 German defence spending placed renewed emphasis on
the army, and the rate of capital ship construction fell back from four to two per
year. When Tirpitz embarked on his naval programme he assumed the Reichstag
would refuse finance for additional navy shipyards. He therefore encouraged
Krupp and the private builders to expand by awarding them navy orders, believ-

[36] Owen, 'Krupp', 75–6.

[37] Epkenhans, 'Grossindustrie', 67–8. The classic source on these questions is E. Kehr,
*Schlachtflottenbau und Parteipolitik, 1894–1901. Versuch eines Querschnitts durch die innenpolitischen,
sozialen, und ideologischen Voraussetzungen des deutschen Imperialismus* (Berlin, 1930).

[38] Krupp circular no. 750, 28 Feb. 1910 Appendix: *Rheinisch-Westfälische Zeitung*, 24 Feb. 1910.
KAE W.A. IV. 1280.

[39] Epkenhans, 'Grossindustrie', 69–78. Owen, 'Krupp', 77–83.

[40] Müller to Rötger, 21 Mar. 1905, KAE FAH. IV. C7.

[41] Krupp von Bohlen to Eccius, 20 Aug. 1909, KAE FAH. IV. C239.

[42] The relevant decisions are recorded in the board minutes, KAE W.A. 41/2–184, 185.
Memorandum, 'Die Entwicklung der Artillerie-Werkstätten während des Krieges', n.d., KAE W.A.
IV. 1342.

ing they would be able to sustain themselves subsequently by winning commercial shipbuilding contracts at Britain's expense. In the event, they largely failed to do so, and the decline in navy work after 1912 forced them into desperate straits. In 1914 only half of Krupp's new armour-plate capacity was being used,[43] and the Germania yard shared in the plight of the rest of the industry. Having previously blocked the formation of a shipbuilding cartel, which Tirpitz greatly feared, the company in 1912–14 successfully led negotiations for one, and on the eve of war discussions were beginning with British builders.[44] Yet the navy had pointed out the threat to industrial capacity if orders fell, and Wilhelm was aware of the connection.[45] That he acquiesced in the change of emphasis hardly suggests that German defence policy was determined by Krupp's interests.

Krupp's relations with the army were at once more guarded and less profitable than those with the sister service. The army took 12.8 per cent of the firm's artillery and munitions orders in 1910–14, against the navy's 43.3 per cent.[46] Army purchases failed to compensate for diminished naval demand, and despite the vast increase on the eve of war in total defence spending the volume of Krupp's orders fell, workers in the artillery division having to be laid off in 1913.[47] There was a long-standing rivalry between Essen and Spandau, which had first claim as an army purveyor. Munitions and artillery components went out to tender, Krupp getting no special consideration and having to compete with Rheinmetall, which became a near obsession.[48] Once the army had encouraged Rheinmetall to enter the artillery sector as an alternative domestic contractor, the Düsseldorf firm also took on Krupp in export markets.[49] Ehrhardt patented a hydraulic recoil gun before Krupp did, but only, so the latter alleged, with assistance from a former Krupp employee who had done the essential work before defecting. Although Krupp's own quick-firer soon outsold Ehrhardt's, it challenged Rheinmetall's patent in the courts, suggested to the War Ministry an exclusive contract, and appealed to Wilhelm II: all of which expedients failed.[50] The two firms were unable to negotiate a compromise and the Krupp directors began secretly purchasing Rheinmetall shares, acquiring by 1913 a big enough minority vote to hamper the latter's investment decisions.[51] By this stage the War Ministry was embarrassed by the competition it had fostered, as was the Foreign Ministry, because of the lack of inter-firm co-operation in winning

[43] Ehrensperger memorandum, Mar. 1914, KAE W.A. IV. 1957.

[44] Epkenhans, 'Grossindustrie', 82–92.

[45] V. R. Berghahn, *Rüstung und Machtpolitik: Zur Anatomie des 'Kalten Krieges' vor 1914* (Düsseldorf, 1973), 61.

[46] Details of artillery production in KAE W.A. VII f. 1070.

[47] Ibid., and memorandum, 'Die Entwicklung der Artillerie', cited in n. 42 above.

[48] 'Kriegsdenkschrift' cited in n. 23.

[49] On Rheinmetall, *90 Jahre Rheinmetall, 1889–1979* (Düsseldorf, 1979) and H. Ehrhardt, *Erinnerungen eines 89-jährigen Mannes und Erfinders* (Zelle-Mehlis, 1928).

[50] Menne, *Krupp*, 172–81. 'Denkschriften zu dem Patentstreit zwischen Fried. Krupp und Fahrzeugfabrik Eisenach/Rheinmetall (Ehrhardt)', KAE W.A. IV. 1608. Memorandum by Budde, 10 June 1901, KAE FAH. III. C177. F. A. Krupp note on conversation with Wilhelm II, 30 Dec. 1897, KAE FAH. III. B251.

[51] Rötger to Hartmann, 13 Jan. 1906, KAE W.A. IV. 2847a. Menne, *Krupp*, 284.

export orders.[52] Unlike Tirpitz for armour-plate, therefore, the army broke the stranglehold of a single private supplier for artillery and munitions. The authorities failed, however, to harness Krupp and Ehrhardt into working jointly for German interests abroad. Conversely, Krupp cared far less about broader defence policy than it did about market share and eliminating competition, but even over the latter it failed to win backing from the Emperor and the military authorities. It could influence the design of particular projects, but not the general scale and direction of the armaments drive. Having responded to government prompting to expand shipbuilding capacity at the turn of the century, when official priorities altered it found itself stranded. In the German 'military-industrial complex' the official rather than the private partner dominated.

* * *

The German case encapsulates more general trends. Private production was gaining on the state sector, but more so in navy than in army weapons, and it was in warship-building that the conditions for a military-industrial complex— high capitalization, rapid innovation—were most fully met. In any case, the state could subcontract to the private sector while still controlling overall policy. These circumstances weaken the force of the military-industrial-complex thesis as an explanation of land armaments competition.

In Britain, home to the biggest private firms apart from Krupp, the contrast between land and sea was particularly sharp. Army and navy guns and shells came from the Royal Arsenal at Woolwich; explosives from Waltham Abbey; and infantry weapons from Enfield. The army bought in revolvers from Webley, rifles from the London Small Arms Company and BSA, and Maxim guns from Vickers, but in 1909–14 four-fifths of its artillery pieces and their ammunition still came from the Royal Ordnance Factories.[53] In the explosives sector, the War Office since the 1890s had attracted new firms into its circle of suppliers, but then failed to keep them busy with new orders, while using Waltham Abbey to hold prices down.[54] Similarly, the 18-pounder and 13-pounder quick-firers for the field and horse artillery were a composite design incorporating an Armstrong barrel, a Vickers recoil system, and Royal Ordnance sighting and elevating gear.[55] When Vickers and Armstrong pleaded that they and Woolwich should monopolize production in order to recover development costs, the War Office insisted on the rival Coventry Ordnance Works taking a share of orders.[56] An inter-departmental committee under Sir George Murray, the Permanent Under-Secretary of the Treasury, recommended that state plants were needed to ensure economy and good design, but that work should be contracted out in order 'to

---

[52] Rötger memorandum on conversation with Einem, 27 Oct. 1907, KAE FAH. IV. C11. Krupp to Jagow, 16 Aug. 1913, PAAA R. 927.

[53] J. D. Scott, *Vickers: A History* (London, 1962), 97.

[54] R. C. B. Trebilcock, 'A "Special Relationship": Government, Rearmament and the Cordite Firms', *Economic History Review*, NS 19 (1966), 364–79.

[55] A. W. Wilson, *The Story of the Gun* (Woolwich, 1985 edn.), 65.

[56] 'Correspondence with WO *re* Horse and Field Artillery Requirements', VA #800.

create an additional source of power in emergency'.[57] In practice both state and private capacity were run down before 1914, because of the lack of government business. The 1905–7 re-equipping with quick-firers was a once-for-all adjustment to technical change, and there was no land armaments expansion on the eve of war. The War Office left the private firms the crumbs after assuring the needs of the Royal Ordnance Factories, it reserved the right to favour interlopers, and accepted no responsibility to manufacturers when trade was slack. Although the army wished to 'nurse' the private sector in order to maintain reserve capacity, it was constrained by *laissez-faire* principles and Treasury requirements.[58]

The navy spent much more on equipment and ordered more from private industry. Between 1884 and 1914 total War Office spending less than doubled but the Admiralty's nearly quadrupled.[59] Construction and repair expenditure rose from £3.4 to £19.3 million, and the share of private constructors as against the Royal Dockyards from 10 to 47 per cent.[60] All the navy's armour-plate was of private manufacture.[61] For the private shipyards, warship construction developed from a sideline into a cornerstone of their prosperity: Vickers, Britain's largest arms firm, received £55,000 of War Office contracts annually in 1910–14 but £3 million from the Admiralty.[62]

At the turn of the century, the private firms became more concentrated in ownership and vertically integrated, in an analogous process to the Krupp-led regrouping in Germany. With the onset of the naval race with France and Russia in the 1880s, a larger share of warship-building went outside the Royal Dockyards, and more breech-loading guns were needed than Woolwich could provide. The Admiralty responded by drawing in new armour-plate and ordnance manufacturers. The biggest beneficiary was Vickers, which during the 1890s ousted Armstrong-Mitchell as the industry leader and became an all-purpose supplier. Starting with armour-plate and naval guns at its works in Sheffield, in 1897 it purchased Maxim-Nordenfeld's machine-gun and light-artillery plants, and the shipyard at Barrow-in-Furness. Armstrong merged with Whitworth, its traditional competitor as a gunsmith, and moved into plate production. Vickers's rivals as armour manufacturers, John Brown and Charles Cammell, joined with the Laird and Fairfield shipbuilders to set up the Coventry Ordnance Works in 1905.[63] Once the regrouping was completed, however,

[57] Noel-Baker, *Armaments*, i. 59. D. French, *British Economic and Strategic Planning, 1905–1915* (London, 1982), 46–7. O. F. G. Hogg, *The Royal Arsenal: Its Background, Origin, and Subsequent History* (London, 1963), ii. 911–12.

[58] French, *Planning*, 47. Trebilcock, 'Special Relationship', 373–5.

[59] McNeill, *Pursuit*, 287.

[60] S. Pollard and P. Robertson, *The British Shipbuilding Industry, 1870–1914* (Cambridge, Mass., 1979), 218–19. Percentages mine.

[61] S. Pollard, '*Laissez-Faire* and Shipbuilding', *Economic History Review*, NS 5 (1952), 107.

[62] Scott, *Vickers*, 99.

[63] For this regrouping, McNeill, *Pursuit*, 262–97; Scott, *Vickers*, chs. 5, 6; Trebilcock, *Vickers Brothers*, chs. 2, 3; K. Warren, *Armstrongs of Elswick: Growth in Engineering and Armaments to the Merger with Vickers* (Basingstoke, 1989), chs. 8, 14; Grant, *Steel and Ships*, 36 ff.

cohesion as much as competitiveness distinguished the British scene. Armstrong and Vickers pooled designs and parcelled out the leading export markets. The arms and shipbuilding firms were interlocked in ownership, and they shared directors. The armour-plate concerns formed a cartel for handling Admiralty work, and were linked with their American, French, and German opposite numbers in the Harvey steel syndicate, which set prices for exports outside the members' home markets and divided orders between them.[64]

There appeared to be further cohesion between industry and state. The arms firms and the Admiralty's design and procurement branches exchanged personnel at the most senior level.[65] At the turn of the century perhaps a quarter of a million people worked in the navy and its supply industries,[66] a dozen MPs were on the boards of armaments firms,[67] and Sir Edward Grey, like his two predecessors as Foreign Secretary, owned armaments shares.[68] The scares of 1884 and 1888 set a pattern for navalist agitation, the Conservative press pointing to foreign danger but also advocating warship construction as a bulwark against depression and anarchy at home. The navalists showed their power in 1894 when Gladstone found himself isolated in Cabinet in opposing the Spencer naval programme, and resigned as Prime Minister. As a result, Britain had already pulled ahead of France and Russia by the time of the entente with Paris in 1904 and the destruction of the tsarist fleet by the Japanese, and in 1906–7 the new Liberal Government reduced expenditure without much opposition, only to change direction when the dreadnought rivalry with Germany touched off the greatest scare of all.

The question remains, however, of where the centre of gravity in the British military-industrial complex lay. The Admiralty believed the national interest was to maintain a strong private warship-building industry, and in 1905 it decided to reduce battleship and cruiser construction in the Royal Dockyards to a minimum, keeping them going for repairs, as a control on prices, and as an insurance against strikes.[69] The initiative for contracting out came from the Government, and the interchange of personnel gave the leading firms a parastatal quality akin to Krupp's. The Admiralty permitted Vickers to be the sole private manufacturer of submarines, on condition that the company kept the specifications secret.[70] It insisted on its own designs for hulls, armour, and everything except marine engines, and private work was supervised by navy over-

[64] Pollard and Robertson, *Shipbuilding*, 99–100. Scott, *Vickers*, 86–7.

[65] A. J. Marder, 'The English Armament Industry and Navalism in the Nineties', *Pacific Historical Review*, 3 (1938), 245–6; Noel-Baker, *Armaments*, i. 170–80; Trebilcock, *Vickers Brothers*, 46; Warren, *Armstrongs*, 182.

[66] W. Ashworth, 'Economic Aspects of Late Victorian Naval Administration', *Economic History Review*, NS 22 (1969), 492.

[67] Marder, 'Navalism', 246.

[68] R. C. B. Trebilcock, 'Legends of the British Armaments Industry, 1890–1914: A Revision', *Journal of Contemporary History*, 5/4 (1970), 3–19. A. J. Marder, *The Anatomy of British Sea Power: A History of British Naval Policy in the Pre-Dreadnought Era, 1880–1905* (London, 1964), 27.

[69] Marder, *Anatomy*, 41–2.   [70] Trebilcock, *Vickers Brothers*, 106.

seers.[71] Like the War Office, the navy encouraged Coventry Ordnance as a counter to Vickers and Armstrong. In 1909 the First Lord of the Admiralty remarked that his department's dealings with the latter firms were 'far more cordial than the ordinary relations of commerce', but the Vickers brothers' contacts with politicians and officials tended to be few and formal, and the arms firms were guaranteed neither a smooth flow of orders nor influence on wider aspects of policy.[72] They appear not to have subsidized the British Navy League, which in 1901 had only 15,000 members, against 600,000 for its German counterpart.[73] The most formidable agitations, such as those of 1894 and 1909, linked the arms firms with the press, the Unionist party, and the Sea Lords themselves, but to build such coalitions it was necessary for there to be a credible external threat. To maintain the interests of the shipbuilders against economy-minded Cabinets, in other words, the Admiralty needed wider backing. In any case, the British naval-industrial complex, like the German, exercised such power as it possessed in favour of naval preparedness: it was tangential to the origins of the pre-1914 race on land.

* * *

In France, as in Germany and Britain, it was in naval armaments that the private sector staged its breakthrough. In the 1870s and early 1880s capital expenditure by the army was in the ascendant, as the country re-equipped after defeat and fortified its truncated eastern frontier. Thereafter naval spending moved decisively ahead, faltering at the turn of the century before the warship construction budget doubled in 1906–13.[74] The French admirals bought in all their armour-plate, from Schneider et Cie at Le Creusot and from the Société des forges et d'aciéries de la marine et d'Homécourt at Saint-Chamond. Naval guns came from private industry as, by the twentieth century, did one in two capital ships.[75] The state yards became assembly locations for privately manufactured armour, turrets, engines, and electrical equipment. The private builders were on the west coast, with the exception of the Forges et chantiers de la Méditerranée, near Toulon, which was much the biggest exporter. Even the private yards were small, costly, and slow, and needed tariffs and state bounties to keep them going.[76]

The army ventured much less far along the privatization road. It halted its post-1870 re-equipment drive precisely when industrial recession and the rise of the Lorraine steel industry were squeezing the arms and metallurgical firms of the interior. At this moment a law of 1885 established almost complete freedom for armaments exports, in order to combat unemployment and the Anglo-German domination of foreign markets, and to create a reserve of private capacity. Forges et chantiers de la Méditerranée and the three big producers in the

[71] Pollard, '*Laissez-Faire*', 106.   [72] Noel-Baker, *Armaments*, i. 62. Scott, *Vickers*, 51, 80.
[73] Marder, *Anatomy*, 54.   [74] Crouzet, 'Recherches', 83–4.
[75] F. Crouzet, 'Remarques sur l'industrie des armements en France (du milieu du XIXe siècle à 1914)', *Revue historique*, 251 (1974), 410–14.
[76] Ibid. 417–18. M. A. Perpillou, *L'Industrie des constructions navales* (Paris, n.d.), 34–8.

centre of the country, Saint-Chamond, Schneider, and Châtillon-Commentry, began turning out complete artillery pieces, and all were profitable and expanding before 1914.[77] Schneider, none the less, was the market leader and the nearest French approach to a complete-cycle producer. In 1897 it bought the Canet artillery workshops at Le Havre, and in 1907 it added one of the big four private warship yards. Eugène Schneider was a director of the Crédit lyonnais, a founder of the Banque de l'union parisienne, and a parliamentary deputy.[78] Saint-Chamond and Châtillon-Commentry specialized in fortress work, the Société française des munitions made rifles, and Hotchkiss, at Saint-Denis outside Paris, made machine guns.

There existed the usual matrix of state and private interrelationships. Colonel Dupont, one of the developers of the 75 mm, went to Châtillon-Commentry; Colonel Rimailho, designer of the army's 155 mm heavy cannon, to Saint-Chamond.[79] The arms firms, the banks, and the Foreign Ministry collaborated highly effectively in winning foreign orders. The French firms were weaker, however, than in Britain or Germany. The warship-builders needed state support; in 1914 the workforce in the state arsenals was three times that doing defence work in the private sector;[80] in 1912 the Schneider plant at Le Creusot was worth barely one tenth of the capital invested in the Krupp installations.[81] Only in 1912–14 did the War Ministry order large numbers of complete heavy guns from Schneider, preferring until then to buy in components.[82] The army had rifle plants at Châtellerault, Tulle, and Saint Étienne—the latter of which was also a machine-gun manufacturer—and an artillery foundry at Bourges,[83] but on the eve of war the arsenals were operating at well below capacity and there were no plans to expand them.[84] French private industry probably had less influence than British or German on weapons design and production volume, and was geared to export and to naval markets rather than the shrunken and unreliable land armaments one. Although army spending on equipment recovered in 1906–7 and on the eve of war, its 1870s peak was never regained.

* * *

In the Habsburg monarchy the naval budget rose from a tenth to a quarter of defence spending between 1900 and 1913–14, much of the increase going to pri-

---

[77] Crouzet, 'Remarques', 415–20. Law of 14 Aug. 1885, *Bulletin des lois de la République*, 310 (1885), 464–6.

[78] *Notes sur les établissements de MM. Schneider et Cie* (Nevers, 1900). J.-A. Roy, *Histoire de la famille Schneider et du Creusot* (Paris, 1962), ch. 6. C. Beaud, 'Les Schneider "marchands de canons" ', European Univ. Institute Colloquium Paper 304/91 Col. 16 (Florence, 1991).

[79] Crouzet, 'Remarques', 419.

[80] J. F. Godfrey, *Capitalism at War: Industrial Policy and Bureaucracy in France, 1914–1918* (Leamington Spa, 1987), 2.

[81] Ibid. 257   [82] Crouzet, 'Remarques', 413.

[83] J. Clarke, 'Land Armaments in France: The Tradition of "Etatism" ', in B. F. Cooling (ed.), *War, Business, and World Military-Industrial Complexes* (Port Washington, NY, 1987), ch. 2. Y. Cayre, *Histoire de la manufacture d'armes de Tulle, de 1690 à 1970* (1970), 208–18.

[84] Godfrey, *Capitalism*, 45.

vate contractors.[85] The navy had a yard at Pola, but the Stabilmento tecnico at Trieste was the Monarchy's pre-eminent warship-builder. The firm had been founded in 1857 with an interest-free loan from Ferdinand Max, the then naval commandant and the Emperor's brother; it continued to benefit from dynastic favour and navy contracts.[86] In 1890 the Skoda steel and engineering firm at Pilsen moved at the navy's behest into shipboard artillery, and was soon followed by Wittkowitz in Moravia as an armour-plate producer.[87] The navy hoped thus to end its dependence on German special steels and heavy guns, which hampered it in winning parliamentary support. Skoda had become a competitor of Krupp, the suspension of whose supplies in the Austro-Prussian War of 1866 had prevented the Austrian flagship from putting to sea.[88] The new armaments complex figured prominently in the 1909 decision to build all-big-gun dreadnought battleships, the Stabilmento, Skoda, and Wittkowitz agreeing to start work on two vessels at their own risk until the navy won parliamentary credits. Business and naval leaders thus collaborated to pre-empt a legislative decision, the maintenance of activity in the shipyards being a leading motive, as it was in the next battleship order at the end of 1913.[89]

The Habsburg armament complex was concentrated in the more advanced 'Austrian' portion of the Dual Monarchy, although the Hungarian Government could be won round to naval building if its own half won sufficient orders, particularly for the Danubius yard at Fiume. In 1913 Skoda beat off Krupp and Vickers to win a contract for a Hungarian artillery plant at Györ.[90] A further feature of the complex was its concentrated ownership and its control by the banks. Skoda held one-third of the capital of the Stabilmento, and when the latter required a second yard in 1897 33 per cent of the extra share capital needed came from the Creditanstalt of Vienna, which led the reconstruction of Skoda itself as a limited liability company two years later. In 1910 the same bank provided one-third of an increase in Skoda's own share capital.[91] The Creditanstalt belonged to the Austro-German banking consortium known as the Rothschild group, which had a monopoly of state loans; another member of the consortium, the Boden Creditanstalt, managed the Emperor's private fortune. The head of the group, Albert de Rothschild, owned Wittkowitz, and in 1910 was thanked by the heir to the throne and naval enthusiast, Franz Ferdinand, for his role in

[85] L. Höbelt, 'Die Marine', in A. Wandruszka and P. Urbanitsch (eds.), *Die Habsburgermonarchie 1848–1914* (Vienna, 1985), v. 721.

[86] *50 Jahre Schiffbau, 1857–1907: Stablimento Tecnico Triestino* (Vienna, 1907).

[87] *Fünfundzwanzig Jahre der Aktiengesellschaft vormals Skodawerke in Pilsen* (Prague, 1925). G. Otruba, 'Emil Ritter von Skoda', in K. Bosl (ed.), *Lebensbilder zur Geschichte der Böhmischen Länder*, i. (Munich, 1974), 197–233. V. Prúcha, 'Development of the Skoda Works and its Role in Czechoslovak Industry up to the Year 1938', European Univ. Institute Colloquium Paper 309/91 Col. 21 (Florence, 1991). *100 Jahre Eisenwerke Witkowitz, 1828–1928* (1928).

[88] K. Skoda, 'Emil Ritter von Skoda', *Neue Österreichische Biographie*, iv (Vienna, 1927), 165. Report on Krupp relations with Vienna military authorities, 1893–1905, KAE W.A. VII f. 635.

[89] See Ch. 3, sect. 2, below.   [90] Höbelt, 'Marine', 754. Otruba, 'Skoda', 221.

[91] B. Michel, *Banques et banquiers en Autriche au début du 20e siècle* (Paris, 1976), 146, 180. E. März, *Österreichische Industrie-und Bank-politik in der Zeit Franz Josephs I* (Vienna, 1968), 303, 342.

dreadnought construction.[92] The naval-arms industry therefore had disguised but intimate connections with the Vienna banking and dynastic establishment. It bought off the Hungarians and was highly efficient, comfortably outdoing Italy in warship quality and construction times. For all these reasons it was a formidable competitor with the army for government finance.

The army produced munitions near Wiener Neustadt and rifles and artillery in the Arsenal at Vienna. The private small-arms industry was overshadowed by the Österreichische Waffenfabrik at Steyr, which had delivered rifles in the nineteenth century and manufactured the Schwarzlose machine gun, which the army adopted in 1908. None the less, the firm was troubled by a persistent shortage of government orders, for which exports did not compensate. In 1912 the Boden Creditanstalt discreetly purchased it.[93] Skoda supplied the army with fortress cupolas, and in conjunction with the War Ministry developed a mobile 30.5 cm mortar for assaulting reinforced concrete defences. The Skoda chief joined the board of Daimler, who provided the mortar with a motorized transport. In 1911 the War Minister ordered a consignment of mortars before receiving parliamentary sanction, Skoda starting work on them at its own risk.[94] But there was no more general private breakthrough into land artillery. Skoda supplied the gun carriages (*Lafetten*) for the M1905 8 cm quick-firer, but the steel-bronze barrel came from the Arsenal. The gun was inferior in performance and its production was slow. The army's heavy guns, also of bronze, lacked recoil systems and protective shields: by 1914 Skoda and the War Ministry had designed replacements, but these were only beginning to come into use.[95] In short, although Steyr and Skoda were among the leading European armaments companies, Steyr languished from lack of orders until the eve of war, and Skoda suffered from the military's conservatism and commitment to an in-house producer. The navy was much more dependent on the private sector; but a private sector that the state itself, acting through the Rothschild banks, had nurtured into life.

* * *

Every other European country had to rely at least in part either on imports or on local production by foreign-owned subsidiaries. Italy was unique among the Great Powers in the weakness of its indigenous defence industry. The army could produce its own small arms and artillery in workshops at Turin, Naples, and Terni;[96] the navy had an arsenal at La Spezia, which was its principal base, a shipyard at Castellamare, and docks at Naples and Venice.[97] Italy's civilian

---

[92] Michel, *Banques*, 99–128, 162, 351.

[93] Strachowsky, 'Waffen-Industrie', 137–44. Doppler, *Steyr-Werke*, 35–8. Michel, *Banques*, 162.

[94] W. Wagner, 'Die k. und k. Armee', in Wandruszka and Urbanitsch (eds.), *Habsburgermonarchie*, v. 450. H. Seper, '100 Jahre Steyr-Daimler-Puch A.G.', *Blätter für Technikgeschichte*, 26 (1964), 30, 83.

[95] G. E. Rothenberg, *The Army of Francis Joseph* (West Lafayette, 1976), 111, 174. Otruba, 'Skoda', 217–18.

[96] J. Whittam, *The Politics of the Italian Army* (London, 1977), 161. L. Segreto, 'Armament Industry and Italian Economic Development (1880s–1939)', European Univ. Institute Colloquium Paper 306/91 Col. 18 (Florence, 1991).

[97] Warren, *Armstrongs*, 71.

shipbuilding and engineering industries, however, were weaker than those north of the Alps, and when the Navy Ministry in the 1880s began to build a modern armaments complex, it had to turn for help from abroad. Schneider had a share in the Terni steel works, set up in 1884 to make fortress cupolas and armour-plate, and kept alive by interest-free loans and the navy's willingness to pay higher prices than for imports.[98] The Armstrong-Pozzuoli plant was set up to deliver naval guns, the unenthusiastic British company being warned that otherwise it stood to lose business. Warship hulls were built by the Orlando yard at Livorno, by Odero at Genoa, and by Ansaldo, just west of Genoa at Sestro Ponente.[99]

The pattern established in the 1880s was complicated by the pre-war upsurge in expenditure. In 1905-12 the navy placed 691 million lire of orders with the metallurgical industries, of which 85 million were outside Italy; the army placed respectively 507 and 81 million.[100] The authorities encouraged foreign armour producers to bid against Terni; new plants built by Ehrhardt and Schneider ended Armstrong's naval gun monopoly.[101] In 1905, with naval encouragement, Vickers, Orlando, and Odero set up the Vickers-Terni company, which produced warship guns and field artillery. Vickers held the largest shareholding and took 10 per cent of the profits, in practice shipping in from Britain much of the output of a company that had been intended to increase Italian self-sufficiency.[102] Both Vickers and Armstrong belonged to the so-called 'Trust', which included most of the armaments industry. The Trust was centred on the Banca Commerciale Italiana, which had a large shareholding in Vickers-Terni and controlled the older Terni concern, which in turn controlled the Orlando and Odero yards. The BCI was vilified, in fact unfairly, for being German-dominated; it did, however, enjoy connections with Giovanni Giolitti, who was Prime Minister for most of the pre-war decade.[103]

In Italy by the eve of war the old armour-plate and naval-gun monopolies had therefore been broken and foreign companies without indigenous partners were handicapped in seeking contracts. Independent producers were gaining prominence, including Fiat, which made Revelli machine guns and submarines, and Ansaldo, the leading non-Trust concern. Ansaldo produced ships, artillery, projectiles, and armour-plate, pleading in its favour 'the emancipation of the country from a dangerous enserfment to foreigners in the field of naval armaments'. Its owners, the Perrone family, bought out Armstrong's interests in the company, and although they had a technical co-operation agreement with Schneider,

[98] R. A. Webster, *Industrial Imperialism in Italy, 1908–1915* (Berkeley, 1975), 56–8. Report by French military attaché, 25 Nov. 1910, SHA 7.N. 1369.

[99] Warren, *Armstrongs*, chs. 10–11.

[100] G. Rochat and G. Massobrio, *Breve storia dell' esercito italiano dal 1861 al 1943* (Turin, 1978), 156.

[101] Webster, *Imperialism*, 55. Warren, *Armstrongs*, 122.

[102] L. Segreto, 'More Trouble than Profit: Vickers' Investment in Italy, 1906–39', *Business History*, 27 (1985), 317–19. Trebilcock, 'European Industrialization', 268. Webster, *Imperialism*, 73.

[103] Ibid. 78, 126–8, 145–60.

this was approved by the War Ministry and was not reinforced by interlocking shareholdings.[104] But the Italian yards still built slowly, and were held back by shortages of armour-plate. Of the forty-eight 12″ guns needed for four dread-noughts ordered in 1913, forty-five were ordered in Italy but only eighteen made there, the others being subcontracted back to Britain because the Italian firms were unable to perform the task.[105] Despite state protection through tariffs, high prices, and preferment of indigenous firms, Italy had still failed by 1914 to cre-ate a naval armaments complex that was either independent or adequate to meet the country's needs.

The same could be said of land armaments. On the eve of war the General Staff still contemplated going abroad for a new howitzer order, in order to escape the slow delivery and inferior steel of Italian industry, although in the end they went to Ansaldo.[106] French firms won orders for siege howitzers and fortress cupolas.[107] The field-gun modernization saga, however, best demonstrated Italy's vulnerability. The 75A gun, approved by Parliament in 1901 for production in state arsenals, lacked a recoil mechanism and was immediately rendered obsolete. In 1907 a secret deal made by the War Minister for Krupp, rather than the ar-senals, to supply quick-firers caused a scandal. In 1912 an order for another 480 guns to complete the re-equipping went to a consortium of Trust firms, who successfully played the nationalist card against Krupp even though their gun's designer was Colonel Deport of Châtillon-Commentry. The consortium imme-diately fell behind schedule, and in 1914 the Italian army, uniquely, had neither a standard quick-firing model nor a full quick-firer complement. Italy was one of the best examples in Europe of successful wirepulling by business interests to gain state subsidy and protection, by exploiting the authorities' desire to assure their independence in armaments. But domestic industry still needed foreign expertise, patents, and capital, and even with this assistance its warship and artillery capacity was choked by 1913–14. Not only was Italy marginal in European diplomacy: it was a laggard in the armaments race.

* * *

Neither of these things was true of the remaining Great Power. Whereas Italy, moreover, had a unusually weak state sector, Russia's armaments industry remained state-dominated until the last years before the war. The tsarist Industry Minister explained to Parliament that state enterprises would not go bankrupt and could be depended on to fulfil their orders.[108] Important parts of state production, however, operated under foreign licence, and much of the plant

---

[104] Webster, *Imperialism*, 76, 81–2. Reports by French military attaché, 21 Feb. 1910, SHA 7.N. 1369, and 11 July 1913, SHA 7.N. 1370. Warren, *Armstrongs*, 123–5.

[105] Webster, *Imperialism*, 165.

[106] French attaché reports, 31 May 1909 and 6 July 1910, SHA 7N 1369; and 10 Mar. 1912, SHA 7N 1370.

[107] See further discussion in Ch. 3, sect. 2, and Ch. 4, sect. 2, below.

[108] K. F. Shatsillo, *Russkii imperializm i razvitie flota nakanune pervoi mirovoi voiny (1906–1914 gg)* (Moscow, 1968), 210.

was antiquated. Although the service ministries agitated for modernization, they made little headway.

Land armaments may be assessed first. The leading private concern was Putilov in St Petersburg. It had its own shipyard, and produced munitions and artillery. It had technical agreements with Schneider, but was Russian-owned. It was also badly managed, overextended, and plagued with debt.[109] No other private firm could produce complete guns, but the army had first-class arsenals at St Petersburg, Briansk, and Kiev, and could draw on the Navy Ministry's Obukhov works and that of the Mining Ministry at Perm. Perm, Putilov, and Obukhov manufactured the 76 mm quick-firing field guns that Russia, in contrast to Italy, adopted early and successfully. Heavy artillery came from the same three plants and the army's own establishments, although partly because of repeated changes in specification production was tardy. Shells were mostly contracted out, but explosives were state-produced, using chemicals purchased from Germany. Small arms came from army arsenals, notably Tula, which made Maxim guns under licence from Vickers. Private-sector penetration had therefore not gone far, and once re-equipment with the Mosin magazine rifle was completed the arsenals were reduced to a very low level of output and most of their workers were laid off. Despite years of War Ministry complaints, expansion of small-arms, fuse, and explosives capacity began only in 1913–14.[110]

In naval armaments too the private sector was small and weak. Five private concerns could do important naval work, including the Putilov and Nevskii yards at St Petersburg and Naval' at Nicolaiev, adjoining the Black Sea. These three were operating at one-quarter of capacity for a decade before 1908, when Nevskii pulled out of shipbuilding. Naval' was beset by creditors and on the verge of a similar decision before it was saved by an upturn in orders.[111] Warship-building was therefore largely a state-owned operation, and concentrated round St Petersburg. The Admiralty and Baltic yards, on opposite banks of the Neva, were the biggest in Russia; the Izhora plant made armour-plate, and Obukhov made naval guns from French and British specifications. The state yards at the turn of the century were poorly equipped, heavily indebted, and incompetently run by officers of mediocre ability. It took twice as long to build a capital ship in Russia as in Britain, Austria, or Germany, and even with cheap labour it cost up to one-third more. When in 1904–5 most of the navy went to the bottom of the ocean there was no money to replace it, and little physical capacity.[112]

[109] R. Girault, 'Finances internationales et relations internationales (à propos des usines Poutiloff)', *Revue d'histoire moderne et contemporaine*, 13 (1966), 217–36.

[110] L. S. Beskrovny, 'Proizvodstvo vooruzheniia i boepripasov dlia armii v Rossii v period imperializma (1898–1917 gg)', *Istorichiskie Zapiski*, 99 (1977), 88–139. P. W. Gatrell, *Government, Industry, and Rearmament in Russia, 1900–1914: The Last Argument of Tsarism* (Cambridge, 1994) is fundamental on Russian armaments: ch. 1 gives a survey of the industry. I am indebted for the opportunity to have seen a copy of this book in typescript.

[111] Shatsillo, *Russkii imperializm*, 226–31.

[112] Ibid. 210–17. Gatrell, *Last Argument*, ch. 1. French naval attaché reports, 1 Feb., 10, 23, and 25 Mar., and 20 Apr. 1911, SHM BB7 121. For shipbuilding times, report of 1 Nov. 1913, SHM SS(Ea) 160.

There were two lines of response. The state yards were kept in being to provide a yardstick for judging commercial tenders, but in 1908 were given more autonomy and permitted a regulated profit, although they were expected to finance investment without recourse to state aid. This was unrealistic, and they were in grave financial difficulty before the boom in government orders after 1911 allowed them to modernize and to expand their labour force.[113] Even now, they were quickly overwhelmed. In 1911 Turkey ordered battleships from Britain with 13.5″ guns: Obukhov could not match this, and it was decided to build new Black Sea battleships with only 12″ armament. Their gun turrets and plate had to be imported.[114] The second new departure after 1905 was to expand the foreign presence in the Russian defence industry. Naval guns, turrets, fire-control systems, boilers, and turbines already copied French and British designs, and the wireless equipment came from Telefunken. Putilov's artillery used Schneider and Krupp designs,[115] Hotchkiss provided machine guns, and Saint-Chamond furnished fortress cupolas.[116] The Navy Ministry rarely purchased complete warships from abroad, however, preferring to order from home industry even if it cost more. In 1907 the Council of Ministers tightened up further, resolving that henceforth all naval programmes must be realized 'in Russian factories, from Russian materials, and with Russian workers'.[117] The Industry Ministry, echoing the wishes of Russian business, wanted as much as possible built at home, as did the Finance Ministry in order to save foreign exchange.[118] Due to the Government's reluctance to import or to expand state capacity commensurately with the new volume of naval orders, and given the continuing technological dependence on the West, the period after 1909 witnessed the emergence of a huge new private shipbuilding industry on the shores of the Baltic and Black Seas, in which British, French, German, and Austrian firms formed partnerships with domestic producers.[119] It came too late to provide a fleet before the outbreak of war. None the less, in Russian naval armaments, a generation later than elsewhere, private-sector interests staged a breakthrough, and it was in shipbuilding that business interests most discernibly influenced policy. They strengthened the authorities' mercantilist predilections, but failed to overcome Finance Ministry tight-fistedness until the economy and state revenues recovered after 1909 from war, revolution, and depression. Land armaments production, in contrast, remained state-dominated, was starved of funds and manpower, and changed very slowly, except for Putilov, down to the out-

---

[113] P. W. Gatrell, 'After Tsushima: Economic and Administrative Aspects of Russian Naval Rearmament, 1905–1913', *Economic History Review*, NS 43 (1990), 255–70. French naval attaché, 15 Apr. 1912, SHM BB7 121.

[114] Shatsillo, *Russkii imperializm*, 224. French naval staff monthly bulletin for Mar./Apr. 1914, SHM SS(Ea) 160.

[115] French naval attaché, 1 Feb. and 23 Mar. 1911, SHM BB7 121.

[116] Note by French 2nd Bureau, 7 Oct. 1909, SHA 7.N. 1539. Note by Section technique of French War Ministry, 15 May 1912, SHA 7.N. 1486.

[117] K. F. Shatsillo, 'Inostrannyi kapital i voenno-morskie programmy Rossii nakanune pervoi mirovoi voiny', *Istorichiskie Zapiski*, 69 (1961), 73.

[118] Gatrell, 'After Tsushima', 261. [119] See Ch. 6, sect. 1, below.

break of war. Little here supports a military-industrial complex interpretation of Russian participation in the Continental arms race.

* * *

Outside the charmed circle of Great Powers the smaller countries might have state arsenals, such as Serbia's Kragujevac, or dockyards, as did the Ottoman Empire. To equip their forces to the highest standards, however, they had to look to the Western European armaments concerns. Belgium, despite its advanced industrialization, exemplifies the predicament. Its defence output was centred on Liège, close to the German frontier. The two state arsenals in the city were diminutive, and orders went mainly to the private sector. The latter included, in small arms, the Fabrique nationale d'armes at Herstal, in which the DWMF had a substantial holding; and the American producer, Browning. Cockerill, at Seraing, manufactured field and fortress artillery, but could not satisfy requirements alone.[120] The crucial order for quick-firing field guns went to Krupp after it outperformed Saint-Chamond in trials, and Krupp also won a contract for heavy coastal guns in the massive new fortress ring being planned round Antwerp. There was no obstacle, it will be seen, to Krupp supplying a potential enemy.[121]

In the later nineteenth century, there had emerged a pattern of international arms trading that in some ways has persisted ever since: East Asia, Latin America, Russia, and the Balkans being the largest markets. Western European governments fostered private industries that were too big for their peacetime needs, in order to secure reserve capacity. Arms sales brought political influence, jobs, and tax revenue for the supplier; for the purchaser, dependence on a private company was preferable to dependence on a government. All the main Western and Central European companies were exporters, but British, French, and German firms dominated, and in warships Armstrong and Vickers held much the largest share of the trade.[122] Krupp had led the field in land artillery, with Armstrong its only serious rival, until the emergence of the French exporters in the 1890s. In the pre-war decade Krupp was far ahead of Ehrhardt, and Schneider led Saint-Chamond. In 1885–1914 Schneider exported over 40,000 cannon to twenty-three countries, and Krupp's sales were of comparable magnitude.[123] The moral and pragmatic arguments against the trade had all been developed by 1914, although as yet they made little impact. To sell arms, it was alleged, was to treat death-dealing instruments as if they were an ordinary commodity; it caused instability and war; weapons were sold by bribery in the client country and sustained manipulative interests in the exporting one: in short, the traffic debauched both parties to it.[124]

---

[120] French military attaché reports, 23 Dec. 1909, SHA 7.N. 1156 and 15 Mar and 22 Dec. 1911, SHA 7.N. 1157.

[121] French attaché report, 27 Jan. 1906, SHA 7.N. 1155. Report by Belgian commission of inquiry into the Antwerp (Lower Scheldt) purchase, 5 June 1913, AGRB, Papiers de Broqueville, #307.

[122] Trebilcock, *Vickers Brothers*, 122.

[123] Manchester, *Krupp*, 114–15. 'Verzeichnis der von der Gussstahlfabrik und von Grusonwerk von 1847 bis 1912 gefertigten Kanonen', KAE Library S3WT1/3. Roy, *Schneider*, 89.

[124] Noel-Baker, *Armaments*, i, *passim*.

Arms sales presented dilemmas as well as opportunities for governments, especially if weapons went to politically unstable regions or to potential enemies. The authorities mostly opted, however, for freedom of export over national security considerations. Krupp had sold to Austria before the war of 1866; in the American Civil War Armstrong sold to both Union and Confederacy. In 1911–12 Italy fought an Ottoman opponent much of whose fleet had been built or modernized by Italian firms; meanwhile, Armstrong and Vickers were each building a super-dreadnought for a Turkish sultan against whom the General Staff in London was preparing war plans. In 1914 the Russian fleet included twenty-three vessels built in Germany, and it was embarrassed when Berlin cut off electrical, wireless, optical, and explosive supplies.[125] Krupp was developing the *M-Gerät* to smash Belgian fortresses that the same firm had helped upgrade.[126] Armour-plate producers co-operated across the diplomatic fault lines in the Harvey and Krupp steel syndicates; in 1901 Vickers licensed the DWMF to manufacture Maxim guns, and in 1902 Krupp licensed Vickers to make Krupp time fuses.[127] The armaments industry was cosmopolitan and profit-oriented, and official Europe gave it its head. Germany sold to Russia and Belgium; France and Britain to Turkey and Italy; and both sides competed in the Balkans. This same cosmopolitanism, however, makes it difficult to invoke the arms trade as a cause, rather than a facilitator, of intra-bloc competition.

Governments did not merely tolerate arms sales: they promoted them. The French did so most aggressively, and after the turn of the century forced Germany on to the defensive. The Balkans was the arena in which arms sales brought most political influence, and here Britain sold little[128] and Austria-Hungary's presence was on the wane, clearing the field for a Krupp–Schneider duel in which both firms were supported by their Foreign Ministries.[129] In Berlin the Ministry supplied Krupp with attaché and consular reports about possible opportunities, and the company briefed the military authorities about its sales.[130] The Foreign Ministry consulted the military before authorizing exports, but generally permitted them.[131] It urged accommodation on Krupp and Ehrhardt when possible, and observed neutrality when it was not, backing whichever performed better in trials. This normally meant Krupp and Ehrhardt repeatedly accused the Ministry of favouritism.[132] The French and British firms

[125] Noel-Baker, *Armaments*, i. 190–1. Shatsillo, *Russkii imperializm*, 225.

[126] Manchester, *Krupp*, 196, 317.   [127] Scott, *Vickers*, 86–8.

[128] Trebilcock, 'Legends', 6.

[129] R. Poidevin, 'Fabricants d'armes et relations internationales au début du XXe siècle', *Relations internationales*, 1 (1974), 39–56; and the same author's *Les Relations économiques et financières entre la France et l'Allemagne de 1898 à 1914* (Paris, 1969) are highly informative. See also L. Hilbert, 'Der Zunehmende Waffenexport seit den 1890er Jahren', in F. Klein and K. Otmar von Aretin (eds.), *Europa um 1900* (Berlin, 1989), 59–72.

[130] Krupp–Foreign Ministry correspondence in KAE FAH. IV. E61. Krupp briefings of War Minister in KAE FAH. IV. E63.

[131] For the regulatory process at work during the First Balkan War, PAAA R. 927, Waffenverkäufe, 1912–13.

[132] Marschall to Bülow, 23 Feb. 1906, Kiderlen-Wächter to Bülow 12 Feb. 1906, Tschirschky to

made market-sharing deals more readily, and the Essen–Düsseldorf duel damaged German effectiveness. The Foreign Ministry organized press campaigns against the French and sometimes made diplomatic *démarches*, but in the Balkan armaments competition Germany was outclassed.

Like the Germans the French monitored their exports, and the French Foreign Ministry, the Quai d'Orsay, briefed the arms firms on commercial possibilities.[133] The firms requested diplomatic backing, often received it, found it effective, and gave their thanks. This backing was given through representations by diplomatic and military missions, press manipulation, arranged visits to plants in France, and bribes. France's greatest advantage over Germany, however, was the larger size and lower interest rates of the Paris capital market. The authorities could withhold quotation from foreign loans they disapproved of, and encourage bond issues that they wanted to succeed. They co-operated with bankers and industrialists in tying loans to military and civilian contracts.[134] In Bulgaria financial pressure helped Schneider win the main quick-firing order in 1904; in Greece France squeezed out Germany as a land supplier and gained on it in the naval sector. Schneider entered the Romanian artillery market in 1912, presaging a change of allegiance by a country hitherto allied to the Central Powers. In Serbia Franco-German financial co-operation broke down in 1903, partly because of artillery rivalry. Raymond Poincaré, then Finance Minister, wrote to the Quai d'Orsay that 'the nation that wins the loan and war material orders will consolidate its influence on the Serb Government'.[135] After months of manœuvring against Krupp and Skoda, Schneider won the quick-firer re-equipment contract in 1906, and the French Groupe Naville took the lead in a 4 per cent loan, which was followed by further artillery loans in 1909 and 1913. Although Serbia was already moving in an anti-Austrian direction, this was a turning-point in the Balkan arms race.

* * *

The mid-nineteenth-century upheaval in armaments technology was followed by another at the century's end. As weaponry grew more costly and more complex, state arsenals and dockyards lost their quasi-monopoly. Even in naval armaments, however, the new private firms did not usurp control over defence policy, although regular orders were needed to sustain them and political constituencies agitated on their behalf. In land armaments the private-sector presence and the pace of innovation were much weaker. Everywhere there was a spending upsurge on field-artillery renewal, but by the onset of the great pre-war expansion this renewal was largely complete. Artillery sales exacerbated tensions in the Balkan peninsula, but these tensions originated in local political and territorial rivalries that were independent of the exporting Powers. Examination

Rheinmetall, 8 Dec. 1906, Krupp to Bülow, 6 Nov. 1906, PAAA R. 925. Krupp to Jagow, 16 June 1913, PAAA R. 927.

[133] Prefects' returns on arms exports in AN F7 12810.
[134] For what follows, Poidevin, *Relations*, 317–27, 674–5.
[135] Ibid. 325. See further Ch. 2, sect. 2 below.

of the industrial wing of the armaments complex does not suggest it had decisive influence on the great pre-war acceleration. For a complete picture to be given, however, it must be seen in conjunction with the military establishment.

3. Armies and governments

The analysis thus far has questioned whether technological change could modify armaments policy unless in conjunction with political pressures. As a vehicle for applying such pressures, the private armaments industry seems inadequate. Technological dynamism and incitement by the private manufacturers might seem plausible explanations for the Anglo-German naval race, but the resurgence of the Continental arms race demanded a redirection of resources towards a more conservative and state-dominated land armaments industry. If we seek a military-industrial lobby, therefore, it may be within the public sector that we shall find it.

'The situation is extraordinary', reported the American President's special envoy to Europe in May 1914, 'It is militarism run stark mad.'[136] 'Militarism' may mean a pretension by the military leadership to determine government policy; or it may refer more broadly to military claims on economic resources, and to military influence on political behaviour and on social institutions and values. 'Militarization', by contrast, is the measure of how far such aspirations have succeeded. It may be quantifiable—defence spending as a percentage of net national product, the proportion of 21-year-olds conscripted—but it also implies a more elusive permeation of mentalities.[137] Although the influence of the military in politics is likely to reflect their status in society as a whole, it is on civil–military relations in the narrow sense that attention here will concentrate. The role of navies as a rival claimant will be left to later chapters.

The 'military' for this purpose means the upper ranks of the officer corps. As career soldiers commissioned to exercise command, they had chosen to specialize in managing violence. They tended to form self-selecting oligarchies—promotion in France for example, until 1899, was decided by 'classification commissions' in which civilians had little say. In Prussia, until 1902, to become a regimental officer required a character testimonial by the commander and a unanimous 'judgement of worth' by one's fellows.[138] Everywhere, aristocrats were concentrated in the senior posts, although except in France this applied in civilian government also.

[136] House to Wilson, 29 May 1914. C. M. Seymour (ed.), *The Intimate Papers of Colonel House* (4 vols., London, 1926–8), i. 255.

[137] V. R. Berghahn, *Militarism: The History of an International Debate, 1861–1979* (Cambridge, 1981), chs. 1, 6. B. Bond, *War and Society in Europe, 1870–1970* (London, 1984), 58–70. G. F. A. Best, 'The Militarization of European Society, 1870–1914' in J. R. Gillis (ed.), *The Militarization of the Western World* (London, 1989), 13–29.

[138] R. Girardet, *La Société militaire dans la France contemporaine (1875–1939)* (Paris, 1953), 197. M. Kitchen, *The German Officer Corps, 1890–1914* (Oxford, 1968), 29. A. Bucholz, *Moltke, Schlieffen and Prussian War Planning* (New York, 1991), 141.

This picture, however, is misleadingly static. The nineteenth-century military revolution was not only technological, it was organizational. The wars of 1866 and 1870 had shown that conscript armies could overwhelm professional ones, provided that they had superior numbers and were thoroughly prepared. The Prussian formula for victory was a short-service peacetime army, rapidly reinforced on mobilization by a trained reserve, and meticulous planning by the Great General Staff (GGS). The formula was imitated, more or less, by the other Powers apart from Britain. As the officer corps expanded, however, it became less exclusive, and the staff system encouraged professionalization and specialization that weakened its cohesiveness. In the Prussian officer corps between 1865 and 1914 the proportion of noblemen fell from 65 to 30 per cent. Most corps commanders remained aristocrats, but by 1913 70 per cent of the GGS were commoners by birth—which is not to say that they did not submit to the army's aristocratic ethos.[139] In Austria-Hungary, too, aristocratic preponderance was slipping; in Russia in 1895–1912 it fell from three-quarters to a half.[140]

The new General Staffs trained up the intellectual cream of their armies for war preparation. Their concerns, however, were largely with intelligence, strategic planning, tactical doctrine, and training. Finance, manpower, transport, and equipment lay more in the domain of War Ministries, and in all the Powers after 1906 parliamentary approval was required for the necessary legislation and for budgetary estimates. The essential question is that of the effectiveness of the professional military—the leaders of the officer corps in the War Ministry, the General Staff, and the senior command positions—in extracting the manpower and finance needed to give their planning significance. It varied over time. The 1880s and early 1890s witnessed a land race that foreshadowed that of 1912–14. The Continental alliances were falling into place; there were simultaneous crises in Western and in Eastern Europe; and diplomatic and military alignments coincided. The armies of the Powers enjoyed generous funding and made rapid progress. But from the mid-1890s Franco-German and Austro-Russian antagonisms eased, and naval and colonial rivalries, which cut athwart the axes of the alliance system, came to the fore. Army planning continued, but supplies of men and money diminished. By 1900 the Continental armies stood on the threshold of stagnation or worse; ten years later the cycle had completed another turn. The concern here is with the framework in which priorities were set, and the discussion should start at the birthplace of the nineteenth-century revolution in military organization, in Berlin.

* * *

The German Empire was Prussian-dominated. There was an all-German navy, under the Imperial Navy Office and Navy Secretary, but Prussia, Saxony,

---

[139] K. Demeter, *The German Officer Corps in Society and State, 1640–1945* (London, 1965), 28. Bucholz, *War Planning*, 3.

[140] I. Deák, *Beyond Nationalism: A Social and Political History of the Habsburg Officer Corps, 1848–1918* (New York, 1990), 163. A. K. Wildman, *The End of the Russian Imperial Army: The Old Army and the Soldiers' Revolt* (Princeton, 1980), 21–3.

Bavaria, and Württemberg kept separate armies, General Staffs, and War Ministers, the Prussian Minister representing them in the imperial Parliament. The Prussian King became German Emperor and had command authority over the smaller armies (Bavaria's only in time of war), which copied Prussian training, organization, and equipment. The GGS drew up imperial war plans, and district commands under its mobilization section and line commands under its railway section extended its authority throughout the land.[141]

The imperial constitution replicated the uneasy amalgam of autocratic and representative principles to be found in its Prussian exemplar. According to article 63 the Emperor 'determines the peace-time strength, the structure, and the distribution of the imperial army', but article 60 prescribed that the peacetime strength was to be regulated by legislation.[142] This followed the Prussian distinction between the sovereign's 'command sphere' of untrammelled authority and the 'military administration sphere' in which his actions required ministerial countersignature and parliamentary consent. The first included training, discipline, appointments, and military operations; the second included size, recruitment, supply, equipment, and everything costing money. The Emperor's command powers were thus circumscribed; they were exercised not through a hierarchy of subordinate authorities but through a multiplicity of conflicting and coequal ones, the so-called *Immediatstellen*, some forty in number, each able to report to him without intermediary.[143] This decentralization created opportunities for great confusion in the absence of co-ordination, which Wilhelm failed to provide. He took his command powers seriously and decided the basic features of defence policy, as well as intervening in detail in the drafting of army laws and the design of battleships. Yet he was normally in Berlin continuously only from January to May, spending one-third of his reign on his yacht, and much of the rest of it hunting. He combined lack of application, posturing, and erratic judgement with inconsistency, a penchant for meddling, and an inability to delegate.[144] Although in the end he normally backed his Ministers, they could never be sure that they enjoyed his confidence without, at the least, wearying bureaucratic infighting.

In 1883 the War Ministry lost its personnel responsibilities to the Emperor's Military Cabinet, which became an *Immediatstelle*. The Chief of the General Staff (CGS) also gained the right of direct access.[145] The changes seemed to strengthen two rival power centres to the Ministry, neither of which came under parliamentary surveillance. The Military Cabinet, from which a Naval Cabinet

[141] Reichsarchiv, *Der Weltkrieg, 1914–1918: Kriegsrüstung und Kriegswirtschaft* (Berlin, 1930), i. 1–2. H. Meier-Welcke and W. von Groote (eds.), *Handbuch der deutschen Militärgeschichte 1648–1939* (Frankfurt, 1968), v. 53–5.

[142] G. A. Craig, *The Politics of the Prussian Army, 1640–1945* (London, 1964), 219.

[143] Meier-Welcke and von Groote, eds., *Handbuch*, v. 62.

[144] Bucholz, *War Planning*, 135. H. H. Herwig, *The German Naval Officer Corps: A Social and Political History, 1890–1918* (Oxford, 1973), 28. G. A. Ritter, *The Sword and the Scepter: The Problem of Militarism in Germany*, ii (Coral Gables, Fla., 1970), 119–23.

[145] Craig, *Politics*, 226–32.

was split off in 1889, handled the sovereign's correspondence with the army authorities. Its chief belonged to the so-called military entourage and the 'Imperial Headquarters': Wilhelm ordinarily saw him three times a week, whereas he saw the Imperial Chancellor and the Chief of the General Staff only once. Yet the Cabinet was too small to rival the administrative and policy functions of the GGS and War Ministry, and General von Lyncker, its chief after 1908, was self-effacing. It was concerned to maintain the exclusiveness of the officer corps, and for this reason opposed expansion, but that the War Ministry shared such views, for technical as well as social reasons, was politically much more significant.[146]

The GGS might seem a far more dangerous competitor to the Ministry. Under Helmuth von Moltke the elder, its chief in 1857–88, it earned the veneration due to an institution that supposedly had won the unification wars. The terminology needs clarification. The 'general staff' was an élite within the Prussian officer corps, numbering about 650 men in 1914.[147] Its members were recruited exclusively from successful graduates of the staff course at the War Academy, entrance to which was by competitive examination among serving officers. The 'troop general staff' comprised staff officers serving with the commanders of divisions, army corps, and fortresses: they alternated between this and service with the 'Great General Staff' in Berlin. It is to the latter that the term 'General Staff' will refer when used here. Staff officers with the line units did not exercise command, but supervised an enormous range of duties on the commander's behalf, with the intention that central planning and doctrine should be informed by line experience but should also guide the unit commands. The Great General Staff and the troop general staff were the army's brain and nerves.

It was understood that the Chief of the General Staff would direct operations if war came. On him, in the hour of supreme emergency, the destiny of the fatherland rested, and he and the GGS had primary responsibility for preparedness in so far as this did not impinge on the military budget. Terms of service were long. Count Alfred von Schlieffen held the post from 1891 to 1906 and Helmuth von Moltke (nephew of the earlier chief) from 1906 to 1914. By the latter date Moltke had five deputies, heading sections dealing with mobilization, concentration, and operational planning; other subdivisions existed for foreign intelligence, military history, staff training, manœuvres, and cartography. Troop training and tactical doctrine also came within the GGS's purview. It was not stinted for funds, and its intelligence service was unrivalled. Prussia had led the Powers into exchanging military attachés, themselves staff officers who

---

[146] W. Deist, 'Die Armee in Staat und Gesellschaft, 1890–1914', in M. Stürmer (ed.), *Das Kaiserliche Deutschland: Politik und Gesellschaft, 1870–1918* (Düsseldorf, 1970), 312–15. Craig, *Politics*, 238–41. I. V. Hull, *The Entourage of Kaiser Wilhelm II, 1888–1918* (Cambridge, 1982), 247–8.

[147] Meier-Welcke and von Groote (eds.), *Handbuch*, v. 71, for this figure and an explanation of the terminology; cf. W. Bronsart von Schellendorf, *The Duties of the General Staff* (4th edn., London, 1905).

reported to their chief, and who constituted a military information-gathering system in parallel with the older diplomatic one. Section IIIb of the GGS, specializing in military intelligence, supplemented the attachés' efforts by means of espionage, frontier observation, and monitoring the military press, as well as by preparing appraisals.[148]

The annually revised mobilization and concentration plan, however, was the core of GGS concern. By the 1890s it was in four parts. Mobilization meant the movement of reservists, horses, weapons, and supplies to concentration points, where they joined their units and raised them to war strength before progressing to a railway embarkation station. Prussia had a territorial mobilization system, each army corps having a separate military district in which its new recruits and its reservists resided and were called up for service and for training. The second stage was the military travel plan, the trains rolling at uniform speeds to the border railheads; the third the concentration of detrained forces on the frontier; and the fourth deployment prior to operations. Arden Bucholz has underlined the importance of the second stage as the one most easily accelerated by technical changes such as longer rail lengths, more and stronger locomotives, and better signalling. By the twentieth century, when Germany faced a possible two-front war with far larger forces than in 1870, the GGS's mobilization and railway sections, staffed by technicians of overwhelmingly middle-class origin, had become its innermost sanctum, sole possessors of a philosopher's stone of power and knowledge.[149]

It is tempting, given the prominence of the Schlieffen–Moltke war plan in 1914, to overstate the CGS's role. In peacetime his command and inspection functions were largely confined to the general staff. His constitutional position was advisory.[150] The elder Moltke had clashed with Bismarck by favouring preventive war against France in 1875 and Russia in 1887, but had bowed to the Chancellor's will. His successor, Waldersee, tried to use the military attachés as an independent diplomatic network, but in 1890 Wilhelm ruled that they must keep to technical matters and leave political reporting to their ambassadors, who were to scrutinize their dispatches. Both Schlieffen and the younger Moltke normally steered clear of foreign policy and deferred to the civilians. Not military interference but the divorce between diplomacy and strategic planning became the hallmark of German decision-making. Schlieffen planned for victory in a two-front war by enveloping the French via Luxemburg and Belgium (and, until Moltke's alterations, the Netherlands too). He sounded out the Foreign Ministry about the violations of neutrality, but was not challenged. Because of the immense prestige of the GGS, its responsibility for national safety, and its access to the Emperor, the plan rested on a technical judgement, derived from railway

---

[148] von Schellendorf, *The Duties of the General Staff*, 170. H. H. Herwig, 'Imperial Germany' in E. R. May (ed.), *Knowing One's Enemies: Intelligence before the Two World Wars* (Princeton, 1984), ch. 3.
[149] Bucholz, *War Planning*, 150–1, 166–74. See, however, the comments in H. F. A. Strachan, 'Germany in the First World War: The Problem of Strategy', *German History*, 12 (1994), 237–49.
[150] Meier-Welcke and von Groote, eds., *Handbuch*, v. 70.

capacities and inferences from military history, with little admixture of political circumspection. The GGS's sovereignty in its own domain, however, was offset by its lack of say in others: not only diplomacy, but also the material aspects of war preparation that came under the War Ministry.[151]

This is not to deny the Great General Staff all influence on armaments policy. Schlieffen helped to introduce light field howitzers, and the younger Moltke the *M-Gerät*. But it frequently dissented from the Ministry over finance and legislation, the Chancellor and the Emperor interceding when necessary between the two. In 1881 Bismarck backed the elder Moltke in favouring a modest strength increase that the Minister opposed. By the time of the 1887 army bill, all three desired expansion. The 1893 bill, however, was far less than Schlieffen wanted against the Franco-Russian alliance, but the Minister and Chancellor thought it adequate and he failed to impose his views. When he devised his war plan he feared it lay beyond the army's capacity.[152]

In the land arms race in manpower and *matériel*, the War Ministry was pivotal. Its central department prepared the budget; its general war department had sections for each main arm. The Minister, normally a general on the active list, swore potentially contradictory oaths to the King-Emperor and to the Prussian and imperial constitutions. He held an invidious intermediary position between Emperor, Chancellor, GGS, and Military Cabinet, and had to struggle for resources against the Navy and Finance Offices. Bismarck and his successors as Chancellor periodically asserted their right to intervene in policy details, and budgetary and legislative proposals needed their support. As the army's principal spokesman in the imperial legislature, however, the Minister was best placed to set priorities among his services' needs and to judge what was politically feasible.[153]

The 1871 constitution tried to base autocracy on consent, in an urbanizing and industrializing society. The upper house of Parliament, the Bundesrat, represented the constituent states; the lower house, the Reichstag, was elected by universal male suffrage. Imperial budgets and legislation needed Reichstag consent, but ministers were neither members of it nor responsible to it. They were appointed by the Chancellor, who himself was appointed and dismissed by the Emperor, irrespective of the parliamentary majority. Without such a majority, however, the system could not work, and although the authorities contemplated tearing up the constitution and ruling by decree, they refrained from doing so. There was much friction, but no breakdown.

The army was central to the constitutional question. It absorbed most of the budget; it conscripted the young men of the nation; it was the ultimate guarantor of the autocracy; and it was controversial for historical reasons dating from

[151] Craig, *Politics*, ch. 7. Ritter, *Sword*, ii, ch. 7. J. Snyder, *The Ideology of the Offensive: Military Decision Making and the Disasters of 1914* (Ithaca, NY, 1984), chs. 4, 5.

[152] Reichsarchiv, *Weltkrieg*, i. 12–20, 43–5.

[153] Meier-Welcke and von Groote, eds., *Handbuch*, v. 63–6. H. O. Meisner, *Der Kriegsminister, 1814–1914: Ein Beitrag zur militärischen Verfassungsgeschichte* (Berlin, 1940).

the 1848–9 revolutions and the 1860s 'era of conflict' between Crown and Parliament. The Prussian army bill of 1860 proposed to increase the standing army and extend service in it from two years to three. Conversely, it restricted the autonomy of the *Landwehr*, a citizen force, as well as reducing it in size and denying it offensive weapons. The liberal majority in Parliament did not necessarily oppose military expansion, but it did object to bolstering the authority of the officer corps and the Crown. As Minister President from 1862 Bismarck implemented the reforms extraconstitutionally and in 1866 split the liberals by securing the passage of an indemnity bill that retrospectively sanctioned the necessary expenditure. His achievement helped provide the manpower needed for the elder Moltke's victories, and set precedents after 1870 both for the military system of the Empire and for the weakness of its parliamentary control.[154]

Legislation in 1871 generalized the Prussian system. On reaching 20, conscripts did three years of full-time service in the standing army. They followed it by four years in the reserves, during which time they were liable for recall from civilian life for two periods of training. After five years in the reorganized *Landwehr*, now with regular officers and NCOs, they served in the *Landsturm*, a territorial force, until the age of 42. If well-to-do they might become 'one-year volunteers', paying for their food, clothes, and equipment, but doing only twelve months' active service before becoming reserve officers. New recruits joined up each year on 1 November and first did individual basic training. By 1 April they could join their units for exercises in formation, culminating in September with the imperial manœuvres. The beginning of November was also when those who had completed their active service were released, and as successive cohorts of young men passed through the system, the trained reserve grew. In wartime the field army would comprise the peacetime units of the active army, brought up to war strength by the younger reservist classes; reserve formations, which in peacetime existed only as cadres but would be made up by reservists and *Landwehr*; and some mobilized *Landwehr* units. The occupation army, composed of the remaining *Landwehr* and *Landsturm*, was for home defence and garrison duty and to replace casualties. Between 1 April and 30 October the army was at maximum peacetime readiness, the new recruits now trained and disciplined to fight in their formations, and reservists called up for summer exercises. This was also the time of year when the most food was available on the land to sustain the soldiers and the 800,000 horses that the German army expected to use for cavalry and for transport. In all the European armies it was well understood that these six months, especially the weeks following the harvest, were the most likely season for the outbreak of war.[155]

According to the constitution, all German men were personally liable to serve. How many actually did so depended on government policy and negotiations with the Reichstag. Legislation in 1874 set the army's peacetime strength for seven years and implicitly bound Parliament to vote the requisite funds, thus compro-

---

[154] Craig, *Politics*, ch. 4.
[155] Meier-Welcke and von Groote, eds., *Handbuch*, v. 49–51. Bucholz, *War Planning*, 60–2, 162.

mising its powers in the annual negotiations over the budget. It also, however, set a precedent for the army's peacetime strength and for its unit composition (the number of army corps at one extreme and of infantry battalions, artillery batteries, and cavalry squadrons at the other) to be determined by legislation rather than decree. After further septennial laws in 1881 and 1887, the government in 1893 agreed to a five-year term, or *Quinquennat*. At the same time, it secured an increase in peacetime strength but provisionally reduced service in the active army to two years (except in the cavalry and mounted artillery), followed by five years in the reserves and service until 39 in the *Landwehr*. This arrangement survived until the great pre-war expansion.[156]

It would be wrong to see the Reichstag as consistently opposing military demands. At first, its main concern was for a shorter review period. In 1893 it wanted a smaller increase than was requested, but the authorities called an election and a more sympathetic legislature was returned. The government could have asked for, and obtained, more manpower than it did. And yet, even leaving aside the one-year volunteers and those exempted for physical unfitness and family reasons, the army failed to call up all the able-bodied men of military age. Those in excess of what was needed to maintain the legislatively determined peacetime strength went into the *Ersatz* reserve, in which they were liable to periodic call-up checks and three exercises of ten, six, and four weeks respectively before ending their duty in the *Landwehr* or *Landsturm*. In 1908 alone 90,000 men went into the *Ersatz* reserve, and of 10.4 million men aged between 20 and 45 in 1914, 5.4 million lacked proper military training.[157] In practice, therefore, Germany did not operate universal service. To have done so would have meant a much larger standing army, which would have been costly and might have appeared provocative, unless the term of service were further shortened, but this would have made the army more akin to a militia, less suitable for an offensive war or for keeping control at home. Universal service would also have necessitated a still larger and less aristocratic officer corps, and more recruiting from the socialist urban workforce. In 1911 42.5 per cent of the population lived in country areas, but 64.15 per cent of reservists. Only 5.84 per cent of reservists came from big cities, and the army was drawing disproportionately on a shrinking rural base.[158] Its budget and manpower grew between the late 1880s and late 1890s, but thereafter the navy surged ahead.[159] Responsibility for this situation lay neither with the General Staff—which favoured expansion—nor the Reichstag, so much as with the War Minister, the Chancellor, and the Emperor himself.

* * *

Austria-Hungary's armed forces, with the dynasty and the administration, formed the unifying carapace of a multinational polity. The ethnic make-up of

---

[156] Reichsarchiv, *Weltkrieg*, 1–41.

[157] Meier-Welcke and von Groote, eds., *Handbuch*, v. 52.

[158] M. Kitchen, *A Military History of Germany: From the Eighteenth Century to the Present Day* (Bloomington, Ind., 1975), 162. Report by French military attaché, 2 Feb. 1914, SHA 7.N. 1112.

[159] Bucholz, *War Planning*, 137.

the Monarchy's common army corresponded almost exactly to that of the population generally. More than half of the officer corps were German, but recruitment to it appears to have been ethnically blind, there was no promotion bias, and it included many Hungarians, Czechs, Poles, Croats, and Serbs.[160] By 1914 the loyalty of portions of the army was beginning to be doubtful, but its discipline as yet was little impaired.

The constitutional settlement known as the *Ausgleich*, or 'Compromise', of 1867 had much more impact on the army's effectiveness. It divided the Monarchy into two halves, each with an elected parliament, a Cabinet, and a Prime Minister. Franz Joseph reigned as Emperor of the 'Austrian' portion and King of the 'Hungarian' one.[161] The resulting organism is better understood as an alliance, or as resembling the post-1945 European Community, than as a single entity. The ruler appointed three common Ministers for Foreign Affairs, Finance, and War. In addition to the common army and navy each half of the Monarchy had its own War Ministry and its own army: the Austrian *Landwehr* and the Hungarian *Honvéd*. In this diffuse power structure it was even harder than in Germany for the military to act as a cohesive pressure group.

Franz Joseph kept himself well briefed, but allowed his ministers considerable latitude, intervening as an arbiter in interagency disputes. He conducted correspondence through his Military Chancellery, whose head, General Arthur Bolfras, was 74 in 1912 and typified the Emperor's liking for conservative men of his own generation. Franz Joseph had a steadiness that Wilhelm II lacked, and bitter experience had made him cautious. He knew little about military innovations, and gave a low priority to keeping pace with them. He wished to avoid creating domestic turbulence by excessive financial and legislative demands. Quietism in foreign policy, armaments policy, and domestic policy was all of a piece.

In 1900, however, Franz Joseph had reached the age of 70, and his nephew, the Archduke Franz Ferdinand, was a heartbeat away from the top job. From 1898 the heir apparent had a right to copies of correspondence from the three War Ministries; in 1906–8 he created his own Military Chancellery in his palace of the Belvedere; in 1913 he became General Inspector of the armed forces, empowered to intervene with Franz Joseph and the two governments and demand reports from all military authorities. His advisers constituted a government-in-waiting, and his relations with Franz Joseph—who described him as a 'rash fool'[162]—were often strained. His greatest influence was on military appointments rather than policy. Once in office, however, men furthered by him owed their primary loyalty to Franz Joseph, and tended to support the Emperor in case of discord. Franz Ferdinand's preferences were for greater preparedness (though more for building up the navy than the army), and against concessions

---

[160] Deák, *Beyond Nationalism*, 179, 183–7.

[161] S. R. Williamson, *Austria-Hungary and the Origins of the First World War* (Basingstoke, 1991), chs. 3 and 4, has a good account of the political system and the role of the dynasty.

[162] Deák, *Beyond Nationalism*, 71.

to the Hungarians; but he generally shared Franz Joseph's aversion from risking force in foreign affairs. His representations were heard out, but he could not deflect the Emperor if the latter had made up his mind.[163]

Given the restrictions on Franz Ferdinand, and Franz Joseph's willingness to delegate, the initiative lay with the General Staff and War Ministry. The 'General Staff' in Austrian parlance took in the equivalent of the troop general staff and the GGS in Germany. Friedrich Beck, the CGS from 1881 to 1906, became if anything more powerful than Schlieffen.[164] Officially he was subordinate to the War Minister, but he took orders direct from the Emperor and had independent access to him. In 1902 he forced the resignation of a minister with whom he disagreed. The Vienna General Staff had all the responsibilities of the GGS, as well as others that in Berlin would belong to the War Ministry. Its crucial sections were the second (operations), sixth (the Evidenzbureau—intelligence), and seventh (railways). The Evidenzbureau exchanged information with the Germans and was reasonably well informed about the Monarchy's enemies, although it underestimated Russian military recovery after 1905 and Serbian strength in 1914.[165] Railway transport and concentration plans were directed against Russia, Serbia and Montenegro, and Italy, as well as combinations of the three, and were revised in an annual cycle. Beck corresponded with his German and Italian counterparts (though consultation with Schlieffen ended in 1896), and as the prospective director of operations if war broke out he advised on military preparedness and the strategic aspects of foreign policy. Railways, mobilization, fortifications, doctrine, and weaponry all came within his purview. Much of his strength, however, depended on his personal relations with the sovereign: a 'quiet, cautious, enormously dedicated middle-class German . . . [he] became, in time, the Emperor's friend'.[166] Before Beck's retirement at the age of 76, Franz Joseph allowed him the rare privilege of conversing with him while sitting. Under Beck's successor, Franz Conrad von Hötzendorf, the CGS gained the right of direct communication with military attachés and senior commanders. Conrad, however, was Franz Ferdinand's nominee, and his appointment marked the arrival of a more assertive generation, with whom the Emperor was out of sympathy. After 1906 the Austrian General Staff gained more power on paper but probably had less in reality, whereas under the younger Moltke, the Emperor's man, put in against warnings from Wilhelm's advisers, the importance of the German General Staff grew.

---

[163] S. R. Williamson, 'Influence, Power, and the Policy Process: The Case of Franz Ferdinand, 1906–1914', *Historical Journal*, 17 (1974), 417–34, reaches slightly different conclusions.

[164] Bronsart von Schellendorf, *General Staff*, 64 ff. Deák, *Beyond Nationalism*, 110–13. F. Käs, 'Versuch einer Zusammenfassten Darstellung der Tätigkeit der Österreichisch-Ungarischen Generalstabes in der Zeit von 1906 bis 1914: Unter Besonderer Berücksichtigung der Aufmarschplänen und Mobilmachungen', Ph.D. thesis (Vienna, 1962), 15–38. On Beck, see Wagner, 'Armee', 378–85. Rothenberg, *Army*, chs. 8–9. I am indebted to conversations on this subject with Mr Scott Lackey. For Beck's annual reports, KAW Gstb Operationsbureau 741.

[165] N. Stone, 'Austria-Hungary', in May (ed.), *Knowing*, ch. 2.

[166] Deák, *Beyond Nationalism*, 60.

Conrad lost ground as the War Minister's influence revived. As in Germany the Minister was customarily a serving general, and the military establishment's public face. He found himself in the storm centre of the Dual Monarchy's politics. The annual budget process illustrates the complexity of his task. It began with liaison about requirements with the commanders and the General Staff, and preparation of a draft in the Ministry. Proposals went to the two governments and back to the military and naval chiefs before discussion in the Common Ministerial Council (*Gemeinsamer Ministerrat* or 'GMR'), where the common Ministers met the Austrian and Hungarian Premiers and Finance Ministers, sometimes in the presence of the Chief of the General Staff and the *Marinekommandant*, the head of the common navy, who was formally subordinate to the War Minister but in practice largely independent. The GMR was chaired by the Foreign Minister rather than Franz Joseph himself and it usually conceded much less than the War Ministry wanted, the Hungarian Government being the more tight-fisted but the Austrians sometimes equally stubborn. Once Franz Joseph and the GMR had agreed the budget it went forward to the Delegations, which were not a true common legislature, but an infrequently convened assembly of two committees elected by the Vienna and Budapest Parliaments and deliberating separately. If the governments were in agreement the Delegations' consent to the budget was a foregone conclusion, although the two Parliaments had still to raise the money. The Hungarians were the principal obstacle. They held their share of common taxes (36.4 per cent from 1907) below what their share of the economy merited, and held out for more military orders than their industry could supply. But in the Austrian half there was also resistance to higher expenditure. The critical problem, however, was winning approval from the Parliaments for manpower bills.[167]

The army law of 1868 had declared a universal liability to service, but fixed an annual recruitment quota (*Rekrutenkontingent*) of 95,000. Most conscripts did three years active service in the common army and seven in the reserve; a minority did two years in the *Landwehr* or *Honvéd*; those not called up went into the *Ersatz* reserve, and received minimal instruction. In 1882 the common army adopted a territorial mobilization system on the German pattern, and this, coupled with the building of the Carpathian railways, gave it an advantage over Russia in mobilization and concentration times. A new law in 1889 raised the quota to 103,000, but this was the last increase until 1912.[168] In 1906 Austria-Hungary conscripted only 0.29 per cent of its citizens, compared with Russia's 0.35 per cent, Germany's 0.47, and France's 0.75. In 1914 France, with a smaller population, could field an army approaching twice the size.[169] From the turn of the century, as unrest grew in both halves of the Monarchy, political deadlock

[167] Williamson, *Austria-Hungary*, 44–6. Wagner, 'Armée', 371–3. W. Hetzer, 'Franz von Schönaich: Reichskriegsminister von 1906–1911', Ph.D. thesis (Vienna, 1968), 43.

[168] Rothenberg, *Army*, 81, 109–10.

[169] N. Stone, 'Army and Society in the Habsburg Monarchy, 1900–1914', *Past and Present*, 33 (1966), 107.

denied the army extra manpower and finance. In 1907 manhood suffrage was introduced for elections to the lower chamber of the Austrian Reichsrat, but the authorities still found it difficult to maintain a stable majority, and for long periods they ruled by decree. In Budapest a restricted franchise buttressed Magyar dominance and nationalist pressure drove ministers into single-mindedly pursuing Hungarian interests. Despite the efficiency of the Habsburg armaments industry and the versatility of its strategic planners, in manpower and equipment the Austro-Hungarian army was falling further behind.

* * *

Before the 1905 revolution, Russia was simpler and more autocratic than Austria-Hungary or Germany. There was no national parliament, and the sovereign's decrees had the force of law. Nor was there a Cabinet or Prime Minister, the so-called Committee of Ministers never presenting the Tsar with a united front. Government was therefore by one-to-one transactions between the Tsar and his ministers, but neither Alexander III (1881–94) nor Nicholas II (1894–1917) were well equipped for their role. Alexander was forceful, but immature and swayed by prejudice; Nicholas less overbearing, although he could be equally determined to get his way. In the later part of his reign he was increasingly away from his desk and from St Petersburg and absorbed in family life. He was conscientious in detail, but had no appetite for systematic discussion of major issues.[170] None the less, the political influence of the military would largely depend on their relations with the dynasty, and the soldierly traditions of the Romanovs might seem favourable. Officers held senior civil-service positions in St Petersburg and were appointed to provincial governorships. Nicholas had received a military education, wore uniforms and medals, and relished ceremonial and parades. On the other hand, the War Ministry was obstructed by dynastic meddling. The officers of the imperial suite, in Nicholas's household, reviewed the performance of candidates for the top commands. Romanov grand dukes were inspectors-general of the various arms, and Grand Duke Nicholas (Nikolai Nikolaevich), the Tsar's uncle and Inspector-General of Cavalry, had a pervasive influence on defence policy.[171]

There was less rivalry than in Vienna or Berlin between the War Ministry and the General Staff. It is true that the staff corps was exceptionally well entrenched as an officer élite. By comparison with the civilian professions, most Russian officers experienced slow promotion and small rewards. Many were condemned to spend their lives in provincial fastnesses with little to console them beyond duelling and drinking.[172] The two escape routes were the Guards and the staff. In 1912 the latter included only 2 per cent of all officers, but 62 per cent of corps commanders. Among them figured Grand Duke Nicholas and General Vladimir

[170] H. Rogger, *Russia in the Age of Modernization and Revolution, 1881–1917* (London, 1983), chs. 2–3. D. C. B. Lieven, *Nicholas II: Emperor of all the Russias* (London, 1993), chs. 4–5.

[171] W. C. Fuller, *Civil–Military Conflict in Imperial Russia, 1881–1914* (Princeton, 1985), xxi. 30. N. Stone, *The Eastern Front, 1914–1917* (London, 1975), 19.

[172] J. Bushnell, 'The Tsarist Officer Corps, 1881–1914: Customs, Duties, Inefficiency', *American Historical Review*, 86 (1981), 753–80.

Sukhomlinov, the War Minister in 1909–15. The staff were virtually synonymous with the High Command, and entrance to them, via competitive examina-
tions and the Nicholas Academy, was ferociously selective, although the rewards
for staying the course were great.[173] Until 1906, however, the 'Main Staff'
(*Glavny Shtab*) in St Petersburg was a section within the War Ministry. Its
responsibilities included intelligence, mobilization, and concentration planning,
but also more mundane administration. Its chief was a second-rate official, subordinate to the Minister, without direct access to the Tsar and without a designated role in time of war. His influence was resisted by the inspectors-general
and by the corps and divisional staffs, who were liable to challenge the authority of the centre rather than accept subordination to it.[174]

Military influence therefore largely meant that of the War Ministry, but this
had diminished since its apogee under D. A. Miliutin (1861–81), the reforming
partner of Tsar Alexander II. After defeat in the Crimea and under the influence
of Prussia's victories, the two men wanted a smaller, cheaper, better equipped
standing army that could be rapidly reinforced by a trained reserve. Miliutin
remodelled the War Ministry bureaucracy and the Main Staff, and laid the foundation of the staff as a military élite. He created permanent army corps, each
with a recruiting catchment area, and divided the country into military districts,
whose commanders would mobilize reserves when needed. Finally, the military
law of 1874 established the principle of universal liability to service, though in
practice with sweeping exceptions. Active service was for six years and reserve
service nine: in 1888 the figures became four and eighteen.[175]

After Miliutin, progress faltered. This resulted from Russia having too much
manpower rather than too little. Under the 1874 regime only 25–30 per cent of
each conscript class did service, those with even elementary education doing a
much shorter term. Those not drafted went into the militia, where they were
neither trained nor assigned to units.[176] The war strength of the Russian army
on mobilization was only half as big again as that of France or Germany, but its
peacetime strength of around one million at the turn of the century was almost
twice theirs.[177] The standing army, in other words, was large in relation to the
trained reserve, partly because of Russia's size, its long and open frontiers, and
the requirements of domestic policing (30,000 troops were used to suppress
unrest in 1901 and 160,000 in 1903).[178] The military authorities contended that
the poorly educated Russian conscript needed a longer training than elsewhere,

[173] M. Mayzel, 'The Formation of the Russian General Staff, 1880–1917: A Social Study', *Cahiers
du monde russe et soviétique*, 16 (1975), 311–16. P. Kenez, 'A Profile of the Prerevolutionary Officer
Corps', *California Slavic Studies*, 7 (1973), 138–40.
[174] Wildman, *Imperial Army*, 17. Bronsart von Schellendorf, *General Staff*, 86–93. Fuller, *Conflict*,
7.
[175] Ibid. 7–11. A. J. Rieber, 'Alexander II: A Revisionist View', *Journal of Modern History*, 43
(1971), 42–57. J. C. H. Keep, *Soldiers of the Tsar: Army and Society in Russia, 1462–1874* (Oxford,
1985), ch. 15.
[176] Wildman, *Imperial Army*, 25–6. W. M. Pintner, 'The Burden of Defence in Imperial Russia,
1725–1914', *Russian Review*, 43 (1984), 255.
[177] Stone, *Eastern Front*, 37. Fuller, *Conflict*, 53.   [178] Wildman, *Imperial Army*, 31.

and slower mobilization necessitated larger standing forces. For the same reason it was decided in the 1880s to concentrate the standing army on the western frontier, almost half of it being garrisoned in the Kiev, Warsaw, and Odessa military districts. The million-strong standing army indicated not high militarization but weakness, and it meant that more expenditure than elsewhere had to go on routine maintenance and administration rather than on equipment and training.[179]

This diversion was the more serious because of the War Ministry's declining share of state expenditure in the quarter-century before the Russo-Japanese war. It lost ground to railway-building (much of which was not strategic), education, and debt service. Within the defence budget the share of the fleet rose to nearly 30 per cent by 1901–5. Military expenditure increased in most years, but not in step with the growth of the economy and total public spending. Although large-scale manœuvres were introduced, roads and fortresses were improved, and the army was re-equipped with magazine rifles and quick-firing field guns, Russia failed to hold its relative position. It spent a higher percentage of its national product on defence than did France and Germany, but its expenditure per soldier in 1893 has been estimated at 40 per cent of the French and one-quarter of the German level.[180] It acquired fewer modern field guns than either of the other two Powers, and had smaller weapons stockpiles. It lacked modern siege and fortress artillery, and many of its fortresses were in disrepair. The problem, apart from the size of the standing army, was the bureaucratic primacy of the Finance Ministry, whose priority was economic growth, to be encouraged by commercially viable railways, foreign investment, and low taxes. Alexander III gave priority to internal consolidation over foreign adventurism; Nicholas backed the Finance Ministry under Sergei von Witte (1892–1903), and was mesmerized by the Asian rather than the European theatre. The Finance Ministry opposed borrowing for weapons replacement, and in 1894–1908 held the War Ministry to successive budget-capping regimes. Rather than attempt a showdown in which Nicholas would rule against them, War Ministers acquiesced.[181]

The consequences of underfunding showed not only in equipment shortages but also in the style and tone of Russian military life. Almost half the men were illiterate, and although the best of the officer corps were up to the highest international standards, their average calibre of recruitment and professionalism was among the lowest in Europe and their social status was diminishing. Lack of provision by the centre forced regiments to concentrate on domestic economy rather than war preparation. After basic training, discipline, and drill imparted by the NCOs in the first four months, new recruits learnt little more. They had to make their own boots and uniform, and except in summer they worked as cobblers, tailors, cooks, gardeners, and stable hands, or did part-time jobs in the civilian economy. The maximum period of readiness was very brief, and for much of the second part of the year regimental strengths fell from 1,800 to 300 as men went into employment or on leave. Officers weighed down with book-keeping had little

---

[179] Fuller, *Conflict*, 15, 53.   [180] Ibid. 53, 57–8.   [181] Ibid. 58–70.

opportunity to inculcate the martial virtues even into their own men, let alone Russian society as a whole, with its undercurrents of radicalism and contempt for authority. The erosion of their political influence coincided with a loss of faith in themselves.[182]

* * *

In the more liberal Powers—France, Italy, Britain—there was greater scope than in the conservative monarchies for civil–military conflict. In Germany, Austria-Hungary, and Russia the officer corps lacked traditions of political intervention, and loyalty to the sovereign formed part of their professional ethos. Any military *coup* would come with the sovereign's authorization; and at times, against German socialists or Hungarian nationalists, one seemed on the cards. The French Third Republic, founded in the wake of national disaster in 1870, faced much more serious problems of legitimacy and potential confrontation between civilian politicians and the military leadership. Yet for a quarter of a century the relationship was surprisingly harmonious, and the French army was arguably the most successful in Europe in maintaining its claim on national resources. Only at the turn of the century did the consensus in favour of military preparedness break down.

The Republic's birth had been precarious. The fundamental laws of 1875, passed by a royalist legislature, were intended to create a powerful presidency that would keep the seat warm for a monarchical restoration. This hope was thwarted when the electorate returned a republican majority, and confirmed their verdict when a royalist President, Marshal MacMahon, dissolved the Chamber and held new elections in the '16 May' crisis of 1877. MacMahon's resignation allowed the republicans to take over central and local government and create a new political system, led by anticlerical bourgeois politicians from provincial towns, amid Europe's crowned heads and aristocracies. Within France, it was the army that now seemed out of place, as a refuge for the sons of Catholic, upper-class families and a bastion of hierarchy and traditional values.

The officer corps coexisted with the Republic without being republicanized. In 1877 the senior commanders were split: most would probably have followed MacMahon in suppressing Parliament, but the Marshal was too scrupulous to attempt it. In 1887–9 there was a second test when General Boulanger, who had championed preparedness against Germany, was dismissed as War Minister and led a protest movement of by-election candidatures and street demonstrations. But he too held back from a *coup*, and probably would have had less support than MacMahon if he had tried one. Finally, in 1899, during a demonstration in Paris at the height of the Dreyfus affair, the nationalist leader Paul Déroulède appealed to the local commander to march on the presidential palace, but was handed over to the police for his pains. Several corps commanders might have been willing to see the Republic overthrown in 1899, but they waited for civil-

---

[182] J. Bushnell, 'Peasants in Uniform: The Tsarist Army as a Peasant Society', *Journal of Social History*, 13 (1980), 565–76.

ians to take the initiative.[183] The army leadership, in short, might not exert itself to save the regime, but it would not kill it. Military traditions were of passivity and neutrality, and of professional rather than political engagement. While the Republic showed that it could keep order and that it took defence seriously, it had little to fear. What resulted was a stand-off. There was no wholesale purge of the officer corps, and overtly republican officers remained few. Politicians interfered little in military routine and professional advancement, but officers kept out of politics. Laws were passed to bar them from standing for the Chamber and to disenfranchise all those doing active service: conscripts while with the colours, and officers and NCOs throughout their careers.[184]

After MacMahon's discomfiture, French Presidents were selected from among the republican politicians and took a minimalist interpretation of their powers. They could do little without the countersignature of a responsible minister, or defy a parliamentary majority. They failed to constitute a strong independent executive to which the General Staff could answer. Nor could the Prime Minister fulfil this role. French Cabinets lasted on average for nine months, and defence ranked low on their agenda. Long-term planning had seemed essential to Prussia's success, yet politicians feared that an established, permanent military leadership might escape their scrutiny and show praetorian tendencies. They fumbled with this dilemma for forty years.

Although France moved towards Prussian systems of planning and recruitment this was a halting, incomplete espousal rather than a slavish imitation. Legislation in 1880 created a new staff corps, alternating between desk and line service after passing through the École de guerre. An intellectual élite with the usual career benefits, they were disliked as privileged and arrogant. From 1871 there was a General Staff of the Minister, which dealt with intelligence and war planning, but as in Russia it was an integral part of the War Ministry and its chief changed with and was selected by each Minister, few of whom held the post for more than a year. His role in wartime was not specified, and it was assumed the Minister would act as commander-in-chief.[185]

The French, therefore, did not strip the War Minister of his functions. On the contrary, his load was crushing. Yet there were no fewer than seventeen Ministers in 1871–88, and the portfolio changed hands more frequently than any other. It had little appeal to politicians, but little to military men either, the senior generals preferring the stability of a corps command. Hence the job went to generals of junior ability and rank, who selected even more junior men as General Staff chiefs.[186] By the time of the Boulanger affair, which coincided with renewed tension with Germany, there was an evident need for greater

---

[183] D. B. Ralston, *The Army of the Republic: The Place of the Army in the Political Evolution of France, 1871–1914* (Cambridge, Mass., 1967), 73, 172, 222. D. Porch, *The March to the Marne: The French Army, 1871–1914* (Cambridge, 1981), 12–15. M. Larkin, 'La République en Danger? The Pretenders, the Army and Déroulède, 1898–99', *English Historical Review*, 100 (1985), 100–4.

[184] Ralston, *Army*, 63–5.   [185] Ibid. 88–91, 141–4.

[186] Ibid. 150–3. Porch, *March*, 46–51, 255.

continuity, while retaining civilian control. Charles de Freycinet, Minister in 1888–93, achieved a settlement that lasted until the Dreyfus case.

De Freycinet continued to separate the wartime command from peacetime planning. He resurrected the Conseil supérieur de la guerre, which comprised the senior commanders, as an element of continuity (and of military influence). The Minister was to consult it on all important questions, including mobilization and concentration, organization, and armaments. Its Vice-President (the Minister normally chaired it himself) would be the generalissimo, or commander in the north-eastern theatre, in the event of war. Its other members had inspection powers over the army corps and authority over their preparedness. The General Staff was reorganized in 1890 as the General Staff of the Army (EMA), with four sections, among which the Second Bureau dealt with intelligence, the Third with operational planning, and the Fourth with railways. Its chief (the CEMA) would be chief of staff to the generalissimo in war. In peacetime he remained subordinate to the Minister, who countersigned his directives, but he no longer changed with each new Cabinet. Although Chiefs of Staff still found it difficult to prevail over bureau chiefs in the War Ministry, de Freycinet's reforms enhanced the autonomy and stability of the military élite and in some ways made it stronger than in the conservative monarchies.[187]

Although the army remained subject to parliamentary control, the National Assembly was generous with resources for it, and relaxed in its surveillance. It rarely trimmed the estimates much, or probed them seriously. In the 1870s and 1880s vast sums were spent on steel breech-loaders, magazine rifles, and frontier fortresses, although the latter were only partially rebuilt when high explosive shells made them outdated.[188] The French caught up with Germany in railways, completing ten double-tracked lines to the north-eastern frontier by 1895.[189] In manpower, too, the army did well, although here there were balances to strike between external defence and internal order. The 'old army' that had been so outclassed in 1870 had none the less suppressed the Paris Commune; whereas the performance of the levies raised during the fighting had shown that mere numbers and enthusiasm counted for little without preparation and training. The authors of the Republic's 1872 recruitment law believed a longer service period was needed than in Prussia, and would promote social cohesion. They opted for a five-year term. But to maintain five entire conscript classes under arms simultaneously would create a larger and a costlier standing army than was needed or the country could afford. Hence the principle of universal personal liability was as usual enunciated, but a lottery would determine who actually served, and

[187] A. Mitchell, 'The Freycinet Reforms and the French Army, 1888–1893', *Journal of Strategic Studies*, 4 (1981), 19–28. Ralston, *Army*, 181–94. Porch, *March*, 51–3. Bronsart von Schellendorf, *General Staff*, 99–102.

[188] Ralston, *Army*, 115–34. Crouzet, 'Recherches', 55–7. Doise and Vaïsse, *Diplomatie*, chs. 1–2. A. Mitchell, ' "A Situation of Inferiority": French Military Reorganization after the Defeat of 1870', *American Historical Review*, 86 (1981), 49–62.

[189] J.-C. Jauffret, 'La Défense des frontières françaises et l'organisation des forces de couverture (1874–1895)', *Revue historique*, 279 (1988), 377.

exemptions remained for the educated and better off. Those who escaped the full conscription term served only six months. In consequence the new standing army was bigger than before 1870, but its reserves were poorly trained and undermanned.

The problem was exacerbated by the 1873 organic law, which opted for eighteen army corps in order to keep parity with Germany; and by the 1875 law on cadres and effectives, which raised each infantry regiment from three battalions to four, partly to provide additional officer posts. The army needed peacetime employment for the regular officers who would command the reservist units formed on mobilization, and provided it by creating more units than the peacetime strength merited, thus saddling itself with under-strength companies that were unsuitable for training and for seasoning new recruits and would be at low readiness in the event of an emergency. The German solution was one-year volunteers and the reserve officer system, but the French disliked the privileged status of one-year volunteers and abolished them in 1889, at the price of a continuing organizational weakness.[190]

The deficiencies of the 1870s restructuring were partially addressed a decade later. By the time of the 1889 recruitment law most French soldiers served in garrisons near their place of origin and the army was moving towards a territorial mobilization system, which reduced the barriers between it and civil society. So did the 1889 law itself, another achievement of de Freycinet, which finally broke with tradition and approximated to the European norm. The Chamber wanted shorter service and to end the inequalities of the 1872 law: the army wanted a more uniform composition of reservists, all serving the same term, and a faster build-up in response to Germany's 1888 *Septennat*. The law made a bonfire of exemptions and established a three-year term for two-thirds of the recruits, the remainder doing one. Henceforward France called up a higher proportion of each age cohort than anywhere else in Europe, and having dug deep into the nation's purse for re-equipment the army now conscripted unparalleled numbers of its sons. It also did more to organize and train the reserves. An 1892 law created reserve regiments; one of 1893 strengthened the cadre of regular officers who would command them in war. On mobilization not only would reservists join the existing active units to bring them up to strength, but reserve divisions would be formed that were composed entirely of reservists under regular officers.[191] By 1899, finally, the *couverture*, or covering force, which would protect the frontiers and interior units during mobilization, was estimated to outnumber Germany's, thus safeguarding against surprise attack.[192] There were flaws in the French achievement—obsolescent fortresses, inadequate heavy artillery, too few reserve officers and NCOs—but measured against the military monarchies to the East the Republic had performed well. By the 1890s, however,

[190] R. D. Challener, *The French Theory of the Nation in Arms, 1866–1939* (New York, 1955), 32–44. Ralston, *Army*, 29–62. Porch, *March*, 23–32.
[191] Porch, *March*, 31–2. Challener, *French Theory*, 46–60. Ralston, *Army*, 96–115.
[192] Jauffret, 'Défense', 378.

the defence consensus was threatened by reviving pacifism and anti-militarism on the Left and by a *détente* with Germany, after years of strain and effort.[193] From the vantage point of what lay ahead, the later nineteenth century would seem a sort of golden age.

* * *

The Franco-Russian–Austro-German parallelogram was the centre-piece of the European land military system. Italy and Britain were the flanking Powers. In Rome the Chamber of Deputies made and unmade ministries with a similarly bewildering rapidity to that in Paris, although War Ministers normally had a longer tenure. As serving generals they were subject to the King's commands, and the constitution gave Victor Emmanuel III (1900–46) control over foreign and defence policy. In practice he did not exercise it. A cynical, misanthropic ruler, he was kept informed and influenced appointments, but generally confined himself to giving advice when asked.[194]

As in France, collective supervision by the Council of Ministers was weak, and inter-departmental liaison notoriously deficient. The Foreign Ministry failed to tell the military the terms of the Triple Alliance; the military held staff talks without briefing the diplomats. None the less, it was the civilians who had the final say, and there was less fear than in France of the army overthrowing the regime. The nearest approach to a civil–military crisis was the prime minister-ship of General Pelloux in 1898–1900, at a time of acute social conflict caused by depression and food shortages. With the sympathy of King Umberto I, Pelloux sought power to rule by decree and arrested his parliamentary critics, only to resign after a disappointing election. As this was followed by Umberto's assassination, the threat of military involvement in politics receded, although the army continued to be used against brigandage and social unrest, and the possi-bility that it might become a sorcerer's apprentice could not entirely be ruled out.[195]

The Italian royal household was less interventionist than in Eastern Europe, and the Chief of the General Staff, whose post was created in 1882 as a 'dowry' to Italy's partners for her admission to the Triple Alliance, was emphatically sub-ordinate to the War Minister, in conjunction with whom he drew up mobiliza-tion and concentration plans. The first two CGS's pressed unavailingly for greater authority; the third, General Saletta (1896–1908), was a safer, less polit-ical figure, who concentrated on military preparations. War Ministers were caught between General Staff demands for greater resources and resistance from their Cabinet colleagues.[196] Sometimes they successfully insisted on extra fund-ing as their condition for taking the post, but in general the army had to accept what the politicians were willing to give to it, which was not particularly gener-

---

[193] Girardet, *Société militaire*, 194, 213 ff.
[194] R. J. B. Bosworth, *Italy and the Approach of the First World War* (London, 1983), 21, 44. J. Gooch, *Army, State, and Society in Italy, 1870–1915* (Basingstoke, 1989), 205.
[195] Ibid., ch. 6. Bosworth, *Italy*, 44–6.
[196] Bronsart von Schellendorf, *General Staff*, 73–9. Gooch, *Italy*, 46–7, 69, 100.

ous. Italy had the smallest population of the Powers and the lowest army spending. Its defence industries lacked raw materials, expertise, and capital, and needed foreign assistance. Naval spending was growing at the army's expense. This helps explain the demoralization of the officer corps, who were competing with armies that theirs could never match. Nor had they the sustenance of a victorious tradition: the Risorgimento battles had been won by the French and by Garibaldi's irregulars; the professional army was beaten by the Austrians at Custozza in 1866 and by the Ethiopians at Adowa thirty years later. Although there was continuing tension on the northern frontier and an unfinished task of national unification in Istria, the Trentino, and Nice, military preparedness and upholding national honour came lower down the political agenda than in France, and Italy's politicians preferred to use diplomacy rather than an army whose limitations they well understood.

None the less, Italy shared in the nineteenth-century military revolution, a series of measures between 1871 and 1882 aligning it with the German model. Ricotti-Magnani, the War Minister in 1870–6, wanted a larger first-line army and a trained reserve. New recruitment laws required service to be done in person and reduced the period with the colours to three years. A militia was created, freeing the active army for field operations. A peacetime command structure was formed of twelve army corps and regional military districts, where reservists would muster before joining their regiments; but, as each regiment contained men from at least two regions and was stationed in a third, Italy did not adopt a true territorial mobilization system, which it feared would encourage particularism. Army spending reached a nineteenth-century peak in 1888–9 at a time of tension with the French, but there was much still to do. 'Category I' recruits, doing the full term of service, in practice served less than three years, and the peacetime strength of 190,000 in 1880 was small in relation to Italy's population and the standing armies of the other Powers. Like the French, the Italians committed themselves (to satisfy their alliance partners) to more units than their peacetime strength could adequately maintain, thus impeding instruction and readiness. Fortress construction and weapons acquisition were slow. In the 1890s the army was diverted more and more to internal peacekeeping, defeated at Adowa, and tainted by Pelloux's premiership. Expenditure was cut, manpower became short, and officers ran into a promotion blockage. The army's position was vulnerable at the best of times, and now became a great deal worse.[197]

* * *

The British army's budget was higher than that of Italy or Austria-Hungary, and not far short of that of France. It counted, however, for very little in the Continental military balance. Its peacetime strength in NCOs and men rose from 213,555 in 1895 to 252,686 in 1910, of whom only about half were stationed in the British Isles and two-thirds of the remainder were in India. The real

[197] Ibid., chs. 2–4. Whittam, *Politics*, chs. 7–9.

difference from the Continental countries showed in the weakness of the first-
class army reserve, whose size in 1910 was 135,712, giving a war strength of
388,398.[198] In the same year the Territorial Army, created in 1908 to replace the
Militia and Volunteers, numbered some 280,000, very few of whom, however,
were willing to serve overseas.[199] Before the Haldane reforms Britain's forces
available for a Continental expedition totalled 80,000, and it would take two
months to send them; in contrast, Germany's occupation army numbered 1.7
million men and its field army 2.1 million.[200]

The Committee of Imperial Defence (CID), set up by the Cabinet in 1902 to
keep the Empire's strategic needs under review, reaffirmed the government's
acceptance of the Royal Navy's 'blue water' doctrine. If Britain commanded the
seas around its coasts it would be safe from Continental invasion, and only minor
raids were possible, which territorial forces could deal with; if it did not, it could
be starved out anyway.[201] The regular army's purpose was not primarily for
home defence, and the navy rather than the army profited from the invasion
scares and the upturn in defence expenditure that began in the 1880s. Imperial
policing, however, necessitated extended overseas tours of duty, and therefore
favoured the institution of a long-service volunteer army that best responded
anyway to anxieties about civil liberties and avoiding conscription. It is true that
Britain had moved closer towards Continental practice as a result of the reforms
of Edward Cardwell, whose 1870 Army Enlistment Act had shortened the term
of service to what became six years with the colours and six in the reserve. To
compensate for the faster turnover, he hoped to stimulate recruitment by a measure of territorialization, dividing Britain into sixty-six military districts with two
militia and two regular battalions headquartered in each. In the event the reserve
grew less than Cardwell had hoped, and the quality of the intake remained poor.
A volunteer army cost more per soldier than did a conscript one, but pay
remained very low by civilian standards and governments paid the minimum that
they could get away with. Most of the rank and file of the army had previously
been urban unskilled labourers. Two-thirds of them could not meet educational
standards set for 11-year-olds. In its weaponry and equipment the British regular army was similar to its Continental counterparts, but its social composition
was anomalous.[202]

British officers, too, were a distinctive breed. Those abroad were likely to have
benefited from frequent campaigning experience. But those at home were poorly
paid in comparison with civil servants and the expenses of their gentlemanly
lifestyle, and the career remained difficult for men without private means.

[198] E. M. Spiers, *The Army and Society, 1815–1914* (London, 1980), 36. *Encyclopaedia Britannica*,
11th edn., xxvii, 'United Kingdom of Great Britain and Northern Ireland', 606–8.

[199] Ibid. 607.

[200] C. Barnett, *Britain and her Army, 1509–1970: A Military, Political and Social Survey*
(Harmondsworth, 1979), 364. Meier-Welcke and von Groote (eds.), *Handbuch*, v. 57.

[201] M. Howard, *The Continental Commitment: The Dilemma of British Defence Policy in the Era of
Two World Wars* (Harmondsworth, 1974), 21.

[202] Spiers, *Army and Society*, 37–48, 60.

Cardwell's abolition of the purchase of commissions did little to broaden the intake. Britain had a Staff College, at Camberley, but demand for places there was low as there was no élite staff corps and the War Office employed few Camberley graduates.[203] The Office acquired an Intelligence Department in 1873, but as an information-gathering rather than a strategic-planning agency. A General Staff on Continental lines appeared unnecessary given Britain's island position, its freedom from alliances, and the army's involvement predominantly in small imperial wars that were difficult to foresee but could be won by improvisation.[204] It was resisted both by military conservatives and civilian liberals, in a political system in which civilian control was unusually complete. The peacetime office of commander-in-chief was abolished in 1904. Notoriously, the War Office exercised close financial scrutiny over every unit and delegated little responsibility. The Secretary of State took the key financial decisions on the advice of his civilian officials; the professional soldiers in the Office were not privy to the deliberations and there was no requirement to consult them. The completed estimates were haggled over with the Treasury, the War Office normally being beaten down, and the Cabinet arbitrating.[205]

There is another side, however, to this picture of military obscurantism and impotence. Traditionally, neither the War Office nor the Admiralty had done much strategic planning and they had not consulted one another about it. When war broke out with the Boer Republics in 1899 there were no operational blueprints and strategic appraisals, or even enough maps. The CID, however, although at first it favoured Admiralty views, included the Directors of Military and Naval Intelligence and gave an opportunity to professional soldiers to be consulted on high policy and place their opinions on record.[206] This development was carried much further by the Esher Committee in 1903–4, which staged a *coup d'état* against the War Office establishment with the backing of the Prime Minister, Arthur Balfour, and of the King. Esher wanted an equivalent of the Great General Staff for the British Empire, and envisaged an expanded CID secretariat in the role. He failed to achieve it, although the secretariat was strengthened and made permanent and authorized to present memoranda and collect information, arguably becoming still more the navy's mouthpiece in the process. Within the War Office, the Army Council was created, on the model of the Board of Admiralty, to act as the supreme administrative body. Of its seven members, four were military, one of them the holder of the new post, established on Esher's recommendation, of Chief of the General Staff. The General Staff itself followed in 1906, and was avowedly influenced by German practice. Its

---

[203] Ibid., ch. 1. T. Travers, 'The Hidden Army: Structural Problems in the British Officer Corps, 1900–1918', *Journal of Contemporary History*, 17 (1992), 523–44.

[204] Spiers, *Army and Society*, ch. 8. J. Gooch, *The Plans of War: The General Staff and British Military Strategy, 1900–1916* (London, 1974), ch. 1.

[205] W. S. Hamer, *The British Army: Civil–Military Relations, 1885–1905* (Oxford, 1970), chs. 1–2.

[206] J. P. Mackintosh, 'The Role of the Committee of Imperial Defence before 1914', *English Historical Review*, 77 (1962), 490–503. N. d'Ombrain, *War Machinery and High Policy: Defence Administration in Peacetime Britain, 1902–1914* (Oxford, 1973).

responsibilities included intelligence, war plans and preparations, and advice on policy, as well as ensuring continuity in executing it. Under the CGS (who functioned as a *primus inter pares*) came a Director of Military Operations (DMO), with the chief intelligence and planning role. The 'General Staff List', also dating from 1906, had most of the features of a Continental staff corps. The military leadership now had the machinery to define and to prepare a new strategic role of European intervention.[207]

* * *

This chapter has tried to probe beneath the statistics set out in the Introduction, and to place pre-war armaments competition in the context of the revolutions in military technology and organization that were initiated in the mid-nineteenth century. It has tested the hypothesis of a long-term 'Continental drift' towards armaments acceleration, impelled by autonomous technological change or by a military-industrial complex. Neither explanation fits well chronologically with the land armaments take-off in the quinquennium before 1914. The major waves of technological innovation came in the 1860s and at the close of the nineteenth century; further developments were coming on stream by 1910, but insufficiently to provide a comparable stimulus to equipment budgets. Large, integrated private armaments firms had gained ground relative to government arsenals and shipyards in Western Europe, and were disseminating weaponry and expertise to the southern and eastern peripheries of the Continent. They helped unsettle the Balkan power balance, but were much less significant in stimulating competition between the central alliance blocs. Their energies were channelled more towards naval than land armaments, and their petitioning of governments was mainly confined to pricing, export promotion, and doing down competitors. They did not decide the broader scale and pace of arms production. In any case, hardware was a relatively small component of pre-1914 budgets, and the 'arms race' should be envisaged as a competition in preparedness, in which war plans, training, mobilization arrangements, and unit strengths counted for as much as rifles and shells.

The examination of the military establishments has shown the limits to influence by the other partner in the complex. It is easy to be captivated by the General Staff mystique, especially in Germany; but Germany was atypical. The mid-century breakthrough into breech-loading weapons and railway deployments was paralleled by advances in deep-future-orientated planning and mass recruitment and training. Austria-Hungary in 1868, France in 1872–5, Russia in 1874, Italy under Ricotti, even Britain under Cardwell, inclined towards Prussian models of territorial mobilization, standing peacetime army corps, trained reserves, and short service with the colours by a much wider section of the population than before. All, too, introduced specialized staff corps and agencies for intelligence-gathering and operational planning, expert in mass railway movements to the frontiers in the opening concentration. These changes, however,

---

[207] Gooch, *Plans*, chs. 2–4.

except in Britain, were mostly complete by the turn of the century. The GGS, it has been argued, moved into a new phase in the 1890s, planning ever larger and faster deployments on railways carrying ever higher traffic densities;[208] the French, Austro-Hungarian, and Russian short-service systems, now in operation for a generation, were yielding more territorials and reservists for transport on the strategic networks all three Powers had laid out since the 1870s. Organizational evolution, if gradual, was cumulative, and did not cease after the elder Moltke's innovations had been imitated elsewhere. But it is as difficult to link the resurgence of land armaments competition after 1900 to organizational as it is to technological tides of change, and essential to see military lobbying in context. Even in Germany, extra conscripts and finance needed parliamentary approval, and the decision about how much to claim rested with the constitutionally responsible War Minister and Chancellor rather then the Military Cabinet or Great General Staff. In Vienna, although Beck had a stronger position than Schlieffen, the Hungarians' special position complicated ratification. In the other Powers General Staffs were constitutionally subordinate to War Ministers and administratively were sections of War Departments. Legislatures rarely begrudged finance, but they were sensitive about military service obligations, and could not be taken for granted. Even Bismarck did not defy the Reichstag after unification as he had the Prussian legislature prior to it, although it is true that over armaments he did not feel the need. In the later nineteenth century German manpower and financial demands were modest, and this helped restrain the other Powers.

In the years before the Franco-Russian alliance there was a flurry of military activity. Army laws were passed in Germany in 1887, 1888, and 1893, and in France and Austria-Hungary in 1889. But thereafter the competition settled down at a higher level of preparedness. Bigger standing armies with bigger reserves now disposed of magazine rifles, smokeless powder, concrete fortresses, and double-tracked railways, and, soon afterwards, quick-firing guns. Instead of war, the outcome was a precarious equilibrium. For a while international politics focused on colonial rivalries, and navies further raised their budgetary shares at armies' expense. This suggests again, however, that the underlying forces so far analysed are inadequate for an understanding of the European armaments system. To technological and military and industrial pressures within each country should be added domestic civilian politics and international crises and diplomacy. It is to these factors, and to the first major pre-war diplomatic confrontation, that the spotlight will now turn.

[208] Bucholz, *War Planning*, chs. 3–4.

Continental Equilibrium? 1904–1908

1. The Diplomatic Revolution and the First Moroccan Crisis

The essential starting-point for the diplomatic origins of the First World War is the Great-Power realignment of 1904–7. Britain reached ententes, or understandings, with France and Russia, and although these began as efforts to liquidate extra-European disputes, they led on to habitual consultation and co-operation. The 'encirclement' of which the German leaders now began to speak was neither so rigid nor so threatening as they supposed, but their near isolation among the Powers, and their inability to break out of isolation by peaceful means, marked a fundamental change. The first Moroccan crisis, in 1905–6, was more a milestone in diplomacy than in defence policies, and in the period covered by this chapter land armaments remained in approximate equilibrium. By the end of it, none the less, there was evidence that a much more dangerous situation was coming into being.

Ten years earlier, Britain rather than Germany had been isolated, in a more fluid international context. The alliances were less constant points of reference than they appeared. The partners in the 1879 Austro-German combination were linked to Italy by the Triple Alliance of 1882 and to Romania in 1883. Russia attached itself to Germany and to Austria-Hungary in 1881–7 in the Three Emperors' Alliance, and to Germany in 1887–90 by the Reinsurance Treaty—Berlin's failure to renew which opened the way to the 1891–4 Franco-Russian alliance and military convention. Yet between 1896 and 1909 Austro-German staff conversations ceased; and at the turn of the century Franco-Russian military liaison was directed against Britain as well as against the Central Powers.[1] Conversely, the Italian Government made clear from the start that the Triple Alliance did not apply against London, and in 1902 it secretly promised the French to stay neutral if Germany attacked them or even if they were 'provoked' into declaring war themselves.[2] In 1887 and again in 1895 the Germans warned Vienna that they did not feel the Near East was worth a European war,[3] and in 1898 the French felt let down by the Russians in the Fashoda crisis with Britain.[4] The alliance treaties were subject to renewal, which could not be taken for granted. They were con-

---

[1] G. E. Rothenberg, *The Army of Francis Joseph* (West Lafayette, 1976), 157. C. M. Andrew, *Théophile Delcassé and the Making of the Entente Cordiale: A Reappraisal of French Foreign Policy 1898–1905* (London, 1968), 125.

[2] L. Albertini, *The Origins of the War of 1914* (Eng. edn., 3 vols., London, 1952–7), i. 45, 129.

[3] Ibid. 53, 90.

[4] Andrew, *Delcassé*, 123.

tingent defensive arrangements against the possibility of hostilities, and entailed neither continuous diplomatic support nor unconditional loyalty.

At the turn of the century, moreover, international conflict centred less on clashes between the two alliance blocs than on extra-European rivalries that set France, Russia, and Germany individually against Britain. Britain competed with the Franco-Russian alliance in a Mediterranean naval race. Britain and France collided over Siam in 1893 as well as over the Upper Nile in the Fashoda affair. Britain and Russia were potentially at odds along an arc of territory stretching from Constantinople to China; and it was against St Petersburg that the British sought an alliance with Germany between 1898 and 1901 and signed one with Japan in 1902. Finally, Britain and Germany were at loggerheads in Southern Africa and over Germany's project for a Berlin to Baghdad railway. In contrast, the animosities within Europe between Austria-Hungary and Russia, Austria-Hungary and Italy, and Germany and France had temporarily eased. Vienna and St Petersburg agreed in 1897 to freeze the Balkan *status quo*; Italy was hostile to the French rather than the Habsburgs; between 1887 and 1905 there was no Franco-German crisis and French bitterness over the loss in 1871 of Alsace-Lorraine had lost some of its sting. The Germans passed their navy laws of 1898 and 1900 at a moment of prosperity and financial surplus, and of diplomatic advantage.[5] In 1903 they remained relaxed and confident about their international position, and failed to anticipate the reshuffling of the cards.[6]

During the South African War of 1899–1902 the British perceived the danger of all the Continental Powers combining against them. In consequence they tried to reduce the number of their enemies. Their new position was not necessarily anti-German, although the Admiralty was becoming worried about Tirpitz's build-up. Meanwhile Théophile Delcassé, the French Foreign Minister from 1898 to 1905, had ambitions to control the decaying Sultanate of Morocco as part of a grand design in the Mediterranean. At first he saw Britain as the biggest obstacle, until Wilhelm II demanded a definitive renunciation of Alsace-Lorraine as the price for German co-operation. Delcassé was not prepared to pay this price, and from now on he pursued his Moroccan objective by trying to sideline Berlin rather than London. In 1902 he gained support from Italy. In the 1904 Entente Cordiale France dropped its anti-British claims in Egypt; Britain accepted France's rights to keep order in Morocco and advise on reforms there, provided that Paris respected other Powers' commercial freedom and the Sultan's formal independence (although a secret article envisaged that this might be terminated). In addition Britain promised diplomatic support for France's Moroccan objectives.[7]

[5] S. Förster, *Der doppelte Militarismus: Die deutsche Heeresrüstung zwischen Status-Quo-Sicherung und Aggression, 1890–1913* (Stuttgart, 1985), 77. P.-C. Witt, *Die Finanzpolitik des deutschen Reiches von 1903 bis 1913* (Lübeck, 1970), 74–5. P. Winzen, *Bülows Weltmachtkonzept: Untersuchungen zur Frühphase seiner Aussenpolitik 1897–1901* (Boppard, 1977), 427–33.

[6] E. N. Anderson, *The First Moroccan Crisis, 1904–1906* (Chicago, 1930), 135.

[7] G. Monger, *The End of Isolation: British Foreign Policy 1900–1907* (London, 1963); Andrew, *Delcassé*, chs. 5, 7–11; Anderson, *Moroccan Crisis*, ch. 6.

The Entente Cordiale was hastened by the outbreak in February 1904 of the Russo-Japanese war, followed by a succession of Russian defeats and a revolt against the tsarist autocracy. Britain and France feared their ties to Tokyo and St Petersburg would embroil them in a conflict that neither wanted. Germany, meanwhile, disastrously overplayed its hand. In October 1904 the Russian Baltic Fleet sailed for the east, coaled by the German HAPAG shipping line and promised naval protection by Wilhelm. When it fired on British trawlers on the Dogger Bank there was a Russo-British war scare, settled by arbitration; and during the winter there was a panic fear in Berlin that the British would attack the German navy. Negotiations for a Russo-German alliance failed, however, when Wilhelm rejected Russian insistence that France must be associated with it. His attempts to forestall encirclement by diplomacy seemed to be frustrated at a moment of possibly unrepeatable military advantage.[8]

* * *

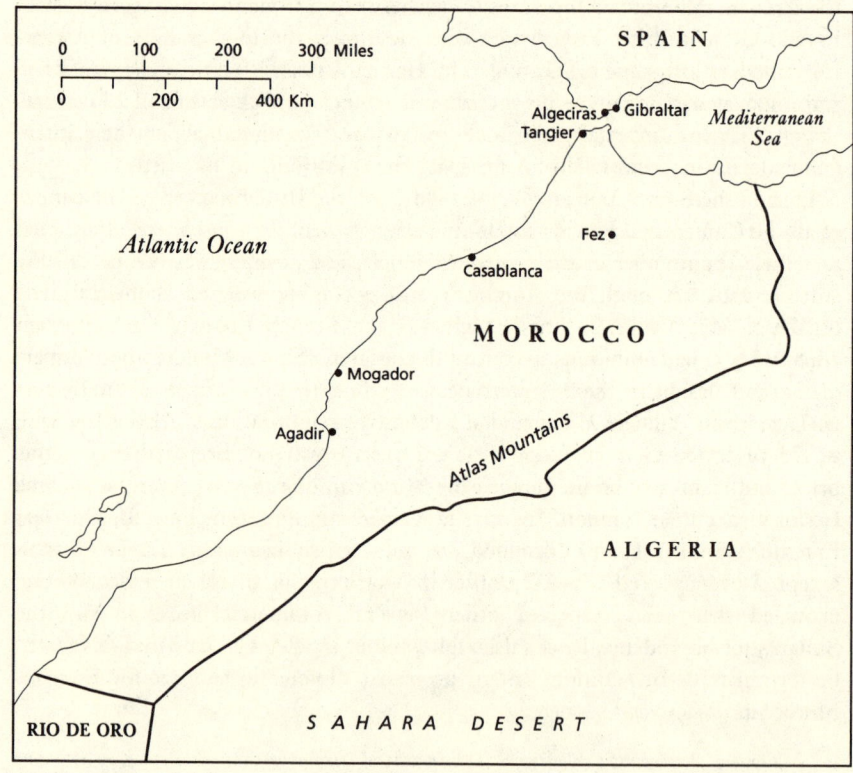

Fig. 5. Morocco

[8] Anderson, *Moroccan Crisis*, ch. 9; Andrew, *Delcassé*, ch. 12; J. Steinberg, 'Germany and the Russo-Japanese War', *American Historical Review*, 75 (1970), 1965–86.

This was the setting for the most serious Western European crisis for a generation.[9] On 31 March 1905 Wilhelm landed at Tangier. Amidst excited scenes he declared his support for the Sultan's independence and for an 'Open Door', or equal access, for foreign investment and trade. The German Government demanded an international conference, which Delcassé, with British backing, resisted until he found himself isolated in the French Cabinet and resigned on 6 June. None the less, when the Algeciras Conference finally convened in January–April 1906, Berlin gave way on the most contentious points. The three main issues to be considered in the year of tension that followed the Tangier incident are Germany's initiative, the Anglo-French response, and German disengagement.

The Germans began the crisis as a diplomatic offensive, unaccompanied by military preparations, and they did not intend to provoke a war. Their objectives were commercial and political. The colonialist societies and the Pan-German League had constructed a 'Morocco myth' of boundless natural resources, which the nationalist press had propagated. German businessmen wanted to co-operate in Morocco with their French counterparts, but the Quai d'Orsay was obstructing them and they lobbied the German Foreign Ministry to intervene. In return for a loan in 1904 the French insisted on supervising the collection of customs duties, French officers had taken control of the Tangier police, and in January 1905 a mission to the Sultan demanded sweeping reforms. Rebellion was sapping the sovereign's control over the countryside, and his advisers urged him to resist further encroachment. Delcassé evidently wanted a *de facto* protectorate, and the Germans were encouraging the Sultan to resist him even before the Tangier incident, itself the consequence of a rapid decision that Wilhelm agreed to reluctantly. Officially their position was defensive: they were upholding Morocco's independence and their own economic rights under the 1880 Madrid Convention, and they wanted no Moroccan territory.[10] The Emperor insisted on this last point, and his Chancellor, Bernhard von Bülow, had to go along with it, although hoping to keep open the territorial possibility later if French dominance could be prevented now.[11] For Bülow's leading adviser, however, the Counsellor at the Foreign Ministry, Friedrich von Holstein, the real issue was that Germany must not be trampled on, or it might face more dangerous challenges elsewhere. The Chancellor came to share this view. Holstein was worried about encirclement, and wanted to show France that advantages in Morocco were better obtained in Berlin than in London. Wilhelm himself was infuriated by the failure of his advances to St Petersburg, blamed Delcassé, and was receptive to the Bülow–Holstein policy of teaching France a lesson.[12]

[9] Anderson, *Moroccan Crisis*, remains the best general account.

[10] P. Guillen, *L'Allemagne et le Maroc de 1870 à 1905* (Paris, 1967), 824–7, 838–9, 851–68, 880–9.

[11] A. Moritz, *Das Problem des Präventivkrieges in der deutschen Politik während der Ersten Marokkokrise* (Frankfurt, 1974), 111. Bülow to Wilhelm, 26 Mar. 1905, in *Die Grosse Politik der Europäischen Kabinette, 1871–1914*, ed. J. Lepsius *et al.* (40 vols., Berlin, 1922–7), xx/1 (Berlin, 1925), doc. 6576; Bülow to Tattenbach, 30 Apr. 1905, ibid. xx/2 doc. 6643.

[12] Moritz, *Präventivkrieges*, 130, 154–7; Guillen, *L'Allemagne*, 856.

This did not mean that the lesson would be taught by force, although in the army war was contemplated.[13] In April 1904 Schlieffen had told Bülow that Russia could do little in a Franco-German war, and Germany's prospects would be favourable. In May 1905 he sent Wilhelm a press cutting suggesting a preventive attack; but the Emperor minuted that he would never agree. Holstein concluded that, because Russia could not help France, Germany could safely press for Delcassé's removal.[14] Even in Morocco itself, Bülow advised the Emperor, the French were unlikely to use force if there was any chance that Germany would get involved, and he doubted the strength of Britain's commitment.[15] France was expected to cave in rather than to fight, and it is unlikely that Wilhelm would have gone ahead otherwise.

As the Germans sensed the measure of French weakness, however, their language became more threatening and they raised the stakes. Schlieffen reported in April that the French Cabinet had instructed the War and Navy Ministers to take no precautions that might be seen as war preparations.[16] From this and from clandestine messages that the Prime Minister, Rouvier, was willing to drop Delcassé, Bülow knew he was running no risk, especially when Rouvier said that war was out of the question and would only serve British interests.[17] Military measures were unnecessary, either to emphasize Germany's demands or as a precaution against hostilities. The most significant step taken during the crisis was the decision to accelerate re-equipping with the *Gewehr 98* infantry rifle and the *Feldkanone 96 n/A* quick-firer, but it would require several months to take full effect, and the French were not informed of it, although they did find out.[18] As early as February 1904 Wilhelm had vetoed as 'thoroughly inopportune' a Bülow proposal to send a warship to Tangier,[19] and Bülow and Holstein viewed the Tangier incident itself as a less provocative alternative to a naval demonstration.[20] After Delcassé fell from power Bülow rejected new suggestions to send a vessel, and when Schlieffen announced that the French were calling up reservists Holstein told him that 'The Chancellor wishes—and I unreservedly agree with this—still to prevent countermeasures, as if that once begins both sides will increase them reciprocally . . . and we hope for a good outcome.'[21] Germany's preferred objective was not war with France but better relations, to be achieved as part of a Continental bloc with Russia against Britain. The more France appeared susceptible to threats, however, the more Bülow was willing to make them.

[13] Gebsattel report, 30 Mar. 1906, KAM MKr 42.   [14] Moritz, *Präventivkrieges*, 173, 218.
[15] Bülow to Wilhelm, 26 Mar. 1905, *GP* xx/1, doc. 6576.
[16] H. Raulff, *Zwischen Machtpolitik und Imperialismus: Die deutsche Frankreichpolitik, 1904/06* (Düsseldorf, 1976), 128.
[17] Radolin to Bülow, 8 May 1905, *GP* xx/2, docs. 6657–8.
[18] Reichsarchiv, *Weltkrieg*, i. 80. Pendézec note, 27 May 1905, Commission de publication des documents relatifs aux origines de la guerre de 1914, *Documents diplomatiques français, 1871–1914* (41 vols., Paris, 1929–59), 2nd ser., vi, doc. 457.
[19] Tschirschky to Bülow, 3 Apr. 1904, *GP* xx/1, doc. 6513.
[20] Guillen, *L'Allemagne*, 839.   [21] Moritz, *Präventivkrieges*, 137, 164.

The Chancellor guessed rightly that his antagonist felt vulnerable. For the first few months Paris was in disarray. The French had antagonized the Russians by remaining neutral in the Far Eastern war, and after the Japanese victory at Mukden, shortly before Tangier, the attaché in St Petersburg warned that Russia could give no help against Germany for the next three years. The CEMA, General Pendézec, shared this view, advising the Quai d'Orsay that the country could not withstand a surprise attack and would suffer a worse débâcle than in 1870.[22] The armed forces had been in turmoil since the turn of the century, and legislation in March 1905, passed over military protest, reduced service with the colours from three years to two.[23] Press articles by General Négrier complained that the frontier garrisons were dangerously under strength and the fortresses unprepared.[24] The High Command was split over the 'Vengeur' documents, purportedly emanating from the GGS and recently sold to French intelligence. They may have been bogus, and most corps commanders distrusted them. However, they alerted the EMA to the possibility that the Germans might sweep through Belgium both north and south of the Sambre–Meuse river line.[25] Under the existing War Plan XV French troops would not concentrate far enough north to meet this; and the EMA feared that the frontier *couverture* was too weak to protect mobilization. The commander-in-chief designate, Bruyère, was sceptical about the revelations, but a CSG meeting on 18 February, which Rouvier attended, agreed that the defences must be improved.[26]

All of this accounts for Delcassé's political isolation, although his failure to communicate with the Cabinet and with Parliament contributed. Even his most loyal subordinates thought that France was outmatched and he should negotiate, the Berlin Embassy advising that Germany did not seek war but would fight for its Moroccan interests.[27] The French Government refrained from extraordinary precautions, explained away exercises and manœuvres as routine and long-scheduled, and instructed its frontier units to avoid incidents, thus encouraging Bülow to step up his intimidation.[28] Yet the Foreign Minister rejected a conference and turned for help from London, which was unexpectedly forthcoming. Sir John Fisher, the First Sea Lord, advised that a German port in Morocco would damage British interests; Lord Lansdowne, the Foreign Secretary, was becoming convinced that Germany wished to destroy the entente.[29] Lansdowne told Delcassé that Britain would join him in opposing a German port, and in

[22] M. Paléologue, *Un grand tournant de la politique mondiale (1904–1906)* (Paris, 1934), 317–18.
[23] This is discussed in sect. 2 below.　　　　　　　　[24] *DDF* 2nd ser. vi. 605–6.
[25] Raulff, *Machtpolitik*, 191–2. J. K. Tannenbaum, 'French Estimates of Germany's Operational War Plans', in E. R. May (ed.), *Knowing One's Enemies: Intelligence before the Two World Wars* (Princeton, 1984), 153–6.
[26] *DDF* 2nd ser. vi. 606. *Conseil supérieur de la guerre*, 18 Feb. 1905, SHA 1.N. 9.
[27] Paléologue, *Tournant*, 301–6, 316–18, 327; Bihourd to Delcassé, 28 Apr. 1905, *DDF* 2nd ser. vi. doc. 369.
[28] Raulff, *Machtpolitik*, 128.
[29] A. J. Marder, *From the Dreadnought to Scapa Flow: The Royal Navy in the Fisher Era, 1904–1914* (London, 1961), 115. S. R. Williamson, *The Politics of Grand Strategy: Britain and France Prepare for War, 1904–1914* (Cambridge, Mass., 1969), 34.

May he suggested that the two Powers should stay in continuous consultation and discuss how to respond to German aggression, while warning Paris against seeking German goodwill through giving way.[30] In effect, Britain and Germany were contending for French allegiance.

With Delcassé's resignation France seemed menaced with satellite status, Balfour commenting that 'it could not be counted on at present as an effective force in international politics'.[31] Delcassé wanted to take up what he supposed to be an offer from London of military and naval talks, but an intercepted cable suggested that if he tried to negotiate a British alliance Germany would declare war. In the Cabinet on 6 June he and Rouvier (whose contacts with Berlin had been revealed to the Foreign Minister by monitoring of German Embassy communications) had a showdown. Delcassé said that Germany was bluffing and France should respond to the British invitation; Rouvier insisted that if it did so Germany would attack and British seapower could not protect France from defeat in three weeks. The *couverture* was under strength, fortresses and weaponry needed renovation, army morale was poor, and strikes and uprisings might sabotage mobilization. Rouvier's assessment catalogued French weaknesses with little attention to Germany's, but the War and Navy Ministers confirmed French unreadiness. Rouvier had support not only in the Council of Ministers but also in the Chamber, where the deputies believed war to be imminent and were 'sweating with fear'. He disliked Delcassé, distrusted Britain, and felt Morocco was not worth a fight, but the determining consideration was the danger of another defeat.[32]

Within six months, however, it was Bülow who was backing away from war. After June 1905 the crisis became more militarized, and the Entente Powers were the beneficiaries, although the change was as much psychological, in the French self-assessment, as in measurable strength. The new French measures should be seen as responses to Bülow's war of words and the revelations in the February CSG, rather than to Germany's own meagre steps. The acceleration of the enemy's field artillery re-equipping was known to French intelligence and was expected to give Germany qualitative parity and numerical superiority in guns per army corps. Completion was not expected, however, until June 1906.[33] To Rouvier's fury and stupefaction, however, the Germans refused his offer of bilateral talks and insisted on a conference, which he grudgingly conceded. Although they gave ground over the conference agenda, this was in a fruitless effort to entice him into the Treaty of Björkö, another Russo-German alliance project, negotiated during a Baltic interview between Wilhelm and Nicholas II in July. By the end of the year his position differed little from Delcassé's, the public and

[30] Lansdowne to Bertie, 22 Apr. and 17 May 1905, *British Documents on the Origins of the War, 1898–1914*, ed. G. P. Gooch and H. V. Temperley (11 vols., London, 1926–38), iii (London, 1928), docs. 90, 94.

[31] Anderson, *Moroccan Crisis*, 232.

[32] Paléologue, *Tournant*, 342–57. *DDF* 2nd ser. vi. 601–4. Andrew, *Delcassé*, 297–300.

[33] Jules Cambon to Delcassé, 22 May 1905; Pendézec note, 27 May 1905, *DDF* 2nd ser., vi, docs. 449, 457. Pendézec note, 8 June 1905, SHA 7.N. 103.

the Chamber moving with him. Already on 6 June he had asked his War Minister to 'get our frontier, our armaments, and our troops in a fit state as soon as possible, assuring him that no credit necessary would be refused'.[34] He ordered surveillance of Germany's frontiers to give warning of mobilization, leave was curtailed, and supplies were readied.[35] A trial mobilization took place at Nancy, although some harvest leave was granted, and in September the most senior conscript class was released on schedule.[36] But during the winter the French moved on to medium-term as well as short-term measures. Frontier units were reinforced, reservists were trained intensively, munitions were replenished, and over 200 million francs of extraordinary credits were authorized, large sums being spent on machine guns, fortresses, and field artillery.[37] The EMA examined how to reinforce the frontiers, and decided to ship the 19th corps from Algeria if necessary.[38] A new Conseil supérieur de la défense nationale (CSDN), set up to co-ordinate the Ministries dealing with national security, began work in 1906.[39] According to the German attaché the French military were preparing for war 'in every direction', and using the crisis to remedy the deficiencies evident before Tangier.[40] General Brun, who replaced Pendézec during the crisis as CEMA, envisaged that if Germany invaded the French army would initially retreat, but that then, even without Russian or British help, it might launch a decisive counterstroke.[41]

In addition to building up his own strength, Rouvier cast about for foreign assistance. His soundings in St Petersburg were discouraging. The French attaché, Moulin, maintained his view that Russia would give little help, and that to repair its army would take at least three years. According to General Polivanov, the Polish frontier had been stripped of artillery, munitions, and seasoned troops.[42] Even the Russians' willingness to help seemed questionable after Nicholas's encounter with Wilhelm at Björkö, of which they gave Paris only a vague and disingenuous account. Whatever Rouvier's earlier inclinations to an understanding with Berlin, however, he ruled out a Franco-German alliance, and as Nicholas, stiffened by his advisers, refused to enter an agreement with Germany without the French the Björkö treaty never took effect.[43] In addition, by the time the Algeciras Conference met, peace had been signed with the

[34] *DDF* 2nd ser. vi. 603.
[35] Paléologue, *Tournant*, 366. Radolin to Bülow, 5 July 1905, PAAA R.6760.
[36] Ibid.; Berteaux to Cdr of 20e Corps, 1 Sept. 1905; *EMA* note on the conscript class, 2 Sept. 1905, SHA 7.N. 103.
[37] Paléologue, *Tournant*, 423. GGS report on France, 4 Dec. 1906, KAM Gstb 489. Mutius reports, 7 June and 11 Aug. 1906, PAAA R.6748. Moltke to Bülow, 23 Jan. 1906, *GP* xxi/1, doc. 6942.
[38] Notes by EMA, 1st Bureau, 24 June 1905, SHA 7.N. 103; and 8 Sept. 1906, SHA 7.N. 104.
[39] EMA 1st Bureau, 25 Aug. 1905, SHA 7.N. 103. Report to the President of the Republic, 3 Apr. 1906, SHA 2.N. 1.
[40] Mutius reports, 6 Jan. and 7 June 1906, PAAA R.6748.
[41] Paléologue, *Tournant*, 408–9.
[42] Moulin reports, 27 June and 23 Sept. 1905, *DDF* 2nd ser. vii, docs. 148, 450; 7 Oct. 1905, ibid. viii, doc. 29.
[43] Anderson, *Moroccan Crisis*, ch. 15.

Japanese. This notwithstanding, Palitsyn, the Chief of the newly created General Staff, and Lamsdorff, the Foreign Minister, warned of Russia's reluctance to fight over Morocco.[44] Moulin advised that France should profit from the Russians' desperate need to raise finance in Paris in order to press them into spending more on armaments, and Rouvier did so urge them, as well as exploiting their dependence to obtain stronger support for France at Algeciras than the Tsar might otherwise have given.[45] But although the Russians said they could still mobilize in Europe, Moulin warned that they could not do more than stand on the defensive, leaving France to bear the full weight of a German attack.[46]

Russia's predicament made it the more imperative to approach the British, and Rouvier's most signal policy reversal was his willingness by the end of 1905 to open naval and military contacts. He found the new Liberal Government receptive. Whereas the Admiralty envisaged amphibious attacks against the German coast, the army strategists were coming to believe that rapid assistance to the French left flank might yield decisive results at small cost.[47] Conversations between the Director of Military Operations and the French military attaché, beginning in January 1906, led to contingency plans to send 100,000 British troops between day 4 and day 15 of mobilization. The talks were authorized by Sir Edward Grey, the incoming Foreign Secretary, and by Sir Henry Campbell-Bannerman, the Prime Minister, but they were not reported to the full Cabinet. They were designed to buttress France without provoking war. There was no commitment to a British intervention, and the EMA did not modify its planning to allow for one. Grey's concern was to forestall a Franco-German bargain at Britain's expense, and although he hoped that a future Franco-British-Russian alignment could contain Germany without war, he thought that at present there would be a 'doubtful issue' between France and Germany on land and the entente was not strong enough to deter aggression.[48] He asked the Secretary for War, Richard Burton Haldane, to examine how Britain might assist if Germany attacked France in the spring,[49] but Britain's preparedness measures were low-key. In July 1905 it announced naval manœuvres in the Baltic, Lansdowne telling the Germans that these were long planned and not a demonstration, although

---

[44] Moulin report, 27 Jan. 1906, *DDF* 2nd ser. ix/2, doc. 77; Spring-Rice to Grey, 7 Feb. 1906, *BD* iii, doc. 272.

[45] Moulin report, 27 Jan. 1906, SHA 7.N. 1477; Rouvier to St Petersburg, 1 Feb. 1906, AMAE NS Russie 38. D. W. Spring, 'Russia and the Franco-Russian Alliance, 1905–1914: Dependence or Interdependence?', *Slavonic and East European Review*, 66 (1988), 572, 585–6. Anderson, *Moroccan Crisis*, 321.

[46] Moulin report, 6 Mar. 1906, *DDF* 2nd ser. ix/2, doc. 371.

[47] Williamson, *Strategy*, 44–51. J. McDermott, 'The Revolution in British Military Thinking from the Boer War to the Moroccan Crisis', in P. M. Kennedy (ed.), *The War Plans of the Great Powers, 1880–1914* (London, 1979), ch. 4. Gooch, *Plans*, ch. 9.

[48] Grey memorandum, 20 Feb. 1906, *BD* iii, doc. 299. On the talks see Williamson, *Strategy*, ch. 3; J. W. and P. F. Coogan, 'The British Cabinet and the Anglo-French Staff Talks, 1905–1914: Who Knew What and When did he Know it?', *Journal of British Studies*, 24 (1985), 110–31.

[49] Grey to Haldane, Jan. 1906, NLS Haldane MSS 5907.

the Liberal Government probably welcomed the timing.[50] In January 1906 Fisher told the French naval attaché that, although he neither wanted nor expected war, he had concentrated all available torpedo boats and submarines at Dover, on the pretext of a training exercise. The Atlantic squadron was being held in British ports, and other units could be quickly recalled.[51] Hence Grey had grounds for his belief that 'the present disposition of the fleet is satisfactory as regards possibilities between France and Germany'. The Foreign Secretary wished to avoid alarming Berlin while there was a chance of success at Algeciras, and he asked the Admiralty not to authorize unusual movements without consulting him about the political implications.[52] He told the German Ambassador that Britain would undertake only 'precautions' rather than 'aggressive preparations' and that he assumed that Germany would do the same.[53]

While the British secured the Straits of Dover and the French their eastern frontier, the Belgians restocked and reinforced their fortresses at Liège, Namur, and Antwerp, updated their mobilization procedures, and prepared to cut communications.[54] They told the French they could call up 180,000 men, 80,000 to garrison the fortresses and 100,000 to campaign in the field.[55] With the British attaché they discussed arrangements for landing British troops.[56] Yet despite the activities of its adversaries the German Government had done little further to increase its preparedness by the time Algeciras began. Wilhelm said afterwards he had not spent an extra mark or moved a soldier or gun,[57] though this was certainly exaggerated. His Admiralty Staff had advised its warships to observe Britain's coast 'with the greatest care', and directives in November approved the navy taking precautions appropriate to times of tension but advised that, if possible, Germany must avoid war. A visit by a warship to Tangier while the conference was in progress was cancelled. Tirpitz profited from the crisis to present a new naval bill to the Reichstag, but it provided only for a modest increase.[58]

German policy on land tells the same story. In June 1905 Schlieffen reported 'war preparations' by France on its eastern border. Bülow told the French Ambassador that he accepted that the measures did not imply warlike intent, although they might support such interpretations.[59] The attaché in Paris reported that the preparations had been exaggerated, apparently accepting the assurances given by the EMA at face value.[60] During the winter British, French,

[50] Anderson, *Moroccan Crisis*, 294. Bihourd to Rouvier, 30 July, 11 and 25 Aug. 1905, *DDF* 2nd ser. vii, docs. 282, 333, 382.

[51] Mercier de Lostende report, 6 Jan. 1906, ibid. viii, doc. 308.

[52] Grey to Tweedmouth, 16 Jan. 1906, *BD* iii. 203.

[53] Grey to Lascelles, 31 Jan. 1906, ibid., doc. 264.

[54] Gérard to Rouvier, 20 and 31 Jan. 1906, *DDF* 2nd ser. ix/1, docs. 26, 105. Barnardiston to Grierson, 31 Mar. 1906, *BD* iii. 221(11).

[55] De Favereau note, 23 Jan. 1906, MAEB NIDMB 7.

[56] Barnardiston reports, Jan.–Apr. 1906, *BD* iii, docs. 221 (1–12).

[57] De Laguiche report, 10 June 1906, SHA 7.N. 1108.   [58] Moritz, *Präventivkrieges*, 228.

[59] Schlieffen to Bülow, 26 June 1905, PAAA R.6760. Bihourd to Rouvier, 29 June 1905, *DDF* 2nd ser. vii, doc. 156.

[60] Radolin to Bülow, 5 July 1905, PAAA R.6760.

and Belgian diplomatic and military reporting uncovered little in Germany except some unusual purchases, recalls of reservists, and revision of mobilization procedures.[61] Numerous German arms firms wished to sell to France, and Bülow had no objection.[62] Moltke, too, took a relaxed view. The French, he reported, were not calling up reservists, moving interior units to the frontier, or preparing mobilization: they had taken only 'precautionary measures' against a possible breakdown at the conference and German attack.[63] Bülow considered that the measures were for domestic political purposes, and the Chief of the Military Cabinet told the French attaché that Germany was not surprised by French precautions or influenced by alarmist newspaper stories.[64] When a (subsequently discredited) report arrived of a French trial mobilization on the frontier Bülow drafted a message that Germany had no intention of attacking and that 'in accordance with our peaceful policy no special military measures of any kind have so far been ordered on the German side, as the French General Staff will certainly well know'. A trial mobilization might cause the German public to demand a response that would increase the danger of 'an unnecessary great crisis', and he briefed his Paris Ambassador that 'such a French military measure must necessarily lead to a sequence of further events'.[65]

Partly because they feared an unintended escalation, the German leaders failed to respond to measures that, in the assessment of German army circles, had moved the balance in France's favour.[66] By the spring of 1906 Bülow was no longer willing even to threaten war, asking Moltke to postpone discussion of a military convention with Italy for fear of indiscretions to Paris.[67] He told his officials that he would fight rather than accept a French diplomatic victory at Algeciras, but nor did he seek a German one, preferring mutual accommodation.[68] It is true that he was still confident about Germany's prospects, expecting France to be isolated and Britain to mediate. But in fact Grey and Rouvier liaised over tactics, and although Grey was prepared to restrain the French in order to avoid fighting, the Germans never forced him to choose. By February the conference was deadlocked over the State Bank and the police of the Moroccan ports, and a confrontation was widely predicted, but it was Germany that was isolated, even Austria-Hungary playing a conciliatory role. Although Bülow upheld the Open Door, the police were placed for five years under French and Spanish control, and international supervision over both this arrangement

[61] Grey to Lascelles, 31 Jan. 1906, *BD* iii, doc. 264; Carteron to Rouvier, 29 Dec. 1905, Lefaivre to Rouvier, 31 Dec. 1905, Crozier to Rouvier, 2 Jan. 1906, *DDF* 2nd ser. viii, docs. 291, 302, 307; Barnardiston to Grierson, 14 Feb. 1906, *BD* iii. 221(4).

[62] Raulff, *Machtpolitik*, 174.

[63] Moltke to Bülow, 23 Jan. 1906, *GP* xxi/1, doc. 6942.

[64] Bülow to Moltke, 24 Jan. 1906, ibid., doc. 6943; Laguiche to Etienne, 28 Jan. 1906, *DDF* 2nd ser. ix/1, doc. 86.

[65] Cdr. of XVI Corps to Moltke, 6 Jan. 1906; Bülow to Radolin, 7 Jan. 1906; Moltke to Bülow, 8 Jan. 1906, *GP* xxi/1, docs. 6937–9.

[66] Gebsattel report, 30 Mar. 1906, KAM MKr. 42.

[67] Moritz, *Präventivkrieges*, 50.   [68] Note by Mühlberg, 25 Dec. 1905, *GP* xxi/1, doc. 6900.

and the Bank was perfunctory. Yet not only did the Chancellor still refrain from military measures, but by the end he wanted to avoid all risk of hostilities.[69]

Tactical misjudgements were partly responsible for this snatching of defeat from the jaws of victory. Bülow spurned Rouvier's offers of bilateral talks and underestimated British commitment. In the autumn of 1905 concessions were made to France in the hope of including it in the Björkö treaty and realigning Europe at London's expense. Even when this failed, however, Bülow did not resume his earlier hectoring. He now paid less attention to Holstein than to Wilhelm, who told him before Algeciras that Germany's chances in a war were as unfavourable as could be: he therefore could not risk one, though nor could he accept dishonour.[70] In public the Emperor blustered, but in private he said he would not fight, not only to his War Minister and his generals, but also to French and British intermediaries.[71] He was concerned, or so he said, about the Socialists, who had threatened a general strike against mobilization, and wrote to Bülow that they must be dealt with before Germany fought a war. He expected Britain to intervene and destroy the fledgling High Seas Fleet, as did the Admiralty Staff and Tirpitz.[72] Even on land, however, he though the prospects in 1906 were 'especially unfavourable'.[73]

Wilhelm took this view in spite of Russia's paralysis, which was confirmed in June 1905 by Schlieffen and in March 1906 by Moltke, who estimated that in a European war the Russian divisions facing Germany and Austria-Hungary would be down from fifty-five to thirty-eight, and their concentration would be very slow.[74] The military expected Britain to intervene, however, and with Russian, British, and Belgian help France would have a slight numerical advantage over Germany, whose assistance from Vienna in a war over Morocco would be luke-warm.[75] Schlieffen's valedictory memorandum in December 1905 noted the approximate equality of the Western balance; Moltke considered a conflict with France would be a long and wearing 'people's war'. Wilhelm also felt he could not 'with a light heart' take the plunge when the artillery and infantry were being re-equipped and the Metz forts not ready.[76] His War Minister, General Karl von Einem, claimed in his memoirs to have urged hostilities, but actually seems to have persuaded Wilhelm to complete the artillery replacement rather than pre-pare more directly.[77] Nor could the process be further accelerated, because if Krupp and Ehrhardt suspended work on foreign orders this would be noticed and might 'cause war at a moment when we do not want it'.[78] According to the Bavarian military attaché, military circles thought the moment favourable in that Russia had collapsed and France was unready, but war was not desired before

[69] Anderson, *Moroccan Crisis*, chs. 16–17.
[70] B. von Bülow, *Memoirs*, ii (London, 1931), 202.
[71] K. von Einem, *Erinnerungen eines Soldaten, 1853–1933* (Leipzig, 1933), 112–14.
[72] Förster, *Militarismus*, 146–7. Moritz, *Präventivkrieges*, 226–7.   [73] Ibid. 90.
[74] Schlieffen to Bülow, 10 June 1905; Moltke to Bülow, 7 Mar. 1906, PAAA R.10449.
[75] Moritz, *Präventivkrieges*, 103–4.   [76] Ibid. 87, 90, 94.
[77] Einem, *Erinnerungen*, 111; Förster, *Militarismus*, 148.
[78] Einem to Caemmerer, 7 Jan. 1906, PAAA R.794.

all the quick-firers had been deployed. Some wanted to fight thereafter, but a war over Morocco would lack popular support.[79] Most of the press and the Reichstag called for a peaceful solution, and this they obtained.[80]

The crisis witnessed a remarkable reversal of roles. In 1905 Germany blackmailed a divided and inexperienced French Cabinet, which was mesmerized by its own unpreparedness. In 1906 entente diplomacy was backed by precautionary steps, and Germany confined itself, apart from naval measures, to an artillery re-equipment that harmed its readiness in the short term. Now Germany was preoccupied with its weaknesses while the French regained confidence, Britain replacing Russia as a *de facto* guarantor of their independence. Despite the tsarist débâcle, an approximately equal military balance survived in Western Europe, to which the Germans reconciled themselves rather than risk a conflict that neither Wilhelm nor his advisers (Schlieffen probably excepted) desired. The retired Generals Goltz and Bernhardi called for preventive war,[81] but they did not speak for Einem or Moltke.

At one level the crisis was Moroccan, but all agreed that Morocco alone did not justify a European conflagration: Germany upheld the Open Door and the Sultanate's nominal independence, but failed to shake the Anglo-French and Franco-Spanish agreements, and Algeciras allowed continuing French financial and administrative penetration. In the underlying struggle over the European alignments, Bülow failed to reduce France to a satellite of a Russo-German bloc, and failed to break the Franco-British entente. On the contrary, he strengthened the latter; and in 1906 renewed staff talks and a huge French loan resuscitated the Franco-Russian alliance, to be complemented in the following year by an Anglo-Russian *rapprochement*. Hence the crisis reinforced the trend to German diplomatic isolation. In the sphere of armaments, by contrast, the peripheral competitions between Britain and Germany and Austria-Hungary and Italy retained their dynamism, intensified by North Sea and Adriatic war scares in the winter of 1904/5. There was a burst of French and German re-equipment, but by 1908 the central Continental balance was reverting towards equilibrium. The forces making for stability must next be considered.

2. European Armies from Morocco to Bosnia

Russia's dramatic military revival after 1910 was an essential element in the take-off of the land arms race; its failure to recover earlier helped restrain its enemies. Between February 1904 and the Treaty of Portsmouth in September 1905 the Empire suffered 400,000 killed and wounded, and lost almost its entire Baltic and Pacific fleets. The war cost more than five times the average expenditure on the armed forces in the years before its outbreak.[82] Yet by summer 1905 the Russians had half a million men in East Asia and outnumbered the exhausted

---

[79] Gebsattel reports, 22 Dec. 1905 and 30 Mar. 1906, KAM MKr. 42.
[80] Moritz, *Präventivkrieges*, 232, 255.   [81] Ibid. 215.
[82] W. C. Fuller, *Strategy and Power in Russia, 1600–1914* (New York, 1992), 406.

Japanese. They were forced to negotiate by the withering of their credit abroad and by revolution at home. Nicholas's promise in October 1905 of a constitution helped to split the opposition, and urban unrest was broken by the end of the year, although in the countryside it lasted longer. Mutiny in the armed forces reached its climax in the winter of 1905/6, affecting elements of one third of the army in European Russia, and it was 1907 before the police pinched out the revolutionary networks in the barracks.[83] The domestic ferment lingered until the eve of the Bosnian crisis.

Some of the army high command, at least, were keen to learn from the bitter experience of the Manchurian campaign, but domestic policing duties, lack of money, and the diversion of resources to the navy gave them little chance to do so. The new governmental structure did not help. The Fundamental Laws of 1906 moved Russia along the road towards the Austro-German model of limited autocracy, but the Tsar kept absolute control of foreign and defence policy. Laws and budgets required his approval, he nominated half the members of the upper house of the legislature, and he appointed and dismissed ministers. The lower house, the Duma, at first contained radical majorities and the authorities could not work with it until, in 1907, they unilaterally modified the electoral system. Even if the Duma did reject the naval or military estimates, however, those of the previous year could be reinstated or a budget approved by the upper house could take effect.[84] The problem for the army reformers was therefore less the democratic element in the new arrangements than the organization of the executive. There was now a Council of Ministers, but it could deliberate on foreign and defence policy only with permission from the Tsar and the Ministers responsible. This meant sometimes, but often not. The Council of State Defence (SGO), chaired by Grand Duke Nicholas, included representatives of the War, Navy, Foreign, and Finance Ministries, and briefly fulfilled a co-ordinating role until it clashed over priorities with the sovereign.[85] Co-ordination was the more imperative because of the creations of army and navy general staffs on the German model, whose chiefs enjoyed independent access to the Emperor, as did newly created inspectors for each arm, and the heads of the military districts. A reduced version of the Main Staff continued in the War Ministry, headed by General Polivanov: the new General Staff (known as the Stavka) had as its first chief one of Grand Duke Nicholas's protégés, General Palitsyn. If to this intricate fabric is added the Tsar's military household, it will be evident that the new War Minister, A. F. Rediger, faced numerous competing influences.[86]

In the aftermath of defeat the military leadership accurately diagnosed much of what had gone wrong. The army needed larger stocks and a bigger output of munitions, high explosive rather than shrapnel shells, and more machine guns

[83] W. C. Fuller, *Civil–Military Conflict in Imperial Russia, 1881–1914* (Princeton, 1985), ch. 5.

[84] Rogger, *Russia*, 218–19.

[85] K. F. Shatsillo, *Russkii imperializm i razvitie flota nakanune pervoi mirovoi voiny* (Moscow, 1968), 15; Fuller, *Conflict*, 232–3.

[86] Ibid. 159. A. K. Wildman, *The End of the Russian Imperial Army* (Princeton, 1980), 65. Moulin reports, 10 July and 25 Dec. 1905, SHA 7.N. 1477.

and field howitzers. The infantry must attack in dispersed order, and be thoroughly trained in new tactics. The middle-aged reservists sent to Manchuria had fought poorly, and a younger, more homogeneous army was required, which could be attained by conscripting a higher proportion of each age cohort, as in France and Germany.[87] To some extent this programme was implemented. Active service was reduced in 1906 to three years in the infantry and four in the mounted arms; the recruitment contingent rose from 320,732 in 1903 to 469,718 in 1906, increasing peacetime strength to 1,305,227 in 1907 and paving the way for a rejuvenated force.[88] The officer corps was purged and the troops' conditions were improved.[89] Each infantry division received sixteen Maxim guns and the army adopted a Krupp-designed field howitzer. The Germans estimated that the Bologoe–Siedlitz railway, opened in 1907, could shorten mobilization and concentration by up to three days.[90]

Despite these improvements, in 1908 the army was still completely unready for European war, in the opinion of both Bülow and Grey and according to French, German, and Austrian military observers.[91] The Russians themselves were the gloomiest of all. In April 1906 Palitsyn told the French he might be able to fight defensively in a year's time; in July 1907 he refused to promise them an offensive against Germany on the outbreak of war or even to prepare one.[92] Rediger told the German plenipotentiary in April 1908 that the army was in no state to fight any war whatever.[93] The immediate reason was the dislocation of mobilization and concentration by the Manchurian campaign and by internal security needs. In 1904–5 the Russians had improvised with nine partial mobilizations, biting deep into their European order of battle.[94] In December 1907 the GGS thought equipment and munitions stocks were still one-quarter below regulation levels. The fifty-two infantry divisions available were still many fewer than pre-war and almost exactly equal to the German and Austro-Hungarian forces, so great was the diversion of manpower to internal needs. The GGS expected a purely defensive initial Russian concentration.[95] After the 1905 revolution many more recruits evaded call-up altogether, and for several years training was interrupted and major manœuvres suspended. Palitsyn complained that deployment of units outside the military districts impeded mobilization, and Rediger protested that aid to the civil power was hampering the army's task of

[87] Moulin reports, 15 and 27 June, 1 Sept., 26 Nov. 1905; 2 and 20 Jan. 1906, ibid.

[88] GGS report on Russian military developments in 1906 (n.d.) KAM Gstb 207; EMA, 'Armée russe: notice' (Dec. 1909), SHA 7.N. 1537.

[89] K. Neilson, 'Watching the "Steamroller": British Observers and the Russian Army before 1914', *Journal of Strategic Studies*, 8 (1975), 199–217; Fuller, *Conflict*, 158.

[90] GGS report on Russian heavy artillery, Mar. 1909, KAM Gstb 208; and GGS annual report for 1907, 19 Dec. 1907, KAM Gstb 207.

[91] R. Ropponen, *Die Kraft Russlands: Wie Beurteilte die politische und die militärische Führung der Europäischen Grossmächte in der Zeit von 1905 bis 1914 die Kraft Russlands?* (Helsinki, 1968), 213–33.

[92] Franco-Russian staff conversations, 21 Apr. 1906, *DDF* 2nd ser. x, doc. 119; French attaché telegram, 9 July 1907, SHA 7.N. 1537.

[93] Hintze telegram, 14 Mar. 1909, PAAA R.10450.   [94] Wildman, *End*, 44–5.

[95] GGS annual report, 19 Dec. 1907, KAM Gstb 207.

external defence, but the Prime Minister, Stolypin, overruled him. Only in March 1908 did Nicholas order units back to headquarters, ending the army's counter-revolutionary deployment except for guard duty.[96]

To war and revolution should be added the consequent financial crisis. Most of the cost was met by foreign credit and an unsupported expansion of the note issue. Russia was kept on the gold standard only by the 1906 French loan, and budget deficits continued until 1910, partly because of a deep and prolonged depression. The Government could borrow no more at home or abroad, and to increase taxes might spark off more unrest. Until economic recovery replenished the coffers, according to the Finance Minister, Kokovtsov, Russia must secure itself not by rearmament but by diplomacy and 'an appropriate orientation in our foreign policy'.[97]

Financial stringency, however, is inadequate to explain the army's predicament. Recovery in ordinary revenue began as early as 1906, but Asia and the navy rivalled the claims of European preparedness. Some members of the General Staff wanted to keep a large presence in East Asia, where there was a fortification race with the Japanese until a *détente* treaty was signed in 1907. The Caucasus front with Turkey was a further distraction.[98] The fleet, however, was the most dangerous competitor. New building was urgent if the state and private yards were not to close, and the naval staff doubted whether what was left of the Baltic Fleet could delay a German advance upon St Petersburg.[99] The navy quickly formulated a rebuilding schedule, and orchestrated propaganda, as well as subsidizing pressure groups. The Council of Ministers was willing to approve two dreadnoughts, but in the Council of State Defence Kokovtsov insisted on a plan and on a rationale, to be co-ordinated with the War Ministry. In April 1907 the majority of the SGO, including Grand Duke Nicholas, supported the War Ministry's contention that, in view of the army's needs, the Baltic Fleet should confine itself to coastal defence. The Navy Minister, however, supported by the Foreign Minister, Izvolsky, insisted that the fleet was essential to Russia's Great-Power status, and should be capable of a wider role. The Tsar felt likewise, overriding the Council of State Defence and approving a programme of four battleships and three submarines in the Baltic, as well as fourteen destroyers and three further submarines in the Black Sea. Normally a mild-mannered man, when the navy was at issue he would lose his temper and bang his fist upon the table. Grand Duke Nicholas challenged the decision unavailingly, and the dispute effectively terminated the SGO's co-ordinating role.[100]

[96] Fuller, *Conflict*, ch. 5.

[97] D. Geyer, *Russian Imperialism: The Interaction of Domestic and Foreign Policy, 1860–1914* (Leamington Spa, 1987), 255–6. A. L. Sidorov, *Finansovoe polozhenie Rossii v gody pervoi mirovoi voiny (1914–1917)* (Moscow, 1960), 18–24.

[98] Moulin report, 25 Oct. 1905, SHA 7.N. 1477. GGS annual reports on fortification, 1 Dec. 1907 and 3 Dec. 1908, KAM Gstb. 489.

[99] K. F. Shatsillo, 'O disproportsii v razvitii vooruzhennykh sil Rossii nakanune pervoi mirovoi voiny, 1906–1914', *Istorichiskie Zapiski*, 83 (1969), 124.

[100] Shatsillo, *Russkii imperializm*, ch. 2.1. Shatsillo, *Rossia pered pervoi mirovoi voiny (vooruzhenye sily tsarizma v 1905–1914 gg)* (Moscow, 1974), 32–42.

The cost of the 1907 programme was 124 million roubles over four years. The Duma refused money for it until maladministration ended in the Admiralty yards, and although the four battleships were laid down in 1909, work soon halted for lack of funds.[101] The Baltic Fleet received a number of destroyers, but nothing bigger except for two cruisers, both ordered abroad. The army's needs, conversely, Rediger estimated at 425 million roubles in one-off and 75 million in extra recurrent expenditure. When he raised the issue early in 1908, however, Kokovtsov, supported by the Emperor, at first offered only 7 million for the Caucasus. Deteriorating relations with Austria-Hungary strengthened Rediger's case, and in March 1908 the Council of Ministers authorized him to seek 299 millions from the Duma over the period 1908–15, mainly for replenishing stores and for artillery, machine guns, telephones, and telegraph equipment. In June the legislature approved the first 92 millions, but the army was still getting less than had been promised to the navy, and waiting longer.[102] As the Bosnia crisis approached, its stores had not regained the pre-war level, and the completion of re-equipping with quick-firing guns was delayed by two years.[103] The fortress artillery was completely outdated, and the heavy field and siege artillery were only beginning to be modernized.[104] Even given Kokovtsov's difficulties, more could have been spent, but neither the new General Staff nor the Council of State Defence enhanced Rediger's effectiveness as a lobbyist. The navy had greater public relations skills and benefited from Nicholas II's favour, but resistance first by Kokovtsov and then the Duma denied the funds that Russian shipbuilding and heavy industry desperately needed. Recovery by both services had a long way to go, and the obstacles to rearmament remained stronger than its protagonists.

* * *

The same was true in Russia's traditional competitor. New challenges in the south-west and south-east were distracting the Habsburg army from the frontier with the Russians in Poland. The essential brake on its progress, however, was that in 1903–6 it became the object of a trial of strength between the Vienna Government and Hungarian nationalism. The precipitant was a new army bill, passed by the Austrian Reichsrat in 1902 on condition that the Hungarian Parliament did likewise.[105] It envisaged a modest increase in the common army's annual recruitment contingent to 125,000 from the 1889 figure of 103,000. In Budapest, most of the ruling Liberal Party wished to maintain the ties with Vienna that the opposition groups wished to loosen or sever. When the army bill was introduced its critics proposed amendments that would magyarize the com-

[101] Report by de Laurens Castelet (French naval attaché), 8 Jan. 1910, SHM BB7 120.

[102] Shatsillo, *Rossia*, 39–42.

[103] Undated (but late 1906) GGS report on Russian development, KAM Gstb 207.

[104] GGS report on Russian heavy artillery, Mar. 1909, KAM Gstb 208.

[105] On the army bill crisis, Rothenberg, *Army*, ch. 9; N. Stone, 'Army and Society in the Habsburg Monarchy, 1900–1914', *Past and Present*, 33 (1966), 95–111; N. Stone, 'Constitutional Crisis in Hungary, 1903–1906', *Slavonic and East European Review*, 45 (1967), 163–82.

mon army regiments recruited from the Hungarian half of the Monarchy, most notably through Hungarian replacing German as the language of command. Their filibustering blocked not only the reform but also the military budget, and denied authority for recruitment even at the existing level, starving the army of men and funds.[106] Franz Joseph and the Liberals worked out a compromise, the so-called *Neunerprogramm*, which was mostly implemented by the common War Minister, Pitreich, in 1904. It allowed Hungarian not as the language of command but as the 'regimental language' for routine use, and permitted the *Honvéd* to acquire artillery. None of this helped, and in elections in January 1905 the opposition won a majority. Franz Joseph tried to impose his will through a minority government and the General Staff made plans for intervention. The 'April Pact' of 1906, however, brought the opposition into government while keeping German as the language of command but increasing the *Honvéd*'s autonomy. The Hungarians promised to increase the common army contingent in the case of 'unconditional necessity', but subsequently denied that such a need existed and the army waited six more years for a manpower increase.[107]

During the tensions with St Petersburg in the 1880s the army had greatly improved its readiness in the north-east. Its development had then ground virtually to a halt and it had already spent a decade urging a new recruitment law, which Pitreich told the GMR was indispensable.[108] Beck entitled his annual report for 1905 'The Standstill in the Army's Development Resulting from the Hungarian Crisis', warning that the Budapest politicians sought to destroy its unity. Yet the price of resistance was to lose extra recruits and to be deprived even of the existing levy: training was suffering, and financial stringency permitted the army merely to study new weapons instead of introducing them.[109] True, the Russians' predicament was worse still. Before the Far Eastern War, Beck had judged them stronger than he was, but after it broke out he dismissed them as a threat for the next few years and the Foreign Minister, Goluchowski, agreed with him.[110] The lack of an external menace, however, facilitated the Hungarian assault from within, and the Habsburg military-industrial complex was too anaemic to sustain the army unaided.

New flashpoints in the Balkans and the Adriatic might come to the rescue. The two were linked via the principality of Montenegro, which adjoined the Monarchy's southern frontier in Herzegovina and Dalmatia, and whose forces on Mount Lovcen overlooked the Habsburg naval anchorage at Cattaro. On its own Montenegro mattered little: it was small and desperately impoverished, with an

[106] R. Kiszling, 'Die Österreichisch-Ungarische Armee in den letzten Decennien vor 1914', *Österreichische militärische Zeitschrift*, 2 (1964), 31.

[107] W. Hetzer, 'Franz von Schönaich: Reichskriegsminister von 1906–1911', Ph.D. thesis (Vienna, 1968), 19, 27.

[108] GMR, 19 Nov. 1903, HHStA PA XL 302.

[109] Beck memorandum, 15 Dec. 1905, KAW Gstb Operationsbureau 741.

[110] Ibid., and Beck memorandum, (?)14 Dec. 1904, same source. Goluchowski in GMR, 29 Sept. 1906, HHStA PA XL 305.

army of only 17,000 men.[111] Traditionally, however, it had been subsidized by the Russians and in 1903–5 the Italians began to open it up as a second front, sending a secret military mission and selling artillery.[112] Serbia in contrast had ten times the population (2.5 million) and a war strength of 250,000, although its army's regulation peacetime strength was only 20,000 and in practice less. In 1905 the Evidenzbureau thought that Serbia's army was in very poor condition, and Conrad two years later that it was 'parterre'; the GGS considered it weak in discipline, training, mobilization readiness, and modern weapons, and the least impressive of the Balkan forces. Most observers thought its Bulgarian rival superior.[113] Until the twentieth century Serbia did not seem dangerous, especially as Austria-Hungary was its largest export market and supplied its armaments and loans.

An officers' coup in 1903, however, brought a more assertive dynasty to the throne in Belgrade. In 1906 negotiations to renew the existing trade treaty broke down, and the Austrians boycotted Serbian imports. They demanded that their tenders for Serbian public contracts should be judged purely on commercial grounds. The Serbs refused, maintaining that their sovereignty was at issue, especially over quick-firing artillery.[114] They concluded a 95 million franc loan agreement (most of the money coming from French investors), which was tied to an order from Schneider for sixty batteries of field and twenty-five of mountain guns.[115] The proceeds also went on building railways to the Austro-Hungarian frontier, on rifles and cartridges, on the state arsenal at Kragujevac, and on the Oblicevo powder plant.[116] The loan was a crucial step towards armaments independence, and Vienna tried its hardest to prevent it, insisting on Skoda's inclusion in the Serbian artillery commission's trials.[117] Indeed, the commission's reports, which the Serbian Government refused to publish, apparently recommended Schneider much less emphatically than did the Government's communiqué.[118] Although the Austro-Hungarian attaché reported that French bribes had influenced the outcome, Skoda does seem to have performed badly, the French had the advantage of being able to lend the money, and Krupp, who insisted on all the order or nothing, ruled themselves out as a compromise choice.[119] All the same, Serbia was re-establishing its independence,

[111] Evidenzbureau report for 1907, KAW Gstb Operationsbureau 742.

[112] GGS annual report, 5 Dec. 1906, KAM Gstb 207. Pitreich memorandum, 'Die Rüstungskredit', GMR, 25 Nov. 1905, HHStA PA XL 304.

[113] GGS annual report, 19 Dec. 1907, KAM Gstb 207. Evidenzbureau report for 1905, KAW Gstb 741; F. Conrad von Hötzendorf, *Aus meiner Dienstzeit, 1906–1918* (5 vols., Vienna, 1921–5), i. 539. Moltke memorandum, (?)23 Feb. 1908, PAAA R.945.

[114] W. S. Vucinich, *Serbia between East and West: The Events of 1903–1908* (Stanford, Calif., 1954), 188, 197.

[115] Ibid. 198. R. Poidevin, 'Les Intérêts financiers français et allemands en Serbie de 1895 à 1914', *Revue historique*, 182 (1964), 55–8. Pomiankowski to Beck, 26 Nov. 1906, KAW Gstb 1906 25–8.

[116] Pomiankowski to Beck, 26 Nov. and 11 Dec. 1906, ibid.　　　　[117] Vucinich, *Serbia*, 190.

[118] Pomiankowski to War Ministry, 10 Apr. 1906, KAW KM Präs 1906, 47–7, and 25 Oct. 1906, KAW Gstb 1906 25–8.

[119] Vucinich, *Serbia*, 192–5.

and the 1906 artillery deal, coupled with Italy's deliveries to Montenegro in the previous year, mark the beginning of a Balkan armaments race.

These developments failed, however, to break the stalemate within the Dual Monarchy, although the General Staff quickly saw the potential threat. Beck in 1905 wanted to reinforce Bosnia-Herzegovina and the Sanjak of Novibazar, a strip of territory under Ottoman rule that separated Montenegro from Serbia, and in which the Habsburgs kept a garrison.[120] Only one narrow-gauge railway ran down to the Sanjak and the Serbian frontier, while Herzegovina and the Dalmatian coast had no rail links at all. Beck, and later Conrad, wanted more troops and greater preparedness, but except at Cattaro nothing much was done.[121]

Rivalry with Italy was little more effective as a stimulus, although a war scare in 1904–5 had a catalytic effect. It was an alert rather than a crisis and no specific issue was in dispute, but it changed perceptions and helped to militarize the relationship.[122] The Austrians were worried by the nationalism of the Zanardelli Government, by Italy's *rapprochement* with France, by its activism in the Balkans, and by its frontier defence works.[123] Japan's surprise attack on Russia was seen as a possible precedent—unrest among the 800,000 Italians under Habsburg rule or cross-border raids by irredentist agitators might set Italian public opinion ablaze. In the spring of 1904 it was reported that Italy intended to establish a naval presence in the Adriatic, whereas previously it had concentrated its fleet against the French in the Ligurian Sea.[124] The moment was propitious for the Habsburg leadership to introduce an armaments increase.

The result was a programme to raise immediate frontier readiness, which was largely implemented; and a quest for medium-term credits for army re-equipment and for warship building, which had much less success. Pitreich warned the Austrian and Hungarian Premiers that military preparations over the previous quarter century had been largely in the north-east, but now a crisis was possible in the Balkans and there might be a sudden war with Italy, the army being able to face neither contingency with reasonable confidence.[125] Funds voted in the summer allowed him to increase stocks of *matériel*,[126] and in November he requested authority to call up 1,636 *Ersatz* reservists. The numbers were small, but extra frontier guards would reassure the local inhabitants and deter irredentist attacks, as well as securing Austria-Hungary's strategic concentration, the frontier railways, and the Pola and Cattaro naval bases against surprise attack.

---

[120] Beck to Franz Joseph, 15 Dec. 1905, KAW Gstb Operationsbureau 741.

[121] P. F. Sugar, *The Industrialization of Bosnia-Hercegovina, 1878–1918* (Seattle, 1963), 71–80, 233–4. Conrad to Franz Joseph, 31 Dec. 1906 and 14 Jan. 1908, KAW Gstb Operationsbureau 742.

[122] M. Behnen, *Rüstung-Bündnis-Sicherheit: Dreibund und informeller Imperialismus, 1900–1908* (Tübingen, 1985), 100 ff. and 187 ff.

[123] Pitreich memorandum, GMR, 25 Nov. 1905, HHStA PA XL 304; and Pitreich in GMR, 23 Apr. 1905, HHStA PA XL 302.

[124] M. Vego, 'Zur Beginn des Rüstungswettlaufes zur See zwischen Ö-U und Italien, 1904–05', *Marine—Gestern, Heute* 9 (1982), 54–9.

[125] Pitreich to Prime Ministers, 28 Mar. 1904, HHStA PA XL 302; Pitreich to Goluchowski and others, 28 Apr. 1904, KAW KM Präs 1904 37–3.

[126] Pitreich to Prime Ministers, 21 Nov. 1904, KM Präs 1904 25–9.

He was supported by Goluchowski, who considered the measures an insurance against Italian adventurism and Serbian attempts to undermine Habsburg authority. With the support of the Common Ministerial Council he implemented his programme early in the new year, using the special provisions of a law of 1888 that allowed him to dispense with parliamentary sanction. He thereby increased his peacetime strength without awaiting the blocked military law, and reinforced the south-west without weakening himself elsewhere.[127]

This was a small success, but one that Pitreich found it difficult to follow through, even though the Monarchy's inner circle were united in wanting to do more. The General Staff revived contingency planning against Rome in 1903, and Beck's annual reports emphasized the threat.[128] Goluchowski advised that Italian public opinion might force a confrontation desired by responsible statesmen on neither side, and that Austria-Hungary could not risk being defenceless. Franz Joseph shared the general mistrust.[129] The Austrian and Hungarian Governments, however, baulked at major expense. The navy needed to replace its small and under-armed capital ships and the army to acquire quick-firing artillery,[130] but deadlock over recruitment was matched by deadlock over re-equipment. In March 1904, citing the dangers on the southern borders, Pitreich asked for 400 million crowns for field guns, howitzers, and warships, to be raised by a long-term loan. The Austrian Government led the opposition, questioning the seriousness of the threat from Italy and jibbing even at an immediate instalment for munitions and frontier defences.[131] Although the Delegations voted in June for a 450-million crown extraordinary credit, of which 88 million for the army and 75 million for the navy were to be made available in 1905, the two governments had still to consent to each instalment. When Pitreich asked for a mere 10 million for the army and 12.5 million for the navy the Austrians said they could not find the money and in consequence Hungary withheld its share.[132] In 1905 the Hungarians could give nothing because of their political crisis and the Austrians, although now better placed, in their turn refused to contribute.[133] By November Pitreich had received only 1.7 million for the army and 12.2 million for the navy, and his Ministry was verging on insolvency. Field-artillery re-equipment was shelved, and munitions workers were laid off. Meanwhile, as he protested, Italian armaments proceeded unabated.[134]

[127] Pitreich to Prime Ministers, KM Präs 1904, GMR, 28 Nov. 1904, HHStA PA XL 303. Pitreich circular, 22 Dec. 1904, KAW KM Präs 1904 25–9.

[128] Beck to Franz Joseph, Dec. 1904 and 15 Dec. 1905, KAW Gstb Operationsbureau 741.

[129] GMR, 23 Apr. and 5 May 1904, HHStA PA XL, 302–3.

[130] A. E. Sokol, 'Der Flottenbau der k.u.k. Kriegsmarine, 1895 bis 1914', *Marine—Gestern, Heute*, 8 (1981), 8–13. Rothenberg, *Army*, 127, 149.

[131] Pitreich to Prime Ministers, 28 Mar. 1904, HHStA PA XL 302; and GMR debates, 15, 16, and 23 Apr., 5 May 1904, ibid. 302–3.

[132] Pitreich in GMR, 25 Nov. 1905, ibid. 304. Pitreich to Prime Ministers, 22 June 1904; Böhm-Bawerk and Lukács to Pitreich, 19 and 28 Aug. 1904, KAW KM Präs 1904 37–3.

[133] Pitreich to Gautsch and Fejerváry, 29 June 1905; Fejerváry and Gautsch to Pitreich, 7 July and 23 Dec. 1905, KAW KM Präs 1905 37–3.

[134] Pitreich in GMR, 25 Nov. 1905, PA XL 304.

That year, 1905, was the nadir, and two years later Conrad felt strong enough to advocate a preventive war against Italy, even though little, apart from greater immediate solvency, had changed. In 1906, however, compromise with the Hungarians and the arrival of a younger generation in positions of authority offered a possible fresh start. There were new Austrian and Hungarian Premiers, Aehrenthal replaced Goluchowski, Schönaich replaced Pitreich, and Conrad replaced Beck. The appointments testified to Franz Ferdinand's influence and portended greater vigour and an end to drift. Schönaich, however, who generally enjoyed Franz Joseph's support, had a sounder and more cautious sense than did Conrad of political constraints, and friction between the two men divided the army's leadership. Conrad was a nervous obsessive, with a wide and detailed knowledge of his forces and outstanding energy, expressed in an outpouring of memoranda and his voluminous memoirs. More than Beck, he trusted in decisive action and armed might to resolve conflicts of interest, both against the Hungarians at home and through preventive wars abroad. His nightmare was a battle on three fronts against St Petersburg, Belgrade, and Rome, and he wished to cripple the Italians while Russia was weak. He argued that hostilities with Italy were inevitable and the timing alone was at issue. Serbia he wanted to absorb.[135] Aehrenthal, by contrast, believed that Italy must be kept 'in a certain fear of us' by military and naval preparations, but like Franz Joseph he opposed preventive war.[136] The military effort against Rome was intended for deterrence rather than aggression.

That Italy rather than Russia was the main preoccupation strengthened the navy's case for more resources at the army's expense. The Italian fleet in 1904 had twice as many warships as Austria-Hungary's, although it also had eight times the length of coastline to defend. Both Powers had six modern ships of the line, although the Habsburg ones were more lightly gunned.[137] Pitreich had accepted that the navy should benefit from the 1904 armaments credit, but when he proposed to cut its ordinary budget in compensation the *Marinekommandant*, Sterneck, resigned. His successor, Montecuccoli, was a skilled and ambitious political operator, whose hand was strengthened by a 127–million lire Italian naval law, voted in June 1905. In response he wanted a long-term programme on the German model, including twelve battleships.[138] Pitreich opposed this if it would mean starving the army; Goluchowski, however, supported Montecuccoli, and threatened resignation to get his way. The Common Ministerial Council agreed in September 1906 to finance three battleships and one cruiser,[139] and in 1910–11 the three semi-dreadnought battleships of the Radetzky class entered service as, briefly, the most powerful warships in the Mediterranean. The navy's supporters were Franz Ferdinand, the Austrian Government, and Goluchowski and Aehrenthal, who felt it was needed to

[135] Conrad, *Dienstzeit*, i. 307–10, 513. Conrad to Franz Joseph, 14 Jan. 1908, KAW Gstb Operationsbureau 742.

[136] Conrad, *Dienstzeit*, i. 575. Aehrenthal in GMR, 30 Apr. 1908, HHStA PA XL 312.

[137] Vego, 'Beginn', 54. Höbelt, 'Marine', 717.

[138] Montecuccoli to Franz Joseph, 6 July 1905, KAW KM Präs 1905 37–3.

[139] GMR, 29 Sept. 1906, HHStA PA XL 305.

overawe Italy; it continued to be handicapped by the scepticism of the Hungarians and of Franz Joseph himself.

The new army leadership after 1906, meanwhile, made little more headway than their predecessors. Conrad pleaded for more machine guns, artillery, fortifications, and training, and above all for more men.[140] Schönaich obtained little, apart from a 15-million crown artillery credit in April 1908.[141] Although the new quick-firing guns were ready to be distributed, he lacked the necessary personnel. Machine guns, artillery, and Montecuccoli's warships would need crews to operate them, and it would be dangerous further to thin out the infantry.[142] Schönaich wanted to raise the combined common army and navy contingent from 103,000 to 158,000, but to reduce the number of exemptions in order to improve the recruits' quality.[143] As the Hungarian Government still set unacceptable political conditions, however, he resorted to a *Notbehelf*, or emergency redistribution of men within the existing contingent.[144] This was anathema to Conrad, who felt that rather than make do the army should pin responsibility where it belonged.[145] Franz Ferdinand, who preferred a smaller army over concessions to Budapest, also disliked the measure, and a commission he presided over greatly reduced its scope.[146] As approved in September 1907 it transferred approximately 5,000 men from the infantry and *Jäger* regiments into the navy, the field and mountain artillery, and siege-howitzer and machine-gun units.[147] Schönaich could now begin distributing the M1905 quick-firer and introduce the Schwarzlose machine gun, reorganize the light artillery, and create an independent heavy field artillery, while the *Honvéd* and the *Landwehr* acquired their own batteries.[148]

By 1907–8, therefore, there were at last some signs of movement. Both Schönaich and Conrad were agreed, however, that the priority was the southwest and secondarily the Balkans: hence they needed mountain artillery and mobile siege guns, and teams of pioneers to assault the Italian strong-points.[149] Although Conrad was beginning to warn about the speed of Russian recovery,[150] the north-east continued to be neglected.[151] Austro-Hungarian military modernization, such as it was, benefited the navy more than it did the army, and was directed against the Habsburgs' partner in the Triple Alliance.

* * *

[140] Conrad to Franz Joseph, 31 Dec. 1906, KAW Gstb Operationsbureau 742.

[141] Schönaich to Bolfras, 1 Apr. 1908, KAW KM Präs 1908 37–2. GMR, 30 Apr. 1908, HHStA PA XL 312.

[142] Pitreich to Prime Ministers, 26 Sept. 1906, KAW KM Präs 1906 26–1.

[143] Schönaich to Conrad, 4 Dec. 1907, KAW KM Präs 1907 26–1.

[144] Hetzer, 'Schönaich', 36. Schönaich to Franz Joseph, 2 May 1907, KAW KM Präs 1907 49–19.

[145] Conrad comments on preceding, n.d. ibid.

[146] Commission proceedings (21 May 1907) in ibid.

[147] Schönaich to Franz Joseph, 18 Sept. 1907, KM Präs 1907 47–19.

[148] Hetzer, 'Schönaich', 99. GGS annual report, 1 Apr. 1909, KAM Gstb 204.

[149] Conrad to Franz Joseph, 31 Dec. 1906, KAW Gstb Operationsbureau 742. Schönaich to Franz Joseph, 2 May 1907, KAW KM Präs 1907 49–19.

[150] Conrad, *Dienstzeit*, i. 572.   [151] Ibid. 550.

In Italy too there was a delayed response to the 1904 war scare, and the navy profited earlier and more. The episode confirmed a reorientation that was already under way. In 1901–2 the War Ministry changed its planning target from France to Austria-Hungary; the navy refocused on the Adriatic soon afterwards.[152] The scare probably agitated the Italian public more than it did the Austrian, because of the Italians' sense of military inferiority. It began with rumours of Habsburg military preparations, followed by the Delegations' votes for Pitreich's re-equipment credit, and his frontier protection measures. The Government in Rome called out 86,000 reservists, ostensibly for internal security during the autumn elections, but it hesitated over raising military spending.[153] Although the army received 11 million lire in 1905 to shorten to two months its period of low strength (*forza minima*) during the winter, this had long been contemplated anyway.[154] It carried out some fortification work, replenished stocks, and increased frontier strengths.[155] But the Finance Minister resisted doing more, and was supported by the Foreign Minister, Tittoni, and the Premier, Giolitti.[156] Possibly the Habsburg countermeasures had a sobering effect.[157] The navy, in contrast, on paper had the advantage over Austria-Hungary but its bases in the Adriatic were unmodernized and many of its ships could not operate there. Its 127-million lire credit, voted in 1905, was for a long-term programme down to 1917, including four battleships. The Habsburg fleet was explicitly the yardstick of comparison and Adriatic superiority the objective.[158]

The army's inglorious record and its unstable leadership contributed to its Cinderella status. Between 1898 and 1908 there were ten War Ministers. The choke points, as usual, were men and money. The call-up ratio fell in 1896–1906 from 26.3 per cent to 18.2 per cent, absenteeism due to emigration being a major cause. Until 1905 the period of the *forza minima* could be up to six months, to the detriment of preparedness and training.[159] Debt repayments constrained the public finances, and the left-leaning administrations of Zanardelli and Giolitti had alternative priorities such as social welfare and railway nationalization. When they came to office they agreed not to cut military spending or peacetime strength, but they fixed a total for army and extraordinary spending within a 'consolidated' budget that they held to even after the war scare.[160] Among the losers were the railways, the Italians in 1908 having only three concentration

---

[152] Behnen, *Rüstung*, 214, 227.

[153] Ibid. 117, 187–8. Goluchowski in GMR, 28 Nov. 1904, HHStA PA XL 303.

[154] G. Rochat and G. Massobrio, *Breve storia dell'esercito italiano dal 1861 al 1943* (Turin, 1978), 153. Behnen, *Rüstung*, 188. Messier de Saint James (French military attaché), 30 May and 20 Sept. 1905, SHA 7.N. 1368.

[155] St James, 10 Feb. 1906, ibid.

[156] St James, 25 Aug. 1904, ibid. Behnen, *Rüstung*, 118.

[157] St James, 30 Jan. 1905, SHA 7.N. 1368.   [158] Behnen, *Rüstung*, 230–1.

[159] Piero del Negro, 'La leva militare', in Stato Maggiore dell'Esercito (Ufficio Storico), *L'esercito italiano dall'Unità alla Grande Guerra (1861–1918)* (Rome, 1980), 456, 459.

[160] Rochat, *Esercito*, 151–2. M. Mazzetti, 'L'esercito nel periodo giolittiano', in Stato Maggiore, *Esercito*, 248.

lines leading to the frontier, against their enemies' seven.[161] The continuing absence of a territorial mobilization system further slowed things down, and Saletta thought the Austrians could deploy much faster than he.[162]

In addition there was a less measurable malaise. Italy was spared a domestic upheaval comparable to those in Austria-Hungary and Russia, but there was increasing social protest (suppressed by the army) and anti-militarism. After 1903 there was much talk of an officer crisis. NCOs felt they lacked a career structure; their superiors complained about accommodation, pensions, and a promotion blockage, as well as sensing that they were not appreciated and that the army was in decay.[163] The most immediate stimulus to reform, however, was the War Ministry's mishandling of quick-firing artillery. The 75A field gun of 1901, manufactured in Italy to a Krupp design, had neither a hydraulic recoil system nor a protective shield. By 1904 it was recognized to be inadequate, with the implication that 60 million lire had been wasted. When the War Ministry signed contracts in January 1907 for 600 (later reduced to 428) Krupp quick-firers, there was fury in the press and in the Chamber that a foreign order of this magnitude was made without consulting Parliament so soon after the 75A fiasco, especially as the new gun too was said to be defective.[164] Giolitti took advantage of the scandal to initiate a parliamentary commission of inquiry into the entire administration of the army and the demoralization in its ranks, taking the unusual step of replacing General Viganò as War Minister by a civilian politician, Senator Casana.[165]

Rearmament was moving up the agenda anyway. The Moroccan crisis and Conrad's appointment both caused disquiet in Italy, and a debt conversion had released some money. In the spring of 1907 Viganò introduced a bill to generalize two-year service while increasing the contingent, and one for a 200-million lire credit.[166] The appointment of the inquiry commission was intended to help the passage of the latter, as well as to cleanse the Augean stables at the War Ministry. In fact only 60 millions were voted, half for north-eastern fortifications and half for Krupp guns. But a second credit in July 1908 provided 223 millions over ten years for fortification and for field, mountain, siege, and coastal artillery. Higher salaries were voted for the officers, and better lodging, rations, and training for the men.[167] The commission's reports laid the basis for structural reforms, and a new leadership took over, Casana being joined in 1908 by General Pollio, who replaced Saletta when the latter retired as CGS. A Supreme Council of State Defence was created as a co-ordinating body, though one with limited

[161] Behnen, *Rüstung*, 195.   [162] Ibid. 211–16. Gooch, *Italy*, 124.

[163] Whittam, *Italian Army*, 150–3. Rochat and Massobrio, *Esercito*, 151. Col. Jullian (French attaché), 6 Mar. 1908, SHA 7.N. 1369.

[164] St James, 25 Aug. 1904, SHA 7.N. 1368; Jullian, 24 Oct. 1907, SHA 7.N. 1369.

[165] St James, 10 May 1907 and 10 Mar. 1908, SHA 7.N. 1369.

[166] St James, 28 Feb. and 20 Mar. 1907, ibid.

[167] Rochat and Massobrio, *Esercito*, 154; GGS 9 Abt. report for 1907, KAM Gstb 204. Jullian, 5 June and 12 and 13 July 1908, SHA 7.N. 1369.

effectiveness. Further legislation reduced exemptions from military service, and in 1908–10 the call-up ratio rose from 25 to 33 per cent.[168]

By 1907–8, therefore, the Italian army, like the Austro-Hungarian one, was over the worst and attracting more recruits and funds. It had also found a purpose. Although the Triple Alliance was renewed in 1907, Italy's fortification and railway programmes were unambigously directed towards the north-east. In June 1907 the Chamber voted almost unanimously in favour of a resolution calling for unconditional command of the Adriatic, as well as for four dreadnought battleships, although work on them was delayed for another two years.[169] Italy emerged from its military stagnation not as a dependable ally of Vienna but poised to commit itself in earnest to the Adriatic arms race.

Russia's disablement allowed the Austrians to divert resources to the rivalry with Italy; but it also contributed to the Hungarian crisis that brought the Habsburg army to the verge of bankruptcy. The paralysis in the Dual Monarchy helps in turn to explain the neglect of the Italian army until Conrad's appointment. To an extent there was a virtuous (or vicious) circle, constraints on armaments expansion in one Power meshing with those in its potential enemies. The 1904 war scare, at least on land, heightened perceptions of hostility but had only small material effects, and the Russian, Austro-Hungarian, and Italian armies followed parallel courses through stagnation to incipient recovery. It is now necessary to compare this trajectory with the impact of the much more serious Moroccan crisis on Germany and its Western adversaries.

* * *

Belgium would be Germany's first antagonist in a Continental campaign. In the later nineteenth century there had been growing confidence that the country could rely on the Great-Power guarantee of its integrity given in the London Treaty of 1839. The army's size and quality, relative to those of France and Germany, had diminished. Military service was more acceptable to the francophile liberals than to the clerical Right, which opposed subjecting Flemish youth to the degradations of the barracks. Much reliance was placed on the imposing, but outdated and incomplete fortress system of General Brialmont, which included barriers at Liège and Namur to a German advance through the Sambre-Meuse valley.[170] On the eve of the Moroccan crisis the army was suffering from the impact of the 1902 recruitment law, which had weakened the compulsory recruitment system while failing to introduce an adequate voluntary one.[171] During the crisis, Parliament voted for a new line of fortifications around Antwerp, which remained a major item of expense, of questionable utility, for the next decade.[172] After Algeciras, however, there was no big increase in

[168] Negro, 'Leva militare', 456–7.   [169] Behnen, *Rüstung*, 236.

[170] E. H. Kossman, *The Low Countries, 1780–1940* (Oxford, 1978), 517–18; C. Terlinden *et al.*, *Histoire militaire des Belges* (Liège, 1931), 307–8.

[171] L. de Vos, *Het Effectief van de Belgische Krijgsmacht en de Militiewetgeving, 1830–1914* (Brussels, 1985), ch. 8. Discussion of recruitment in AGRB Lesaffre MSS 10, cahier 1. On the artillery, Lt.-Col. Siben (French attaché), 27 Jan. 1906, SHA 7.N. 1155.

[172] Siben, 25 Jan. 1906, ibid.

funding or new legislation.[173] French appraisals found the Belgian army mediocre: Liège and Namur could put up a serious resistance, but the artillery was defective and mobilization slow.[174] The GGS thought the Belgian army small, its guns outdated, and its training and discipline poor.[175] There was growing criticism of the 1902 law, but in January 1908 the War Minister said it must be given another year's trial.[176] A further alert would be needed to concentrate minds.

* * *

After Morocco the British army was a potential element in the European military equation. Innovations in 1906–8 enhanced its war preparedness and its Continental striking power. It too, however, laboured under manpower and financial shortages, and was losing ground to the sister service. Before 1905 the army was beginning to define a new strategic mission for itself, but had progressed little with the reorganization that its South African discomfiture had shown to be necessary. The reforms of Balfour's Secretaries for War, St John Brodrick (1900–3) and Arnold-Forster (1903–5), were abortive, or worse. Haldane, their Liberal successor (1905–11), was a more skilful politician with more workable plans. His principal monuments were the Territorials and the British Expeditionary Force. The 1907 Territorial and Reserve Forces Act replaced the old auxiliary forces by a Territorial Force and a Special Reserve, the latter being a manpower reservoir for the regular army. In the Territorial Force, however, by 1913 only 1,090 officers and 17,778 NCOs and men had volunteered to serve abroad on mobilization.[177] Their contribution was essentially to home defence, and for the Continent it was the Expeditionary Force that mattered. The GGS estimated that before Haldane Britain would have been able to get barely 100,000 men on the mainland by day 18 of mobilization, but now 166,000 (115,000 of them combatants) could be in the Channel ports by day 15.[178] According to Haldane himself, an inquiry he ordered during the crisis revealed that some 80,000 men could be ready in two months; by 1911 160,000 fighting troops could reach France in fifteen days.[179] This was an overstatement, and British mobilization and concentration were not perfected until the eve of war, but Haldane's regrouping of the regular army into six large divisions raised the number of artillery batteries immediately available on mobilization from forty-two to sixty-three and brought the peacetime and wartime organization into closer correspondence.[180]

---

[173] Siben reports, 27 Jan. 1906, 27 Jan. 1907, 25 Jan. 1908, ibid.
[174] Siben, 27 Jan. 1907, ibid.
[175] GGS, 'Die Taktik der Belgischen Armee', Jan. 1908, KAM Gstb 223.
[176] Siben, 25 Jan. 1908, SHA 7.N. 1155.
[177] E. M. Spiers, *Haldane: An Army Reformer* (Edinburgh, 1980), 186. In 1913 NCOs and men totalled 236,389. Ibid. 184.
[178] Summary of GGS description of British military position, 9 Apr. 1908, KAM Gstb 146.
[179] R. B. Haldane, *Before the War* (London, 1920), 165–8. Haldane to Lloyd George, 10 Nov. 1909, NLS Haldane MSS 5908.
[180] Spiers, *Haldane*, 82–4.

Furthermore, although the British did not acknowledge it, Continental intervention was seen increasingly as the Expeditionary Force's primary task. Just before the Tangier incident the first DMO, Grierson, visited Paris and told French officials that Britain would fight alongside them in a war against Germany. On his return, he ordered a war game in which British forces came to Belgium's assistance.[181] Haldane was aware of General Staff contingency planning and the conversations with the French while he was incubating his reorganization.[182] In 1908 the General Staff testified explicitly that the army was needed to maintain the balance of power and make Britain's friendship more valuable to its Continental neighbours. To a CID subcommittee on the military needs of the Empire, meeting in 1908–9, it recommended sending one cavalry and four infantry divisions to reinforce the French left flank. The subcommittee left the decision whether to send such an expedition to the government of the day, but commended the plan as 'valuable' and asked the staff to work out the detail.[183]

By enhancing their ability to intervene in Western Europe the British might seem to have been encouraging an arms race. In fact the GGS was more worried by the Royal Navy's alternative strategy of blockade and coastal raids than by a possible deployment athwart the main German axis of advance.[184] After the Haldane reforms the Expeditionary Force was a disciplined army with quick-firing field guns and an adequate rifle, but it remained deficient in machine guns, munitions stocks, and heavy artillery, and had a very small trained reserve. It remained tiny in relation to Germany's field force. It is true that some General Staff officers suggested a six-division expedition could tip the Franco-German balance, but there were private doubts about this, and Haldane's reforms were driven by pressures for retrenchment rather than a precise calibration of strategic needs.[185] The size of the Expeditionary Force depended on the number of troops available in the home islands, and in a voluntary system manpower depended on money, of which there was not enough.

Compulsory service was championed by the National Service League, which grew, or so it claimed, from 10,000 to 270,000 members in 1907–14, among them over eighty MPs. However, even the NSL advocated only short-term training for home defence, not obligatory service abroad, and as both main party leaderships opposed its nostrums conscription was not practical politics.[186] Leaving aside the infringement of civil liberties, Haldane objected to compulsion on practical grounds. Conscripts could not be sent on extended tours of duty overseas; to train and command a mass conscript army would require a large officer corps that would take years to establish; and Britain could not finance both a first-class

[181] Williamson, *Strategy*, 46.   [182] Spiers, *Haldane*, 78.

[183] Howard, *Commitment*, 45–6.

[184] This is discussed further below; cf. A. Offer, *The First World War: An Agrarian Interpretation* (Oxford, 1989), chs. 15–17.

[185] Howard, *Commitment*, 42; Spiers, *Haldane*, ch. 3.

[186] R. J. Q. Adams and P. P. Poirier, *The Conscription Controversy in Great Britain, 1900–1918* (Basingstoke, 1987), 10–13, 20, 23, 39, 41.

navy and an army of Continental size.[187] Whereas St John Brodrick had shortened the term of service, which had added to the reservists at the cost of instability in the standing army, Haldane returned to Cardwell's formula of seven years with the colours and five in the reserves. Recruitment to the regular and territorial armies held up well until 1910, but both then started to fall below establishment, and in the last years of peace the General Staff was becoming disenchanted with the voluntary system.[188] Haldane, however, belonged to a radical government that wanted to spend more on social reform, and Liberals and Unionists agreed that the army estimates must be cut back. They had risen from £18.156 million to £29.813 million between 1896–7 and 1905–6: by reducing effective strength and by economizing on overseas commitments Haldane held to a £28 million ceiling. His success enabled him to fight off radical pressure for further cuts, but at the price of freezing British army spending while the Royal Navy and the Continental army budgets rose.[189] His reforms achieved a one-off augmentation in 1907–8 in Britain's military capabilities in Western Europe, but then reached a plateau. No more than in Belgium were developments in Britain adequate to break the Western European armaments equilibrium without movement in Paris or Berlin.

* * *

The civil–military consensus of the early Third Republic had been fraying anyway before the Dreyfus affair destroyed it and brought the French Radicals to power in the governments of Waldeck-Rousseau (1899–1902), Combes (1902–5), and Clemenceau (1906–9). Not only had the General Staff wrongfully convicted an innocent man and obstructed the course of justice; Dreyfus's supporters felt the army had shown it was unreliable as a defender of the Republic against clerical and conservative enemies. In consequence they curtailed the independence that Freycinet had given to the High Command. Louis André, the War Minister in 1901–4, immediately clashed with the generalissimo and the CEMA, who resigned when André removed two staff officers whom he thought implicated in the Dreyfus case. The next two Chiefs, Pendézec and Brun, were less senior than their predecessors, and there were nine generalissimos between 1898 and 1911. The CSG met less frequently than hitherto and the Minister strengthened his position relative to the army leadership.[190]

At lower levels there was no wholesale purge, but André abolished the *Commissions de classement* and took sole responsibility for officer promotion. He was determined, according to his memoirs, to protect republican officers: for information on individual candidates he and his advisers turned to the freemasons, who built up a system of military files at their Paris headquarters. When the link was disclosed in Parliament there was an outcry, and André resigned, but his methods had divided the army and encouraged men to inform on colleagues. After 1904 the prefects reported regularly on the party and religious

---

[187] Spiers, *Haldane*, 164; Haldane, *Before the War*, 171–5. [188] Spiers, *Haldane*, 173–86.
[189] Ibid., ch. 3. [190] Ralston, *Army*, 160, 289–300.

affiliations of candidates for advancement, and the apolitical career structure was gone for good.[191]

This was only one of many grievances. Officers' incomes were barely adequate to support a family in bourgeois style, and both salaries and pensions were less than in the German army or for French civilian officials. The Radicals made it harder to use private soldiers as personal servants and axed facilities such as tennis courts, as well as requiring Saint-Cyr cadets to spend one year in the ranks. Officers were expected to exercise a 'social role' and attend to the 'civic' education of their conscripts, which some resented as a distraction from their mission. There was growing rowdiness and insubordination among the men, and hostility to the army from outside. All of this contributed to an Italian-style moroseness: applicants to Saint-Cyr halved in 1897–1907, and resignations became more frequent.[192]

A further hallmark of the Radical ascendancy was the two-year service law of 21 March 1905. It fixed the term of duty as two years with the colours, eleven in the reserves, six in the territorial army, and six in the territorial reserve. In emergency, those under arms could be retained for longer than two years, and reservists recalled. Almost all exemptions were eliminated, those unfit for armed service being required to do auxiliary service, and families dependent on a single breadwinner being subsidized. Under the 1889 system almost two-fifths of each conscript class qualified for some exemption and over half the infantry did no more than ten months active service: now almost everyone would complete the full term.[193]

Professional military opinion almost unanimously opposed the law, on the grounds that two years was too little to make a soldier, especially a mounted one. None the less, it passed with big majorities. Its supporters wished to lessen and to equalize the conscription burden, especially as Germany in 1893 had set a precedent. They assumed that in a war reservists rather than the standing army would take the main weight.[194] The EMA acknowledged that the law would create a larger and more homogeneous reserve, although this would do little for the cavalry, who needed high peacetime strengths for training and for frontier protection.[195] To train the reserves, however, France would require extra NCOs, of whom Germany had three times the number.[196] The law did not diminish France's wartime strength, but it would reduce the peacetime standing army, even if there were fewer exemptions, because only two rather than three conscript classes would normally be under arms. The predicted fall was from 580

[191] Ibid. 266–80. D. Porch, *The March to the Marne* (Cambridge, 1981), ch. 6. R. Girardet, *La Société militaire dans la France contemporaine (1875–1939)* (Paris, 1953), ch. 7. L. André, *Cinq ans de ministère* (Paris, 1907).

[192] Porch, *Marne*, chs. 5, 7. Ralston, *Army*, 287–8.

[193] Ibid. 301–11. Text of the bill in AN C7257.

[194] Ralston, *Army*, 301. André, *Cinq ans*, 170–8. Porch, *March*, 192–6.

[195] Pendézec to Berteaux, 1 Dec. 1904, 30 Jan. 1905, Pendézec note of 1 Mar. 1905, SHA 7.N. 103.

[196] Ralston, *Army*, 301.

to 512,000.[197] Moreover, because of the declining birth rate France's recruitment cohorts were shrinking rapidly, and the gap with Germany widening. Given the extent of Russia's defeat, the law appeared to signify a relaxation of effort when France needed to intensify it.

At this point the Moroccan crisis supervened. It failed to insulate the army from domestic pressures. When Clemenceau became Prime Minister he gave the War Ministry to General Picquart, who had been dismissed from the General Staff during the Dreyfus affair, and humiliated the High Command in other ways, such as placing prefects before generals in status lists. It was harder for the army to remain a symbol of national unity when on the one hand it was used to enforce, against Catholic demonstrations, the 1905 separation of Church and State, and on the other was deployed in strike-breaking. In 1908 the main trade union federation, the CGT, voted for a general strike in the event of war. There was increasing desertion, anti-militarist propaganda, and unrest among the troops, culminating in 1907 when discipline in several units in the south of France broke down during mass protests by winegrowers and both the generalissimo and the deputy chief of staff resigned in indignation over the army's condition.[198]

None the less, French war preparation was moving into higher gear. Weapons expenditure had bottomed out in 1903–4 after the 75 mm re-equipping, André being unable, in the absence of a credible external threat, to challenge Finance Ministry insistence that excessive spending would damage French creditworthiness.[199] Morocco's main effect, apart from measures to raise immediate readiness, was to make the Chamber more generous. In October 1906 a new long-term programme for *matériel* was approved, although it would be subject to votes on annual instalments. Equipment spending reached a new peak in 1906–7 before tailing off, though not to pre-crisis levels.[200] The army had the advantage of there being only one obvious enemy. Mobilization preparations against Britain were downgraded in 1908.[201] The Quai d'Orsay did not disclose the 1902 neutrality agreement with Rome, and in 1908 when drawing up its Plan XVI the EMA still earmarked three corps for either the Alps or the north-east, but the latter was the main theatre and defence work against Italy was minimal.[202] A second advantage was that the navy was a lesser competitor than elsewhere. In 1902–5, under the administration of Camille Pelletan, the fleet had become disastrously disorganized. In 1906 a new programme was adopted for six pre-dreadnought battleships, but for three more years the construction budget showed no big increase.[203] Clemenceau told the newly established CSDN that

[197] Pendézec to Berteaux, 19 Dec. 1904, SHA 7.N. 103. EMA note for CSG on cadres law, n.d. but late 1906, SHA 7.N. 104.

[198] Ralston, *Army*, 281–5. Porch, *March*, 86–7, 105–24.   [199] André, *Cinq ans*, 192–3.

[200] Millerand to Finance Minister, 23 Jan. 1912, SHA 7.N. 134. F. Crouzet, 'Recherches sur la production d'armements en France (1815–1913)', *Revue historique*, 509 (1974), 83.

[201] Note by Lt.-Col. Bernard, 24 Nov. 1908, SHA 7.N. 105.

[202] Brun in CSG, 15 Feb. 1908, SHA 7.N. 10. Col. Beltranelli note, 3 Feb. 1908, SHA 7.N. 105.

[203] Crouzet, 'Recherches', 63, 83–4. J. Doise and M. Vaïsse, *Diplomatie et outil militaire* (Paris, 1987), 144. Testimony of Navy Minister to Chamber Marine Commission, 7 Feb. 1906, AN C7258.

he considered British help certain and that in a war the French fleet should, in conjunction with the Royal Navy, go quickly on to the attack. None the less, the decision would come on land, where, given that the Russian alliance was 'without practical utility', the army must observe great caution.[204]

The army continued to face major problems. The reduction in peacetime strength following the 1905 law took effect in 1907, and though less than expected it brought numbers below regulation.[205] There was no NCO increase; and a law in 1908 shortened reservist and territorial training.[206] During the winter inexperienced recruits made up more than half the standing force.[207] In future a higher proportion of its war strength, too, would be inadequately prepared, and it was coming closer to resembling a militia. In response the EMA wished to revise the 1875 cadres law in order to ensure that each unit had enough officers, while not reducing the number of units available on mobilization. By suppressing some infantry and cavalry contingents they would provide regular officers to command reservist formations and release 6,800 men for the field artillery and engineers, while trying to maintain infantry company strengths. A bill along these lines (resembling Schönaich's *Notbehelf*) was ready by October 1906, but there was a long delay before it went to the Chambers.[208]

A cadres law was the more necessary because the French artillery's turn-of-the-century superiority was slipping. Much of the 1905–7 re-equipment funding went to the fortresses on the eastern frontier, for munitions, wireless, raisable turrets, and hardening with reinforced concrete, although little was done opposite Belgium and Luxemburg.[209] In 1907, moreover, the CSG decided urgently to provide the entire French metropolitan infantry with machine guns, as it understood that Germany was about to do likewise.[210] But the field artillery remained a one-club arm. The 75 mm could shoot four or five times faster than the German 77A 96, but the only other French field weapon, the 1904 Rimailho 155 mm CTR (canon à tir rapide), was a failure, with insufficient range and mobility to be an answer to the German 10.5 cm field howitzer.[211] Because of the 75 mm's rapidity of fire, when the French acquired it they switched from six-gun to four-gun batteries, their field guns per army corps falling from 138 to 92 but still exceeding the firepower of the Germans' 144 (126 field guns and 18 howitzers). The new German 77n/A gun, whose introduction was accelerated during the Moroccan crisis, was not as light, rapid, or robust as the 75 mm but

[204] CSDN, 31 Dec. 1906, SHA 2.N. 1.

[205] EMA note for CSG on cadres law, Sept. 1907, SHA 7.N. 105.

[206] Ralston, *Army*, 314–15.   [207] Porch, *March*, 193.

[208] Pendézec to Berteaux, 19 Dec. 1904, SHA 7.N. 103. Fournier, 'Note pour le Direction de la Cavalerie', 19 Oct. 1906, SHA 7.N. 104. EMA note for CSG on cadres law, Sept. 1907, SHA 7.N. 105.

[209] Mutius to Prussian War Ministry, 11 Aug. 1906, PAAA R.6748. Reports by GGS 4 Abt., 30 Aug. and 4 Dec. 1906, 2 Dec. 1907, 2 Dec. 1908, KAM Gstb 489.

[210] CSG, 27 Sept. 1907, SHA 1.N. 9.

[211] Doise and Vaïsse, *Diplomatie*, 132, 135. Villemejane note on the Rimailho, 2 Sept. 1905, SHA 7.N. 103. M. Lachmann, 'Probleme der Bewaffnung des Kaiserlichen Deutschen Heeres', *Zeitschrift für Militärgeschichte*, 6 (1967), 27.

closed most of the qualitative gap without there being any offsetting reduction in the gap in numbers. The EMA urged that France should increase its 75 mm provision without delay, to 128 or 138 per corps.[212] In January 1907 the Government promised Parliament it would act quickly,[213] but the War Ministry arsenals were still geared up to produce Rimailhos, and the cadres law was required to make men available for field gun teams.[214] When Europe returned to crisis at the end of 1908 nothing had been done, and the EMA lamented 'our manifest numerical inferiority to the German artillery'.[215]

Despite these weaknesses, the preparatory documentation for Plan XVI was moderately optimistic. The army envisaged neither British nor Belgian help, but counted on numerical superiority unless France had to fight Italy as well. The Germans were expected to mobilize and concentrate faster, but France would adopt a defensive–offensive posture, using its transverse railways to position its reserves for a counterstroke.[216] German assessments of France, by the military attaché and the GGS, were more complimentary than those of the French themselves. They doubted that the Radicals had greatly harmed the officer corps, or that indiscipline was serious.[217] Under the 1905 law France was calling up 80 per cent of each conscript class against Germany's 54 per cent; it had superior transport and could concentrate faster in the decisive theatre with an army of comparable size. It was disadvantaged by the fall in peacetime strength and by Germany's lead in field artillery, but Moltke expected the cadres law to redress the latter.[218] The two armies were not far from equivalence, but French military development was gradual, and no more than British or Belgian did it offer much incentive to the Germans to redouble their efforts.

* * *

The German military and political chiefs were well aware—to the point of over-confidence—of Russia's enfeeblement. In April 1908 Bülow thought that the Russians were not to be reckoned with militarily for seven or eight years, and that their denials were bluff.[219] As for the Adriatic competition, the Germans took for granted that Austria-Hungary was the stronger Power and that Italy knew it: Moltke recognized that the rivalry was a potential distraction but still supposed that the Habsburgs could field a reliable army of one and a half million men. The navy welcomed the build-up of the Italian fleet and saw little danger of it clashing with the Austro-Hungarian one.[220] In the West, the GGS had

[212] Villemejane to Berteaux, 30 Jan. 1905; Villemejane note for the Direction de l'artillerie, 8 June 1905; Villemejane note for acting CEMA, 30 Sept. 1905, SHA 7.N. 103; EMA note for CSG on cadres law, n.d. but late 1906, SHA 7.N. 104.
[213] Beltranelli note, 9 Mar. 1907, ibid.					[214] Fournier note, 13 Sept. 1906, ibid.
[215] EMA note, 'Augmentation de l'artillerie', Oct. 1908, SHA 7.N. 105.
[216] CSG, 15 Feb. 1906, SHA 1.N. 10.
[217] Hugo to Radolin, 12 Aug. 1905, PAAA R.6747. Mutius report, 29 Apr. 1906, PAAA R.6748.
[218] Oberstleutnant Staabs in Reichstag Budget Commission, 15 Mar. 1905 (on railways), KAM Militärbevollmächtiger 1. Moltke memorandum, Feb. 1908, PAAA R.995.
[219] Podewils conversation with Bülow, 13 Apr. 1908, GSM MAI 700.
[220] Lerchenfeld dispatch, 21 May 1908, GSM Bayerische Gesandtschaft Berlin 1080. Behnen, *Rüstung*, 247. Moltke memorandum, Feb. 1908, PAAA R.995.

a poor view of the Belgians and although Moltke expected Britain to support the French, he actually welcomed this as an opportunity to hurt an otherwise inaccessible adversary. Over both Britain and France, he thought, Germany retained a qualitative edge.[221] Bülow believed that France had passed its peak and that from now on demographic trends would favour Germany.[222] A favourable external environment was one reason for the War Ministry to curb the army's expansion.[223]

Curbed it indeed was, and before 1912 German peacetime strength (which through the annual recruitment contingent determined the size of the trained reserve and therefore wartime strength) grew very slowly indeed. In 1897–8 it was 557,436, and as some 30–40,000 able-bodied men were not called up each year an increase of some 60–80,000 was possible. In fact for the 1899 *Quinquennat* the Government requested only 27,437 officers and men and the Reichstag shaved 7,000 off this figure. The 1905 *Quinquennat* provided for an even smaller increase of 10,229 by 1910. Despite Germany's much larger population, its peacetime strength and that of France were comparable.[224] The army budget, by contrast, after declining in 1901–4, rose sharply until 1909.[225] This supports the view that Western European armaments competition before 1912 was in equipment rather than in manpower, but although Morocco loosened the purse-strings it did so only temporarily. Throughout this period limits on expansion were imposed by the Reich's financial difficulties and by naval encroachment on army spending.

As Einem pointed out, there was no need for a financial crisis, the problem being not lack of wealth but the political obstacles to raising revenue.[226] The constitution allowed the imperial government to levy direct taxes, but the state governments and the fiscal conservatives in the Reichstag forced it to rely on tariffs, levies on consumption, and profits from state enterprises. If these were insufficient it could ask the States for 'matricular contributions', or borrow. In fact income rarely covered expenditure, and during recessions the pressure was acute. When Tirpitz started his naval programme the economy was growing strongly and Reich finances were buoyant, but the navy law of 1900 was followed by a downturn. The states withheld matricular contributions and the deficit deepened, with a consequent increase in debt service payments. There was no consensus on how taxes should be raised, and Bülow evaded the issue, despite a joint request from Tirpitz and Einem in 1903 that he should find new sources of income. As over 90 per cent of the Reich budget went on the armed forces, moreover, there was little scope for protecting them by making economies elsewhere.[227] Within a total expenditure that was frozen in 1901–3 the navy's share

[221] Moltke memorandum, ibid.   [222] Bülow circular, 1 July 1908, HHStA PA III, 167.

[223] Einem, *Erinnerungen*, 83.

[224] Förster, *Militarismus*, 96–8, 106. Reichsarchiv, *Weltkrieg*, i. 76.

[225] Witt, *Finanzpolitik*, 380–1.   [226] Einem, *Erinnerungen*, 65.

[227] P.-C. Witt, 'Reichsfinanzen und Rüstungspolitik, 1898–1914', in H. Schottelius and W. Deist (eds.), *Marine und Marinepolitik im Kaiserlichen Deutschland, 1871–1914* (Düsseldorf, 1972), 146–77, gives an overview.

rose until it stabilized at one-fifth of total defence outlays. In 1907–9 it jumped again.[228] Tirpitz agitated more effectively; and the army acquiesced.

The change in armaments priorities dated back to 1896–7. The Germans were humiliated when they supported the Afrikaners diplomatically against the British, the Emperor sending the demonstrative 'Kruger telegram' to congratulate the President of the Transvaal but lacking the naval strength to support the gesture. Contingency planning for war against Britain began. Tirpitz was appointed to the Navy Office and Bülow to the Foreign Ministry, whence he moved in 1900 to the Chancellorship. In a secret memorandum to the Kaiser in 1897 Tirpitz advocated not a commerce-raiding navy but a battlefleet that could apply power-political leverage between Helgoland and the Thames. In 1898 Britain had thirty-eight first-class battleships and Germany seven; the 1898 navy law would raise the seven to nineteen and that of 1900 to thirty-eight, but by 1907 Tirpitz was thinking of sixty, and he wanted more durable, better armed ships than the British ones, with superior gunnery and tactics. His aim, once Bülow's diplomacy had traversed the 'danger zone' during which London might launch a pre-emptive strike, was a fleet too strong for the Royal Navy to attack without risking unacceptable losses, and which would have a reasonable chance of victory if war came. Ultimately he may have wanted parity. The 1898 and 1900 laws were only a beginning, although by determining a statutory fleet size and a building programme they implicitly bound the Reichstag to find the necessary finance. Their passage was a triumph of parliamentary management. In 1900 the navalist coalition embraced all the parties except the socialist SPD, but Tirpitz's cultivation of the Catholic Centre Party, which held a balancing position between Right and Left, was the key to his achievement.[229]

The War Ministry, if not the General Staff, was the readier to go along with Tirpitz's ambitions because limiting army growth coincided with its own agendas. When the Treasury Secretary asked the War Minister, Gossler, to show the 'greatest restraint' over the 1899 army law, Gossler replied that it was 'self-evident' that there would be no big increases but only piecemeal improvements and that Germany should not participate in the arms race. He wished to minimize strain on the finances, but also to preserve the social homogeneity of the officers and men in order to ensure the army's domestic reliability. He told the Reichstag that innovation could slow down, in view of the *détente* with France and Russia, and that the army was large enough. The legislature acknowledged his right to come back later for the 7,000 men knocked out of the bill, but he chose not to, after another Treasury appeal to show restraint because of the 1900 navy law. Command and logistics in the army, he felt, were already becoming unmanageable, and it would contain too many reservists on mobilization. He

[228] Witt, *Finanzpolitik*, 380–1.

[229] P. M. Kennedy, 'Strategic Aspects of the Anglo-German Naval Race', in his *Strategy and Diplomacy, 1870–1945* (London, 1984), ch. 5. J. Steinberg, *Yesterday's Deterrent: Tirpitz and the Birth of the German Battle Fleet* (New York, 1965). I. N. Lambi, *The Navy and German Power Politics, 1862–1914* (Boston, 1984), ch. 9. V. R. Berghahn, *Der Tirpitz Plan: Genesis und Verfall einer innenpolitischen Krisenstrategie unter Wilhelm II* (Düsseldorf, 1971).

overrode Schlieffen's protests that one could 'never be strong enough on the battlefield'. Schlieffen pleaded that the French had more infantry battalions, a better field gun, and fortresses that could withstand German bombardment. He wanted three more army corps, faster re-equipment, and greater reliance on reservist formations to expand the field force. But except for an expansion of the heavy artillery, the CGS's wishes for the 1899 *Quinquennat* were set aside.[230]

The War Ministry argued that quality rather than numbers counted most against the French. The broader reasons for its position were manifested in the planning for the next military bill. Einem, Gossler's successor, postponed the *Quinquennat* from 1904 to 1905, giving priority to a pensions increase. He envisaged a growth in peacetime strength of only 10,339 over the five years, and sought no quid pro quo from the Reichstag for an accompanying bill that would make two-year service permanent for all except the mounted arms. He considered the army's existing organization adequate to meet 'all eventualities', telling Schlieffen that the current peacetime strength was broadly sufficient and there was no need to create new units, which there were not enough officers to lead. The relative tranquillity of international politics when Einem took over was one reason for his restraint, and the Russian disaster in Manchuria confirmed his assessment.[231] Although he regularly expressed concern about Reich finances, money was not the main reason why he opposed growth. Both the *Quinquennat* and the two-year service bill (which would necessitate more NCOs and training) entailed extra expenditure, as did re-equipment with the quick-firing field gun.[232] After about 1902 competition from Tirpitz eased. When Schlieffen challenged Einem's priorities, therefore, the Minister's defence rested not on financial but on personnel considerations. He was short of infantry officers, and would not relax standards by admitting 'democratic and other elements'. Without more officers, extra infantry units (which Schlieffen wanted, whereas Einem saw the cavalry as a higher priority) would be a source of weakness, and to lower requirements for the men 'in my opinion must be avoided under all circumstances'. He told the Reichstag that he opposed a broader officer recruitment and wanted as few socialists as possible in the army, as they might be unreliable.[233] None the less, the shrinkage of its rural catchment area was pushing it towards an invidious choice.[234] Einem's was for technical and organizational improvements rather than for additional infantrymen.

The 1905 *Quinquennat* provided for the army's peacetime strength (excluding NCOs and officers) to rise from 495,500 to 505,839 by 1909–10. It would provide more positional artillery (*Fussartillerie*), twenty-eight new squadrons of reconnaissance cavalry, and extra pioneers and telegraph troops; and it would simplify mobilization by creating organizational cadres for units that otherwise

---

[230] Reichsarchiv, *Weltkrieg*, i. 59–71; Anlagen, docs. 16–21. Förster, *Militarismus*, 89–115.

[231] Reichsarchiv, *Weltkrieg*, i. 72–9; Anlagen, docs. 22–6.

[232] Reichstag Budget Commission, 16 Feb. 1904, KAM MKr. 5577.

[233] Einem to Schlieffen, 19 Apr. 1904, Reichsarchiv, *Weltkrieg*, i; Anlagen, doc. 26. Förster, *Militarismus*, 111, 133.

[234] Cf. Ch. 1, sect. 2, above.

would exist in peacetime only on paper.[235] Essentially it was an anti-French measure, although Bülow preferred not to publicize this.[236] Einem defended it on the grounds that Germany could not maintain superiority over all potential enemies but must do so in at least one direction. The bill was expected to give Germany a slight advantage over France in peacetime strength, although Einem acknowledged that, even in a war with France alone, Germany must leave troops on the eastern frontier and that while the Franco-Russian alliance lasted it would have to fight in the West with numerical inferiority.[237] The War Ministry did little, therefore, to provide the manpower needed for Schlieffen's projected offensive, the preamble to the *Quinquennat* saying that the country lacked the money to maintain universal military service when the population was growing.[238]

While the Socialists acknowledged Einem's moderation, not even the ultranationalists of the Pan-German League called on him to ask for more, and the news of Russian defeats led the Reichstag to press for further economies. The Centre Party, seeking to lever the Government into financial reform, wanted a further postponement of the bill to 1906, which Bülow refused on the ground that it would be interpreted abroad as weakness.[239] For the same reason he resisted pressure from the Centre to reduce the cavalry increase, conceding, however, that it would not be implemented fully for five years.[240] This compromise permitted the bill to become law on 15 April 1905, along with its two-year service counterpart. It passed through Parliament during the hiatus between the outbreak of the Far Eastern war and the start of the Moroccan crisis. Yet it set the pace of army development for the six years down to 1911, during which Germany's external situation drastically deteriorated, and it accentuated the contradiction between War Ministry policy on the army's size and equipment and the GGS operational plans.

This brings us to the Dogger Bank and Tangier. In the winter of 1904/5 the German leaders and public feared that the Royal Navy would launch a preemptive attack. Memories of the destruction of the Danish fleet a century earlier lent a name to this 'Copenhagen complex'; the benign reaction of the British press to Japan's surprise attack on Port Arthur intensified it, as did imprudent statements by British officials. Bülow, Tirpitz, and Wilhelm treated the danger seriously—it now seemed unlikely that they would negotiate the initial 'danger zone' of naval building surreptitiously.[241] After Algeciras, however,

[235] Einem to Bavarian War Minister, 22 May 1904, KAM MKr 1130.

[236] Bülow to Einem, 15 June 1904, PAAA R.852.

[237] Einem to Bavarian War Minister, 22 May 1904, KAM MKr 1130. Einem in Budget Commission, 3 and 7 Mar. 1905, ibid.

[238] Reichsarchiv, *Weltkrieg*, i. 77.

[239] Förster, *Militarismus*, 134–43. Lerchenfeld to Bavarian Foreign Minister, 13 Mar. 1905, KAM MKr 1130.

[240] Bülow to Spahn, 11 Mar. 1905, BA Nachlass Bülow 107. Reichstag Budget Commission, 14 Mar. 1905, KAM MKr. 1130.

[241] J. Steinberg, 'The Copenhagen Complex', *Journal of Contemporary History*, 1/3 (1966), 23–41; Marder, *Dreadnought*, 111–13; Bülow to Büchsel, 9 Feb. 1905, PAAA R.2283; Lerchenfeld dispatch, 12 Feb. 1904, GSM, Bayerische Gesandtschaft Berlin 1076.

Anglo-German tension eased, and despite the formation of the Anglo-Russian entente Russia's continuing weakness meant that Bülow had few worries about the international scene. Radical diplomatic realignment did not yet imply a radical readjustment of defence priorities.

If Germany's external circumstances worsened after 1904, so did its domestic financial dilemma. Neither economic growth between the 1901–2 and 1907–8 recessions, nor a tax increase in 1906, halted the growth of Reich debt. They were offset by big increases in army and navy demands, and the 1907 estimates again envisaged heavy borrowing. Bülow's efforts to grasp the nettle of financial reform antagonized the Right and destroyed the Conservative–National Liberal bloc on which he had relied to manage the Reichstag. A new Conservative–Catholic combination supported a reform that raised taxes and prescribed expenditure limits but rejected his proposed inheritance tax, thus contributing to his departure from office in July 1909.[242]

In this unpromising environment the growth in army spending lost impetus. By contrast the naval *Novelle* (supplementary law) of 1906 was modest, but that of 1908 raised naval spending from one-fifth to one-quarter of the defence budget, and held it there until 1912. Because of the 'Copenhagen' scare and the Moroccan crisis Wilhelm and the Navy League pressed Tirpitz to speed up capital ship construction, but the Secretary resisted. He did not want an unsustainable rate that could later leave the shipyards idle, preferring to stabilize on a three-ship tempo. He feared he would antagonize his Reichstag allies, and even provoke a British attack, if he asked for too much. In his 1906 *Novelle* he restricted himself to six additional heavy cruisers.[243] When the bill was almost ready for submission to the Reichstag, however, he learnt that the British were building what became HMS *Dreadnought*, the first turbine-driven all-big-gun battleship, which with its ten 12″ guns would be faster and more heavily armed than any vessel afloat. He decided, while remaining within the existing programme of warship numbers and replacement rates, to seek authority to follow Britain's lead.[244]

The consequences did not show themselves immediately. Tirpitz delayed construction while making new designs, and launched his first two dreadnoughts only in 1908. The 'dreadnought leap', however, nearly doubled capital ship-construction costs, and necessitated higher spending on repair and maintenance, larger crews, and the enlargement of the Kiel Canal between the North and Baltic Seas.[245] In addition, the Admiral hoped to shorten the battleship replacement period from twenty-five to twenty years, and to make the three-ship tempo permanent, thus aiming for a sixty-battleship fleet. In 1905–6 he and his budget

---

[242] Witt, 'Reichsfinanzen', in Schottelius and Deist (eds.), *Marine*, 158–65.

[243] A. von Tirpitz, *Politische Dokumente: Der Aufbau der deutschen Weltmacht* (Stuttgart, 1924), 10–11. Tirpitz to Bülow, 27 Sept. and 8 Nov. 1905, BA Rklei R.43 F/950.

[244] H. H. Herwig, 'The German Reaction to the Dreadnought Revolution', *International History Review*, 13 (1991), 272–83.

[245] Witt, *Finanzpolitik*, 142.

chief, Capelle, judged this politically unfeasible;[246] but in the autumn of 1907 an ambitious new *Novelle* seemed possible after all. A *détente* with Britain after Algeciras made a 'Copenhagen' attack seem less likely. New Reichstag elections weakened the Socialists and reduced the leverage of the Centre's balancing position, with the result that the Catholics competed with the Progressives to be the main supporters of a new law. Economic recovery had boosted revenue, and the Finance Ministry unexpectedly predicted a budget surplus. Tirpitz easily passed his new law in March 1908, misleadingly portraying it as a moderate and essential riposte to Britain. It set a twenty-year replacement period for battleships and cruisers, and a four-ship tempo for 1908–11. In 1912–27 the rate would fall to two ships annually unless new legislation prevented it, but if the British maintained a three-ship tempo, by the end of 1911 Germany might have nine dreadnoughts to their fourteen.[247]

Einem was little disposed to compete, and after Algeciras the pressure on him from the General Staff diminished. This was despite the radicalization of the Western offensive plan in a memorandum Schlieffen handed to his successor on leaving office. It envisaged that seven-eighths of the army (thirty-three and a third corps) would exploit the close-knit Dutch and Belgian railway networks in order to outflank and overwhelm the French and British in thirty to forty days.[248] Schlieffen knew that this plan might well exceed Germany's strength, and his memorandum advocated truly universal conscription.[249] Yet in November 1905 he had accepted that the army would undergo no major changes in the near future, and Einem was privately scathing about him.[250] When Moltke took over in 1906 he was initially preoccupied with the danger of a British invasion, and he wanted to double-track the railways to the north, update the coastal fortifications, and prepare second-line units that could be moved into position.[251] The Moroccan crisis persuaded Bülow to authorize railway work, the island of Borkum was fortified, and extra guns were deployed along the Baltic.[252] To some extent the alerts of 1904–6 therefore distracted Germany from the competition with the Franco-Russian alliance, although much less than the Adriatic rivalry was distracting Austria-Hungary. But initially Moltke lacked the authority of his formidable predecessor. His appointment had been widely criticized, and reflected Wilhelm's predilection for a court general with a famous name. Moltke

[246] Capelle memorandum, (?)May 1906, BA-MA Nachlass Tirpitz N 253/23.

[247] J. Steinberg, 'The *Novelle* of 1908: Necessities and Choices in the Anglo-German Naval Arms Race', *Transactions of the Royal Historical Society*, 5th ser, 21 (1971), 25–43; Tirpitz, *Aufbau*, 39–47; Von Burkhard dispatch, 11 Nov. 1907, KAM MKr 761/1.

[248] Bucholz, *War Planning*, 209–10. G. Ritter, *The Schlieffen Plan: Critique of a Myth* (London, 1958), 37 ff.

[249] Ritter, *Sword*, ii. 207. Förster, *Militarismus*, 165.

[250] Reichsarchiv, *Weltkrieg*, i; Anlagen, docs. 23, 27.

[251] Moltke to Einem, 27 Apr. 1906, ibid., doc. 28. Moltke memorandum (approved by Wilhelm), July 1906, KAM MKr. 43.

[252] Bülow to Wilhelm, 9 Jan. 1906, BA Rklei R.43 F/107. Memorandum on Reich fortifications (n.d.), p. 47, KAM MKr. 4605/2. Gebsattel to Bavarian War Ministry, 14 Mar. 1906, KAM MKr. 43.

doubted his own abilities, and lacked familiarity with mobilization planning.[253] He agreed with Einem that 'the army's structure can be regarded as fixed for a long period', and the priority was its 'internal development' within the existing framework. He did not press for additional army corps, and in general differed little from Einem's position.[254]

Moltke may have disagreed with the War Minister over the urgency of re-equipment, but he did not press his case. In June 1906, after consulting the new CGS, Bülow made a rare intervention in army planning. He feared, according to his memoirs, that the French were gaining the technological edge and that the German army was becoming hidebound. He told Einem that he was worried about France's revanchism and intensified military spending. He asked what was needed to keep pace, and seemed willing to seek more funds.[255] Einem, however, opposed any further quickening of field gun, rifle, and machine gun acquisition, arguing that this would damage quality. Only if war was close (which Bülow denied) would he feel justified in seeking to amend the *Quinquennat*: it tied his hands but it also tied the Reichstag's, and he wanted a 'calm and constant further development'. Einem was sceptical about the Chancellor's sincerity, and he may have wished to assert his authority over Moltke. None the less, his response shows his unwillingness even to explore opportunities to expand the army faster, and his fear of greater dependence on the deputies.[256] He had stepped up rifle and field-gun acquisition during the crisis, but would do no more. Moltke wanted extra telephones, wirelesses, automobiles, airships, and machine guns, as well as fortress and siege artillery, but in January 1907 he told Bülow that the new military budget satisfied the most urgent needs, and the *Quinquennat* provided adequate manpower. He was much less assertive than Conrad was towards Schönaich, and allowed the moment of opportunity, if it was one, to slip by.[257]

Despite surface immobility, under Einem the German army made considerable strides. In addition to a new rifle, cartridge, and uniform, the field artillery adopted the 15 cm field howitzer 02 and the 10 cm *Kanone* 04. Distribution of the Mo8 machine gun, developed by Spandau and the DWMF, began towards the end of Einem's tenure, as did that of the 98/09 quick-firing field howitzer.[258] On the western frontier and the northern coast there was substantial fortification expenditure,[259] and both the French and Russian military attachés commented

[253] Bucholz, *War Planning*, 214–25. Gebsattel to Bavarian War Ministry, 3 Jan. 1906, KAM MKr. 43.

[254] Moltke to Einem, 12 Apr. 1907, Reichsarchiv, *Weltkrieg*, i; Anlagen, doc. 33.

[255] Bülow to Moltke and Einem, 1 June 1906, PAAA R.794; and Reichsarchiv, *Weltkrieg*, i; Anlagen, doc. 29. Bülow, *Memoirs*, ii. 218–21.

[256] Einem to Moltke, 18 June 1906, PAAA R.794; and Reichsarchiv, *Weltkrieg*, i; Anlagen, doc. 30. Förster, *Militarismus*, 166–9.

[257] Moltke to Tschirschky, 9 Oct. 1906, PAAA R.794; Reichskanzlei minute, 21 Jan. 1907, ibid. Moltke to Einem, 12 Apr. 1907, Reichsarchiv, *Weltkrieg*, i, Anlagen; doc. 33.

[258] Einem, *Erinnerungen*, 84–90. BA-MA Einem Nachlass N.324/3.

[259] Memorandum on Reich fortifications (n.d.), pp. 37–47, KAM MKr. 43. Details in correspondence on the estimates, Einem to Bülow, 21 July 1906, KAM MKr. 5580. Einem to Bülow, 25 July 1907, KAM MKr. 5581; and 31 July 1908, KAM MKr. 5582.

on the advances made in equipment and training.[260] Although the War Minister opposed any faster weapon replacement, he defended himself against cut-backs, and there are signs that he was becoming more forceful. When in September 1906 Bülow asked all departments to lower costs, Einem successfully resisted.[261] He refused to postpone items of expenditure in order to alleviate the states' matricular contributions,[262] and when in February 1907 the Chancellor called publicly for the army estimates to be reduced, he was incensed.[263] Asked to make room for Tirpitz's 1908 *Novelle*, he protested that Germany's security depended on the army and it was dangerous to strengthen the fleet at its expense.[264] None the less, he accepted a 3 per cent cut in the following budget round, whereas the navy escaped any reduction.[265] Now that field-gun re-equipment was completed army spending began falling anyway, and Einem did not seek to prevent it. Nor did he stop the rival service from gaining further ground.

Einem's continuing conservatism is equally evident over manpower. He was willing to postpone the next *Quinquennat* from 1910 to 1911, and he agreed with Moltke in not wishing to use it to create extra divisions or army corps. He secured Wilhelm's consent to an increase next time of only 9,000 in peacetime strength, even smaller than in the law of 1905. Machine guns, wireless, airship, automobile, and foot artillery units would gain the benefit. He defended the figure on the grounds that a maximum of only 17,000 more men were available annually anyway: a figure that the army laws of 1912 and 1913 would show to be a gross underestimate.[266] In short, although by 1908 the Russian, Austro-Hungarian, and Italian armies were beginning to step up the pace, the German one, like the French and British, was slowing down. Naval competition and the 1907–8 recession helped to draw out Einem's re-equipment, and his and Moltke's long-term planning envisaged little change.

* * *

Closer examination supports the impression given by the budgetary statistics of equilibrium between the European armies in 1904–8. The Russian and Austro-Hungarian forces were in crisis; the French and Italian ones experienced a malaise, as did the British before Haldane. All acknowledged that the German army remained the strongest, but it was hobbled by the Reich's financial difficulties, by the naval build-up, and by the restraint of its own leaders, and was inadequate to the task that Schlieffen set for it. Serbia and Belgium were beginning to re-equip, but were woefully short of men. The crises of 1904–6, and the chaos in Russia, prompted Austria-Hungary to divert resources against Italy, and

[260] Moulin to French War Ministry, 10 Dec. 1907 (for Russian view), AMAE NS Allemagne 105. Reports by de Laguiche (French attaché), 12 Feb. 1907, SHA 7.N. 1108 and 17 Feb. 1909, SHA 7.N. 1109.

[261] Witt, *Finanzpolitik*, 166.

[262] Burkhard to Bavarian War Ministry, 9 Dec. 1906, KAM MKr. 5580.

[263] Förster, *Militarismus*, 169–70; Gebsattel to Bavarian War Ministry, 1 Mar. 1907, KAM MKr 42.

[264] Förster, *Militarismus*, 170–1.   [265] Witt, 'Reichsfinanzen', 163.

[266] Reichsarchiv, *Weltkrieg*, i. 96–7. Gebsattel to Bavarian War Ministry, 18 June and 29 Sept. 1908, KAM MKr. 1131.

Germany to do so against Britain. In all the Powers except France there was unusual financial stringency, because of the 1901–2 and 1907–8 recessions, the South African and Russo-Japanese Wars, revolutionary or quasi-revolutionary unrest in Russia and Hungary, and radical governments in Italy and Britain. In Austria-Hungary, Italy, and France there were serious manpower shortages, for which Schönaich's *Notbehelf* and the French cadres bill were inadequate remedies. Shorter terms of service were introduced in Russia, France, and Italy, and confirmed in Germany; and everywhere, except in Russia, the peacetime strength, on which the wartime strength largely depended, stagnated or fell. Everywhere, except in France, armies lost relatively in money and men to navies.

The picture was not, however, one of unrelieved torpor. Quick-firing field artillery, adopted earliest in France, was taken up elsewhere. In Serbia and Italy it became a political *cause célèbre*. Machine guns were more generally distributed after the Russo-Japanese War, and there were smaller investments in mountain guns, howitzers, field telephones, wireless, and airships. Fortifications and railways were under construction or being upgraded. France and Germany engaged self-consciously in technological, qualitative competition, which was spurred on by the Moroccan crisis, as was reorganization in Britain. By 1908–9, however, innovation in all three Powers was again decelerating. It was in the East, where Russia and Austria-Hungary were at last emerging from domestic turmoil, and Italy from the military doldrums, that the break-out into intensified land armaments competition would first take place.

3. Armaments Diplomacy and the Second Hague Peace Conference

In the lull that followed Algeciras there occurred the most serious pre-war effort to limit armaments by negotiation. This effort, at the Second Hague Peace Conference of June–October 1907, was abortive, and was followed by new rounds of expansion. Much of the European political class objected even to the principle of discussing limitation, and insisted on untrammelled sovereignty in defence policy.

The first Hague Conference, in 1899, had included armaments limitation as a main agenda item. The modern peace movement had emerged in Europe in reaction to the Napoleonic wars and, more strongly, to those of the mid-nineteenth century. It advocated disarmament as part of a complex of proposals, notably that for settling disputes by arbitration. In Western Europe it had grown sufficiently for politicians to pay lip service to its nostrums, and, beginning with Anglo-Russian proposals in 1816, arms limitation began to figure in diplomacy. In issuing the appeal that led to the convening of the 1899 conference, however, the tsarist Government was aware of the activities of the peace societies but much more concerned about the cost of supplying its army with quick-firing guns. The idea began as one of agreeing on a moratorium with Vienna. Subsequently it broadened out, but when the conference met the Russians suggested limits on peacetime strengths and military budgets, and prohibiting or suspending the introduction of new explosives and weapons. It was agreed to ban poison gas and dum-dum bullets and (for five years) the dropping of projectiles from balloons. An anodyne resolution declared that arms limitation was desirable, and called on governments to study it. Objections from the German military delegate halted more serious negotiation, but although Germany attracted odium in consequence there was little more enthusiasm elsewhere. The British Prime Minister, Lord Salisbury, thought that modern weapons were 'a serious deterrence' to hostilities.[267] The conference refined the law of war and set up a Permanent Court of Arbitration, but it left intact states' legal right to resort to force. Although it invited the Powers to take in hand the armaments question, there was a notable absence of follow-up.[268]

The initiators of the second conference began by omitting armaments altogether. The American President, Theodore Roosevelt, who was seeking pacifist support for his re-election campaign, launched the idea. His 1904 circular to the Powers said nothing about arms limitation. After the Russians picked up the baton their April 1906 invitation proposed to concentrate on the peaceful settlement of disputes, 'leaving untouched those questions which might affect the limitation of naval and military forces'.[269] After their East Asian disaster they wanted no restrictions on their rearmament, the General Staff assuming there would be no suggestions for 'the reduction of effectives or budgets'.[270] The German Foreign Ministry accepted this programme, and neither Tirpitz, Einem, Moltke, nor the Chief of Naval Staff objected to it.[271]

The impetus for discussing armaments came from the British Liberal Government, which felt that its naval strength would permit a humanitarian gesture without endangering national security. In the 1906 election the Liberals had asserted that armaments were costly and dangerous, and that negotiated reductions could free resources for social reform. They inherited from the Unionists the Cawdor memorandum, which envisaged laying down at least four capital ships annually. With most of the Russian navy at the bottom, the Admiralty could defend this only by invoking a two-Power standard against France and Germany, which Campbell-Bannerman found 'almost a preposterous combination'.[272] In addition, Britain had HMS *Dreadnought* and three dreadnought

[267] Quoted in C. D. Davis, *The United States and the Second Hague Peace Conference: American Diplomacy and International Organization, 1899–1914* (Durham, NC, 1975), 6.

[268] On the 1st conference see M. Tate, *The Disarmament Illusion: The Movement for a Limitation of Armaments to 1907* (New York, 1942); J. Dülffer, *Regeln gegen den Krieg? Die Haager Friedenskonferenzen von 1899 und 1907 in der Internationalen Politik* (Frankfurt, 1981); C. D. Davis, *The United States and the First Hague Peace Conference* (Ithaca, NY, 1962); T. K. Ford, 'The Genesis of the First Hague Peace Conference', *Political Science Quarterly*, 51 (1936), 354–81; D. L. Morrill, 'Nicholas II and the Call for the First Hague Conference', *Journal of Modern History*, 46 (1974), 296–313.

[269] Davis, *Second Hague Conference*, 112–13, 135–7; Tate, *Illusion*, 322.

[270] Moulin to French War Ministry, 27 Jan. 1906, SHA 7.N. 1477.

[271] Tschirschky to Wilhelm, 11 Apr. 1906, GP xxiii/1, doc. 7805.

[272] A. T. Sidorowicz, 'The Liberal Government and the Second Hague Peace Conference' (unpublished TS, LSE), 2–8. I am indebted to Mr Sidorowicz for permission to cite his

battlecruisers building before anyone else had laid down an all-big-gun ship. In July 1906 the Liberals announced they would start work on three capital ships in 1906–7 but two in 1907–8, and three only if the Hague Conference failed to agree on arms limitation. Fisher believed that Britain was far enough ahead of Germany to maintain supremacy even if it stopped building altogether,[273] and Grey and Campbell-Bannerman agreed that they were running no risk. Financial retrenchment seemed urgent, and inside and outside Parliament there was agitation for cuts. The Government accepted the Vivian resolution in the Commons, which asked for arms reduction to be entered on the Hague agenda, and Grey formally requested this at the same time as the Government made its building proposal.[274]

Although an inter-departmental memorandum in April 1907 recommended that Britain should propose limits on spending or on warship numbers and size, the Admiralty dissented from this view. It opposed trying to freeze the *status quo*, even at so favourable a moment, on the grounds that verification and enforcement would raise insuperable difficulties, and that Germany and Russia were likely to object.[275] In contrast, Grey and Campbell-Bannerman hoped to mobilize public opinion as a means of pressure on the Continental Powers;[276] but the Foreign Secretary's policy had a harder edge. He insisted on Britain retaining its 'offensive' capacity to drive other Powers from the seas, and instructed his conference delegates to reject any restrictions on the right of blockade.[277] His goal was not 'disarmament' but lower 'expenditure on armaments', and he hoped for an Anglo-German agreement to limit naval building for five years.[278] He told the Germans that Britain had large naval spending 'in suspense', and must proceed with it if there was no accord.[279] He seems to have expected them once more to refuse to discuss the issue, and the failure of the conference to be followed by a big expenditure increase: Berlin would have been placed in the wrong with British and German taxpayers, and it would be easier to carry the naval budget with Liberal MPs.[280]

The British initiative, then, was ambiguous and self-interested, and failed to set a basis for serious discussion. Given Einem's belief that reorganization was completed, however, the German army had reason to desire a halt, even though

research. See also his 'The British Government, the Hague Peace Conference of 1907, and the Armaments Question', in B. J. C. McKercher, ed., *Arms Limitation and Disarmament: Restraints on War, 1899–1939* (Westport, Conn., 1992), 1–19.

[273] Marder, *Dreadnought*, 129.

[274] Sidorowicz, 'Liberal Government', 10–18. A. J. A. Morris, 'The English Radicals' Campaign for Disarmament and the Hague Conference of 1907', *Journal of Modern History*, 43 (1971), 371–80.

[275] Sidorowicz, 'Liberal Government', 33.

[276] Ibid. 17. Grey to Bertie, 24 July 1906, BD viii, doc. 161.

[277] Grey minute on Lascelles dispatch, 16 Aug. 1906, ibid., doc. 163. Tate, *Illusion*, 337.

[278] Grey to Nicolson, 15 Feb. 1907, BD viii, docs. 178–9.

[279] Grey to Lascelles, 12 Mar. 1907, ibid., doc. 184.

[280] Grey to Durand, 6 Nov. 1906; Grey to Knollys, 12 Nov. 1906; Grey to Nicolson, 15 Feb. 1907, ibid., docs. 167, 168, 178. Metternich to Bülow, 8 Feb. 1907, GP xxiii/1, doc. 7840. Paul Cambon to Pichon, 28 Nov. 1906 and 22 Apr. 1907, AMAE C-Administrative 57.

the GGS interpreted Britain's behaviour as the 'culmination' of encirclement.[281] The decisive obstacle was the navy, Tirpitz telling the British naval attaché that 'you, the colossus, come and ask Germany, the pygmy, to disarm. From the point of view of the public it is laughable and Machiavellian, and we shall never agree to anything of the sort.'[282] Wilhelm believed that Germany could not limit its sovereignty over land and naval armaments—Britain was trying to perpetuate its 'colossal superiority', and disarmament proposals were 'utopian' and 'dangerous'.[283] Hence the Germans opposed placing armaments on the agenda, arguing that to do so would pointlessly increase friction between the Powers.[284] While Bülow shared this opinion, he and the Foreign Ministry were anxious to forestall a British public relations victory. He persuaded Wilhelm not to boycott the conference, but not to participate in discussion of arms limitation. Announcing this position in the Reichstag, he told his delegates not to go beyond renewing the 1899 armaments resolution. His aim was to sabotage disarmament (and any restriction on the right to go to war) without incurring public obloquy or diplomatic isolation.[285]

To achieve his objectives, Bülow would need support from other capitals. The Austrians, if anything, were even more intransigent than their allies. Franz Joseph feared that discussing arms limitation would disseminate antimilitarism.[286] Conrad insisted that the Monarchy's defences were so run down that it must reject any restriction on its right to arm.[287] Aehrenthal told the British that discussion would be a waste of time, and that armaments policy was for each Power to decide.[288] The Italians, however, were initially more sympathetic to arms limitation, partly because it enjoyed public support. Their Foreign Minister, Tittoni, suggested that it might be discussed but that no resolution on the subject would be binding: a compromise that both the British and the Germans rejected.[289] By the time the conference met the Italians had changed their views, possibly because of their new desire for naval expansion, and they sided with their allies.[290]

Given the uncertainty in Rome, however, the Germans needed backing in the opposite camp, and Russia held the balance. The Tsar had abandoned his 'illu-

[281] GGS 9 Abt., 1907 annual report (n.d.), KAM Gstb. 204.

[282] Marder, *Dreadnought*, 131.

[283] Minute on Stumm to Bülow, 10 May 1906, GP xxiii, doc. 7809. Szyögyény to Aehrenthal, 20 Feb. 1907, HHStA PA III 164.

[284] Tschirschky to Metternich, 4 Feb. 1907, GP xxiii, doc. 7839.

[285] Bülow, *Memoirs*, ii. 289. Bülow to Tschirschky, 5 Aug. 1906; Tschirschky to Wilhelm, 20 Aug. 1906; Wilhelm minute, 15 Aug. 1906; Bülow in Reichstag, 30 Apr. 1907, GP xxiii, docs. 7839, 7812, 7813, 7815, p. 221 n.

[286] De Reverseaux to Pichon, 30 Jan. and 4 Mar. 1907, DDF 2nd ser. x, docs. 404, 426.

[287] Conrad to Schönaich, 16 Feb. 1907, KAW K.M. Präs 1907 70–28, Karton 1265.

[288] Goschen to Grey, 23 Mar. 1907, BD viii, doc. 190. Crozier to Pichon, 11 Apr. 1907, AMAE C-Administrative 57.

[289] Barrère to Pichon, 2 Apr. 1907; Tornielli *aide-mémoire*, 5 Apr. 1907; Geoffray to Pichon, 8 Apr. 1907, Bompard to Pichon, 9 Apr. 1907, ibid.

[290] Barrère to Pichon, 9 Apr. 1907, ibid. Mérey to Aehrenthal, 20 Aug. 1907, KAW K.M. Präs 1907 70–28 Karton 1266; Aehrenthal to Prime Ministers, 13 Nov. 1907, ibid., Karton 1267.

sions' of 1899.[291] Izvolsky asked the French if Russia could really pledge to freeze expenditure when its army and fleet needed to be reconstituted.[292] He told the Germans that 'disarmament was an idea just of Jews, socialists, and hysterical women', and that he sympathized with Berlin's position.[293] Rather than oppose the British initiative outright, however, he preferred 'a first-class burial' at The Hague.[294] The Russians were caught between the alliance blocs, and as conference conveners had an interest in preventing a débâcle. A tour of the capitals by Professor Martens, the legal adviser to their Foreign Ministry, revealed no common ground, and the final Russian circular in April 1907 explained that Britain and America reserved the right to raise the topic of armaments and that Russia, Austria-Hungary, and Germany reserved the right to stay aloof.[295] This formula threatened to align the three conservative monarchies, and caused alarm in Paris. Pichon liaised urgently with St Petersburg to secure an understanding that if the issue of arms limitation was raised the Russian chairman would propose simply a renewal of the 1899 resolution and nothing more.[296]

Against this incipient conservative bloc, Grey had hoped to co-operate with America and France, but he found Pichon much more cautious than he was, wishing merely for Paris and London to give backing if Washington took the lead.[297] Anxiety about the Russian alliance was only part of the explanation. The French Marine Minister had publicly opposed a naval freeze, and the Government would approve his stand unless Germany set an example.[298] It is true that in April 1907 an inter-departmental commission reported that the navy could stay with its present tonnage in capital ships and the army its present peacetime strength: indeed, the latter could allow its effectives gradually to diminish.[299] The Finance Minister, Caillaux, thought such an arrangement would be in France's interest, as the falling birth rate would reduce the effectives anyway. But Clemenceau assailed the document, insisting that without enforcement procedures any agreement would be valueless. At his insistence the CSDN agreed to suppress it and to discourage discussion of the matter.[300]

If France would not join a liberal coalition, neither would the Americans. Roosevelt had been alarmed by the laying down of HMS *Dreadnought*, and wanted to explore negotiated limits on the size of capital ships as an alternative to asking Congress for huge new appropriations. For a time he seemed willing

[291] Schoen to Bülow, 28 Jan. 1907, GP xxiii/1, doc. 7835.

[292] Bompard to Pichon, 14 Apr. 1907, DDF 2nd ser. x. 467.

[293] Schoen to Bülow, 18 Feb. and 18 Mar. 1907, GP xxiii/1, docs. 7853, 7879.

[294] Schoen to Bülow, 11 Feb. 1907, ibid., doc. 7843.

[295] Benckendorff to Grey, 3 Apr. 1907, BD viii, doc. 191.

[296] Bompard to Pichon, 19 Apr. 1907; Jules Cambon to Pichon, 20 Apr. 1907; Pichon to Bompard, 27 Apr. 1907; Bompard to Pichon, 15 June 1907, AMAE C-Administrative 57.

[297] Pichon to Paul Cambon, 4 Dec. 1906, ibid. Grey to Bertie, 5 Dec. 1906, BD viii, doc. 170.

[298] *Le Matin*, 17 May 1906, AMAE C-Administrative 57. Bertie to Grey, 1 June 1906, BD viii, doc. 160.

[299] Dülffer, *Regeln*, 294.

[300] CSDN, 6 Feb. 1907, SHA 2.N. 1.

to grasp the nettle.[301] As the conference approached, however, he became more estranged from London and preoccupied by tension with Japan, which pushed him towards dreadnought rearmament. Although the Americans reserved the right to raise the subject of arms limitation, they warned that they would leave the initiative to Britain rather than exercise it themselves.[302]

By the eve of the Hague meeting the cause of arms limitation was in disarray. The evidence of the Martens mission was that most of the Powers would agree to a non-binding discussion in order to humour pacifist opinion, but only London and possibly Washington expected practical results.[303] The American stalking-horse refused to move, and in the Foreign Office there was an inclination to back off.[304] Grey was reluctant to embarrass Russia, and after Bülow's Reichstag declaration he decided to avoid further controversy.[305] British opinion was becoming cooler and he had already partially succeeded in smoking the Germans out. He told the British delegation that the Government would like a discussion, but as Germany would boycott it it could not be serious, and he did not intend to cause friction or ill-will. If there was a negotiation, the delegates could suggest regular communication by the Powers of their naval programmes to each other before presenting them to Parliament, to facilitate discussion before they were publicly committed.[306] In any case, in its first few weeks the peace conference did not pursue the issue.

Grey had told the Commons that an armaments resolution must be in a form the conference could accept,[307] and the initial British draft merely reaffirmed the 1899 wording with the rider that it was 'more urgent than ever' for governments to consider the issue.[308] The Germans and Austrians wanted this toned down to: 'it is highly desirable that the Governments should resume the serious study of this question.'[309] In a plenary session on 17 August their wording was carried without a vote, the introductory speech by the chief British delegate having been cleared with the Germans beforehand.[310] The Russian chairman closed the proceedings after twenty-five minutes. Disarmament thus received Izvolsky's 'first-class burial', the British and Americans failing even to fix a date for a successor meeting. Tirpitz introduced his *Novelle*, and the Liberal Cabinet approved the third 1907–8 capital ship. Henceforth the British navalists could argue that negotiation had been tried and failed.

To an extent the conference had polarized the liberal and dynastic states. In

[301] Davis, *Second Hague Conference*, 141. Jusserand to Bourgeois, 30 May 1906, AMAE C-Administrative 57.

[302] Davis, *Second Hague Conference*, ch. 9. White to Haldane, 14 Sept. 1906, NLS Haldane MSS 5907. Jusserand to Pichon, 9 May 1907, AMAE C-Administrative 57.

[303] Schoen to Bülow, 12 Mar. 1907, GP xxiii/1, doc. 7874.

[304] Paul Cambon to Pichon, 14 May 1907, AMAE C-Administrative 57.

[305] Paul Cambon to Pichon, 3 May 1907, ibid. Grey to Nicolson, 1 May 1907, BD viii, doc. 194.

[306] Grey to Fry, 12 June 1907, ibid., doc. 206.

[307] Metternich to Bülow, 24 July and 2 Aug. 1907, PAAA R.179.

[308] Davis, *Second Hague Conference*, 216.

[309] J. B. Scott, *The Hague Peace Conferences of 1899 and 1907* (2 vols., Baltimore, 1909), i. 662–9.

[310] Bülow to Auswärtiges Amt, 5 Aug. 1907, PAAA R.179.

America and Britain the peace movement had considerable weight—as did its navalist enemies. France sent delegates to The Hague who sympathized with the movement's objectives, despite Clemenceau's views. In the Italian Chamber the movement had some influence. The German Peace Society, in contrast (which urged its government to act on the armaments resolution), had only 10,000 members, against perhaps 300,000 in the analogous French organizations. The Catholic Centre and the National Liberal parties supported the German Government's position, and Wilhelm and Bülow spoke disparagingly of the peace activists, as did Franz Joseph and Izvolsky.[311] Even the Western Powers, however, were half-hearted about armaments limitation, and public support for it faltered as the conference neared. France and Britain could not risk a Russo-German line-up, and there were insufficient Anglo-American common interests. Ironically, there was some basis for attempting land armaments limitation in Western Europe, where the German army was approaching steady state, some French leaders were resigned to dwindling peacetime strength, and Haldane was retrenching in Britain. But the French, German, and British Admiralties opposed a naval treaty, and navies were the crux of the debate in 1907, as armies had been in 1899. In Eastern Europe, the Austrians and Russians wanted no restrictions on their military recovery. There was no consensus in favour of concerted limitation, and the land armaments equilibrium was precarious. Between 1907 and 1912 in both halves of Europe it would be dislocated, and the conditions for a Continental arms race brought into being.

[311] R. Chickering, *Imperial Germany and a World without War: The Peace Movement and German Society, 1892–1914* (Princeton, 1975), 59, 229–30, 242, 244, 345, 371, 384 ff.

3

The Breakdown of Equilibrium in the East: From the Bosnian Crisis to the Balkan Wars, 1908–1912

1. The Annexation Crisis

Austria-Hungary's annexation on 5 October 1908 of the Ottoman provinces of Bosnia and Herzegovina ushered in six months of European tension. It resulted in a trial of armed strength, in the Balkan if not the broader Continental arena, and it set a menacing precedent. Austria-Hungary, Serbia, Montenegro, the Ottoman Empire, and Bulgaria all raised their armies above normal peacetime levels and at the peak called out between them perhaps a quarter of a million extra men. By throwing into harsh relief the prevailing balance of forces, the crisis stimulated armaments development from the Baltic to the Adriatic. It ended a decade of Austro-Russian *détente* and revived the confrontation in the East between the two alliance blocs. Its profoundest impact was reserved, however, for relations between the Habsburg Monarchy and the South Slavs.

* * *

Austria-Hungary had occupied and administered Bosnia-Herzegovina since 1878, after receiving a mandate from the European Powers at the Congress of Berlin. It claimed now to be responding to the Young Turk revolution. Since the regime installed in Constantinople in July 1908 was introducing a constitution, the provinces needed one too, and to grant it Vienna must have sovereignty.[1] The change might seem purely formal; and simultaneously with the declaration the Austrians withdrew their garrison in the adjoining Ottoman territory of the Sanjak of Novibazar. Having initially refused additional compensation to the Turks, they eventually agreed to pay an indemnity in return for recognition of the annexation. But their action raised much larger issues. It affronted South Slav nationalism by asserting Habsburg control in perpetuity over territories that formed the heartland of the medieval Serbian kingdom and contained two-thirds of a million Serbs.[2] Moreover, by violating the treaty of

---

[1] Aehrenthal to Hardinge, 28 Sept. 1908, *BD* v, doc. 288. B. E. Schmitt, *The Annexation of Bosnia, 1908–1909* (Cambridge, 1937) is the best account of the crisis. I am indebted to Professor Roy Bridge for his advice on this chapter.

[2] The population in 1908 was 1.57 million, of whom 674,000 were Serbs, 334,000 Croats, and 548,000 Muslims. F. Conrad von Hötzendorf, *Aus meiner Dienstzeit 1906–1918* (5 vols., Vienna, 1921–5), i. 13.

Fig. 6. The Balkans in 1914 (the shaded area shows the territories lost by the Ottoman Empire in 1912–13)

1878 it challenged the other signatories and the authority of the 'Concert of Europe'—the conference machinery through which the Powers handled crisis management. This made it possible that resistance to the annexation from Serbia and Montenegro would win wider backing, and that European peace would be threatened.

Behind the Austrian initiative lay the generational shift in the Vienna leadership in October 1906 and the arrival at the Foreign Ministry of Alois Lexa von Aehrenthal. A cool, unscrupulous negotiator, he wanted better relations with St Petersburg, in order to reduce his dependence on Germany, but also to enhance the Monarchy's Balkan position. In January 1908 he announced that he had won a railway concession in the Sanjak of Novibazar: he had been casual about consulting the Russians, who considered that it violated previous agreements and threatened to shift the Balkan balance in Austria-Hungary's favour.[3] None the less, Izvolsky tried to reinvigorate the flagging co-operation between the two capitals by dropping his objections to the railway and by seeking Aehrenthal's support for a line of his own. Beyond this, he wanted assistance in revising the status of the Turkish Straits, to allow passage for Russian warships. He suggested that the Straits and Bosnia-Herzegovina might be discussed in a spirit of 'friendly reciprocity'.[4] On 15–16 September 1908 he met Aehrenthal privately in Moravia, at the castle of Buchlau, and reached an understanding that afterwards each man accused the other of misrepresenting. It seems, however, that Izvolsky promised benevolence towards the annexation in return for Aehrenthal's support over the Straits. Aehrenthal was surprised by the extent of Russia's subsequent hostility, although he partly courted it by moving faster and more unilaterally than Izvolsky expected, while using Buchlau to wrongfoot him. Izvolsky's resentment that 'the dirty Jew tricked me, he lied to me, he put me in it'[5] was one factor in the following events.

Aehrenthal seized a chance to annex while he felt he could discount Russian opposition. But his underlying concern was the Monarchy's vulnerability in the face of South Slav agitation, Serbian assertiveness, and the decline of the Ottoman counterbalance to Belgrade. Although in the past he had toyed with the idea of partitioning Serbia, in October 1908 he judged the circumstances unfavourable, and he had the limited objective of securing the annexation in order to give more freedom to the Habsburg authorities in the provinces and to demoralize pan-Serb agitators.[6] The Sanjak garrison had been intended to bar a Serbian–Montenegrin union, but it was a small and scattered force of only 2,400 men that could be attacked from three sides. Even Conrad advised that it lacked military significance, and by withdrawing it Aehrenthal could signal that the annexation did not presage further expansion.[7] The Young Turk revolution

[3] F. R. Bridge, *From Sadowa to Sarajevo: The Foreign Policy of Austria-Hungary, 1866–1914* (London, 1972), 297 ff. Schmitt, *Bosnia*, 7–8.

[4] Schmitt, *Bosnia*, 9.   [5] Bülow, *Memoirs*, ii. 395.   [6] Conrad, *Dienstzeit*, i. 107–8.

[7] Ibid. 99. Girodon to Picquart, 14 Oct. 1908, *DDF* 2nd ser. xi, doc. 493. Aehrenthal in GMR, 19 Aug. 1908, *Österreich-Ungarns Aussenpolitik von der Bosnischen Krise 1908 bis zum Kriegsausbruch 1914*, ed. L. Bittner and H. Übersberger (9 vols., Vienna, 1930; henceforth *ÖUA*), i, doc. 40.

meanwhile increased the risks of friction with the Ottoman authorities and of Turkish–South Slav co-operation. On 19 August the Joint Council of Ministers decided the Monarchy was in a *Zwangslage* (a situation of compulsion)[8] and must act.

The cost of action was expected to be low. Aehrenthal thought the Turks too disorganized to fight; Conrad confirmed that the Russians were too, and that the Monarchy had such superiority over Italy that war with her would be 'almost desirable'. The two Prime Ministers agreed to the annexation on condition that it did not lead to a clash with a Great Power, and Aehrenthal judged that, with German support, France tied down in Morocco, and Russia internally fragile, such a clash was improbable. Serious Serbian and Montenegrin opposition was not envisaged.[9] It is true that Schönaich wanted a partial mobilization to raise the XV Corps in Bosnia from 20,000 to 64,000 men, and warned the Foreign Minister against being underinsured militarily. Insurrection rather than Serbian attack, however, was the danger he foresaw, and the civilians opposed his suggestion because it would be expensive (if it continued into the spring it would cost 100 million crowns) and would cause uncertainty at home, as well as seeming provocative.[10] Schönaich ordered the commanders of the XV Corps and the Zara military district to be ready for rapid mobilization if necessary, but the troops were not reinforced.[11] Political exigencies took precedence over military security, in keeping with Aehrenthal's restricted goals.

The Austrians failed to anticipate the vehemence of the South Slav response. There were huge demonstrations in Belgrade, and the Serb Parliament, the Skupshina, called for compensation or for the annexation to be revoked. For the Serbian Government compensation meant a land bridge through Bosnia between Serbia and Montenegro, or at least an assurance that the annexed provinces would remain autonomous.[12] The Russians promised to support Serbia's claims, although not at the risk of war. Montenegro also wanted territory, and to cancel article 29 of the 1878 treaty, which restricted its fortifications and forbade it a navy.[13] Both Serbia and Montenegro backed up their demands by military measures, from which the Austrians had deliberately refrained. Montenegro mobilized all its able-bodied men, garrisoned the frontier, and positioned artillery above Cattaro, as well as shipping in Russian and Italian munitions.[14] The Serbian Government obtained a 16-million dinar emergency credit from

---

[8] GMR, 19 Aug. 1908, *ÖUA* i. doc. 40. See also F. R. Bridge, 'Izvolsky, Aehrenthal, and the End of the Austro-Russian Entente, 1906–8', *Mitteilungen des Österreichischen Staatsarchivs*, 29 (1976), 315–62, esp. 331.

[9] GMR, 19 Aug. and 10 Sept. 1908, *ÖUA* i, docs. 40, 75.

[10] Ibid., 10 Sept. 1908, doc. 75. Schönaich to Franz Joseph, 30 Aug. 1908, KAW KM Präs (1908) 76–7. Conrad, *Dienstzeit*, i. 111.

[11] Schönaich to Defence Ministers, 4 Oct. 1908, KAW KM Präs (1908) 76–7. Conrad to Aehrenthal, 13 Oct. 1908, Conrad, *Dienstzeit*, i. 601.

[12] Schmitt, *Bosnia*, 46–7. Schoen minute, 20 Oct. 1908, *GP* xxvi/1, doc. 9100.

[13] Schmitt, *Bosnia*, 71–2, 234.

[14] Conrad, *Dienstzeit*, i. 601. GGS annual report, 3 Dec. 1908, KAM Gstb. 489.

Parliament for foreign military orders.[15] It set up what purported to be a pan-Serb propaganda agency, the Narodna Odbrana, and was reported by Austrian military intelligence to be organizing bands of irregulars.[16] It called up reservists and expanded the army from the normal 10–12,000 winter strength to over 30,000.[17]

Aehrenthal countered by appealing to the Powers, but with only limited success. On 6 November he complained about Belgrade's reinforcement of its standing army, the emergency credit, the foreign arms orders, troop movements towards the Bosnian border, and the creation of guerilla bands.[18] The Powers instructed their representatives to take up the last two points, while mostly ignoring Serbian counter-protests. In response the Serbs promised that only guard detachments would remain on the frontier, and guerrilla bands would not be allowed to form or to cross it, but the larger problem remained unresolved.[19] Conrad reported that he had about 20,000 men available for field operations in Bosnia-Herzegovina and Dalmatia: the solitary narrow-gauge railway from northern Bosnia could move about 9,000 every 24 hours. Seaborne reinforcements could be intercepted by Italy. On the other hand, Montenegro could concentrate 25,000 troops anywhere on the border within eight to ten days: an estimate he later shortened to two days. By the spring, he thought, the Montenegrins might have 40,000 available on mobilization and the Serbs 160,000. In the opening stages of a war the Monarchy's enemies might shatter its prestige and its armies' morale by overrunning territory that it would be difficult and costly to regain. He lamented that pre-annexation precautions had been rejected, and that his forces remained 'on a peace footing'.[20]

Conrad's pleas were slow to have an impact, perhaps because he evidently envisaged military preparations as leading to a war, rather than as being precautions or a deterrent. If Serbia mobilized, he argued, Austria-Hungary should implement a 'Case B' ('Balkan') mobilization, and overwhelm its enemy.[21] But his main immediate anxiety was Montenegro, as he thought Serbian and Austro-Hungarian mobilization speeds were comparable. Aehrenthal, in contrast, doubted whether Montenegro would attack.[22] He ordered that Austrian warships should pull back from the Montenegrin coast, once it was clear that Montenegro's measures had only a 'demonstrative character'. Schönaich agreed, saying that 'provisionally on our side no military measures have been taken' and that his border troops would simply observe Montenegro's actions, 'so that the

[15] Descos to Pichon, 24 Oct. 1908, AMAE NS Serbie 8.
[16] Captured Serbian War Ministry document, 28 Sept. 1908, KAW KM Präs (1908) 51–7. Kageneck report, 3 Dec. 1908, PAAA R.8618.
[17] Schmitt, *Bosnia*, 46–7. Conrad, *Dienstzeit*, i. 601. Lippe to Bülow, 6 Oct. 1908 and Tschirschky to AA, 8 Oct. 1908, *GP* xxvi/1, docs. 9090, 9093. Whitehead to Grey, 6 and 8 Oct. 1908, *BD* v, docs. 315, 344. Summary of attaché report, 12 Oct. 1908, KAW KM Präs (1908) 51–7.
[18] Aehrenthal circular, 6 Nov. 1908, *ÖUA* i, doc. 513.
[19] Schmitt, *Bosnia*, 74–6. Ratibor to AA, 18 Nov. 1908, *GP* xxvi/1, doc. 9118.
[20] Conrad, *Dienstzeit*, i. 100–3, 125–7. Conrad to Franz Joseph, n.d. but *c*.16 Oct. 1908, KAW KM Präs (1908) 76–7.
[21] Conrad to Schönaich, 6 Oct. 1908, ibid.   [22] Conrad, *Dienstzeit*, i. 124–6.

Prince [of Montenegro] may be deprived of any basis for the assertion that through our military measures he is disturbed or obliged to take special precautions'.[23] Against Serbia too, Aehrenthal was reluctant to take steps that might make the Monarchy seem the aggressor in the eyes of Europe,[24] and he had the sovereign's support. Unlike Serbia or Turkey, Franz Joseph told the British Ambassador in October, he had taken 'no military measures whatever . . . I know that in the present state of affairs any abstention from all special military preparations is dangerous. But I have preferred to run the risk rather than to take measures which might cause excitement or offer a pretext for aggression'.[25]

This overstated the case. While minimizing any immediate appearance of provocation, the Monarchy was preparing to bring the crisis to a head. Both the British and the French suspected that the Government was already doing what was open to it without informing the public or the legislatures. This included moving the Danube flotilla downstream and stepping up production of rations and munitions, as well as keeping on some of the retiring conscript class and calling up members of the youngest cohort of reservists, neither of which measures required publicity or special authorization.[26] On 30 October Schönaich warned his officials that 'current political circumstances' would necessitate a 'heightened war readiness' in the spring, and that they should be able to order mobilization from 1 March.[27] In mid-November he prevailed upon Franz Joseph with Conrad's arguments about the need for greater readiness in the south-east if the Monarchy was not to risk irrecoverable loss of territory to enemy attack. The Emperor agreed to another *Notbehelf*, designed to double the mountain artillery at the cavalry's expense. In addition, fifteen infantry battalions and one cavalry squadron were to be transferred into the annexed provinces, the Powers being informed that this was not a mobilization but a defensive precaution, necessitated for border security and by the winter weather.[28]

Schönaich soon perceived the possibility of profiting from the tension to raise the army's permanent, as opposed to short-term, preparedness. At the end of October he requested an armaments credit, initially of 47 million crowns for tinned meat, munitions, and frontier guards. But the figure was raised sucessively to 164 millions, the extra being earmarked for field kitchens, mountain howitzers, bridging equipment, machine-gun detachments, and fortifications against Italy as well as in the Balkans, expenditure on all of which would continue into 1910.[29] Schönaich also tried to end the manpower deadlock, offering

---

[23] Aehrenthal to Schönaich, 21 Oct. 1908; Schönaich to Aehrenthal, 22 Oct. 1908, KAW KM Präs (1908) 51–17.

[24] Conrad, *Dienstzeit*, i. 124. [25] Goschen to Grey, 19 Oct. 1908, *BD* v, doc. 397.

[26] Ibid. and Goschen to Grey, 9 Oct. 1908, *BD* v, doc. 345. Girodon to Picquart, 14 Oct. 1908, *DDF* 2nd ser. xi, doc. 493.

[27] Schönaich circular, 30 Oct. 1908, KAW KM Präs (1908) 55–15.

[28] Schönaich to Franz Joseph, 14 Nov. 1908, KAW KM Präs (1908) 76–7. GGS 9 Abt., annual report, 1 Apr. 1909, KAM Gstb 204. Kiderlen-Wächter minute, 17 Nov. 1908, *GP* xxvi/1, doc. 9117. Kageneck report, 3 Dec. 1908, PAAA R.8618.

[29] Schönaich to Prime Ministers, 30 Oct. and 30 Nov. 1908, KAW KM Präs (1908) 37–13. Schönaich to Finance Ministers, 12 July 1909, KAW KM Präs (1909) 37–5.

the Hungarians new linguistic concessions in return for a higher recruitment contingent and thereby irrevocably antagonizing Franz Ferdinand.[30] This latter initiative failed, but he succeeded in his bid for the credit, which Aehrenthal recommended 'in the warmest and most earnest fashion'.[31] The benefits for the army included eleven new batteries of mountain guns and a central reserve of heavy field artillery.[32] Re-equipment with quick-firers was completed ahead of schedule, and the Monarchy gained an advantage over its neighbours in machine guns.[33]

With a metre of snow on the ground by December, even Conrad accepted that there would be no war before 1 March, and the situation temporarily stabilized.[34] The ensuing deadlock, however, was embarrassing and expensive, and damaged business confidence and domestic morale. Aehrenthal told Bülow on 8 December that he could not remain patient indefinitely, and if need be he would seek a 'decisive resolution', although he would try to localize a war by promising to respect Serbian and Montenegrin independence and integrity.[35] Absorbing Serbia into the Monarchy, he told Conrad, was impracticable, and even if force were needed to secure the annexation he did not wish to penetrate far into enemy territory.[36] It was therefore central to his planning that, although mobilization should be possible after 1 March, Austria-Hungary's preparations in the meantime should seem defensive. This meant continuing to fight off the CGS, who complained bitterly in his memoirs that the Foreign Minister objected even to the slightest military precaution as a provocation and an encroachment on his own authority.[37]

Nor was occasion for further escalation given by the South Slavs. Aehrenthal began softening up the ground in February, warning that Serbian preparations were 'of a very serious character' and causing 'great disquietude'. If they continued, Austria-Hungary would lose patience.[38] The Serbs, however, claimed that they had taken no threatening steps and that their frontier dispositions were normal, leaving them 'completely open' to an attack. Although they called up some of their oldest reservists on 9 March, this was in response to Aehrenthal's diplomatic offensive, and militarily Serbia appears to have been little better prepared than in the autumn.[39] Grey told Aehrenthal that he was unaware of any Serbian 'offensive steps or provocation beyond general recruitment at home'.[40] According to the Austrians' own military intelligence, most of the Serbian extraordinary credit was used to pay reservists rather than for new equipment and the

---

[30] Schönaich to Conrad, 15 Nov. 1908, KAW KM Präs (1908) 49–39. Hetzer, 'Schönaich', 105–13. Conrad, *Dienstzeit*, i. 133–6.

[31] Aehrenthal to Prime Ministers, 18 Feb. 1909, KAW KM Präs (1909) 37–5.

[32] GGS 9.Abt. annual report, 1 Apr. 1909, KAM Gstb 204.

[33] GGS annual report for 1911, n.d., KAM Gstb 576.   [34] Conrad, *Dienstzeit*, i. 129.

[35] Aehrenthal to Bülow, 8 Dec. 1908, *ÖUA* i, doc. 703.

[36] Conrad, *Dienstzeit*, i. 138, 141.   [37] Ibid. 101.

[38] Schmitt, *Bosnia*, 155. Cartwright to Grey, 17 Feb. 1909, *BD* v, doc. 575.

[39] Whitehead to Grey, 19 Feb. 1909; Serbian Note, 25 Feb. 1909, *BD* v, docs. 588, 610. Schmitt, *Bosnia*, 180.

[40] Grey to Cartwright, 19 Feb. 1909, *BD* v, doc. 585.

state of the country's finances was 'delicate'.[41] In February the War Minister resigned because he was refused more money.[42] Schönaich noted that Serbia was unlikely to be ready until 1 May—two months later than his own preparedness date[43]— and the mood in Belgrade was reported to be sober and restrained.[44] Exasperation with the stalemate rather than Serbian acts of brinkmanship provoked the sudden heightening of Austrian preparedness that heralded the climax of the crisis.

Conrad's lobbying was one factor in this new development; but only when it meshed with Aehrenthal's diplomatic schedule. In spite of the reinforcement at the end of 1908, the CGS deemed the garrison of the annexed provinces too small. The Montenegrin frontier, held by the 18th Infantry Division with 13,200 men and outdated fortifications and artillery, was particularly at risk, and it would be dangerous for the Monarchy to mobilize without stronger defences.[45] With Schönaich's backing he appealed to Franz Joseph, and Aehrenthal reluctantly agreed to a further strengthening of the units already in Bosnia-Herzegovina under the guise of a 'spring exercise'. Fourteen additional infantry battalions would join them. There would be no public placarding, and the letters sent to the men's homes would avoid the phrase 'up to war strength' (although for the reinforced units this was what was intended), in order to prevent 'unnecessary anxiety to the population and financial circles'.[46] No sooner had the Foreign Minister agreed in principle to the measures, however, than on 16 February he postponed them to mid-March, even though both Conrad and Schönaich wanted them implemented by the start of the month.[47]

There followed several weeks of civil–military contention, and a race between Habsburg military preparations and British-led endeavours to mediate. Until mid-February Britain as well as Russia supported Serbia's demands, but rumours of an impending Habsburg ultimatum impelled Grey to cut loose. He proposed that the Powers should both restrain the Serbs and prevail upon the Austrians to offer compensation. When the Germans refused to rein in their ally, the French and British turned to Izvolsky. Eventually on 27 February the Russian Foreign Minister advised the Serbs to avoid anything that might lead to war with Austria-Hungary, and to acquiesce in whatever satisfaction the Powers might provide.[48] Aehrenthal was aware of these moves,[49] and he held back on reinforcement partly to see what Russia could deliver. But he also needed to clear himself with Bülow, whom he informed that if necessary he would fight to

---

[41] Military attaché report on Serbian financial situation, 17 Jan. 1909, KAW Gstb (1909) 25–8.

[42] Descos to Pichon, 20 Feb. 1909, AMAE ns Serbie 8.

[43] Forgách to Aehrenthal (seen by Schönaich), 6 Feb. 1909, KAW KM Präs (1909) 51–7.

[44] Forgách to Aehrenthal, 11 Feb. 1909, ibid.

[45] Conrad to Franz Joseph, 5 Feb. 1909; Schemua report on situation in Herzegovina, 9 Jan. 1909, KAW KM Präs (1909) 76–57.

[46] Schönaich and Conrad to Franz Joseph, 13 Feb. 1909; Schönaich to Aehrenthal and other Ministers, 14 Feb. 1909, ibid.

[47] Schönaich to Franz Joseph, 24 Feb. 1909, and enclosures, ibid. Conrad, *Dienstzeit*, i. 145. Conrad to Schönaich, 26 Feb. 1909, KM Präs (1909) 76–57.

[48] Schmitt, *Bosnia*, ch. 10.   [49] Forgách to Aehrenthal, 7 Mar. 1909, *ÖUA* ii, doc. 1135.

maintain the annexation, which was essential to forestall the emergence of a greater Serbia aligned with the entente. The cost and risk even of a localized Balkan war would outweigh any likely gains, and he preferred to avoid one, but the existing situation was untenable. After negotiating a settlement with Turkey and awaiting the Italian elections in March he would require Serbia to drop its compensation claims and halt its military preparations. Only if Belgrade refused would he send an ultimatum, hoping that Russia and the other Powers would accept that his policy was not aggressive.[50]

The Foreign Minister therefore preferred a diplomatic solution, and wanted to postpone military measures that might complicate one and unsettle domestic public opinion. Conrad, by contrast, argued that war was inevitable and that Bosnia must be reinforced in advance. If Serbia and Montenegro intended to fight (and he believed that Serbia was secretly beginning mobilization), the less delay the better.[51] The course of events strengthened his hand, Aehrenthal warning the German Ambassador that if the crisis dragged on until the end of March he would demand that Serbia give a binding declaration of peaceful intentions or face imminent invasion.[52] Although the Serbs dropped their territorial demands, two notes sent by them on 10 and 14 March were thought disappointing and insulting by most of the Powers, and the tension went up a further notch.[53] On 13 March Aehrenthal finally agreed to the proposed new reinforcement of the annexed provinces, as a precaution against surprise attack rather than as the first stage of mobilization, but also as a means of pressure.[54] The Austrian public was growing impatient with the length of the crisis and the resulting economic uncertainty.[55] The Foreign Minister himself was becoming exasperated with the Serbs, and more willing to use force against them, telling the Germans that if he did so he would not partition the country or annex it, but he would impose an indemnity, hold Belgrade as a pledge, and probably replace the ruling dynasty.[56] Although he wished not to seem aggressive to the other Powers, to whom he looked to impose a settlement, he needed to impress them with a sense of urgency.[57] He ordered that the new measures were to be portrayed as exercises and to cause the minimum disturbance to civilian rail traffic,[58] but in fact the barracks in Bosnia were jammed and the railways almost wholly reserved for military trains.[59] Perhaps as many as 30,000 men joined the 26,000 sent in November, and the garrison of Bosnia-Herzegovina and Dalmatia reached treble its pre-crisis size.[60]

[50] Aehrenthal to Bülow, 20 Feb. 1909, *GP* xxvi/2, doc. 9386.

[51] Conrad, *Dienstzeit*, i. 150, 154–5.   [52] Schmitt, *Bosnia*, 171, 174, 182.

[53] Ibid. 180. Conrad, *Dienstzeit*, i. 155. Schönaich to Franz Joseph, 13 Mar. 1909, KAW KM Präs (1909) 76–57.

[54] Aehrenthal to Prime Ministers, 13 Mar. 1909, ibid. Szögyény to Bülow, 15 Mar. 1909, *GP* xxvi/2, doc. 9434.

[55] Cartwright to Grey, 18 Mar. 1909, *BD* v, doc. 717. Crozier to Pichon, 15 Mar. 1909, *DDF* 2nd ser. xii, doc. 101.

[56] Schmitt, *Bosnia*, 209.   [57] Cartwright to Grey, 18 Mar. 1909, *BD* v, doc. 715.

[58] Conrad, *Dienstzeit*, i. 155.   [59] Grenard to Pichon, 23 Mar. 1909, *DDF* xii, doc. 129.

[60] Käs, 'Generalstab', 217–23.

Nor did Habsburg preparations stop here. On 22 March Franz Joseph approved heightened readiness for the VII and XIII Corps, to increase frontier security.[61] The Austrians' attitude hardened further when they obtained a copy of a dispatch from the Serbian Minister in St Petersburg, which suggested that Izvolsky intended to drag out the conflict and wear them down financially. In contrast to the cost of the extraordinary measures, the War Ministry estimated that of a three-month Balkan campaign at 800 million crowns, which the common Finance Minister thought affordable. In the light of this Schönaich dropped his opposition to using force and Aehrenthal decided to seek partial mobilization.[62] On 26 March the Emperor agreed to call up all reservists in the annexed provinces,[63] and on 29 March the Joint Council of Ministers recommended a 'yellow' mobilization against Serbia and Montenegro. According to Conrad (who probably misjudged him) Aehrenthal now 'reckoned on war'.[64]

Yet within forty-eight hours there was a peaceful outcome. For at the same time as sabre-rattling on the frontier, Aehrenthal had been exploring a British suggestion for a revised and more accommodating note that Serbia would be compelled to sign. He insisted that the Serbs must reverse their military measures, or he would give way to his military and send an ultimatum.[65] The British accepted his right to make the demand, but they pleaded that the Serbian submission note should not be humiliating, or prejudge the position of the Powers. Only at the end of March did a German warning to St Petersburg break the impasse, and Russia's collapse and Britain's acceptance of Aehrenthal's terms may have come just in time. But on 30 March the Powers' *démarche* in Belgrade went ahead and the following day the Serbs swallowed the dish prepared for them, which was essentially of Austrian concoction. They dropped their opposition to the annexation, agreed to return to their pre-crisis military deployments and force strengths, and promised to live in future as a good neighbour of the Monarchy. By doing so they ended the confrontation's most acute phase.[66]

Aehrenthal had gained essentially what he started with: the annexation. Subsequently, he described the crisis as a textbook example of the need for strength to impose one's will.[67] His military preparations had been slow and cautious, taken initially as defensive safeguards but increasingly as part of a strategy of coercion, albeit one with limited aims. Their adoption did not signify that a 'military party' had triumphed, or that policy was slipping out of civilian control. The Serbs and Montenegrins, conversely, had used military measures in the hope of reversing the annexation, or at least of winning territorial compensations at Austria-Hungary's expense. Both countries were obliged to drop their claims.

[61] Conrad, *Dienstzeit*, i. 160.

[62] Serb Minister in St Petersburg to Foreign Minister, 8 Mar. 1909, KAW KM Präs (1909) 51–7. Conrad, *Dienstzeit*, i. 162. Kageneck report, 27 Mar. 1909, PAAA R.8619.

[63] Burián to Schönaich, 27 Mar. 1909, KAW KM Präs (1909) 76–57.

[64] Käs, 'Generalstab', 141, 218. Conrad, *Dienstzeit*, i. 162.

[65] Cartwright to Grey, 18 Mar. 1909, *BD* v, doc. 715. On Britain's role, F. R. Bridge, *Great Britain and Austria-Hungary, 1906–1914: A Diplomatic History* (London, 1972), 128–34.

[66] Schmitt, *Bosnia*, ch. 13.   [67] GMR, 14 Sept. 1909, HHStA PA XL, 308.

Aehrenthal was mistaken, however, in his hopes that South Slav aspirations could be permanently dashed, and he had refrained from seeking permanent restrictions on Serbian sovereignty and military power.[68] Moreover, in a separate agreement on 7 April, in return for Montenegro withdrawing its forces from the border, he agreed to reduce the restrictions imposed by the 1878 treaty on the principality's military development.[69] Although Austria-Hungary could now cancel its own extraordinary measures and send home the reservists, short-term disengagement left its adversaries free to expand as a long-term threat.

Conrad had perceived the danger, and although he agreed that permanent military restrictions on the Serbians were not feasible, he had intended to destroy their forces through war.[70] Until the last moment he pleaded for hostilities, and his chagrin was the greater because temporarily war had indeed seemed imminent. In a retrospective memorandum he presented an analysis that he would reiterate down to 1914. The outcome was an 'illusory success' that would merely postpone the confrontation with the Monarchy's enemies until the latter were ready. In a few years' time Austria-Hungary would face either 'a many-front war or . . . far-reaching concessions'. It must rearm as quickly as possible. There was a dismal cogency in this Social Darwinist prescription, but its premiss was that only the 'incorporation' of Serbia into the Monarchy would resolve the problem.[71] Franz Joseph had seen strength in the military arguments and Aehrenthal himself had expected a war to be victorious and to bring domestic advantages. The decision, he confessed, had been finely balanced. But he had repeatedly assured the other Powers that war was not his preference and that he had no designs on Serbian independence and integrity. It would be difficult to justify spending 800 million crowns if annexing or partitioning Serbia was impracticable and would create new 'tinder' for the future.[72] Given this, the 31 March note gave as much as war could, and more cheaply. The Foreign Minister's decision was supported by the two Prime Ministers and by Schönaich, who congratulated him on the result, passing over opposition from 'hotheads' in the War Ministry.[73] In his own retrospective comments Aehrenthal cited the expense and risk of military action and the danger of provoking a hostile Russo-Turkish-Italian alliance. The Monarchy must seek no more Balkan gains and avoid armed clashes with St Petersburg and Rome.[74] Thus had the poacher turned gamekeeper. He agreed, however, that at least half the money saved by not going to war should be devoted to the army and navy, especially the latter.[75] In Vienna, as in Cetinje and Belgrade, the stage was set for a new round in the arms race.

* * *

[68] Cartwright to Grey, 19 Mar. 1909, *BD* v, doc. 720.   [69] Schmitt, *Bosnia*, 240.

[70] Kageneck report, 18 Mar. 1909, PAAA R.8619.

[71] Conrad to Franz Joseph, 3 Apr. 1909, KM Präs (1909) 76–7. Conrad, *Dienstzeit*, i. 163.

[72] Tschirschky to Bülow, 28 Mar. 1909, *GP* xxvi/2, doc. 9493.

[73] Schönaich to Aehrenthal, 30 Mar. 1909, HHStA Nachlass Aehrenthal 3.

[74] Unsigned memorandum by Aehrenthal, 15 Aug. 1909, KAW Gstb Operationsbureau 738.

[75] Tschirschky to Bülow, 28 Mar. 1909, *GP* xxvi/2, doc. 9493.

Both Aehrenthal and Conrad saw the crisis in a European as well as local perspective. The Foreign Minister judged that the broader conjuncture favoured a diplomatic success, and Great-Power pressure had indeed made an ultimatum to Belgrade unnecessary. The same conjuncture, however, led Conrad to advocate a preventive war, and in 1909 would probably have permitted one without escalation. The Continental armaments context might impinge on the crisis in two ways: through arms sales, and through the danger of Habsburg military measures triggering retaliation elsewhere. In fact arms sales were significant but did not cause a serious confrontation, while outside the Balkans the level of militarization remained low. Both sides recognized that there would be an Austro-German advantage in a collision between the two alliances, a recognition that gave Russia and France no incentive to make military preparations and Austria-Hungary and Germany no need.

The diplomacy of arms sales centred on supplies to Serbia and Montenegro, the Habsburg local authorities having been ordered to stop war material being exported to either, or being transported through the Monarchy.[76] At the time of the annexation, however, the Steyr plant was in the middle of a large order for Belgrade, converting rifles into repeaters; unless it completed the contract by February it would face a daily fine. To escape the penalty the authorities blocked the delivery rather than the manufacture of the firearms, 34,000 rifles and 10,000 carbines ordered prior to the crisis arriving only after it had finished.[77] The ban on transit caused more difficulty. During October the Austrians detained twenty-nine railway wagonloads of 75 mm field guns and munitions dispatched by Schneider-Creusot. With support from the French Embassy the company applied for a re-export licence, which Aehrenthal granted, pointing out that the consignments could get to Serbia by another route and that to keep them would allow Schneider to claim compensation. The War Ministry acquiesced, on condition that restitution was delayed for as long as was possible without incurring legal proceedings.[78] The embargo was hurting domestic industry (or so the Hungarians complained) and, given Serbia's alternative channels of supply, it had little purpose. It exposed the Monarchy to the embarrassment of numerous claims for damages from German firms, and in November its scope was restricted.[79]

The spotlight now moved to Serbian supplies via the Ottoman Empire and Salonika. Schneider used this route for a new consignment, including eleven mountain batteries. When the company owning the railway from Salonika into the interior made difficulties, the French consul intervened. As usual, the Quai d'Orsay gave strong support to business interests, and the French won many of the Serbian arms orders, including one for 25 million cartridges from the Société

[76] War Ministry to border commands, 10 Oct. 1908, KAW KM Präs (1908) 51–7.
[77] War ministry comments on Gstb report concerning Steyr, 16 Oct. 1908, ibid.
[78] Schönaich to Aehrenthal (with enclosures) 26 Oct. 1908, KAW KM Präs (1908) 51–7. Pichon to Crozier, 22 Oct. 1908 (and subsequent correspondence), AMAE NS Serbie 8.
[79] Schönaich to Aehrenthal, 17 Nov. 1908; Foreign Ministry minute, 18 Dec. 1908, KAW KM Präs (1908) 51–7; Schönaich to Hungarian Trade Minister, 9 Feb. 1909, KM Präs (1909) 51–7.

française des munitions.[80] They were helped by the German Government's warning (not always heeded) to its own firms not to get involved.[81] The French asserted in Vienna that their motives were commercial, and it is true that they impartially applied pressure to the Serbian Government when the latter tried to alter payment conditions.[82] However, in March 1909 Turkey agreed with the Austrians to close the Salonika channel, despite being lobbied by the Russians to allow the passage of 100,000 Belgian rifles.[83] Only one, slower route remained, via the Black Sea and Bulgaria. Aehrenthal had succeeded in delaying shipments while avoiding serious conflict with France and Russia, although such a conflict over arms sales was anyway unlikely.

The larger problem was whether the militarization of Balkan international politics would spill over into Europe as a whole. In general it did not, although the Bosnian affair coincided with a Franco-German mini-crisis, the Casablanca deserters dispute, and with Anglo-German friction over the 1909 British naval estimates.[84] In addition, the Bosnian conflict had a subplot, in the shape of Turkey's confrontation with Bulgaria, which on declaring independence in October had reinforced its standing army to 110,000 men. The Turks mobilized the reservists of their three European army corps, totalling 164,000, and imported German and Austrian munitions and rifles.[85] They wanted financial compensation, and when Bulgaria found the Ottoman demands too high, it too carried out a limited mobilization. Russia overcame the deadlock by offering to buy the Turks out in return for reimbursement from the Bulgarians, and the Ottomans accepted the deal. Aehrenthal drew the lesson that a successful Bulgarian bluff had forced Istanbul to drop its territorial claims and had elicited the Russian financial scheme: in other words, that military pressure got results.[86] The other Powers, however, did not follow Turkey's example. The French army may have banned leave on the eastern frontier and made a few mobilization preparations; the British navy may also have taken some precautions, although the army did nothing.[87] A German Crown Council on 17 March considered possible measures, but until then only the navy took steps, such as sowing mines and buying Cardiff coal.[88] In Italy there was a storm of protest against the annexation, and Tittoni, who had privately agreed not to oppose it, refused to sanction it publicly and called for a conference. The Chamber voted for an increase in defence spending, a former prime minister, Fortis, causing a sensation by declar-

---

[80] Telegram from French Minister at Belgrade, dispatch from French consul at Salonika, 4 Nov. 1908, Foreign Ministry internal memorandum, 13 Nov. 1908, AMAE NS Serbie 8.

[81] De Berckheim dispatch, 22 Dec. 1908, ibid.

[82] Crozier to Pichon, 6 Apr. 1909; Pichon to Descos, 29 Jan. 1909, ibid.

[83] Schmitt, *Bosnia*, 121–2.   [84] See Ch. 4, sect. 1, below.

[85] GGS 1. Abt. annual report, 3 Dec. 1908, KAM Gstb 489.   [86] Schmitt, *Bosnia*, 137.

[87] Nelidov to Izvolsky, 1 Apr. 1909, B. von Siebert (ed.), *Diplomatische Aktenstücke zur Geschichte der Ententepolitik der Vorkriegsjahre* (Berlin, 1921), 114. This report is uncorroborated by French and British evidence. For War Office inactivity, *BD* v. 761 n. cf. Bridge, *Great Britain and Austria-Hungary*, 123.

[88] Goschen to Grey, 18 Mar. 1909, *BD* v, doc. 709. Russian naval attaché in Berlin (Bob) to Osten-Sacken, 31 Jan. 1909, HS E.74#170.

ing that it was against Austria that this must be directed, and Giolitti by demonstratively shaking his hand.[89] In mid-January Tittoni felt 'consternation' over reported Austrian frontier reinforcements.[90] None the less, the Italians seem to have done little beyond intensifying some of their railway and fortification building and their field artillery renewal.[91] In the Adriatic the crisis intensified Italo-Austrian rivalry in medium-term re-equipment rather than heightening immediate readiness.

The key question in the Bosnian crisis, as during the Balkan Wars and in 1914, was whether the conflict would set Austria-Hungary against Russia, supported by Germany on the one hand and France and Britain on the other. In fact the Russians took a few, apparently purely defensive, precautions. They alleged that the Austrians were making preparations in Galicia, but there is little corroborative Austrian evidence, and none that Germany was doing anything in the East. On 14 December the Russian Foreign Ministry told the Austro-Hungarian Ambassador in St Petersburg, Berchtold, that Russia had taken 'defensive measures', but its 'principal interest' was to prevent an Austro-Serb war and it had warned Serbia and Montenegro to remain passive.[92] In February Berchtold reported that Russian military circles were 'horrified' at the thought of war, but that wire had been ordered for the Polish fortresses, and the 33rd Infantry Division and the 33rd Artillery Brigade, which had been moved to the Caucasus to deal with internal unrest, were now returning to the Kiev military district, in turn permitting four infantry regiments to move up to the Austrian border. The consul in Kiev reported intensified training and stock replenishments. Neither Berchtold nor the German military attaché, however, regarded the movement of the units as of great significance.[93]

Instead, it was the Russians who took fright, Izvolsky telling Berchtold that he had learned that Austria-Hungary was preparing to mobilize in Galicia, whereas Russia was doing nothing similar and the 33rd Division was merely resuming its normal location. All rumours of Russian preparations were baseless, and even if Austria-Hungary occupied Belgrade, Russia would remain 'absolutely quiet'.[94] Aehrenthal replied that no military measures had been taken against Russia and none were planned, and he accepted that the Kiev troop movements were 'internal measures'.[95] Izvolsky repeated his allegations to the German Ambassador, emphasizing that 'Russia had not deployed a man more than previously on the Galician frontier and had not spent a rouble on armaments purposes. Russia neither could nor would wage war now.'[96] Actually his agitation

[89] Schmitt, *Bosnia*, 98.   [90] Barrère to Pichon, 15 Jan. 1909, *DDF* 2nd ser. xi, doc. 607.
[91] Conrad to Schönaich, 4 Jan. 1909, KAW KM Präs (1909) 33–8. Conrad, *Dienstzeit*, i. 124, 127.
[92] HHStA, Nachlass Berchtold, 1, vol. i, 162.
[93] Berchtold to Aehrenthal, 24 Feb. 1909, *ÖUA* i, doc. 1051; Berchtold to Aehrenthal, 6 Mar. 1909, *ÖUA* ii, doc. 1132; Kageneck report, 23 Feb. 1909, *GP* xxvi/2, doc. 9390. Posadowsky to German War Ministry, 10 Mar. 1909, PAAA R.10425.
[94] Berchtold to Aehrenthal, 15 Mar. 1909, *ÖUA* ii, doc. 1224; cf. Nicolson to Grey, 12 and 20 Mar. 1909, *BD* v, docs. 675, 728.
[95] Aehrenthal to Berchtold, 17 Mar. 1909, *ÖUA* ii, doc. 1256.
[96] Pourtalès to Bülow, 18 Mar. 1909, *GP* xxvi/2, doc. 9452.

seems to have been unfounded. Conrad told the German attaché in Vienna that at present military measures against Russia were not intended, although 'in Galicia we are, so to speak, prepared'.[97] The British and French also believed that Russian information about Austria-Hungary was exaggerated, and Izvolsky may have been misled by his Vienna military attaché.[98] Militarization in Eastern Europe halted at a level far below that of 1912–13, let alone that of the Sarajevo crisis, and outside the Balkans Bosnia remained a diplomatic affair. Given the balance of Balkan strength, Austria-Hungary was likely to prevail unless Russia took up the South Slav cause, but Nicholas II was unwilling to exceed verbal backing, or even go that far if Germany stood behind Austria-Hungary. The two central topics for investigation are therefore Russian restraint, and Berlin's solidarity with Vienna.

Izvolsky was handicapped from the start by the Buchlau meeting and the preceding correspondence, which in March Aehrenthal threatened to publish, on the eve of the decisive phase of the crisis.[99] He was isolated from his colleagues, having kept informed neither the Council of Ministers nor Stolypin, the Premier, who apparently learned about Buchlau from the Austrian press.[100] Still more serious was Izvolsky's isolation from his allies. The British at first agreed with him that a European treaty such as that of 1878 should not be unilaterally overthrown. But Germany backed Austria-Hungary in rejecting a conference, which Wilhelm expected to be a 'second Algeciras'.[101] On 27 February Grey spelled out to Izvolsky that unless Serbia renounced its territorial claims there would be war; and it would renounce them only on Great-Power insistence. Britain could not fight for Serbian territorial compensation, and a conflict involving most of the 'Continent of Europe' would be quite disproportionate to the interests at stake. The Quai d'Orsay was even blunter: France and Russia should do everything possible to avoid war over an issue that did not engage Russia's 'primordial interests' and that French public opinion would not comprehend.[102]

This warning was the more compelling because the French authorities had just approved a 1,400-million rouble Russian Government loan, 1,220 million of which was to be subscribed in Paris, and for which Kokovtsov had nowhere else to go. The money was essential to amortize a Russo-Japanese War loan that was coming to maturity, and to cover a projected budget deficit.[103] In addition, the

[97] Kageneck report, 23 Feb. 1909, ibid., doc. 9390.

[98] Grey to Nicolson, 7 Dec. 1908, *BD* v. 478. Girodon to Picquart, 14 Oct. 1908, *DDF* 2nd ser. xi, doc. 493.

[99] Aehrenthal to Berchtold, 8 Mar. 1909, *ÖUA* ii, doc. 1146. M. de Taube, *La Politique russe d'avant-guerre et la fin de l'Empire des Tsars* (Paris, 1928), 225–8.

[100] V. N. Kokovtsov, *Out of my Past* (Stanford, Calif., 1955), 214–18.

[101] Schmitt, *Bosnia*, 57.

[102] Grey to Nicolson, 27 Feb. 1909, *BD* v, doc. 621. Pichon to Touchard, 25 Feb. 1909, *DDF* 2nd ser. xii, doc. 55.

[103] Caillaux to Pichon, 21 Jan. 1909, *DDF* 2nd ser. xi, doc. 615. D. W. Spring, 'Russia and the Franco-Russian Alliance 1905–1914', *Slavonic and East European Review*, 66 (1988), 569–70. D. Geyer, *Russian Imperialism: The Interaction of Domestic and Foreign Policy, 1860–1914* (Leamington Spa, 1987), 262.

French army could give assistance that the British navy could not (and was under no treaty obligation to provide). Neither member of the Franco-Russian alliance, however, thought much of the other's military prowess. The French did not trust the Russian CGS, Palitsyn, whom they found evasive. The upshot of his September 1908 staff conference with his French opposite number, Brun, had been that the Russians could mobilize on their western frontier only half of the 800,000 soldiers specified in the 1893 military convention. The Quai d'Orsay therefore expected part of the new loan to be used for strategic railways.[104] In November the French consul in Warsaw reported that there were still no preparations in the Polish fortresses.[105] The EMA considered that the Russian army was demoralized and 'in the middle of reorganization'; the most to be expected of it was a defensive action against Austria-Hungary and a 'timid offensive' in East Prussia.[106] A further study thought it would make little difference for France if Russia stayed neutral.[107] Sukhomlinov, who replaced Palitsyn during the crisis, told the French attaché on 8 March that he would need at least a year for his planned reorganization of the army, and until then 'he asks, he even begs' that there should be no war, which was wanted neither by the Tsar nor by his ministers.[108]

None of this encouraged the Entente to go with Russia to the brink, and Izvolsky was unsupported when the crisis reached its culmination. At the end of February, recriminating against Paris, he began his retreat. He warned the Serbs to drop their demand for territorial compensation, and helped draft their note of 10 March, which entrusted the settlement of the question to the Concert. This was not enough for Aehrenthal, or for the Germans, who now moved into the diplomatic front line, proposing that the Powers should recognize the annexation and Russia force the Serbs to quieten down. Izvolsky was willing to extricate himself by this procedure, but he still wanted a conference, which in the climactic note of 21 March the Germans refused. Before inviting the Powers to recognize the annexation, said Bülow, he must have Russia's unequivocal assurance that it would accept. Failing this, Germany would withdraw and let matters take their course: in other words, let Austria-Hungary invade Serbia. Although without a time limit, the note read like an ultimatum, and the Russian Council of Ministers agreed on 23 March to recognize the annexation unconditionally, thus opening the way for Serbia and the other Powers to do likewise without a conference being convened.[109]

'We were compelled to chose', explained Izvolsky to his ambassadors, 'between an immediate decision on the annexation question and an irruption of

---

[104] Brun–Palitsyn meeting, 24 Sept. 1908, *DDF* 2nd ser. xi, doc. 455. Pichon to Touchard, 23 Jan. 1909, AMAE Russie NS 58.
[105] Consul-general in Warsaw, 12 Nov. 1908, SHA 7.N. 1537.
[106] 'Concentration russe', 28 Oct. 1908, ibid.
[107] EMA 2nd Bureau, 'Rôle possible de l'Autriche-Hongrie . . .', SHA 7.N. 1538.
[108] Matton to War Ministry, 6 Mar. 1909, SHA 7.N. 1535.
[109] Schmitt, *Bosnia*, chs. 10–12.

Austrian troops into Serbia.'[110] Strictly this was not a choice between war and peace but one of whether to accept humiliation now in order to avert a unpalat-able choice between a disastrous intervention on Serbia's behalf and an even greater humiliation. The Russians accepted that their vital interests were not at stake, as Serbian independence and integrity would survive the annexation, as would a Balkan balance of power.[111] On the other hand, the Navy, War, and Finance Ministries all consistently opposed a European war. At the time of the Sanjak railway crisis the military chiefs had advised that Russia was unready for one, Stolypin fearing a new revolution and commenting that 'a policy other than pacific and exclusively defensive would at the moment be the delirium of a Government that had lost its reason'.[112] The General Staff believed that war against Austria-Hungary alone was 'not hopeless', but that they must not fight Germany too: an opinion that Berchtold relayed to Vienna.[113] Rediger admitted to the German attaché that it was 'ruled out' that the Tsar would fight over Serbia, as the frontier fortifications and all classes of artillery were outdated or faulty, and army reform needed eight to ten years.[114] It is true that on 8 March the Duma voted another 40 million roubles for army stores, but only after a devastating exposé in secret session by its leading military expert, Guchkov, which the government spokesmen did not challenge.[115] Not only was Russia financially vulnerable, but neither the 1907 naval programme nor the 1908 army credit had yet had much effect. The Russians were acutely conscious of their weaknesses, and freely admitted them to their adversaries.

Even so, at first the Russian leaders hinted that pan-Slav opinion might force them into irrational action. Nicholas raised the possibility in a letter to Wilhelm, as did Izvolsky to the French and British.[116] Stolypin too, although a much steadier figure, told the British Ambassador on 17 February that if Austria-Hungary used force against Serbia public opinion would force his government to mobilize, making general war imminent.[117] In the second half of March, when the Council of Ministers debated the issue of war and peace three times, Izvolsky proposed as a 'security measure' a partial mobilization of the Kiev military district, entailing a call-up of the reservists resident in it. But the military almost unanimously rejected this as a 'half-measure', and after it was ruled out on 20 March the hapless Foreign Minister made 'policy only according to instructions'.[118] Rediger told

---

[110] S. Sazonov, *Fateful Years, 1909–1916* (London, 1928), 18.

[111] Ibid. 20.

[112] Schmitt, *Bosnia*, 8.

[113] Berchtold to Aehrenthal, 22 Nov. 1908, *ÖUA* i, doc. 629.

[114] Posadowsky report, 10 Dec. 1908, *GP* xxvi/1, doc. 9149.

[115] Hintze to Wilhelm, 13 Mar. 1909, *GP* xxvi/2, doc. 9428. Posadowsky to War Ministry, 10 Mar. 1909, PAAA R.10425.

[116] Nicholas to Wilhelm, 28 Dec. 1908, *GP* xxvi/2, doc. 9187. Izvolsky to Nelidov, 23 Oct. 1908, Siebert, ed., *Aktenstücke*, 73. Nicolson to Grey, 15 Feb. 1909, *BD* v, doc. 571.

[117] Nicolson to Grey, 17 Feb. 1909, ibid., doc. 576.

[118] Hintze to AA, 14 Mar. 1909, PAAA R.10450. Hintze to Wilhelm, 3 Apr. 1909, *GP* xxvi/2, doc. 9505.

the assembled ministers, as he had everyone else, that the army could not fight even a defensive war.[119]

This latter judgement reflects the Russians' high, even exaggerated, assessment of their potential enemies, the consequence of which was that in part they deterred themselves. According to their Ambassador in Berlin, the German 'war party' saw hostilities as a tactic to divert attention from an ill-judged interview given by Wilhelm II to the *Daily Telegraph*, which had caused domestic uproar. He warned that Russia should not supply them with a pretext. The military attaché advised that the German army had reached organizational perfection a decade earlier and thanks to Einem's re-equipping was on the verge of technical perfection too. The naval attaché thought the fleet was 'in complete battle readiness', and the financial attaché that Germany could fund at least a year of fighting.[120] Yet, as has been seen, Izvolsky professed to fear not only a German but also an Austrian attack. Probably he did so as a means of exculpation *vis-à-vis* his partners, pleading with the British Ambassador that 'the military preparations in Galicia were . . . ominous, the immediate readiness of Germany for war was undoubted, and Russia was alone . . . all was in readiness for an invasion of Russia by Austrian forces . . . there was not a shadow of doubt that if Austria were getting the worst of the conflict Germany would then step in'. Although he acknowledged that Russia could defeat the Austrians in a one-to-one match, in doing so it would wear down its armies before Germany struck. At the 23 March Council of Ministers he accepted the advice of the responsible ministers that although three to four years hence Russia might speak with a different voice, war now would undermine all the progress made in redressing the finances, reorganizing the army, and subduing unrest.[121] From mid-March he dropped his threats of irrational action in his conversations with the German and Austrian Ambassadors, but precisely this change of tune (and a request to Berlin to take a hand) prompted Germany's forceful note on 21 March, as French weakness had encouraged Bülow to step up the pressure in 1905.[122] It is difficult not to conclude that Izvolsky panicked and played a bad hand badly. After his partial mobilization ploy was rejected, there was nothing to do but disengage. None the less, although Aehrenthal's restraint saved him from his nightmare of acquiescing in an Austrian attack on Serbia, acquiesce is probably all he would have been able to do.

The Russians were correct at least in the perception that Germany would support Austria-Hungary in a war against them, even one arising from a Habsburg expedition against Serbia. Conversely, French and British support was doubtful, and Russia alone could not take on the Central Powers. With German backing, Aehrenthal could push Izvolsky to the wall without taking destabilizing military

[119] V. A. Sukhomlinov, *Erinnerungen* (Berlin, 1924), 221. Pourtalès to Bülow, 18 Mar. 1909, *GP* xxvi/2, doc. 9452.

[120] Osten-Sacken to Izvolsky, 5 Feb. 1909 (with inclosures), HS E.74#170.

[121] Nicolson to Grey, 23 and 24 Mar. 1909, *BD* v, docs. 753, 761.

[122] Berchtold to Aehrenthal, 15 Mar. 1909, *ÖUA* ii, doc. 1224. Pourtalès to AA, 17 Mar. 1909, *GP* xxvi/2, doc. 9451. Szögyény to Aehrenthal, 31 Mar. 1909, *ÖUA* ii, doc. 1427.

precautions in Galicia, and he seems to have been confident that the Russians would not fight on Serbia's behalf. Indeed, they had said as much, not only via Berchtold, but possibly also in a personal message from Nicholas to Franz Ferdinand.[123] Before forcing the issue, however, he reinsured himself in Berlin, not only through his correspondence with Bülow but also by permitting an exchange of views between Conrad and Moltke. This he had previously forbidden, and even now, presumably to maintain civilian control, he refused a face-to-face meeting. All the same, Moltke's letter to Conrad of 21 January 1909, endorsed by Wilhelm and Bülow, gave the Foreign Minister what he required. Russian intervention against an Austro-Hungarian invasion of Serbia, it said, would be the *casus foederis* for Germany: when Russia mobilized Germany would do likewise with its entire army, which would mean war with France as well. Aehrenthal welcomed this 'loyal and binding declaration', which extended the defensive terms of the 1879 alliance to cover offensive military action, but he correctly foresaw that German diplomacy in St Petersburg would make war with Belgrade 'superfluous' by forcing Russia, and therefore Serbia, to give way.[124]

Like the Austrians and Russians, the Germans knew that the military balance favoured them, and Bülow did not think the crisis very dangerous. He told Wilhelm that Russia would be unlikely to get involved in an Austro-Serb conflict and France would do all possible to avoid war over the issue.[125] Reports from the St Petersburg Embassy confirmed Russia's unpreparedness, and were obligingly corroborated by the tsarist military, though even when Palitsyn tried to bluster to the contrary his statements were discounted.[126] On 29 January Moltke provided a consolidated survey, which Bülow welcomed as 'extraordinarily important and valuable': according to the CGS, the Habsburg armies could 'very quickly' gain superiority in the south-east. Russia could still field only fifty-four divisions on the western frontier against sixty before 1904, its heavy artillery had not been modernized, and the stocks lost in Manchuria not been fully replenished. It needed peace. The French army was efficient and not to be underestimated, but against it Germany would have 'full prospects of success'.[127] In short, as Izvolsky put it, the Central Powers were the stronger combination.[128]

It does not follow that the Germans' blank cheque to Austria-Hungary in January 1909 bears comparison with that of July 1914. For a start, they did not expect Aehrenthal to cash it, taking seriously his protestations that he did not want war, and that even if he fought one he would respect Serbia's independence and integrity.[129] In such a war Bülow thought Russia unlikely to intervene, and

[123] Aehrenthal to Bülow, 20 Feb. 1909, *GP* xxvi/2, doc. 9386. Wilhelm to Bülow, 5 Nov. 1908, *GP* xxvi/1, doc. 9087.

[124] Conrad, *Dienstzeit*, i. 379–85. Aehrenthal to Bülow, 20 Feb. 1909, *GP* xxvi/2, doc. 9386. Cf. N. Stone, 'Moltke–Conrad: Relations between the Austro-Hungarian and German General Staffs, 1909–14', *Historical Journal*, 9 (1966), 201–28.

[125] Bülow to Wilhelm, 22 Feb. 1909, *GP* xxvi/2, doc. 9388.

[126] Hintze to Wilhelm, 1 Nov. 1908, PAAA R.10425.

[127] Moltke to Bülow, 29 Jan. 1909; Bülow to Moltke, 9 Feb. 1909, PAAA R.995.

[128] Nicolson to Grey, 24 Mar. 1909, *BD* v, doc. 761.

[129] Schoen to Pourtalès, 25 Jan. 1909, *GP* xxvi/2, doc. 9369.

he still saw Britain, rather than France and Russia, as the more immediate threat. Despite, or perhaps because of, Moltke's optimism, the GGS did not advocate preventive war. Austria-Hungary's encirclement in the Balkans and Germany's in Europe were still new developments, and moderate solutions to them not yet exhausted. However, as Germany's sole reliable and effective Great-Power ally, Austria-Hungary needed to be supported and Bülow probably hoped to show the Russians the price of their entente with Britain, while not permanently antagonizing them. The Germans seem to have believed their description of the 21 March intervention as a friendly one, and to have been surprised by the resentment it caused. Limited objectives therefore helped to keep the conflict diplomatic rather than military, as did congruent perceptions of the strategic balance. None the less, if after April 1909 the measures taken for immediate readiness could be countermanded, the crisis intensified the competition for medium-term preparedness between the Habsburg Monarchy and its Balkan, Italian, and Russian neighbours. To the resulting displacement of the armaments equilibrium we must now turn.

2. From Bosnia to Balkan Wars

There followed a diplomatic lull in Eastern Europe until the next great upheaval in the autumn of 1912. In the interim there was a quickening in the regional armaments system. Austria-Hungary remained at the hub. Italy, Serbia, and Montenegro all felt themselves in competition with Vienna, where the sentiment was reciprocated. Russia, however, was still a secondary target for Habsburg planners, and tsarist rearmament was directed against Germany and the Ottomans as much as against the Dual Monarchy. Austro-Italian rivalry remained more intense than Austro-Russian. By 1912 Italy's imbroglio in Libya and the tsarist military renaissance had started a reorientation, but the Agadir crisis and the Balkan Wars rather than Bosnia relaunched inter-bloc armaments competition and set the stage for war.

Although the annexation had roused Serbia more powerfully than Montenegro, it was the latter's rapid mobilization that had most preoccupied the Habsburg military. Conrad continued to fear for Herzegovina, with its woefully inadequate railways,[130] and the Montenegrins did something to exacerbate the threat. They bought four mortars from the stocks of the Italian War Ministry, which claimed ignorance of the transaction.[131] Russia appears to have increased its subsidy, and in 1909 delivered 10,000 rifles and fifty-six artillery pieces.[132] Under a military law of 1908 the army was gradually reorganized into four

---

[130] Conrad to Aehrenthal, 17 Mar. 1911, KAW Gstb Operationsbureau 738.
[131] Report from Austrian military attaché in Rome, 7 Oct. 1910; Italian Ambassador to Austrian Foreign Ministry, 12 Nov. 1910 KAW KM Präs (1910) 47–5.
[132] Conrad to Franz Josef, 21 Feb. 1910, KAW Gstb Operationsbureau 742.

divisions with eighty nondescript guns, although most of the officers and men were still untrained.[133]

During the same period the Serbian army progressed from being one of the weakest to being one of the strongest Balkan forces, although few foreign observers realized this and the change came mainly in *matériel*. There was a post-crisis effort, followed by a relaxation.[134] In 1908 the Serbs were still adjusting to the late nineteenth-century transformation in rifle and artillery firepower, whereas the Austrian army had virtually completed the transition. They drew the obvious conclusion from the crisis that Austrian and German armaments firms were unreliable, and excluded them from new bidding rounds.[135] They also aimed for greater self-sufficiency, engaging Schneider to install a munitions workshop at Kragujevac and approaching another French firm for assistance with explosives manufacture.[136] The greatest contribution to the army's renovation, however, came from a Serbian state loan worth 150 million francs that was agreed with a predominantly French banking consortium in November 1909.[137]

The Franco-Serbian relationship handsomely benefited both sides. German houses took part in the loan, but only to the tune of 25 per cent, Paris and Belgrade agreeing to confine German orders largely to railway equipment. British attempts to win a privileged share for Vickers were resisted, and three-quarters of the resulting military orders went to French suppliers. It is true that the Serbs resented high French prices and tried to beat them down by threatening to go elsewhere: the Quai d'Orsay insisted on French firms getting their due.[138] In the winter of 1910/11 an order for fifteen mountain batteries was on the verge of going to Krupp rather than Schneider, but it was cancelled after a spectacular public row between the German Minister (who was actually an Ehrhardt lobbyist) and the Serbian War Minister.[139] In all the Serbs bought forty batteries of Schneider quick-firing field guns, ten of howitzers, and six of mountain guns, as well as 176 machine guns from the DWMF. Kragujevac converted 50,000 rifles to repeaters, using barrels from Steyr.[140] The French War Ministry was willing, indeed, to manufacture rifles in its own arsenal at

[133] De Salis to Grey, 10 Jan. 1913, K. Bourne and D. Cameron Watt, eds., *British Documents on Foreign Affairs: Reports and Papers from the Foreign Office Confidential Print* (henceforth *BDFA*), series IF *Europe, 1848–1914*, ed., J. F. V. Keiger, and D. Stevenson (35 vols., Frederick, Md., 1987–91), xv, doc. 33.

[134] Annual reports by British Legation in Belgrade, 31 Mar. 1909, 30 Jan. 1911, 25 Jan. 1912, *BDFA*, IF xvi, docs. 51, 53, 56.

[135] Loukitch to Director of Châtellerault, 20 June 1912, AMAE NS Serbie 9.

[136] De Thomarson to War Ministry, 8 Oct. 1908; Descos to Pichon, 9 Nov. 1910 and 5 Jan. 1911; Descos to Poincaré, 27 July 1912, ibid.

[137] Poidevin, 'Les Intérêts financiers français et allemands en Serbie de 1895 à 1914', *Revue historique*, 59–61; Gellinek report, 15 Nov. 1909, KAW Gstb (1909) 25–8.

[138] D'Apchier le Maugin to Pichon, 24 Nov. 1909; British Embassy note, 24 Nov. 1909; and French reply, 27 Nov. 1909; Pichon to Descos, 22 Dec. 1909, AMAE NS Serbie 8.

[139] Descos to Pichon, 9 and 30 Nov. 1910, 27 Feb., 1 Mar., and 12 Apr. 1911, ibid. Gellinek report, 9 Mar. 1911, KAW KM Präs (1911) 47–7.

[140] Annual report for Serbia, 25 Jan. 1912, *BDFA*, IF xvi, doc. 56; Gellinek report, 21 Feb. 1910 KAW KM Präs (1910) 47–7. Evidenzbureau report, 6 Feb. 1911, KM Präs (1911) 47–7.

Châtellerault, although the Serbs decided not to take this up.[141] From the loan 56 million francs went to railway building and rolling stock, which would speed up Serbian deployment on the northern and eastern frontiers,[142] and as tension once more mounted in 1912 the Skupshina voted a further 21 million francs for weaponry.[143] By now the army was vastly better provided for than four years before.

All the same, in June 1912 the French attaché still considered that only 'in a few years' time' would Serbia possess 'an army to be reckoned with'. The General Staff remained 'very inferior'. The standing army reached 35,000 in summer, but in the winter it fell to 8–9,000 and only one-third of the recruits did the legal term of service (one and half years in the infantry), the rest doing only six months.[144] In 1909 Conrad expected speedy action on Serbian War Ministry plans to increase the first-line divisions from five to eight (or twelve), standardize the length of service, and accelerate mobilization.[145] Instead, the reorganization bill was not published until the end of 1911, and had not passed the Skupshina by the outbreak of the Balkan War. It indeed provided for a uniform twenty-month service and enlarged the recruitment contingent from 17,000 to 27,000, but foreign observers doubted if the country could afford it.[146] Disputes over reorganization and the budget had caused the resignation of a succession of War Ministers; military spending had jumped in 1908–9 but then held steady, apart from the proceeds of the loan. The annexation crisis hastened a re-equipment that had already begun, and encouraged improvements in peacetime strength and officer training, but obstacles to further development persisted.

* * *

In Italy the Inquiry Commission had been at work since 1907, and Parliament had already voted more recruits and extraordinary credits. The main new developments after Bosnia were legislation in 1909–10 for a major military reorganization and the start of an Adriatic dreadnought race. As each side assumed the other to be gathering its forces before the next renewal date for the Triple Alliance, these years marked the apogee of Austro-Italian armaments competition before the impetus of the Italian build-up was lost in the sands of Libya, and Vienna redirected its attention towards the north-east.

It is easier to describe the contours of Italian policy than to find evidence for its motives. Military and naval budgets in 1908–11 showed an acceleration in the upward trend that had begun in 1906–7. In addition to the extraordinary army credits of 60 and 223 million lire voted in 1907 and 1908, another 125 million

---

[141] Foreign Ministry memorandum on Châtellerault affair, n.d., AMAE NS Serbie 8, p. 206.

[142] Annual report for Serbia, 31 Mar. 1910, 25 Jan. 1912, *BDFA*, IF xvi, docs. 51, 56.

[143] Descos to Poincaré, 31 July, 24 Aug. 1912; French War Ministry to Loukitch, 26 Aug. 1912, AMAE Serbie 9. Adamkiewicz to Foreign Ministry, 26 July 1912, KAW KM (Präs) 1912 51–7. See further discussion in Ch. 5, sect. 1.

[144] 'Notice sur l'armée serbe', 24 June 1912, SHA 7.N. 1568.

[145] Conrad, *Dienstzeit*, i. 232.

[146] Annual report for Serbia, 25 Jan. 1912, *BDFA*, IF xvi, doc. 56. Gellinek report, 5 Oct. 1911, KAW KM Präs (1911) 47–7.

were voted in July 1909. Of these totals, some 186.8 million lire were scheduled for fortification, 145.8 million for field artillery, and 22.3 million for small arms and machine guns; 10 million were added for aviation in 1910 and in July 1909 another 440 million over six years for naval construction. The financial ceiling of the first years of the century had been decisively left behind.[147]

In addition to receiving extra money, the army was restructured under Casana (War Minister in 1907–9), Spingardi (1909–14), and Pollio (CGS in 1908–14), following broadly the reports of the inquiry commission. Legislation in 1909 facilitated officer promotion and benefited NCOs. Regular officers were assigned to the second-line 'mobile militia'. The cavalry and the Alpine regiments were regrouped, and the field, mountain, fortress, and coastal artillery strengthened. An independent heavy field artillery was created, equipped with Krupp 144 mm howitzers and Italian 120 mm cannon. A further law in 1910 confirmed the adoption of two-year service for all, and the army's budgetary strength was raised from 205,000 to 225,000 men, although its actual strength was higher. In the same year, however, the inquiry commission was dissolved, and in 1911, apart from a 50 million lire field artillery credit, the pace of innovation fell off.[148]

Notable gaps remained. Conrad was impressed by the railway improvements in the north-east, but the coastal lines up from the south remained vulnerable to naval bombardment, and their shortcomings would delay Italian concentration.[149] So would Spingardi's decision, taken against the commission's advice, to reject territorial mobilization, which would have had the danger of concentrating big-city recruits in cohesive units.[150] Machine guns were adopted more slowly than in other armies, as was quick-firing artillery.[151] The Krupp field guns were an improvement on the 75A but there was persistent dissatisfaction with them.[152] For Spingardi, however, manpower shortages were the army's Achilles' heel. Italian infantry strengths had always been very low, in 1906–9 averaging sixty-seven men per company. The creation of new specialized units made them even lower, as did the need for higher strengths on the frontier and the precipitate introduction of a two-year term. Public-order duties were a further distraction from war preparation. Yet by October 1910 Spingardi no longer felt he could request even the 5 million lire needed for 10,000 more men—a sign

[147] G. Rochat and Massobrio, *Breve storia dell'esercito italiano dal 1861 al 1943* (Turin, 1978), 154. Jullian to French War Ministry, 18 June 1909, 25 June 1910, SHA 7.N. 1369. French naval attaché reports, 10 July 1909, 10 Jan. 1910, SHM BB7 123 bis.

[148] Jullian reports, 6, 9, 15, 19 July, and 2 Dec. 1909, 7 Mar. 5 June, 9 July, 26 Sept. 1910, SHA 7.N. 1369. De Gondrecourt report, 25 Jan. 1912, SHA 7.N. 1370. Reports by Austrian military attaché, 17 June and 2 July 1910, KAW KM Präs (1910) 47–5. Rodd to Grey, 25 Jan. 1910, PRO FO/881/9610.

[149] Ibid. and Conrad to Franz Joseph, 3 Nov. 1910, KAW Gstb Operationsbureau 738.

[150] P. del Negro, 'La leva militare', in Stato Maggiore dell'Esercito (Ufficio Storico), *L'esercito italiano dall'Unità alla Grande Guerra (1861–1918)* (Rome, 1980), ch. 13.

[151] Austrian military attaché, 17 Jan. 1910, KM Präs (1910) 47–5.

[152] Jullian report, 10 Apr. 1911, SHA 7.N. 1370.

of returning financial constraints at the same time as the reforming impulse was running out of steam.[153]

Yet all observers recognized that much had been done. The Krupp scandal and the officer crisis had forced the army up Giolitti's political agenda at a time when rapid economic and demographic growth provided money and men. The annexation crisis led to changes in war planning, a project being approved for a landing in Dalmatia.[154] It also stimulated the nationalistic and anti-Habsburg mood. The French military attaché reported a 'fever of patriotism' when the Chamber voted the 1909 army credit, even though only one speaker named the adversary (Austria-Hungary) against whom it was directed. All preparations against France, conversely, had ceased.[155] In private Spingardi was frank about the sense of threat he felt, despite superficially correct relations. If Franz Ferdinand replaced Franz Joseph, he feared a conflagration that was in neither country's interest.[156] Although the Italians detected a slackening of Habsburg frontier preparations against them, they did not reciprocate.[157] The Vienna Evidenzbureau reported continuing strengthening of Italy's frontier forces, espionage, railway work, and fortifications.[158] Conrad cited the latter first among the 'military measures that Italy is taking quite explicitly for a war against the Monarchy'[159]—in fact the inquiry commission's fortification recommendations had been defensive, and the GGS interpreted the Italian efforts as being designed to interdict a descent from the Alpine passes across the Veneto plain. By 1911 the Germans felt the necessary work had more or less been accomplished,[160] and Conrad feared that without modern heavy mortars his army would face in the Italian theatre 'challenges . . . that with the available means simply cannot be surmounted'.[161]

Preparation on land was accompanied by the opening of the dreadnought race, Italy making the first move. The Navy Minister, Mirabello, was reportedly seeking an extraordinary credit even before the annexation crisis touched off a navalist agitation in the Italian press, subsidized by businesses suffering from the construction slowdown. Two months after the crisis ended it was reported— probably incorrectly, but with 'profound effect'—that Austria-Hungary intended to build four dreadnoughts. Mirabello used the scare to win Giolitti's and Tittoni's imprimatur for a programme of four dreadnought battleships, three scout cruisers, and twelve destroyers. The first battleship, the *Dante Alighieri*,

[153] Jullian reports, 9 May and 2 Dec. 1909, SHA 7.N. 1369. Spingardi to Tedesco, 30 Oct. 1910, ASC Carte Brusati VI. 4. 36, No. 248.

[154] J. Gooch, *Army, State, and Society in Italy, 1870–1915* (Basingstoke, 1989), 134–5.

[155] Jullian reports, 26 Oct. 1908 and 18 June 1909, SHA 7.N. 1369.

[156] Spingardi to Tedesco, 30 Oct. 1910, ASC Carte Brusati VI. 4. 36, No. 248.

[157] M. Mazzetti, *L'esercito italiano nella triplice alleanza: Aspetti della politica estera, 1870–1914* (Naples, 1974), 249.

[158] e.g. Conrad to Schönaich, 26 Mar. 1911, KAW KM Präs (1911) 76–72.

[159] Conrad, *Dienstzeit*, ii. 76.

[160] Jullian report, 25 May 1908, SHA 7.N. 1369. GGS 4. Abt. annual report, 5 Dec. 1911, KAM Gstb 489.

[161] Conrad to Schönaich, 26 Mar. 1911, KAW KM Präs (1911) 76–72.

was laid down almost immediately; three more in 1910; and two supplementary vessels early in 1912. There were accompanying harbour works at Venice, Taranto, and Brindisi. The Italian navy may have been motivated by what the French attaché described as 'megalomania', wanting all-big-gun ships because the other Powers had them and to keep the yards busy, but the shore works left no doubt that naval expansion too was anti-Austrian, and Bosnia and the dreadnought alert gave Mirabello the support he needed. To the Austrian leaders themselves the point was no less clear.[162]

After 1908, then, Italian military and naval development gathered pace. Giolitti's support was essential, and the new departure had Victor Emmanuel's sympathy, but Spingardi was an accomplished parliamentarian and with Pollio he provided direction and continuity. By 1910 the organization was in place for Italy to present a much more formidable challenge to the Habsburg Monarchy, although it would take time for the new units to be created and for modern guns and battleships to enter service. Although the Italian leaders appear to have seen their efforts as defensive, and to have continued to feel vulnerable to their neighbour, Conrad could assert with plausibility that their armaments were systematic, offensive, and dangerous.

* * *

Table 9. *Austro-Hungarian military and naval expenditure, 1907–1912* (mn crowns)

	Common Army	Landwehr	Honvéd	Navy	TOTAL
1907	350.49	50.66	42.69	63.38	507.22
1908	422.60	56.76	45.16	73.35	597.87
1909	523.36	76.62	59.28	100.36	759.62
1910	453.42	68.60	59.25	100.65	681.92
1911	411.84	69.69	55.64	120.67	657.83
1912	489.76	75.91	45.02	170.20	780.89

Source: A. Wandruszka and P. Urbanitsch (eds.), *Die Habsburgermonarchie 1848–1914*, v (Vienna, 1985), 591.

Expenditure on the Austro-Hungarian common army had been virtually static in 1903–7, but rose sharply in 1908–9, fell back in 1910–11, and then again forged ahead. Expenditure on the navy also jumped during the annexation crisis, fell back less thereafter, and in 1911–12 made a rapid ascent. The naval budget grew two and a half times, and its share of defence spending doubled. The statistics show the effects of the 180-million crowns armaments credit in 1908–10; of the post-Bosnia relapse; and of the five-year land and naval programme agreed in 1911 and known as the Schönaich Pact, which set the financial framework for the military service bill that at last became law in July 1912. Most of the 180-million credit was not used for immediate crisis readiness but went into

---

[162] French naval attaché, 20 Dec. 1908, 20 May and 10 July 1909, 10 Jan. 1910; French consul at La Spezia, 27 Apr. 1909, SHM BB7 123 bis; naval attaché, 10 Dec. 1910, SHM BB7 124. P. Halpern, *The Mediterranean Naval Situation, 1908–1914* (Cambridge, Mass., 1971), 190.

re-equipment of lasting value. None the less, there were grounds for Conrad's feeling that after the 'victory' in the annexation crisis these were locust years, which Austria-Hungary used less well than did its enemies. When the Monarchy's leaders changed the pace and the direction of its rearmament in 1912–13, they did so with a desperation that helps explain their later decision to fight.

Under Montecuccoli, who was its commander and administrative chief from 1904 to 1913, the navy benefited from stable leadership. The army lacked it. Schönaich clashed with Conrad during the crisis, and afterwards their relationship deteriorated. In addition, the War Minister was caught in the crossfire between Franz Joseph and Franz Ferdinand, and the attacks made on him were veiled criticisms of the Emperor. After years of jarring confrontation, Schönaich wanted to end the log-jam in the army's development. Given that coercing the Hungarians had been rejected, he saw no alternative to seeking an agreement that could be carried by the more moderate politicians in Budapest. Franz Ferdinand and Conrad objected to this logic, as well as to the financial strait-jacket in which the Austrian and Hungarian Governments confined the common armed forces. In the budgetary discussions in the Joint Council of Ministers, however, the two Prime Ministers deferred to Aehrenthal, with whom Schönaich generally co-operated. Both Aehrenthal and Schönaich sensed the limits to their authority in what, for all its pomp and circumstance, was a subtle, consensual system. Both were exasperated by Conrad's incessant memoranda, and questioned the gravity of the Italian threat that he paraded as his leading rationale. The prevailing policy was therefore one of accommodation with the Hungarians at home and restraint towards Italy abroad.

In the autumn of 1911, however, Franz Joseph agreed to replace Schönaich with Franz Ferdinand's candidate for Minister, Moritz von Auffenberg, although soon afterwards replacing Conrad himself with Blasius Schemua. Early in 1912 Aehrenthal died and Count Leopold Berchtold became Foreign Minister, working relatively harmoniously with Auffenberg and Schemua in pressing for faster rearmament, which the Hungarian Government was increasingly isolated in resisting. Under the Schönaich–Conrad leadership the 1908 credit relieved equipment shortages and the principal theme was the struggle for manpower, leading to the Schönaich Pact; in 1912 hardware became the first priority, and Auffenberg and Schemua, though still seeing Italy as the most immediate antagonist, felt growing anxiety about the Russian threat.

The Joint Council of Ministers approved the Schönaich Pact in January 1911. Subject to ratification by the Delegations, the navy would receive an extraordinary construction credit of 312.4 million crowns between 1911 and 1916, principally for six destroyers, three cruisers, and four dreadnought battleships. Over the same period the ordinary budget of the army and navy would go up by 345.3 million, the two services deciding how to distribute this sum between them. Third, 100 million crowns would be made available in five equal instalments from 1911 to 1915. The total of 757.7 million, however, would be the absolute limit to extra funding over the next five years. It would have to pay for the proposed military service law and for all cost overruns, as well as for all fortification work, Schönaich's requested additional 155 million for this latter purpose being rejected. The service law and overruns were expected to cost 320 millions, and 25 million of the third 100 million would go to the navy, thus leaving only 100 million for fortification and for all the army's other equipment and extraordinary needs. Whereas the two governments met Montecuccoli's initial demand of 321.2 million for shipbuilding and shore works almost in full, they agreed to meet the army's manpower needs but bit heavily into its requests for *matériel*.[163] Conrad, who claimed not to have been consulted and to have first learnt about the Pact in the press, exploded and asked to resign. This Franz Joseph refused, but he allowed Conrad to brief the Joint Council on his own estimate of the army's requirements.[164] It was of no avail. The army's expenditure was set in concrete, whatever the conduct of its rivals, and until the Balkan Wars its leaders were unable to break out.

Although the Monarchy's budgetary problems were real enough, opposition to army spending was as much a political choice as a financial necessity. In the debates leading to the Schönaich Pact the Hungarian Ministers said that their financial position was 'uncommonly difficult' and that military spending was seen as 'unproductive'; the Austrians that they had supposed the 1908 credit to be a once-for-all measure, that they were reaching the limits of their borrowing capacity, and that they faced 'bankruptcy'.[165] Aehrenthal had wanted after the crisis to spend on armaments half of what had been saved by not going to war (and ended up by spending much more than that), but by August 1909 he was worried by the budget deficits in both halves of the Monarchy and reluctant to raise taxes when there were already complaints about higher prices.[166] The Monarchy's leaders therefore sensed they were financially constrained—and Franz Joseph himself thought the Italians had more money[167]—but the Austrian *Landwehr* Minister, for example, acknowledged that even with the Pact the call-up ratio and military expenditure per capita would be lower in Austria-Hungary than in the other Continental Powers.[168] The same Finance Ministers who now resisted Schönaich had agreed to raise the 1908 credit from 47 to 180 million crowns, and in 1912 were to agree to a further 250 million. When convinced more money was essential they disgorged it, albeit under protest. For the time being they were unconvinced.

The comparison with the navy underlines the point. Montecuccoli could capitalize on his service's reputation for efficiency in building and in maintaining its ships, and on the romance of high technology and overseas expansion into the Levant. He had support from the press and from the Austrian Navy League,

[163] GMR, 20 Nov. 1910, 6 Jan. 1911, HHStA PA XL 310.
[164] GMR, 5 Mar. 1911, ibid.   [165] GMR, 17 May 1910, HHStA PA XL 309.
[166] Tschirschky to Bülow, 28 Mar. 1909, *GP* xxvi/2, doc. 723. Aehrenthal memorandum, 15 Aug. 1909, KAW Gstb Operationsbureau 738.
[167] Conrad, *Dienstzeit*, ii. 115.
[168] Georgi to Finance Ministers, 21 Nov. 1911, FAW 84.850/II-1911.

whose patron was Franz Ferdinand, and which rose to 44,617 members by 1914.[169] Even the Hungarian Prime Minister conceded that money for ship-building was more popular than money for military service.[170] Montecuccoli promised the Hungarians that one dreadnought would be built in their Danubius yard, and that they would get their share of orders.[171] Indeed, he presented the Joint Council with a *fait accompli*, pleading a national emergency. In July 1909, a month after the Italians passed their dreadnought law, the Stabilmento tecnico reported that it had nearly finished the Radetzky class of battleships and would have to lay off workers, but that it could lay down three dreadnoughts for build-ing to the navy's specifications at the firm's risk and without payment for the time being.[172] Because of a new political crisis in Hungary the Delegations were unable to meet, but Aehrenthal and the two Prime Ministers authorized Montecuccoli to negotiate with the Stabilmento, Skoda, and Wittkowitz. If noth-ing were done, the Admiral warned, Italy would have Adriatic superiority by 1912 and might launch a surprise attack. Aehrenthal thought Italy might pull out of the Triple Alliance unless Austria-Hungary remained strong. These consid-erations swayed Franz Joseph, and the first two dreadnoughts were laid down in July and August 1910, the expense being approved in the Schönaich Pact.[173] However much Montecuccoli might protest that he had not compromised the Delegations' freedom of action, he had actually done precisely that, and followed Mirabello's example in exploiting a sense of crisis in order to loosen the purse-strings.

Schönaich showed less determination and less tactical skill. He was hampered by his budget overruns, which the two Prime Ministers deeply distrusted. None the less, the Pact was aptly named in that it reflected his priorities rather than Conrad's. It gave the War Ministry more or less what had been estimated as the cost of the military service law, and it was its neglect of equipment that caused the CGS's onslaught. Now that the 1908 credit had provided quick-firers, field kitchens, and machine guns, manpower seemed to Schönaich the crying require-ment.[174] Almost half the new field guns had to be mothballed, for lack of crews to operate them. He wanted soldiers to guard the Balkans, for coastal fortresses, mountain artillery, railways, and telegraphs; and he wanted sailors for Montecuccoli's warships. It was becoming difficult to man the Galician strong points, and some units in the interior were so under strength as barely to per-mit training.[175] Yet a third *Notbehelf*, in December 1910, moved 1,103 men out of stud farms and garrison duty into mountain artillery in the south-east, the Tyrolean defences against Italy, and a regrouped heavy field artillery whose

[169] Halpern, *Mediterranean*, 155.
[170] Khuen-Héderváry in GMR, 17 May 1910, HHStA PA XL 309.
[171] Halpern, *Mediterranean*, 160 ff.
[172] Bienerth to Austrian Finance Minister, 9 Sept. 1910, FAW FM Präs (1910) #1738.
[173] Ibid. and GMR, 18 Sept. 1909, HHStA PA XL 308; 17 May and 20 Nov. 1910, HHStA PA XL 309. Cf. Höbelt, 'Marine', 719.
[174] Schönaich in GMR, 17 May 1910, HHStA PA XL 309.
[175] Schönaich to Franz Joseph, 3 Sept. 1909, KAW KM Präs (1909) 49–26.

wartime strength would rise from 108 to 168 guns.[176] Naturally this was only a temporary expedient, and no substitute for the elusive military law.

To obtain the law, Schönaich and Aehrenthal were willing to implement the promises made to the Hungarians in April 1906, including greater use of Magyar in the common army. They were also willing to introduce two-year service, whereas Conrad and Franz Ferdinand still opposed both measures.[177] Schönaich had little enthusiasm for a shorter term of duty, but was willing to trade it for a higher recruitment contingent, on condition that he got money for extra NCOs, training grounds, and ammunition for shooting practice.[178] He prepared bills both for a continuing three-year term and for a two-year one, the Austrian and Hungarian Governments opting for the second, despite its higher cost, because of its political acceptability—another sign that finance was not their overriding preoccupation.[179] With this, however, the War Ministry and the two governments had settled the organizational framework of the military reform, and it .remained to get it through the legislatures.

The loser in the bargain was Conrad, and the army's needs for fortification and *matériel*. Schönaich was an older, more phlegmatic, perhaps more humane man than the CGS, and responsible for peacetime administration. He had to heed demands for better living conditions and career advancement that took second place in Conrad's eve-of-war mentality.[180] As the prospective Commander-in-Chief, however, Conrad feared becoming the scapegoat for disasters caused by others' neglect.[181] He admitted the necessity for higher infantry strengths, especially in the annexed provinces. But he also wanted heavy attack artillery, more machine guns and bigger munitions stocks, re-equipping of the technical troops, strategic railways, and Balkan and Tyrolean defence works. His main target remained Italy, and he demanded an emergency programme to make ready for a confrontation in 1912. In the event of war he wanted to be able to disrupt the enemy concentration by attacking immediately, and he estimated that 1,000 million crowns were required for the two armed services, although he isolated 260 millions worth of immediate needs.[182] Schönaich felt this latter would be difficult to justify to the Delegations in addition to the Pact, and would overstrain the Monarchy's finances. In February 1911 Franz Joseph decided against it.[183] On the other hand, both the War Minister and the Emperor had agreed

[176] Schönaich to Conrad *et al.*, 6 Aug. 1910, KAW KM Präs (1910) 49–33.

[177] G. E. Rothenberg, *The Army of Francis Joseph* (West Lafayette, 1976), 160–1.

[178] Schönaich in GMR, 17 May 1910, HHStA PA XL 309.

[179] Schönaich to Franz Joseph, 3 Sept. 1909, KAW KM Präs (1909) 49–26; Schönaich to Prime Ministers, 30 July 1910; Schönaich to Franz Joseph, 22 July 1910, KM Präs (1910) 26–1. GMR, 22 Sept. and 6 Oct. 1910, HHStA PA XL 309.

[180] Schönaich to Conrad, 10 Sept. 1909, KM Präs (1910) 37–2; Conrad to Schönaich, 19 Sept. 1910, KM Präs (1910) 33–8. W. Hetzer, 'Franz von Schönaich: Reichskriegsminister von 1906–1911', Ph.D. thesis (Vienna, 1968), 148.

[181] Conrad in GMR, 5 Mar. 1911, HHStA PA XL 310.

[182] Conrad to Schönaich, 19 Nov. 1910, KAW KM Präs (1910) 76–51; Conrad to Franz Joseph, 13 Feb. 1911, KAW KM Präs (1911) 76–51.

[183] Schönaich to Conrad (draft), June 1911, KM Präs (1911) 76–51.

with Conrad on a ten-year 'minimum programme' of fortification, entailing 10.44 million crowns of expenditure in Poland, 53.12 million in the Balkans, and 88.57 million against the Italians.[184] But when Schönaich argued in the Joint Council that this was an essential accompaniment to two-year service, the two Prime Ministers were unconvinced and he did not persist.[185] Deprived of both an armaments credit and the minimum programme of fortification, Conrad pleaded before the Joint Council that two-year service had been conceded without adequate return. He asked for 60 million crowns to be made available by postponing just one dreadnought. This too was refused.[186]

The Prime Ministers considered that the Schönaich Pact was a high enough insurance premium and they must now look to budgetary stability. To ask for more, according to the Hungarian Premier, would endanger the military service bill.[187] That Montecuccoli and Schönaich prevailed over Conrad, however, owed much to Aehrenthal. The CGS as usual weakened his position by his offensive rationale, lamenting that there had been no war with Italy in 1907 or Serbia in 1909.[188] The Foreign Minister, by contrast, had backtracked from his earlier willingness to build up the armed forces, both for financial reasons and because of his scepticism about the doctrine of preventive attack.[189] He feared that intensified fortification would create an 'element of anxiety' and in conjunction with naval building might cause Italy to be 'carried away with emotion'.[190] When Schönaich submitted a long account of Italy's build-up since the turn of the century, the Foreign Minister took a very cool view of it, commenting that it went little beyond what the Monarchy itself had done during the same period.[191] The precautions taken in 1901–4 had strengthened the Monarchy's position only at the price of calling forth further Italian land and naval reinforcements. Austria-Hungary was a *status quo* Power, with few conflicts of interest with Rome, and it should avoid war unless compelled to it. It must keep strong, because Italy was unreliable; but Aehrenthal did not want an Austro-Italian arms race.[192] In October 1910 he felt relations were improving and was confident that Rome would stay in the alliance if the Monarchy remained vigilant. Even at sea, he was willing to make allowances for Italy's less favourable coastal configuration, without the protective inlets and archipelagos of the Adriatic eastern shore.[193] In short, the Foreign Minister was unusual among the statesmen of his generation in the sophistication of his understanding of the relationships between armaments and diplomacy, not only in international crises but also in more normal

---

[184] Schönaich to Conrad, 7 Jan. 1910, KAW KM Präs (1909) 33–8; Schönaich to Franz Joseph, 5 Feb. 1910, KM Präs (1910) 33–8.
[185] GMR, 17 May and 6 Oct. 1910, HHStA PA XL 309.
[186] GMR, 5 Mar. 1911, HHStA PA XL 310.   [187] Ibid.
[188] War Ministry summary of Conrad memoranda, with draft for Schönaich to Franz Joseph, 16 July 1909, KAW KM Präs (1909) 49–26.
[189] Aehrenthal memorandum, 15 Aug. 1909, KAW Gstb Operationsbureau 738.
[190] GMR, 17 May and 6 Oct. 1910, HHStA PA XL 309.
[191] Aehrenthal to Schönaich, 28 Feb. 1910, KAW KM Präs (1910) 76–51.
[192] Aehrenthal memorandum, 15 Aug. 1909, KAW Gstb Operationsbureau 738.
[193] GMR, 6 Oct. 1910, HHStA PA XL 309; 5 Mar. 1911, ibid. 310.

times. He made allowances for Italian insecurities, and saw the danger of an action–reaction cycle leading to an avoidable confrontation. Conversely, he believed that strength was necessary to hold in check the potential adversary. He backed the Schönaich Pact, but opposed anything beyond it, including Conrad's pleas in March 1911. The CGS continued, however, to urge intensified preparations, assigning ever greater prominence to the fortress-smashing Skoda 30.5 cm mortars.[194] In October 1911 he advocated using Italy's war in Libya as the occasion for launching an attack, at a moment when his own position was vulnerable because of a rift with Franz Ferdinand. Aehrenthal complained that Conrad was exceeding his authority and Franz Joseph sent a letter rebuking him. A month later the General lost his post.[195]

Conrad's experience in 1911 shows the impotence of the CGS against a determined Foreign Minister who enjoyed the Emperor's backing. That of the Auffenberg–Schemua–Berchtold regime in 1912, by contrast, shows the dependence of the central organs of the Monarchy on the constituent governments, and that even when supported by Franz Joseph and the Foreign Ministry the military did not necessarily get their way. The examples of the military service bill, the south-eastern railways, and the proposed 250 million crowns re-equipment credit all bear this out. True, the recruitment law, or *Wehrgesetz*, had the backing of both Prime Ministers, but not yet of the Parliament in Budapest, which early in 1912 passed a resolution to restrict the Emperor's power under article 43 to call up by decree the first class of reservists and the first three classes of *Ersatz*-reservists in an emergency. Decree powers had been used in 1904–5 and 1908–9 and were deemed essential for crisis management. Franz Joseph, Schemua, Auffenberg, and Berchtold refused to budge over the issue.[196] They must keep the article, warned Schemua, so as to have a *de facto* mobilization prerogative without recourse to what might be a deadlocked legislature.[197] In April a new government was formed in Budapest, which succeeded in carrying the bill. Probably the critical reason for this was the acceptance by the veteran politician Stephen Tisza, the President of the Lower House, that the mounting perils in the Balkans now made the law essential for Hungary's safety.[198]

The *Wehrgesetz* reduced the normal term of service from three years to two, while raising the recruitment contingent from 139,000 to 181,000 men, of whom 136,000 would enter the common army. By 1918 the contingent was to rise to

---

[194] Conrad, 'Bemerkung', 2 June 1911, KAW KM Präs (1911), 37–2. See 1911 Aehrenthal correspondence in KAW Gstb Operationsbureau 738.

[195] Conrad notes on meeting with Franz Joseph, 30 Sept. 1911, ibid. 739. J. Mann, 'FML Blasius Schemua: Chef des Generalstabes am Vorabend des Weltkrieges, 1911–1912', Ph.D. thesis (Vienna, 1978), 24–6. Rothenberg, *Army*, 163–4.

[196] J. Ullreich, 'Moritz von Auffenberg-Komarów: Leben und Wirken, 1911–1918' Ph.D. thesis (Vienna, 1961), 41–51. Auffenberg to Khuen-Héderváry, 27 Feb. 1912, 4 and 5 Mar. 1912, KAW KM Präs (1912) 26–1. HHStA Nachlass Berchtold, 3, i. 41–2.

[197] Schemua to Auffenberg, 27 Feb. 1912, KAW Gstb (1912) 52–2.

[198] Rothenberg, *Army*, 164–5. J. Leslie, 'The Antecedents of Austria-Hungary's War Aims: Policies and Policy-Makers in Vienna and Budapest before and during 1914', *Wiener Beiträge zur Geschichte der Neuzeit*, 20 (1993), 324.

236,300, most of the addition going to the *Landwehr* and *Honvéd*. The authorities kept their powers under article 43.[199] Two-thirds of the extra soldiers in the common army would go to undoing the imbalances created by the *Notbehelfe* and to raising strengths in existing units, especially in the infantry; the rest would be used to create new detachments, especially mountain batteries in Bosnia-Herzegovina and pioneers and fortress artillery against Italy.[200] Schemua believed that the measure was inadequate and work must start at once on a successor, but he feared his troops were degenerating into a 'Miliz-Armee', and he and Auffenberg had been desperate for some relief.[201]

The authorities continued to be preoccupied with the southern frontiers, including the railways in Bosnia-Herzegovina whose inadequacies the events of 1908–9 had demonstrated. Strategic railways, lacking commercial viability, would overstretch the central and the Bosnia-Herzegovina budgets, and the Austrian and Hungarian Governments must be called upon to pay for them. Schönaich had already asked for two new lines, at least one of which should be normal (rather than narrow) gauge.[202] Neither government, however, wished to finance railways that would primarily benefit the other, and they were deadlocked over the route of the connection to the Montenegrin frontier. In October 1911 Auffenberg and Aehrenthal pleaded for an end to the impasse, followed in May 1912 by Franz Joseph himself, but the Joint Council referred the question for yet further study. When the Balkan 'jack-in-the-box', as Aehrenthal called it, next burst open, the Monarchy was no better placed for rapid reinforcement than it had been four years before.[203]

Auffenberg and Schemua inherited Conrad's Italophobia. The War Minister felt that the false reassurance provided by the Italian alliance hindered the army from getting the money it needed; and yet if war broke out with Russia or Serbia he feared that Rome would join the enemy within weeks.[204] Schemua, similarly, wanted to exceed the Schönaich Pact restrictions on the budget for *matériel*, but although he wanted to strengthen Cracow and Lemberg, the south-west, followed by the Balkans, was his priority.[205] In December 1911 Auffenberg asked for extra credits for artillery and for aircraft, and 40 million crowns for fortifications against Italy. The Hungarians objected that supplementary demands would jeopardize the passage of the recruitment law, and questioned the gravity of the threat, a scepticism that Aehrenthal still shared.[206] From the following spring, however, the military were furnished with a more plausible case for expansion. Mounting tension in the Balkans caused by the Italo-Turkish war

[199] Ibid. Text of the law (5 July 1912) in KAW KM Präs (1912) 26–1.
[200] Auffenberg directive, 8 Aug. 1912, KAW Gstb (1912) 52–2.
[201] Schemua to Auffenberg, 22 Jan., 3 June 1912, KAW Gstb (1912) 52–2.
[202] Schönaich to Austrian Premier, 12 May 1911, KAW KM Präs (1911) 81–11.
[203] GMR, 26 Feb. and 28–9 Oct. 1911, 6 May 1912, HHStA PA XL 310.
[204] Auffenberg to Franz Joseph (draft), 20 Nov. 1911, KAW KM Präs (1911) 76–93.
[205] Schemua to Auffenberg, 3 Feb. 1912, KAW Gstb (1912) 45–1. Schemua memoranda on fortification, 17 Feb., 7 Mar., and 25 July 1912, KAW Gstb (1912) 41–3.
[206] GMR, 6 Dec. 1911, HHStA PA XL 310.

in Libya was accompanied by the re-emergence of a frontier of insecurity in the north-east. In February–March 1912, during a Turkish–Persian frontier dispute, the Russians concentrated forces on the Ottoman border. Action against Turkey might embroil Russia in a conflict with the Central Powers, and the Evidenzbureau detected preparations in the Warsaw, Kiev, and Odessa military districts.[207] The Russians denied that they were preparing mobilization against Austria-Hungary, but there were rumours of war between the two Powers and for a time, according to one St Petersburg official, the atmosphere had been 'overcharged with electricity'. Both the Foreign and the War Ministries in Vienna boosted their expenditure on intelligence-gathering, and the General Staff instructed its attaché not to be sidetracked by Russian assurances but to monitor all military activity.[208]

Against this backdrop Auffenberg returned to the charge, applying for a 250-million crown credit. When Berchtold arrived from the St Petersburg Embassy to replace Aehrenthal as Foreign Minister and chairman of the GMR, Schemua briefed him on Russia's March 1912 military measures.[209] In his opening audience with Franz Joseph the new Minister cautioned that 'European peace today rests on a very fragile foundation. This gives the external situation a character of insecurity that previously we did not know, and that should induce us to give heightened attention to the Monarchy's defences.'[210] He agreed in principle to Auffenberg's new programme, and on 8 and 9 July supported it in two dramatic sessions of the Joint Council.

By now the Council was in significantly more sombre mood. Berchtold saw several 'black spots' on the horizon: Libya, Anglo-German and Franco-German hostility, and Austro-Russian conflict over the Balkans and Ruthenia. Any might lead to war, and diplomacy was powerless to keep the peace without battle-ready armed forces. The international situation was 'precarious' and worsening, and the Monarchy might have to stand firm at the risk of cataclysmic conflict or cease to be an independent Power. The Libyan War increased the likelihood of fresh turmoil in the Balkans, where Austria-Hungary might need again to raise its frontier strength if it wished to remain a 'power factor'. Auffenberg wanted 25 million crowns for aviation, 55 million for fortification, and 170 million for artillery, saying that Austria-Hungary must be prepared for war with either Italy or Russia. Both eventualities would mean war with Serbia and Montenegro as well, and in both the Habsburg forces would be 'heavily outnumbered'. Since 1909 Belgrade had increased its combat-worthy field divisions from two to five, and the Monarchy's relative position had never been less favourable. To leave things as they stood would be 'utterly irresponsible'. It was, however,

[207] Hohenlohe to War Ministry, 16 Mar. 1912; Urbánski memorandum, 30 Mar. 1912, KAW KM Präs (1912) 47–2.

[208] Schemua to Hohenlohe, 30 May 1912; Hohenlohe to Schemua, 8 May 1912, KAW Gstb (1912) 25–7. For intelligence spending, HHStA PA XL 310, pp. 413, 423.

[209] Schemua note on audience with Franz Joseph, 19 Mar. 1912, KAW Gstb Operationsbureau 739.

[210] HHStA Nachlass Berchtold 3, i. 1.

Berchtold's position that decided the Austrian Government representatives, who agreed that if the new demands were necessary for the Monarchy's Great-Power status they must be met, even though credit was tightening all over Europe, partly because of higher armaments expenditure elsewhere. Despite the risk to the Monarchy's 'financial war preparedness' they were willing to grant the 250-million credit and a fifth dreadnought for Montecuccoli. It was the Hungarians who dug their heels in, using the sophist's argument that there was no point in investing in greater readiness in two or three years' time if the situation was critical now, but objecting in reality to the political embarrassment of another military request so soon after the recruitment law's stormy passage. At the end of the session Auffenberg went ahead with an order for twenty-four 30.5 cm mortars that he had authorized on his own initiative and Berchtold proclaimed that he had acquitted his responsibilities before history. But the credit remained blocked.[211]

The Schönaich Pact and the *Wehrgesetz* were the biggest stimulus in years to the Habsburg Monarchy's defence effort, and although the Hungarians resisted additional militarization the central authorities and the Austrian Government had formed a common front. The Stabilmento tecnico needed to be kept occupied, and the warship firms were roped in to pre-empt the Delegations over dreadnought-building, but the Monarchy's leap into the new naval era would have been neither so speedy nor so decisive had it not been for the Italian challenge. The army, in contrast, was handicapped by Aehrenthal's suspicion that, whereas dreadnoughts would intimidate Italy and make hostilities less likely, Conrad's schemes might cause an unnecessary war. Hence it languished until the resurgence of the Balkan and the Russian perils. After the change of position by the Foreign Minister the Hungarian obstacle too was about to crumble, and by the autumn of 1912 Austria-Hungary was poised on the verge of an inter-bloc arms race.

* * *

Table 10. *Russian military and naval expenditure, 1908–1912* (mn roubles)

	War Ministry	Navy Ministry	Extraordinary defence exp.	TOTAL
1908	462.5	93.5	52.0	608.1
1909	473.4	92.2	64.9	630.5
1910	484.9	112.7	50.0	647.6
1911	497.8	121.0	50.6	669.3
1912	527.9	176.1	110.5	814.5

Source: P. W. Gatrell, 'Industrial Expansion in Tsarist Russia, 1908–1914', *Economic History Review*, NS 35 (1982), 104–5. Discrepancies in the totals are due to rounding. The totals given in Table 1 are slightly higher because they include retrospective expenditures on the Russo-Japanese War.

[211] GMR, 8–9 July 1912, HHStA PA XL 310.

Developments in Russia between 1908 and 1912 undermined the military equilibrium not only in Eastern Europe but in Europe as a whole: in the land arms race the government in St Petersburg can most justifiably be said to have fired the starting shot, although it is doubtful if it realized what it was doing. The expenditure statistics obscure as much as they illuminate the significance of what was happening, but again we must begin with them. Army spending moved upwards fairly smoothly, but with accelerations in 1907–8 and 1911–12, the latter inaugurating a dramatic expansion down to the outbreak of war and being matched by a doubling of the extraordinary budget. After falling in 1905–7, naval spending began its pre-war ascent in 1910 and by 1912 was nearly twice its 1909 level. Whereas there was little to show for the money poured into the fleet, moreover, the army was radically restructured at marginal extra expense. The military reorganization of 1910 will form the centre-piece of the following discussion, but it must be located in the context of the February 1910 ten-year defence expenditure programme and of the supplementary naval programmes for the Black and Baltic Seas approved in 1911 and 1912.

The first point to address is the navalist bias to Russian policy, which persisted in the face of War and Finance Ministry protests that it inhibited a rational assessment of the empire's needs. It was a bias in favour of a dreadnought battlefleet rather than a coastal defence force of mine-layers, torpedo boats, and submarines. Already before the Bosnian crisis the 124-million rouble naval programme of June 1907 contrasted with the army's 92-million re-equipment allocation a year later.[212] After the crisis the navy led the pressure for a long-term plan. In 1909 the Tsar provisionally approved a naval schedule submitted by the new Navy Minister, Voevodsky, but the Council of Ministers referred it to a special commission composed of the Premier, the Foreign, Finance, War, and Navy Ministers, and the army and navy chiefs of staff. This body produced the ten-year programme. Out of 1,413 million roubles in total, 715 million would go to the army: 373 million for fortification (mainly in Poland), 114 million for railways (mainly in the Far East), 81 million for siege artillery, and 147 million for other *matériel*, including field artillery and machine guns. But 698 million would go to the navy (31 million for the Pacific, 51 million for the Black Sea, and 614 million for the Baltic). Given that Russia was primarily a land power, and that the army's ordinary budget was four times the navy's in size, this was a remarkable tribute to the admirals' influence.[213]

The programme would remain a paper schedule unless it was translated into legislation, and here again the navy led the way. A law of May 1911 approved 150 million roubles for a Black Sea reinforcement of three battleships, nine destroyers, and six submarines over four years.[214] A further law in June 1912

[212] K. F. Shatsillo, 'O disproportsii v razvitii vooruzhennykh sil Rossii nakanune pervoi mirovoi voiny, 1906–1914', *Istorichiskie Zapiski*, 83 (1969), 127–8.

[213] A. L. Sidorov, 'Iz istorii podgotovki tsarizma k pervoi mirovoi voine', *Istoricheskii Arkhiv* (1962), 2, 120–2, 132–3, 141–3. K. F. Shatsillo, *Russkii imperializm i razvitie flota nakanune pervoi mirovoi voiny (1906–1914 gg)* (Moscow, 1968), 65–9.

[214] Ibid. 132–3.

authorized 448.5 million of Baltic spending by 1917 on shore works, four battle-cruisers, four light cruisers, thirty-six destroyers, and eighteen submarines, as well as two more light cruisers for each of the Black Sea and Pacific theatres.[215] These sums exceeded the outlays envisaged for the army and navy combined in the relevant portion of the ten-year programme, and propelled Russia's naval construction budget into second position to Britain's. As soon as the four battle-cruisers were launched, moreover, the Tsar and the Navy Ministry intended to lay down four more.[216] Meanwhile, the army continued to finance its extraordinary expenditure from the 1908 credit, and only in May 1912 did a new law raise it to the level envisaged in the 1910 schedule.[217]

The navy had transformed its political position. Its 1907 construction programme had been halted by the Duma's denial of funds to the 'Tsushima Ministry' and by its own incompetent planning.[218] But Admiral I. K. Grigorovich, who became Minister in 1911, reformed his department's administration and ended direct access by his assistant minister and the Chief of Naval Staff to Nicholas II. He won the Duma's confidence, and outmanoeuvred Kokovtsov, who after the assassination of Stolypin in 1911 became Premier as well as Finance Minister.[219] Kokovtsov remained committed to a balanced budget and to covering expenditure increases out of extra revenue derived from economic growth rather than from higher rates of taxation. He was concerned not to over-borrow, so that Russia would remain creditworthy in the event of hostilities.[220] In the 1909 special commission he warned that the navy's plans would push up either taxes or borrowing unacceptably, and that the destruction of the economy would finish Russia as a Great Power.[221] He cut the navy down to 648 million from over 1,000 million, maintaining that there would be no war for at least ten years.[222] But by the time he became Prime Minister such optimism was less convincing, and it became harder for him to represent single-mindedly the Treasury view. In addition, good harvests after 1909 and industrial growth of more than 7 per cent per annum gave him a budget surplus, thereby weakening his defences against the armaments lobbyists. After a long and severe depression the recovery was spectacular, and strongly oriented towards capital goods, the output of iron, steel, and machinery rising by up to three-quarters between 1908 and 1913. In comparison with earlier Russian booms, moreover, this one was more sustainable and broadly based. Consumer demand as well as government orders underpinned it, and an indigenous banking sector was becoming more

---

[215] Ibid. 76–7. Reports by Captain Durand, 12, 20, and 22 June 1912; and Captain Gallaud, 5 Dec. 1912, SHM BB7 121 dossier 1310.

[216] Durand report, 12 June 1912, ibid.

[217] K. F. Shatsillo, *Rossia pered pervoi mirovoi voiny (vooruzhennye sily tsarizma v 1905–1914 gg)* (Moscow, 1974), 93–4.

[218] De Laurens Castelet report, 8 Jan. 1910, SHM BB7 120 dossier 1390.

[219] Ibid. Aubrey Smith to Buchanan, 30 Apr. 1911; Grenfell to Buchanan, 8 Jan. 1913, *BDFA*, series IA, *Russia, 1859–1914*, ed. D. C. B. Lieven (6 vols., Frederick, Md., 1983), vi, docs. 66, 133.

[220] Kokovtsov, *Out of my Past*, 457–60. Geyer, *Russian Imperialism*, 256–7.

[221] Shatsillo, *Russkii imperializm*, 326 ff.

[222] Ibid. and Sidorov, *Finansovoe polozhenie*, 54–5.

prominent. Russia's growing preponderance in the armaments balance rested on a profounder revitalization of its national energies that attracted worldwide attention.[223]

Naval expansion required a political justification. The Black Sea law was an action–reaction response to a Turkish threat: it was an unwelcome distraction from the larger objectives of the Russian leadership, which found expression in the Baltic plans. The law of 1907 and the ten-year programme both emphasized the Baltic, the 1909 special commission agreeing that in the Black Sea the existing capital ship strength would suffice for another decade.[224] Yet the most recent battleship there dated from 1900, the fleet was too variegated in its armament to be able to function as a squadron, the crews were poorly trained, and the coal burned so inferior that on manœuvres the ships could not see each other and had to break line.[225] This could be tolerated while the Ottoman fleet was even more decrepit, but after the 1908 revolution the Young Turks invited a British naval mission to the Golden Horn, as well as ordering four destroyers and a cruiser from Germany. Despite being warned that if they sought command of the Black Sea they would face an expensive naval race with Russia and would lose, in 1911 they signed contracts with Vickers and Armstrong for two dreadnought battleships, the first to be delivered by April 1913. Sazonov and Stolypin were convinced that Russia must respond, and the War Ministry acquiesced. It was the navy that dragged its feet, proposing that the Turks should be discouraged by diplomacy and insisting that the Black Sea must not siphon off funds from the main shipbuilding programme. Although Stolypin prodded Voevodsky into drafting what became the 1911 law, the three battleships it envisaged would not be ready until at least 1915, thus bestowing on the Turks a period of opportunity that might last more than two years.[226]

In the Baltic, by contrast, the navy achieved the 1912 law only by overcoming much domestic resistance. Already in the 1909 special commission it pressed for eight battleships and the development of Reval as an ice-free forward base for Kronstadt. It wanted not only to control the eastern Baltic and the Gulf of Finland, but to be strong enough to threaten the German coast.[227] Stolypin and the War Ministry, more navalist than the navy against Turkey, preferred a smaller force, sufficient to prevent an enemy landing and defend St Petersburg.[228] The naval spokesmen denied there was a meaningful distinction between a defensive and an offensive capacity, and Izvolsky supported them by asserting that warships could support diplomacy and that a navy was essen-

---

[223] Geyer, *Russian Imperialism*, 257, 260. P. W. Gatrell, *Government, Industry, and Rearmament in Russia, 1900–1914: The Last Argument of Tsarism* (Cambridge, 1994), 161, 176, 187. M. E. Falkus, *The Industrialization of Russia, 1700–1914* (London, 1972), ch. 9. See generally R. Ropponen, *Die Kraft Russlands* (Helsinki, 1968), *passim*, and W. C. Wohlforth, 'The Perception of Power: Russia in the Pre-1914 Balance', *World Politics*, 39 (1987), 353–81.

[224] Shatsillo, *Russkii imperializm*, 337.

[225] Ibid. 121–3.

[226] Ibid. 109–36; M. Kent (ed.), *The Great Powers and the End of the Ottoman Empire* (London, 1984), 86–9.

[227] Shatsillo, *Russkii imperializm*, 332.   [228] Ibid. 323, 331.

tial to keep Russia as a world Power of the first rank.[229] Hardly had the Council of Ministers agreed to the February 1910 programme than the measure got bogged down in the Duma, yet in April 1911 Nicholas endorsed a twenty-year Baltic plan costed at 2,192.5 million roubles, the first five years of which became the basis of the 1912 law.[230] Although the Council of Ministers was anxious about the compatibility between this and the army's intentions, the Government put on a show of solidarity in the Duma. Kokovtsov, who three years earlier had denounced such outlays, assured the Budget Committee that they could be financed without higher taxes or borrowing.[231] Together with spokesmen for the Foreign, War, and Navy Ministries he testified that the law was 'necessary for the defence of the Baltic, for the greatness of Russia, for her foreign policy, for the functioning of her diplomatic alliances and ententes'.[232]

The Navy Ministry planners regarded Germany as the primary Baltic enemy, possibly in combination with Sweden,[233] but in contrast to the Black Sea law it is difficult to see the Baltic programme as a reaction to an intensified external threat. Its Duma critics pointed out that Russia could never match the German fleet, and felt that money spent on battleships would be wasted.[234] It was true that there was an urgent need for orders if private firms were not to withdraw from shipbuilding and the state yards not to lay off workers and cut capacity. For Nicholas himself the Baltic battlecruisers may have been a status symbol, necessary to keep up with the other Powers and shore up dynastic prestige after the disaster in Asia. The naval planners, however, developed a more sophisticated justification. A first objective was to defend the capital and the politically unreliable Baltic littoral and Finland; but to do this they must dominate the eastern Baltic with advance bases and a modern battlefleet. Furthermore, warships in the Baltic, unlike in the Black Sea where the Straits were closed to their passage, could range more widely in support of Russian interests. In addition, they could provide cheap diplomatic leverage, as even a small force could hold the balance between the British and German fleets. This argument appealed to Izvolsky, although Kokovtsov countered that it was the army that made Russia's friendship valuable, and the Kadets, the main liberal party in the Duma, opposed a Baltic fleet on the grounds that it might presage a conservative and anti-British foreign-policy realignment. All the Ministers agreed, however, with the generalized argument that naval strength was essential to Russia's remaining a first-class Power. Once money became available, and Grigorovich provided leadership and competent administration, there was an irresistible impulse for growth.[235]

There turned out, however, to be much cogency in the forebodings of the critics. After 1911 the navy overtook the army in spending on equipment, and in 1914 the army was underprovided for the sake of expenditure on warships

---

[229] Ibid. 343, 346.
[230] Ibid. 70–6.
[231] Kokovtsov, *Out of my Past*, ch. 26. O'Beirne to Grey, 12 June 1912, *BDFA*, IA vi, doc. 101.
[232] Durand report, 12 June 1912, SHM BB7 121 dossier 1310.
[233] Shatsillo, *Russkii imperializm*, 332.
[234] O'Beirne to Grey, 12 June 1912, *BDFA*, IA vi, doc. 101.
[235] Shatsillo, 'O disproportsii', 128–9; Shatsillo, *Russkii imperializm*, 79–89.

that were mostly uncompleted. When the war broke out army munitions needs forced the suspension of naval construction. The four Baltic pre-dreadnought battleships started in 1909 were completed by the end of 1914, but not one of the 1912 ships, and of the 1911 Black Sea vessels only four destroyers and two submarines were operational.[236] Naturally the timing caught the Russians out, but there had been warnings that to build a battlefleet would take years and that there were more pressing priorities. The Duma insisted, moreover, with the navy's concurrence, on concentrating all construction in Russian yards, even though it cost perhaps 60 per cent more to build a battleship in Russia than in Britain and up to twice as long,[237] especially as the programme required a huge prior investment in infrastructure. Impressive though the spending figures were, in 1911–14 Russia's main achievement was to magnify its shipbuilding capacity, rather than to build ships.

The War Ministry enjoyed more favour than the navy in the Duma, if less in the Council of Ministers and with Nicholas. Sukhomlinov, who became Minister in 1909, was a man of conservative reputation and dictatorial instincts, but his assistant, Polivanov, worked well with Guchkov and the Octobrist party in Parliament.[238] After the *coup* of 1907 the Duma voted practically everything the army asked, granting money faster than officials could place the orders.[239] An inquiry in 1917 found that less than one-thirtieth of the total cut from the Ministry estimate between 1908 and 1913 was the responsibility of the legislature, the great majority of the deductions being made by inter-departmental conferences and the Council of Ministers.[240]

The relationship between the War and Finance Ministers was particularly bitter. Sukhomlinov thought Kokovtsov narrow, verbose, and self-seeking; Kokovtsov that Sukhomlinov was incompetent, irresponsible, and corrupt.[241] Although the Finance Ministry grip gradually relaxed, only new external perils could break it. Worsening relations with Vienna in 1908 helped elicit the re-equipment credit of June. After the annexation crisis, a law of March 1909 released 40 million roubles to implement the 1908 targets.[242] Sukhomlinov's efforts to raise the targets further, however, remained fruitless until, as in Austria-Hungary, the deteriorating situation in the spring of 1912 forced a reconsideration. A special conference of War Ministry, General Staff, and military district representatives agreed that it was urgent to improve the army's equipment and its mobilization arrangements, and to modify the concentration plan. Legislation in May approved 70 million roubles for stores and artillery. Yet even now, when the Ministry asked for a further increase for 1913 of up to 108

---

[236] Shatsillo, 'O disproportsii', 128–9; Shatsillo, *Russkii imperializm*, 78, 355.

[237] Grenfell to O'Beirne, 22 June 1912, *BDFA*, IA vi, doc. 104.

[238] Knox to O'Beirne, 27 May 1912, ibid., doc. 99.

[239] Nicolson report, 30 Dec. 1909, ibid., doc. 103 (p. 385). Nicolson to Grey, 7 May 1909, ibid., doc. 70. Janin to Vignal, 17 Feb. 1911, SHA 7.N. 1485. Sukhomlinov, *Erinnerungen*, 278.

[240] Sidorov, *Finansovoe polozhenie*, 76.

[241] Sukhomlinov, *Erinnerungen*, 271–7; Kokovtsov, *Out of my Past*, 229 ff., 313–15.

[242] Posadowksy to War Ministry, 10 Mar. 1909, PAAA R.10425. Conrad, *Dienstzeit*, i. 243.

million roubles, Kokovtsov launched a frontal attack. The Council of Ministers cut the figure to 65 million and would have cut it by more had not Nicholas accepted that German rearmament meant that the army as well as the navy must be expanded. After the outbreak of the Balkan War, Sukhomlinov was given all (and more than) he needed.[243]

Like the Hungarians in Vienna, the Finance Ministry was increasingly isolated, but it held down spending until the new Balkan upheaval in 1912 burst the dam. Admittedly, the War Ministry's failure to use fully such credits as it did receive hindered Sukhomlinov in fighting for extra. The cause was partly bureaucratic inefficiency, but also the incapacity of Russian industry promptly to fulfil contracts.[244] This is not to say that nothing was done. Infantry training was improved and large-scale manœuvres resumed.[245] Re-equipment with quick-firers was virtually completed, investments made in machine guns, wireless, lorries, and aviation; and in 1908 funds were voted for 146 batteries of field howitzers.[246] None the less, Russian army corps remained inferior in field artillery to those of the Central Powers, and larger calibre pieces were neglected.[247] In 1914 Germany had 575 heavy field guns, Russia 240, and France 180.[248] The Russian fortress artillery was way below regulation strength and much of it was decades old.[249] The GGS believed that its fortresses could resist tsarist assaults, whereas the Russian strongholds in Poland could not withstand Germany's siege guns.[250] As for strategic railways, Russian state expenditure was mainly in Asia, on the Amur railway and on double-tracking the Trans-Siberian. In the West activity was at a low ebb, and Sukhomlinov himself did not press for new lines.[251]

The War Minister's railway priorities point to his concerns in the reorganization of 1910, which was the major development of this period. The Tsar stipulated that the reorganization should not mean higher costs or manpower needs, and in fact it modestly reduced the army's peacetime strength.[252] It could therefore be implemented by imperial command, without requiring legislation, although it enjoyed Duma support anyway.[253] It affected the army's unit composition, its mobilization, its peacetime deployment, its wartime concentration,

---

[243] Shatsillo, *Rossia*, 94. Sidorov, *Finansovoe polozhenie*, 70–2.   [244] Ibid. 81.

[245] See esp. Ropponen, *Kraft*, 235 ff. K. Neilson, 'Watching the "Steamroller" ', *Journal of Strategic Studies*, 8 (1975), 207–12.

[246] Sukhomlinov, *Erinnerungen*, 339–40. Nicolson report, 30 Dec. 1909, *BDFA*, IA vi, doc. 103, pp. 390–1.

[247] A. M. Zaionchovksy, *Podgotovka Rossii k imperialisticheskoi voine (Plany voiny)* (Moscow, 1926), 86.

[248] Stone, *Eastern Front*, 38.

[249] Nicolson report, 30 Dec. 1909, *BDFA*, IA v, doc. 103, p. 390. Cf. report by Austrian military attaché, 29 Mar. 1910, KAW KM Präs (1910) 47–2.

[250] GGS 7. Abt. report on Russian heavy artillery, Mar. 1909, KAM Gstb 208.

[251] GGS 1. Abt. report on Russia in 1911 (n.d.), KAM Gstb 208; annual report 2 Dec. 1909, ibid. Matton reports, 6 Mar. and 15 Apr. 1910, SHA 7.N. 1535.

[252] Shatsillo, 'O disproportii', 131. Shatsillo, *Rossia*, 49.

[253] Ibid. 48. EMA 2nd Bureau, 'Déplacements de troupes: Russie: renseignements de presse', 1910, SHA 7.N. 1537.

Fig. 7. The Polish Marches.

and the frontier fortresses. Before considering the political motives for the reorganization, it is necessary to address the technical problems facing Sukhomlinov, and the solutions that he adopted.

Sukhomlinov believed that the complexity and lack of uniformity in the army's composition impeded command. Companies had eleven different strengths; battalions between four and ten companies each; and army corps between sixteen and sixty-eight battalions and fifty-six and 168 guns. Peacetime unit strengths were too low, and in much of the infantry there were only fifty men per company. Yet the expansion of the army on mobilization would be proportionately much smaller than in France or Germany. Whereas other armies formed units composed exclusively of reservists only on mobilization, the Russian one already had such units organized in peacetime. When mobilized, in the judgement of the British attaché, they would swell so much as to be ineffectual. It would be better to merge them with the other active units, even if on paper doing so weakened the army's order of battle. Beyond this, Sukhomlinov wished to increase the army's peacetime and wartime size—which were smaller in relation to the population than in other European countries—and to provide extra artillery and technical troops.[254]

The reorganization started to address these weaknesses. It increased the peacetime strength of the infantry in the field army by suppressing the independent reserve formations and fortress infantry units. Sukhomlinov's assumption was that Germany and Austria-Hungary could not fight a long campaign and would therefore concentrate on developing their front-line forces; and Russia must do likewise. He created seven new active peacetime divisions, and seventeen rifle brigades, raising the number of army corps from thirty-one to thirty-seven (twenty-seven in European Russia). Thirty-five reserve divisions would be created on the outbreak of war. The composition of infantry regiments was standardized, and they, the field artillery, and the field howitzer batteries were strengthened at the reserve units' expense. A heavy field artillery was to be created, and a siege artillery train. The numbers of sapper, balloon, and railway companies were increased. Sukhomlinov was creating the framework for a more skilled and technologically based army, and he followed Western practice in sharpening the distinction between first- and second-line forces. He raised Russia's wartime strength by about 10 per cent to 3.268 million men. Without the funds for artillery and other equipment that were being withheld by Kokovtsov or being directed to the navy, however, his work would be incomplete.[255]

The structural changes must be seen in conjunction with those in mobilization. Nicholas approved the reorganization in May 1910 for completion by 1 September, the date set for the introduction of the new mobilization schedule 19. Like Italy, and unlike Austria-Hungary, France, or Germany, Russia had

[254] Zaionchovsky, *Podgotovka*, 83–6. Nicolson report 30 Dec. 1909, *BDFA*, IA v, doc. 103; and 22 Mar. 1911, ibid. vi, doc. 62. For an overview of the reorganization, W. C. Fuller, *Strategy and Power in Russia, 1600–1914* (New York, 1992), 423–33.

[255] Zaionchovsky, *Podgotovka*, 87–9; Ropponen, *Kraft*, 200–6; Shatsillo, *Rossia*, 48–9.

hitherto lacked a territorial mobilization system. Only one new recruit in eight was assigned to a unit stationed in his home military district. Each infantry regiment and artillery brigade was intended to comprise recruits from areas dominated by Great Russians, from areas dominated by White Russians or Ukrainians, and from areas dominated by other ethnic groups. Because so much of the army before 1910 was positioned near the western border, on mobilization huge numbers of reservists would be transported over long distances. They would join their units within striking range of enemies who would be ready before them. Sukhomlinov believed that Russia could keep pace with Germany only by remodelling its system from the bottom up, rather than continuing with large forward deployments in peacetime. In consequence the 1910 reform endowed most of European Russia with a territorial mobilization system, recruiting areas being assigned to each regiment, division, and corps. In Poland, Transcaucasia, and the Baltic provinces local recruits did not exceed one third of unit strengths on mobilization, but elsewhere the new system was remarkably standardized. Of those called up 97 per cent would join units assigned to their region, thus expediting the process and giving the men a stronger sense of fighting for their homes.[256]

Territorial mobilization was bound up with the army's new peacetime deployment (the geographical distribution of its active units), to which Sukhomlinov gave special attention and which attracted some of the keenest interest abroad. Breaking with the inheritance of Alexander II and Miliutin, he redistributed forces from the western military districts to the central ones, Warsaw and Vilna losing ninety-one and thirty-seven battalions respectively and Moscow and Kazan gaining twenty-eight and fifty-one. Of the army's infantry formations 35 per cent, not more than half at reinforced strength, would henceforth be deployed between the frontier and the Western Dvina/Dnieper line, compared with 47 per cent, mostly at reinforced strength, hitherto. Units were spread more evenly through the Empire, in keeping with a territorial mobilization system, and a reserve of 320 battalions was created in the Kazan military district, at the head of the railway lines to Asia. Henceforth mobilization would proceed in the interior, and when it was completed units at full strength, rather than unincorporated reservists, would be transported to the deployment zone. This was another move towards Western European practice, faster mobilization and better railways reducing the need for a large peacetime presence in the Polish salient. By 1910, according to the British military attaché, ten lines linked central Russia to the western frontier, six of them double-tracked; twenty years earlier the figures had been six and two. The implications of reorganization for the army's striking power in Europe were therefore equivocal—accelerated mobilization, but carried out deeper in the heartland; greater protection against a spoiling attack, but an earlier concentration in Asia rather than the West.[257]

---

[256] Zaionchovsky, *Podgotovka*, 113–20.

[257] Ibid. 107–12. GGS 1.Abt. annual report on Russia for 1910, n.d., KAM Gstb 208. Wyndham to Nicolson, 6 Apr. 1910, *BDFA*, IA vi, doc. 14.

The fourth point to consider is indeed the revised strategic concentration (*sosredotochenie*) or disposition of the mobilized units after transport to the frontier and before the opening of hostilities. Schedule 19, whose principal author was the Quartermaster-General in the General Staff, V. N. Danilov, was the most pessimistic and defensive Russian war plan between 1880 and 1914. After the annexation crisis Danilov did not question Austro-German solidarity. Romania, Sweden, and the Ottomans might join the enemy, and there could be simultaneous hostilities with China and Japan. Conversely, he expected Britain to stay neutral in a European war, and possibly France too. Russia might face the entire German army; and even if Moltke's forces were divided between East and West the Central Powers could mobilize faster than the Russians and would probably seek to envelop the Polish salient by a rapid pincer attack. If Germany's main blow was directed against France and Austria-Hungary's against Italy, Danilov was willing to contemplate an offensive, but pending clarification of the enemy's intentions the Russian concentration could no longer be in the western tip of the salient but must be across the neck of it, along the Brest-Litovsk—Bialystok line. Most of Poland, including Warsaw and the Vistula bridgeheads, would initially be abandoned. More forces would be concentrated against Germany than against the Habsburgs, but although Danilov envisaged an eventual counterstroke its axis was not specified. The priority was to mobilize and concentrate in safety, even if this meant allowing similar freedom to the enemy. Admittedly he was criticized by General Alekseev, the Chief of Staff in the Warsaw military district, who would be Chief of Staff for the whole of the Austrian front in the event of war. Alekseev expected Russia to face fewer enemies simultaneously, and doubted that Germany's main effort would be in the East: he wanted to concentrate further forward and attack in Galicia. At first Sukhomlinov favoured Alekseev's ideas, but he allowed Danilov to prevail.[258]

The final aspect of the reorganization concerned the Russian fortresses. In February 1909, while still Chief of the General Staff, Sukhomlinov ordered many of them to be demolished or downgraded, on the Baltic and Black Seas, the Vistula line in western Poland, and the Narew line in the north. This decree, issued unexpectedly and without consultation, caused consternation in military circles and among Russia's allies. Sukhomlinov maintained in his defence that artillery and aviation deserved priority. There was no money to modernize or even to repair many fortresses, and without modernization they would be too vulnerable, uselessly bottling up field troops. Unlike Germany, Russia had not installed quick-firing long-range guns, the radius between the central citadels and their outlying strong-points was too short, and the defences needed armour protection for their artillery, anti-storming cupolas, and concrete rather than brick roofs against plunging fire. In short, the adaptation to high explosive had largely passed them by, and Sukhomlinov wished to husband his resources for a chain of new or updated strong-points in the new zone of concentration to the east of

---

[258] Zaionchovsky, *Podgotovka*, ch. 12. J. Snyder, *The Ideology of the Offensive: Military Decision Making and the Disasters of 1914* (Ithaca, NY, 1984), 166–72.

the salient. Thus the February 1909 order declassified the western fortresses except for Kovno, Ossoviets, and Brest-Litovsk, and announced the creation of a new one at Grodno. There appears to have been a ministerial revolt against it, led by Stolypin and Kokovtsov, particularly because the French had not been notified. Many in the army, including Grand Duke Nicholas, wished to modernize the abandoned fortresses, and there were polemics in the military press. In a new and this time definitive decree in May 1910 Sukhomlinov relented. A dozen fortresses in European Russia would be conserved. Those on the Bug–Narew line would mostly be declassified, but Vistula bridgeheads would be maintained at Osseviets and Novogeorgievsk. This arrangement appeared to maintain the option of an attack across the river, although it was inconsistent with the new peacetime deployment and strategic concentration. The same resources would have to be distributed among more numerous fortresses, and modernization would be slower. None the less, during 1910 and 1911 demolition proceeded.[259]

This account of the reorganization has emphasized the role of Sukhomlinov: by 1910, in the words of a perceptive French observer, the previously 'polycephalic' army administration had been concentrated in the hands of an autocratic Minister who was jealous of his authority.[260] Nicholas had clipped the wings of the Council of State Defence in 1907, and abolished it two years later. On becoming Chief of the General Staff in 1908 Sukhomlinov renounced the CGS's right of independent access to the Emperor, whereas on becoming War Minister he secured an order that confirmed the Minister's sole right to report direct to Nicholas on army questions.[261] He replaced his first CGS, Mishlaevski, after six months, accusing him of deceit and incompetence. His second, Gerngross, less able but conscientious and loyal, died at his desk in 1911, and was replaced by Zhilinski.[262] Between them, Sukhomlinov and Danilov, who became head of the Minister's Chancellery in March 1911, squeezed out the possibility of a powerful CGS on German or Austrian lines.[263] In 1912 Sukhomlinov was able to remove another rival, his own assistant Polivanov, whom Kokovtsov tried vainly to defend.[264] The War Minister enjoyed sufficient confidence from Nicholas to be able to resist supervision over him by his Cabinet colleagues except in financial matters. His new peacetime deployment appears to have been introduced without reference to Stolypin and Kokovtsov, and despite their reservations.[265]

[259] Zaionchovsky, *Podgotovka*, ch. 8. Kokovtsov, *Out of my Past*, ch. 21. Stone, *Eastern Front*, 31. Matton reports Nos. 125 (?15 Apr. 1910) and 145 (6 July 1910), SHA 7.N. 1535. Wehrlin note on Russia's military intentions, Apr. 1910, ibid. Fuller, *Strategy*, 432–3.

[260] Janin to Vignal, 10 Dec. 1910, SHA 7.N. 1485.

[261] Sukhomlinov, *Erinnerungen*, 203, 207, 293.

[262] Ibid. 284–5. Louis dispatch, 18 Oct. 1909, SHA 7.N. 1536.

[263] Janin to Vignal, 12 Nov. 1910 and 17 Mar. 1911, SHA 7.N. 1485.

[264] Kokovtsov, *Out of my Past*, 309, 315. Sukhomlinov, *Erinnerungen*, 287–90. Knox to O'Beirne, 27 May 1912, *BDFA*, IA vi, doc. 99.

[265] Kokovtsov, *Out of my Past*, 253, 321.

The accumulator of this power was an ambiguous and controversial figure. In 1915 Sukhomlinov was dismissed and imprisoned on corruption charges, and two years later an inquiry found him guilty of negligence and treason. The officer corps was split between his protégés and his enemies. Yet he was responsible for much of the progress in the army down to 1914, and his detractors played up their criticisms for motives of opportunism.[266] Like Einem he opposed a broader citizen army, and resented civilian guard duties, wanting a professional force that would devote itself to war preparation.[267] Despite the assurances of the French Embassy in St Petersburg that he was loyal, there was good reason for the suspicion felt towards him in Paris.[268] Sukhomlinov saw the army as an instrument to be forged for the general purposes of Russian greatness, and not specifically for the Franco-Russian alliance. Danilov complained in retrospect of the 'suffocating' French influence on Russian strategy: the War Minister saw the French as financially necessary but considered their interest to be purely egotistic, and resented their 'pivotal role' despite their 'paltry military worth in war'.[269] His cultural and ideological kinship was with Germany, but he accepted that an armed clash with Vienna would also mean one with Berlin. Looking back on when he assumed office in March 1909, he commented:

the Tsar, Stolypin, the diplomats, and naturally also we military men demanded that the army should again become an instrument of high policy and enable Russia to reoccupy its place among the peoples of the world as a Great Power. My army reform was therefore not conditioned by any particular foreign policy constellation, although it naturally took the French alliance as a starting point; general considerations that without a combat-ready army no policy could be pursued . . . brought my plans to maturity. An army build-up is neither more nor less than the creation of an instrument that in all conceivable political conditions and conjunctures may be used by the State authorities peacefully or as a means of war.

From a 'purely defensive weapon' the army was to be turned into a 'first-class offensive' one, and because of the heightened likelihood of war with Germany, comparability with the latter must be the starting-point for all reforms.[270]

The 1910 reorganization should not be seen, however, as a reaction to Germany's intervention over Bosnia, for the planning had begun earlier and the Russians' dispositions were influenced by Asian rather than Balkan factors. In contrast with French planners who could focus on the Vosges, Russian ones felt ringed with enemies. There was a continuing need to garrison the interior against social unrest. In a European war two army corps would be needed to hold down Finland and protect the capital, the Swedes might land on the Baltic coast, and neither Balts nor Poles were dependable. A German military mission was

[266] Stone, *Eastern Front*, 25–7; Fuller, *Conflict*, 237–44.

[267] Sukhomlinov, *Erinnerungen*, 249. Fuller, *Conflict*, 242–58.

[268] Matton report, 6 Jan. 1912, SHA 7.N. 1487. Louis dispatch, 11 May 1912, AMAE NS Russie 41.

[269] Spring, 'Franco-Russian Alliance', 576. Sukhomlinov, *Erinnerungen*, 240–1.

[270] Ibid. 228, 331, 333.

helping to reorganize the Turkish army—much to Nicholas's resentment—and Russia might have to defend the Caucasus.[271] Already in the winter of 1907/8 Grand Duke Nicholas had advocated a redeployment towards the heart of the Empire so that the army could be used either in Europe or Asia, and Palitsyn had worked out the idea in detail. Sukhomlinov's thinking closely followed Palitsyn's, and he took particularly seriously the dangers in the Far East, which he did not believe Izvolsky's 1907 agreements with Britain and Japan had secured. He went beyond Palitsyn in his wish to abandon the western frontier fortresses and to concentrate as well as mobilize in the interior—views he adopted under the influence of Danilov and the fortification expert Major-General Vitner, who had no enthusiasm for fighting Germany on France's behalf.[272] Despite Sukhomlinov's tendency to measure himself against the German army, the reorganization originated as a general precautionary measure that was not expected to touch off an inter-bloc arms race.

As the reorganization proceeded, however, there was a return of confidence. When Sazonov replaced Izvolsky at the Foreign Ministry he considered that Russia's 'complete lack of military preparedness' had explained Germany's 'provocative action' in 1909; like Stolypin and Sukhomlinov he felt that European 'complications' must be avoided until the defences were made good.[273] Although Ministers did not expect war for at least a decade,[274] they shared Sukhomlinov's and the navy staff's belief that strong armed forces were needed to support diplomacy as well as to safeguard the country against attack, and they expected such support to be available soon. Bosnia was a wounding blow to national pride, but there was balm in the awareness, as Stolypin put it, that the army was progressing and 'in two to three years' time' (Izvolsky thought three to four) Russia 'would be able to face any likely combination and speak in European affairs with a very different voice'.[275] The Premier told the French Ambassador that 'we desire peace, but it is necessary for countries that are ill disposed to us more and more to feel our strength'.[276] Soon after the reorganization was initiated Sukhomlinov told the French attaché, Colonel Matton, that the Russians themselves were surprised at the acceleration of mobilization and concentration, and the Germans were very unhappy. During the Agadir crisis of 1911 he observed that if there was war 'you will see what progress our army has made'.[277] In the following February Matton reported that the Russians would never permit another humiliation like Bosnia, and soon afterwards they flexed their muscles in the Turco-Persian border dispute.[278] In May Sukhomlinov got

---

[271] Janin to Vignal, 27 Oct., 16 and 27 Nov., 24 Dec. 1910, 31 Mar. and 13 May 1911, SHA 7.N. 1485. Report by Captain Renty, 10 Oct. 1910, SHA 7.N. 1478. Zaionchovsky, *Podgotovka*, 184.

[272] Fuller, *Strategy*, 424–9.

[273] Sazonov, *Fateful Years*, 32.   [274] Sidorov, *Finansovoe polozhenie*, 61, 70.

[275] Nicolson to Grey, 7 May 1909, *BDFA*, IA v, doc. 280 [Stolypin]. Nicolson to Grey, 24 Mar. 1909, *BD* v, doc. 761 [Izvolsky].

[276] Louis dispatch, 6 Nov. 1910, *DDF* 2nd ser. xiii, doc. 14.

[277] Matton report, 17 Feb. 1911, ibid. doc. 157; and Louis dispatch, 26 Aug. 1911, ibid. xiv, doc. 211.

[278] Matton report, 6 Jan. 1912, SHA 7.N. 1487.

his re-equipment credit, and a new recruitment law, which reduced the categories of exemptions, allowed him to improve the quality of the annual intake without yet increasing its size.[279] By now, moreover, the danger of a European confrontation seemed to be eclipsing that in Asia. Sukhomlinov suspended demolition of the Polish fortresses and began upgrading their artillery.[280]

The clearest sign of reappraisal was Plan 19 Altered, a modified version of the 1910 mobilization schedule that Nicholas approved in May 1912. At a meeting in February of military representatives, Alekseev renewed the call for an offensive into Galicia. France seemed a stronger partner after the Agadir crisis, and Britain was thought more likely to intervene. The Russian military detested Austria-Hungary, and had excellent intelligence about its weaknesses, although they still feared that unless they struck first its relatively quickly mobilizing armies would penetrate into Russian Poland and foment insurrection. On the other hand, they respected Germany and had no desire to fight it, but Danilov was worried about a German standing-start attack, and wanted extra forces opposite East Prussia. In addition, the French were pressing for an early blow against Germany to relieve the strain in the West, and in the 1911 staff talks Zhilinski promised an offensive on day 15. Plan 19 Altered was a compromise between Danilov's cautious anti-German orientation and Alekseev's more adventurous anti-Austrian one, but there was an evident change of emphasis. Variant A of the plan, which would apply unless countermanded, assumed that Germany's main forces would go west: sixteen army corps would be assigned against the Habsburg Monarchy and nine against Germany, and both forces would attack. Variant G, which envisaged a massive German onslaught and a defensive concentration on the northern Polish frontier, would apply only if specifically authorized.[281]

* * *

The 1910 reorganization was pivotal in the origins of the European land arms race not only because of its effect on Russian capabilities but also because of its impact on the other Powers and on the balance between the Triple Entente and the Austro-German alliance. The British attachés expected from the start that it would strengthen Russia militarily, and although the Director of Military Operations, Sir Henry Wilson, had a low opinion of Russian capacities, the Foreign Office believed by 1912 that Russia was much stronger than four years previously, and that the danger of war had correspondingly increased.[282] The French, in contrast, at first felt great anxiety, not least because St Petersburg kept them in the dark. In March 1910 the 2nd Bureau still had only 'extremely vague information'.[283] The French Ambassador feared that the new concentration would prolong from nineteen to thirty days the delay before the Russians

[279] GGS report on changes in Russia, second quarter of 1911, n.d., KAM Gstb 208.
[280] Fuller, *Strategy*, 437.
[281] Ibid. 442–5. Shatsillo, *Rossia*, 87. Snyder, *Ideology*, 172–81.
[282] Nicolson annual report, 30 Dec. 1909, *BDFA*, IA v, doc. 328. Wyndham to Nicolson, 6 Apr. 1910; Nicolson report, 22 Mar. 1911, ibid. vi, docs. 14, 62. Ropponen, *Kraft*, 239.
[283] Wehrlin note, 18 Mar. 1910, SHA 7.N. 1535.

could invade Germany, and that Moltke could reduce his eastern covering force to a single corps.[284] French General Staff appraisals were similar.[285] The EMA wanted a strong Russian presence west of the Vistula, which would force Germany to station more troops in the East in peacetime. They also wanted better railways up to the river and fortified crossing points, to facilitate an early offensive from the tip of the salient.[286] All of this ran counter to Danilov's and Sukhomlinov's plans.

Subsequent disclosures gave the French little reassurance, and the rift in the alliance became more open. The Russian attaché in Berlin told his French opposite number that Germany would strike first in the East and that France could not be counted on: the Russians still intended to attack, but would be ready to do so with all their forces only two weeks after their ally. The EMA replied that France would launch an immediate offensive—though it is difficult to reconcile this with the counterstroke conception of Plan XVI. It was evident that the westernmost fortresses would be levelled and the Russian concentration take place further to the rear, and that Bosnia had shaken St Petersburg's confidence in Paris. Nor were there any plans for new western strategic railways.[287] In May 1910 the new peacetime deployment was attacked in the prestigious and semi-official Paris daily, *Le Temps*. In fact the article had not been government-inspired, but the Russians protested and the French Ambassador in Berlin warned that the reorganization could be seen as undermining the alliance. Pichon agreed: 'we must have "sureties".' Laffon de Ladébat, the CGS, speculated that the Russians might intend simply to wait upon events. If they did attack it could be fifteen to twenty days later than France did and this was 'far too much. No precision, in spite of all our efforts.' Pichon asked his ambassador to speak 'very clearly', and Izvolsky promised a formal briefing from Gerngross.[288]

From now on, the French War Ministry began to view the reorganization more favourably, although the Quai d'Orsay took longer to fall into line. The autumn conversations between the Chiefs of Staff went well, Gerngross promising to cross the German frontier on about day 20.[289] Admittedly, the Russo-German summit meeting at Potsdam in October–November 1910 caused renewed anxiety. Sazonov dropped his opposition to the German-financed Berlin–Baghdad railway in return for German undertakings not to support the

---

[284] Nicolson to Grey, 8 May 1909, *BDFA*, IA v, doc. 71.

[285] 'Résumé des conclusions de l'étude de juin 1909 . . .' (note submitted to CGS, n.d., SHA 7.N. 1537). EMA 2nd Bureau, 'Note sur le stationnement de l'armée russe . . .' and 'Étude sur la situation militaire de la Russie . . .', Dec. 1909, SHA 7.N. 1535.

[286] Wehrlin note, 18 Mar. 1910, ibid. EMA 2nd Bureau note, 10 Feb. 1910, SHA 7.N. 1538.

[287] Pellé to Brun, 23 Jan., 6 and 24 Mar. 1910, *DDF* 2nd ser. xii, docs. 399, 453, 467. Pellé to Vignal, 7 Mar. 1910, SHA 7.N. 1537. Wehrlin note, 18 Mar. 1910, SHA 7.N. 1535. Matton report No. 125 (?15 pr. 1910), ibid.

[288] Jules Cambon to Pichon, 30 May 1910, *DDF* 2nd ser. xii, doc. 504. Laffon de Ladébat note, 22 May 1910, SHA 7.N. 1538 (with minute by Pichon); Pichon to Louis, 2 June and Louis to Pichon, 16 June 1910, AMAE NS Russie 40.

[289] Gerngross/Laffon de Ladébat conversations, 20–1 Sept. 1910, *DDF* 2nd ser. xii, doc. 573.

Austrians in further Balkan expansion.[290] Once again the French were not consulted, Pichon recording the 'emotion' in the Paris press and the Government's
'astonishment'. He quizzed the War Minister, Brun, about 'the offensive value
of our allies'. In contrast to earlier assessments, however, Brun now thought the
new deployment neither enhanced nor diminished Russia's effectiveness:
Germany would have to keep 'a serious portion' of its forces in the East, and the
tsarist army would be able to launch an offensive 'within a very acceptable time
limit'.[291] Although Pichon was still doubtful, by 1913 the EMA considered that
the 1910 reforms had 'in no way diminished the military value of the Russian
alliance'.[292]

Within this context of a recovery of nerve, moreover, the Franco-Russian staff
talks led to firm commitments, in contrast to the previous evasiveness. In July
1912 the two navies agreed to exchange information: there was little scope for
joint operational planning, but the Central Powers suspected that the understanding amounted to more than it did.[293] On land, Zhilinski gave his pledge in
1911 that as far as possible the two sides would attack Germany simultaneously
and that he would attempt to start on day 15. He admitted that the army would
not have its full complement of field artillery until 1913 or of machine guns until
1914, and that there was not the slightest chance of success against Germany for
another two years, but he had emphatically broken with Gerngross's suggestion
of day 20 and Danilov's belief that the earliest feasible was day 23. The 2nd
Bureau still questioned whether the offensive would materialize, but in 1912
the Russians repeated the promise, specifying an attacking force of 800,000
men.[294]

Given this Russian commitment, it was not surprising that by 1912 the issue
of strategic railways was coming to the fore. During the reorganization they were
a low priority for Sukhomlinov, and the Russian General Staff feared that they
would be taken over by German invaders.[295] Conversely, the French had already
tried to tie railway building to the 1909 loan, and now that Russia was mobilizing further into the interior the EMA considered rapid transit to the frontier to
be more critical than ever.[296] The 2nd Bureau began defining what it wanted,
and Lt.-Col. Janin, who was attached to the Nicholas Academy in 1910–11,
examined construction priorities and ways of raising throughput on existing

[290] J. A. Head, 'Public Opinion and Middle Eastern Railway Negotiations: The Russo-German
Negotiations of 1910–11', *International History Review*, 6 (1984), 28–47.

[291] Pichon to Paul Cambon, 11 Dec. 1910; Pichon to Brun, 7 Dec. 1910, AMAE NS Russie 40.
Brun to Pichon, 14 Dec. 1910, *DDF* 2nd ser. xii, doc. 83.

[292] Pichon to Louis, 15 Dec. 1910, AMAE NS Russie 40. 'Note sur la transformation de l'armée
russe . . .', June 1913, SHA 7.N. 1538.

[293] Franco-Russian naval convention, 16 July; Quai d'Orsay circular, 10 Aug.; Louis to Poincaré,
28 Aug. 1912, AMAE NS Russie 41.

[294] Sukhomlinov, *Erinnerungen*, 254–63. Janin note on the value of Russian co-operation, Dec.
1911, SHA 7.N. 1538.

[295] Matton report No. 125 (?15 Apr. 1910), SHA 7.N. 1535. Snyder, *Ideology*, 174.

[296] Pichon to Touchard, 23 Jan. 1909, AMAE NS Russie 58. Note by EMA 2nd Bureau, 8 July
1912, SHA 7.N. 1538.

lines.[297] Yet the 2nd Bureau's information was that Russia would do little until 1913, and what they learnt of Plan 19 Altered left the French dismayed.[298] In the July 1912 staff conversations, Joffre, the new French CGS, asked Zhilinski for all lines to the frontier to be double-tracked and some to be quadrupled, the two men agreeing on a list of desirable projects. Invited to comment on what the Prime Minister, Raymond Poincaré, should emphasize when he visited Russia in August, Joffre pointed to the railway improvements, and mentioned nothing else.[299] Poincaré took a memorandum with him and spoke to Kokovtsov, who set out his own building plans and said that he would need to borrow in Paris in order to implement them.[300] The exchange prefigured the Franco-Russian railway loan negotiations of 1913–14, which were central to armaments diplomacy in the last year of peace.

It is now time to look at the other side of the hill. Moltke and Conrad corresponded optimistically in February 1910 about the eastward displacement of the Russian concentration, Conrad thinking it would delay a Russian offensive and Moltke that it would facilitate a German one.[301] However, Conrad with his Italian fixation may have been atypical. The Evidenzbureau thought the reorganization had decisively improved Russian mobilization and striking power,[302] and as 1912 went on Auffenberg and Schemua began to reckon seriously with the danger. The evidence from Vienna is of mounting apprehension but of no sudden movement of fear.

In Berlin there was a more dramatic turnaround. The GGS was informed early and fully, and Moltke sent Bülow a remarkably accurate assessment of Russian intentions as early as May 1909. His first impression was that he could send more troops against the French and would have more time to seek a decision in the West. The German press was advised not to gloat over the redeployment, the leadership regarding it as a favourable development and not wishing to prejudice the Russian debate.[303] By the end of 1910, however, at the same time as the 2nd Bureau of the EMA became more optimistic, the 1st Division of the GGS judged that the reorganization would significantly increase Russian preparedness. The military had reported to the Foreign Ministry in August that Russia's peacetime deployment opposite the eastern frontier would alter little; the 1st Division concluded that in a war the new Kazan reserve would probably be directed against Germany, and 'there can be no talk of an allevia-

[297] Note by EMA 2nd Bureau, 30 May 1910, SHA 7.N. 1535. Janin to Vignal, 10 and 23 June 1911, SHA 7.N. 1485.

[298] EMA 2nd Bureau, 'Plan d'études de voies ferrées nouvelles en Russie', Mar. 1911, SHA 7.N. 1535. EMA 2nd Bureau note of 8 July 1912, SHA 7.N. 1538.

[299] Sukhomlinov, *Erinnerungen*, 262. Joffre to Paléologue, 30 July 1912, AMAE NS Russie 41.

[300] EMA 3rd Bureau, 'Note sur l'action militaire de la Russie en Europe', 3 Aug. 1912, SHA 7.N. 1538. Kokovtsov, *Out of my Past*, 334–5.

[301] Conrad, *Dienstzeit*, ii. 57–9.

[302] Ropponen, *Kraft*, 241.

[303] Moltke to Bülow, 29 May; Schoen press directive, 2 June 1909, PAAA R.10450.

tion . . . rather of intensified pressure'.[304] The reports from St Petersburg caused Wilhelm to demand that Germany should do more, although at first he was dissuaded by Bülow's successor, Bethmann Hollweg, and by Moltke.[305] Subsequently, the latter modified his view. By the end of 1911 he was advocating an army increase, on the grounds that Russia could concentrate twice as quickly as five years previously: 'It is not correct to assert that Russia will for long remain unready for a European war'. According to the War Minister, Heeringen, the changed deployment had seemed at first 'a weakening relative to Germany', but had proved to be the opposite. The central army of seven corps could quickly reach the frontier, and with the halving of Russia's mobilization and concentration times 'our situation in the east has taken on a quite different appearance and therewith our general position compared with 1910 has altered very significantly to our disadvantage'.[306] Although these were pieces of advocacy, they confirm the military perception of an altered balance. When Tsar and Kaiser met at Baltic Port in June 1912 Kokovtsov protested that Germany's armaments were making it impossible for him to resist the pressure to retaliate, although Russia's 1910 fortress and deployment programmes had shown her purely defensive intentions. Bethmann replied that 'there was nothing left . . . but to keep in check the inevitable march of events, hoping that all countries would have so many interests in common as to view armaments as a measure of prevention without allowing them to be actually applied'. Nicholas told Kokovtsov that Wilhelm had assured him he would not let Balkan complications cause a world conflagration. 'Nevertheless', the Tsar concluded, 'we must get ready. It is a good thing we succeeded in adopting the naval programme; besides, we have to prepare our land defence.'[307]

* * *

We may leave Bethmann and Kokovtsov at Baltic Port, two men of prudence fumbling for a terrain of restraint as the shadows from the Victorian sunset lengthened. German perceptions of the Russian reorganization moved inversely to those of France, and in retrospect it seemed the opening of an eastern arms race. One half of the four-Power, two-bloc competition of 1912–14 may now be seen as virtually *in situ*. Two points should be reiterated. One is the erosion of internal obstacles to expanded armaments. In Vienna by 1912 the War Minister and the CGS formed a united front with a new Foreign Minister and the Austrian Government. Even Hungary had accepted dreadnoughts, the Schönaich Pact, and the 1912 military law. In St Petersburg Kokovtsov loosened his control as the army and navy unified their leadership and honed their lobbying skills with the advent of Sukhomlinov and Grigorovich. The second point is the

[304] GGS 1. Abt. annual report on Russia for 1910, KAM Gstb 208. Report to Kiderlen-Wächter, 'Die Reorganisation der russischen Armee', Aug. 1910; report by GGS 1. Abt., 14 Nov. 1910, PAAA R.10450.
[305] See Ch. 4, sect. 1, below.
[306] Moltke to Bethmann Hollweg, 2 Dec. 1911, PAAA R.789. Heeringen to Bethmann Hollweg, 22 Mar. 1912, BA Rklei R.43F/953.
[307] Kokovtsov, *Out of my Past*, 321–3.

realigned axis of effort. In 1908–11 Austria-Hungary's chief 'enemy' for purposes of defence policy was its ally, Italy, and in managing this antagonism Aehrenthal preferred to hold land (though not naval) armaments in check. Higher preparedness also seemed necessary in the Balkans, although after the impetus given by the annexation the Serbian and Montenegrin build-ups lost steam. By 1912, however, in Austrian calculations the possibility of war with Russia was regaining prominence. In St Petersburg, Turkey became more significant for the naval planners after 1910 and it was the Young Turks who initiated the Black Sea race. But the main weight of naval resources was directed to the Baltic, albeit with a view to possible realignment in favour of Germany as well as to hostility. The army's 1910 reorganization, like the Baltic naval programme, was initially ambiguous, and designed to meet Asian as much as European exigencies. Hence the difficulty for France and Germany in reading its significance. By 1912, however, as Russian confidence grew, a defensive war plan was replaced by a recklessly offensive one, discussion turned to the strategic railways, and France was promised 800,000 men on day 15. The Franco-Russian alliance had survived its time of testing, and Germany's situation had unmistakably worsened.

Russia's experience differed from Austria-Hungary's in the role played by its ally. Moltke refrained from pressing Vienna to redirect resources from south-west to north-east, although in his 1909 talks with Conrad he urged an Austrian attack in Galicia and promised a concurrent eastern offensive. French policy, however, had a single-mindedness that the Russian lacked. There was an anti-Austrian animus, especially after Bosnia, at the Russian court and in the élite, as well as rising Germanophobia in the Duma and the press, but the Tsar and Foreign Minister still wished to keep relations with Berlin below danger level, and Danilov and Sukhomlinov had a healthy respect for German strength. To an extent the Russians edged in spite of themselves into a contest with Germany in these years, although such a contest was the logical culmination of French efforts, an immediate offensive from the left bank of the Vistula persisting as a lodestar for the EMA. The Russians wished to reconstruct their forces after war and revolution, and to have the wherewithal to back up their diplomacy in crises. They hoped to modify the balance of power and were dissatisfied with the status quo, but they did not want war, and there was no Conrad in St Petersburg. Indeed, the Austrian leaders too, apart from the CGS, wished to intimidate rather than fight Serbia and Italy, and had no wish or incentive to engage in armaments rivalry with Russia. The Russians began from their hostility to Austria and accepted the French alliance as a counter to German support for the Ottomans and Habsburgs. But under French influence their resurgence after 1910 took on an anti-German as well as an anti-Austrian edge. By the end of 1912 the inter-bloc arms race in the East was taking off. The annexation crisis had encouraged it, but was not in itself a fault-line in armaments policies. For such a break a further crisis was needed, and this need the Balkan Wars supplied.

4

The Breakdown of Equilibrium in the West, *1908–1912*

1. The Western European Triangle before the Second Moroccan Crisis

In Western as in Eastern Europe, until the Agadir crisis of 1911, diplomatic and military lines of tension still coincided only partially. As Habsburg armaments efforts remained directed against Italy and Serbia rather than against Russia, so German rivalry with France on land remained less acute than German rivalry with Britain at sea. Competition between the two great Continental military blocs proceeded in slow motion. This chapter will focus on the events of 1911, and the extent to which they marked a watershed in armaments policies. It will concentrate especially on Germany's reorientation of priorities from the naval to the land race, which became manifest in 1911–12 although its origins dated back further. Already before Agadir the German navy was losing the initiative against Britain; and the army was beginning to revolt against the constraints placed on it while the capacities of its potential enemies grew.

* * *

Tirpitz's 1908 *Novelle* led to an unanswerable increase in British building rates, which undermined the Admiral in Berlin and eased the way for the army's rival bid. The Liberal Government laid down three dreadnought battleships or battle-cruisers in 1906–7 and in 1907–8, and two in 1908–9. But it laid down eight in 1909–10 and five each in 1910–11 and 1911–12. With two further ships being started at Australia's and New Zealand's expense, this totalled eighteen in 1909–11, against eight in the previous three years.[1] Initially the Liberals had slackened off construction—and offered, if Germany would negotiate, to slacken off more. They had been supported by the Sea Lords, including Fisher, who had unofficially urged the Unionist opposition to moderate its attacks. But the *Novelle* was an unprecedented challenge to Britain's superiority. In the Cabinet debates in early 1908 the Admiralty fended off Treasury and Radical pressure for new reductions. It won approval to lay down one battleship and one battle-cruiser in 1908–9, in order to maintain building capacity for the possibility of a much bigger increase, unless Germany desisted, in the following year. The

---

[1] J. T. Sumida, *In Defence of Naval Supremacy: Finance, Technology, and British Naval Policy, 1889–1914* (Boston, 1989), 186, 190.

Radicals in the Commons pressed for a division, whose outcome showed that they were comfortably outnumbered by Liberal moderates who believed that enough retrenchment was enough. Radical influence suffered further when in April 1908 Campbell-Bannerman was replaced as Premier by Asquith, who had just promised the Unionists that the Government would build what was necessary to preserve Britain's lead. The Radicals' defeat in the struggle of 1908 foreshadowed their defeat in the greater struggle that followed.[2]

Construction capacity was the crucial issue. The Government had hitherto maintained that Britain could produce dreadnoughts significantly faster than could Germany: an assumption the Unionists challenged.[3] In October 1908 Tirpitz placed orders early for two of the four capital ships scheduled for 1909–10, but he did so in order to profit from low prices and to protect the shipyards in a recession while heading off the formation of a shipbuilders' cartel. The completion dates were not brought forward.[4] The Admiralty, however, was coming to suspect that the Germans were secretly exceeding the *Novelle*'s provisions. According to Reginald McKenna, the new First Lord, they had laid down four dreadnoughts in 1907, two in 1908, and just ordered four more. They would have thirteen in commission by the spring of 1911 and probably twenty-one by the spring of 1912, although according to the published schedule there would be twenty-one only by February 1914.[5] McKenna and the Sea Lords now followed the Unionists in assuming that the only safe guide to the likely size of Germany's fleet was Germany's ability to build it, which they estimated generously. They knew that supplies of armour-plate and gun mountings (rather than hulls) were Britain's weak point. They had information that Krupp had greatly increased its resources in both areas (which was true) and was stockpiling nickel. As McKenna vouched that Germany's capacity to build dreadnoughts equalled Britain's it appeared that the Royal Navy had levelled the playing field to its own disadvantage and risked losing in an equal fight.[6]

There was little evidence that Germany would moderate its challenge by negotiating. Grey had always insisted that a *rapprochement* was conditional on a reduction in naval spending, but he failed to achieve this either at The Hague in 1907 or through bilateral contacts in the following year. In April 1908 he told Clemenceau that there were about twelve months in hand to measure the progress of German construction: if Tirpitz made the advances that were

---

[2] A. Sidorowicz, 'Social Reform, Free Trade, and the Quest for Peace, 1907–1914' (TS, 1991), ch. 4, A. J. Marder, *From the Dreadnought to Scapa Flow* (London, 1961), 135–9. R. F. Mackay, *Fisher of Kilverstone* (Oxford, 1973), 386–90. A. J. A. Morris, *Radicalism against War, 1906–1914: The Advocacy of Peace and Retrenchment* (Totowa, NJ, 1972), 122–32.

[3] R. Williams, *Defending the Empire: The Conservative Party and British Defence Policy, 1899–1915* (New Haven, 1991), 89–92.

[4] McKenna, 'Navy Estimates, 1909–10', BLO Asquith MSS 21. McKenna to Asquith, 3 Jan. 1909, CCAC, McKenna MSS 3/19.

[5] Marder, *Dreadnought*, 151–5, cf. J. Steinberg, 'The *Novelle* of 1908', *Transactions of the Royal Historical Society*, 5th ser. 21 (1971), 40–1. Tirpitz to Bülow, 17 Mar. 1909, *GP* xxviii, doc. 10272.

[6] Sea Lords to McKenna, 18 Jan. 1909, CCAC Fisher MSS 1/7. McKenna to Asquith, 3 Jan. 1909, CCAC McKenna MSS 3/19. Marder, *Dreadnought*, 151.

expected, Britain must respond or there would be a panic that would overthrow the Liberal Government.[7] Before Edward VII and Sir Charles Hardinge, the Permanent Under-Secretary of the Foreign Office, met Wilhelm II at Cronberg in August, Grey advised that in the absence of agreement a fresh construction effort was inevitable. But the summit went badly, Wilhelm insisting that the programme specified in the Navy Law was a matter of honour, over which he would go to war.[8] Nothing more resulted from an alternative channel opened by Grey between the German Ambassador, Count Metternich, and the leading Cabinet Radical and new Chancellor of the Exchequer, David Lloyd George. Lloyd George had told the Commons that Britain had the larger responsibility for the naval race and he wanted to divert armaments spending into social welfare. He suggested to Metternich a 3:2 ratio, which was probably more favourable to Tirpitz than the Cabinet would have accepted. But when he followed up by visiting Germany in the summer he cast about in vain for an interlocutor.[9] The negotiating track was leading nowhere, and despite the warnings of British retribution there were no signs that the Germans were slowing down. In October 1908, moreover, the *Daily Telegraph* published its notorious interview with Wilhelm, in which he said that although he personally was well disposed towards Britain his subjects were not and he was growing tired of being misrepresented. Even without the Admiralty's suspicions of a secret acceleration, strategic, diplomatic, and domestic political developments were all pushing the Liberals towards an increase.

When the Cabinet began considering the 1909–10 estimates, discussion centred not on the necessity for a response to the *Novelle* but on its timing and its size. 'The rate at which we have to build new Dreadnoughts is practically ruled by what is being done or projected in Germany, in order that we may be certain of a substantial superiority in 1911 or 1912', reported Asquith to the King.[10] To Grey he commented that 'nobody here understands why Germany would need or how she can use 21 Dreadnoughts, unless for aggressive purposes, and primarily against ourselves'.[11] The Admiralty claimed six ships rather than four because of the evidence of German acceleration,[12] but Winston Churchill assailed McKenna's projections and Lloyd George argued that Tirpitz was speeding up in order to combat the recession (which he himself had suggested that McKenna should do). He wrote to Churchill that the Admirals 'are procuring false information to frighten us'.[13] The Cabinet approved 'in substance' McKenna's opening request for six dreadnoughts, but delayed commitment to

[7] Sidorowicz, 'Social Reform', 87.

[8] Ibid. Wilhelm to Bülow, 13 Aug. 1908, *GP* xxiv, doc. 8226.

[9] M. G. Fry, *Lloyd George and Foreign Policy*, i. *The Education of a Statesman, 1890–1916* (Montreal, 1977), 93–7. D. Lloyd George, *War Memoirs*, i (London, 1933), 11–31.

[10] Asquith to Edward VII, 19 Dec. 1908, BLO Asquith MSS 5.

[11] Asquith to McKenna, 1 Jan. 1909, CCAC McKenna MSS 3/3.

[12] Asquith to Edward VII, 19 Dec. 1908, BLO Asquith MSS 5.

[13] Cited in R. S. Churchill, *Winston S. Churchill*, ii. *Young Statesman, 1901–1914* (London, 1967), 516–17; cf. Fry, *Lloyd George*, i. 106–7.

two of them, which did not need to be laid down before March 1910, in the lingering hope that diplomacy might render them unnecessary. Early in 1909, however, by which time further soundings had proved fruitless, the Sea Lords prevailed on McKenna to raise his demand to eight ships, the absolute maximum that he believed Britain could build.[14] Asquith's compromise, reached in a Cabinet meeting on 24 February that began with a briefing on the aggravation of the Bosnian crisis, was for four dreadnoughts to be laid down anyway, and for Parliament to authorize the Government to lay down four more by April 1910 if necessary. Powers would be taken to ready gun mountings and other materials in advance, and the firms producing or able to produce mountings and turrets would be invited to expand capacity, with an assurance of Admiralty contracts. This would re-establish Britain's industrial lead, and if all eight ships were ordered Britain would have twenty by April 1912, providing 'more than the necessary margin of superiority'.[15]

There were differing interpretations of what the compromise meant. McKenna was uneasy, and Fisher and the Sea Lords wanted an earlier and firmer commitment. New evidence arrived from two Argentinian visitors to Germany that twelve or thirteen dreadnoughts were in progress there and Krupp was finishing one hundred 11" and 12" guns.[16] H. H. Mulliner, the Managing Director of the Coventry Ordnance Works, provided corroborating information. Much of his evidence was tainted, as it came from Ehrhardt, and Mulliner was an interested party, in that the Cabinet's decision allowed his firm to join Armstrong and Vickers as a turret and mountings supplier. None the less, he was called upon to brief the CID, and the Admiralty and the Prime Minister took him seriously.[17] Asquith pledged to McKenna that the extra ships would be laid down if (as he thought probable) they were shown to be needed. Grey told Fisher that Britain should build as fast as possible until the situation was well in hand, and if only four were ordered immediately it was because of capacity limits.[18] A footnote in the estimates gave notice that the Government would order the extra ships if national safety required it, which was for the Admiralty to judge. Strictly the Cabinet was not committed to order the 'footnote four', although materials for them would be gathered now: in practice the Sea Lords controlled the position. Although Tirpitz gave an assurance that Germany would not have thirteen dreadnoughts earlier than the end of 1912 the British Government decided in July to go ahead, after receiving news of Italy's and especially Austria-Hungary's intentions to build all-big-gun ships, which the

---

[14] McKenna to Asquith, 1 Jan. 1909, BLO Asquith MSS 21.

[15] Asquith to Edward VII, 24 Feb. 1909, BLO Asquith MSS 5.

[16] McKenna to Asquith, 25 Feb. 1909; Sea Lords to McKenna, 4 Mar. 1909, CCAC McKenna MSS 3/19.

[17] Ottley to McKenna, 25 Feb. 1909, ibid. 3/14. 'Navy Estimates' (minutes of conference of 23 Feb. 1909), BLO Asquith MSS 21. Marder, *Dreadnought*, 156–9.

[18] Asquith to McKenna, 2 Mar. 1909, CCAC McKenna MSS 3/19; note by Grey, 4 Mar. 1909, CCAC Fisher MSS 1/17; cf. *Fear God and Dread Nought: The Correspondence of Admiral of the Fleet Lord Fisher of Kilverstone*, ii. *Years of Power, 1904–1914*, ed. A. J. Marder (London, 1956), docs. 165, 167.

Admiralty suspected had been orchestrated with Berlin. The information facilitated a decision that most of the Cabinet were probably steeled to anyway.[19]

The February compromise was symptomatic of a larger change in British politics and the collapse of resistance to armaments increases. Asquith's public warning that Britain could no longer count on building dreadnoughts faster than Germany apparently silenced the Radicals, who never regained their earlier influence. The 'footnote four' were voted through by 290:98, only thirty-seven Liberal MPs joining the Irish and Labour opposition.[20] In concentrating on their critics within the Liberal Party, however, Asquith and McKenna opened their flank to Unionist charges that they were not doing enough, especially when the latter admitted he had miscalculated the pace of German construction. Hence the Opposition, briefed by Mulliner and egged on by Fisher, pressed for the supplementary ships to be ordered at once, and launched the biggest navalist agitation of the pre-1914 years.[21]

The Liberals regained the initiative, however, with Lloyd George's 'People's Budget', introduced in April 1909 to finance both the navy and social reform, to combat the fiscal crisis caused by the recession, and to increase direct taxes as an alternative to Unionist demands for protective tariffs. Lloyd George may have acquiesced in higher naval estimates because they would strengthen his hand in a prospective confrontation with the House of Lords: at any rate, he could argue that having clamoured for eight capital ships the wealthy should now pay for them. Although the Lords threw out the budget the Liberals and their allies did well enough in the extraordinary election of January 1910 to be able to get it through. In conjunction with economic recovery it raised government revenue by more than 30 per cent between 1908–9 and 1913–14, naval spending going up from £32.2 to £48.8 million over the same period.[22] By the time of the estimates debate in the winter of 1910/11 McKenna could report that if Germany stuck to the *Novelle* and dropped back to two ships a year from 1912 Britain too could afford to relax.[23]

By this stage it was becoming clear that the Admiralty's fears had been exaggerated. The German capital ships laid down after 1908 were not completed ahead of time, and in April 1912 Tirpitz had only nine dreadnoughts available. Britain's fifteen at this date, however, were fewer than the twenty McKenna had thought possible if eight ships were laid down in 1909–10, and in the first year of the World War the 'footnote four' gave Britain a precarious advantage.[24] The Unionists may have been right to fear that in the first years of the naval

[19] Marder, *Dreadnought*, 159–71. Williams, *Defending*, 158–9.

[20] Morris, *Radicalism*, 165–6. H. Weinroth, 'Left-Wing Opposition to Naval Armaments in Britain before 1914', *Journal of Contemporary History*, 6 (1971), 110–18.

[21] Williams, *Defending*, 162–74. A. J. A. Morris, *The Scaremongers: The Advocacy of War and Rearmament, 1896–1914* (London, 1984), ch. 13.

[22] B. R. Mitchell and P. Deane, *Abstract of British Historical Statistics* (Cambridge, 1962), 398. Fry, *Lloyd George*, 115–16. B. K. Murray, *The People's Budget, 1909/10: Lloyd George and Liberal Politics* (Oxford, 1980), 127–30.

[23] Fry, *Lloyd George*, 123–4. Marder, *Dreadnought*, 214–15.

[24] McKenna to Asquith, 3 Jan. 1909, CCAC McKenna MSS 3/19. Marder, *Dreadnought*, 177–9.

revolution the Liberals had run excessive risks. In 1909 the Cabinet had to make decisions that bore critically on British national security, in a fast-moving technological competition against a formidable adversary whose capabilities and intentions were obscure. In these circumstances there was much to be said for the Grey and McKenna policy of building until Britain was out of trouble,[25] and effectively this was what the British Government did. From now onwards the Admiralty abandoned the two-Power standard and pursued a 60 per cent margin over Germany, although the new policy was not publicly admitted until 1912. It operated in a more sympathetic public climate, and the taming of the Lords broke resistance to the fiscal underpinnings of Liberal policy.

At first sight the acceleration crisis supports a military-industrial complex interpretation of British policy-making. Much more than on land, industrial capacity was central. In both Britain and Germany the 1908–9 recession played a role, in that Tirpitz and McKenna tried to place orders counter-cyclically, and concern to alleviate working-class distress was one reason why Radical opposition to the estimates faded away. Mulliner briefed both Liberals and Unionists and, as the director of a newly established enterprise that badly needed orders, he had much to gain. Yet his earlier warnings had been ignored, and essentially both the Admiralty and the Cabinet were reacting to what they thought the Germans were doing. Both the Liberal Imperialist and the Radical wings of the Government, including Grey as well as Lloyd George,[26] would have preferred to keep down taxes or spend money on social reform, but the evidence of German intentions and the failure of diplomacy moved Grey and enough members of the Cabinet to back McKenna for Asquith to be forced to address the issue if he wished to avoid a split. This he did through his crab-like motion towards ordering eight capital ships. Britain secured its numerical superiority, and in this sense it 'won' the naval race.

* * *

Tirpitz denied there was a race at all, maintaining that he was simply executing the Navy Law.[27] But he wished to get through the danger zone as fast as possible, and the 1908 *Novelle* would assist him in doing so, while not increasing the ultimate target of fifty-eight capital ships.[28] The essence of the Tirpitz Plan, as he reminded Wilhelm, was the risk principle of deterring attack, and given the Royal Navy's worldwide commitments he did not need numerical parity in order to implement it.[29] In the mean time the Germans rebuffed British approaches with the plea that a law that had received parliamentary sanction could not be overturned at foreign behest. The strengths it specified were premissed on

[25] Grey note of 4 Mar. 1909, Fisher, *Fear God*, doc. 165.

[26] Grey speech to Iron and Steel Institute, reported in *The Times*, 15 May 1908. Fry, *Lloyd George*, 93.

[27] Tirpitz to Henry of Prussia, 28 Jan. 1907, V. R. Berghahn and W. Deist (eds.), *Rüstung im Zeichen der Wilhelminischen Weltpolitik* (Düsseldorf, 1988), doc. vii/7.

[28] Undated Navy Office memo (*c*.Apr. 1911?), 'Ganz Geheim', BA-MA Tirpitz MSS N. 253/24b.

[29] Draft for Tirpitz conference with Wilhelm, 24 Oct. 1910, Berghahn and Deist (eds.), *Rüstung*, doc. vii/11.

Germany's absolute requirements for protecting its coastline, colonies, and trade, and could not be made dependent on British construction.[30]

After the acceleration crisis, in contrast, Germany was willing to take the initiative, and there was a move from confrontation to negotiation in the North Sea. The reappraisal seems to have begun with Bülow himself. By 1908 the naval programme, so far from consolidating support for the authorities, had divided their Reichstag supporters over how to pay for it. The Chancellor needed to check the growth of naval spending if he was to contain a deepening financial crisis, and he was coming to regret the fleet's expansion at the army's expense.[31] The fortune of Germany, he told the Bundesrat, 'lay in the strength of the army. It must, above all, be kept strong.'[32] In addition, the naval build-up had failed to yield the expected diplomatic pay-off. Bülow was probably influenced by Metternich's reports that the Liberals were determined to maintain Britain's lead,[33] and by the advice of Albert Ballin, the head of the Hamburg-Amerika shipping line and a friend of the Emperor, that the naval programme was the main cause of tension with London and Germany could not match Britain's financial strength.[34] Having previously rejected internationally agreed limits on Germany's armed forces, in July 1908 the Chancellor for the first time raised with Wilhelm the possibility that naval building might be eased in return for a British pledge not to support a French attack on Germany, but the Emperor said no.[35] After the Cronberg meeting, in which he thought Wilhelm's behaviour dangerously provocative, Bülow urged that Germany could not outspend Britain, and that a race might lead to a war against the Triple Entente in which the Royal Navy could inflict much more damage than could Germany in return. They should not refuse negotiation in principle, but do what was necessary to protect the fleet during the next four critical years.[36]

By September Bülow had secured Wilhelm's agreement not to go beyond the 1908 *Novelle*, and Tirpitz's to forgo a further Navy Law if Britain gave a political quid pro quo.[37] But he had little to offer in naval reductions, and he envisaged a high political price. His authority over Wilhelm was faltering—and was diminished further by the *Daily Telegraph* episode—and a hard-hitting correspondence in the winter of 1908/9 showed that much still separated him from the Navy Secretary. Bülow wanted to shift the emphasis away from battleships towards mines, submarines, and coastal defences. These would cost less money, and be less likely to incite a preventive attack. Tirpitz insisted (as did McKenna in Britain) on the primacy of the battlefleet. To relax the building tempo would

---

[30] Bülow to Metternich, 22 Sept. 1908, *GP* xxiv, doc. 8248.

[31] M. Epkenhans, *Die Wilhelminische Flottenrüstung 1908–1914* (Munich, 1991), 31 ff. 5. Förster, *Der doppelte Militarismus* (Stuttgart, 1985), 187–9.

[32] I. N. Lambi, *The Navy and German Power Politics, 1862–1914* (Boston, 1984), 296.

[33] A. von Tirpitz, *Politische Dokumente: Der Aufbau der deutschen Weltmacht* (Stuttgart, 1924), 72.

[34] Ibid. 67. Bülow to Wilhelm, 15 July 1908, *GP* xxiv, doc. 8216.

[35] B. von Bülow, *Memoirs* (London, 1931), ii. 309.

[36] Ibid. 312, 314. Bülow to Metternich, 5 Aug. 1908, *GP* 24, doc. 8220.

[37] Bülow to Wilhelm, 26 Aug. 1908, ibid. 8239. Tirpitz, *Aufbau*, 86.

prolong the danger period, and might give the appearance of submitting to threats. He was willing to make concessions over Germany's naval strength only in exchange for reciprocal concessions over Britain's, and not for a political agreement that could easily be broken. Specifically, he would agree to a three-ship tempo over ten years if Britain would accept a four-ship one. But at this point British Ministers made statements in the March 1909 estimates debates that contradicted Tirpitz's private assurances, and the naval scare in London hardened all the German leaders against negotiating.[38]

A new hostility to Britain therefore characterized the final round of discussions during Bülow's Chancellorship. Tirpitz backed off from a 4:3 ratio, and Wilhelm wished to retract a pledge given by Metternich that Germany would introduce no new *Novelle* in 1912.[39] At an inter-departmental conference on 3 June 1909 Bülow agreed that it was not the time to seek an agreement. Tirpitz seemed to want to wait and let Germany get stronger. Moltke, in contrast, was pessimistic about the fleet's prospects in a war with Britain, and was anxious to avoid one. He favoured a mutual slowdown. Bülow's deputy, Theobold von Bethmann Hollweg, also supported an agreement, perhaps by slackening the tempo within the framework of the Navy Law. Even if Bülow had little manœuvring room at present, the acceleration scare had not ruled out all possibility of a diplomatic approach.[40]

This helps explain the rapid shift in policy after Bethmann replaced Bülow in July. Inexperienced in foreign affairs, the new Chancellor hoped that by retrenchment and mending fences with the British he could remedy the damage that the naval programme had inflicted. Germany should press on and get through the danger zone, but it should simultaneously negotiate in order to reduce tension and to win time. He believed that he must take the lead, thus putting London in the wrong if it failed to respond. Tirpitz apparently accepted this analysis, and agreed with Wilhelm on an offer to build eleven rather than fourteen capital ships between 1910 and 1914 if Britain built sixteen—a 1.45:1 rather than a 4:3 ratio.[41] Bethmann had made more progress in a month than had Bülow in a year, and the arrival of a novice whom Tirpitz may have thought he could manipulate seems insufficient to explain the softening in the latter's position. The Navy Secretary may have been shaken by the confirmation that Britain would lay down eight dreadnoughts, and Australia and New Zealand two more. The British were not (as he had supposed) near their financial breaking point, whereas he himself was under pressure to cut back.[42] At all events, on 21

[38] Bülow to Tirpitz, 30 Nov. 1908, Bülow to Metternich, 11 Dec. 1908, Bülow to Tirpitz, 25 Dec. 1908, 11 and 27 Jan. 1909; Tirpitz to Bülow, 17 Dec. 1908, 4 and 20 Jan. 1909, 4 Feb. 1909; Bülow to Metternich, 19 Mar. 1909, *GP* xxiv, docs. 10235–6, 10241, 10251, 10256, 10238, 10247, 10254, 10257, 10276.

[39] Wilhelm to Bülow, 3 Apr. 1909, ibid., doc. 10294. Tirpitz, *Aufbau*, 151.

[40] 3 June 1909 conference, *GP* xxviii, doc. 10306.

[41] Epkenhans, *Flottenrüstung*, 52–3. Bethmann memorandum, 13 Aug. 1909, *GP* xxviii, doc. 10325.

[42] Epkenhans, *Flottenrüstung*, 54. Wermuth circular to Ministers, 26 Aug. 1909, Berghahn and Deist (eds.), *Rüstung*, doc. viii/6.

August Bethmann told the new British Ambassador, Goschen, that he was willing to slow down German building as part of a package deal.[43]

Now that Berlin at last seemed willing to talk seriously, however, London was embarrassed. Grey replied that he would welcome proposals on naval expenditure and for a political understanding that was compatible with the ententes. Bethmann insisted that Germany must complete its naval programme, but it might drop back to a three-ship tempo in return for a promise of non-aggression. He also proposed that the two sides should exchange information. The naval and political negotiations must be simultaneous, and the latter was his principal concern. Grey gave higher priority to expenditure reductions, and the Cabinet agreed with him that a threat to the ententes (which a neutrality pledge would certainly constitute) was unacceptable. The ententes were necessary not only to contain Germany in Europe but also to protect the Empire against France and Russia. Rather than abandon them it would be easier to carry on the naval competition. There was therefore little prospect of the discussions succeeding even before 17 November, when Grey cited the forthcoming British elections as a reason to interrupt them.[44] This must have been a bitter disappointment for Bethmann after his success in bringing the Reich bureaucracy in line, and when the British renewed the dialogue in the following July they found dispositions in Berlin less favourable.

The Liberal Government was now willing to declare that Britain had no hostile intentions against Germany, but this would not satisfy Bethmann's political needs.[45] Navally, on the other hand, there seemed more of a negotiating basis. Tirpitz's relations with Bethmann had soured, and he was, so he later complained, frozen out of the talks. In any case, by the summer of 1910 he was once again willing to accept a 3:2 building ratio between the two fleets, and Grey suggested to the Commons in March 1911 that a 30:21 dreadnought balance by the spring of 1914 would give an adequate margin.[46] The British had come to accept that the German Government would not change the Navy Law, and they had reason to be accommodating, if only to ensure that the 1908 *Novelle* was not replaced by one less favourable. Conversely, the scheduled fall to a two-ship tempo after 1912 made it harder for Bethmann to offer additional concessions.[47] To drop below a two-ship tempo would result in shipyards going bankrupt and would complicate the authorities' financial planning, as more ships would have to be started later if the legislative targets were still to be met.[48] By May 1911 neither Bethmann nor the Navy Office wanted an accord, and he sent a

[43] Goschen to Grey, 21 Aug. 1909, *BD* vi, doc. 186.

[44] Grey to Goschen, 1 Sept. 1909; Goschen to Grey, 15 Oct. 1909; Goschen to Grey, 4 Nov. 1908; Grey to Goschen, 17 Nov. 1909, ibid. docs. 194–5, 200, 204, 205. D. W. Sweet, 'Great Britain and Germany, 1905–1911', in F. H. Hinsley (ed.), *British Foreign Policy under Sir Edward Grey* (Cambridge, 1977), 229–35.

[45] Grey to Goschen, 29 July 1910, *BD* vi, doc. 387(i).

[46] Tirpitz memorandum, 23 Sept. 1910, *GP* xxviii, doc. 10408. Epkenhans, *Flottenrüstung*, 68.

[47] Goschen to Grey, 12 and 16 Oct. 1910, *BD* vi, docs. 399, 403.

[48] Cf. Bethmann *aide-mémoire*, 10 May 1911, *BD* vi, doc. 464(i).

communication that Grey described as 'unsatisfactory and discouraging', effectively breaking off the exchanges.[49]

There was greater progress only towards sharing information about naval building. By the summer of 1910 the navies and Foreign Ministries on both sides were willing in principle to take up the idea. As clarified by the Admiralty, it would entail six-monthly visits by the two naval attachés to inspect the vessels under construction, and reciprocal communications about the types and numbers of ships to be built each year, with dates of laying down and delivery.[50] Both sides, naturally, hoped to use the procedure to their advantage. For the British, who could find out less through open channels about the Germans than the Germans could about them, the attraction was obvious, although they argued that the scheme would be of mutual benefit as a confidence-building measure that would make scares less likely. Bethmann and Wilhelm were sceptical, and Tirpitz feared that the Germans would be wrongfooted, as their estimates appeared each autumn, whereas Britain's were published in the following spring.[51] Hence the German leaders wanted the exchange of plans to be simultaneous and binding for the next financial year. The British would agree to restrict the publication period to the four months between 15 November and 15 March, but not to the information being binding. On the same day, 1 July 1911, as the Germans accepted these conditions in principle, their gunboat, the *Panther*, dropped anchor off Morocco, and in the ensuing furore even this minimum product of the negotiations was temporarily lost.[52]

With the exception of the Haldane mission to be discussed below, July 1911 marked the end of the most sustained pre-1914 essay in armaments diplomacy. In its way it was remarkable, Bethmann pointing out the absence of historical precedent for a treaty limitation on naval armaments.[53] Bülow highlighted the technical obstacles, including those of determining a standard of measurement of naval power and of taking account of ententes and alliances.[54] Actually both sides were agreed on the dreadnought battleship as the basic unit, but the alliance question was more disruptive. The British were building against Austria-Hungary as well as Germany; the Germans were beginning to feel anxious about the Russian Baltic Fleet.[55] In addition, because of the Navy Law, the Germans wanted a long-term commitment that the British, anxious to retain flexibility after the 1909 panic, refused. But with the transition to dreadnoughts gaining

[49] Navy Office memorandum, 'Ganz geheim', n.d. but *c*. Apr. 1911; Tirpitz memo on discussion with Bethmann, 4 May 1911, BA-MA NL Tirpitz N. 253/24*b*. Bethmann *aide-mémoire*, 10 May 1911, *BD* vi, doc. 464(i). Asquith to Edward VII, 17 May 1911, BLO Asquith MSS 6.

[50] Captain Watson to Tirpitz, 24 Aug. 1910, *BD* vi, doc. 397(i).

[51] Goschen to Grey, 16 Oct. 1910; Bethmann memorandum, 16 Dec. 1910; ibid. docs. 403, 424(i). Tirpitz to Bethmann, 17 Mar. 1911, *GP* xxviii, doc. 10436.

[52] Goschen to Grey, 24 Mar. 1911; Admiralty to Foreign Office, 16 May 1911; Grey to Goschen, 1 June 1911, *BD* vi, docs. 454, 465, 469. Marder, *Dreadnought*, 229.

[53] Note on conversation between Bethmann, Schoen, and Goschen, 5 Nov. 1909, *GP* xxviii, doc. 10355.

[54] Goschen to Grey, 10 Dec. 1908, *BD* vi, doc. 108.

[55] Navy Office memorandum, 'Ganz geheim', cited in n. 49 above.

momentum the destabilization caused by the new technology became less severe. As more German battleships entered service Tirpitz was less exposed to a preventive attack, and as the British learned more about German building capacities the Royal Navy had less reason to fear its superiority vanishing overnight, although it was still being pressed hard. During the negotiations the two sides moved closer to consensus over battleship ratios, perhaps without realizing that they were doing so.

Consensus was facilitated by the waning of Tirpitz's ambitions. In 1908–9 he had envisaged a supplementary *Novelle* in 1912,[56] but after Britain resolved to lay down the 'footnote four' he was willing to renounce a further law if London would agree to a 4:3 ratio in completed ships by 1914. By 1910 he was willing to settle for 3:2, and when the Navy League began to agitate for a new *Novelle* the Navy Office withheld its backing.[57] Capelle doubted if the Reichstag would approve a bill before the next elections,[58] and Wilhelm's role in policy diminished after the *Daily Telegraph* affair. But whereas Tirpitz now looked to negotiations to bind the Royal Navy, and no longer intended simply to build his way out of the danger zone, the German civilians were less interested in a naval agreement than in prising apart the Triple Entente. Rather than the Navy Secretary, it was Britain's refusal to be separated from its partners that frustrated their objective. In short, the negotiations demonstrated Tirpitz's growing vulnerability to the combination of forces that was about to unseat him from his political primacy.

* * *

At the same time as the naval balance moved to Germany's disadvantage, so did that on land. There was little change in Britain between the Bosnian and the Agadir crises, as Haldane's budget remained constant and his BEF reorganization was largely completed. In Belgium and France, however, there were important developments.

The garrisoning of the huge new Antwerp fortifications would add to the strain on a Belgian army that had been enfeebled by the 1902 recruitment law.[59] During the Bosnian crisis the War Minister, Hellebaut, came out in favour of general and compulsory military service.[60] He was encouraged by King Leopold, who felt that Belgium needed to be strong to meet its international obligations, and that the country would not support an increase in effectives if the wealthy could still buy exemption.[61] A parliamentary commission endorsed Hellebaut's view, and a new recruitment bill passed in December 1909.[62] It was fiercely

[56] Metternich note, 4 June 1909, *GP* xxviii, doc. 10308.
[57] Epkenhans, *Flottenrüstung*, 90.
[58] Capelle to Tirpitz, 29 July 1910, BA-MA Tirpitz MSS, N. 253/24*a*.
[59] Terlinden, *Histoire militaire des belges* (Liège, 1931), 310.
[60] Report by Captain Duruy, 24 June 1909, SHA 7.N. 1156.
[61] E. Carton de Wiart, *Léopold II: Souvenirs des dernières années, 1901–1909* (Brussels, 1944), 37, 125, 212, 231.
[62] Foreign Ministry note on Leopold conversation with Clemenceau, 5 May 1909; note on conversation with German Minister, 2 July 1909, MAEB NIDMB 8.

resisted by the Flemish Catholics, and, although it may have been as much as was feasible politically, its effects would be gradual. The purchase of substitutes was abolished, and the annual recruitment levy was to rise from 13,000 to 20,000 men, leading eventually to peacetime and to wartime strengths of 42,000 and 180,000 respectively. The fifteen months of military service, however, remained shorter than in Belgium's neighbours, and the army budget was not increased.[63] Re-equipment with quick-firers was completed, and in 1910 the number of active field artillery batteries was raised from thirty-four to fifty-two,[64] but neither French nor German commentators thought highly of Belgian effectiveness.[65]

In France, after the fall in numbers caused by the introduction of two-year service, the army's peacetime strength held steady[66] and the main innovations were qualitative. Reservist exercises were intensified, and tactics and training improved.[67] During the annexation crisis distribution of the 1907 Puteaux-Saint Étienne machine gun was hastened, a 'complementary programme' of work on the eastern fortresses was drawn up, and new mobilization instructions issued.[68] Although Germany had the edge in dirigibles, in heavier-than-air flight the French secured a lead in pilot training and in airframe and engine manufacture that inspired great national enthusiasm. In 1911 the Germans thought the French had over a hundred aircraft and seventy-seven military pilots, although both armies were still uncertain about the new invention's utility.[69]

Artillery, however, was the nodal point of Franco-German rivalry, and the arm in which the EMA felt most vulnerable. The first attempt to tackle Germany's new superiority in field guns formed part of a more general cadres bill, introduced by Picquart in 1907. As well as raiding the infantry and cavalry to find men for field-artillery expansion, the bill was intended to minimize the damage to training and preparedness caused by lower peacetime strengths, to raise the officer complement of active and reserve units, and improve officers' promotion prospects.[70] When this omnibus measure got bogged down, Picquart extracted the artillery component and submitted it to the Chamber in November 1908,[71] at the height not only of the Bosnian crisis but also of the Casablanca deserters incident, caused when the French authorities in Morocco detained

---

[63] Duruy report, 15 Dec. 1909, SHA 7.N. 1156.

[64] Duruy report, 24 Apr. 1911, SHA 7.N. 1157.

[65] Duruy report, 1 Feb. 1911, ibid. GGS 3. Abteilung reports on Belgian army, Feb. and Mar. 1910, KAM Gstb. 221.

[66] GGS report on French recruitment, 13 Nov. 1910, KAM Gstb. 163. CSG minutes, 18 Oct. 1909, SHA 1.N. 10.

[67] GGS report on reservist exercises, May 1910, KAM Gstb 163. GGS report on French 1909 manœuvres, 10 Dec. 1909, KAM MKr 991.

[68] CSG minutes, 30 Dec. 1908, SHA 1.N. 10. Report of high commission on fortresses, 21 Mar. 1908 (approved in May), SHA 7.N. 106. Picquart to corps commanders, 30 Jan. 1909, ibid.

[69] EMA 2nd Bureau report on German airships, 25 May 1909, SHA 7.N. 672. GGS report on French military aviation, 20 May 1911, KAM Gstb. 164. Testimony by Picquart to Army Commission, 4 Feb. 1909, AN C7341.

[70] CSG minutes, 18 Oct. 1909, SHA 1.N. 10. GGS annual report on French army, 5 Dec. 1909, KAM Gstb. 162.

[71] Ibid. Text of the bill (24 Dec. 1908) in SHA 7.N. 49.

German and Austrian defectors from the Foreign Legion. Germany asked for the men to be handed over, and the officials responsible to be disciplined. Clemenceau's Government stood firm, and the dispute went to arbitration, but at its height Asquith was 'extremely perturbed' and contemplated British intervention in a Continental war, while Grey made covert preparations to give France naval assistance.[72] Perhaps assisted by these developments, the artillery bill became law on 24 July 1909, and had been fully implemented by the end of 1910.

The law was a very significant addition to French strength. Its cost was relatively low: 67 million francs in one-off expenditures and 15 million in recurrent ones. But it raised the number of field-artillery batteries in metropolitan France from 508 to 670, partly at the expense of fortress and coastal guns. The normal peacetime provision per army corps would rise from twenty-three batteries with 90 guns to thirty with 120. Only on mobilization would six extra batteries be created and the total number of guns rise to 144, the same as in a German corps.[73] To maintain more than thirty batteries in peacetime was not thought possible, given the army's manpower shortage, and the French artillery on mobilization would therefore be more improvised and less cohesive than its German counterpart, although the French believed their four-gun batteries to be superior to Germany's six-gun ones.[74] Four-gun batteries were easier to supply with munitions but more extravagant with men; after much debate it was decided to keep them, although doing so meant fewer guns per corps.[75] The measure was also intended to increase munitions stocks, a matter of great concern to Clemenceau personally, and in this it had some success.[76] It therefore helped to restore parity in field artillery, but failed to restore it completely. Most of the reinforcement consisted of 75 mm guns; and France still lacked an equivalent of Germany's light field howitzer, while the 155 cm Rimailho batteries were increased only from eighteen to twenty-one. On the eve of the Agadir crisis Moltke was impressed by France's continuing weakness in heavy artillery, and observed that French counter-battery doctrine was one of simply 'neutralizing' enemy guns whereas Germany intended to destroy them. The Germans were confident that they still enjoyed superiority, and French military intelligence appears to have agreed with them.[77] None the less, the Russian military

---

[72] The affair is summarized in Pichon circular telegram, 2 Nov. 1908, *DDF* 2nd ser. xi, doc. 522. See Williams, *Defending*, 161; Sweet, 'Great Britain and Germany', 225, cf. n. 44 above.

[73] GGS report on French army budget, August 1910, KAM Gstb. 163.

[74] GGS annual report on French army, 5 Dec. 1909, KAM Gstb. 162.

[75] Hearings of Chamber Army Commission, June to Nov. 1908, AN C7341.

[76] CSG minutes, 15 May and 9 June 1909, SHA 1.N. 10. But by 1910 the French believed their munitions endowment was superior: see report on German field artillery by EMA 2nd Bureau, 5 May 1910, SHA 7.N. 672. The Germans disagreed: see report on munitions provision of French and German artillery, 20 May 1911, KAM Gstb. 164.

[77] GGS report on French artillery tactics, 20 Jan. 1910; and on French field artillery regulations, 7 Apr. 1911, KAM MKr. 991. EMA 2nd Bureau report on German field artillery, 4 Nov. 1910, SHA 7.N. 672.

reorganization was not the only source of anxiety for German planners. They retained their qualitative advantage in the West, but by a finer margin.

* * *

Such was the strategic context for the 1911 *Quinquennat*, the last expression of Germany's steady-state policy before the great expansion. Einem's preparations for it before he left office in August 1909 largely tied the hands of his successor, Josias von Heeringen. Einem had decided neither to seek a big increase in peacetime strength nor to create new units in the principal arms. He told the Reichstag commission on financial reform that he would seek only technical improvements and that the recent spate of armaments innovation was ending. In 1909 expenditure had dropped, and he expected to keep it at the new level.[78] Moltke wanted a larger strength increase and to respond to the French artillery law by improving the reserves, but on neither issue did he make much headway.[79] Indeed, Wilhelm took pride in having retaliated against the French law neither with counter-increases nor with threats, in contrast to Britain's reaction to the naval *Novelle*.[80]

Heeringen built up a reputation for frankness, seriousness, and command of his brief, but he lacked his predecessor's presence and parliamentary skills.[81] He was matched against a formidable new Treasury Secretary, Adolf Wermuth, who generally enjoyed Bethmann's backing. Under Wermuth's stewardship in 1909–11 the budget was restored to balance and the increased revenues from economic recovery and the 1909 tax increases were used to reduce the Reich's indebtedness. Bethmann wished to avoid both additional direct taxes, which would divide the Government's supporters, and higher consumption taxes, which would strengthen the SPD. Wermuth's mantra was therefore 'no uncovered expenditure': spending must be met from current revenue. In the interests of 'financial war preparedness' the Reich must ease the pressure on the bond markets so that in emergency it could raise large short-term credits.[82] On taking over he advised all departments that Germany's domestic stability, international prestige, and strategic readiness depended on expenditure cuts.[83] But he believed that the army mattered more than the navy for national security, and he complained about Tirpitz's irresponsibility.[84] From now on the navy would no longer be treated with special favour, although in the 1910 and 1911 estimates the army budget remained tightly controlled.[85]

[78] Förster, *Militarismus*, 195–6. Budget Commission minutes, 13 Jan. 1909, HSMA M1/6 Bd. 126.

[79] Reichsarchiv, *Weltkrieg*, i. 107.

[80] Wilhelm to Bülow, 11 Aug. 1908, *GP* xxiv, doc. 8224.

[81] Förster, *Militarismus*, 197. Gebsattel to Bavarian War Minister, 4 Apr. 1911, KAM MKr. 42.

[82] R. Kroboth, *Die Finanzpolitik des deutschen Reiches während der Reichskanzlerschaft Bethmann Hollwegs und die Geld- und Kapitalmarktverhältnisse (1909–1913/14)* (Frankfurt, 1986), 114–17, 319–20. P.-C. Witt, *Die Finanzpolitik des deutschen Reiches von 1904 bis 1913* (Lübeck, 1970), 316 ff.

[83] Wermuth circular, 26 Aug. 1909, Berghahn and Deist (eds.), *Rüstung*, doc. viii/6.

[84] Witt, *Finanzpolitik*, 318. A. Wermuth, *Ein Beamtenleben: Erinnerungen* (Berlin, 1922), 278–80.

[85] Lerchenfeld to Bavarian Ministry of State, 17 Oct. 1910; Wermuth to Bundesrat plenipotentiaries, 29 Oct. 1910, KAM MKr. 5584.

In addition, Heeringen had to contend with Wermuth over the new *Quinquennat*. The War Minister agreed to delay the measure to 1911, but he dug his heels in when Bethmann and Wermuth wanted to postpone it for yet a further year.[86] None the less, he agreed that the main expenditure increase would come only in 1913–14, after the naval expansion had passed its peak, and even then would be modest. The army's peacetime strength would rise by 10,875 to 515,321 by 1915, there would be more machine-gun detachments, some reinforcement of the field artillery in response to the new French law, and larger reinforcements of the foot artillery and communications troops. This was still a measure in the Einem tradition of gradual technical improvement within an unchanged basic framework, and as a percentage of the able-bodied population the annual recruitment levy would continue to fall.[87]

That tradition, however, was increasingly questioned. Heeringen advised the Emperor that there was no military case for a large increase, but asked if there was one on other grounds. Wilhelm, concerned about the friction with St Petersburg since the annexation crisis, asked the War Minister to prepare variants of the bill in which peacetime strength would rise by 30,000 and even 51,000 men, with the formation of two new army corps.[88] But this was unanimously opposed, at least by the most senior officials. Erich von Ludendorff, the Chief of the Operations Division in the General Staff, wanted a bigger bill but was ignored.[89] Heeringen reported that he and Moltke did not foresee a deterioration in Germany's circumstances sufficient to justify a more ambitious measure, although he agreed that Russia's military reorganization might change the position.[90] Bethmann judged the international situation to be 'generally quiet', and with Wermuth's approval said he refused to conjure up a war scare just to get through an unnecessarily large bill.[91] He put domestic financial and political stability foremost, although he too was impressed by the evidence of Russian hostility and military preparations, and acknowledged that there was limited time in which to get the German army ready.[92] Wilhelm agreed to the bill going forward as drafted, but warned that he expected Bethmann to support a much bigger increase later if circumstances demanded it, which the Chancellor promised to do.[93]

The caution of the *Quinquennat* was therefore conditioned on an optimism about Russia that for none of the German élite was unqualified. Bülow's questioning of the naval priority had become much more generalized, and the army was losing patience with the abnegation of the Einem years. According to the Bavarian plenipotentiary, its leaders resented Tirpitz's absorption of resources,

---

[86] Förster, *Militarismus*, 197. Reichsarchiv, *Weltkrieg*, i. 102.

[87] Ibid. 99. Heeringen to Bavarian War Ministry, 28 May and 2 June 1910, KAM MKr. 1132.

[88] Reichsarchiv, *Weltkrieg*, i. 101 ff.

[89] Förster, *Militarismus*, 199. [90] Reichsarchiv, *Weltkrieg*, i. 111.

[91] Ibid. 102. Lerchenfeld to Bavarian State Ministry, 17 Apr. 1910, GSM Bayerische Gesandtschaft Berlin Nr. 1082.

[92] Bethmann to Wilhelm, 15 Sept. 1910, BA Kl.Erw 342–1.

[93] Reichsarchiv, *Weltkrieg*, i. 104.

which had created great international difficulties without winning corresponding advantages, and would help Germany little in a war.[94] In May 1910 Moltke and Heeringen pressed jointly for more field howitzers in response to the French artillery law, only to run up against a Wermuth veto.[95] In the previous winter they had resisted cuts in the strategic railway budget, Moltke advising that the western network was inferior to France's and that the eastern one was also inadequate. Heeringen warned that he could not accept financial stringency in the longer term, and that he would need more men.[96] Moreover, there was evidence that if the army did press its case it would enjoy public support. Tirpitz never again benefited from such sympathy in the Reichstag as he had in 1908, and during the Bosnian affair conservative newspapers and politicians began pressing for an army increase.[97] When Bethmann and Heeringen presented the new *Quinquennat* at the end of 1910 they made it clear that if necessary they would ask for extra, and the leader of the National Liberal party urged them to do so. Outside the Reichstag there were calls for the army to spend more on equipment and on raising unit strengths.[98] The bill passed in March 1911 without significant amendments and with record majorities. None the less, the contradiction between the army's strategy—the Schlieffen Plan—and its force structure was becoming more glaring than ever, and the Russian military reorganization, which the Germans had had such difficulty in interpreting, was the potential trigger for a shift from sea to land priorities that would snatch from Tirpitz the initiative he had held for the previous ten years. The conditions for a German reorientation were falling into place; and Germany was the axis on which European armaments turned.

2. Agadir and After

The realignment of German policy towards a land competition between the Continental blocs took place after Agadir. There were successive stages in the winters of 1911/12 and 1912/13. Tirpitz's last legislative victory, the 1912 naval *Novelle*, fell short of his construction objectives and failed to prevent a relapse from a four-ship to a two-ship building tempo, but it raised the High Seas Fleet to unprecedented battle-readiness, which the Royal Navy promptly countered. The parallel 1912 army law cost more in money and in manpower than did its naval counterpart, and was balanced by organizational and legislative changes in the French camp. On land as well as at sea, however, the race was in efficiency and readiness as much as in men and in *matériel*. It was in 1913–14 that the race in personnel and in equipment reached its climax, but in a context now, because of the earlier transition, of an inter-bloc confrontation and hair-trigger readiness.

---

[94] Gebsattel to Bavarian War Ministry, 1 Apr. 1910, KAM MKr. 1132.
[95] Heeringen to Wermuth, 18 May 1910; Wermuth reply, 26 May, HSMA M1/6 Bd. 277.
[96] Wermuth to Bethmann, 30 Nov. 1909; Moltke to Bethmann, 21 Dec. 1909; Heeringen to Bethmann, 12 Jan. 1910, BA R43F/107.
[97] Epkenhans, *Flottenrüstung*, 83 ff.   [98] Förster, *Militarismus*, 200–4.

Simultaneously, Agadir touched off a chain of wars and crises in the Eastern Mediterranean that kept Europe on tenterhooks down to the summer of 1914. Italy's attack on Libya in September 1911 led on to the Balkan States' attack on Turkey in the following year, and pushed Rome away from France and back towards the Triple Alliance. As the central arms race between the Austro-German and the Franco-Russian blocs took off, the peripheral races in the Adriatic and the North Sea went into lower gear. Italy's diplomatic *rapprochement* with its alliance partners was mirrored by tightening bonds between Britain and France. All of these repercussions, in greater or lesser degree, can be traced back to the scorching summer of 1911. In Grey's words: 'The consequences of such a foreign crisis do not end with it. They seem to end, but they go underground and appear later on.'[99]

Why did the ripples from Agadir spread so wide? As usual we must distinguish between the impact of the crisis on immediate military readiness and that on medium-term development. It began with a mechanism of escalation, linking the French decision in April to send an expedition to the Moroccan capital, Fez, with the arrival of the *Panther* at Agadir on 1 July and the war scare that followed Lloyd George's Mansion Speech on 21 July. Subsequently, however, the militarization of the conflict was held in bounds. Its medium-term impact can be witnessed in the first phase of the German armaments reorientation, or *Rüstungswende*, the contemporaneous developments in Britain and France, and the effect on Italy of the Libyan War.

* * *

The Fez expedition consisted of a column of 15,000 troops that advanced to the outskirts of the city between 11 and 21 May.[100] As the French gave out, in the first of the bogus pretexts of 1911, the European community in Fez might be endangered by the rebellion in the interior of the country against the Sultan, Moulay Hafid, who had appealed for aid. In fact the danger to the Europeans was still remote and the German Minister in Tangier denied that there was one.[101] The Sultan's 'appeal' was drawn up by the French consul for him to sign and was backdated after the decision in Paris had been taken. Probably the main purpose of the expedition was to protect not the Europeans but Moulay Hafid. If he were overthrown much of French influence was likely to go with him, and it was symptomatic that Paris acted ostensibly in his name.

The Franco-German Moroccan agreement of February 1909, signed in the midst of the Bosnian crisis, had traded German recognition of French political predominance for French pledges not to discriminate against German businesses, and to associate with them in joint undertakings.[102] Since then, although the

[99] E. Grey, *Twenty-Five Years 1892–1916* (London, 1925), i. 241.

[100] J.-C. Allain, *Agadir, 1911: Une crise impérialiste en Europe pour la conquête du Maroc* (Paris, 1976), ch. 9, and G. Barraclough, *From Agadir to Armageddon: Anatomy of a Crisis* (London, 1982), ch. 8, for the origins of the expedition.

[101] Seckendorff to Bethmann, 10 Apr. 1911, *GP* xxix, doc. 10530.

[102] Allain, *Agadir*, ch. 7. E. W. Edwards, 'The Franco-German Agreement on Morocco, 1909', *English Historical Review*, 78 (1963), 483–513.

French still paid lip-service to the Algeciras principles, their control over the Moroccan Government had grown apace. A loan in 1910 tightened their grip on the public finances, and their military mission expanded its role. By weakening Moulay Hafid's legitimacy and fuelling the revolt against him, they justified yet further control. The French army advanced piecemeal from Algeria in the east and Casablanca in the west, bringing more and more of the country under *de facto* occupation. By the winter of 1910/11 the Germans were afraid that even their commercial rights were being relegated, the new Foreign Minister, Alfred von Kiderlen-Wächter, regarding Moroccan railway contracts as a 'touchstone' of French sincerity.[103] In the fragile and inexperienced Monis ministry that now took office in Paris, however, Kiderlen's opposite number, Cruppi, neglected warnings from his Berlin Ambassador, and gave the military and the more irresponsible Quai d'Orsay officials their head. The Germans' interests were challenged more aggressively, and Cruppi sent the Fez expedition without consulting them, not anticipating 'direct opposition' from Berlin.[104] It is true that the Germans were partly to blame, as their attitude towards the expedition was equivocal. Kiderlen warned on 28 April that if French troops stayed Germany would regard Algeciras as finished and resume its liberty of action, but in subsequent weeks, while the British urged that the expedition should be withdrawn, he failed to clarify his views.[105] This notwithstanding, in 1911 as in 1905 Germany's brinkmanship was a defensive response to a French forward policy that presaged a Moroccan hegemony in disregard of the Reich's legitimate concerns.

That some action was appropriate does not mean that sending a gunboat was the right one. The *Panther*'s arrival was a spectacular demonstration of armed diplomacy against a Great Power. In Paris, according to the British Ambassador, it produced 'a great sensation' and indignation comparable to that provoked by the Tangier incident.[106] Yet its military significance was negligible. Ostensibly Kiderlen was responding to a plea from local German businessmen—a plea that in fact was stage-managed by the Foreign Ministry and reached Berlin after the warship reached Agadir.[107] South Morocco was a convenient pressure point because of its mineral wealth and because of Pan-German interest in the region, but its remoteness appealed to Kiderlen as a means of containing the incident. Plans to send two ships were scaled down as too provocative; the *Panther* and

---

[103] E. Oncken, *Panthersprung nach Agadir: Die Deutsche Politik während der zweiten Marokkokrise 1911* (Düsseldorf, 1981), 102.

[104] Bertie to Grey, 25 Apr. 1911, *BD* vii, doc. 216. On French decision-making, C. M. Andrew and A. S. Kanya-Forstner, 'The French "Colonial Party": Its Composition, Aims, and Influence, 1885–1914', *Historical Journal*, 14 (1971), 123–5; J. F. V. Keiger, *France and the Origins of the First World War* (London, 1983), ch. 2; M. B. Hayne, *The French Foreign Office and the Origins of the First World War, 1898–1914* (Oxford, 1993), ch. 9.

[105] Kiderlen memorandum, 28 Apr. 1911, *GP* xxix, doc. 10545. M. L. Dockrill, 'British Policy during the Agadir Crisis of 1911', in Hinsley (ed.), *Grey*, 271.

[106] Bertie to Grey, 2 July 1911, *BD* vii, doc. 345.

[107] J. S. Mortimer, 'Commercial Interests and German Diplomacy in the Agadir Crisis', *Historical Journal*, 10 (1967), 440–56.

the vessels that succeeded it hardly had the capacity to organize a landing, and had no instructions to do so. Such action, Kiderlen feared, would mean a direct conflict with France and Britain, which he wanted to avoid. He consulted neither the army nor the Colonial Office, and the navy only in order to instruct the crews to protect German nationals and show the flag, while exercising the greatest restraint.[108] Nor was the *Panther*'s spring exactly the application of military power to support negotiation, as the Germans made no explicit demands and had not yet formulated them. According to their ambassador in Paris they considered Algeciras had been so infringed that their action was necessary to calm German public opinion.[109] But the German Foreign Ministry accepted that an independent sultanate was unviable, and its objective was to press France into offering 'a hellish pound of flesh', probably in the Congo, but not to partition Morocco.[110] Indeed, although Kiderlen was—realistically—cutting his losses in the Maghreb, he seems to have had no great knowledge of or interest in Central Africa either. He had warned in May that if the Government did nothing it would lose credit with all but the Socialists in the forthcoming Reichstag elections, but it appears that his and Bethmann's principal anxiety was lest Germany lose prestige and influence by signing agreements and then allowing them to be overturned without its consent.[111] This preoccupation with Great-Power status makes more comprehensible his strategy of forcing France to offer compensation rather than asking for it himself. The *Panther* was a 'Faustpfand' (a pledge) to be left at Agadir until the French were more forthcoming.[112] He would thump the table, and wait and see.

Kiderlen's failure to spell out his objectives to the other Powers helps explain why what he intended as a limited operation got out of control. His tactical assumptions were almost immediately exploded, and he was plunged into a far more dangerous crisis than he had expected, from which he extricated himself only by paying precisely the ransom in international and domestic credibility that he had hoped to avoid. His first miscalculation concerned the French. The Monis ministry was replaced in June by that of Joseph Caillaux, who as Finance Minister in the previous government had been sceptical about the Fez expedition and willing to offer Central African compensation. As Premier, however, he had no intention of giving up the occupation of central Morocco. He kept his nerve and kept his head, and refused to be intimidated. His government agreed to bilateral negotiation but still made no definite offer of compensation, with the result that on 15 June it was Kiderlen who offered to abandon all but Germany's economic rights in Morocco but demanded part of Gabon and the entire French Congo. The French had decided to cede as little territory as possible, and

[108] Allain, *Agadir*, 326–33. Oncken, *Panthersprung*, 136–44.
[109] Paul Cambon to Grey, 1 July 1911, *BD* vii, doc. 340.
[110] Zimmermann memorandum, 12 June 1911, *GP* xxix, doc. 10572.
[111] Kiderlen memorandum, 3 May 1911; Bethmann to Wilhelm, 20 July 1911, ibid., docs. 10549, 10613.
[112] Kiderlen memorandum, 3 May 1911, ibid.

although agreeing in principle to compensation in Central Africa they rejected this demand.[113]

At this point, the Foreign Minister's second miscalculation became evident. His action was not primarily intended to test the Anglo-French entente.[114] None the less, he supposed that London would do little to help Paris, and was vindicated in as much as the Liberal Cabinet at first defined British interests cautiously. It agreed that there should be no German port on the Mediterranean coast of Morocco (Agadir lay on the Atlantic) and no fortified German port anywhere; but it considered that France was partly responsible for the situation and should be encouraged to give ground.[115] It was the demand for the entire French Congo, combined with irritation over Germany's failure to respond to British soundings, that set the alarm bells ringing. On 19 July the Cabinet agreed that the Congo concession was one that the French could not be expected to (and probably were not intended to) accept. But it still authorized Grey to tell them that Britain would not oppose a German presence in Morocco in all circumstances, Caillaux retorting that for Britain to permit one would violate the 1904 agreement.[116] The lack of information about Kiderlen's plans was now straining Anglo-French as well as Anglo-German relations. If (as the German evidence suggests) he wished to abandon Morocco and get the best possible Central African compensation, all three capitals could perhaps be satisfied. If he wanted a political presence in the sultanate he might be able to drive London and Paris apart. But if he intended to inflict on France a humiliation that would jeopardize its Great-Power status, the entente would come back into play.

It was because of this last possibility that the Liberal Government raised the temperature. On 21 July, with Cabinet approval, the Foreign Secretary warned Metternich that if Franco-German negotiations broke down Britain must be brought in. If Germany meant to land and establish itself at Agadir the British would be obliged to protect their interests there (which Grey envisaged might mean sending ships). Independently of this conversation Lloyd George, who was scheduled to speak at the Mansion House that evening, decided to insert a statement that it would be an intolerable humiliation if peace were secured at the price of Britain being treated, in a matter in which it had vital interests, as if it were of no account. It must maintain its place and prestige among the Great Powers, and national honour and the security of its foreign trade were not party questions.[117] The passage was cleared beforehand with Churchill (who was now Home Secretary), Asquith, and Grey: its message was similar to the latter's advice to Metternich that the British could not be ignored. Both Lloyd George and Grey believed that the greatest danger was to leave their position vague. Germany and France seemed to be adopting irreconcilable postures, and

---

[113] Allain, *Agadir*, ch. 12. J. M. A. Caillaux, *Mes Mémoires*, ii (Paris, 1943), 112–21.

[114] Oncken, *Panthersprung*, 134.

[115] Asquith to George V, 4 July 1911, PRO CAB/41/33.

[116] Ibid., 19 July 1911. Grey to Bertie, 19 and 20 July, Bertie to Grey, 21 July 1911, *BD* vii, docs. 397, 405, 408.

[117] Grey to Goschen, 21 July 1911; extract from Mansion House speech, ibid., docs. 411, 412.

Kiderlen should be encouraged to back off before he committed himself to claims that Britain must join France in resisting.[118] It has to be said that a private warning was better calculated to achieve this aim than a public speech, and Grey and Asquith probably seized on Lloyd George's invitation because it was an opportunity to undercut the Radicals in the Cabinet rather than after careful appraisal of its effect in Berlin. Kiderlen, like the French before him, had acted without adequately preparing the diplomatic terrain. Now it was Britain's turn to feel that it was not treated as befitted its status, and the Germans correctly interpreted the Mansion House speech as a public calling into line.

Kiderlen's response to Grey's conversation with the ambassador was conciliatory. He authorized assurances that Germany wanted no Moroccan territory, and would not land at Agadir. But he reacted to the speech much more sharply, and the consequence was a naval alert on both sides of the North Sea, followed by six weeks of acute anxiety. The escalation process had reached its climax. But even now the crisis remained much less militarized than its Balkan counterpart of 1912–13 or even that of 1908–9. All three main governments concerned had entered it with limited objectives, and none regarded it as acceptable or desirable that it should lead to war. All understood that military and naval measures might exacerbate the situation, though all also understood that such measures might lend emphasis to diplomacy and be necessary as precautions should diplomacy fail. There was a balance to strike, and it was struck more in favour of preparedness in the entente camp, more in favour of restraint—at least, after the sending of the *Panther*—in Berlin, but on all sides with war avoidance as the preferred outcome.

This is not to say that no one advocated taking greater risks, and Caillaux's moderating role in Paris was particularly significant. At the Foreign Ministry de Selves had a penchant for independent action and for heeding his more Germanophobe officials. While conversations proceeded between Kiderlen and the French Ambassador in Berlin, Jules Cambon, the Premier made clandestine contact with the German Embassy in Paris and increasingly took crisis management into his own hands. He agreed with the Navy Minister, Delcassé, not to send warships to shadow the *Panther*, although a gunboat was made ready at Casablanca for immediate dispatch.[119] Meanwhile de Selves and Paul Cambon, the Ambassador in London, suggested to Grey without Caillaux's knowledge that both Britain and France might send warships, but the Foreign Secretary objected.[120] Caillaux and Grey were at one with Kiderlen at least in wishing to prevent any further escalation on the spot.

In the second half of July the arena for possible naval measures shifted northwards. Here too restraint was evident. Already on 14 July Kiderlen had spoken

[118] W. S. Churchill, *The World Crisis, 1911–1914* (London, 1923), 46–7. Grey, *Twenty-Five Years*, i. 224–5. Lloyd George, *War Memoirs*, i. 41–4. K. M. Wilson, 'The Agadir Crisis, the Mansion House Speech, and the Double-Edgedness of Agreements', *Historical Journal*, 15 (1972), 513–32.

[119] Allain, *Agadir*, 351–2.

[120] Paul Cambon to Grey, 1 July 1911; Grey to Bertie, 4 July 1911, *BD* vii, docs. 340, 355. Caillaux circular, 4 July 1911, *DDF* 2nd ser. xiv, doc. 18.

to the British Ambassador, saying that if the conversation were disclosed he would at once be dismissed. There was a prospect that British and German naval squadrons would meet on 29 July in Norwegian waters at Molde Fiord. As Wilhelm would be present and had the ceremonial title of an admiral in both fleets he would wish for joint manœuvres, banquets, and toasts, with the danger that each side would try to overawe the other. Kiderlen urged, therefore, that the Royal Navy should postpone its arrival; and in London, where the Foreign Office had already been considering the problem, it was decided to cancel the visit, while denying any connection with Morocco.[121] All the same, after the Mansion House speech there was near panic in Whitehall. On the evening of 22 July the Admiralty lost track of the German fleet, and did not regain contact until the following day.[122] Between 21 and 24 July Sir Charles Ottley, the Secretary of the CID, twice warned that the German fleet was concentrated at sea and in a position to launch a surprise attack (although the Admiralty did not expect it to do so), while Britain's forces were dispersed. The Home Fleet had taken no precautions, and the First Sea Lord, Sir Arthur Wilson, had gone to Scotland for a weekend's shooting.[123] On 25 July Metternich warned Grey that 'If the British Government . . . should have had the intention to embroil the situation and lead towards a violent explosion, they could not have chosen a better means than the speech of the Chancellor of the Exchequer.'[124] Grey warned Lloyd George and Churchill that the fleet might be attacked at any moment, and told McKenna that for practical purposes the German fleet was mobilized.[125] Only now were defensive precautions taken, while Churchill arranged armed guards for the magazines and issued general warrants to open the correspondence of suspected agents. In his memoirs he caught the drama of the hour: 'So now the Admiralty wireless whispers through the ether to the tall masts of ships, and captains pace their decks absorbed in thought.'[126] Yet although the navy remained at readiness, Admiralty complacency left a galling aftertaste.

In Germany there were different consequences. When the Royal Navy called off its visit to Scandinavia the Kaiser's entourage saw 'with terror—war before their eyes'.[127] So far from being poised for an attack, the High Seas Fleet was scattered, but the Admiralty Staff told Kiderlen that there was no need to concentrate it, and the Emperor agreed. The upshot was that while the British moved to high preparedness the Germans remained as before, and it was only

---

[121] Goschen to Nicolson, 14 July, Nicolson to Goschen, 18 and 26 July 1911, *BD* vii, docs. 632, 633, 638.

[122] C. E. Callwell, *Field Marshal Sir Henry Wilson: His Life and Diaries* (2 vols., London, 1967), i. 97–8.

[123] Nicolson to Grey, 24 July 1911, *BD* vii, 636. Marder, *Dreadnought*, i. 242–3.

[124] Grey, *Twenty-Five Years*, i. 230.

[125] Churchill, *World Crisis*, 48. Grey to McKenna, 24 July 1911, *BD* vii, doc. 637.

[126] Churchill, *World Crisis*, 49. However, Mr Nicholas Lambert, of Wolfson College, Oxford, is conducting research that casts doubt on the extent of the British naval measures.

[127] W. Görlitz, *Der Kaiser . . . Aufzeichnungen des Chefs des Marinekabinetts Admiral Georg von Müller über die Ära Wilhelms II.* (Göttingen, 1965), 87. Kiderlen to Treutler, 26 July, Wilhelm to Bethmann and Bethmann to Wilhelm, 27 July 1911, *GP* xxix, docs. 10629–31.

later that they realized what their potential adversaries were doing.[128] Perhaps this was fortunate. At any rate, British intervention probably assisted in deterring Germany from pressing demands that Caillaux could not concede. After sending the *Panther* Kiderlen apparently believed at first that he could safely bluff, telling Bethmann that 'we . . . should in any event act very forcefully'. Germany must be willing to fight, although he was convinced that France would not 'pick up the gauntlet'. Wilhelm, however, objected to starting down such a road without being consulted. He authorized continuing negotiations, without threats.[129] On 29 July Kiderlen agreed with the Emperor that Britain was likely to support France in a war with Germany, which would therefore be inopportune. Three days later he told Jules Cambon that he would accept a French protectorate in Morocco.[130] He was now deprived of the instrument that he himself had said was necessary and that he believed could have been wielded safely.

This notwithstanding, the Central African negotiations were far from settled, and during August tension remained high. Kiderlen wanted a common frontier between the German Cameroons and the Belgian Congo, so as to improve Germany's chances of a share of the latter if it were partitioned. But for such a land bridge the French would have to accept a *coupure*, or separation, of Gabon and the French Congo from the rest of their African colonies. Caillaux secretly agreed to this at the end of the month, but de Selves still opposed it.[131] Moreover, when the Foreign Ministry's interception of the German Embassy's cables uncovered Caillaux's parallel contact the Premier's position was badly shaken, and on 4 August he sent a virtual ultimatum that unless an agreement were in sight by the end of the following week both Paris and London would send warships to Agadir.[132] The follow-up, however, showed that the restraining mechanisms established in July were still operating. Caillaux explained that he had meant only that hotheads might demand that ships were sent.[133] Grey, who feared that such action would result in German mobilization, obtained from Caillaux a promise not to take it without consulting him. If war broke out, the Foreign Secretary emphasized, it must seem to be Germany's responsibility.[134] Conversely, Wilhelm was infuriated by Caillaux's message of 4 August, and ordered Kiderlen to liaise with the naval authorities. But the reconcentration of the fleet was not brought forward from the scheduled date of 15 August, and all that was done was to recall a few naval reservists. Kiderlen told Capelle, who was deputizing while Tirpitz was on holiday, that Germany could not fight over Morocco and anything that could be represented as a mobilization measure was

[128] Ibid., doc. 10630, and Oncken, *Panthersprung*, 289.

[129] Bethmann to Wilhelm, 15 and 20 July, Bethmann to Foreign Ministry, 21 July 1911, *GP* xxix, docs. 10607, 10613–14. Oncken, *Panthersprung*, 283.

[130] Görlitz, *Der Kaiser*, 87. Barraclough, *Agadir*, 134; though Oncken, *Panthersprung*, 168 ff. has a different emphasis.

[131] Allain, *Agadir*, 302. [132] Schoen telegram, 4 Aug. 1911, *GP* xxix, doc. 10686.

[133] Kiderlen to Jenisch, 9 Aug. 1911, ibid., doc. 10697.

[134] De Selves to Paul Cambon, Paul Cambon to de Selves, 22 and 23 Aug. 1911, *DDF* 2nd ser. xiv, docs. 202, 205.

'in the highest degree undesirable'.[135] Capelle shared his wish to keep things cool: 'Suggestions are constantly being made to me to execute this or that mobilization preparation. If I gave way on one, I fear there would be no halting.'[136] The navy knew it could not beat the British,[137] and Tirpitz preferred to use the crisis to get a new *Novelle*. Contrary to French fears, Kiderlen did not intend to reinforce at Agadir, and he wished to avoid provocation; while Grey restrained Caillaux, and Caillaux, on the whole, restrained de Selves.

These dress rehearsals prepared the Powers for more difficult decisions. In the second half of August negotiations were suspended while Kiderlen went on holiday with his mistress to Switzerland, finding time for a much publicized foray across the French border. Jules Cambon returned to Paris, where a meeting between Caillaux and his Ministers and Ambassadors on 22 August decided to accept the *coupure*.[138] When discussions resumed the two sides concentrated first on Morocco, a joint communiqué on 20 September making known that in principle the issues there were resolved. Attention switched to Central Africa, where Germany was given two narrow (and militarily indefensible) corridors through French territory. On 4 November the agreements embodying this arrangement were signed.

After the September communiqué all perceived that the danger had diminished, but it was preceded by a hardening of opinion and what one historian has called a 'war psychosis'.[139] For Germany, war over Morocco or the Congo was fantastic, as Kiderlen and the Emperor periodically reminded themselves.[140] France had a much larger stake in the sultanate, but little in the tropics. Once Kiderlen had ceased demanding the entire French Congo and the French had granted the *coupure*, the two sides converged. But until agreement was reached neither government could be sure that the negotiations would succeed or that its opponent intended them to. Like the British, the French distinguished between acceptable concessions and humiliation: at a certain point, they warned Britain and Russia after the 22 August meeting, they would send troops and warships to southern Morocco rather than give way. What would then be at issue would be not colonial territory but their own and others' perception of France's international standing.[141] Churchill's remark that 'great commotions arise out of small things, but not necessarily concerning small things' is apposite.[142] On 4 September Pellé, the French military attaché in Berlin, reported that German opinion had been calm at the beginning of the crisis but was increasingly strained, not only officers but also businessmen appearing to desire war. Caillaux

[135] Kiderlen to Jenisch, Admiralty Staff to Wilhelm, 8 Aug. 1911, *GP* xxix, docs. 10691–2. Tirpitz, *Aufbau*, 201–2.

[136] Ibid. 27.

[137] Memoranda by Commander of High Seas Fleet (Holtzendorf), 16 Sept. 1911, BA-MA NL Tirpitz N. 253/25a; and 25 Oct. 1911, ibid. 25b.

[138] Allain, *Agadir*, 402.   [139] Ibid. 375.   [140] Tirpitz, *Aufbau*, 201, 203.

[141] De Selves to Paul Cambon and Louis, 27 Aug. 1911, *DDF* 2nd ser. xiv, doc. 202, cf. de Selves to Louis, 3 Sept. 1911, ibid., doc. 249.

[142] Churchill, *World Crisis*, 55.

told the British Ambassador that although he believed that neither government nor the majority of either people wished to fight there was increasing irritation in France and less fear of Germany than a few years earlier.[143] Moreover, the normal rhythms of the military year now required decisions on whether to go ahead with the autumn manœuvres, and whether to send home the reservists called up for summer exercises and to release the oldest conscript class. Not to do so would give priority to military preparedness, even if this imperilled a negotiated solution.

The September tension spilled out across Europe. In Norway the Government was criticized (mistakenly, according to its supporters) for not having taken precautions. In Sweden, manœuvres were terminated, and warships returned to port.[144] In Italy, in contrast, manœuvres on the French border went ahead, for fear of the impact on foreign perceptions and Italian public opinion if they were cancelled.[145] In the Netherlands, where a Dutch vessel had clashed with a German torpedo boat in the Ems estuary, the War Minister foresaw that the climax would come in late September, when the French and German conscript classes were scheduled for discharge. As this moment approached the Dutch cancelled the manœuvres of their 3rd Division, and two reservist classes that had been called up for exercises were kept under arms. At Maastricht leave was ended and the Rhine bridges were put under guard.[146] In Belgium initial inactivity reflected Hellebaut's influence. Subsequently the War Minister seems to have been overborne by General Jungbluth, the head of Albert's military household and the prospective commander-in-chief, whose reputation was liberal and Anglophile. The annual manœuvres were cancelled, on the pretext of foot-and-mouth disease. The 1909 conscript class, due for release on 15 September, was retained indefinitely, Liège and Namur were reinforced, and the frontier bridges manned and primed for demolition. The Government was on the point of calling up three classes of reservists when a telegram from Kiderlen reported that the Franco-German dispute was about to be settled. The measures decided in Brussels were, on paper, the most extensive anywhere, and all commentators took for granted that both Dutch and Belgian precautions benefited the Triple Entente.[147]

On 21 August it was Britain's turn to call off cavalry manœuvres, ostensibly

---

[144] Spring-Rice (Stockholm) and Wingfield (Christiania) to Grey, 2 and 6 Sept. 1911, PRO FO 425/354, docs. 184, 188.
[145] Correspondence between Spingardi, Giolitti, and Brusati, Aug.–Sept. 1911, ACS Carte Brusati VI. 4. 36, docs. 290, 291, 297.
[146] Acton to Grey, 14 and 19 Aug., Johnstone to Grey, 12, 19, and 22 Sept. 1911, PRO FO 425/354, docs. 47, 53, 97, 102, 106.
[147] Bridges to Hardinge, 26 July; Watson to Grey, 2 and 5 Sept.; Bridges to Watson, 22 Sept.; Bridges to Villiers, 19 Oct. 1911, PRO FO 425/354 docs. 26(i), 85, 87, 101, 141(i). Duruy to Messimy, 3, 7, 15 Sept. 1911, *DDF* 2nd ser. xiv, docs. 253, 279, 323. GGS annual report, 5 Dec. 1911, KAM Gstb. 489.

because of drought. This, of course, was another pretext.[148] War, wrote Lloyd George to Grey, 'is so much in the reckoning as to render it urgently necessary for us to take every step which would render the issue of war more favourable, always provided that such a step does not include the chance of precipitating war'.[149] With a volunteer army the question of the senior conscript class did not arise, and the most obtrusive steps, such as calling up reservists, were avoided. None the less, the new Director of Military Operations, Sir Henry Wilson, was twice sent to consult with the EMA in Paris, and briefed Ministers on the Continental military balance. Tunnels and bridges on the principal railway lines were put under guard, and preparations for sending the BEF intensified.[150] In mid-September Grey asked the Admiralty to keep the fleet assembled and 'in such a condition and position that they should welcome a German attack'. Only at the end of the month did he agree to suspend the special precautions for the Home Fleet and the railways, provided that they could at once be reimposed.[151]

In this atmosphere of anticipation, the French and German Governments approached their September deadlines. Probably in late August Caillaux reminded the newly appointed Joffre that Napoleon had supposedly not given battle unless he reckoned on at least a 70 per cent chance of victory. He asked whether France could assume this now. Joffre, embarrassed, eventually said that it could not, the Premier concluding, 'well then . . . we shall negotiate'.[152] Actually, the decision to negotiate had already been taken, but Caillaux's awareness of military weakness may have encouraged the concessions that ensured success. He and Messimy were particularly impressed by France's deficient heavy artillery and the unsatisfactory organization of the High Command. Both matters could be remedied, but the remedies would take time.[153] In addition, the Prime Minister had been shocked by Britain's warning in July that it would not necessarily fight to prevent Germany from installing itself in Morocco, and he was never told precisely how far and in what circumstances London would back him.[154] As for the Russians, they followed up the 1910 Potsdam meeting by signing an agreement with Germany in mid-August on railway concessions in the Ottoman Empire and Persia. Izvolsky promised military assistance in a conflict, but urged France to settle without fighting as the Russian army was not ready and the Russian public would not understand a war over Morocco. It is true that in the annual Chiefs of Staff meeting Zhilinski promised to bring forward his offensive against Germany to day 15, and on 8 September Nicholas reaffirmed his loyalty to the alliance and the military convention. None the less, the

---

[148] Allain, *Agadir*, 375. Haldane to Grey, 11 Sept. 1911, PRO FO/800/102.

[149] Lloyd George to Grey, 1 Sept. 1911, *BD* vii, doc. 642.

[150] Nicolson to Goschen and Grey, 12 and 26 Sept. 1911, PRO FO/800/350. Callwell, *Wilson*, i. 96, 104.

[151] Grey to Nicolson, 17 Sept., Nicolson to Grey, 22 and 26 Sept. 1911, PRO FO/800/350.

[152] J.J.-C. Joffre, *Mémoires du Maréchal Joffre, 1910–1917* (2 vols., Paris, 1932), ii. 15–16. Caillaux, *Mémoires*, ii. 145.

[153] Ibid. 123–9. A.-M. Messimy, *Mes Souvenirs* (Paris, 1937), 74–88.

[154] Caillaux, *Mémoires*, ii. 130–9.

Russians' contradictions suggested that their attitude, like Britain's, would depend on the circumstances in which negotiations broke down.[155]

Perhaps for these reasons, French military activity was purposive but low-key. The main development came on 24 August, when the manœuvres scheduled for the northern *départements* were cancelled, supposedly again because of foot-and-mouth disease. The German military attaché, Winterfeldt, recognized that the cancellation (which followed Caillaux's meeting with his ministers on 22 August and was accompanied by approaches to St Petersburg and London) was significant. Military preparations had quietly been taking place for weeks, and the French army and the press were confident, although the Government would not provoke war.[156] On 1 September Joffre and Messimy told Winterfeldt's British counterpart that preparations had been 'intensive'.[157] According to the GGS much of the information received from the French border regions had been exaggerated or false, but there had been inspections, trial mobilizations, and restrictions on leave, and the fortress stores had been replenished. Even so, the French were neither mobilizing in earnest, nor preparing to do so, confining themselves rather to 'precautionary measures'.[158]

The Germans, like the French, had no reason to expect unqualified support from their allies. Kiderlen had not consulted Vienna before dispatching the *Panther*, and the crisis had little bearing on Austrian interests. In 1902 Italy and France had secretly promised each other mutual sympathy over Libya and Morocco.[159] The German leaders knew that critical choices were impending, and in the army and navy there were advocates of preparedness; but in the end decisions were taken for both services that entailed deliberate acquiescence in security risks and a gamble on negotiation. The navy had taken limited precautions in mid-August, although on 13 September the Foreign Ministry agreed to the release of marine reservists.[160] Three days later Holtzendorff, the Commander of the High Seas Fleet, warned that after 1 October the intake of the new class of conscripts (especially stokers) would make the fleet no longer operational, although the British would remain at high readiness.[161] The Chief of the Admiralty Staff advised that unless the situation were clarified soon more visible and costly steps would be necessary, including faster repairs, postponing annual refits, keeping on reservists with special skills, concentrating U-boats in the North Sea, and reinforcing the garrison of Helgoland. As a result of the diplomatic breakthrough, however, Bethmann ruled that these measures were not needed, almost simultaneously with Grey's instructions to the Sea Lords to 'ease

---

[155] Buchanan to Grey, 24 Aug., Bertie to Grey, 1 and 2 Sept., Buchanan to Grey, 7 Sept. 1911, *BD* vii, docs. 496, 499, 500, 505. De Selves circular, 14 Aug., Louis to de Selves, 25 Aug.; de Selves to Louis and Louis to de Selves, 1 Sept.; Louis to de Selves, 8 Sept. 1911; Russo-French staff conversations, 31 Aug. 1911, *DDF* 2nd ser. xiv, docs. 172, 208, 234–5, 283, 232.

[156] Allain, *Agadir*, 375. Winterfeldt reports, 19 and 24 Aug. 1911, *GP* xxix, docs. 10715, 10723.

[157] Col. Fairholme to Bertie, 1 Sept. 1911, *BD* vii. 643(i).

[158] Moltke to Heeringen, 1 and 19 Sept. 1911, KAM Gstb 164.

[159] Oncken, *Panthersprung*, 287.   [160] Ibid. 303.

[161] Holtzendorf memorandum, 16 Sept. 1911, BA-MA Tirpitz MSS N.253/25a.

off' the precautions taken by the Home Fleet.[162] In retrospect Zimmermann, the Under-Secretary for Foreign Affairs, believed that Britain's naval measures had been prudential rather than offensive, but if it had become known that Germany was increasing its preparedness the Royal Navy might have attacked. Any international dispute might lead to serious conflict, and 'Premature military measures . . . would in most cases certainly bring about this outcome . . . that it was possible to lead the Moroccan crisis to a peaceful outcome I attribute in the first instance to the fact that last summer we refrained from any military preparations.'[163]

On land it seems that during the summer little was done. The British attaché in Berlin reported during July that he had seen no unusual activity, or abnormal rail traffic.[164] The rumours reaching the French were mostly discounted by Pellé, a very acute observer, who during September stressed repeatedly that he had no evidence of 'visible' war preparations. Military grain purchases, possibly resulting from the poor harvest, were the only slightly worrying step. On 14 September he reported that units had been moved from the western frontier to the interior for manœuvres, which would not have happened if German intentions were seriously threatening.[165]

The attaché was correct to underline the significance of this development, which resulted from a decision at the highest level. On 28 August Wilhelm had written to Bethmann that the cancellation by the French of their manœuvres meant that their 1st and 6th Corps would remain in their normal locations. But if Germany ordered mobilization during its own forthcoming manœuvres the units involved in them would have to travel back to their garrison points, thus clogging up the railways and adding two or three days to their mobilization times. None the less, after consulting Moltke and Heeringen he decided that the manœuvres should go ahead. Bethmann and Kiderlen confirmed this decision, which meant that for several days the western frontier would be 'militarily almost defenceless'. Metz would be specially protected against a standing-start attack, but to cancel the manœuvres on the pretext of dysentery or foot-and-mouth disease would heighten tension and might lead to war. The negotiations could be dragged out if it was necessary to win time.[166] Heeringen similarly advised the Bavarian Government not to cancel manœuvres without consulting him, for fear that this would be seen in France as a war preparation, with 'a political consequence directly contrary to the one intended'.[167]

---

[162] Tirpitz to Bethmann (with enclosures), 21 Sept.; Bethmann to Tirpitz (?) 27 Sept. 1911, BA R.43F/1267/2. Nicolson to Grey, 24 Sept. 1911, PRO FO 800/350.

[163] Zimmermann to Chief of Admiralty Staff, 26 Jan. 1912, *GP* xxix, doc. 10673.

[164] Lt.-Col. Russell to Goschen, 27 July 1911, *BD* vii, doc. 432(i).

[165] Pellé reports, 4, 7, 10, 14, 20 Sept. 1911, SHA 7.N. 1110.

[166] Wilhelm to Bethmann, 28 Aug.; Heeringen memorandum, 31 Aug. 1911, *GP* xxix, docs. 10724, 10726. G. Granier, 'Deutsche Rüstungspolitik vor dem Ersten Weltkrieg: General Franz Wandels Tagebuchaufzeichnungen aus dem preussischen Kriegsministerium', *Militärgeschichtliche Mitteilungen*, 38 (1985), 137.

[167] Gebsattel to Bavarian War Minister, 4 and 5 Sept. 1911, KAM MKr. 41.

On 3 September Wilhelm confirmed both this decision and that the reservists would be sent home, although in August he had feared precisely that the French were stalling until the men had gone.[168] On the following day the Foreign Ministry agreed to the release of the senior conscript class.[169] Kiderlen told Jules Cambon that the class would go as soon as the manœuvres were completed—'we shall not keep on one'—and that he trusted Paris would see this as an earnest of Germany's confidence in a peaceful outcome. There would be 'extraordinary emotion' in Germany, however, if France's own class were retained. In a further conversation, which he asked to be kept 'rigorously secret', he explained to the French representatives how he had prevailed over strong pressures from 'the military party' on the issue. For France to keep on its own class now, Pellé commented, might have the most serious consequences, and perhaps transform the balance between the war and peace advocates.[170] De Selves waited for French military intelligence and the Quai d'Orsay's agents to confirm the stand-down, but on 14 September he made clear that the French senior class would also be released as normal, a disclosure that Moltke's own intelligence soon corroborated.[171]

After the *Panther*'s spring—which was an impulsive and ill-considered gesture rather than a serious application of armed force to support diplomacy—the Germans acted consistently to keep the crisis below the threshold. The panic in July did not hasten the High Seas Fleet's return from Scandinavia; Caillaux's threat on 4 August rattled Wilhelm, but Kiderlen still kept naval precautions to a minimum. In September Bethmann shelved the recommendations of the Admiralty Staff. On land there were decisions in quick succession to proceed with manœuvres and to release the reservists and the senior conscript contingent. It was the entente, with Britain's naval alert, the cancellation of manœuvres by both Paris and London, and other less dramatic steps, that placed the higher premium on readiness, and the contrast requires explanation. On 3 September 100,000 people attended a peace demonstration in Berlin, but in the final weeks most of German opinion was growing more intransigent, and the SPD's Jena Congress rejected motions for a general strike to prevent war.[172] More influential on the Government than Socialist pressure was probably the fall on the Berlin Bourse in September. Kiderlen had enquired earlier in the summer whether the German banks were able, without borrowing, to make up for the Government's inability to finance even two months of war expenditure, and had been told that the answer was no. Caillaux got wind of this, and probably helped engineer the liquidity crisis through withdrawals of French and Russian short-term funds.[173] The decision to proceed with manœuvres, however, preceded the

---

[168] Ibid.; and cf. Granier, 'Rüstungspolitik', 136.   [169] Oncken, *Panthersprung*, 303.

[170] Jules Cambon to de Selves, 7 and 8 Sept. 1911, *DDF* 2nd ser. xiv, docs. 276, 290. Pellé to Messimy, 7, 8, 10 Sept. 1911, SHA 7.N. 1110.

[171] Pellé to Barthélemy, 25 Sept. 1911 (ibid.). De Selves circular, 14 Sept. and de Farges to de Selves, 15 Sept. 1911, *DDF* 2nd ser. xiv, docs. 315, 319. Moltke to Heeringen, 19 Sept. 1911, KAM Gstb. 164.

[172] Allain, *Agadir*, 379–82.   [173] Ibid. 363–7.

financial panic, and German restraint must be traced back to the consistent preference of the Berlin leadership for negotiation. In the end Kiderlen issued his
joint communiqué with the French before the German manœuvres ended on
24 September, at what militarily was an exceptionally disadvantageous time. The
Emperor, though taunted with the sobriquet of 'William the Timid' in the conservative press, backed Kiderlen and Bethmann against the 'military party pushing for war', on condition that a peaceful settlement was possible without
'humiliation'.[174]

According to the Bavarian military plenipotentiary, senior army figures were
arguing by September that Germany should strike before the Russian military
reorganization was completed, while Britain was plagued by strikes, and France
by anti-militarism.[175] But before the crisis stronger civilian control had been
imposed on mobilization preparations, Zimmermann and Heeringen agreeing in
June that these should be preceded by full discussion between the Foreign, War,
and Navy Ministries and authorized by imperial command, in order to ensure
that they were undertaken only if the military-political situation made them
absolutely necessary and that the Chancellor could take responsibility.[176] In any
case, neither Heeringen nor Moltke wanted war without a 'convincing ground',
and the German leaders were agreed that if they wished for Austrian and Italian
aid they must not seem the aggressors. Heeringen opposed half measures such
as retaining reservists and cancelling manœuvres, which he considered would
seem threatening to the outside world while adding little to readiness.[177] General
Wandel, the Director of the General War Department in the War Ministry,
agreed that warning measures would simply impede smooth mobilization.[178] On
the other hand, according to the War Minister, 'if it is serious, then full mobilization straightaway'.[179] As for Moltke, he wrote to his wife on 19 August that
if the Germans crept out of the crisis with their tail between their legs and did
not make energetic demands that they were prepared to back up at the point of
the sword, he would despair of the future of the Reich and resign.[180] Yet in practice he did nothing of the kind, and the letter, which may be a suspect text, called
neither for war nor for preventive war. Nor did Moltke use his influence as the
Government's principal military adviser in order to push for one. On the contrary, in a circular on 1 September to the civilian authorities and corps commanders on the frontiers he noted how in previous crises since 1905 there had
been a tide of reports on enemy short-term measures, which were often exaggerated and could lead to unnecessary alarms. All such reports must be processed
in the GGS, which had been able to show repeatedly that disturbing rumours

---

[174] Gebsattel to Bavarian War Ministry, 4 Sept. 1911, KAM MKr. 41.
[175] Gebsattel to Bavarian War Ministry, 3 Sept. 1911, ibid.
[176] Oncken, *Panthersprung*, 212.
[177] Gebsattel to Bavarian War Ministry, 3 Sept. 1911, KAM MKr. 41.
[178] Granier, 'Rüstungspolitik', 137.
[179] Gebsattel report cited in n. 175 above.
[180] H. von Moltke, *Erinnerungen, Briefe, Dokumente, 1877–1916*, ed. E. von Moltke (Stuttgart, 1922), 362.

were incorrect, and was able to distinguish between precautions and war pre-parations. With this, he began a series of regular bulletins on the steps taken by Germany's potential antagonists: a practice he repeated in the 1912–13 Balkan crisis and in July–August 1914. The bulletins were cautious and sober, and min-imized the significance of French activity rather than raising the alarm. And Moltke, like Heeringen, went along with the decision to leave the western fron-tier vulnerable during the climactic September days.[181]

The growing impatience in the military, then, was not translated into an assault upon civilian leadership. One returns to the fundamental preference in both France and Germany for a compromise settlement, provided that its terms were not adjudged humiliating. What might be so adjudged depended on the Western European leaders' perceptions of each other and of themselves, and the transmutation of such perceptions was perhaps Agadir's most ominous legacy. In Britain, Lloyd George's and Churchill's view of Germany had become more sombre, and the peace party in the Liberal Cabinet was enfeebled.[182] The smart-ing wounds of outraged nationalism were manifest in the French and German treaty ratification debates. According to the Bavarian military plenipotentiary, 'even after a peaceful ending to the present Moroccan crisis there would remain so much injury, so much bitterness, and such irritability that the possibility of war within the next year seems to have come very close'.[183] The repercussions were to dominate the armaments politics of 1911–12.

* * *

The period of the four-ship tempo between 1908 and 1911 saw the navy take its highest-ever share of German defence spending, although within tighter overall restrictions than before Bülow's financial reform. In Tirpitz's words, Wermuth ringed the Treasury 'with barbed wire',[184] and by 1911 he achieved a surplus. In the protracted, tortuous, and bitter inter-departmental struggle that followed Agadir, however, Treasury control was dealt a fatal blow, and despite the SPD successes in the January 1912 elections the new Reichstag was more willing than its predecessor to approve defence expenditure. But whereas Tirpitz led the move to cash in on the Moroccan crisis, it was the army rather than the navy that benefited. Compared with the Navy Secretary's initial ambitions, his 1912 *Novelle* was a major defeat; whereas Heeringen's objectives for the 1912 army law were largely accomplished. Without the Moroccan crisis this redressing of the armaments balance might not have happened at all, and certainly neither so quickly nor emphatically.

On the eve of Agadir it had seemed that no new naval bills were in prospect, and that Tirpitz was resigned to returning to two ships a year. His office was budgeting accordingly, and when the Navy League conference on 28 May called

---

[181] Moltke circular to frontier corps staff, 1 Sept., and Moltke to Heeringen, 1 and 19 Sept. 1911, KAM Gstb 164.

[182] B. B. Gilbert, 'Pacifist to Interventionist: David Lloyd George in 1911 and 1914. Was Belgium an Issue?', *Historical Journal*, 28 (1985), 866–79.

[183] Gebsattel to Bavarian War Ministry, 3 Sept. 1911, KAM Mkr. 41.

[184] V. R. Berghahn, *Germany and the Approach of War in 1914* (London, 1973), 98.

for accelerated battlecruiser building he protested to Wermuth that he was foreign to the agitation.[185] By 3 August, in contrast, he expected such vehement
public reaction to the crisis that 'The possibility of a *Novelle* thereby moves
nearer . . .', and he feared that if he waited he would miss the tide. He accepted
the recommendation of the Admiralty Staff that the fleet needed extra battlecruisers and larger guns if it was to keep pace with Britain. He thought a continued four-ship tempo would be provocative and feared that he lacked the
necessary personnel, but he welcomed a three-ship one. Indeed, he and Capelle
had already thought of challenging the existing schedule, possibly in 1913, and
although Capelle was sceptical about the strength of public feeling Tirpitz moved
ahead.[186]

By the time the Navy Secretary broached the topic with Bethmann on
30 August, his ideas had expanded. As well as faster replacement of the outdated
armoured cruisers by battlecruisers, he wanted to raise the number of active
squadrons from two to three, the extra ships coming partly from the care-and-
maintenance fleet, the *Materialreserve*, but also from new building. There would
be a three-ship rather than a two-ship tempo in 1912–17, resulting in six additional capital ships. A *Novelle* would counter the domestic discontent and the
damage to Germany's prestige caused by the Moroccan crisis,[187] and, as the
British naval attaché commented, new orders would protect capacity and
employment in the yards.[188] Capelle and the Navy Office feared that if they
dropped back to two ships a year they might never rise again, with the danger
that their cherished objective of a sixty-ship battlefleet would slip permanently
out of reach. The creation of a third squadron, in contrast, reflected the priorities of Admiral Holtzendorff and the line commanders. Because of Wermuth's
financial squeeze and Tirpitz's construction priority, the navy's operational
readiness had been neglected. The officer corps was further stretched every year
to command bigger and more complex vessels, and for several weeks each
autumn while the new recruits were trained the fleet was disabled. In short, the
navy's *matériel* had grown faster than its ability to use it. Holtzendorff wanted
more cruisers, battlecruisers, and torpedo boats, but in the light of the 1911 war
scare he placed the emphasis on readiness. The reserve divisions should be made
more combat-worthy, the autumn disruption truncated, and shortages of specialized personnel remedied. Nor were the fleet commanders satisfied with the
role of cannon fodder that Tirpitz's Risk Theory assigned to them: they aspired
to a less sacrificial destiny.[189]

Tirpitz used both Capelle's and Holtzendorff's lines of argument against the

---

[185] Capt. Watson to Goschen, 28 May 1911, *BD* vi, doc. 470(i). Wermuth to Tirpitz, 19 June
1911, BA-MA Tirpitz MSS N.253/24b. Tirpitz to Wermuth, 24 June 1911, ibid.
[186] Tirpitz, *Aufbau*, 200–6. CAS to Tirpitz, 22 June and 8 July 1911, BA-MA Tirpitz MSS
N.253/24b.
[187] Tirpitz, *Aufbau*, 207–9.
[188] Watson to Goschen, 27 Nov. 1911, PRO FO/435/354 doc. 181(i).
[189] Berghahn, *Germany*, 99–100. Holtzendorf memorandum, 16 Sept. 1911, BA-MA NL Tirpitz
N.253/25a. Görlitz (ed.), *Der Kaiser*, 91.

civilians, but the latter approach made more headway. His opening discussion with Bethmann was discouraging. The Chancellor was worried about the cost and about the danger of war with Britain, and it was agreed to wait until the end of the Moroccan dispute. Wilhelm, in contrast, incensed by the Mansion House speech and the press criticisms made of him, was already committed to a new *Novelle*, telling von Müller, the Chief of the Naval Cabinet, that the people wanted one and if Bethmann, Kiderlen, and Wermuth demurred they would have to go. In a meeting at Rominten on 26 September he showed himself receptive to Tirpitz's contention that the Risk Theory should be superseded as the public justification of the naval programme by the open pursuit of a 2:3 ratio relative to Britain in capital ships. The aim was now 'a good defensive chance' against a British attack— to be able to survive one, in other words—and not simply deterrence by threatening Britain with a Pyrrhic victory. The combination of a third active squadron with a three-ship tempo down to 1917 would bring this objective within Germany's reach, and a public offer of a 2:3 ratio (which Tirpitz expected London to reject) would prepare German opinion to favour it. The Emperor, enthused, took to minuting '2:3' on dispatches from the London Embassy.[190]

Rominten marked the end of the phoney war, and with his master's backing Tirpitz was able to impose himself. In mid-October Wilhelm threatened to dismiss Bethmann unless a *Novelle* was introduced immediately: the Chancellor compromised by scheduling one for the spring. Tirpitz's sense of urgency was directly linked to Agadir and the outbreak of hostilities between the Ottoman Empire and Italy. He wanted to exploit public anxiety in order to demonstrate to the Reichstag that only a 2:3 ratio would do. At the moment he agreed with Holtzendorff and the Admiralty Staff that Germany's prospects in a war were 'thoroughly unsatisfactory', but he was confident that he could narrow the gap.[191] The first draft of the *Novelle* provided for an active battlefleet of a flagship plus three squadrons of eight battleships each, as well as twelve battle-cruisers, all to be fully manned and permanently in service. Two more squadrons would make up the reserve fleet, of which four battleships would be continuously available and the rest have nucleus crews. In 1912–17 three ships would be laid down in most years, and by 1920 the predicted ratio in capital ships would be 95:61. But it was thought that Britain would have neither the money nor the manpower to keep more than fifty-seven ships constantly operational, whereas the German fleet would rise from a current figure of twenty-one battleships and larger cruisers to thirty-seven. The preamble openly acknowledged that to preserve peace after the Moroccan crisis the fleet must be strong enough to have a reasonable chance of successfully resisting attack, and with the attainment of the 2:3 ratio Tirpitz believed he could bargain from strength.[192]

---

[190] Ibid. 89–90. Tirpitz, *Aufbau*, 209, 213–15. Jenisch to Kiderlen, 28 Sept.; Metternich to Bethmann, 27 Sept. 1911, *GP* xxxi, docs. 11308–9. Wilhelm to Bethmann, 30 Sept. 1911, BA-MA Tirpitz MSS N.253/25b.

[191] Tirpitz, *Aufbau*, 217–26. Görlitz (ed.), *Der Kaiser*, 93–8.

[192] Tirpitz to Bethmann, with inclosures, 3 Nov. 1911, BA R.43.F/951/1.

With the commitment to a *Novelle*, however, the Navy Secretary had reached his apogee, and from here on the draft bill would be stripped of much of its content. The reasons for the change of fortune included the new mood of German public opinion, as well as the navy leadership's internal divisions, Bethmann and the Foreign Ministry's diplomatic and Wermuth's financial reservations, and the emergence of the army as a formidable competitor. Between them, these forces were too powerful for Tirpitz to overcome, enjoying as he did only fitful patronage from Wilhelm.

The public indignation unleashed by Britain's intervention in the Moroccan crisis took the German authorities by surprise. Disappointment at the terms of the November settlement added fuel to the flames. In the Reichstag ratification debates the parties outbid each other in their attacks, but that by the Prussian Conservative spokesman, Heydebrand, attracted most attention, as a warning that the Government was estranging its traditional following.[193] On 9 November, moreover, a speech in the House of Commons by the Unionist MP, Captain Faber, disclosed that the British army had had plans during the crisis to send six divisions across the Channel. The impression created, wrote Bethmann to Metternich, was that 'while France in November made no war preparations, Britain seems to have been ready to strike every day'.[194] It was a short step to the conclusion that Germany must strengthen its own forces. The head of the Navy League wrote to Bethmann that Britain's 'unmistakable war threat' had provoked the strongest movement of opinion since 1870. In recent weeks 125 meetings held all over the country had demanded faster naval building to prevent any repetition. Wilhelm believed the Reichstag would support a bill, and the speeches in the ratification debates bore out his view.[195]

By late November, however, Bethmann expected pressure for an army as well as a naval increase. General August Keim appealed for the creation of a German Defence League (Deutscher Wehrverein—DWV), which was launched in January 1912 and by May had 33,000 members. By 1914 it had 100,000, as well as 260,000 corporate subscribers, and among the hypertrophied German patriotic associations ranked second only to the Navy League. Comparisons with the French army formed the basis for its programme for the German one. The French implemented truly universal conscription, which Germany did not, they trained their reservists more thoroughly, employed the more manœuvrable four-piece battery, and had more machine guns, lorries, and aircraft.[196] The publish-

---

[193] Förster, *Militarismus*, 211–16.

[194] Bethmann to Metternich, 22 Nov. 1911, *GP* xxix, doc. 10657; and same date, *GP* xxxi, doc. 11321.

[195] Koester to Bethmann, 3 Nov. 1911, BA R.43.F/951/1. Tirpitz, *Aufbau*, 228–9.

[196] M. S. Coetzee, 'The Mobilization of the Right? The *Deutscher Wehrverein* and Political Activism in Württemberg, 1912–14', *European History Quarterly*, 15 (1985), 431–52. R. Chickering, 'Der "Deutsche Wehrverein" und die Reform der deutschen Armee, 1912–14', *Militärgeschichtliche Mitteilungen*, 25 (1979), 7–34. A. Keim, *Erlebtes und Erstrebenes: Lebenserinnerungen von Generalleutnant Keim* (Hanover, 1925), ch. 8. Pingaud to French Foreign Ministry, 5 Mar. and 12 Apr. 1912, AMAE NS Allemagne 104. Pellé to War Ministry, 25 Dec. 1911, SHA 7.N. 1110; and 4 Feb. 1912, SHA 7.N. 1111. Förster, *Militarismus*, 221 ff.

ing success of General Bernhardi's *Germany and the Next War* was another straw in the wind. War, it argued, was a 'biological necessity', and Germany had the right to seek European hegemony by destroying French power for all time. Intensive preparation should be the main aim of policy.[197] The French representatives in Berlin observed the trend, Pellé interpreting the army bill as a reaction against France's diplomatic victory.[198] If Agadir at first directed German nationalism towards naval armaments and against Britain, by 1912 it was directed towards land armaments and with France as the enemy.

It is more difficult to trace the effects of public opinion on official policy. The DWV was frequently referred to in the Reichstag debates on the army bill. Unlike the Navy League, however, it kept aloof from government patronage. Keim had led the radical wing of the Navy League during the civil war that racked that organization in 1905–8, and left it after Wilhelm intervened personally against him. Before the Moroccan crisis Kiderlen had met Heinrich Class, the Pan-German leader, and encouraged him to propagandize for a settlement colony. The outcome of the crisis therefore deepened the divide between the Government and the radical Right. The Pan-German League contained both navalist and pro-army tendencies, and it decided to launch the DWV as an ostensibly independent organization. Keim and the retired generals round him, in contrast to the War Ministry, were more concerned with strengthening the army against foreign threats than with its role as a buttress of social and political order at home. They foresaw an imminent 'next war', in which a fatherland rotted by pacifism and materialism would be ringed by ruthless foes. A cultural regeneration was imperative, as well as military restructuring and expansion. Although the DWV supported the 1912 army bill, it also condemned it as thoroughly inadequate, and immediately demanded more.[199]

The authorities were suspicious of the DWV, which aroused inter-departmental controversy. Heeringen wanted it to be treated like the Navy League as a 'non-political' organization open to serving officers. Tirpitz and the Interior Ministry objected. Bethmann agreed with Heeringen that it should enjoy such status, though officers were covertly to be discouraged from membership.[200] In fact the army bill was drafted before Keim went public, and it embodied the War Ministry's conservative militarism rather than his own more fiery variant. The DWV helped to assure the bill's Reichstag support, but this would probably have been forthcoming anyway. More significantly, it created a rival focus to the battle-fleet agitation, and after the passage of the *Novelle* Tirpitz could discern no public sympathy for further increases. The navalist upsurge after Agadir looked like being the last for a long time.

The navy was additionally handicapped by discord among its leaders. In

---

[197] Ibid. 232. F. von Bernhardi, *Deutschland und der Nächste Krieg* (Stuttgart, 1912).
[198] e.g. Pellé to War Ministry, 26 May 1912, SHA 7.N. 1111.
[199] See sources cited in n. 196 above.
[200] See correspondence between Bethmann, Heeringen, and Delbrück on the DWV, Feb.–Apr. 1912, BA R.43.F/2273.

briefing Wilhelm, Tirpitz had to admit that not all shared his views.[201] The Admiralty Staff endorsed the first draft of the *Novelle*, but Holtzendorff feared that it increased the danger of a war that his fleet should not risk for at least another two years.[202] Müller favoured the bill in principle, but disliked Tirpitz, whom he thought conceited, inconsistent, and difficult. He was probably right in his suspicion that the Navy Secretary was losing his touch, and Müller's proximity to the Emperor permitted him to engineer a series of compromises at Tirpitz's expense.[203]

In opposing the *Novelle* Bethmann enjoyed co-operation from the Foreign Ministry and the Treasury, as well, less directly, as the the army leadership. Even after the Moroccan crisis had subsided, the Chancellor remained afraid of courting a British pre-emptive strike.[204] The problem of assessment was complicated by divided counsels in the London Embassy, where the naval attaché, Captain Widenmann, reported both that the Royal Navy had been mobilized and poised to attack during the crisis, and that none the less Britain would swallow a new law. Metternich took a less dramatic view of the precautionary measures, but advised that although the British would probably accept the passage of the legislation they might seek a pretext to fight rather than let Germany implement it. He believed *détente* was possible if Germany did not accelerate its build-up, whereas the Navy Office thought the *Novelle* would encourage Britain to negotiate. This difference of opinion replicated the disagreements in Berlin. Wilhelm scrawled 'Capital!' on Widenmann's dispatches, refused to reprimand him for straying outside his technical brief, and discounted Metternich as an alarmist. Bethmann, Kiderlen, and Müller, however, appear to have taken the ambassador's warnings seriously, and the army used the danger that the *Novelle* would cause war with Britain as a justification for its own claims.[205]

All the same, it was the domestic implications of a navy bill that probably most harmed Tirpitz. The Navy Secretary mishandled his initial presentation to Bethmann, and exposed himself to damaging counter-arguments. The six extra capital ships, he envisaged, would be financed by a twenty-year loan, the interest and amortization being paid for mainly by an increase in inheritance tax. A pre-election compact on this basis with the Conservatives and the Catholic Centre might allow the government to go to the polls on a patriotic platform. But Wermuth calculated that the tax increase would yield less than Tirpitz needed, and he objected to paying for the *Novelle* by borrowing. He wanted a new financial plan that would allow him to compare the needs of all the spending departments. Tirpitz complained that the Treasury Secretary was inventing difficulties, but the financial constraints were real enough, although Wermuth

---

[201] Notes on audience with Wilhelm, 27 Oct. 1911, BA-MA Tirpitz MSS N.253/25*b*.
[202] CAS to Tirpitz, 24 Nov. and 6 Dec. 1911; Holtzendorf memorandum, 25 Oct. 1911, ibid.
[203] Görlitz (ed.), *Der Kaiser*, e.g. 96.
[204] Oncken, *Panthersprung*, ch. 10, for a general discussion.
[205] Widenmann to Tirpitz, 28 Oct.; Metternich to Bethmann, 1 Nov. 1911, *GP* xxxi, docs. 11313, 11316. W. Widenmann, *Marine-Attaché an der Kaiserlich-Deutschen Botschaft in London, 1907–1912* (Göttingen, 1952).

doubtless exaggerated them. The argument was really a struggle over priorities. Wermuth's were debt repayment and the army, which he consistently argued should have preference. He professed to represent a balance between financial and military imperatives (and insisted that financial strength was necessary for war preparedness anyway); Tirpitz accused him of being a 'finance fanatic', and insisted that financial planning should be subordinated to national security, rather than the other way round.[206]

The financial issue was bound up with electoral and parliamentary management. Tirpitz acknowledged that the next Reichstag was likely to be less supportive, and he wanted a commitment to the *Novelle* before the elections. Bethmann feared the opposition parties would allege that such a commitment meant higher indirect taxes. But Tirpitz's alternative of an extended inheritance tax, so far from uniting the Government's supporters, was likely to reopen the fissures between them. In any case, the Chancellor's soundings indicated that the Conservatives and the Centre would reject it. In two memoranda in November and December, Wermuth pressed home his assault. A three-ship tempo would push the public finances into 'Deroute'. The growth in revenue expected by 1913 would yield at most half of the cost of the defence increases now envisaged. Further borrowing would compromise financial war preparedness, and negotiations on tax increases should await the outcome of the elections. He did not believe that the British had reached their limit, and if Germany introduced a navy bill without a political agreement they would simply raise their own spending. The message was clear: Tirpitz would have to wait, he would get much less than he was asking, and he would have to share with Heeringen.[207]

Whereas Tirpitz had contemplated supplementary legislation even before Agadir, the army had had no such deep-laid plans. The Moroccan crisis did not lead directly to the army's intervention, but by galvanizing Tirpitz it elicited civilian approaches to Heeringen. Early in the autumn Wermuth told the War Minister that a navy bill was being prepared and tried to coax him into presenting demands of his own, but Heeringen refused until Bethmann, too, enquired whether in the changed political circumstances he wished to bring forward a bill.[208] As late as October the War Minister remained unconvinced that he needed to speed up implementation of the 1911 *Quinquennat*. Only in the following month, when it briefly seemed that Tirpitz and the Emperor would secure the immediate introduction of a navy bill, did he feel obliged to act in order not to be pre-empted.[209]

On 19 November a long letter from Heeringen to Bethmann, cleared in advance with Moltke, set out the army's views. Its occasionally threadbare

[206] Tirpitz, *Aufbau*, 208-9, 226-7, 259. Wermuth, *Beamtenleben*, 278-82, 304 ff. Witt, *Finanzen*, 338-44.

[207] Wermuth to Tirpitz and Bethmann, 28 Nov. and 8 Dec. 1911, Berghahn and Deist (eds.), *Rüstung*, viii/7, 8.

[208] Tirpitz, *Aufbau*, 266. Granier, 'Rüstungspolitik', 125.

[209] Reichsarchiv, *Weltkrieg*, i. 119-23. Gebsattel to Bavarian War Ministry, 19 Nov. 1911, KAM MKr. 42.

arguments suggested hasty composition. Like Tirpitz, Heeringen found difficulty in explaining why what had been considered adequate earlier in the year was not so now. But recent events, he said, compelled him to reappraise the *Quinquennat*. He did not oppose a navy bill, but the army should be strengthened too, and if finance was restricted it should take precedence. If Britain attacked before the *Novelle* had been implemented, Germany could strike back only against France. It was on land that the country's destiny would be decided, and an army increase could be pushed through quickly, providing a shield for naval development. When the 1911 law had been drafted there was no immediate danger, but now the Russian reorganization was almost completed, the French were bringing in African troops, and Belgium and Holland seemed more likely to defend their neutrality. Though still strong enough to defeat Germany's enemies, the army no longer seemed adequate to deter them, and within a few years a reinforcement would be imperative.[210] Heeringen told his brother, who was Chief of the Admiralty Staff, that the public mood obliged him to do something and that Germany's strategic environment had decisively worsened, not just because of Agadir but also because Italy could no longer be relied on and its neutrality would liberate three French army corps.[211] It is questionable if he believed that the army needed to be expanded as a shield for the Navy Law, although this reasoning apparently influenced the Emperor and Bethmann. At any rate, it achieved its objective. The Chancellor still hoped that he could fend off a naval increase by securing an agreement with Britain, and he authorized Metternich to speak to Grey before the latter addressed the Commons on 27 November. But Grey's speech, though friendly, contained nothing concrete, and Wilhelm ruled that both land and sea reinforcement must go ahead.[212]

In contrast to the Navy Secretary, the army was pushing on an open door. Wilhelm remembered how he had agreed only conditionally to the 1911 *Quinquennat*, and reserved the right to add to it.[213] Bethmann had told the Reichstag that 'Germany can conduct a strong policy in the sense of *Weltpolitik* only if she maintains her power on the Continent. Only the weight which we can throw into the scales as a Continental power' would allow her to uphold her global interests.[214] Wermuth hoped to use the army to block Tirpitz and perhaps to get his way over the inheritance tax, but the army leaders had no intention of being anybody's cat's-paw. As drafting work began in earnest they clarified their analysis of German's military-political predicament and their justification for seeking extra.

Moltke's fullest statement of his views came in a memorandum sent to Bethmann on 2 December. It identified France as the 'most dangerous enemy'. The French Government did not at present intend war, but nationalist agitation

---

[210] Heeringen to Bethmann, 19 Nov. 1911, BA R.43F/951/1. Summary in Reichsarchiv, *Weltkrieg*, i. 123–5.

[211] Tirpitz, *Aufbau*, 266.

[212] Bethmann to Metternich, 22 Nov. 1911, *GP* xxxi, doc. 11321. Reichsarchiv, *Weltkrieg*, i. 125.

[213] Ibid.   [214] Berghahn, *Germany*, 114.

and reviving confidence, especially within the army, heightened the danger of a surprise. In any case, all the strategic scenarios Moltke envisaged would begin with a German onslaught to the West. In hostilities with Britain Germany would be unable to gain a decision at sea and should therefore occupy the Low Countries; as this would inevitably mean war with France the latter should be attacked forthwith, and France alone, among Germany's enemies, could be broken in the first great battles. However, the French had modernized their equipment, and their wartime strength was not far behind Germany's. They would probably be assisted by a 130,000-strong BEF, and Agadir had shown that Belgium and the Netherlands were likely to increase their forces. Even against such a combination Germany would have little to fear if Russia stayed neutral, and if it did not, Austria-Hungary would intervene. But the war between Italy and Turkey meant that support from one or other belligerent might be lost, and in either case the pressure applied on Russia, via the Habsburgs or the Ottomans, would be diminished. Meanwhile Russia's army was completing its reorganization, and its deployments on its western frontier might be twice as fast as five years ago. Every element in the European strategic complex was interconnected, and the military balance had been moving for years against the Central Powers, but it was on Germany's ability to overwhelm its western neighbour that all turned. It was essential to participate in the general intensification of activity: 'All sides are preparing for European war, which all sides expect sooner or later.' Where Heeringen emphasized German rearmament's deterrent effect, Moltke looked to it as preparation for war, and his stress was less on quality than on numbers.[215]

The Chancellor read and acknowledged Moltke's memorandum, seizing especially on its appraisal of Russia.[216] The army bill, however, as prepared by Heeringen and his officials, did not primarily address Germany's inadequate trained manpower and the growing numerical inequality, and the GGS accepted this, leaving the DWV advocates of massive expansion out in the cold. A memorandum on 29 November by Wandel highlighted the events of 1911 rather than underlying developments. Agadir, he said, had made the world more dangerous, by making war more probable and by worsening Germany's chances if it occurred. Extra troops would be needed to overcome the Belgians and secure the Dutch border; Britain would probably give France naval and military assistance, and Italy was unlikely to commit significant forces. France would probably increase its trained manpower as a result of absorbing Morocco, its High Command was more likely to adopt an offensive strategy, and it respected the German army less; Germany's neighbours might impose a conflict on her, and 'at no time are we safe against war'. Financial and 'other general state interests', however, still imposed limits on peacetime strength, and they could never hope to equal the Russians. More reserves were needed to replenish losses and sustain a long war, but the primary remedies were improved mobilization and

[215] Moltke to Bethmann, 2 Dec. 1912, PAAA R789. cf. Reichsarchiv, *Weltkrieg*, i. 126–35.
[216] Lerchenfeld dispatch, 11 Dec. 1911, GSM Bayerische Gesandtschaft Berlin No. 1083.

organization to maintain the army's qualitative edge. Corps commands could not be improvised, and the XX and XXI Corps should already be established in peacetime. The infantry regiments should be made more uniform by raising more of them from two battalions to three, and all the frontier battalions should be raised to high strength. Every infantry regiment should have a machine-gun company, and the specialized troops, including the aviation units, should be enlarged. The emphasis was partly on technological change, but more on a rapid and secure mobilization.[217]

Wandel's recommendations were close to Heeringen's and Wilhelm's own ideas and were largely incorporated in the army bill.[218] However, the Minister still felt it necessary to observe restraint on financial grounds and because of the officer shortage, the chief economy being in the creation of 'missing' third battalions. In negotiations with the GGS Moltke pressed for higher unit strengths; Heeringen and Wandel urged prudence. None the less, the 1911 *Quinquennat* would now be fully implemented by 1 October 1912, as would most of Wandel's other proposed changes, although the extra machine-gun companies would wait until 1913. To the 10,875 rise in peacetime strength specified in the existing law there would be added another 26,500.[219] In the subsequent discussions with Wermuth Heeringen made some concessions over training grounds and accommodation, but in January he put his foot down. Wilhelm, he pointed out, had decided that the army must have absolute priority over the navy; unlike the laws of 1905 and 1911 this one was an immediate response to threatening political developments, and he would yield no more.[220] From here on the bill remained substantially unchanged.

Tirpitz had much less success. Heeringen rejected overtures for a united front, and the Navy Secretary failed to commit the Government to introduce a *Novelle* in 1911, or to provide for one in the 1912 estimates. Bethmann avoided public reference to the army and navy bills until the Emperor's speech to the new Reichstag, after the elections, on 7 February. As for the content of the *Novelle*, the Chancellor distinguished between the third squadron and additional construction, suggesting that the first of these mattered more. Tirpitz had maintained they were inseparable, but he now began his retreat from the three-ship tempo, Müller mediating the climbdown. The Navy Secretary acknowledged, in the light of the events of 1911, the importance of greater readiness, and in retrospect he highlighted this as the *Novelle*'s leading feature.[221] Within the building programme battlecruisers mattered less than did battleships, two more of which were needed to raise the projected total from fifty-eight to sixty. To replace them automatically after twenty years at the rate of three per annum would consolidate the principle of the 'Iron Budget', or *Äternat*, and end the need for regular

[217] Reichsarchiv, *Weltkrieg*, i, Anlage doc. 41.
[218] Gebsattel to Bavarian War Minister, 19 Nov. 1911, KAM Mkr 42. Heeringen to Bethmann, 4 Dec. 1911, R.43 F.951/1.
[219] Heeringen to Bethmann, 6 Dec. 1911, ibid. Reichsarchiv, *Weltkrieg*, i. 136–7.
[220] Heeringen to Bethmann, 5 Jan. 1912, ibid., Anlagen, doc. 43.
[221] Tirpitz, *Aufbau*, 263–8. Müller to Wilhelm, 23 Dec. 1911, BA R.43F/951/1.

battles with the Reichstag for funds. On 23 December Tirpitz acquiesced in a decision by Wilhelm to drop two of the three battlecruisers in the bill while maintaining the three battleships, the extra money going to the army and thereby benefiting it directly at the navy's expense. The Chancellor wanted more, and was armed with information from the London Embassy that if the building rate were not stepped up an Anglo-German agreement might be possible over African colonies. If the bill confined itself to increases in personnel and auxiliary vessels, he suggested, Germany could drive a wedge into the Triple Entente. In consequence, a second compromise removed the third battlecruiser and purged the bill's preamable of its anti-British edge. The three-ship tempo would now apply only in alternate years between 1912 and 1917, but the *Äternat* was still attainable, and the extra squadron would enhance readiness.[222] Two battlecruisers had been sacrificed to the Treasury and the army, and one to Bethmann's hopes of *détente* with Britain. The anxieties of Holtzendorff and his commanders, and Müller's political manœuvrings, had taken precedence over the Admiralty Staff's call for battlecruisers and Capelle's for the three-ship tempo. Tirpitz, however, was becoming exhausted, and feared, or so he said, that more delay would jeopardize the urgently needed increase in war readiness. By mid-January a new armaments consensus seemed at last to be coming into being.

* * *

At this point the waters were muddied again by the Haldane mission. It emerged from contacts during January between Albert Ballin and the financier and former friend of Edward VII, Sir Ernest Cassel. After high-level deliberations on both sides the Secretary of State for War arrived in Berlin for two days of talks on 8–9 February, at the end of which both he and his German opposite numbers appear to have believed that agreement might be attainable. The mission further delayed the navy bill, and the infighting in Berlin reached a new pitch of ferocity, but the practical results, apart from Tirpitz losing yet another capital ship, were slight. The war-preparedness aspects of the *Novelle* went through, and evoked a prompt British response; there was no political agreement, and the Triple Entente emerged strengthened.

From the outset the two sides were far apart. German expectations were inflated, and the British seem to have handled the discussions more coolly and with greater realism. Agadir had made the Radicals in the Cabinet more vociferous, especially after the disclosure of the staff talks with France. A revolt against Grey in November 1911 obliged him to agree that future conversations should have prior Cabinet approval, but in practice such approval was given and his freedom not much limited. None the less, he had reason to display at least a willingness to talk with Germany if he was to maintain domestic support for the ententes and for the sacrifices needed to uphold naval supremacy. In December he opened conversations with the German Ambassador about relaxing tension

---

[222] Tirpitz, *Aufbau*, 274–6. Görlitz (ed.), *Der Kaiser*, 106–10. Müller to Bethmann, 12 Jan. 1912, BA R43.F/951/1. Second draft of *Novelle* in Tirpitz to Bethmann, 20 Nov. 1911, ibid. See also Tirpitz note, 13 Jan. 1912, BA-MA Tirpitz MSS N253/26a.

and about possible agreements over the Baghdad railway, the Portuguese colonies, and the Belgian Congo. He was not prepared, however, to make more than contingency arrangements about the colonies of the smaller Powers, or to compromise the Anglo-French relationship. He could offer a non-aggression pledge, but for Bethmann this was useless. Churchill, now at the Admiralty, thought it was worth trying to slow down the implementation of the German Navy Law, and that if he could be seen to have negotiated he could more easily ask Parliament for extra money.[223] But Tirpitz had already yielded so much in the internal struggles over the *Novelle* that he had little left to give.

Much of the reason why in Germany the affair raised higher expectations than in Britain lies in amateur diplomacy. Cassel and Ballin persuaded each side that the other had requested an exchange of views; and Haldane glossed over the differences. Both he and Ballin believed that the Anglo-German antagonism was due to overcaution and misunderstanding rather than to genuine conflicts of interest, and they hoped that by improving the atmospherics of the relationship they could make progress on substantive issues. This was a recipe for disillusionment.

The upshot of the initial contacts was that Wilhelm thought the British had proposed to send a Minister to Berlin; and the British that Wilhelm wanted them to do so.[224] Grey was 'willing, but not hopeful' about the idea, but if Wilhelm was its author, it would be a 'wanton rebuff' to reject it.[225] An *aide-mémoire* delivered to Bethmann on 29 January described as 'fundamental' that Britain's naval superiority must be recognized and the present German naval programme and expenditure (as established by the 1908 law) should be delayed or diminished. On these conditions the British were willing to discuss ways of assisting Germany's colonial aspirations and would welcome undertakings that neither would join aggressive combinations against the other (which Britain did not consider the ententes to be). The Germans replied that the 1912 estimates must be included in the 'present . . . naval programme', and gave Cassel a copy of the navy bill.[226] This was an attempt to make the *Novelle* non-negotiable, although by communicating it Bethmann missed the chance to haggle over the three battle-cruisers that had already been struck out. He suggested that concessions might be possible if both sides promised to keep out of wars and combinations against each other, but he dropped the key qualifier 'aggressive'.[227] Meanwhile the British warned that if the *Novelle* went through their naval spending would immediately be raised.

Despite this unpromising start, the Cabinet agreed to send Haldane. During his visit, a speech by Churchill at Glasgow on 9 February distinguished between

[223] Grey to Goschen, 20 Dec. 1911, *BD* vi, doc. 480. Grey, *Twenty-Five Years*, i. ch. 14. J. Steinberg, 'Diplomatie als Wille und Vorstellung: die Berliner Mission Lord Haldanes im Februar 1912', in H. Schottelius and W. Deist (eds.), *Marine und Marinepolitik im Kaiserlichen Deutschland, 1871–1914* (Düsseldorf, 1972), 272.

[224] Ibid. 273.   [225] Grey, *Twenty-Five Years*, i. 250.

[226] Bethmann memorandum, 29 Jan. 1912, *BD* vi, doc. 11347.

[227] Bethmann memorandum, 4 Feb. 1912, ibid., doc. 11351.

the Royal Navy as a 'necessity' to Britain and the High Seas Fleet as being 'from some points of view . . . more in the nature of a luxury'. If competition intensified Britain would have to increase not only the number of ships it built but also the ratio of superiority. This was another warning not to exclude the *Novelle* from negotiations, and it touched a sensitive nerve. Yet Wilhelm made light of it, and the Emperor's expansive humour lent the conversations an unexpected dynamic, the more so as the War Secretary reciprocated.[228] Given Churchill's and Grey's reluctance to go to Germany, Haldane was the obvious choice: he had military expertise and knew the country and the language. His hosts assumed that he had greater powers than he did. It is true that the Cabinet had sent him on an exploratory basis, which encouraged vagueness. Moreover, he was conceited, and, despite his philosophical and legal training, surprisingly inattentive to detail.[229] He told Bethmann that Britain could not let Germany crush France, and suggested non-aggression pledges: the Chancellor said that Germany must have a third squadron at full war readiness. Haldane replied that the Royal Navy would then have to move extra ships into home waters, but that the third squadron was less serious than the *Novelle*'s extra battleships, which Britain would have to counter by laying down two keels to every one. In conversation with Wilhelm and Tirpitz he opposed a 2:3 strength ratio, but not an increase in the proportion of ships in service or the creation of a third active squadron. Instead, he stressed that he wanted the extra battleships delayed, and seemed willing to separate a naval from a political agreement. He took back a 'Sketch of a Conceivable Formula' for a non-aggression accord. Bethmann supposed the British to be willing to accept the *Novelle*'s non-building aspects, and he and Kiderlen were willing to trade the three battleships in the bill for a political formula. After Haldane returned to London, however, there was silence, followed by a rude awakening.[230]

The *Novelle* was the primary issue. On 22 February Grey and Haldane told Metternich that Britain could not make a political agreement if simultaneously there was a substantial increase in Germany's naval strength, and that the Admiralty had found that Tirpitz's bill entailed just such an increase. According to the Sea Lords, it might keep almost four-fifths of the German fleet in permanent full commission, and they would have to raise the proportion of the British navy that was at comparable readiness.[231] It appeared that Britain's objections could not be met simply by postponing the *Novelle*'s new constructions, and if the legislation went ahead there would be no political arrangement. Wilhelm resolved that the bill should mention only the first two of the three

---

[228] Churchill, *World Crisis*, 99–101. Görlitz (ed.), *Der Kaiser*, 114.

[229] Grey to Buchanan, 7 Feb. 1911, *BD* vi, doc. 495. Asquith to George V, 2 Feb. 1912, PRO CAB 41/33.

[230] Diary of Haldane's visit, *BD* vi, doc. 506. Haldane, 'Memorandum of Events between 1906–1915', NLS Haldane MSS 5919. Steinberg, 'Diplomatie', 277–80. For German accounts of the visit, *GP* xxxi, docs. 11359–62; Tirpitz, *Aufbau*, 286–9.

[231] Grey memorandum, 22 Feb.; Grey to Goschen, 24 Feb. 1912, *BD* vi, docs. 523–4(i). Metternich to Bethmann, 22 Dec. 1912, *GP* xxxi, doc. 11370.

extra battleships, a decision on the third being left open, and Müller again secured Tirpitz's consent, thus reducing the extra ships to the absolute minimum needed to attain the magic figure of sixty.[232] Although Bethmann and the Emperor made this unilateral gesture of goodwill, however, both men felt that the British had repudiated Haldane's statements and shifted their position, and the negotiation never regained its initial momentum.[233]

Not all the blame for the Germans' sense of letdown lies with Haldane, as the Admiralty had been slow to clarify its views. But the preparedness aspects of the navy bill, which Bethmann supposed were less provocative than the building schedule, caused consternation in Whitehall. For Churchill the creation of the third squadron was 'a serious and formidable provision'. At present, while the first and second squadrons of the High Seas Fleet were congested with reservists during the winter months, the pressure on the Royal Navy eased; but in future twenty-five capital ships would be in full commission throughout the year and 'this exposes us to constant danger, to be warded off by vigilance approximating to war conditions'. The Cabinet was advised that the most dangerous feature of the German bill was neither the extra battleships nor the third squadron, but the manpower increase, which was more than was needed for either. There would, said Churchill, be an 'extraordinary increase in the striking force of ships of all classes immediately available throughout the year': between twenty-five and twenty-nine fully commissioned German battleships would be available in all seasons, whereas at present in home waters Britain had only twenty-two. Even if the construction programme in the bill were modified, the Cabinet decided, such an increase in British expenditure would be needed as to make a political agreement an 'absurdity if not a mockery'.[234]

The issue in the naval rivalry had become preparedness rather than new building. Indeed, on the latter a preliminary agreement had already been reached. On 28 January Kiderlen sent to London a memorandum setting out conditions for an exchange of information that were acceptable to both sides. The Admiralty envisaged the disclosure each year of the numbers and cost of warships under construction, so as to indicate the 'scale of warlike preparation' without vouchsafing sensitive technicalities or giving a detailed breakdown of spending. Tirpitz regarded this as harmless, and a safeguard against new accusations that he was secretly accelerating.[235] Now that he had lost the battle for the three-ship tempo the rivalry could begin to stabilize, although at much higher levels of readiness. This was the prospect emerging by the end of January, although Grey and Bethmann kept the negotiations running for a while yet. On 1 March Haldane warned that unless the *Novelle* were scaled down Britain would intro-

---

[232] Tirpitz, *Aufbau*, 292, 299.

[233] Wilhelm to Bethmann, 27 Feb., ibid. 306–8. Bethmann memorandum, 28 Feb. 1912, *GP* xxxi, doc. 11376.

[234] Churchill, *World Crisis*, 95–7, 101–3. Asquith to George V, 15 and 21 Feb. 1912, PRO CAB 41/33.

[235] Admiralty to Foreign Office, 12 Dec. 1911; note to Kiderlen, 28 Jan. 1912, *BD* vi, docs. 478, 489(i). Tirpitz, *Aufbau*, 280.

duce supplementary estimates and move warships from the Mediterranean to the North Sea. This was the last straw for Wilhelm, who sent a warning over Bethmann's head to Metternich that such a redeployment would be answered by a three-ship tempo and ultimately by mobilization.[236] Even Tirpitz acknowledged that this time the Emperor had gone too far, and Bethmann tendered his resignation, insisting that Germany should continue to talk, if only to throw blame for the failure on to London. He was permitted to continue seeking a neutrality agreement, and a German note on 6 March offered to confine the bill's provisions to one extra capital ship in each of 1913 and 1916, without setting a date for the third. A counter-resignation threat from Tirpitz prevented the Chancellor from offering more. But in any case the British still refused an unconditional neutrality pledge, and on 19 March Metternich spelled out that only such a pledge would do. Effectively this was the end, and Bethmann ceased attempting to delay the publication of the bill.[237] So, in an atmosphere of recrimination, the *Novelle* went forward to the Reichstag, but the Liberal Government responded not, as the Chancellor feared, with a preventive strike, but with its own measures to heighten readiness. None the less, binding undertakings on strength ratios and on British neutrality were off the agenda for good.

* * *

The navy bill was presented to the Reichstag in April 1912 and became law, with little change, in June. The target numerical strength of the fleet in battleships was to rise from thirty-eight to forty-one, but thanks to Haldane's visit the laying-down dates of only two of these (in 1913 and 1916) were specified. The battlecruiser target would remain constant at twenty. The British expected the number of fully crewed battleships, however, to rise from seventeen to twenty-five; that of battlecruisers from four to eight.[238] Bethmann estimated the total cost down to 1917 to be 206 million marks, which was little more than half of what Tirpitz had first asked for, and less than half the cost of the army law. Yet when set against the 2,000 million marks of the 1908 *Novelle*, the new bill offered an enormous increase in fighting power for a comparatively small outlay.[239] The objective of the *Äternat* was still attainable, and the letter of the law continued to provide for a three-ship tempo after 1917, but official spokesmen in the legislature placed the emphasis on readiness.[240] An additional step towards this readiness was the redeployment from Kiel to Wilhelmshaven being planned by the naval authorities. The High Seas Fleet's cruiser reconnaissance force would lead the way, followed by battlecruisers and the new third squadron. Although

---

[236] Metternich to Bethmann, 1 Mar.; Wilhelm to Metternich, 5 Mar. 1912, *GP* xxxi, docs. 11380, 11387.

[237] Tirpitz, *Aufbau*, 315–30. Metternich memorandum, 6 Mar.; Grey to Goschen, 15 Mar. 1912, *BD* vi. 529, 539.

[238] Text of the bill in PRO CAB 37/111, doc. 84.

[239] Bethmann circular, 5 Mar. 1912, BA R.43 F/952. Tirpitz in Bundesrat, 14 Mar. (reported in Kühn to Bethmann, 16 Mar. 1912), BA R.43 F/953.

[240] Minutes of Prussian Council of Ministers, 4 Mar. 1912, BA R.43 F/952. Tirpitz in Bundesrat, 14 Mar. (see n. 239). Tirpitz to Bethmann, 27 Mar. 1912, R.43 F/953.

the Admiralty Staff justified the redeployment as a precaution against surprise attack, Bethmann rightly saw it as a 'high political measure', and it would further reduce the Royal Navy's warning time.[241]

Readiness was also the keynote of the army's legislation. A separate bill established two new army corps from October 1912, one opposite Belgium and Luxemburg and the other in East Prussia. The main bill raised the 515,321 peacetime strength designated in the 1911 law to 543,497 men and 28,890 officers. Most of the extra money and new units would go to the infantry, which was to increase from 634 battalions to 651, and the field artillery, which would go up from 592 batteries to 633. Strength levels in existing units would be raised.[242] The Agadir experience continued to dominate the thinking of the War Minister, who told the Prussian Council of Ministers that on land as well as at sea the decisive battles would probably come quickly and organization could not be improvised. He wrote to Wermuth about 'the raising of the army's striking power, to which the entire present bill is directed'. Higher strengths were needed on the frontiers to ensure that the infantry stationed there could perform their duties during the autumn changeover, and that railways, fortresses, and mobilization could be protected against standing-start attack.[243] In the Bundesrat on 14 March he said the French nationalist ferment and the military and political changes in Russia made improvements in Germany's capacity an 'absolute State necessity'. On the other hand, he still denied that there was scope for calling up a larger portion of the age cohort, and he could have asked for higher expenditure than he did. After Heeringen addressed the Bundesrat Bethmann asked him whether he was sure the bill contained everything that was needed; on reflection, he asked for, and obtained, merely one additional cavalry regiment.[244] The contrast with Tirpitz's treatment could hardly be plainer.

Bethmann was not alone in being willing to give Heeringen more. In the January elections the SPD had jumped from 43 to 110 seats and every other party had lost ground. None the less, both army bills were passed with large majorities that included all the major groupings except the Socialists. After Agadir the right-wing parties had become more chauvinistic and aggressive, while the Centre and even the Progressives were more sympathetic to army spending. The National Liberals followed the DWV in wanting all able-bodied men to be trained.[245] The Government therefore had an easy ride. Another strategic appraisal, prepared by the War Minister for his confidential briefing of the Reichstag Budget Commission, stressed the need to guarantee peace by restoring French respect for Germany. The Germans now knew about the Anglo-French staff conversations and were certain that two French army corps would be redirected from the Italian border. Austria-Hungary could no longer

[241] Bethmann note, 4 May; CAS to Bethmann, 11 June 1912, PAAA R.2284.
[242] Heeringen to Bavarian War Minister, 21 Feb. 1912, KAM MKr. 1134.
[243] Heeringen to Bavarian War Minister, 12 Jan. 1912, ibid. Heeringen to Wermuth, 11 Mar. 1912, HSMA M 1/6 Bd. 285.
[244] Kühn to Bethmann, 16 Mar.; Wahnschaffe memorandum, 25 Mar. 1912, BA R.43 F/453.
[245] Förster, *Militarismus*, 234–44.

give adequate protection against a Russian advance, and larger forces must be stationed in the East.[246] The bill declared that Germany's readiness must be enhanced by calling up and training more able-bodied men, remedying deficiencies in organization, and facilitating the transition to a war footing.[247] In private testimony Kiderlen put the diplomatic case that Germany's influence in disputes arising from its global expansion depended on its military and naval might. Heeringen, however, was concerned with the army's importance for defence and as a deterrent to aggression. He opposed shorter service, or a militia as advocated by the Socialists, because it would not serve these purposes. Only if a strong and prepared army existed on the frontiers in peacetime could he take responsibility for Germany's security. This, of course, glossed over the reality that German strategy was offensive.[248]

The 1913 army law would show that Heeringen could have asked for many more men than he did; and already in 1912 he would have had parliamentary support in doing so. Meanwhile, the Treasury Secretary was fighting a losing battle. Wilhelm and Bethmann committed themselves to the army and navy bills without a systematic comparison of departmental spending plans and without a long-term financial programme. Wermuth was presented with a *fait accompli*, and protested that he simply could not find the money.[249] His case was weakened, however, by the budget surplus recorded in 1911, and the Interior Ministry and the Prussian Finance Ministry, as well as the armed services, challenged his assessment.[250] Bethmann wanted to rely on the same combination of political parties for the army and navy bills and for the finance bill, but to press for a Reich inheritance tax would antagonize the Right, and neither the Chancellor nor the majority of Ministers were willing to support Wermuth in seeking it.[251] Once this became clear, in March 1912, Wermuth resigned and was replaced by his deputy, Kühn, the 'no uncovered expenditure' principle departing with him. The navy bill would cost 130.4 million marks in non-recurrent spending and 79.6 million annually in recurrent; the army legislation would cost 144 million and 296.5 million respectively. The money would be found in the first year by diverting funds from debt amortization and by partially revoking a tax concession on spirits, among other expedients. Beyond that, the Basserman-Erzberger law passed by the Reichstag required the the introduction of a Reich property tax by April 1913, but there was no agreement yet about its nature.[252]

The Government left the political parties to sort out the fiscal problem, but

[246] Heeringen to Bethmann, 22 Mar. 1912, BA R.43 F/953.

[247] Heeringen to Bethmann, 21 Feb. 1912, BA R.43 F/952.

[248] Budget Commission sittings, 30 Apr., 1, 2, 7 May 1912, HSMA M 1/6 Bd. 126. Wenninger to Bavarian War Minister, 27 Mar. 1912, KAM MKr. 1134.

[249] Wermuth, *Beamtenleben*, 309. Wermuth to Bethmann, 26 Jan. 1912, BA R.43 F/951/1.

[250] Wermuth to Bethmann, 13 Feb., Lentze to Wermuth, 16 Feb., Michaelis to Wahnschaffe, 21 Feb. 1912, BA R.43 F/952.

[251] Minutes of Prussian Council of Ministers, 4 Mar. 1912, ibid. Kühn to Bethmann, 16 Mar. 1912, BA R.43 F/953.

[252] Förster, *Militarismus*, 255, 246. Witt, *Finanzpolitik*, 346–55. French Foreign to Finance Minister, 5 Mar. 1913, MFF F30 258/II.

its commitment to debt reduction and to 'financial war preparedness' had evidently relaxed while the army was increasing its appetite. Early in 1912 the GGS asked for 320 million marks to modernize the eastern fortresses at Graudenz and Posen; the War Ministry scaled this down, but proposed a 200 million equipment schedule. Kühn wanted to hold expenditure at previous levels, but Heeringen offered only a small reduction and with the outbreak of the Balkan Wars in the autumn he insisted that he could make no more cuts on financial grounds and that military security must take precedence.[253] Already in the spring of 1912 the French attaché reported the heightened level of activity. A special railway fund was being created that had all the appearance of a war chest. The defence industries were working flat out, munitions stocks were being accumulated, and aircraft purchases speeded up.[254] Although Heeringen was making preparations on the eastern frontier, Germany's efforts in the first phase of the *Rüstungswende* were essentially a response to Agadir and Libya and directed against its Western European enemies. It took the new Balkan crisis at the end of the year to open the highway to *matériel* expenditure and a much larger manpower increase, thus completing the discomfiture of the retrenchment camp.

* * *

Britain's response to the German armaments increases came mainly at sea, and it stayed aloof from the competition in army budgets and manpower that gripped the Continent after Agadir. The BEF was not expected to keep pace with the German army, and Haldane held War Office spending steady. German forecasts that 130,000 British soldiers would be disembarking in the Channel ports by day 15, however, were not far wide of the mark.[255] By 1908 the Anglo-French staff talks had agreed on 110,000 by day 18, though not on where to put them. A CID subcommittee set up in October of that year favoured sending the BEF to the French left flank, but the General Staff envisaged sending only four out of six divisions immediately, and the Admiralty had no plans for their transport.[256] When Sir Henry Wilson became Director of Military Operations in 1910 the men could be mobilized in a few days, but arrangements for horse supply were quite inadequate and railway timetabling had not been completed even within the UK. The new DMO was a forceful and abrasive organizer with a rare first-hand knowledge of Continental military conditions, and he at once began work on faster mobilization and concentration.[257]

During the Moroccan crisis Haldane sent Wilson to Paris for conversations with the EMA, which were supposedly unofficial and non-binding. The Wilson–Dubail memorandum of 21 July envisaged that by day 15 six British infantry divisions, one cavalry division, and two mounted brigades (in all some

[253] Reichsarchiv, *Weltkrieg*, i. 146–50.
[254] Pellé to War Ministry, 21 Jan., 4 and 29 Feb., 7 and 19 Mar. and 26 Apr. 1912, SHA 7.N. 1111. Allizé to Poincaré, 19 Mar. 1912, AMAE NS Allemagne 104.
[255] GGS memorandum on 'Das Englische Expeditionskorps', May 1912, KAM Gstb 146.
[256] Williamson, *Strategy*, 108–13.
[257] Callwell, *Wilson*, i. ch. 6. IWM, Wilson diaries, eg. 25 Oct. 1910, 10 Jan., 11 Mar. 1911.

67,000 horses and 150,000 men) would be deployed on the French left flank.[258] But Wilson still could not give a date for the mobilization of the BEF, and was radically dissatisfied with its equipment and organization.[259] Nor was the Admiralty yet ready to get it across the Channel, as was manifested in a special meeting of the CID convened on 23 August. This was a celebrated confrontation, in which the First Sea Lord, Sir Arthur Wilson, was no match for his namesake. The Admiralty said it could not undertake troop transports at the same time as confining the Germans to the North Sea; it intended a close blockade (despite the vulnerability of surface ships to mines and torpedoes) and raids on the German coast (dismissed by the CIGS, Sir William Nicholson, as 'madness'). Yet the feebleness of the opposition allowed the DMO to get away with assumptions that should have been questioned more rigorously. He contended that Russia would count for little in a Franco-German war, and that six British divisions could tip the balance between sixty-six French and eighty-four German ones. The Admiralty doubted this, and pointed out that once British forces had been committed they could not be withdrawn without great damage to national pride. The temptation would be to reinforce them, at the price of mounting sacrifices. Wilson may have constructed his theory as a ruse to get Ministers committed, and he assumed incorrectly that the Germans would stay east of the Sambre–Meuse line, where they would have to funnel forty divisions against thirty-seven to thirty-nine French ones along thirteen through roads. When asked if the Germans would not pass further west, he avoided being pinned down.[260] None the less, the Admiralty's performance on 23 August, following on its alleged complacency in the July alert, resulted in McKenna's replacement by Churchill in October 1911. Inter-service discussions on the passage of the BEF ensued, while Wilson completed his transport and logistical arrangements to the last detail. In 1914 Ministers were still not committed to sending all six divisions, but all was prepared for them to do so immediately.[261] The army had been moving in this direction before Agadir, but the crisis strengthened the political backing for its strategy and brought the navy into line.

For the navy, the *Novelle* rather than the Moroccan crisis was the turning-point, although Agadir brought Churchill to the Admiralty and accomplished his Damascus conversion to the gospel of war preparedness. He took over intending 'to prepare for an attack by Germany as if it might come next day'; every morning until war broke out he marked the position of the High Seas Fleet on a map in his room.[262] Unlike McKenna, he wanted a long-term building programme for capital ships, although one not embodied in legislation and therefore modifiable at will. He hoped thereby to improve labour and financial management, and impress upon the Germans that they had no hope of catching up. In

[258] S. R. Williamson, *The Politics of Grand Strategy* (Cambridge, Mass., 1969), ch. 7. Wilson–Dubail memorandum, 20 July 1911, *BD* vii, doc. 640.

[259] Wilson to CIGS, 16 Aug. 1911, IWM Wilson MSS 3/5.

[260] CID minutes, 23 Aug. 1911, PRO CAB/38/19.

[261] Williamson, *Strategy*, 307–16.   [262] Churchill, *World Crisis*, 72, 77.

his 18 March 1912 speech to the House of Commons on the 1912–13 estimates, he abandoned the pretence of a two-Power standard and acknowledged that Britain was building against Germany alone. The objective was 60 per cent superiority while Tirpitz adhered to the present (1908) naval law, to be achieved by a 4-3-4-3-4-3 dreadnought programme in 1912–17. As a result of the *Novelle* Britain altered this in July to 4-5-4-4-4-4: or twenty-five capital ships to Germany's fourteen, instead of twenty-one to twelve.[263]

In addition, Britain's naval strength was reorganized and redistributed. On 1 May 1912 Churchill created a new command known as the Home Fleets, responsible for defending the British Isles. The First Fleet, comprising the newest and most powerful battleships, fully crewed, consisted of four squadrons. Two were already in home waters and a third was moved there from Gibraltar, whither the fourth (composed of pre-dreadnoughts transferred from Malta) was now relocated. Twenty-eight battleships (rising to thirty-three) would be available in home waters—though this figure included four (rising to eight) at Gibraltar, three and a half sailing days away. The creation of the third squadron would therefore raise the always-ready element of the High Seas Fleet to near parity with Britain. Churchill predicted that in April 1914 the Royal Navy would have only twenty-seven dreadnought battleships and battlecruisers against twenty-one: this would be the 'worst moment' before his building programme widened its lead.[264] Holtzendorff, similarly, expected the High Seas Fleet to be much readier to fight by the autumn of 1914 than it was in 1912, especially as the Helgoland defences and the enlargement of the Kiel Canal would have been completed. For the next two years Germany would continue to gain, as the Dreadoughts laid down during the four-ship tempo period became operational.[265] None the less, the building race was becoming less significant in the total equation, as was indicated by Churchill's suggestion in March 1912 of a one-year 'naval holiday' or freeze on capital-ship construction, which Wilhelm courteously declined.[266] A dangerous moment was approaching for the Royal Navy, but unless the Germans accelerated again there would be light beyond that, and by 1914 both sides would have completed the transition from mixed to all-dreadnought active fleets. Conversely, Tirpitz had much stronger defensive capacity, and less reason to fear surprise attack than in the early dreadnought period. After vast expenditure the outlines of a *modus vivendi* were emerging, although one that the two sides were unable to embody in a formal accord.

* * *

The pressure on Britain in the North Sea had repercussions in the Mediterranean that necessitated a joint Anglo-French response. Churchill's redeployment, undertaken at the moment when Austria-Hungary and Italy were

---

[263] Churchill, *World Crisis*, 105–10. Marder, *Dreadnought*, i. 283–5.

[264] Ibid. 287–9. Churchill, *World Crisis*, 111–17. Churchill memoranda, 15, 22, and 25 June, 6 July 1912, PRO CAB/37/111. Admiralty memorandum, 26 Aug. 1912, PRO CAB/37/112. The 'worst moment' phrase comes from Churchill's memorandum of 6 July 1912.

[265] Holtzendorf memorandum, 25 Oct. 1911, BA-MA Tirpitz MSS N.253/25b.

[266] Marder, *Dreadnought*, i. 284.

acquiring modern battleships, left British interests there potentially exposed. The majority of the Cabinet questioned whether these interests were essential, and were willing to rely on French protection; the Unionists were more critical of the 'abandonment' of the Mediterranean, as were the War and Foreign Offices. In July the Cabinet agreed to another of Asquith's compromise formulae. The first requirement was an acceptable margin of superiority in home waters, but subject to this Britain should seek to maintain a Mediterranean one-Power standard, equal to the largest local navy other than France. Four battle-cruisers would be stationed at Malta, and conversations with the French navy were authorized.[267]

The British insisted that the naval conversations, like those between Wilson and Dubail, were purely about contingency planning, but the French, rattled by the Haldane mission, were determined to exact a political price. The resulting exchange of letters between Grey and Paul Cambon on 22–3 November helped satisfy French wishes for a continuing basis of diplomatic co-operation now that the Morocco provisions of the 1904 entente had been fulfilled. Neither side was obliged to implement the plans agreed between them, but if either feared unprovoked aggression or a threat to the peace they would consult on whether to take joint action, and if such action resulted the plans 'would at once be taken into consideration'. In fact, although there had been brief contacts during the two Moroccan crises and the Casablanca deserters affair, before July 1912 the two navies had had no sustained discussions. But by February 1913 arrangements had been reached for Britain to take responsibility for the Straits of Dover, the eastern Channel, and France's northern coast; for French responsibility west of the Isle of Wight and Cherbourg; and in the Mediterranean for France to operate west of Malta and Britain to bottle up the Austrian navy to the east. In this way the British covered themselves during the danger period before they could strengthen their Mediterranean fleet, and negotiated a wider ranging contingency agreement as a result of the strain imposed on them by the *Novelle* in the North Sea. Once more Tirpitz's policies had tightened the bonds between Britain and Germany's Continental enemies.[268]

Whereas the French army still prepared on the assumption that there would be no co-operation with the British, the navy assumed the opposite, although it had plans to go it alone if need be. The 1913 agreements meshed in with the redirection of building and deployment policy under the ministries of Vice-Admiral Boué de Lapeyrère (1909–11) and Théophile Delcassé (1911–13).[269] While the army's preoccupation with Germany was becoming more single-minded than ever, the navy was redefining its mission so that Germany was no longer its principal antagonist. Boué de Lapeyrère's staff advised him that the goal of parity with the High Seas Fleet was unattainable and should be abandoned in favour of Mediterranean supremacy over the combined

[267] Ibid. 287–98.   [268] Ibid. 298–308. Williamson, *Strategy*, chs. 11–13.

[269] Generally on the navy see P. G. Halpern, *The Mediterranean Naval Situation, 1908–1914* (Cambridge, Mass., 1971), ch. 3.

Austro-Hungarian and Italian forces.[270] He drew up an appropriate building programme but failed to get it through Parliament, although he did secure funds in 1910 for the first true French dreadnoughts. Delcassé, in contrast, obtained a programmatic law in March 1912, directed towards Mediterranean dominance and assistance to Britain against Germany. In addition to four dreadnoughts laid down in 1910–11, thirteen more would be started by 1917 with a target of twenty-eight battleships by 1920, although only eight would be in permanent full commission.[271]

That this was a Mediterranean programme was underlined by the redistribution of the French fleet away from the Channel and the Atlantic in 1911–12. British Ministers feared that the redistribution would suggest that Delcassé was relying on the Royal Navy to protect the northern coast, but in fact it developed from an independent policy. The outmoded and outnumbered French warships would be unable to achieve much against Germany unassisted, and if Britain were on France's side they would be superfluous in the Channel anyway. But in the Mediterranean they could play a valuable role. The French army acquiesced on the condition that absolute priority was given to escorting the troopships from North Africa that would begin the transport of the 19th Corps towards the north-eastern border.[272]

This brings us to French land armaments development in the era of the *réveil national*—the nationalist revival, or reawakening. There was no one turning-point as dramatic as in Germany. French naval spending increased after the law of 1912, but its Mediterranean orientation had already been defined. The army's rehabilitation had been in progress since Algeciras. As the early fears about the Russian military reorganization subsided, however, there was growing evidence that the balance on land was altering in favour of the Triple Entente. After Agadir, German observers rightly detected a heightening of French self-confidence. Moreover, the crisis precipitated changes that were already impending in organization, command, and planning. To an extent this was still a pre-arms race, in which competition showed itself in administrative structures and intentions rather than in manpower and *matériel*. But as in Germany, the framework and direction were established for a subsequent expansion.

An earlier generation of writers viewed events after Agadir though the prism of domestic politics, as a reaction against the Radical ascendancy of the André years. New men with new ideas reasserted the army's independence from civilian supervision and steered it towards a vainglorious offensive strategy.[273] There is truth in this interpretation, but it neglects external factors, foremost among which was the crisis itself. The German army law of 1912 was justified by its initiators as a reaction against a prior recovery in French military prowess, and the French responded to it by continuing with a package of measures that had been decided in the previous year.

---

[270] Bienaimé testimony to Marine commission, 15 Nov. 1910, AN C7420.
[271] Text of the bill in ibid.   [272] Marder, *Dreadnought*, i. 305. Halpern, *Mediterranean*, 61 ff.
[273] D. Porch, *The March to the Marne* (Cambridge, 1981), preface.

In the first weeks of the Moroccan tension the French army leadership was in disarray over the use of reserve formations in the front line and over heavy artillery. It lacked confidence in its commander-in-chief, as he did in himself. All three issues came to a head on 19 July in the Conseil supérieur de la guerre. Caillaux's War Minister, Messimy, was a young career soldier turned politician. The British attaché thought him impulsive and exaggeratedly patriotic:[274] he had a reputation for harshness. But in 1911 he showed good judgement and decisiveness, in delicate circumstances. The CSG Vice-President, and therefore commander-in-chief designate, was General Michel. Messimy thought him inadequate to his responsibilities, and decided he must go, but agreed to use the CSG meeting to test out Michel's authority.[275]

The artillery question was the first item on the agenda.[276] According to a presentation by General Dubail, since the 1909 law France had nearly caught up with Germany in the number of field guns per army corps. It had no equivalent, however, of the German light field howitzers, which could be used for counter-battery fire from concealed positions, hitting the French crews behind their gun shields. In addition, it remained massively outnumbered in heavy field artillery. Dubail believed France must acquire its own field howitzer and a heavy artillery force of 216 guns, composed partly of Rimailhos and partly of a new 120 mm cannon. Traditionally the French High Command had distrusted heavy artillery as an impediment to mobility, but improved supply and the introduction of tractors that could pull the guns reduced the force of this objection, and the EMA felt that action was essential and urgent. Messimy agreed, and the meeting voted in favour of heavy artillery. It also decided to adopt a light field howitzer, overriding Michel, who wanted to rely on more Rimailhos.[277]

The commander-in-chief designate's second defeat was over reserve formations. This was a politicized question, the Right arguing that reservists should be employed only to bring active units up to war strength rather than to form units in their own right, because they were older, family men, less recently trained and therefore less suitable for the front line. The Left, notably the Socialist leader, Jean Jaurès, in his *L'Armée nouvelle*,[278] favoured a short-service militia, partly because it would be difficult to use for domestic repression but also because it implied a defensive, non-provocative, strategic posture and would exploit scarce French manpower to the maximum. Michel, who argued that reserve formations were nearly equivalent in value to active units, seemed to be moving towards this view. Until now, he said, the French army when campaigning had completely separated active from reserve formations and kept the latter well in the rear. This practice dated from the period of five-year service and made no sense now that there was a two-year term. He suggested a 'demi-brigade' system, in which each brigade would contain one regiment of active men

---

[274] Col. Fairholme to Bertie, 1 Sept. 1911, *BD* vii, doc. 643(i).
[275] Messimy, *Souvenirs*, 75–6.   [276] CSG minutes, 19 July 1911, SHA 1.N. 10.
[277] Porch, *March*, ch. 12. Joffre, *Mémoires*, i. 10.
[278] J. Jaurès, *L'Armée nouvelle* (Paris, 1911).

and one of reservists, with equal complements of officers. This would allow the army to lengthen its front line and maintain a larger mobile reserve, while mobilizing as rapidly as before. The concentration could be extended northwards, against a German envelopment attempt through Belgium. But opposition was unanimous. Dubail said that the system would overturn the army's organization completely and delay concentration by five days. Only active formations, composed of young, vigorous men, were thought capable of offensive operations, it being alleged (in fact erroneously) that the Germans followed the same principle. Once again the Minister supported Michel's critics, and on 28 July Jules-Césaire Joffre took over the latter's duties, Messimy profiting from the occasion in order to restructure the High Command.[279]

Messimy's decrees restored to the army leadership some of the peacetime authority lost since the Dreyfus affair, but left Joffre well short of the independence of a Moltke, even if he had been disposed to use it, which he was not. The new Commander was a placid but unimaginative colonial soldier, trained as an engineer. Although not known himself as a political or anti-republican general, he asked that his deputy should be General de Castelnau, a notorious clerical, and Caillaux and Messimy accepted the political fall-out that the appointment would cause. The existing structure was designed to minimize potentially dangerous concentrations of military power, and the designated corps commanders on the CSG were unable to train and organize their staffs in peacetime or inspect their prospective units. The Chief of the Army General Staff (CEMA) could not give orders to the War Ministry services, and the commander-designate, who lacked an organized peacetime staff of his own, also lacked authority over the General Staff, and therefore over mobilization and concentration planning. The reorganization abolished Michel's former post of Vice-President of the CSG, Joffre becoming Chief of the Army General Staff (CEMGA) and thereby both commander-designate and the officer with chief responsibility for planning. Dubail continued, confusingly, as CEMA, and therefore in potential conflict with de Castelnau. The CSDN, which had been inactive since 1908, was expanded and required to meet regularly. Finally, members of the CSG were allowed to create nucleus staffs and regained the right of inspection over their wartime commands. The changes should have made it easier for the High Command to introduce a standardized tactical and strategic doctrine, but the French army continued to lack one before 1914. Joffre remained responsible to the War Minister and to Parliament, and his strategic planning was subject to civilian overview. He was still unable to impose his will on the War Ministry services, and with respect to the artillery, in particular, this had serious consequences. Effective leadership required a strong War Minister who could co-operate with Joffre, and in 1911–12 these preconditions were met. But if the army received stronger direction after Agadir, it did so because of a change

---

[279] On the reserves question, CSG minutes, 19 July 1911, SHA 1.N. 10. Joffre, *Mémoires*, i. 7–11. J. Snyder, *The Ideology of the Offensive* (Ithaca, NY, 1984), ch. 3.

of heart among the civilians rather than a resurgence of military autonomy. Such resurgence as did occur was largely on sufferance.[280]

The new leadership immediately reviewed strategic planning. In addition to checking mobilization arrangements, in September 1911 Joffre adopted a 'Variant No. 1' of Plan XVI. The intention was still not to hold the Germans on the frontier, but to launch a counter-offensive after rolling with the blow. The EMA had a copy of Germany's 1907 mobilization plan and expected a primary offensive in the West, probably, to judge from German frontier fortification and railway building, from the Eifel into Belgium, although they were uncertain exactly where and in what strength the thrust would come. Plan XVI envisaged a front-line deployment of only thirty-eight active divisions (and four reserve ones) against Germany's sixty-five. From this flowed the defensive–offensive conception, which entailed holding the enemy until Russia and Britain could bring their forces to bear. Joffre feared that if the initiative were left to Germany it might win in the first month, given the French tendency to panic at early reverses; moreover, the battle would devastate French territory. By transferring almost all the forces designated against Italy, together with more troops from North Africa, and (despite the 19 July CSG) including more reserve formations in the front line, he planned to increase the divisions on the frontier to fifty-eight, rising to sixty-three, which would allow him to extend his concentration towards Belgium, and give him near numerical parity.[281]

The second stage was a new concentration that would replace Plan XVI altogether, and this, as the GGS correctly divined, would entail abandoning the defensive–offensive concept in favour of a strategic offensive. By the autumn of 1911 the EMA had in its pocket not only Variant No. 1 but also the Wilson–Dubail memorandum and Russia's promise to attack by day 15, giving it confidence that the Triple Entente was gaining the edge. Its political assumptions encouraged optimism. The EMA complained about the lack of guidance from the Foreign Ministry in previous planning rounds, which had meant, for example, that for years it had targeted unnecessary forces against Italy. But after discussion in the CSDN Joffre reached an understanding with de Selves. If Germany provoked a war with France Russia was expected to give 'the most active and complete assistance'. Italy would be unlikely to join its allies, and most of the troops stationed in the Alps could be sent north. There was confidence that 'we can count entirely on the assistance of England' (although in practice Joffre did not do so). Germany was expected to violate at least part of Belgium, and thereafter France could follow suit: Luxemburg could be occupied pre-emptively, as the British were unlikely to object. Joffre now had the guidance

---

[280] Messimy, *Souvenirs*, 71–82. Porch, *March*, 171–6. Caillaux to Fallières, 2 July 1911, SHA 2.N. 1. GGS 'Die Umgestaltung des Oberbefehls über das Französiche Heer', Oct. 1911, KAM Gstb 164, for a German analysis.

[281] Joffre, *Mémoires*, i. 7, 16–25, 102.

that he needed, and on 27 October he asked Dubail to study ways of accelerating concentration and detraining forces further northwards as the revised basis for planning.[282]

The new buoyancy was manifest in a study of 9 January 1912 by the CSDN secretariat. France, it considered, could concentrate as fast as Germany and attain a numerical superiority that the 'probable' addition of the BEF would make decisive. 'This superiority would allow us to take the offensive and carry the war into enemy territory . . . the Triple Entente has sufficient resources to dominate the forces of the Triple Alliance on land, and even if England defects Russia and France would be able to conduct the struggle without disadvantage.'[283] This optimism was conveyed through the CSDN machinery to the civilian leadership, and it informed the preparations for Plan XVII. It continued into the Balkan crisis of the following winter. Contrasting as it did with French prognoses in the first Moroccan and Bosnian crises, and even with Joffre's doubts in 1911, it was of considerable significance. There were some solid reasons for it: British and Russian military assistance seemed more likely and likely sooner, and Italy was bogged down in Libya. But it is difficult to see either these developments or Joffre's juggling with the numbers as objectively justifying the change of strategy. Although the new commander was not an extreme exponent of the cult of the offensive that was permeating the French officer corps, it is difficult to ignore an undercurrent of irrationality, or at least of a change in self-perception, in the origins of the new mood.

Furthermore, although Joffre's guiding principle was 'to proceed to battle with all my forces', and concentrate everything in the north-east for an opening attack,[284] there was no obvious direction for the advance. He told the CSDN in October 1911 that France's military interest was to take the initiative in moving into Belgium, but he acknowledged that if he did this Britain would give no help, and indeed at the height of the Agadir crisis the General Staff and the Quai d'Orsay had agreed that France would enter the country only after Germany had done so.[285] At a further meeting in January 1912 the civilians present endorsed the EMA's thinking, including the commitment to a strategic offensive, but there was unanimous agreement that France should not go into Belgium first.[286] Reconnaissance by French officers meanwhile suggested that the hilly terrain of southern Belgium and Luxemburg was unsuitable for large-scale operations anyway. Yet Joffre saw little purpose in an offensive into Alsace, and to enter Lorraine between Strasbourg and Metz would be to move forward along narrow lines of communication and to court a German flank attack. He kept his options open, and Plan XVII specified a revised concentration (though one that could be modified) but not a commitment to any particular advance. By his own admis-

---

[282] Joffre, *Mémoires*, 103–13. CSDN minutes, 11 Oct. 1911, SHA 2.N. 1. Foreign Ministry/EMA 3rd Bureau note on conference of 16 Oct. 1911, ibid.

[283] CSDN, Section d'études, 'Note de présentation', 9 Jan. 1912, ibid.

[284] Joffre, *Mémoires*, i. 143.   [285] CSDN minutes, 11 Oct. 1911, SHA 2.N. 1.

[286] CSDN minutes, 9 Jan. 1912, SHA 2.N. 1. Joffre, *Mémoires*, i. 117.

sion, if he penetrated Alsace-Lorraine he would encounter serious obstacles and be unlikely to achieve an early breakthrough; whether he attacked in Belgium would depend on what the Germans did and how quickly he could improvise. He would attack, moreover, with at best parity in infantry and a serious disadvantage in field and heavy guns.[287]

This raises the question of the men and the equipment needed for the revised strategy. In 1911–12 there were large increases in neither. The most important legislation of the period was the infantry cadres law, introduced by Messimy and passed under his successor, Alexandre Millerand, at the end of 1912. Messimy considered the question of effectives to be of 'dominating importance', and that 'we are obliged . . . to measure out men like droplets. In fact we no longer have any flexibility in our recruitment resources.'[288] According to the EMA the situation of the *couverture* in 1912 was 'particularly critical', because of the disappointing 1911 intake and forces being distracted to pacify Morocco.[289] The infantry cadres bill (which was accompanied by bills for the engineers and cavalry) was intended to alleviate the consequences of a projected decline in peacetime effectives from 495,309 to 439,428 by 1931.[290]

Messimy asked his services to prepare the bill in September 1911, when the Agadir tension was still high.[291] He rejected any 'profound modification' in the army's organization, which would disrupt mobilization. Like Heeringen, he and his advisers opposed socialist proposals for a short-service militia. Nor, however, did they wish to modify two-year service, partly because of the economic burden of a longer term. Messimy believed that France was calling up the maximum possible of each age cohort, and must look to improve quality. The 'essential purpose' was to reinforce officer provision in order to ameliorate training and unit cohesion in peacetime and to strengthen the command in wartime both of active and of reserve formations.[292] The bill increased the number of native units from the colonies, and in January 1912, over opposition from the settler lobby, Messimy introduced limited conscription for North African Muslims.[293] Ten new infantry regiments would be created on the north-eastern frontier, but they would be largely composed of pre-existing battalions. Company strengths were to be set at one of three levels: 160 on the frontiers, 100 in the fortresses, and 118 in the interior. The EMA recognized that these figures were too low, but regarded them as preferable to the alternative of reducing the number of units. However, each regiment would be assigned a 'complementary cadre' of officers, thus strengthening the quota where appropriate and

---

[287] Ibid., ch. 9.

[288] Messimy note on military reforms, 12 Dec. 1911, SHA 5.N. 4. Messimy in Chamber Army Commission, 21 Dec. 1911, AN C7421.

[289] Joffre *et al.* to Millerand, 25 Oct. 1912, SHA 7.N. 134.

[290] Note on effectives, 1912–31, by Cabinet du Ministre, Oct. 1912, SHA 5.N. 4.

[291] Messimy note for EMA, 13 Sept. 1911, ibid. Text of the bill in AN C7419.

[292] Messimy note on military reforms, 12 Dec. 1911, SHA 5.N. 4. Messimy in Army Commission, 21 Dec. 1911, AN C7421.

[293] Messimy, *Souvenirs*, 91. Winterfeldt report, 14 Feb. 1912, PAAA R.6753.

allowing all regiments to constitute reserve formations. It was envisaged that on mobilization each active regiment would form a reserve regiment and assign officers to it, but there would be an increasing proportion of reservists as opposed to serving men even in the active regiments.[294] In effect the army was moving willy-nilly towards accepting Michel's ideas in modified form, but the cadres law was not a remedy for its shortage of peacetime manpower, and the GGS regarded it as a stopgap.

Moltke correctly divined that there was an increase in French assertiveness. Modern research has stressed the limits of the French nationalist revival, as a phenomenon largely confined to the Parisian intellectual and political élite and a conservative reaction against the post-Dreyfus Radical predominance.[295] But the Germans took it seriously, and the fear of conflict with a truculent neighbour was used to justify their 1912 army bill. Winterfeldt reported on French bellicosity at the time of Agadir, and the army's sense of superiority over Germany. The heightened national consciousness after 1911 was no 'straw fire', and there was a growing conviction that war was inevitable. The change was evident in the press and theatre, in spy scares, and in anti-German economic campaigns, and the further international tension at the end of 1912 accentuated it.[296]

It is in this context that Millerand's tenure as War Minister must be situated.[297] The Caillaux Government fell as another delayed repercussion of the Moroccan crisis, de Selves bringing it down by resigning in January 1912 when the Premier's clandestine contacts with the German Embassy were publicly exposed. The successor ministry, under Raymond Poincaré, represented a shift to the centre right, but it posed as a cabinet of political heavyweights and a government of national unity. Millerand himself was a former socialist who had estranged himself from his *confrères* by accepting office at the time of the Dreyfus case. He was the first War Minister for many years to belong to the front political rank, and was eloquent, patriotic, and hardworking. None the less, there was something in his critics' accusation that he was a publicity seeker who accomplished little of substance,[298] in this perhaps epitomizing the Poincaré ministry's preoccupation with national self-conciousness and morale.

Millerand wished to rebuild the army's independence, confidence, and discipline after years of political interference. He established good relations with Joffre, whom he strengthened by completing the High Command reorganization. Dubail's post was suppressed, and de Castelnau retitled Deputy Chief of the General Staff.[299] Millerand ended reporting by prefects on officers' opinions and insisted that advancement must be by merit, reinstating the system of promotion committees. Weekly military parades returned to garrison towns, and drums

[294] EMA presentation note for CSG on cadres bill, Sept. 1911, SHA 7.N. 108.

[295] J.-J. Becker, *1914: Comment les Français sont entrés dans la Guerre* (Paris, 1977), chs. 1–2.

[296] Winterfeldt reports, 19 Feb. and 11 May 1912, 13 Jan. 1913, *GP* xxxi, docs. 11515, 11522, 11532(i).

[297] M. M. Farrar, 'Politics versus Patriotism: Alexandre Millerand as French Minister of War', *French Historical Studies*, 11 (1980), 577–609.

[298] Winterfeldt report, 11 May 1912, *GP* xxxi, doc. 11522.   [299] Joffre, *Mémoires*, i. 27–8.

and bugles as markers of the barracks day. There were restrictions on the wearing of civilian dress, officers regained the right to impose punishments, and regimental co-operatives were forbidden to sell alcohol. It was symptomatic that Millerand eventually lost office because of his desire to reintegrate the notoriously anti-Dreyfusard officer du Paty de Clam, an error of judgement that testified to his desire to rehabilitate the army as a whole.[300]

Millerand's main legislative initiative was the military aviation law of March 1912, which doubled from 11 to 22 million francs the credits assigned to aviation for that year. It committed France to a force of 334 machines and to additional trained pilots, aircraft being assigned to the eastern fortresses as well as to each field army. Poincaré and Millerand were responding to press and parliamentary agitation, and were highly sensitive to public perceptions. In the CSG it was admitted that, even in their reconnaissance function, aircraft were handicapped relative to dirigibles by their shorter range. But it was felt that France's capacity in airships (where Germany had the lead) could be reinforced only if the more glamorous arm were reinforced as well.[301]

The War Minister had other achievements to his credit, including the passage of the infantry cadres bill and a decree in August 1912 that created 141 new infantry machine gun sections.[302] None the less, in manpower policy he followed Messimy's lead, and there was no spectacular budgetary increase. The cadres law, with annual recurrent costs of 14.5 million francs and non-recurrent ones of 3.15 million, was cheap.[303] There was a moderate increase in equipment spending, but a five-year programme worth 246.6 million francs that had been prepared under the preceding ministry was cut back to 50.7 million.[304] On taking over Millerand told the Chamber Army Commission that he thought the equipment of the French and German armies was roughly comparable,[305] but privately the French leaders well understood their continuing weakness. In correspondence with Poincaré Senator Charles Humbert made blistering criticisms of French artillery and fortifications, which, at least as far as Verdun was concerned, the Premier admitted were largely vindicated.[306] Joffre estimated that Germany spent half as much again on equipment in 1912.[307] But Millerand did little to remedy the problem, or to foster weapons innovation. The 50.7 million

[300] Porch, *March*, ch. 9. GGS report on Millerand's disciplinary measures, July 1912, KAM Gstb. 165. GGS annual report on foreign armies, 14 Jan. 1913, KAM Gstb. 167. Chronological history of Millerand's ministry (n.d.), AN Millerand MSS 470 AP.9.

[301] CSG minutes, 25 Jan. and 26 Feb. 1912, SHA 1.N. 10. Note 'Aviation' (n.d.), AN Millerand MSS 470 AP.10. GGS memoranda on French army development, Nov. 1912, KAM MKr. 991, and on French military aviation, Apr. 1912, KAM Gstb. 165.

[302] French War Ministry note on artillery measures since Feb. 1912, AN Millerand MSS 470 AP.10.

[303] War Ministry Secretariat for Cabinet du Ministre, 27 Jan. 1912, SHA 5.N. 4.

[304] War Ministry, 1st Bureau, to Millerand, 29 Nov. 1912, AN Millerand MSS 470 AP.10. Porch, *March*, 187. Joffre, *Mémoires*, i. 51–2.

[305] Millerand in Chamber Army Commission (?Jan. 1912), AN C7421.

[306] Humbert to Poincaré, Poincaré to (?)Millerand, 26 Sept. and 20 Oct. 1912, AN Millerand MSS 470 AP.10.

[307] Joffre, *Mémoires*, i. 52.

credit went to increasing field-gun munitions, and the expenditure heads cut from the five-year programme were training grounds and heavy artillery.[308] Joffre and Messimy had identified precisely these latter as the highest priorities, and the GGS perceived them as France's most serious areas of deficiency.[309] This was the more so as in a meeting on 25 February Joffre had pleaded that the best chance of victory lay in an offensive at the outset into Luxemburg and Belgium, which Poincaré ruled out on political grounds, the idea of a *démarche* to London being wisely dropped.[310] For all Millerand's desire to restore the army's independence it remained subordinate to the civilians in matters of high policy, and Joffre would now be attacking in the hills and forests of Lorraine with only the horizontally firing 75 mm field guns against a skilled and well-positioned enemy.

This sceptical interpretation of Millerand's tenure is borne out by his treatment of the German army law. Pellé kept the War Ministry thoroughly briefed about it, and warned of the rising francophobia across the Rhine, interpreting the law as being intended to enable Germany to outface France in a future crisis or for possible aggression a few years hence.[311] Jules Cambon thought there was no immediate threat, but that the passage of the measure was a warning.[312] French military intelligence estimated that German covering forces on the common frontier would rise by about 12,000 men, and that Germany was widening its lead both in effectives and in per capita expenditure.[313] Asked by Millerand how to riposte, the EMA prepared a memorandum on the 'Reinforcement of French Military Power'.[314] It considered that France, unlike Germany, could not call up a higher proportion of the age cohort, and it ruled out a longer term of service except possibly in the mounted arms.[315] Essentially, the army should continue with the existing piecemeal measures. When Millerand addressed the Chamber, accordingly, his remedy was to carry on as at present, and to vote the infantry cadres law.[316] It took the further stimulus of the German 1913 army bill to call forth a radical French response. The significance of the nationalist revival and the Poincaré ministry was for French domestic politics and for German perceptions. None the less, in conjunction with closer co-operation with the Russians,[317] the decisions taken after Agadir had recast the framework for

---

[308] 'Pièce No. 2' attached to letter of 29 Nov. 1912 cited in n. 304 above.

[309] Messimy in CSDN, 9 Jan. 1912, SHA 2.N. 1. Moltke, memorandum on French tactics, 12 Oct. 1912, KAM MKr. 991.

[310] Minutes of conference of 21 Feb. 1912, SHA 2.N. 1. G. Pedroncini, 'Stratégie et relations internationales: La Séance du 9 janvier du Conseil supérieur de la défense nationale', *Revue d'histoire diplomatique*, 91 (1977), 143–58.

[311] Pellé report, 21 Jan., 12 May, 9 June 1912, SHA 7.N. 1111.

[312] Jules Cambon to Poincaré, 26 May 1912, AMAE NS Allemagne 104.

[313] EMA 2nd Bureau note on the *couverture*, 13 June 1912; and on French and German military spending, Aug. 1912, SHA 7.N. 673.

[314] EMA 1st Bureau report on reinforcement of French military power, 31 May 1912, SHA 7.N. 134.

[315] Note on Millerand statement to the Chamber of Deputies, 19 June 1912, AN Millerand MSS 470 AP.9.

[316] Ibid.

[317] See Ch. 3 above.

French strategic planning, and the concomitant increases in manpower and in equipment spending would soon follow.

3. Italy and the Libyan War

In Western Europe the Agadir crisis redirected German armaments policy away from the North Sea and towards the Meuse; in the East it permitted Habsburg armaments policy to be reorientated towards Galicia, as a result of the break in the impetus of the Austro-Italian arms race caused by the Libyan War. Libya proved to be a very different conflict from the one the Italians had envisaged, and as in 1915 and in 1940 their forecasts of a simple, speedy operation went astray. Apart from Morocco, Libya was the last portion of the southern Mediterranean shore to be free from European domination, and its geographical proximity and Roman heritage made it an obvious magnet for Italian nationalism. Military plans had been updated since the 1890s, diplomatic sympathy had been promised by all the Powers, and cultural and economic penetration had proceeded on the ground. On the other hand, the Turkish administration was being reinvigorated, and by the summer of 1911, the fiftieth anniversary of Italy's unification, the press was advocating a resort to arms. Unless Giolitti and his Foreign Minister, San Giuliano, seized the initiative, their conservative opponents might play the patriotic card.[318]

Before the dispatch of the *Panther* there is no indication that Italy had set a date for attacking Libya or gone beyond contingency plans. But on 28 July San Giuliano wrote to Giolitti envisaging a military expedition within the next few months. The main reason was that once France had 'tunisified' Morocco it might renege on its support. Action should be taken before the impending renewal of the Triple Alliance, to prevent Vienna from using Libya as a bargaining point. San Giuliano expected force would be needed, although it was not his preference because he foresaw that it would lead to an attack by the Balkan Slavs upon the Ottoman Empire. Giolitti also realized that the attack might cause a Balkan and then a European conflict, and in his memoirs tried lamely to refute the accusation that he had started the avalanche. Both men knew that they were playing with fire, but their and Italy's interests were their main preoccupation, rather than the peace of Europe.[319]

The Italian leaders supposed that they could quickly win a localized war if they forced the issue now, but not if they delayed. To do nothing might make worthless the promissory notes accumulated over a generation. According to their attaché in Constantinople the Turks were distracted by rebellions in Albania and the Yemen and could not offer sustained resistance, but the Turkish

---

[318] R. J. B. Bosworth, *Italy, the Least of the Great Powers: Italian Foreign Policy before the First World War* (Cambridge, 1979), chs. 5–7; Gooch, *Italy*, 138 ff; G. Giolitti, *Memoirs of my Life* (London, 1923), ch. 11; C. J. Lowe and F. Marzari, *Italian Foreign Policy, 1870–1940* (London, 1975), all deal with the background.

[319] F. Malgeri, *La guerra libica (1911–1912)* (Rome, 1970), 385–8 (for San Giuliano's memorandum). Giolitti, *Memoirs*, 257, 351.

army was being modernized and the navy awaited its British dreadnoughts.[320] On 14 September Giolitti and San Giuliano decided to strike. Frantic military preparation followed, and an ultimatum on 28 September declared that as the Turks could not keep order or protect Italian interests, Italy was moving in. By the time that it expired the troopships were under steam. The entire fleet was mobilized, and an expeditionary force of 44,000 was sent against an Ottoman garrison one-sixth of the size. Once the Italians had taken the coastal cities, however, the Turks regrouped in the interior and kept up resistance with the aid of Arab irregulars. The Italians failed to break the stalemate when they extended operations into the Aegean. But by proclaiming Libya annexed they also blocked negotiation. Only the outbreak of the first Balkan War in October 1912 forced Constantinople to come to terms, and under the Treaty of Lausanne Italy gained sovereignty over the territory.[321]

The war suggested that the demise of the Ottoman Empire was imminent, and its consequences included a Russian attempt to secure free passage through the Straits and an Anglo-French agreement over Syria as well as the formation of a league of Balkan states. With the nationalist resurgence and the armaments build-up, it contributed to the mounting European tension. But it brought Italy and Austria-Hungary closer together. In January 1912 the Italians intercepted three French merchant ships. Poincaré protested, and the incident was referred to the Hague Tribunal, but it checked the improvement in Franco-Italian relations. Meanwhile Conrad was dismissed in November 1911 because of his advocacy of preventive war, and even after he returned a year later the Austrian and Italian General Staffs co-operated better than previously. In December 1912 the Triple Alliance was renewed ahead of its expiry date, San Giuliano judging that the Central Powers were still militarily stronger than the entente, that rivalry with France was increasing, and that Paris could not compensate him for changing camps.[322] Pollio, as usual, was not informed of the terms.[323] Italy remained an opportunist member of the Triple Alliance, but the alliance's health improved.

This improvement further showed itself in the alliance's military aspect. Pollio consistently advocated fighting alongside the Central Powers in a Continental war, and at the peak of the arms race with Vienna Italy remained committed in principle to sending troops to fight alongside Germany on the Rhine. In December 1912 Pollio disclosed to Moltke that he could no longer honour the Rhine commitment and would attack in the Alps instead, but this change of tack was a consequence of the drain of resources in Libya, and by 1914 he was again offering three army corps for deployment in Alsace.[324] Moreover, in June 1913

---

[320] D. G. Herrmann, 'The Paralysis of Italian Strategy in the Italian-Turkish War, 1911–1912', *English Historical Review*, 104 (1989), 332–6. Gooch, *Italy*, 138.

[321] Herrmann, 'Paralysis', 336–56, for an excellent discussion.   [322] Bosworth, *Least*, 208–15.

[323] Pollio to Brusati, 24 Dec. 1912, ASC Carte Brusati VII. 2. 42.

[324] M. Palumbo, 'German–Italian Military Relations on the Eve of World War I', *Central European History*, 12 (1979), 347–53. M. Mazzetti, *L'esercito italiano nella triplice alleanza* (Naples, 1974), 534–49.

an Austro-Italian naval convention provided for a united wartime command, and for joint operations against the French North African troop transports.[325] Both the Italians and the French resumed fortification work on their common frontier after several years of neglect, and the Italian General Staff examined the scenario of a French invasion.[326] The navy similarly reconsidered the possibility of war against France, and gave new attention to its west coast rather than its east coast bases.[327] The French 1913 military build-up—in reality directed against Germany—was misunderstood in Italy, and encouraged the political leadership to allow military and naval discussions as a token of loyalty to the Triple Alliance.[328] This did not necessarily mean, however, that Italian civilian, as opposed to military, policy-makers were predisposed to fight alongside Germany and Austria-Hungary in a European conflict.

Probably more important in slowing down the Adriatic arms race than these changes in political orientation was the check to Italy's military development. Even before the war the Italians were industrially and financially overstretched, and they played little part in the climax of the European land arms race. They lost nearly 8,000 dead and wounded in Libya. Giolitti told Parliament that the war cost about 512 million lire, but the true figure may have been three times that, compared with a War Ministry budget in 1909–10 of 399.5 million. Even after the peace treaty Arab resistance continued, and although the expeditionary force peaked in 1912 at about 100,000, in January 1914 it was still half that figure. At the height all but three divisions in Europe sent a regiment each, and the Italians dispatched almost all their infantry machine-gun sections, thus denuding their *couverture*.[329] Company strengths, averaging eighty-eight in 1909–10, now fell to sixty-six or even less.[330] Although the men in Libya were gaining combat experience, there was much discontent and some indiscipline, including in the mainland garrisons.[331] The rundown in army stores had not been made good by July 1914, and the navy's warships were overdue for refit.[332]

It is true that these deficiencies showed themselves only after a lag. Foreign observers agreed that 1913 was the year when progress slowed down.[333] In

[325] M. Palumbo, 'Italo-Austro-Hungarian Military Relations before World War I', in S. R. Williamson and P. Pastor (eds.), *Essays on World War I: Origins and Prisoners of War* (New York, 1983), ch. 3 (pp. 43–4).

[326] Palumbo, 'German–Italian Military Relations', 347. Evidenzbureau annual report on Italy, Dec. 1913, KAW Gstb. Operationsbureau 820. GGS report on fortification developments, 14 June 1913, KAM Gstb. 489. Gooch, *Italy*, 152. However, the fortification work was small.

[327] Halpern, *Mediterranean*, 202, 204. De Gondrecourt to French War Ministry, 8 Dec. 1913, SHA 7.N. 1370. Lt. d'Huart to French Marine Ministry, 30 Dec. 1913, SHM BB7 126.

[328] Gooch, *Italy*, 152.

[329] Malgeri, *Guerra libica*, 364. Gooch, *Italy*, 144, 147–8. De Gondrecourt to French War Ministry, 27 July 1912, 7 Jan. 1914, SHA 7.N. 1370.

[330] R. Cruccu, 'L'Esercito nel periodo giolittiano (1909–1914)', in Stato Maggiore dell'Esercito, *L'esercito italiano dall'Unità alla Grande Guerra* (Rome, 1980), 264. Pollio to Brusati, 10 Sept. 1912, ASC Carte Brusati VI. 3. 35.

[331] Malgeri, *Guerra libica*, 284–90.   [332] Cruccu, 'Esercito', 267. Halpern, *Mediterranean*, 195.

[333] Evidenzbureau annual report on Italy, Dec. 1913, KAW Gstb. Operationsbureau 820. De Gondrecourt to French War Ministry, 29 Nov. 1913, 7 Jan. 1914, SHA 7.N. 1370. GGS annual report on Western Europe, 1 Dec. 1913, KAM Gstb. 576.

1911–12 decrees continued to create new units, and extraordinary credits of 50 and 60 million lire were voted for equipment.[334] Thereafter Libya's demands on funds and manpower halted reorganization. Given the monetary tightness everywhere in Europe, the market for Treasury bills was reaching its limits, and Giolitti held off a bond flotation. Italy found itself in a 'crisis of stagnation' while others redoubled their efforts.[335] In the spring of 1913 Pollio reported that a manpower increase was urgently needed, and Spingardi wanted a programme to raise the budgetary strength to 300,000, build more coastal and frontier fortifications, organize an air force, and increase munitions stocks. The Premier was sympathetic, and the War Ministry drew up a plan for an extra 85 million lire annually in military spending and an extraordinary credit of 600 million. Little was done, however, before Giolitti fell from office in March 1914.[336] Spingardi complained about a 'lamentable deficiency of strength' in some units because of the North African commitment, and yet the Finance Ministry was blocking even a 25,000-man increase, which he found 'simply ridiculous' in view of the enormous reinforcements taking place elsewhere.[337] The reforming impulse of 1907–9 had run its course, and the War Minister was growing weary of office.[338]

It would be wrong, however, to see the 'crisis of stagnation' as simply resulting from the war. Industrial undercapacity had been exacerbated by mistaken procurement decisions. The law of June 1909 should have given Italy dreadnoughts before the Austrians, but the ships entered service more slowly and the navy remained at a disadvantage down to 1914.[339] The bottleneck was less in the shipyards than in the delivery of heavy cannon, turrets, and armour-plate. Terni fell behind with the armour, and Vickers-Terni, Armstrong-Pozzuoli, and Vickers and Armstrong in England were up to a year late in supplying 12″ guns.[340] There was also a liquidity crisis, Ansaldo closing its doors for twenty-four hours in protest against delays in payment by the Marine Ministry.[341] As for land armaments, Italy's transition to quick-firing field guns was still incomplete when the First World War broke out. After the scandal caused by the 1907 award to Krupp, a second order, after much hesitation and with bad grace, went to them in 1909; but by 1911 Giolitti and Spingardi were determined not to resort to Essen again.[342] Of the 1,500 guns needed, Krupp had supplied 861. The choice for the remainder lay between the Schneider 75 mm, which the French firm could produce in conjunction with Ansaldo, or an alternative 75 mm designed by Colonel Deport of Chatillon-Commentry, which a consortium of

[334] De Gondrecourt reports, 25 Jan. and 29 May 1912, SHA 7.N. 1370.

[335] De Gondrecourt report, 29 Apr. 1913, ibid.

[336] Cruccu, 'Esercito', 265–6. Gooch, *Italy*, 149–50. Spingardi to Brusati, 29 Apr. 1913, ASC Carte Brusati VII. 3. 43.

[337] Spingardi to Brusati, 27 Sept. and 4 Oct. 1913, ibid. VI. 5. 37.

[338] De Gondrecourt report, 3 Nov. 1913, SHA 7.N. 1370.

[339] Halpern, *Mediterranean*, 190–3. Rodd to Grey, 18 Feb. 1913, PRO FO/881/10194.

[340] Lt. d'Huart to French Marine Ministry, 30 Dec. 1913, SHM BB7 126.

[341] D'Huart reports, 1 Mar. 1913, ibid.

[342] Col. Jullian to French War Ministry, 8 Feb. and 29 Apr. 1911, SHA 7.N. 1370.

nineteen Italian companies had come together to manufacture.[343] The War Ministry was divided over the Deport gun's cost and technical qualities, and about the consortium's capacity to deliver, but the Council of Ministers was swayed by the argument for favouring national industry, and in March 1913 accepted the design. Whether it was the right decision militarily, commented Spingardi, 'I do not know'.[344] Almost immediately the work was hampered by shortages of steel: progress was soon reported to be 'painful' and the gun of poor quality. In the mean time, part of the Italian field artillery continued to use 75A pre-quick-firers, whose munitions were incompatible with either the Krupp or Deport weapons.[345] The machine-gun story was similar, the War Ministry hesitating between the Maxim-Vickers gun and the Revelli model. It opted for Vickers but reconsidered because delivery was so slow, and by 1914 in this area too, targets had not been met.[346] Doubts over which model to order additionally delayed the modernization of the heavy fieldguns.[347]

* * *

Pollio and Spingardi had expanded the army and improved its morale and organization since the 1907 crisis, but it remained poorly equipped and trained, and it stagnated as other Continental forces underwent intensive development. Italy ceased to press the Austrians on land, and was overtaken by them at sea. But elsewhere in Western Europe, as in Russia and the Habsburg Monarchy, the domestic obstacles to armaments increases had been much weakened, and in France and Germany nationalism was on the march. Even in Britain the ideological opposition to defence expenditure from the Radicals and the fiscal opposition from the House of Lords were consumed in the political firestorms of 1909–11. Bülow and Bethmann Hollweg achieved no revenue breakthrough comparable to the People's Budget, and by 1912 it seemed that Tirpitz would be unable to narrow the British advantage either through diplomacy or through building. Although there was another navalist agitation after Agadir, the Navy Secretary failed to repeat the *coup* that he had pulled off with the 1908 *Novelle*, and for the first time in his career he found himself outclassed. Within the budgetary constraints imposed on the German Government the army formed an alliance with the Chancellor in favour of land expansion, and conditions were emerging in which the North Sea contest could stabilize.

The relative eclipse of the naval rivalry was accompanied by a heightening of inter-bloc competition on land. The German 1911 *Quinquennat* had been a conditional measure, passed on the understanding that more would be required if

[343] De Gondrecourt report, 1 Mar. 1912, ibid.

[344] De Gondrecourt report, 28/30 Mar. 1913, ibid. Spingardi to Brusati, 15 Feb. 1912, ASC Carte Brusati VI. 4. 36.

[345] De Gondrecourt reports, 22 Dec. 1912, 21 June and 3 Nov. 1913, SHA 7.N. 1370. Evidenzbureau annual reports on Italian army, Jan. and Dec. 1913, KAW Gstb. Operationsbureau 820.

[346] Ibid. Cruccu, 'Esercito', 264. GGS annual report on Italian army, 1 Dec. 1913, KAM Gstb. 576.

[347] Ibid. De Gondrecourt reports, 10 Oct. and 18 Nov. 1912, SHA 7.N. 1370.

the menace from the 1910 Russian reorganization were reassessed. Tsarist military progress would probably have forced a reappraisal well before the next law was due in 1916; but in fact the timing of the *Rüstungswende* was decided by Agadir, and the French rather than the Russians were identified as the principal enemy. This was not only because they, after Belgium, were the first target of the Schlieffen Plan, but also because the nationalist revival was seen as making it more likely that Parisian obstreperousness would trigger a European conflict. The reorientation of German armaments policy was justified by reference to the longer-term deterioration in the Reich's position caused by Russia's resurgence and the recovery of French capabilities since Algeciras and the 1909 artillery bill. But it was precipitated by the second Moroccan crisis and its impact on German domestic armaments politics. Once drawn into the Berlin bureaucratic battles, moreover, the army leaders quickly established their superiority, and the law of 1912 whetted their appetite.

In Britain, by contrast, Agadir at first revived the fortunes of the Left, but the Radical revolt was short-lived, and with Haldane's failure and the passage of the *Novelle*, as well as the defection of Churchill and Lloyd George, the Westminster critics of continued naval building and of the tightening of the ententes were marginalized and decapitated. Furthermore, by sparking off the Libyan War, the crisis paralysed Italy's ability and inclination to compete with Austria-Hungary, thereby releasing more of the Dual Monarchy's resources for the re-emerging competition with Russia at the same time as Britain's widening lead encouraged German disengagement from the North Sea race. Finally, in France a military recovery from the post-Dreyfus nadir was already under way, but Agadir strengthened public support for the military and diplomatic consolidation of the Triple Entente, and led to the formation of the Poincaré ministry. The army High Command was reconstructed to assure it more stability and independence; manpower and equipment reforms were pressed with greater vigour; and French strategy was remodelled. As in Germany the Moroccan drama may have hastened changes that were coming anyway, but the timing mattered, and the rapid succession of policy reappraisals in East and West was fundamental to the breakdown of equilibrium. In both halves of Europe by 1912 the scene was set for the culmination of the inter-bloc arms race inaugurated by the outbreak of the Balkan Wars.

5
The Great Acceleration, 1912–1913

1. Balkan Ignition

Events in Eastern and in Western Europe must now be brought to their convergence. Continental diplomacy in the last two years of Great-Power peace centred on the outbreak and the aftermath of the Balkan Wars. With constant turmoil in the Eastern Mediterranean it was understood in every chancellery that the situation was much more strained, and at the climax of the winter crisis of 1912–13 Europe reached unprecedented levels of immediate military readiness. In addition, the crisis spectacularly intensified the drive for medium-term preparedness, expressed in massive spending increases and a string of major army laws. Diplomatic and military developments interacted ever more closely, and armaments competition and crisis management must be seen as aspects of a single phenomenon.

The first of the two Balkan Wars began when Montenegro declared war on Turkey on 8 October 1912, swiftly followed by Bulgaria, Serbia, and Greece. Serbia's advance through Turkish territory to the Adriatic raised the spectre of a clash with Austria-Hungary and caused weeks of anxiety. By the time of the ceasefire on 3 December the Ottomans had been driven back to the Chatalja lines outside Constantinople, losing all their other European possessions except the three besieged cities of Janina, Adrianople, and Scutari. Two conferences now opened in London: the peace conference between the belligerents, and the Conference of Ambassadors, chaired by Sir Edward Grey, comprising the representatives of the Powers. Neither was able to prevent a second round of fighting between 3 February and 15 April 1913, during which Janina and Adrianople fell respectively to Greece and to Bulgaria. Scutari's capture by Montenegro caused a further international crisis, before Habsburg pressure compelled the transfer of the city to the newly created state of Albania. Moreover, the London Treaty of 30 May, ending the First Balkan War, lasted barely a month before the victors fought each other in the Second. For a third time Austrian military intervention seemed conceivable; and in October, when the Dual Monarchy presented an ultimatum to Serbia to evacuate Albania's eastern territories, for yet a fourth.

Vienna therefore faced twelve months of upheaval in the south-east. Until an Austro-Russian disengagement agreement was negotiated in March 1913, this was accompanied by an armed confrontation with St Petersburg. The subsequent trials of strength between the Habsburg Monarchy and its South Slav neighbours prepared the Balkan arena for the explosion of July 1914; but it was events before the disengagement agreement that revolutionized the Great-Power arms race and are the more important in the origins of the larger Continental catastrophe. Consequently, it is to the winter crisis that this section will give most attention, before considering Scutari, the Second Balkan War, and the October ultimatum.

* * *

The pretext for the declarations of war was the Turks' treatment of their subject populations. The truer origin was the competition between the Balkan States for their neighbour's territory, and their encouragement of armed rebellion there.[1] The Ottomans began to call up 100,000 reservists for manœuvres in Thrace on 22 September, and the Balkan Powers ordered mobilization eight days later. On 13 October an ultimatum from Bulgaria, Serbia, and Greece required the Turks to grant autonomy to their European provinces, to agree to local assemblies and militias and to freedom of education, and to demobilize. It was timed to allow two weeks of preparation and was meant to be unacceptable. The operative question is less why the Balkan States attacked than why they did so now, to which the answer is that they were unusually united and their adversary unusually vulnerable. Both developments took their origins from the Libyan War,[2] which the Turks liquidated only on the brink of the new struggle. The Italians had brought hostilities to the Aegean by occupying the Dodecanese in April, and had attacked the Dardanelles. In addition, the war remoulded Balkan diplomacy.

The cornerstone of what became the Balkan League was the Serb–Bulgarian friendship treaty of March 1912, which was followed up by military agreements. In the first instance it was a secret defensive alliance against Austro-Hungarian expansion, but a protocol envisaged a joint attack on Turkey, though subject to a Russian veto. If the two countries disagreed on whether to launch military action, St Petersburg's ruling would be binding. If the war succeeded, Macedonia would be partitioned, except for a 'contested zone', which would either be autonomous or would be divided between Serbia and Bulgaria by the Tsar. Although the initiative for the treaty came from a new government in Bulgaria, hoping to profit from the Italo-Turkish conflict, the Russian ministers in Sofia and Belgrade encouraged and helped to draft it, and the Russian Government immediately received copies of the texts, yet was very slow to provide full details to Paris and London. Russian diplomacy was deeply implicated in the origins of Europe's most serious pre-war crisis.

Sazonov's motives were anti-Austrian rather than anti-Turk. The Bosnian

---

[1] For the origins of the wars, see E. C. Helmreich, *The Diplomacy of the Balkan Wars, 1912–1913* (repr. New York, 1969), chs. 1–6; E. C. Thaden, *Russia and the Balkan Alliance of 1912* (Philadelphia, 1965), chs. 1–4.

[2] On the role of Libya, R. J. Crampton, *The Hollow Detente: Anglo-German Relations in the Balkans, 1911–1914* (London, 1979), ch. 3.

humiliation still rankled, and since coming to the Foreign Ministry he had hoped to check Habsburg aggrandizement by creating a Balkan League. On first learning of the possibility of an agreement, he was inspired by the vision of half a million bayonets barring the Balkans to the Central Powers.[3] His Ambassador to Constantinople had pursued a *rapprochement* with Turkey as a prelude to including it in a Balkan bloc, but the overtures had been rejected.[4] Sazonov defended his actions retrospectively as an effort to control an outbreak that Libya made increasingly likely anyway; but, although he supposed he was safer with the treaty than without it, he had 'started the motor', as Poincaré put it, and unavailingly applied the brake.[5] The Russians were informed of, but had little say in, the follow-up military convention. They opposed the inclusion of Montenegro and Greece, but Bulgaria signed an alliance with Athens in May, and a Serb–Montenegrin alliance followed in October, Russia being consulted over neither.[6] The government in Sofia, like that in Belgrade, correctly calculated that victory was attainable without Great-Power assistance, it feared being pre-empted by the Macedonian revolutionaries, and Bulgarian public opinion was urging it to move.[7]

Having helped to start a process that they could not stop, the Russians appeared thwarted by the outbreak of hostilities. During the summer Nicholas II and the Foreign Ministry warned the Bulgars that Russia was unprepared for war and that it opposed an attack on Turkey. Given that both Sofia and Belgrade thought the moment opportune, however, it could not exercise its treaty veto.[8] Once Sazonov realized that the Balkan allies meant business, he belatedly co-operated with pacification attempts. In a joint *démarche* in Constantinople on 10 October the Great Powers declared that they intended to examine with the Ottomans the reforms to be introduced in Turkey-in-Europe, while maintaining its integrity. Austria-Hungary and Russia warned the Balkan States to keep the peace, and that the Powers would uphold the *status quo*. But the Turks rejected the proposal, and the prospect of European intervention probably encouraged the Balkan allies to cross the brink. Even so, at this stage an Austro-Russian confrontation seemed unlikely to follow.[9]

Neither Concert nor Russian diplomacy, however, were what they seemed. The Powers' *démarche* was not thought likely to ward off the Balkan allies' attack, although it was hoped to contain the fighting. The *status quo* declaration was unconvincing, as it was not expected that the territory Christians conquered would revert to Muslim rule. The Russians wished to obstruct Habsburg expansion, especially in the Sanjak; Berchtold did not aim at such expansion, but at strengthening his claim to compensation if the Balkan States were enlarged.[10] Although Sazonov feared a rerun of the annexation crisis, he did not exclude a

[3] Sazonov, *Fateful Years*, 49 ff. Thaden, *Russia*, 78.
[4] Ibid., ch. 2.
[5] Helmreich, *Balkan Wars*, 147.
[6] Thaden, *Russia*, 56, 101, 103.
[7] Ibid. 104–6, 113.
[8] Ibid. 111–13.
[9] Helmreich, *Balkan Wars*, 125–37.
[10] Ibid. Thaden, *Russia*, 128–30. S. R. Williamson, *Austria-Hungary and the Origins of the First World War* (Basingstoke, 1991), 126.

shift in the Balkan balance to his profit. He told the Bulgarians that he opposed not the principle of a war but the timing—Russia was not yet ready to risk a general conflagration.[11] Even if he and Kokovtsov were sincere in their warnings to desist, however, they were not fully in charge. Sazonov's deputy, Neratov, was less categorical than he was, the military attaché in Sofia apparently urged the Bulgarians on, and Hartwig, the forceful and well-connected Minister in Belgrade, advised the Serbs that they could count on unofficial Russian sympathy and on keeping their gains. The Balkan Powers took the plunge in the knowledge that there were divided counsels in St Petersburg and that if things went badly they were unlikely to be left to their fate.[12]

Further evidence for the Russians' opportunism is to be found in their military measures. In contrast to 1908, two Powers, not one, now played the game of armed diplomacy and St Petersburg rather than Vienna took the initiative. Between September and early November the Russians carried out a 'trial mobilization', approved an extraordinary military credit, and decided to prolong the service of their most senior conscript class.

The mobilization was announced on 30 September and was to take place in four military districts, including Warsaw.[13] Although the Russians denied all connection with the crisis, their communiqué coincided with the Balkan allies' mobilization and had a shock effect.[14] The Austrians were divided over how to interpret it. Schemua reported to Berchtold that 50–60,000 reservists had been called up in the Warsaw military district for weapons training, and soon a further 170,000 would follow, creating an enormous Russian preponderance on the northern border. The motive, he surmised, was to 'cover the rear' of the Tsar's Balkan protégés; but as the mobilization was directed against the German rather than the Austrian frontier this seems questionable.[15] Sazonov made light of it, claiming that he had not been party to the decision, which Sukhomlinov denied.[16] In contrast to Schemua, the attaché in St Petersburg, Hohenlohe, accepted assurances from the Stavka that there would be no permanent increase in frontier strengths and that the men would soon be released.[17] He was instructed to visit the staff daily (as his Russian counterpart was doing in Vienna) to check for abnormal activity: a week later he reported that he had found none (for example, the lights were not on late) and Sukhomlinov had reassured him that the timing of the mobilization was fortuitous and the men had gone home.[18]

[11] Helmreich, *Balkan Wars*, 153; Thaden, *Russia*, 113.   [12] Helmreich, *Balkan Wars*, 155–7.

[13] S. R. Williamson, 'Military Dimensions of Habsburg–Romanov Relations during the Balkan Wars' in B. K. Király and D. Djordjevic (eds.), *East Central European Society and the Balkan Wars* (New York, 1987), 319. See also R. Kiszling, 'Russlands Kriegsvorbereitungen im Herbst 1912 und ihre Rückwirkungen auf Österreich-Ungarn', *Berliner Monatshefte*, 13 (1935), 181–92.

[14] War Ministry summary of report from St Petersburg, 1 Oct. 1912, KAW KM Präs (1912) 51–2.

[15] Schemua to Berchtold, 7 Oct. 1912, ibid. 47–2. Schemua to Berchtold, 18 Oct. 1912, KAW Gstb Operationsbureau 710.

[16] Thurn to Berchtold, 14 Oct. 1912, *ÖUA* iv, doc. 409; Eggeling to Prussian War Ministry, 3 Feb. 1913, PAAA R.10431.

[17] Hohenlohe telegrams, 9 and 10 Oct. 1912, KAW KM Präs (1912) 51–2.

[18] Auffenberg to Hohenlohe, 18 Oct., Hohenlohe to Auffenberg, 24 Oct. 1912, ibid.

By the end of October the Evidenzbureau was satisfied that this was true, and when further rumours arrived of mobilization in Poland Kokovtsov formally denied them.[19] Berchtold told the Delegations that the exercise had been planned in the spring and gave no cause for concern,[20] and the Germans' conclusion seems to have been similar. Sazonov told them while on a visit to Berlin on 8 October that it was 'a regularly recurring measure', which the military authorities advised Kiderlen was 'to a certain extent correct'.[21] According to the German representatives in Russia the mobilization was confined to Poland and entailed no requisition of horses and carts: it was indeed preplanned and was over by mid-October.[22] It was disquieting, none the less, that there had been no official notification and, as the Austrian Foreign Ministry observed, that the Russians had not cancelled the measure in the light of the Balkan conflict.[23] This already contrasted with their previous caution.

It was the steps that followed the trial mobilization, however, that really caused anxiety to the Central Powers, and the second wave of measures unquestionably had Sazonov's support. With the destruction of the Turkish field armies in late October, and the rapid progress of their adversaries, the Powers' initial attachment to the Balkan *status quo* became untenable. Two repercussions pushed the Russians towards armed diplomacy. The first was a panic on 7–8 November, when the Turks fell back to the Chatalja lines and a threat to Constantinople seemed imminent. Sazonov and Grigorovich obtained authority from Nicholas for the Russian Ambassador to call up the Black Sea Fleet if he needed it. Sukhomlinov was asked to prepare a landing force of 5,000 men (which was probably beyond his logistical capacities), Sazonov envisaging intervention if the Christians in the city were massacred or if the Bulgarians reached the Bosphorus. Neither eventuality materialized, and Sazonov was anyway unwilling to act without Franco-British endorsement. But the episode was symptomatic of his growing interest in backing up his diplomacy by contingency planning, admittedly against the Turks or Bulgarians rather than the Austrians or Germans, though with the possibility that hostilities might spread.[24]

The second repercussion of the Turkish collapse was a crisis over the Adriatic. The Austro-Hungarian authorities now reconciled themselves to the enlargement of the Balkan States, but only on certain terms. As spelled out on 3–4 November these included a viable independent State of Albania, no territorial corridor for Serbia to the sea, and guarantees of Serbian good neighbourliness. Only over the second of these was Vienna willing to fight. It argued that a corridor to the Adriatic would jeopardize Albania's survival and contravene self-determination. Nor was it necessary, as Serbia could be given international guarantees of access

[19] Evidenzbureau memorandum, 31 Oct. 1912; Thurn to Berchtold, 15 Nov. 1912, ibid.
[20] Berchtold diary, 7 Oct. 1912, HHStA Berchtold MSS 1.
[21] Kiderlen memorandum, 9 Oct. 1912, *GP* xxxiii, doc. 12256.
[22] Reports by Lucius, Kohlhaas, and Pourtalès, 1, 3, and 7 Oct. 1912, PAAA R.10430.
[23] Tschirschky to Bethmann, 11 Oct. 1912, *GP* xxxiii, doc. 12261.
[24] V. I. Bovykin, *Iz istorii vozniknoveniya pervoi mirovoi voiny: Otnosheniya Rossii i Frantsii v 1912–1914 gg* (Moscow, 1961), 138–42.

to the ports and their connecting railways. The Austrians hoped to restrict Serbia's economic independence (especially its imports of war material), and they feared, improbably, a Russian naval base that could obstruct their maritime passage to the Mediterranean.[25] The Serbs maintained that direct sea access was vital to them, and in the second half of November they occupied the seaboard towns of Durazzo and Alessio. Simultaneously they detained the Austro-Hungarian consul in Prizren, Prochaska, and accused him of having encouraged Turkish resistance. Berchtold agreed to investigate the accusation, but for a time the Serbs prevented communication with the official, and until he was released at the end of the month there were fears for his safety.[26]

Sazonov's response to Austria-Hungary's conditions was to defend Serbia's right to sea access,[27] and for most of November the reports from the Central Powers' representatives in St Petersburg were disquieting. Behind the scenes Sazonov was urging the Serbs to settle for a railway and a port under international guarantee, and warning them that he would not go to war.[28] But he was mindful of the Bosnian humiliation and determined not to repeat it.[29] On 13 November he told Pourtalès that he favoured a corridor, though was willing to consider other solutions: if he was driven into a corner as in 1909, however, he would fight.[30] To add to the uncertainty, foreign observers sensed that Sazonov was not fully in control. In mid-November Nicholas was away at Spala, and was reportedly worked up by the Grand Dukes and his military entourage into a belligerently anti-Austrian mood. Only after 23 November, when the sovereign was back at Tsarskoe Selo, on the outskirts of the capital, did Sazonov indicate consistently that Russia was willing to compromise.[31]

An early consequence of the Balkan conflict was to push Kokovtsov further onto the defensive. Conferring with Nicholas on 19 October, he sensed that neither the Tsar nor the Council of Ministers would back him against Sukhomlinov over the 1913 War Ministry budget, and that for the first time he would have to concede all the army's demands. Nicholas apparently said that in the circumstances he would not forgive himself if he denied Sukhomlinov a rouble. At a meeting on 31 October–2 November the Council of Ministers agreed to a supplementary credit of 66.8 million roubles, to replenish the army's stocks of *matériel* and accelerate the implementation of the 1910 programme. Kokovtsov's

[25] L. Albertini, *The Origins of the War of 1914* (3 vols., London, 1952–7), i. 391–6. Helmreich, *Balkan Wars*, 203–8. W. Deutschman, 'Die militärischen Massnahmen in Österreich-Ungarn während der Balkankriege, 1912/13', Ph.D. thesis (Vienna, 1965), 31.

[26] Grey to Paget, 6 Nov. 1912, *BD* ix(ii), doc. 142. E. Zechlin, 'Die Adriakrise und der "Kriegsrat" vom 8 Dezember 1912', in *Krieg und Kriegsrisiko: Zur deutschen Politik im Ersten Weltkrieg* (Düsseldorf, 1979), 113 ff. Helmreich, *Balkan Wars*, 212–15.

[27] Buchanan to Grey, 8 and 9 Nov. 1912, *BD* ix(ii), docs. 161, 171.

[28] Sazonov to Izvolsky, 9 Nov. 1912, F. Stieve (ed.), *Der diplomatische Schriftwechsel Iswolskis, 1911–1914* (4 vols., Berlin, 1924), ii. doc. 558.

[29] Buchanan to Grey, 13 Nov. 1912, *BD* ix(ii), doc. 195.

[30] Pourtalès to Bethmann, 13 Nov. 1912, *GP* xxxiii, doc. 12375.

[31] Pourtalès to Bethmann, 20 and 23 Nov. 1912, ibid. docs. 12415, 12425. Buchanan to Grey, 27 Nov. 1912, *BD* ix(ii), doc. 291.

memoirs subsequently represented this as a demand announced without warning by Sukhomlinov that the Tsar insisted must go through.[32] In fact, the originator was Sazonov, who wrote to the Premier on 23 October that his task was to defend Russian interests while preserving peace, and he could achieve it only if he could draw on support from the armed forces. He wanted urgently to increase the army's readiness for a confrontation with Austria-Hungary or Turkey. Assistance from Britain and France, he considered, would depend on how far they thought Russia itself was prepared. In similar vein he wrote to Izvolsky that evident military preparedness would support peaceful pressure and diplomatic intervention by Russia to end the fighting. Kokovtsov forwarded the Foreign Minister's letter to Sukhomlinov, who responding by pressing for the credit.[33] Combined diplomatic and military representations overbore Finance Ministry resistance.

Sazonov had decided on a foray into armed diplomacy, admittedly with the aim of asserting Russian interests peacefully. Yet at this stage the Austrians had passed additional credits but had taken very little concrete action, and indeed, as Schemua reminded Berchtold, had decided to release their senior conscript class.[34] It seems to have been in the first week of November, at the time of the Constantinople and Adriatic alerts, that Russia resolved to do the opposite—contrary to the Western Powers in the previous year. On 10 November the French Ambassador reported that the class would be retained until 13 January, which the authorities had the legal right to do although in previous years they had dismissed it in October to save money.[35] The decision increased the Russian standing forces from their normal level by some 350,000 men, of whom 150,000 stood on the Western frontiers.[36] According to Zhilinski, frontier companies whose normal strength was 120 or 130 had been raised to 160 effectives; those whose strength was 140 or 150 had reached 200, and were little short of the wartime level of 215: 'we can therefore easily adjust to any eventuality'.[37] In addition, the Russians told their allies, the army had been reprovisioned, some units moved closer to the frontier in the Kiev military district, and there had been a 'whole series' of other measures.[38] Among them were arms imports, 120 Schneider guns arriving in November as well as German products.[39] Pourtalès, who had previously been relaxed about the situation, now agreed with Hohenlohe that

[32] V. N. Kokovtsov, *Out of my Past* (Stanford, Calif., 1935), 339–44. A. L. Sidorov, *Finansovoe polozhenie Rossii v gody pervoi mirovoi voiny (1914–1917)* (Moscow, 1960), 72. Louis to Poincaré, 24 Dec. 1912, *DDF* 3rd ser. v, doc. 116.

[33] Bovykin, *Otnosheniya*, 136–7.

[34] Schemua to Berchtold, 7 Oct. 1912, KAW KM Präs (1912) 47–2.

[35] Louis to Poincaré, 10 Nov. 1912, *DDF* 3rd ser. iv, doc. 410. Wehrlin and Laguiche to War Ministry, 21 and 28 Nov. 1912, SHA 7.N. 1478.

[36] Louis to Poincaré, 2 Jan. 1913, *DDF* 3rd ser. v, doc. 154.

[37] Laguiche to War Ministry, 16 Dec. 1912, SHA 7.N. 1478.

[38] Sazonov to Izvolsky, 18 Dec. 1912, Stieve (ed.), *Iswolski*, ii, doc. 640, cf. Zhilinski to Nicholas II, 14 Nov. 1912, G. Frantz (ed.), *Russlands Eintritt in den Weltkrieg: Der Ausbau der russischen Weltmacht und ihr Einsatz beim Kriegsausbruch* (Berlin, 1924), doc. 31.

[39] Hohenlohe to Schemua, 29 Nov. 1912, KAW Gstb (1912) 25–7.

St Petersburg was doing everything possible to avoid being caught unprepared, including retaining railway wagons and moving troops up to the frontier.[40] Moltke accepted that keeping on the extra class was not mobilization, but it marked 'an essential increase in Russian war preparedness'. Schemua agreed,[41] and according to the Austrian attaché the Government in Vienna was 'completely panic stricken'. Retaining a class of fully trained men was if anything more dangerous than calling up reservists, who would initially need a period of acclimatization, and the numbers added to the Russian forces were not much fewer than those of the entire Habsburg standing army.[42]

Russia's actions in November were much more significant than the trial mobilization. Yet Sazonov supposed that by avoiding calling up reservists he was observing moderation, and he reassured the French that the retention of the class was not 'a mobilization measure'.[43] In a cliff-hanging exchange at Tsarskoe Selo on 23 November, he and Kokovtsov blocked more drastic steps. According to the Premier (whose memoirs are certainly inaccurate but not easily corroborated by other sources), the two men attended an emergency meeting with Sukhomlinov, Zhilinski, and Rukhlov (the Minister of Communications) on a summons from Nicholas. The Tsar began by stating, incorrectly, that Austrian frontier strengths were more than double their own and because of the slowness of Russian transport it was necessary to do more. Hence he had decided with Sukhomlinov and the commanders of the Kiev and Warsaw military districts to mobilize all of the former and part of the latter, and to prepare the mobilization of Odessa. The telegrams were ready, and, had he not insisted on conferring with his other ministers, would already have gone out. Kokovtsov remonstrated that mobilization without notifying Paris would violate the Franco-Russian convention and run great danger of a war for which the country was unprepared. Instead he proposed to lengthen the term of service, so that the senior class would be kept on from January until July. Sazonov and Rukhlov supported him, and Nicholas and Sukhomlinov yielded.[44]

The clash—which was impassioned—arose from conflicting assumptions that neither side did much to substantiate. Sukhomlinov believed, or affected to believe, that war was inevitable and desirable and the sooner it came the better. Yet that he was preparing, and subsequently undertook, a visit to Berlin and the French Riviera hardly suggests that he thought it imminent. Ernest May has plausibly argued that he well understood the army's weaknesses and that his seemingly irresponsible behaviour was designed to pitchfork the civilians into lower-risk concessions.[45] If he really believed (contrary to the evidence of his

---

[40] Pourtalès to Bethmann, 19 Nov. 1912, PAAA R.10430.

[41] Moltke to Kiderlen, 12 Nov. 1912; von Kageneck report, 13 Nov. 1912, *GP* xxxiii, docs. 12360, 12370.

[42] Laguiche to War Ministry, 13 Dec. 1912, SHA 7.N. 1478.

[43] Louis to Poincaré, 10 Nov. 1912, *DDF* 3rd ser. iv, doc. 410.

[44] For accounts of this episode, Kokovtsov, *Out of my Past*, 345 ff.; E. R. May (ed.), *Knowing One's Enemies* (Princeton, 1984), 17 ff.; L. C. F. Turner, 'The Russian Mobilisation in 1914', in P. M. Kennedy (ed.), *The War Plans of the Great Powers, 1880–1914* (London, 1979), 254–6.

[45] May (ed.), *Knowing*, 23.

memoirs)[46] that Russia was prepared for war, he was isolated at Tsarskoe Selo. It is true that at the Council of Ministers on the following day several participants supported Sukhomlinov and condemned Kokovtsov for being unpatriotic, but this reflected distaste for 'cringing before the Germans' rather than a considered assessment.[47] At a conference on 19 November the commanders of the military districts had reported grave shortages in horses, artillery, and munitions, and unanimously agreed that Russia was not ready, although they did, in view of Austria-Hungary's supposed measures, wish to move the equivalent of four cavalry divisions secretly up to the border.[48] Presumably a variant of this proposal came to Tsarskoe Selo, where Nicholas agreed that 'the very thought of war was folly', but supposed that a limited frontier reinforcement incurred no risk of it, especially if directed against not Germany but only the Dual Monarchy. In this he may have been mistaken, given that Moltke had advised on 19 November, as will be seen below, that any further such Russian measures would have to be viewed as the beginning of mobilization. But what divided him from Kokovtsov and Sazonov was his judgement of what was possible short of war. In addition, Nicholas and the soldiers were looking to guard the frontier against a surprise attack that might disrupt the *couverture*, rather than to strengthen Russia's diplomatic position. The outcome of the conference—a decision to prolong the retention of the senior class—might simultaneously serve both goals.

After 23 November it seemed that civilians and military were approaching harmony, on the basis of the extraordinary credit, the retention of the conscript class, and measures to facilitate mobilization if necessary, but not mobilization itself. The harmony was liable to be disturbed by Russia's ally. At Tsarskoe Selo Kokovtsov protested that the French had not been consulted, but if they had been their influence might well have been provocative. Although St Petersburg was the driving force in the militarization of the crisis, Paris evolved from initial circumspection into a posture more belligerent than the Russians' own. Distinctively absent from the crisis was a French attempt to restrain Russia and Serbia, as had happened in 1909, would happen again in 1913, and once more, if belatedly and ineffectively, in the following July. Poincaré's policy has long been controversial, and appears more adventurist as reported by Izvolsky than in the Prime Minister's memoirs and the Quai d'Orsay files. But the French over Bosnia and the Russians over Agadir had interpreted the alliance strictly defensively: it would operate against German aggression, but not necessarily in a war provoked by either ally's intransigence. In 1912, however, Poincaré failed to reiterate this position. He joined Sazonov in urging restraint on Serbia when requested, but he refrained from unsolicited advice to Russia to be conciliatory. It is true that on first learning of the Serb–Bulgarian treaty he was worried and distrustful. When he visited St Petersburg in August, however, and was fully briefed for the first time, he told Sazonov that France would not aid Russia

[46] V. A. Sukhomlinov, *Erinnerungen* (Berlin, 1924), 342.
[47] Kokovtsov, *Out of my Past*, 349.   [48] May (ed.), *Knowing*, 23.

militarily in the Balkans, even against Austrian aggression, but that if Russia were attacked by Germany or by Austria-Hungary with Germany's backing France would assist. According to Sazonov's notes, Germany must be involved 'on its own initiative', but on this crucial point there remained ambiguity, and Poincaré gave up seeking a Russian commitment to uphold the Eastern Mediterranean *status quo* when Sazonov resisted. Poincaré's acquiescence was symptomatic of his tendency to treat the alliance as a bloc, in which the interests of each member should be defended by the grouping as a whole, and foreshadowed French efforts to strengthen the bloc militarily in 1913. In September he gave a new assurance that, although if Austria-Hungary alone attacked Russia there would be no *casus foederis*, if Germany assisted Austria-Hungary France would be bound to march.[49]

This firmer tone continued after the outbreak of war. In a speech at Nantes on 26 October Poincaré said that the French people 'does not desire war and yet does not fear it'.[50] At the height of the tension over the Adriatic, Sazonov enquired about France's attitude to an Austro-Hungarian attack on Serbia. The official reply was that France could not state its position until it knew Russia's own.[51] Sazonov, however, avoided specifying any course of action, despite repeatedly warning that public opinion might force him to retaliate. It might seem that because he failed to commit himself he was unable to commit his ally; but Poincaré made clear to his Ambassador in St Petersburg that the official response did not mean that France was unwilling to face a confrontation, and he did not want Sazonov to be able to blame a climb-down on Paris.[52] According to Izvolsky, Poincaré's personal opinion was that if Russia went to war because Austria-Hungary attacked Serbia France would follow suit, because the French would know that behind the Austrians stood Germany. In his memoirs Poincaré insisted that his line had been that Russia must be attacked by Germany or by Austria-Hungary supported by Germany, but this failed to stipulate that Russia would forfeit French support if it intervened to protect Belgrade. French influence—especially as mediated by the Russian Ambassador in Paris—presumably contributed to St Petersburg's new willingness to run risks.[53]

Not only did the French give diplomatic assurances: they also urged greater military readiness. The EMA's post-Agadir confidence was evident in a briefing of 2 September, used by Colonel Vignal of the 2nd Bureau to instruct Poincaré.[54] If Austria-Hungary faced no Balkan distraction, it predicted, the Russians would

[49] R. N. L. Poincaré, *Au service de la France: Neuf années de souvenirs* (Paris, 1926–33), ii. 32, 35, 115–19, 200–2. R. Girault, 'Les Balkans dans les relations franco-russes en 1912', *Revue historique*, 513 (1975), 155–84.

[50] Poincaré, *Service*, ii. 281–2.

[51] Note from Russian Embassy in Paris, 12 Nov. 1912, *DDF* 3rd ser. iv, doc. 432, Poincaré to Louis, 13 Nov. 1912, ibid., doc. 443. Grey to Bertie, 15 Nov. 1912, *BD* ix(ii), doc. 209.

[52] Poincaré to Louis, 16 Nov. 1912, *DDF* 3rd ser. iv, doc. 469.

[53] Izvolsky to Sazonov, 17 Nov. 1912, Stieve (ed.), *Iswolski*, ii, doc. 567. Bovykin, *Otnosheniya*, 144. Poincaré, *Service*, ii. 335–40.

[54] 'Note de l'EMA', 2 Sept. 1912, Paul to Jules Cambon, 3 Sept. 1912, *DDF* 3rd ser. iii, docs. 359, 366.

be 'sensibly balanced' by thirteen Habsburg army corps in Galicia and the German forces in East Prussia, leaving France and Germany in the West, unless Britain intervened, with approximately equal numbers. But a campaign against the South Slavs might tie down more than half the Habsburg army, obliging Germany to leave Russia a free hand in Poland or to transport so many soldiers eastward as to be obliged to fight France 'in a state of considerable numerical inferiority . . . In these conditions the Triple Entente would have the greatest chances of success and could achieve a victory that would permit it to redraw the map of Europe, despite Austria's local Balkan successes.' Although Poincaré later denied that Izvolsky had enquired about the French military assessment, it appears that he did communicate to the Ambassador the EMA's optimism.[55] Similarly, when Sir Henry Wilson visited Paris he found his hosts 'of the opinion that it would be better for France if a conflict was not too long postponed', and that if war came over the Balkans they could expect wholehearted Russian support. The French military authorities believed that Russia was becoming 'exceedingly strong', and might soon wish to take an independent line, while they still doubted whether assistance from the BEF would be timely or effective.[56]

Such self-assurance was offset by apprehension that France would be the target of the main German attack. It was feared that Austria-Hungary might neutralize the Triple Entente's advantage by faster mobilization, especially after Russia's decision to retain the conscript class was followed by the raising of Austrian troop strengths in Galicia. On 9 December Poincaré told Izvolsky that Habsburg preparations far exceeded Russia's, and Germany might therefore be able to invade France with overwhelming force. He asked his ambassador, Georges Louis, to ascertain what Russia had done. The reply was that the Stavka was not particularly worried about the Habsburg measures, which it believed might hamper an Austro-Hungarian general mobilization.[57] Not reassured, Poincaré told Izvolsky that Austria-Hungary might crush Serbia before Russia had mobilized, obliging Nicholas to accept a *fait accompli* or start a war in which Germany could safely send all its forces to the West. De Castelnau spoke similarly to the Russian attaché.[58] Once again, however, St Petersburg's replies were anodyne, the Stavka even suggesting that if Serbia were attacked it would take no action: a comment so alarming to Poincaré and Millerand that they called the Council of ministers into emergency session.[59] The French attaché urged the Stavka to call up reservists, but the Russian authorities demurred, on the grounds that Germany had done nothing and that Austria's measures were a 'bluff'.[60] Habsburg preparations, according to General Monkewitz, were purely

[55] Poincaré, *Service*, ii. 205, but see Albertini, *Origins*, i. 373; L. C. F. Turner, *Origins of the First World War* (London, 1970), 36–7.
[56] Nicolson to Grey, 24 Feb. 1913, *BD* ix(ii), doc. 656.
[57] Izvolski to Sazonov, 23 Nov. and 9 Dec. 1912, Stieve (ed.), *Iswolski*, ii, docs. 579, 614. Poincaré to Louis, 9 Dec. 1912, Louis to Poincaré, 10 Dec. 1912, *DDF* 3rd ser. docs. 22, 33.
[58] Bovykin, *Otnosheniya*, 147.
[59] Louis to Poincaré, 14 Dec. 1912, *DDF* 3rd ser. doc. 61. Bovykin, *Otnosheniya*, 148–9.
[60] Wehrlin and Laguiche to War Ministry, 6 and 9 Dec. 1912, SHA 7.N. 1478.

defensive and motivated by 'a chimerical fear of Russian aggression', but for Russia to mobilize or gather forces on the frontier would cause Germany to do likewise and 'then a mere trifle would suffice to set in motion the entire machine'.[61]

The Russian military's resistance to French urgings contrasted with their hawkishness in internal debate. In mid-December Sukhomlinov brought a six-point proposal before the Council of Ministers: (1) in the Kiev and Warsaw military districts the frontier cavalry units should be reinforced at the expense of those in the interior; (2) two cavalry brigades should move from the Moscow district to the southern frontier of the Warsaw one; (3) the Kiev and Warsaw infantry units should be brought up to war strength by calling up reservists for training; (4) the cavalry and artillery units on the Kiev and Warsaw district frontiers should receive more horses; (5) the military guard on railways and bridges in these districts should be strengthened; and (6) exports of horses should be banned. Once again Kokovtsov and Sazonov assailed the plan, on the grounds that any rash step might lead to a war with Austria-Hungary, whom Germany would inevitably support, while Russia could not depend on backing from Britain and France, still had no active Baltic fleet or an army at adequate readiness, and lacked dependable public support. Hence the Council approved only points 1, 4, and 5 of Sukhomlinov's package.[62] The French continued with their representations, de Castelnau saying that he wanted war and Millerand that if the Austro-Serb conflict escalated France was ready,[63] but Zhilinski told Laguiche, perhaps ruefully, that 'the Council of Ministers having decided that there were no grounds, on the basis of either military or political intelligence, to proceed to any mobilization whatever', nothing further would be done.[64] Sukhomlinov, emollient, urged that Paris could remain calm: 'we have quietly made all ready, you will see.'[65] General Monkewitz and General Engel believed that Russia could defeat and dismember Austria-Hungary if war broke out now and agreed that the European conjuncture had moved against the Central Powers. Everything was 'well prepared, it would suffice to press a button to set it in motion'.[66] In response to yet a further French enquiry in January, Zhilinski answered that the conscript class was being kept on for six more months and that there were reinforcements of cavalry and artillery in the Kiev and Warsaw districts—in other words, that the measures agreed at Tsarskoe Selo and the December Council of ministers were going into effect.[67]

Despite the injunctions from their ally, the Russians, with small concessions to the military, cleaved to the Sazonov/Kokovtsov line. There was military readiness, but of a kind held to be non-provocative, though adequate to protect the frontiers and show that Russian diplomacy meant business. The army lead-

[61] Laguiche to War Ministry, 13 Dec. 1912, ibid.
[62] Bovykin, *Otnosheniya*, 152–3. Laguiche to War Ministry, 16 Dec. 1912, SHA 7.N. 1478.
[63] Bovykin, *Otnosheniya*, 149–50.
[64] Laguiche to War Ministry, 16 Dec. 1912, SHA 7.N. 1478.
[65] Wehrlin to War Ministry, 21 Dec. 1912, ibid.
[66] Ibid.
[67] Bovykin, *Otnosheniya*, 154–5.

ers wanted troop movements and reservist call-ups in the frontier districts but accepted that more sweeping measures would impede mobilization. By comparison with the civilians, they were less willing to run the risk of being caught unprepared and more willing to run that of provoking Germany, but they felt better placed than in the Bosnian crisis, and more confident of French support.[68] According to Pourtalès the Stavka thought it could beat the Austrians now, although it would prefer to wait one or two more years.[69] Unfortunately, Germany was also expected to grow stronger in the interim and the Russian attaché there foresaw a critical period in the winter of 1913/14.[70] But in the present crisis the Russians' intelligence services informed them reasonably accurately about their potential enemies,[71] and that neither Central Power wanted war. Although Sazonov had to take precautions, especially given Austria-Hungary's demonstrated proclivity to back up its diplomacy by military measures, he seems to have recognized that large troop movements and call-ups of reservists would be dangerous. There was a balance to strike between deterrence and provocation, and Russia's wavering in its search for it intensified the insecurity felt elsewhere.

* * *

The Triple Entente's main contribution to the militarization of the crisis was the Russian extraordinary measures. But in addition the entente helped the Balkan States, and Britain and France heightened their own preparedness. Although Balkan arms sales bulked less large in the diplomacy of 1912–13 than in 1908–9, this was hardly because of a diminished willingness on the part of the suppliers. It is true that there was some effort to restrain Bulgaria, to which the Paribas bank was allowed to extend a loan in June only after the Russians had assured Poincaré that they could control Sofia. When it became clear that the Bulgarians were bent on war, he attempted to halt the flotation. But once war broke out, France allowed both loans and arms sales, as did Russia, and the Austro-Hungarian War Ministry agreed to deliver 50,000 rifles and 50 million cartridges in the belief that Bulgaria was a potential ally against the Serbs. Only Germany remained aloof.[72]

Montenegro received fifty machine guns from the DWMF in October 1912, and 5,000 horses and 2.4 million cartridges from the Russians during the run-up to the Scutari crisis.[73] Serbia, in contrast, relied mainly on France, the last consignment of the 1910 artillery order from Schneider arriving in January

[68] Hohenlohe to Auffenberg, 19 Nov. 1912, KAW KM Präs (1912) 47–2.

[69] Pourtalès to Bethmann, 20 Nov. 1912, PAAA R.10430.

[70] K. F. Shatsillo, *Rossia pered pervoi mirovoi voiny (vooruzhennye sily tsarizma v 1905–1914 gg)* (Moscow, 1974), 82.

[71] See e.g. Laguiche to War Ministry, 28 Nov. 1912, SHA 7.N. 1478; Fourmier to War Ministry, 7 Dec. 1912, SHA 7.N. 1568.

[72] Poincaré, *Service*, ii. 33, 180, 188–9. Thaden, *Russia*, 118–19. J. Ullreich, 'Moritz von Auffenberg-Komarów: Leben und Wirken, 1911–1918', Ph.D. thesis (Vienna, 1961), 81.

[73] Eckhardt to German Foreign Ministry, 29, 31 July, and 6 Aug. 1912, PAAA R.927. Hubka to War Ministry, 3 Apr. 1913, KAW KM Präs (1913), 47–16.

1913.[74] The war came at an awkward moment for the Serb army, which was equipping itself against the Habsburgs rather than the Turks, and whose reorganization was incomplete.[75] As hostilities drew near the Government obtained from the Skupshina a 21-million franc credit for, among other things, aircraft, mountain guns, and 60,000 rifles.[76] The French army was asked again if it could produce the latter at Châtellerault, the Serbs explaining that they were dissatisfied with the quality of Austrian and German weapons and that Steyr had refused to deliver during the Bosnian affair. The Quai d'Orsay considered the possibility 'highly interesting', and Châtellerault tendered at 85 francs per weapon, but as this was dearer than rival bids negotiations stalled until the outbreak of war.[77] Soon afterwards, however, 40,000 fuses were ordered from Le Creusot, and eight aircraft were delivered, with French-trained pilots.[78] Commentators across Europe saw the outcome of the fighting (not altogether fairly) as a victory for the Balkan allies' Schneider guns over Turkey's Krupp ones.

In September 1912 the Turks impounded French munitions in transit for Serbia. Schneider appealed to the Quai d'Orsay, which protested in Constantinople, apparently to no avail.[79] The French Legation in Belgrade insisted on Schneider's right to receive payment regardless—another indication of the commercial as much as strategic purpose behind French export promotion.[80] Berchtold told Auffenberg that for 'political reasons' he could not prohibit the sale and transport of war material to the belligerents, and he resisted military pressure to apply sanctions to the Serbs for not returning Austro-Hungarian rolling stock. None the less, several consignments of equipment for Serbia were halted in December, Berchtold agreeing to 'internal administrative hindrances' being placed on arms exports, but opposing anything more overt.[81] In February 1913 the Austrians agreed to sell 60,000 rifles to Romania from their own War Ministry stock, although the concession earned them little goodwill as the Romanians found the weapons unsatisfactory.[82] Finally, in June the War Ministry agreed to investigate when Conrad reported in great alarm that Serbia was trying to buy 31,000 rifles from Steyr.[83] In general, therefore, the French and Russians continued to supply the Balkan allies, and Austria-Hungary, except

[74] Fourmier to War Ministry, 1 Feb. 1913, SHA 7.N. 1568.

[75] Gellinek to War Ministry, 6 Oct. 1912, KAW KM Präs (1912) 147–7.

[76] Descos to Foreign Ministry, 19 June and 31 July 1912, AMAE NS Serbie 9.

[77] Loukitch to Châtellerault, 20 June 1912; Foreign to War Ministry, 31 July 1912; War Ministry to Loukitch, 26 Aug. 1912; Descos to Foreign Ministry, 17 Sept. 1912, ibid.

[78] Descos to Foreign Ministry, 23 Dec. 1912, ibid. Fourmier to War Ministry, 22 Dec. 1912, SHA 7.N. 1568.

[79] Schneider to Foreign Ministry, 30 Sept. and 19 Nov. 1912, AMAE NS Serbie 9.

[80] Foreign Ministry to Descos, Descos reply, 18 and 23 Dec. 1912, ibid.

[81] War Ministry to Austrian Railway Ministry and Hungarian Trade Ministry, 11 Dec. 1912; Berchtold to Krobatin, 21 Dec. 1912, KAW KM Präs (1912) 32–19. Conrad to Berchtold (on rolling stock), 20 Mar. 1913, KAW Gstb (1913) 37–7.

[82] See correspondence between War Ministry and Hranilović, KAW KM Präs (1913) 32–5.

[83] Conrad to Krobatin, 21 June 1913, KAW KM Präs (1913) 32–11.

through internal administrative harassment, did little to prevent them. Arms sales formed another aspect of the entente military challenge.

France and Britain's own level of military readiness was much higher than in 1909. A crisis on one side of Europe now had much greater repercussions on the other, in this epitomizing the intermeshing of the diplomatic and armaments systems and the intensifying inter-bloc confrontation. In Britain, German observers saw no evidence of the army taking extraordinary measures,[84] but the Royal Navy in home waters was moved into the highest state of readiness short of mobilization. Leave in the First and Second Fleets was restricted; stocks of coal, ammunition, and provisions were readied; and night shifts worked in the dockyards. The Navy's deployment remained defensive, but such that a rapid transfer from the Channel to the east coast remained possible.[85] The French fleet was concentrated in the Mediterranean and ready for battle. Both forces were on higher alert than the Russian Baltic Fleet, and the Royal Navy's preparedness may have been not far short of that reached during Agadir.[86]

As for the French army, like the German it released its senior conscript class, although this time apparently without a tacit agreement. In late November, according to the GGS, neither side had increased their standing forces.[87] There was intensified training, reservists were called up in the border corps, precautions were taken in the fortresses, and there were frontier troop exercises. But the GGS noted no special mobilization preparations or saw reasons for concern.[88] The attaché in Paris found evidence of unusual activity, but nothing that went beyond precautionary measures. Moltke reported to the Kaiser that 'It can be stated definitely that in France actual war preparations are not being undertaken . . . extraordinary measures indicating mobilization preparations have not been evident'.[89]

Soon after this, however, German anxiety began to grow, principally because of a trial mobilization on 26–7 November. According to the Russian attaché, Millerand had ordered the three eastern corps to prepare the frontier for defence. The purpose was mainly to test the civil authorities' preparations, and the German Ambassador was assured that no 'partial mobilization' was in progress.[90] None the less, Kiderlen told the British Ambassador in Berlin that press reports that France was doing nothing were untrue: 'we have heard of such things; the French call them "*essais de mobilisation*", but we know quite well what that

[84] Moltke report on French military situation, 21 Nov. 1912, KAM MKr. 991; and on British military measures, 29 Nov. 1912, KAM MKr. 1711.

[85] Ibid. Chief of Admiralty Staff to Kiderlen, 28 Nov. 1912, PAAA R.5596; and 14 Dec. 1912, PAAA R.995.

[86] Ibid. and reports on French and Russian fleets, 27 Nov. 1912, PAAA R. 5596. Bovykin, *Otnosheniya*, 146–7.

[87] Wenninger to Bavarian War Minister, 25 Nov. 1912, KAM MKr. 41.

[88] Report on French military situation, 21 Nov. 1912, KAM MKr. 991.

[89] Schoen to Bethmann, 18 Nov., Winterfeldt to Moltke, 24 Nov. 1912, Moltke to Wilhelm, 26 Nov. 1912, *GP* xxxiii, docs. 12407, 12436, 12446.

[90] Report on French military situation, 21 Nov. 1912, KAM MKr. 991; Bovykin, *Otnosheniya*, 150; Schoen to Foreign Ministry, 27 Nov. 1912, PAAA R.6754.

means'.[91] According to the GGS, the French were carrying out trial mobilizations all along the border, and placing bridges and railways under guard.[92] They used German rolling stock to move artillery, although the Reich Railway Ministry decided not to protest.[93] Moltke noted the accelerated training of the new recruits and the faster distribution of machine guns. On 2 January he reported that 'The Government has . . . continued unobtrusively to take precautionary measures for all eventualities', including accumulating fortress provisions and bank cash reserves. By mid-February the mobilization preparations had ceased, but the French army remained in a condition of 'rapid war preparedness', and the GGS feared that it could reinforce its frontier battalions so quickly as to be able to launch a surprise attack.[94] At the same time as Millerand and the EMA were pleading for intensified Russian preparedness, the French themselves reached a peak of activity.

* * *

In the autumn of 1912 the Triple Alliance faced not only a challenge in the Balkans but also a diplomatic offensive and unprecedented military and naval preparedness on the part of its potential adversaries. How did its own efforts compare? The Italians remained bogged down in Libya. Such special measures as they could manage were directed against their Austrian ally and towards intervention in Albania. They speeded up their fortification and railway work, and moved stores into Venetia.[95] French intelligence reported that their northeastern corps had restricted leave, although without calling up reservists.[96] On the other hand, the Triple Alliance was prematurely renewed in December 1912, apparently in part because Pollio feared French landings, and one reason why in the following February he requested that the army should be strengthened was the vulnerability revealed in the crisis. The evidence from Rome is of a lower level of readiness than in the Triple Entente.[97]

There was a similarly low level of activity in Germany, perhaps the lowest in any of the big Continental Powers. The best evidence for what the Germans did and did not do comes from the dispatches of the Bavarian military plenipotentiary, von Wenninger. As of late November, he reported, in view of the 'highly tense' situation Wilhelm had ordered bicycle detachments to be added to each cavalry division and the machine-gun and aircraft units scheduled for formation by the autumn of 1913 to be ready by 1 April. Reinforcement of the army's field howitzer units was likewise brought forward, and Zeppelin orders accelerated. Frontier railways and the Rhine bridges were under guard; on the Russian border there was intensified surveillance, horses were requisitioned, and officers

[91] Goschen to Grey, 7 Dec. 1912, *BD* ix(ii), doc. 352.
[92] Bienerth to Conrad, 18 Dec. 1912, KAW Gstb 1912 25–1.
[93] Wedel to Bethmann, 16 Dec. 1912, and minute of 21 Dec., PAAA R.6754.
[94] Moltke report on French military situation, 10 Dec. 1912, KAM MKr. 991; and 2 Jan. and 18 Feb. 1913, ibid. MKr. 992.
[95] Schemua to Berchtold, 13 Nov. 1912, KAW Gstb Operationsbureau 710.
[96] De Gondrecourt to French War Ministry, 30 Dec. 1912, SHA 7.N. 1370.
[97] J. Gooch, *Army, State and Society in Italy, 1870–1915* (Basingstoke, 1989), 148–9.

were equipped for winter campaigning. The Military Cabinet pensioned off elderly and incompetent commanders, the arsenals stepped up tinned-food production, oats and hay were purchased in secret, and fodder was ordered in Sweden and Antwerp as a test of Germany's ability to circumvent a blockade.[98] A commission in the Interior Ministry began deliberating on civilian grain supply in wartime, and the Reichsbank accumulated gold reserves.[99] French and Russian appraisals corroborate the Bavarian and Austrian sources. According to the Stavka, Germany had limited officers' leave, speeded training of new recruits, and heightened activity in the staffs and factories, but done little more. There had been 'no measure of mobilization strictly defined'.[100] On 21 November the 2nd Bureau briefed Joffre that 'nothing alarming is reported in Germany'.[101]

No call-up of reservists, no trial mobilization, little beyond precautions to increase stocks and accelerate re-equipment: in the midst of the commotion to east, west, and south, Germany appeared an island of calm. One reason was anxiety not to worry the public or the Bourse. In an open letter to the *Oberpräsident* of Königsberg Bethmann wrote that Germany had taken no special measures against Russia and that there was no evidence of Russian measures to which it needed to respond.[102] The Bavarian War Minister instructed his corps commanders to speed up training of their new recruits, check their mobilization arrangements, and raise their military readiness as much as possible, but not to cause public alarm.[103] More significant than opinion management, however, was probably the conviction of the Prussian authorities that more was unnecessary— they could already move quickly and smoothly into operational readiness. Eggeling, the military plenipotentiary in St Petersburg, lamented that because the German army needed to take no crisis precautions it was almost at a disadvantage to one like Russia's that had to check its procedures.[104] According to Wenninger, in October the GGS was 'quite cool' about Russia's measures, and was 'ready' with nothing to be done.[105] In December the Austro-Hungarian Ambassador reported that no special preparations were required in Germany as

[98] Wenninger to Bavarian War Ministry, 25 Nov. and 14 Dec. 1912, KAM Mkr. 1136; and 24 Dec. 1912, KAM Mbvm I. (cf. J. C. G. Röhl (ed.), 'An der Schwelle zum Weltkrieg: Eine Dokumentation über den "Kriegsrat" vom 8. Dezember 1912', *Militärgeschichtliche Mitteilungen* (1977), 77–134, doc. 38. Szyögyény to Berchtold, 17 Dec. 1912, ibid., doc. 29). Reichsarchiv, *Weltkrieg*, i. 163 n.

[99] Wenninger to War Ministry, 24 Dec. 1912, Röhl (ed.), 'Schwelle', doc. 38. J. C. G. Röhl, 'Die Generalprobe. Zur Geschichte und Bedeutung des "Kriegsrates" vom 8. Dezember 1912', in B. Stegmann, B.-J. Wendt, P.-C. Witt (eds.), *Industrielle Gesellschaft und politisches System: Beiträge zur politischen Sozialgeschichte: Festschrift für Fritz Fischer* (Bonn, 1978), 371. See also L. Burchardt, *Friedenswirtschaft und Kriegsvorsorge. Deutschlands Wirtschaftliche Rüstungsbestrebungen vor 1914* (Boppard, 1968).

[100] Wehrlin to War Ministry, 6 Dec. 1912, SHA 7.N. 1478.

[101] 2nd Bureau to Joffre and Foreign Ministry, 19 Nov. 1912, SHA 7.N. 1370.

[102] GP xxxiii. 442 n.

[103] Bavarian War Minister to Corps Commanders, 14 Dec. 1912, KAM Gstb 925.

[104] Eggeling to War Ministry, 6 Dec. 1912, PAAA R.10431.

[105] Wenninger to von Stetten, 25 Oct. 1912, KAM MKr. 44.

the military authorities said they could be ready in a week.[106] Kiderlen wrote to Pourtalès that Berlin would not let itself be disturbed by the 'multiplying reports of Russian armaments . . . and will take no countermeasures. We have matters in order, and if God wills that it starts, within six days our army, even without "preparatory measures", will stand where it should.'[107]

The low level of German militarization must be linked to Berlin's appraisal of its diplomatic position, which to begin with was calm. Kiderlen advised that he had 'every confidence' in the Russian Government, although there was a danger of its being carried away by public opinion. The trial mobilization, though very maladroit, was long planned and not worrying.[108] Bethmann saw no need for anxiety if hostilities started, and agreed that the mobilization had no significance. Wilhelm himself confirmed that Germany had no interest in preserving Turkey-in-Europe and could let matters take their course. When the Emperor's entourage became concerned about his presence at Rominten, only a few kilometres from the Russian cavalry across the border, Bethmann insisted that the notion of a Russian raid to capture Wilhelm was a 'fantasy' and that he need not curtail his stay.[109] The GGS too, as during Agadir, was determinedly unsensationalist. Moltke reported on 12 November that there had been numerous preparations in the Western military districts that would facilitate Russian mobilization, but nothing yet that marked its beginning.[110]

Moltke was concerned, however, that the trial mobilization had not been notified, in contrast to previous practice. Only with prolonged observation could a trial and an actual mobilization be distinguished, and if the Russians were not to carry through the latter covertly they must give early notice. 'Otherwise we should find it necessary, if the occasion arises, to make military preparations, which could then easily lead to serious consequences.' Although these considerations could not be vouchsafed, it might be put to Russia that due notification would obviate unnecessary public alarm.[111] When the issue was raised with Sazonov, however, he agreed that the Germans had a justified complaint but was slow to do anything about it. Eventually Sukhomlinov explained that the Foreign Ministry had neglected to inform the German Embassy but that in future the Stavka would inform the attaché direct.[112] The episode underlined the dangerous ambiguity, in a supercharged atmosphere of international crisis, even of prescheduled measures, and the same ambiguity helps explain why civil–military unanimity crumbled as the external prospect darkened.

---

[106] Szyögyény to Berchtold, 17 Dec. 1912. Röhl (ed.), 'Schwelle', doc. 29.

[107] Kiderlen to Pourtalès, 23 Nov. 1912, PAAA Pourtalès MSS.

[108] Kiderlen to Kühlmann, 20 Oct. 1912, *GP* xxxiii, doc. 12287. Flotow to Berchtold, 2 Oct. 1912, HHStA PA III 170.

[109] Bethmann to Wilhelm, 1 Oct. 1912, Jenisch to Bethmann, and Bethmann to Jenisch, 1 Oct. 1912, Jenisch and Wilhelm to Bethmann, 2 Oct. 1912, *GP* xxxiii, docs. 12192, 12200–2, 12205.

[110] Moltke to Kiderlen, 12 Nov. 1912, PAAA R.10430.

[111] Moltke to Kiderlen, 15 Oct., Kiderlen to Moltke, 18 Oct., Moltke to Kiderlen, 12 Nov. 1912, ibid.

[112] Pourtalès to Bethmann, 23 Nov. 1912, ibid.; Eggeling to Heeringen, 3 Feb. 1913, PAAA R.10431.

After the Ottomans were routed in late October Jules Cambon wrote privately to Poincaré that he had never known the German Government so preoccupied and disturbed:[113] the strategic balance had trembled, and a trial of strength seemed imminent. Kiderlen wished not to surrender his freedom of action to the Austrians or to let them involve him in an unnecessary war, but he was anxious to uphold the the vital interests of his one reliable Great-Power ally. On 7 November he warned Belgrade that Germany backed Austria-Hungary in the Adriatic dispute and was willing to fight if Russia supported Serbia.[114] Wilhelm, in contrast, still saw no danger in a Serb port on the Adriatic, saying that he could not answer to his conscience if he made war to prevent one. It was agreed that Germany would fight if Russia attacked Austria-Hungary, but not if the latter had provoked St Petersburg. The Russians must seem in the wrong if Germany was to have the rallying cry (*eine gute Parole*) needed for its people to support mobilization. Although the distinction would be difficult to draw in practice, this understanding allowed Kiderlen to resume his balancing act, telling Sazonov that he would not put pressure on the Austrians but at the same time asking the latter to specify possible concessions.[115]

It is necessary to bear in mind the fragmentation of the German leadership, and that adjudication between the civilian and military élites rested with the erratic Kaiser and his entourage. For in late November Wilhelm returned from a few days absence from Berlin in a much more intransigent mood, to find a report from Pourtalès that war was possible with Russia and to learn that the Austrians were reinforcing in Galicia. Now, he considered, Europe would see Vienna as the provoked party, and he would consider himself treaty-bound even if Franz Joseph initiated war.[116] Meanwhile Moltke was taking a much more sombre view of the Russian measures. On 19 November he advised that the retention of the senior class, among other actions, had brought Russia to such a pitch of readiness that any further steps, such as trial mobilizations, reservist call-ups, or movements of units, would have to be seen as the beginning of mobilization.[117] Such a development, to judge from his 12 November memorandum, might have dire effects: and three days later he considered asking for reservist call-ups on the Eastern border.[118] While Kiderlen and even Wilhelm blithely repeated that Russia was taking precautions against a Polish uprising, the GGS had abandoned this interpretation and considered Russia's actions 'rather seriously . . . as preparations directed externally'.[119] According to Arthur

[113] Poincaré, *Service*, ii. 285.

[114] Zechlin, 'Adriakrise', 120. Goschen to Grey, 7 Nov. 1912, *BD* ix(ii), doc. 150.

[115] Wilhelm to Kiderlen, 7 Nov. 1912; Wilhelm memorandum, 11 Nov. 1912; Kiderlen to Pourtalès and Tschirschky, 18 Nov. 1912, *GP* xxxiii, docs. 12339, 12349, 12388, 12391.

[116] Wilhelm to Kiderlen, 21 Nov. 1912; Pourtalès to Bethmann, 20 Nov. 1912, ibid. docs. 12405, 12415.

[117] Moltke to Kiderlen, 19 Nov. 1912, ibid., doc. 12344.

[118] E. C. Helmreich, 'An Unpublished Report on Austro-German Military Conversations of November 1912', *Journal of Modern History*, 5 (1933), 206.

[119] Ibid. 207. Kiderlen to Wilhelm, 19 Nov. 1912, *GP* xxxiii, doc. 12395. Bienerth to Schemua, 19 Nov. 1912, KAW Gstb (1912) 25–1.

Zimmermann, the Under-Secretary for Foreign Affairs, the German Government was now 'anxious' about Russia, and Heeringen reported that two cavalry divisions had been concentrated only 20 kilometres from the frontier, even if Bethmann was less worried about them than was his War Minister.[120]

These circumstances underline the danger of Sukhomlinov's prescriptions at the Tsarskoe Selo conference, which met the day after Schemua and Franz Ferdinand arrived secretly in Berlin on 22 November for emergency consultations. Moltke told the Austrians that they could count absolutely on Germany's help. He would attack Russia in parallel with Schemua, although German mobilization would mean war in the West as well, and beating the French would be his first priority. Wilhelm said his evidence was that the Russians did not think they could fight for another two years, but he reiterated that Austria-Hungary could depend on Germany in all circumstances. Vienna must reject a Serbian port and corridor to the Adriatic, and as soon as its prestige demanded it should take 'energetic action' against Belgrade with the assurance of his support. Although the implication was that the Emperor expected an Austro-Serb conflict to remain localized, his language foreshadowed that of 1914.[121]

From being more conciliatory than his civilian advisers, Wilhelm had become more belligerent, and Moltke had moved with him. After the Austrians departed Kiderlen and Bethmann tried to rebalance the line. Whereas the Emperor had urged Austria-Hungary to reject a European conference, an article on 25 November in the semi-official *Norddeutsche Allgemeine Zeitung* recommended that all questions should be settled by the Powers jointly. Berchtold was much annoyed, but Kiderlen refused to issue a counter-commentary.[122] On 26 November he telegraphed to his Ambassador in London, Lichnowsky, that Germany and Austria-Hungary had kept their heads during the trial mobilization and he refused to see aggressive intentions in Russia's later moves.

We could not criticise Austria-Hungary if it took certain purely defensive countermeasures. We ourselves, however, in spite of the possible threat to our security, should abstain from such measures, in order not even to seem to exacerbate the situation. But the danger exists that further Russian military measures would lead to further Austrian ones and thereby a state of tension be created that would lead to a discharge, without there being serious and irreconcilable interests on the two sides that would make such a development only too understandable.

Rather, however, than 'pour oil on the fire' by tackling the Russians directly, he suggested that if Britain reined in St Petersburg, Germany might rein in Vienna. 'It would be regrettable if merely because of reciprocal military measures, which admittedly Russia has started, there should arise a serious threat to European

---

[120] Goschen to Grey, 25 Nov. 1912, *BD* ix(ii), doc. 273. Bethmann minute, 27 Nov. 1912, PAAA R.10430.

[121] Helmreich, 'Military Conversations', 197–207.

[122] Helmreich, *Balkan Wars*, 244. Zechlin, 'Adriakrise', 127–8. H. Hantsch, *Leopold Graf Berchtold: Grandseigneur und Staatsmann* (2 vols., Graz, 1963), i. 350–1.

peace.'[123] He was willing for co-operation between the blocs, and even to run risks with German security, in order to avoid seeming provocative. One reason for Germany's caution was thus a calculated choice by Kiderlen and Bethmann. They stood by this choice when the GGS became more anxious about Russian preparations, and later about French ones also.

The consequence was a struggle for control of policy. Kiderlen had day-to-day responsibility for German diplomacy,[124] and after his 26 November dispatch a message was passed on to Grey.[125] There is no evidence, however, that London tried to restrain the Russians, and Grey instead protested against the Austrian preparations, which Kiderlen, in the absence of British co-operation, did not.[126] On 28 November Kiderlen told the Foreign Affairs Committee of the Bundesrat that Germany would assist Austria-Hungary if the latter were attacked by Russia while in the course of upholding its interests, the issue then being no longer Adriatic Sea access but the Dual Monarchy's survival as a Great Power. This resembled the approach earlier agreed with Wilhelm.[127] Behind the scenes, Moltke appears to have been pressing for tougher language than that in the *Norddeutsche* statement,[128] and to some extent he obtained it in a speech by Bethmann to the Reichstag on 2 December. If Austria-Hungary's existence were threatened, declared the Chancellor, Germany, in fighting alongside Vienna, would be fighting for its own security.[129] Berchtold, however, still suspected that the speech was directed against him as well as against Sazonov, and he correctly supposed that Kiderlen was pursuing a dual strategy, the London Ambassadors' Conference developing out of a German *démarche* to Britain and France. Agreement in principle was reached in early December, when the Serbs agreed to abide by the conference's rulings. As Sazonov, too, was no longer insisting on a territorial corridor, the greatest danger seemed to be past.

What Bethmann dubbed ironically the 'War Council' therefore met when a solution to the Adriatic crisis was opening up and after a fortnight of conflict between Kiderlen's and Bethmann's more even-handed approach and Moltke's and the Emperor's unilateralist instincts. Its immediate origin was as an unexpected consequence of the Chancellor's Reichstag speech, which the British Foreign Office, in contrast to the Austro-Hungarian, interpreted as being essentially a 'warning' to the Russians. Grey thought it gave the impression, probably unintentionally, that Germany would support Vienna in any demands.[130] He instructed his ambassador, Goschen, to speak to Kiderlen, who retorted that Germany remained moderate and calm: despite the 'mobilization' in Russia and

[123] Kiderlen to Lichnovsky, 26 Nov. 1912, *GP* xxxiii, doc. 12437 (also PAAA R.10430).

[124] Zechlin, 'Adriakrise', 120.

[125] Grey to Goschen, 27 Nov. 1912, *BD* ix(ii), doc. 293. Lichnovsky to Kiderlen, 27 Nov. 1912, *GP* xxxiii, doc. 12447.

[126] Grey to Goschen, 19 Dec. 1912, ibid., doc. 398; note from British Embassy, 22 Dec. 1912, *GP* xxiv/1, doc. 12513.

[127] *GP* xxxiii. 445 n.   [128] Bienerth to Schemua, 4 Dec. 1912, KAW Gstb (1912) 25–1.

[129] *GP* xxxiii. 445 n. Hantsch, *Berchtold*, i. 352.

[130] Nicolson to Buchanan and Grey to Bertie, 3 Dec. 1912, *BD* ix(ii), docs. 321–2.

the trial ones in France, it had not moved a man.[131] None the less, British initiatives multiplied. Grey told Lichnowsky that if Austria-Hungary attacked Serbia and Russia invaded Galicia, France would be drawn in and the further consequences were 'unforeseeable'—which the Ambassador assumed meant that the United Kingdom would intervene.[132] George V remarked to Prince Henry of Prussia that Britain would 'in certain circumstances' help the Franco-Russian alliance against the Austro-German one, and this too was relayed to Wilhelm. But the real damage was done by Haldane, who sought out Lichnowsky to warn that if an Austro-Hungarian attack on Serbia over the Adriatic caused a European war, Britain would come in rather than see Germany overthrow France.[133] It was his outrage on reading this that moved the Emperor to convene the Potsdam War Council on the morning of Sunday 8 December, despite his having recognized already that a European war over the Adriatic would pit Germany in a 'struggle for existence' against all three Entente Powers.[134]

Wilhelm's audience at Potsdam comprised Moltke, Tirpitz, Heeringen (the Chief of the Admiralty Staff but not his brother, the War Minister), and Müller. Kiderlen and Bethmann were neither invited nor informed.[135] The Emperor said much the same as he had done to Franz Ferdinand. Vienna must use force against Serbia, and if Russia supported Belgrade Germany would fight as well, sending the whole weight of its army against France while U-boats torpedoed British troopships. On 21 November he had told the Austrian attaché that Vienna could rely on him unconditionally—'Germany's sword already lay loose in the scabbard: you can count on us.'[136] He had reached this position before the British called him to order, but, given that Austria-Hungary was about to prevail in the Adriatic anyway, the scenario he depicted was of doubtful relevance. Whereas the Emperor envisaged a local war that might grow, Moltke seemed unambiguously to want a Continental one, and the sooner the better, on the grounds that such a conflict was inevitable, that the army was losing to its competitors in the arms race, and that Germany lacked the money to catch up. He wanted to strike now, as for France the moment was inopportune, whereas for Germany it had never been better since the formation of the Triple Alliance. Müller, too, wanted an ultimatum to France and Russia, and was disappointed by the meeting's inconclusive outcome. Tirpitz, however, wanted to wait a year or eighteen months (depending on the account) until the enlargement of the Kiel Canal and the defences of Helgoland were completed. To this the meeting deferred, Moltke protesting that in the future the navy would still not be ready, while the army would lose more ground. He consoled himself with the thought

---

[131] Goschen to Grey, 7 Dec. 1912, ibid., doc. 352.

[132] Lichnowsky to Foreign Ministry, 4 Dec. 1912, *GP* xxxiii, doc. 12481.

[133] Röhl (ed.), 'Schwelle', docs. 1–3.

[134] Memorandum by Wilhelm, 11 Nov. 1912, *GP* xxxiii, doc. 12349.

[135] The documentation on the War Council is assembled in Röhl (ed.), 'Schwelle', esp. docs. 4, 14, 22.

[136] Bienerth to Schemua, 4 Dec. 1912, KAW Gstb (1912) 25–1.

that although France might catch up in artillery, Germany could compensate by exploiting its manpower superiority.[137]

The principal significance of the 8 December meeting, as will be discussed below, was in heightening Germany's medium-term preparedness. But it rejected an early war, and was followed by little increase in immediate readiness. By 14 December, indeed, Bethmann decided that Christmas leave could be granted and the border railway guard lifted, although the GGS objected to doing so in the East.[138] And with the War Council there passed the climax of the challenge to the Chancellor's and Foreign Minister's authority. While promising assistance to the Austrians if Russia attacked they had sought a peaceful outcome in the Adriatic. Kiderlen accepted that Austria-Hungary's reinforcement in Galicia was legitimate, but he resisted using force against Serbia and kept Germany's own militarization low. Wilhelm's encouragement to Franz Ferdinand was not supported by his civilian ministers and was quickly overtaken by events. Nor, although Moltke promised Schemua his assistance, did the German General Staff urge the Austrians on to extra preparedness as the French did the Russians. The impulse for the military measures taken by Austria-Hungary in the crisis must be sought not in Berlin, but in Vienna itself.

* * *

Austro-Hungarian military policy was characterized by phased increases in the Monarchy's troop strengths on the south-eastern and north-eastern frontiers. In contrast to 1908–9 the second was as important as the first, Russia was the target as well as Serbia and Montenegro, and the measures undertaken were more extensive and more costly, as well as lasting longer. Normal peacetime strengths were exceeded for almost a year, between October 1912 and August 1913, and never returned to their pre-crisis level. Down to the end of 1912 policy went through four phases: a first of relative inactivity, whose main feature was a 250-million crown special credit; a second of responses to the perils created on the Balkan frontier by the Turkish defeats; a third dominated by the Russian build up in Poland; and a fourth during which the Monarchy's leaders debated whether to move on to the offensive. The defeat of the 'war party' in this last phase made possible the beginnings of disengagement.

The pivotal figure in both diplomacy and defence policy was Berchtold, who could normally carry the Emperor. His personal odyssey in 1912–13 encapsulated the drift of the Vienna élite towards military solutions. After intercepted telegrams in late July disclosed to him the nature of the Serb–Bulgarian agreement he tried unavailingly to head off the assault on the Ottomans. In his view Austria-Hungary was 'satiated' and wanted no more Balkan gains.[139] But if war broke out it must reinforce its frontier garrisons in order to insist on territorial

---

[137] See accounts of the War Council cited in n. 135, and Moltke memorandum, 16 Dec. 1912, Röhl (ed.), 'Schwelle', doc. 27.

[138] Wenninger to Kressenstein, 14 Dec. 1912, ibid., doc. 21.

[139] Williamson, 'Military Dimensions', 318. Stolberg to Bethmann, 27 Sept. 1912, *GP* xxxiii, doc. 12172.

changes being subject to its consent, and to enable intervention.[140] During the summer he agreed to keep on troops who were due for release after a shooting exercise, and to the immediate call-up of the new cohort of reservists in Bosnia-Herzegovina and Dalmatia. But he resisted appeals for more from Potiorek, the Army Inspector in Sarajevo.[141] He failed to carry the Common Ministerial Council even for a warning to Serbia not to invade Turkish territory,[142] and there was little prospect of his supporting a Schemua memorandum that advocated mobilization and occupying the Sanjak if the Balkan States opened hostilities. Berchtold replied that they must wait and see: mobilization would seem provocative, and would hinder his attempts at localization. Thus far, all that had been done, so Schemua told the Germans, was to provide more money for the Evidenzbureau's secret agents.[143]

During the opening round of fighting Austro-Hungarian passivity continued, despite Potiorek's pleas that while he had only 10–12,000 infantry available Serbia and Montenegro would soon have 230,000.[144] Nothing had been done to improve communications to the annexed provinces, which once again were vulnerable. Potiorek was allowed to set up six frontier protection companies, but on 26 October Berchtold reiterated that he intended to rely if possible on the Concert rather than use force to uphold the Balkan *status quo*.[145] Franz Ferdinand and the civilian ministers, who wished to avoid the expense of special measures, agreed with him. Schemua supported Potiorek, but was less forceful than Conrad, and more deferential towards the diplomats.[146] Auffenberg acted as a buffer by containing his subordinates for six weeks, and could have done so for longer, according to his memoirs, if there had been higher peacetime strengths in the south-east. Whereas Potiorek wanted full war strengths Auffenberg suggested a more limited call-up of reservists, but this too was deferred.[147]

The War Minister was constrained by worries about the home front. Mention of 'mobilization' and of 'full war strength' was avoided in the call-up cards, for fear of public anxiety and of upsetting the money markets. Berchtold wished to reassure the Berlin financial community that Austria-Hungary was not seeking 'mobilization credits'.[148] In addition Auffenberg believed, or so he said in retrospect, that war with Serbia was bound to lead to war with Russia, which outnumbered him in men and guns. He told the Common Ministerial Council that the army was unready for such a 'great conflagration', and even for war with

[140] Hantsch, *Berchtold*, i. 290.   [141] Williamson, 'Military Dimensions', 318.

[142] GMR, 14 Sept. 1912, HHStA 310 PA XL.

[143] Schemua memorandum, 28 Sept. 1912; Berchtold commentary, 2 Oct. 1912, *ÖUA* iv, docs. 3869, 3928. Report by Kageneck, 27 Sept. 1912, *GP* xxxiii, doc. 12179.

[144] Deutschman, 'Massnahmen', 20.

[145] Ibid. 35. Berchtold to Schemua, 26 Oct. 1912, *ÖUA* iv, doc. 4185.

[146] Schemua to Berchtold, 18 Oct. 1912, KAW Gstb Operationsbureau 710, allows for the possibility of a diplomatic solution.

[147] M. Auffenberg-Komarów, *Aus Österreichs Höhe und Niedergang: Eine Lebensschilderung* (Munich, 1921), 208. Deutschman, 'Massnahmen', 24–6.

[148] Ibid. 26. Berchtold to Szyögyény, 10 Oct. 1912, HHStA, PA III, 170.

Serbia alone.[149] Schemua, it is true, submitted a memorandum denying that Austria-Hungary's chances against the Russians were 'in any way unfavourable', but his own analysis hardly bore this out.[150] Hence Auffenberg recommended strength increases in the south that he depicted as a minimum, and wanted delayed as long as possible. 'Mobilizations', he wrote afterwards, 'even if implemented partially, can easily start the wheel rolling—often against one's own intention—and in any case are enormously expensive.'[151] Berchtold was clear that he would not cancel military measures because of Russian objections (and Sazonov had said that he would regard troop concentrations on the Serb border as 'understandable'), but he was reluctant to give Potiorek more than what was necessary for internal order. To invade Serbia or 'demonstrate' before Belgrade would be 'senseless'. He equally opposed taking precautions in Galicia 'because he well knew that one step in this direction from Austria-Hungary's side would lead to the same on the other side and then the ball would start rolling'. He deliberately refrained from raising the Polish trial mobilization with the Russian Ambassador, telling the Germans that he would not respond,[152] and on 15 October Franz Joseph ordered the senior conscript class to be discharged.[153] While Berchtold clung to a diplomatic approach, military measures might provoke precisely what he wished to avoid.

This conclusion is not invalidated by the passage during October of the 250-million crowns special credit. Thwarted in July, Berchtold brought it back to the GMR in October, and the Hungarians acknowledged that circumstances had altered.[154] Yet how, they asked, could they tell their legislature that they were departing from the Schönaich Pact because of the present crisis when what was proposed was a six-year credit? For what Auffenberg envisaged was a medium-term programme of expenditure (170 million crowns on artillery, 55 million on fortifications, and 25 million on aviation) to remedy critical areas of backwardness and preserve peace.[155] More than previously, in the light of the trial mobilization, he saw the prospective enemy as Russia, with whom war 'in the next few years' was 'very probable'. Stürgkh too saw the tension as an opportunity to increase the army's preparedness. Berchtold conceded that hostilities were not imminent, and that the programme was not simply a response to the current tension. The crisis made it much more probable, however, that the Monarchy would have to assert itself in order to defend its interests: in other words, it was entering a more dangerous world.

That the credit was for the medium term became still more evident when Montecuccoli joined the bandwagon. He wanted 170 million crowns over the

[149] Auffenberg, *Höhe und Niedergang*, 211, 219. GMR, 14 Sept. 1912, HHStA, 310 PA XL.

[150] Schemua to Auffenberg, 13 Oct. 1912, KAW KM Präs (1912) 47–2.

[151] Auffenberg in GMR, 3 and 8/9 Oct. 1912, HHStA 310 PA XL. Auffenberg, *Höhe und Niedergang*, 207.

[152] Berchtold in GMR, 8/9 Oct. 1912, HHStA 310 PA XL. Tschirschky and Pourtalès to Bethmann, 12 Oct. 1912; *GP* xxxiii, docs. 12268–9.

[153] Mann, 'Schemua', 124.   [154] GMR, 3 and 8/9 Oct. 1912, HHStA 310 PA XL.

[155] Krobatin to Teleszky, 18 Oct. 1912, KM Präs (1912) 37–9.

next three years, mainly for two more battleships. Berchtold defended him, on the grounds that France's naval concentration in the Mediterranean might make the Italians feel so vulnerable that they would go over to the Triple Entente. The Hungarians were promised that they would build one of the battleships, and that part of the army's expenditure would go to their planned artillery factory when it came on stream. It was agreed to seek 125 million for the army over the next three years, and the same again at the end of that time; and that the 54 million of the 1911 programme that was earmarked for 1912–14 would be brought forward for use now. Most of the 41.6 million eventually assigned to the War Ministry for 1912–13 was designated to pay for the 30.5 cm mortars that Auffenberg had already ordered without authorization, as well as for aircraft and fortification work in Bosnia-Herzegovina and Galicia. Very little went to increasing immediate readiness.[156]

We now come to the repercussions of the Turkish collapse. By late October the Serbs and Bulgars had defeated the main Ottoman armies, Montenegro was advancing on Scutari, and Serbia and Montenegro had occupied the Sanjak of Novibazar. Potiorek warned that he still had only 13,000 men for field operations and that it would take him seventeen days to reach war strength, whereas Montenegro could assemble 30,000 in a week.[157] According to Schemua, the Balkan States had mobilized faster and with larger numbers than expected, and in effect constituted a new Great Power on the southern flank. Russia was unlikely to stay out of a war between them and the Monarchy, and if it did so he could deploy in the Balkans only a holding force, without numerical superiority. Territorial expansion would allow the Serbs to increase their war strength from 250,000 to 350,000, and the Montenegrins to go up from 40,000 to 50,000. Ten years of costly and intensive rearmament would be needed if the Monarchy's situation were not to become 'completely hopeless'.[158]

Such was the backdrop to a 'twelve-hour, nerve-racking Council of Ministers' on 28–9 October.[159] The Bosnia-Herzegovina railway question returned to the agenda, and soon afterwards the text of a bill was agreed.[160] Faced with what Berchtold described as 'a critical situation' and a heightened danger of war, the Council at last decided to increase the Monarchy's immediate readiness. Auffenberg received a further special credit of 21.9 million crowns, to be spent on barracks for extra soldiers on the Balkan frontier, cartridges, machine guns, and shells for the 24 cm mortars that would pound the Russian fortresses. A decree of 31 October provided for the two south-eastern army corps (XV and XVI), numbering 40,000, to receive an extra 16,400 men, but even given Serbia's denuded northern defences such a force was unsuitable for a lightning attack.[161]

[156] Auffenberg to Schemua, 31 Oct. 1912, KAW Gstb (1912) 45-1.
[157] Potiorek to Schemua, 23 Oct. 1912, KAW Gstb Operationsbureau 710.
[158] Schemua to Franz Joseph, 7 Nov. 1912, ibid.
[159] Berchtold diary, 29 Oct. 1912, HHStA Berchtold MSS 1.
[160] GMR, 16 and 28 Oct., 8 Nov. 1912, HHStA 310 PA XL. Williamson, *Austria-Hungary*, 66.
[161] Deutschman, 'Massnahmen', 47. Williamson, 'Military Dimensions', 319. Helmreich, *Balkan Wars*, 461.

Although Berchtold set out in the next few days his minimum requirements in the Adriatic, his military measures were more a safeguard against aggression than a credible lever against his enemies.

The next step was much more grave. This was a reinforcement in the northeast. The Austrians intensified their espionage in Russia as well as the Balkans during the crisis,[162] and the Evidenzbureau compared notes with the GGS.[163] Schemua soon concluded that the Russians' preparations might allow them to neutralize Austria-Hungary's faster concentration, and attack before the *couverture* was in place.[164] On 13 November he told the German attaché that there had been no special preparations in Galicia, but these must begin soon.[165] Berchtold took a more relaxed view, encouraged by reassurances from his St Petersburg Embassy. In mid-November, however, both German and Austrian military appraisals became much more alarming, and Hohenlohe reported that Russia was doing everything it could to get ready. If Austria-Hungary used force against Serbia St Petersburg would fight.[166] Berchtold was disturbed by reports (which may have been mistaken) of Russian troop movements towards the frontier, and agreed with Franz Ferdinand that Galician troop strengths must be raised.[167] On 19 November he attended an audience with Franz Joseph and the military. Schemua explained the danger of a Russian attack: higher strengths were required to guard against one and to dissuade St Petersburg from its threatening attitude. Auffenberg said that the situation was the most difficult since 1866, and the Emperor that it was much worse. The meeting rejected Schemua's proposal for an ultimatum to Serbia to halt its march to the coast, but it agreed to send him for consultations in Berlin and to reinforce in Galicia, Berchtold telling the Germans that in view of the Monarchy's transition to two-year service and the release of its senior conscript class it had to protect itself against surprise. Nor did he wish to decide how to respond to Serb provocation while under the shadow of a Russian military preponderance. Kiderlen replied that he would not oppose the decision, and on 21 November the order was signed.[168]

Auffenberg had the sense of a leap in the dark: they would see how Russia reacted, and if it stayed calm they would have a free hand against the Serbs.[169]

---

[162] At least, this may be the significance of a secret fund of 770,000 crowns under the War Minister's personal control, minute of 31 Dec. 1912, KM Präs (1912) 37–3.

[163] Kageneck report, 18 Nov. 1912, *GP* xxxiii, doc. 12393.

[164] Schemua to Franz Joseph, 7 Nov. 1912, KAW Gstb Operationsbureau 710.

[165] Kageneck report, 13 Nov. 1912, *GP* xxxiii, doc. 12370.

[166] Pourtalès to Bethmann, 19 Nov. 1912, PAAA R.10430. Hohenlohe to Auffenberg, 19 Nov. 1912, KAW KM Präs (1912) 47–2.

[167] Tschirschky to Foreign Ministry, 17 Nov. 1912, Kageneck report, 27 Nov. 1912, *GP* xxxiii, docs. 12392, 12455.

[168] Note on audience of 19 Nov. 1912, KAW Gstb Operationsbureau 739. Auffenberg, *Höhe und Niedergang*, 218. Berchtold diary, 19 Nov. 1912, HHStA, Berchtold MSS 1. Williamson, 'Military Dimensions', 320–1.

[169] Kageneck report, 21 Nov. 1912, *GP* xxxiii, doc. 12404.

Within days Sazonov did indeed become more conciliatory over the Adriatic, but it is doubtful whether this was because of Austro-Hungarian action.[170] Sazonov's and Kokovtsov's caution at the Tsarskoe Selo meeting was motivated by fear of Germany rather than the Habsburgs. To begin with, the Austrians proceeded gingerly anyway, waiting, in the interests of secrecy, until after the Delegations had dispersed, blanketing the press, and using their discretionary powers under Clause 43 of the 1912 military law. They called up the first class of reservists and the three youngest classes of *Ersatz* reservists to raise the three Galician corps from 57,000 to 97,000 men: small in comparison to the Russian increase.[171] But once the measure was taken it broke the ice, and others followed quickly, perhaps also because of the assurances given in Berlin to Schemua and Franz Ferdinand and the anger aroused by the Consul Prochaska affair. Extra cavalry units were moved into Galicia, in reaction to reports that six Russian cavalry divisions were being readied.[172] On 23 November another conference presided over by Franz Joseph authorized Auffenberg to create seventy-five new field-gun batteries; orders soon followed for 600 machine guns and for other supplies. The fleet and the Danube flotilla were made ready, and the four most south-easterly corps brought up to the same strengths as in Galicia, bringing the total under arms in the Balkan theatre to perhaps 72,000. Berchtold was losing patience, and there were hopes in the War Ministry that this time the extra forces would be used.[173]

Developments at the beginning of December brought the Monarchy to the brink of a war–peace decision. As in Germany the most serious challenge by the 'war party' came after the ceasefire and agreement in principle to the Ambassadors' Conference. There was simmering unrest in Bosnia-Herzegovina and among the South Slavs in Hungary, which Potiorek wanted to overawe. With the ceasefire began the *Rücktransporte*, or return movements, of the Serbian forces, and according to Gellinek, the attaché in Belgrade, the Serbs looked forward to confrontation with the Monarchy or to war. Until the transports were completed, however, they would have to accept whatever Vienna demanded. By Christmas they were re-establishing their defences on the Danube, but were anxious not to seem aggressive, and King Nikita of Montenegro promised that he was not moving units to the Austrian border.[174] None the less, on 4 December Schemua asked for the troops in the south-east to be raised to full strength (about 100,000 men) because of the *Rücktransporte* and reports of large Serb arms

---

[170] On 11 Dec. Buchanan found Sazonov very calm about the Austro-Hungarian measures. Buchanan to Grey, 11 Dec. 1912, *BD* ix(ii), doc. 371.

[171] Deutschman, 'Massnahmen', 61–4. Kageneck report, 18 Nov. 1912, *GP* xxxiii, doc. 12393.

[172] Deutschman, 'Massnahmen', 65–7. Schemua to Franz Ferdinand, 27 Nov. 1912, KAW Gstb Operationsbureau 710.

[173] Auffenberg, *Höhe und Niedergang*, 220–1. Deutschman, 'Massnahmen', 71–3, 83–90. Kageneck report, 25 Nov. 1912, *GP* xxxiii, doc. 12434. Williamson, 'Military Dimensions', 321.

[174] Deutschman, 'Massnahmen', 96–7. Gellinek to War Minister, 25 Oct., 20 and 26 Nov., 6, 11, 16, 18, 24 Dec. 1912, KM Präs 47–2. Descos to Poincaré, 14 and 18 Dec. 1912, *DDF* 3rd ser. v, docs. 64, 84. Kageneck report, 21 Dec. 1912, *GP* xxiv/1, doc. 12567.

orders in Germany.[175] Potiorek and the military authorities were looking ahead to war, the German attaché being informed that it would be better to attack when the Serbs had come back north, as they could then be beaten more quickly before the Habsburg armies were redirected against Russia.[176] Berchtold, in contrast, told the German Ambassador that, although he could arrange hostilities in twenty-four hours, he preferred to extricate himself peacefully. Although he doubted that reinforcement was needed to ensure diplomatic success, he and Franz Joseph were reluctant to query the military judgement, and were increasingly concerned about South Slav unrest.[177] Yet the effect of the December increases was to replace new and poorly trained recruits by more seasoned reservists, thus enhancing Habsburg striking power. The number of machine-gun detachments on the Balkan frontier rose from five to twenty-four; that of mountain howitzer batteries from two to eight. Simultaneously, there was a dramatic personnel change, Conrad returning as Chief of the General Staff and Auffenberg being replaced by Krobatin.[178] Conrad at once renewed his tireless advocacy of war against Serbia, and Krobatin aligned himself with his subordinate's views. The reshuffle was largely engineered by Franz Ferdinand, who had returned from Germany 'wholly convinced of the necessity for the monarchy to awake from lethargy and proceed forcefully. Should it not do so, its role is played out.'[179]

Austria-Hungary redoubled its efforts as the crisis subsided. By the end of 1912 it had added at least 86,000 men to its standing forces in Galicia and the same again in the Balkans, plus 50,000 in the interior and 6,500 naval personnel. Total expenditure already exceeded that in the annexation crisis and was approaching 200 millions crowns.[180] The scale of these preparations, and the probability that an attack on Serbia would bring a Russian response, caused alarm across Europe. Until two crucial conferences between the Monarchy's leaders on 11 and 23 December, moreover, their purpose remained unresolved.

In the first meeting, Berchtold confronted Franz Ferdinand. The Archduke wanted not war but yet further preparations as a buttress for new political demands. He did not think Russia would interfere, but if it did the Monarchy would have Germany's backing. His comments flowed from what Wilhelm had told him, and Berchtold objected that the German Emperor's views were not those of his ministers, who had refused to support the Monarchy in aggression. The London Conference was likely to decide in Austria-Hungary's favour, and 'warlike measures' would put it in the wrong. Franz Joseph said he wanted to preserve peace, if this was compatible with the Monarchy's prestige; the other ministers present supported Berchtold. Hence the new measures did not presage an ultimatum on the lines of 1909, Berchtold describing them as having 'a purely

[175] Deutschman, 'Massnahmen', 97–8. Kageneck reports, 5 and 7 Dec. 1912, *GP* xxxiii, docs. 12485, 12488.

[176] Kageneck report, 25 Nov. 1912, ibid., doc. 12434.

[177] Tschirschky to Bethmann, 6 Dec. 1912, ibid., doc. 12485.

[178] Deutschman, 'Massnahmen', 99, 103–4.

[179] Berchtold diary, 10 Dec. 1912, HHStA Berchtold MSS 1.

[180] Williamson, *Austria-Hungary*, 132. Conrad minute, 31 Dec. 1912, KAW Gstb 1912 45–1.

defensive character'. Potiorek had only a quarter of the horses that he needed for mobile operations, and was forbidden to buy more.[181] Even if an 'increase in European armaments competition' resulted, the army was entitled to take precautions against the 'nationalist high tide' in the south and Russia's measures in Galicia, but 'considerations of supporting our diplomatic demands come only in second place'.[182]

By the time of the 23 December Crown Council Berchtold's approach was visibly bearing fruit. The Serbs had apologized over Consul Prochaska and dropped their claims to sea access.[183] Potiorek feared the diplomats were forfeiting the last chance to 'reckon with' Serbia without Russian intervention; in the War Ministry there were forebodings that national separatism was infecting the army and that the Czech and Croat contingents might soon become unreliable.[184] At the Council Potiorek wanted to call up all reservists in the south-east; Conrad and Krobatin pressed for war. Berchtold, however, thought that Belgrade was looking for *rapprochement*, and that further measures would seem to presage aggression. An offensive against Serbia would isolate the Monarchy and perhaps antagonize Germany, unless embarked on with a plausible pretext. 'Struggle on two fronts', he confided to his diary. 'From within the pressure is for activity, initiatives, armaments . . . from outside come pleas for calm, concession, disarmament.'[185] But he retained the backing of the Emperor, and Franz Ferdinand reverted to a more pacific mood.

* * *

We come to the play of forces that led to disengagement. Between December and late February Austro-Hungarian and Russian armaments remained at the diplomatic storm centre. All the Powers hoped for a peaceful solution, but in all three eastern monarchies and even in France 'military parties' saw the moment as opportune for war and were not afraid to risk or even to initiate it. Despite the set-backs that they suffered at Tsarskoe Selo on 23 November, at Potsdam on 8 December, and in Vienna on 23 December, the war parties were gaining support, and uncertainty in the Balkans persisted. The London Peace Conference had already broken down when a more nationalist Young Turk Government seized power in Constantinople at the end of January. The Ambassadors' Conference, however, continued with its work despite the renewal of fighting, the main issue being the Albanian borders. Berchtold intended Albania rather than Montenegro to have Scutari, and he wished to limit Serbian expansion in the east of the country, round Dibra and Djakova. Discussions over

---

[181] Hantsch, *Berchtold*, i. 360–5. Berchtold diary, 20 Dec. 1912, Berchtold MSS 2. Potiorek to Conrad, 15 Dec. 1912, KAW Gstb Operationsbureau 710.

[182] Berchtold diary, 27 Dec. 1912, HHStA, Berchtold MSS 2.

[183] Helmreich, *Balkan Wars*, 220–30.

[184] Potiorek to Conrad, 15 Dec. 1912, KAW Gstb Operationsbureau 710. Conversation with Oberst von Boog, 23 Dec. 1912, HHStA PA I 493.

[185] Berchtold diary, 23 and 24 Dec. 1912, HHStA, Berchtold MSS 3.

troop reductions and the haggling in London became intertwined.[186] In the meantime, Serbia and Montenegro carried on with their *Rücktransporte*. At present both were weary from their previous campaigns and faced resistance in their new conquests. But in time their vulnerability would lessen, and this sharpened the appetite of the Viennese advocates of preventive war.[187]

Exchanges at the end of 1912 highlighted the deadlock. Berchtold told the Russians that in Galicia he had responded to their own steps, and merely raised Austro-Hungarian unit strengths to levels similar to those of the other Powers. The reinforcements would be permanent. In the south the measures would continue until outstanding issues had been settled and Belgrade had demobilized.[188] The Russians denied the need for Habsburg 'mobilization' now that Serbia had given up the Adriatic corridor. Austria-Hungary, they alleged, was the only Power to go armed into the conference chamber.[189] Sazonov may have felt that his precautions had antagonized Vienna more than necessary, and he offered to stand down his senior conscript class if Vienna would make the first move.[190] Berchtold considered making a 'gesture' to St Petersburg, but Krobatin advised him that regulars were not able replace reservists at this point. In any case, Berchtold was unwilling to approve reductions purely for military concessions, while Franz Joseph objected to appearing to yield to pressure. Hence Berchtold felt he must maintain untrammelled the Monarchy's 'right of military self-determination'.[191]

In the absence of agreement, the Russians threatened to ratchet up another notch. Sazonov hinted at a public ukase to prolong the retention of the senior conscript class. Beyond this, he had a 'project for mobilizing on the Austrian frontier' and envisaged moving up more men.[192] According to General Tatishchev, the Russian military plenipotentiary in Berlin, mobilizing the Kiev military district was envisaged, and he may have added that Vienna would be sent an ultimatum. The news put Wilhelm 'in a very serious mood', and Moltke warned Tatishchev that Germany would fight alongside its ally, while Zimmermann urged the Austrians to handle the 'mobilization question' with 'great care'.[193] In the event the Tatishchev episode turned out to be a false alarm, probably resulting from a brush between the Russian civilian and military

[186] Helmreich, *Balkan Wars*, chs. 12, 13.

[187] Gellinek reports, 13, 22, 31 Jan., 12, 18 Feb., 3 Mar. 1913, KAW KM Präs 1913 47–7. Fourmier (French attaché) 10, 20, 28 Jan., 3, 24 Feb. 1913, SHA 7.N. 1568.

[188] Berchtold diary, 31 Dec. 1912, HHStA Berchtold MSS 2. Louis to Poincaré, 2 and 3 Jan. 1913, *DDF* 3rd ser. v, docs. 156, 163. Grey to Buchanan, 31 Dec. 1912, *BD* ix(ii), doc. 425. See Berchtold conversation with Russian Ambassador, 27 Dec. 1912, *ÖUA* v, doc. 5088.

[189] Berchtold diary, 24 and 31 Dec. 1912, HHStA Berchtold MSS 2.

[190] Laguiche to Vignal, 19 Dec. 1912, SHA 7.N. 1478. Lucius to Foreign Ministry, 23 Dec. 1912, *GP* xxxiv/1, doc. 12570.

[191] Tschirschky to Foreign Ministry, 28 Dec. 1912; Zimmermann to Tschirschky 3 Jan. 1913; Tschirschky to Zimmermann, 2 Jan. 1913, *GP* xxiv/1, docs. 12580, 12605, 12607.

[192] Grey to Buchanan, 2 Jan. 1913, Buchanan to Grey, 30 Dec. 1912, *BD* ix(ii), docs. 438, 419. Louis to Poincaré, 25 and 27 Dec. 1912, *DDF* 3rd ser. v, docs. 122, 131.

[193] Zimmermann to Tschirschky, 3 Jan. 1913, *GP* xxiv/1, doc. 12605. Röhl (ed.), 'Schwelle', doc. 2. Berchtold diary 2 Jan. 1913, HHStA Berchtold MSS 2.

authorities in which the latter briefly won Nicholas round.[194] The senior conscript class was kept on after 13 January by secret imperial command rather than a public pronouncement.[195] The Austrians maintained their troop strengths, and no mobilization of the Kiev military district followed. Once more Kokovtsov was able to dissuade the Tsar from further steps, and during January Conrad found little evidence of unusual Russian activity.[196] By the end of the month, however, the situation was again deteriorating. The British Ambassador in Vienna conveyed Habsburg exasperation: 'Servia will some day set Europe by the ears and bring about a universal war on the Continent.'[197] According to Pourtalès, Sazonov and Kokovtsov were under attack from the Grand Dukes, the army, and pan-Slav agitation. If Serbia were attacked, Slavophile solidarity—'die Slavophile Gefühlspolitik'—would decide the issue.[198] The tsarist military feared that discipline was cracking, and wanted either war or to release the senior class, but not an indefinite stalemate.[199]

It was the Austrians who took the initiative. They too faced discontent among their troops and Krobatin agreed at the end of January to release those whose families were suffering most hardship or who stood to lose their jobs.[200] But the main consideration was money. On 4 January the GMR approved another 195 million crowns, but only with the greatest reluctance. The Common Finance Minister, Bilínski, insisted that the Monarchy must pay the bill, regardless of whether it could find the money or risked economic collapse, but speculated that fighting might be cheaper than continuing as at present. The Austrian Finance Minister, Zaleski, complained that the army was exploiting the emergency in order to implement measures that were unrelated to it, and that Austria-Hungary's 'financial war preparedness' was jeopardized. The Hungarian Finance Minister, Teleszky, concurred. Ministers were presented with *faits accomplis* and financial control had virtually collapsed, yet the Hungarian Government had entered the crisis with only 50 million crowns in cash reserves, the German and domestic capital markets were inadequate, and access to entente markets was debarred.[201]

In Vienna as in St Petersburg, then, there were growing obstacles to continuing with armed diplomacy. Conrad opposed half measures and a diplomatic solution like that of 1909.[202] Although he preferred localized hostilities against the

[194] Tschirschky to Bethmann, 4 Jan. 1913, *GP* xxiv/1, doc. 12619.

[195] Laguiche to War Ministry, 12 Jan. 1913, SHA 7.N. 1478.

[196] Tschirschky to Bethmann, 4 Jan. 1913, *GP* xxiv/1, doc. 12619. Berchtold diary, 4 Jan. 1913, HHStA Berchtold MSS 2. F. Conrad von Hötzendorf, *Aus meiner Dienstzeit 1906–1918* (Vienna, 1921–5), iii. 69–71.

[197] Cartwright to Nicolson, 31 Jan. 1913, *BD* ix(ii), doc. 582.

[198] Pourtalès to Bethmann and Jagow, 1 and 6 Feb. 1913, *GP* xxiv/1, docs. 12787, 12805.

[199] Pourtalès to Bethmann, 20 Feb. 1913, ibid., doc. 12881.

[200] XV Corps Commander to Krobatin, 27 (?May) 1913, KAW Gstb (1913) 52–4. Deutschman, 'Massnahmen', 138.

[201] GMR, 4 Jan. 1913, HHStA PA XL 311. Kageneck report, 5 Jan. 1913, *GP* xxiv/1, doc. 12621.

[202] Breakfast with Conrad and lunch with Potiorek, Berchtold diary, 26 and 27 Jan. 1913, HHStA Berchtold MSS 2.

Serbs, by now he was clearly willing to risk them with Russia as well.[203] He wanted no reductions in the existing measures, and to add more.[204] But the prevailing mood was against him. When he planned to supply rifles for an Albanian insurrection against Serbia, Berchtold vetoed the idea on the grounds that it would be unneutral and might compromise relations with Italy at a time when the Ambassadors' Conference was proceeding favourably.[205] When he proposed moving four batteries of heavy artillery to Semlin, on the Danube frontier opposite Belgrade, Berchtold objected that they had undertaken to refrain from hostile measures while negotiating, and that if they risked war with Serbia they might antagonize their ally. On Conrad's opinion that defeating Russia would give the Monarchy a hundred years of peace, he commented, 'Who knows whether Germany will stand with us?'[206] The Foreign Minister was consistently more sceptical than was Conrad about Berlin's solidarity, and victory over Russia he saw as leading to a Russian republic that would be still more dangerous.[207] Franz Ferdinand, too, opposed war against St Petersburg, and expected even a localized victory over Serbia to isolate Austria-Hungary in Europe, while incorporating more South Slavs would prove a liability. Only when order had been restored at home could the Monarchy pursue a 'hurrah-policy' abroad. In Berchtold's view, the Archduke's reasoning should rule out resort to arms for all except those who saw it as an end in itself.[208]

The final element in the coalition containing Conrad was Franz Joseph. He too foresaw that further military measures might lead to European conflict, and when Conrad urged that they must envisage fighting Russia he rejoined that 'the duty of sovereigns is . . . to maintain peace'.[209] But if war was best avoided and the *status quo* untenable, the remaining option was de-escalation, and it was with Franz Joseph that originated what became the Hohenlohe mission. According to the British Ambassador the Emperor, depressed and not wishing to die in the midst of blood-letting, sprang the idea on an unprepared Berchtold.[210] Prince Gottfried zu Hohenlohe-Schillingsfurst was one of the most illustrious blooms on the Monarchy's aristocratic bough. A former attaché in St Petersburg and a relative of the present one, he was a personal friend of Nicholas, to whom he carried an autograph letter from Franz Joseph. His instructions, however, allowed him only to explain and defend the Habsburg position, with little scope for bargaining.[211] The crucial issue in his conversations in the Russian capital became the linkage

---

[203] Conrad, *Dienstzeit*, iii. 12–13, 85.

[204] Conrad to Krobatin, 13 Feb. 1913, KAW Gstb 1913 52–4. Kageneck report 14 Jan. 1913, *GP* xxiv/1, doc. 12684. [205] Conrad, *Dienstzeit*, iii. 108–11.

[206] Ibid. 77–9, 106. Berchtold diary, 4 Jan. 1913, HHStA Berchtold MSS 2. Hantsch, *Berchtold*, i. 374–5.

[207] Conrad, *Dienstzeit*, iii. 115–17, cf. Hantsch, *Berchtold*, i. 381.

[208] Ibid. 389–91. Conrad, *Dienstzeit*, iii. 76, 127, 155. Kageneck report, 26 Feb. 1913, *GP* xxiv/1, doc. 12905. Albrecht of Württemberg to Prince of Furstenberg, 2 Feb. 1913, ibid., doc. 12788.

[209] Conrad, *Dienstzeit*, iii. 79, 85.

[210] Cartwright to Nicolson, 14 Feb. 1913, *BD* ix(ii), doc. 618.

[211] Tschirschky to Foreign Ministry, 31 Jan. 1913; Berchtold to Bethmann, 5 Feb. 1913, *GP* xxiv/1, docs. 12766, 12792. Hantsch, *Berchtold*, i. 383–5. Williamson, 'Military Dimensions', 326.

between the military confrontations in Poland and in Bosnia. Hohenlohe said that both sets of Austro-Hungarian measures were purely defensive. Sazonov warned that if there were an attack on Serbia Russian opinion would clamour for him to act. He offered to release the senior conscript class if Austria-Hungary would reverse its Balkan reinforcements. Sukhomlinov, in contrast, was more concerned about Galicia, suggesting that for even a small reduction he would send home all the extra men called up.[212] The Prince reported back that once the Albanian frontier was settled Austria-Hungary should modestly reduce the Galician forces, but that if it did nothing there would be hostilities within two months, 'and in reality over neither Albania nor the Balkan question but as a natural discharge of the quite extraordinary tension that he found in Russia'.[213]

Although Conrad and Krobatin wanted smaller troop cuts than Hohenlohe envisaged, his mission pointed the way. The Habsburg ministers had decided that they could cover the expense of their troop reinforcements until mid-March, but the men had inadequate food, clothing, and shelter, and were becoming demoralized.[214] On the other hand, Sazonov still opposed giving Dibra and Djakova to Albania or forcing Serbia to evacuate them, although he warned the Serbs that he would not fight over the towns. The result was a trade-off. On 18 February Berchtold decided to let Serbia have Dibra if Albania got Scutari; a month later he yielded over Djakova.[215] On 21 February Franz Joseph offered to reduce Galician company strengths from the existing 160 to a level below Russia's normal 120, and in exchange Nicholas asked his ministers to consider releasing the senior class.[216] The Austrians were therefore already turning before they were enjoined to do so by a concerted German intervention. Bethmann, in a letter that Berchtold found insolent, warned that an attack on Serbia would cause a clash between the Triple Alliance and the Triple Entente. But there was a possibility of British policy being reorientated, and 'I would regard it as a mistake of immeasurable magnitude to bring about a violent solution . . . at a moment when a prospect, if still only distant, is opening before us of settling the conflict in fundamentally more favourable conditions for us'. Moltke wrote to Conrad that everyone except Russia would have understood if Austria-Hungary had made the Adriatic a *casus belli*, but it had been hoped that Russia's proposal for simultaneous 'demobilization' would lead to a *détente*. Sooner or later there would be a European war, but it would be hard to find a rallying cry that would carry the German public now.[217] Wilhelm asked Franz Ferdinand if Scutari was

[212] Buchanan to Grey, 5 and 19 Feb. 1913, *BD* ix(ii), docs. 590, 592, 631. Louis to Jonnart, 9 Feb. 1913, *DDF* 3rd ser. v, docs. 343, 366. Thurn to Berchtold, 4, 6 Feb., Hohenlohe/Hoyos conversation, 10 Feb. 1913, *ÖUA* v, docs. 5675–6, 5697–9, 5751.

[213] Berchtold diary, 10 Feb. 1913, HHStA Berchtold MSS 2.

[214] Conrad, *Dienstzeit*, iii. 126, 128. Dumaine to Jonnart, 24 Feb. 1913, *DDF* 3rd ser. v, doc. 443.

[215] Buchanan to Grey, 21 Feb. 1913, *BD* ix(ii), doc. 645. Williamson, 'Military Dimensions', 327. Helmreich, *Balkan Wars*, 284–94.

[216] Louis to Jonnart, 28 Feb. 1913, *DDF* 3rd ser. v, doc. 478. Bethmann to Wilhelm, 24 Feb. 1913, *GP* xxiv/1, doc. 12891. Berchtold to St Petersburg, 22 Feb. 1913, *ÖUA* v, doc. 5910.

[217] Tschirschky to Bethmann, 5 Feb., Bethmann to Berchtold, and Moltke to Conrad, 10 Feb. 1913, *GP* xxiv/1, docs. 12797, 12818, 12824. Conrad, *Dienstzeit*, iii. 167. Hantsch, *Berchtold*, i. 388.

worth fighting over, questioned whether Austria-Hungary's and Russia's extra-ordinary measures were justified, and said that he believed Vienna could reverse them if St Petersburg did likewise.[218] For the first time since the early stages of the crisis, the Germans were pursuing a united line.

The agreement was made public by a communiqué of 11 March. The Russians discharged some 370,000 conscripts from the senior class; Austria-Hungary released 40,000 men in Galicia, although their garrison there remained larger by some 40,000 than before the crisis and their company strengths rose from 97 to 120 or 130. They sent home their 1908 class everywhere except in the XV and XVI Corps,[219] which neither Krobatin nor Berchtold was willing to weaken until Serbia and Montenegro had evacuated Albania.[220] In effect the confrontations in north and south had been decoupled, the Russians standing down their senior class in return for troop cuts in Galicia and Albanian concessions to Serbia. From the beginning of the crisis Sazonov had been willing to tolerate extraordinary Austro-Hungarian measures in the Balkans. He had recommended that Russia should make war only for its own interests, particularly at the Turkish Straits, and not be carried away by sentimental solidarity.[221] If such considerations lay behind the disengagement, however, he attempted to conceal them by calling on Vienna to repudiate aggression against Serbia. When the Austrians jibbed, he published a unilateral declaration to this effect in the Russian text of the com-muniqué.[222] None the less, both Vienna and St Petersburg could now save money and spare their troops, and avoid the choice between a climb-down and yet more dangerous escalation. German pressure had probably contributed to this outcome by reinforcing Berchtold and Franz Joseph against their military, despite the absence of corresponding French pressure on Sazonov. But the upshot was that Austria-Hungary remained armed in the Balkans, whereas Russia was no longer similarly armed in the north.

As the Powers' short-term readiness passed its peak, the impact of the con-frontation on their longer-term preparedness was beginning to manifest itself. Maintaining permanently higher strengths in Galicia would necessitate a new Austro-Hungarian military bill. Russia's disengagement decision may have been connected with a major concession by Nicholas to the military, opposed by Sazonov and Kokovtsov, in the shape of the regulations approved on 2 March for the 'Period Preparatory to War'.[223] Under the 1912 regulations the

[218] Bethmann to Wilhelm, 24 Feb. 1913, *GP* xxiv/1, doc. 12891 n. Conrad, *Dienstzeit*, iii. 156. Williamson, 'Military Dimensions', 327.

[219] Ibid. Kageneck report, 7 Mar. 1913, *GP* xxxiv/2, doc. 12943 (text of communiqué, ibid. 473 n). Kageneck report, 15 Mar. 1913, PAAA R.8624. Berchtold diary, 12 Mar. 1913, HHStA Berchtold MSS 2. Deutschman, 'Massnahmen', 151–3.

[220] Ibid. 154–6. Berchtold to Conrad, 15 Mar. 1913, KAW Gstb Operationsbureau 738.

[221] Pourtalès to Bethmann, 12 Oct. 1912, *GP* xxxiii, doc. 12269. Louis to Poincaré, 21 Dec. 1912, *DDF* 3rd ser. v, doc. 105.

[222] Buchanan to Grey, 4 Mar., Cartwright to Grey, 13 Mar., Buchanan to Grey, 18 Mar. 1913, *BD* ix(ii), docs. 680, 708, 731. Dumaine to Jonnart, 3 Mar., Louis to Jonnart, 9 Mar., Dumaine to Jonnart, 14 Mar. 1913, *DDF* 3rd ser. docs. 501, 543, 585.

[223] May (ed.), *Knowing*, 33–4. See the discussion in M. de Taube, *La Politique russe d'avant-guerre et la fin de l'empire des tsars (1904–1917)* (Paris, 1928), 281–2. Sukhomlinov, *Erinnerungen*, 343.

mobilization order in the Western military districts was simultaneously one to commence hostilities. Now this was revoked to order to give more time for diplomacy, but the armed forces were given more discretion to accelerate an eventual mobilization by a range of preliminary measures. The new regulations, which would be implemented in periods of political tension, were known to Moltke by July 1913.[224] Yet the German CGS was already worried by his inability to distinguish between trial and genuine mobilizations, and after the crisis the Germans appear to have strengthened their arrangements for surveillance of French and Russian extraordinary measures.[225] The Austro-Hungarian General Staff shared the Germans' disquiet at the Russians' facility for concealment, and was the more distrustful in consequence.[226] None of this boded well for the next great clash between the Powers.

* * *

In tracing the pathways to that clash, however, we must first pursue the 1913 Balkan after-shocks and their radicalizing of Habsburg diplomacy. This development at the local level, as well as the heightening of medium-term preparedness at the Continental level, will form the guiding threads of the analysis of the months between the Austro-Russian disengagement and July 1914. The Scutari crisis of April–May 1913 witnessed an even higher level of Austro-Hungarian readiness than the previous December, and a new willingness to take the offensive. In the absence, however, of corresponding militarization elsewhere, it marked a return to the 1908–9 pattern of Austro-Hungarian coercive diplomacy and Russian acquiescence, coupled with German willingness to back Vienna and French restraint upon St Petersburg.

The Scutari affair had a pre-critical and a critical phase. It did not come unexpectedly, as Montenegro had besieged the city since October, assisted from March 1913 by the Serbs. Austria-Hungary and Italy insisted that it must go to Albania. After Berchtold's concession over Djakova Russia agreed, and on 22 March the Ambassadors' Conference recommended that the siege should be lifted. The Austrians sent a naval squadron, including three battleships, to the Albanian coast, soon joined by British, French, German, and Italian vessels. But the Montenegrins carried on regardless, and Scutari's surrender to them on 23–4 April opened the crisis proper.[227]

From February onwards Berchtold was in touch with Conrad about the military options, and it was in part because of Scutari that he resisted extending the disengagement agreement to the south-east. In late March and early April there was a rehearsal debate. Conrad opposed limited operations such as a blockade of Montenegro or an amphibious expedition to take the city, wanting instead to break with the Concert and mobilize for 'Case B[alkan]', which meant full-scale

[224] Moltke to Foreign Ministry, 5 July 1913, PAAA R.10432.

[225] U. Trumpener, 'War Premeditated? German Intelligence Operations in July 1914', *Central European History*, 9 (1976), 66, refers to the sending of 'tension travellers' into Russia in Mar. 1914.

[226] Kageneck report, 7 Feb. 1913, *GP* xxxiv/2, doc. 12943.

[227] Helmreich, *Balkan Wars*, 295–300.

war against Montenegro and Serbia. He expected such a war to lead to one with Russia, but still pressed with Krobatin for full mobilization of the XIII, XV, and XVI Corps.[228] Berchtold and Franz Ferdinand opposed additional measures and wished to keep in with the Concert if possible, although Berchtold shared Conrad's doubts about the efficacy of an international naval demonstration and on 5 April asked him whether Belgrade could be shelled or occupied and how quickly the troops could be made ready—a most significant departure in the Foreign Minister's thinking.[229] Franz Joseph's mood also hardened in the face of Montenegrin defiance. At first he told Berchtold that using force would mean war, and he overruled a proposal by Conrad to intercept Serbian troopships. But by 15 April when the CGS again advocated using force, he replied enigmatically that it must be carefully considered ('Das will sehr überlegt sein').[230] The civilian front against military action was faltering.

The pre-crisis run-in gave other Powers an opportunity to plot their moves. After the Ambassadors' Conference recommended that the siege should be lifted, Austria-Hungary warned that it would coerce Montenegro if it continued to resist. Sazonov spent a day agonizing over whether to recall the liberated conscript class—and the possibility that he might do so may have deterred the Austrians from imposing a blockade—but he settled for a protest.[231] None the less, he told the French that Russian opinion was 'exasperated' by the arrival of the Austrian naval squadron, and a landing would mean war.[232] As in Vienna, late April and early May was the testing time. According to the Stavka the situation was very tense and Russia could not allow Habsburg action against Scutari; there might be an Austro-Russian war that would spread to the West. They wanted an agreement that in such circumstances France and Russia would both concentrate at once against Berlin, rather than wait until tsarist forces had been committed against the Habsburgs.[233] Russian military thinking, like French, was becoming accustomed to the logic of inter-bloc confrontation. However, Sazonov did not oppose the Concert compelling Serbia and Montenegro to comply with its decisions, although he did object to Austria-Hungary doing so unilaterally or as the Concert's mandatory.[234] The French joined in the naval demonstration, with Russian consent, thus reducing the

[228] Conrad, *Dienstzeit*, iii. 157, 160, 170, 189. Hantsch, *Berchtold*, i. 403. Berchtold diary, 27 Mar. 1913, HHStA, Berchtold MSS 2. For Conrad's expectation of Russian involvement, Kageneck report, 11 Mar. 1913, *GP* xxxiv/2, doc. 12955, although this was more likely in the event of war with Serbia than with Montenegro, *Dienstzeit*, iii. 188.

[229] Ibid. 155, 188, 194, 238. Bardolff (for Franz Ferdinand) to Conrad, 7 Apr. 1913, KAW Gstb Operationsbureau 710.

[230] Hantsch, *Berchtold*, i. 394. Kageneck report, 11 Mar. 1913, *GP* xxiv/1, doc. 12955. Conrad, *Dienstzeit*, iii. 159–62, 245.

[231] Helmreich, *Balkan Wars*, 297. Laguiche to War Ministry, 23 Mar. 1913, SHA 7.N. 1478. Conrad, *Dienstzeit*, iii. 186.

[232] Delcassé to Pichon, 26 Apr. 1913, *DDF* 3rd ser. vi, doc. 169. Poincaré, *Service*, iii. 166.

[233] Wehrlin to War Ministry, 8 Apr. 1913, SHA 7.N. 1478.

[234] Doulcet to Jonnart, 20 Mar. 1913, *DDF* 3rd ser. vi, doc. 30.

likelihood that Vienna would go it alone.[235] By the time of a German *démarche* on 8 April, expressing grave anxiety about Russian support for King Nikita, St Petersburg had made up its mind. Sazonov reassured Pourtalès that he would stand by the Scutari/Djakova trade-off. He told the British Ambassador, Buchanan, that if Austria-Hungary coerced Montenegro Russia would have to accept it, as Scutari did not justify a war and most of the country did not want one. The Tsar was angry with Nikita and said he must be left to his fate: only if the action was extended to Serbia would there be a *casus belli*. Significantly, the French thanked Sazonov for his statement to Pourtalès as serving the cause of peace: there would be no encouragement from Paris for intransigence.[236] Nikita was warned to abandon all hope of getting either Scutari or Russian support, and on 11 April Serbia withdrew its forces from the siege,[237] thereby permitting the Austrians to strike at Montenegro without falling foul of the much stronger Russian commitment to its neighbour.

Russia's decision in early April made it unlikely that the conflict would remilitarize Great-Power relations when it reached its climax. The Ottoman surrender caused 'intense joy' in St Petersburg, but the mood in Vienna was likened to that in London after General Gordon's murder in Khartoum.[238] Berchtold reiterated that if the Powers did not act, Austria-Hungary would do so. But rather than agree to his proposals for bombarding or occupying Montenegrin ports, the Concert called on Nikita to hand over Scutari to the commander of the international naval squadron. Nikita's reply was unsatisfactory, and on 1 May Berchtold announced that he would send an expeditionary force.[239]

Krobatin considered that 'the reputation of the Monarchy as a Great Power' was at stake. It was predictable that he and Conrad should demand 'energetic action'. But Berchtold agreed that 'now we must do something', and Franz Ferdinand and Franz Joseph accepted the case for firmness.[240] For the first time a consensus was forming in favour of measures that were not merely a protective safeguard or a support for diplomacy but a prelude to offensive operations. Potiorek wanted to call up all available manpower in Bosnia-Herzegovina at once, so as not to choke the transport routes in an attack. He accepted that an assault on Montenegro was likely to bring in Serbia, but believed that a rapid *fait accompli* was the best means of keeping Russia at bay. Conrad shared his views.[241] On

[235] Poincaré, *Service*, iii. 167–74. Delcassé to Pichon, 2 Apr., Pichon circular, 3 Apr. 1913, *DDF* 3rd ser. vi, docs. 169, 182.

[236] Buchanan to Grey, 9 Apr. 1913, *BD* ix(ii), doc. 820. Delcassé to Pichon, 8 Apr., Pichon to Delcassé, 9 Apr. 1913, *DDF* 3rd ser. vi, 235, 244.

[237] Delcassé to Pichon, 12 Apr. 1913, ibid. doc. 277. Poincaré, *Service*, iii. 172.

[238] Doulcet to Pichon, 25 Apr. 1913, *DDF* 3rd ser. vi, doc. 384. Cartwright to Nicolson, 25 Apr. 1913, *BD* ix(ii), doc. 891.

[239] Berchtold to Mensdorff, 23 Apr., Cartwright to Grey, 27 Apr., 29 Apr., and 1 May 1913, ibid., docs. 877, 892, 900, 919.

[240] Kageneck reports, 24 and 26 Apr. 1913, *GP* xxiv/1, docs. 13202, 13214. Conrad, *Dienstzeit*, iii. 267. Tschirschky to Bethmann, 25 Apr. 1913, *GP* xxiv/1, doc. 13209.

[241] Potiorek to Conrad, 27 and 28 Apr., Conrad to Potiorek, 26 Apr. and 3 May 1913, KAW Gstb Operationsbureau 710. See also Potiorek/Conrad correspondence in KAW Gstb (1913) 52–4.

29 April the GMR agreed that all units in Bosnia-Herzegovina and Dalmatia should bring their horses up to full complement, removing the principal obstacle to making them operationally mobile.[242] On 2 May 12.9 million crowns was assigned for this purpose and 5 million to fortify Cattaro and call up the first three classes of Bosnia-Herzegovina reserves. This meant another 48,000 men, and on the following day Potiorek proclaimed a state of emergency.[243]

A threshold had been crossed. At the meeting of 2 May it was not foreseen that Nikita would yield.[244] Berchtold, exasperated with the Concert's dilatoriness, foresaw 'the possibility, not to say probability' of a war, which might also involve Serbia. It was agreed to mobilize if Nikita defied a three-day ultimatum.[245] Whereas Conrad, however, wanted full-scale operations against both Serbia and Montenegro and to annex the latter, Berchtold, with the Emperor's support, insisted that mobilization must in the first instance be against Montenegro alone and the objective confined to Scutari. He hoped to invade by sea rather than go overland, and to reduce the affront to Russia by intervening jointly with Italy. But negotiations with the Italians proved delicate, and he was willing to launch an amphibious operation without them, while they meanwhile were making frenzied preparations for a parallel landing.[246]

Berchtold and Franz Joseph were still seeking to minimize risk, but the GMR of 2 May witnessed something close to a revolt against them. The Foreign Minister remarked in his diary on Stürgkh's and Bilínski's anger.[247] Krobatin complained that Europe would always hold Austria-Hungary back without itself applying effective coercion: if Montenegro gave way after the Monarchy mobilized, a million crowns would have been wasted. Bilínski, too, dwelt on the cost of mobilization and wanted either a lasting friendship with Serbia or to destroy its independence. Teleszky thought the public would see securing Scutari for Albania as little compensation for a Montenegrin campaign. Zaleski, however, believed that the burden of rearmament since 1906 had already been enormous, and that there were financial arguments for acting now rather than facing greater sacrifice and danger within a few months. Pecuniary considerations must take second place anyway. He believed there would be war with Serbia, and like Bilínski he did not expect Russia to intervene.

The Government of the Austrian half of the Monarchy had moved into the military camp—a development confirmed by its reaction to the news on 4 May that Nikita was evacuating Scutari and entrusting the city to the Powers. Conrad, Krobatin, Bilínski, Stürgkh, and the Hungarian Defence Minister, Georgi,

[242] Krobatin to Bilínski, 1 May 1913, KAW KM Präs 1913 37–4. Kageneck report, 30 Apr. 1913, *GP* xxiv/1, doc. 13247.

[243] GMR, 2 May 1913, HHStA PA XL 311. Käs, 'Generalstab', 240. Conrad, *Dienstzeit*, iii. 294.

[244] Williamson, *Austria-Hungary*, 138–9. Bilínski to Zaleski, 1 May 1913, FAW FM Präs 1913 #1031.

[245] GMR, 2 May 1913, HHStA PA XL 311.

[246] Berchtold diary, 26 Apr.–2 May 1913, HHStA Berchtold MSS 2. Conrad, *Dienstzeit*, iii. 271–95. Tschirschky to Foreign Ministry, 1 and 2 May 1913, *GP* xxiv/1, docs. 13257, 13262; Flotow to Foreign Ministry, 3 May 1913, ibid., doc. 13265.

[247] Berchtold diary, 2 May 1913, HHStA Berchtold MSS 2.

wanted to send a twelve-hour ultimatum. Conrad told the Germans that he was 'absolutely in despair' over the climb-down, which had made a 'shattering impression'. But Berchtold, supported by Franz Joseph, preferred to let Nikita escape. To have humiliated him, he thought, would have discredited Austria-Hungary in the eyes of Europe, and he felt satisfaction at having avoided an unprofitable and inglorious mountain campaign.[248] The measures agreed on 2 May were cancelled. None the less, the crisis was a sinister milestone. Repeated near-mobilizations without the use of force were psychologically bruising, and devastating to business confidence and the Monarchy's finances. On mobilization, Zaleski warned Bilínski, 'the money markets would panic'. The Government had no cash reserve, and even its peacetime borrowing capacity was nearing its ceiling.[249] The War Ministry estimated the cost of three months' mobilization against Montenegro alone at 340.5 million crowns; against both Montenegro and Serbia at 952 million.[250] In some ways a partial mobilization would actually be harder to finance than a general one, as in a limited war there would be more resistance to suspending the central bank statutes.[251] The cost of fighting, however, had to be set against the 180 million spent in the annexation crisis and the (according to Teleszky) 500 million in the present one,[252] as well as against that of medium-term rearmament. If the Russians could be kept out and a short, sharp war could solve the South Slav problem, the option was increasingly tempting.

Ironically, although an attack on Serbia in May 1913 would almost certainly have escalated, it probably was possible to wage a limited war against Montenegro. Nikita was estranged from both his Balkan and his Great-Power backers. Serbia had exhausted its cash reserves and was having to import food. It was making precautionary troop movements to the eastern frontier against Bulgaria. The Serbian premier, Nikola Pašić, wanted to give Vienna no pretext for war over Scutari, and he warned Nikita to expect no support.[253] The Russian Government found itself in an 'abominable' dilemma, and was uncertain what to do if Austria-Hungary used force. Sazonov tried to head the danger off, by applying pressure in Belgrade and Cetinje and pleading that Nikita would yield if given time. He suggested the alternative of joint landings on the Montenegrin coast, but found Britain and France lukewarm.[254] On 1 May he told Buchanan that for the moment he would wait upon events. Russia was not afraid of fight-

[248] Helmreich, *Balkan Wars*, 323–4. Conrad, *Dienstzeit*, iii. 297–8. Berchtold diary, 4 May 1913, HHStA Berchtold MSS 2. Tschirschky to Foreign Ministry, 5 May and Kageneck report, 4 May 1913, *GP* xxiv/1, docs. 13272 and 13318.

[249] Zaleski to Bilínski, 4 May 1913, FAW FM Präs 1913 #1031; KAW KM Präs 1913 76–38.

[250] Krobatin to Finance Ministers, 3 May 1913, ibid. 37–4; and 25 Mar. 1913, ibid. 76–38. Bilínski to Zaleski, 10 May 1913, FAW FM Präs #1106.

[251] GMR, 2 May 1913, HHStA PA XL 311. [252] Ibid.

[253] Gellinek reports, 26 and 27 Apr., 1 May 1913, KAW KM Präs 1913 47–7. Buchanan and Paget to Grey, 1 and 2 May 1913, *BD* ix(ii), docs. 925 and 929. Descos to Pichon, 1 May 1913, *DDF* 3rd ser. vi, doc. 456. Griesinger to Foreign Ministry, 3 May 1913, *GP* xxiv/1, doc. 13263.

[254] Doulcet to Pichon, 25 and 26 Apr. 1913, *DDF* 3rd ser. vi, docs. 384, 393. Buchanan to Grey, 29 and 30 Apr. 1913, *BD* ix(ii), docs. 901, 911.

ing Austria-Hungary, but if Berlin joined in he doubted Britain would help, and against Germany only the Royal Navy could deal a mortal blow. If war were avoided, however, he expected the Balkan Powers to grow stronger year by year as the Habsburg Monarchy declined. Provided Austria-Hungary confined itself to securing the evacuation of Scutari he believed he could hold public opinion in check. According to Buchanan, the Russian army 'to a very large extent actively desires war', but nobody outside St Petersburg wished to fight, and Nicholas desired peace at almost any price.[255] Sazonov informed the French that neither Sukhomlinov nor Zhilinsky wanted hostilities, and that he was avoiding any action that Austria-Hungary might find threatening. Although he warned that if Vienna went beyond strict enforcement and tried to gain predominance over Montenegro there might be 'the gravest consequences', he, like Berchtold, welcomed the denouement.[256]

Nor was there more enthusiasm in Western Europe that grenadiers should die for Scutari. The French Government was alarmed when Sazonov suggested that Nikita should be bought out by financial or territorial compensation, and he dropped the idea. Wilhelm II was said to be against war, and the German Foreign Ministry pressed hard at the Ambassadors' Conference for rapid and effective joint enforcement.[257] It is true that the German attaché told the Austrians that Berlin stood fully behind them, and there was no fresh attempt to restrain Vienna. German officers and reservists were reportedly held in readiness.[258] But Nikita's submission forestalled a dangerous trial of strength that no Power wished to see. All had agreed that Albania should get Scutari, and Sazonov had already decided before the crisis not to recall the senior conscript class. London and Paris gave him no encouragement to intransigence. Habsburg coercive diplomacy scored a signal success, and was encouraged towards further unilateral action at a moment when opinion in Vienna was moving away from armed diplomacy and in favour of limited war.

* * *

Austro-Hungarian attitudes hardened further in the remaining crises of 1913. The most striking feature of the Monarchy's reaction to the Second Balkan War, in July, was a crossover between military and civilian views, Berchtold becoming more hawkish than the army leaders. This tendency was beginning during the interlude after Scutari. During May some 35,000 reservists and 15,000 *Ersatz* reservists were dismissed, but in Bosnia-Herzegovina troop cuts were again postponed.[259] The main pressure to release the troops came from Franz Ferdinand

---

[255] Buchanan to Grey and Nicolson, 1 May; Buchanan to Grey, 15 May, ibid., docs. 925, 928, 975.

[256] Doulcet to Pichon, 1 May; Russian note 4 May 1913, *DDF* 3rd ser. vi, docs. 450, 490. Pourtalès to Bethmann, 6 May 1913, *GP* xxiv/1, doc. 13282.

[257] Poincaré, *Service*, iii. 178–9. Jagow to Lichnowsky and Flotow, 26 and 28 Apr. 1913, *GP* xxiv/1, docs. 13207, 13223.

[258] Conrad, *Dienstzeit*, iii. 275, 294. Jules Cambon to Pichon, 6 May 1913, *DDF* 3rd ser. vi, doc. 509.

[259] Kageneck report, 18 May 1913, *GP* xxiv/1, doc. 13318.

and Franz Joseph.[260] Conrad accepted that poor morale necessitated some reductions, but Berchtold wanted still to be able to threaten Serbia.[261] A compromise was reached whereby the soldiers would be released in rotation. The Emperor regretted the appearance of mobilization that this would create abroad, and would have preferred simply to send the troops home, but reluctantly agreed.[262] In June the commander of the XVI Corps reported that the troops could not understand why they had not got leave, and that there was growing impatience. Krobatin warned that the approaching summer drought in Bosnia would allow fewer horses to be maintained there, and he needed to know whether the Monarchy was going to fight. Berchtold replied that only 'in the most extreme case' would he use force, but he did not wish to exclude it. By now he was the principal obstacle to reversing the Monarchy's military measures.[263]

As both Berchtold and Conrad pointed out, the domestic pressures to release the conscripts had to be set against external uncertainties. The Ambassadors' Conference remained in session until 11 August, agreeing to neutralize Albania and delineating its southern frontier. The Balkan League was disintegrating as a result of arguments over the share-out. Greece and Serbia negotiated an alliance and agreed on their respective gains; Montenegro promised to support them if the quarrel came to blows. Serb–Bulgarian negotiations over territory and over reciprocal demobilization made no progress. On the night of 29–30 June Bulgaria launched the Second Balkan War, the High Command apparently hoping for a speedy victory and King Ferdinand for sympathetic intervention by St Petersburg. But neither calculation was well founded. The Serbs and Greeks halted the attack and fought their way forwards. Romania declared war on 1 July and advanced on Sofia, meeting negligible resistance. The Turks joined in and recaptured Adrianople. By the Treaty of Bucharest on 10 August the Bulgarians ceded many of their conquests.

Once again, Russia and Austria-Hungary had to decide what to do. The Russians had a foot in both camps, and little reason for dissatisfaction with the outcome, although Sazonov was upset at the collapse of the Balkan League and contemplated protecting Bulgaria from Turkey. The news of this possibility led to a academic discussion in Vienna of joint intervention with Russia.[264] But Sazonov had been infuriated by the Bulgarians, whom he considered unreliable and ungrateful. He refused their pleas for aid against the Balkan States, calculating that any loss of influence in Sofia would be outweighed by gains in Bucharest. On the other hand, he feared that a Serbian victory 'might lead to international complications', and wanted above all to keep Austria-Hungary

---

[260] Conrad, *Dienstzeit*, iii. 324. Berchtold diary, 16 and 25 May, 2 June, HHStA Berchtold MSS 2.

[261] Conrad audience with Franz Joseph, 20 May 1913, KAW Gstb Operationsbureau 739. Conrad, *Dienstzeit*, iii. 329.

[262] Berchtold diary, 23, 25, 28 May 1913, HHStA Berchtold MSS 2.

[263] XVI Corps Commander to Potiorek, 18 June 1913, KAW Gstb 1913 52–4. Berchtold diary, 11 June 1913, HHStA Berchtold MSS 2.

[264] Ibid., entries from 24 July to 27 Aug. 1913.

quiet.[265] Neratov told the Germans that if the Austrians mobilized units on the Serbian frontier Russia would have to take special measures, but it was undertaking no trial mobilization. Both France and Britain wished to stay aloof, and St Petersburg let events take their course.[266]

Austria-Hungary had greater capacity to intervene, and more incentive to do so. The units in the annexed provinces were still at war strength, and some 60,000 reservists were available. The cavalry (though not the supply trains) had their full complement of horses and could attack sixteen days after the start of mobilization. Montenegro mobilized in Serbia's support, but the Serbs' own forces had been moved east.[267] In the run-up to war Conrad, predictably, wanted to profit from a Serb–Bulgarian cock-fight in order to settle accounts with Belgrade. Franz Joseph was wary, and Berchtold told Conrad that the Monarchy should adopt 'a waiting attitude',[268] though he warned the Germans that it would not tolerate Russian intervention and reserved its right to act in the event of a decisive Serb victory. When the war began he confirmed that Austria-Hungary would show 'initially complete reserve'. Once it became clear that the tide was turning against Bulgaria, however, he lost his composure. He told the German Ambassador that it was a 'life-and-death question' for the Monarchy to hold on to its South Slav provinces, and it could not do so against an 'over-mighty Serbia'. If Bulgaria were defeated, he would present demands in Belgrade with 'military backing'.[269] Yet when Ferdinand appealed for assistance Berchtold merely advised him to come to terms with Romania. He gave effective help neither in the fighting nor at the peace conference.[270]

Germany bore part of the responsibility for this outcome. Wilhelm thought it would be a mistake for the Monarchy to commit itself as it had done over the Adriatic. Bethmann refused to warn the Romanians to keep out, for fear of driving them towards Russia. The war, he considered, did not affect Austria-Hungary's vital interests and was wearing out its enemies. Vienna should seek a *rapprochement* with Belgrade, and any attempt to expel the Serbs from their new territories would lead to a European conflict. Even Berchtold's hopes of revising the peace treaty were dashed when Wilhelm publicly congratulated King Carol of Romania on the settlement. Simultaneously the Italians gave notice that if an Austro-Hungarian attack on Serbia led to war with Russia they would not feel bound to give support.[271]

[265] Buchanan to Grey, 4 July 1913, *BD* ix(ii), docs. 1110 and 1127.

[266] Pourtalès to Bethmann, 11 July 1913, PAAA R.10432. Laguiche to War Ministry, 26 June 1913, SHA 7.N. 1478. Goschen to Zimmermann, 4 July; Schoen to Foreign Ministry, 5 July 1913, *GP* xxxv, docs. 13484, 13488.

[267] Williamson, *Austria-Hungary*, 145. Potiorek to Conrad, 17 July 1913, KAW Gstb Operationsbureau 710. Hubka report, 24 June 1913, KAW KM Präs 1913 47–16.

[268] Conrad, *Dienstzeit*, iii. 322, 332–3. Ibid. 345, 353. Berchtold diary, 21 June 1913, HHStA Berchtold MSS 2.

[269] Tschirschky to Bethmann, 20 June; Tschirschky to Foreign Ministry, 1 July; Zimmermann to Treutler, 4 July 1913, *GP* xxxv, docs. 13410, 13475, 13483.   [270] Albertini, *Origins*, i. 460–3.

[271] Treutler to Foreign Ministry, 5 July; Zimmermann to Tschirschky, 6 July 1913, *GP* xxxv, docs. 13486, 13490. Helmreich, *Balkan Wars*, chs. 17, 18.

It is doubtful if the messages from Berlin and from Rome were needed. Berchtold was already in a dilemma because of Romania's prospective intervention. To warn it off, as Germany pointed out and as Franz Joseph and Franz Ferdinand agreed, would risk sacrificing a long-standing alliance for the friendship of the untrustworthy Ferdinand. Yet if Romania came in Bulgaria would be beaten, unless Austria-Hungary came to the latter's aid. The obvious solution was for Ferdinand to make concessions, but this he refused to do.[272] While the diplomats wrestled with this conundrum, the military were uncharacteristically muted. Conrad went off on holiday with the advice that the Monarchy should stay out.[273] His change of tack may have been caused by the suicide of Colonel Redl, the former head of military counterintelligence, who had been discovered betraying secrets to the Russians, including mobilization documents and possibly the Schlieffen Plan. The scandal shook Franz Ferdinand's confidence in Conrad, who had initially concealed its magnitude from him, and possibly forced the general to pay more attention to his patron's position.[274] The Archduke counselled Berchtold to resist the influence of the CGS—who saw war as the means to personal salvation—to keep the reservists under arms, keep calm, and not intervene.[275]

The feeling among the reservists was now causing much concern, the commander of XV Corps urging that those who had been under arms for nine months were very depressed and that discontent was spreading. Even Potiorek agreed that it was high time to relax and in late July Berchtold agreed to discreet releases. The War Ministry thought that morale was 'highly worrying', and if the Foreign Minister hesitated further it was willing to appeal to the Emperor. The order to send home the reservists and *Ersatz* reservists in Bosnia-Herzegovina went out on the day after the Bucharest Treaty was signed.[276] When the Hungarian Premier's representative in Vienna, Burián, demanded regardless that the Monarchy should mobilize and force the Serbs to give up territory, Berchtold replied that to do so would antagonize Romania and Germany, and would be both expensive and dangerous.[277]

The exchange was symptomatic of Austro-Hungarian feelings at the end of a ten-month experiment with armed diplomacy. Since October 1912 the Monarchy had remained greatly above its peacetime strength, even after Russia had stood down. By the time of the Scutari crisis the Austrian Government was coming to prefer limited war to the continuing expense; by July even the High Command felt that the reservists should go home. Yet in the Second Balkan War armed diplomacy failed to win even a prestige victory, which lent powerful sup-

---

[272] Helmreich, *Balkan Wars*, 372–5.

[273] Berchtold diary, 8 July 1913, HHStA, Berchtold MSS 2. Williamson, *Austria-Hungary*, 146.

[274] Ibid. A. Sked, 'A Patriot for Whom? Colonel Redl and a Question of Identity', *History Today*, 36 (1986), 9–14.

[275] Franz Ferdinand to Berchtold, 4 July 1913, HHStA Berchtold MSS 4.

[276] XV Corps Commander, 4 July 1913, KAW Gstb 1913 52–4; and further correspondence in this file on troop releases. Berchtold diary, 9 Aug. 1913, HHStA Berchtold MSS 2.

[277] Ibid., 14 Aug. 1913.

port to the military arguments against half measures. As Conrad put it, the Monarchy could not for a third time mobilize its forces and not use them, as neither its prestige, nor its finances, nor its public opinion would tolerate it. Potiorek warned that in the next Balkan crisis there might not be time for another graduated increase, and domestic considerations might not permit one: they should go straight for full mobilization, and maintain permanently larger forces under arms.[278] Meanwhile Berchtold was driven to distraction during the Second Balkan War, and may have undergone a form of breakdown. He told Franz Joseph that the Monarchy's crisis was so fundamental that he no longer felt up to his responsibilities and wanted to be relieved. The Emperor agreed that the external situation was perhaps more difficult than for a hundred years.[279] On 1 August Berchtold advised the Germans that a reconciliation with Serbia was impossible and 'in the not too distant future there would be war'. He complained that hitherto it had been tacitly assumed within the alliance that Vienna would take the lead in making Balkan policy, and he could not tolerate the Monarchy's interests being thwarted.[280] Following the removal of Auffenberg in the previous December, and the radicalization of the Austrian Government in April, the staunchest advocate of restraint was changing sides. The middle road of armed diplomacy was reaching a dead end, and the German Government coming to accept that it must support its ally more strongly. The consequences of these reappraisals became evident in the ultimatum crisis of October 1913.

* * *

After the Treaty of Bucharest the Serbs had demobilized, but from mid-September they were again calling out reservists for weapons training. Five regiments of infantry and one of mountain artillery were put on readiness. Officers on leave were recalled, and troops transported to the Bulgarian and Bosnian borders. By the following month, according to the British Minister, some 123,000 men were on a war footing. In Albania, Serbia faced a rebellion, which it alleged had Austrian support. Dibra's fall to the insurgents precipitated the new round of measures. The Serbs maintained that they had no intention of challenging the frontier set by the Ambassadors' Conference or of permanently stationing troops to the west of it, but their assurances were distrusted.[281] As Serb forces drove the rebels back in the first week of October, it seemed that there might be a *fait accompli* and a 'viable' Albania would be overthrown. Belgrade had already ignored one summons to evacuate eastern Albania, and the Austrians were again obliged to consider acting as the Concert's enforcing agent. They sent a warning on 14 October and, after Pašić gave a dilatory reply, an ultimatum on

---

[278] Conrad, *Dienstzeit*, iii. 329, 406, 410. Potiorek to Conrad, 25 June 1913, KAW Gstb Operationsbureau 710.

[279] Berchtold diary, 16 July 1913, HHStA Berchtold MSS 2.

[280] Hantsch, *Berchtold*, ii. 466–9.

[281] Gellinek reports, 15 Aug., 22 and 28 Sept. 1913, KAW KM Präs 1913 47–7. Crackanthorpe to Grey, 24 and 25 Sept. 8 Oct. 1913, *BD* x(i), docs. 18, 20, 33. Clément-Simon to Pichon, 26 Sept. 1913, *DDF* 3rd ser. viii, doc. 146.

18 October requiring Serbia to withdraw behind the London line within eight days. On 20 October it agreed to do so.[282]

The Serbs were overextended. They faced a hostile Bulgaria on their eastern frontier, and might have to help their Greek allies in a developing confrontation with Turkey in the Aegean. Their conquests had yet to be organized for military recruiting, and parts of them were in armed revolt. Even in Old Serbia the reservists responded poorly to the call-up order. The country was undergoing economic depression and financial crisis, and although the authorities estimated that 600 million francs were needed to pay for the wars, for restocking, and for investment in the new territories, they could raise a loan from a consortium in Paris for only 250 millions. The French Government suspended approval even for this amount because of the Albanian conflict,[283] and decided before the ultimatum to require Serbia to submit, Sazonov associating himself with the message.[284] Once again Russia could look to no support from Paris in subverting a Concert decision. But Sazonov himself felt that 'Serbia had been more to blame than was generally supposed in the events which led up to the recent ultimatum', and Hartwig urged Belgrade to yield, so as to discredit Vienna in the eyes of Europe.[285] Hence the Cabinet in Belgrade agreed to pull out and to abandon talk of 'frontier rectification', possibly even welcoming the ultimatum as a pretext for liquidating an embarrassing overcommitment. Montenegro had also carried out a partial mobilization in early October, but withdrew from Albanian territory without awaiting a similar demand.[286]

If the Entente Powers restrained the Serbs, Austria-Hungary received the strongest support from Germany since December 1912. Berchtold sent the 14 October warning without consulting Berlin, and indicated that he would follow it with an ultimatum and go 'to the limit' if need be: he asked for 'moral' support, and expected that this would suffice, as he believed that Serbia was bluffing and neither France nor Britain wanted to fight. The German Foreign Ministry recommended giving support, in part because of fears that Austria-Hungary would go over to the Triple Entente. Both Wilhelm and his diplomats promised their backing before the ultimatum went ahead, the Emperor minuting that he hoped Belgrade would refuse.[287] On the day that it was delivered, after the dedication of the centenary memorial to the battle of Leipzig, he urged on Conrad a Balkan offensive. 'The other (Powers) are not ready, they will do nothing against you. In two days you must be in Belgrade . . . I have read much

[282] Helmreich, *Balkan Wars*, ch. 20, for an account of the crisis.

[283] Gellinek reports, 27, 28, 29 Sept., 4 and 12 Oct. 1913, KAW KM Präs 1913 47–7. Sevastopoulo and Izvolsky to Neratov, 1 and 18 Oct. 1913, Stieve (ed.), *Iswolski*, iii, docs. 1070, 1093.

[284] Poincaré, *Service*, iii. 306–7.

[285] Crackanthorpe and O'Beirne to Grey, 22 and 28 Oct. 1913, *BD* x(i), docs. 52, 56.

[286] Crackanthorpe to Grey, 20 Oct. 1913, ibid., doc. 48. Gellinek report, 21 Oct. 1913, KAW KM Präs 1913 47–7. Hubka reports, 6, 7, and 21 Oct. 1913, ibid. 47–16.

[287] Stolberg to Foreign Ministry, 15 Oct.; Zimmermann to Wedel, 16 Oct.; Zimmermann to Tschirschky, 16 Oct.; Wedel to Foreign Ministry, 17 Oct.; Zimmermann to Lucius, 20 Oct.; Zimmermann to Tschirschky, 22 Oct. 1913, *GP* xxxvi/1, docs. 14160–2, 14172, 14174, 14193. Helmreich, *Balkan Wars*, 426.

of war and know what it means, but eventually there comes a situation in which a Great Power can no longer look on but must grasp the sword.'[288]

In the event Serbia collapsed so quickly that Vienna had no need for military gestures. But this was the reverse of indicating that Habsburg diplomacy had become pacific. Conrad's doctrine of no half measures had won wide support. On 29 September Berchtold suggested occupying the Serbian town of Sabac until the Serbs left Albania. Conrad replied that they should either say and do nothing, or send an ultimatum and mobilize after twenty-four hours. Berchtold sympathized with the latter, but did not believe that Franz Joseph and Franz Ferdinand would see it through. During the three-week gap between mobilization and hostilities the Powers would intercede; he regretted that they could not send an ultimatum and march in immediately. Just before Belgrade caved in he suggested occupying Serb territory with troops at peacetime strength, but Conrad objected that, though on mobilization Potiorek could deploy 80,000 infantry, at present he had only 25,000. The Foreign Minister and at least some of his officials were inclining to use force if the risks could be limited, and the Austrian attaché in St Petersburg considered that Russia would be unlikely to retaliate against a sudden and rapid attack. Conrad, meanwhile, checked over his mobilization plans, but his advice was not to go further unless the Monarchy meant business.[289] The new Hungarian Premier, István Tisza, agreed that they should not mobilize again without going to war, but the issue was whether Austria-Hungary was still 'a living Power' or in 'laughable decadence', and it must not let the Concert prevent it from imposing its will.[290] When the GMR met on 3 October it rejected Conrad's advocacy of attacking Serbia in order to incorporate it into the Monarchy, but there was widespread acceptance that war was necessary and that the armed forces must be built up in readiness.[291] At a further meeting ten days later the mood was even more intransigent. There was agreement in favour of the ultimatum, and most ministers, except for Tisza, wanted sooner or later to solve the Serbian problem by force. The militarization of the Monarchy's foreign policy was almost complete.[292]

The remaining obstacle was the dynasts themselves. Franz Ferdinand intended to keep on Conrad only until the following spring. He tried unsuccessfully to halt the ultimatum.[293] But Berchtold agreed with the CGS that the Emperor was more inclined to force than was the heir to the throne. He noted Franz Joseph's 'serious mood . . . in view of the Albanian rebellion and the eventual inevitability of an intervention by ourselves against Serbia'. The Emperor approved the ultimatum with the words, 'if they do not give way within eight days we shall begin at once', and according to Krobatin he was 'wholly for

[288] Conrad, *Dienstzeit*, iii. 469–70.   [289] Ibid. 443–5, 455, 462, 465, 474.

[290] Tisza to Berchtold, 13 Oct. 1913, HHStA Berchtold MSS 4; and 9 Oct. 1913, Hantsch, *Berchtold*, ii. 498–9.

[291] GMR, 3 Oct. 1913, HHStA PA XL 311.   [292] Conrad, *Dienstzeit*, iii. 464–6.

[293] Ibid. 440. Conrad to Franz Ferdinand, 26 Sept. 1913, KAW Gstb 1913 1–7. Hantsch, *Berchtold*, ii. 501.

mobilization'. Unlike Conrad, he insisted on a 'legal basis' for action and was satisfied with the diplomatic victory, but he too was hardening in his views.[294]

* * *

The year of conflict in the Balkans had cankered European politics. More men had been called up in time of peace than ever before, and many taboos had been broken. In 1911 France and Germany had both stood down their senior conscript class, but in 1912 Russia kept its class on, and the Austrians partially recalled theirs. 'Trial mobilizations' at times of crisis were a new feature of the scene. There were now two players in the game of armed diplomacy in Eastern Europe, and elsewhere there were greater spillover effects than previously as the two halves of the Continent were drawn more tightly together. France had encouraged Russian military measures in December 1912; Germany had supported Austria-Hungary in November–December 1912 and October 1913. 'War Councils' had become recurrent features of institutional life in the Eastern monarchies. Following Bosnia, Agadir, and the Tripoli war, the turmoil confirmed that Europe was moving into near-permanent crisis. High levels of preparedness were indispensable not only to lend emphasis to diplomacy and as an insurance against attack but also—at least for Austria-Hungary and Russia— in order to be able to safeguard vital interests by active operations. In any future confrontation both sides would be better equipped militarily, and the collision would be more likely to be between blocs than between isolated states. In addition, armaments competition was becoming more dynamic and relentless. The Balkan Wars tipped the European balance drastically against the Central Powers and spurred them into new rearmament efforts, to which France and Russia responded. Both sides' programmes were unprecedented, not only in their scale, but also in their orientation towards superior readiness in time of crisis and earlier and faster mobilization. And from now on the inter-bloc arms race was so interdependent in East and West as to constitute a single phenomenon. By the time of the next great crisis in 1914 not only were both sides ready to undertake military measures but both were willing to fight. In the meantime, the Austrians, or most of them, had reached a point where they were no longer prepared to take new measures on their south-eastern frontier unless in anger, and by October 1913 the target was not Montenegro but Serbia. It is true that over the Albanian borders they were acting to enforce the decisions of the Ambassadors' Conference, and thus inhibited Franco-Russian retaliation. But given their disenchantment with the Concert, even this safeguard might soon fall away. The warning lights were set at red.

2. Continental Response

In the eighteen months before the First World War there was a series of diplomatic *détentes*: between London and Berlin, even between Paris and Berlin, and

---

[294] Berchtold diary, 26 Sept., 13, 17, and 25 Oct. 1913, HHStA Berchtold MSS 2. Conrad, *Dienstzeit*, iii. 445, 464, 474.

between St Petersburg and Vienna. Yet the same months saw the climax of the inter-bloc armaments race. Germany and France passed huge new laws in July and August 1913. The German law provided for an unprecedented increase in peacetime strength and for massive re-equipment. The French one extended military service from two years to three, and it too was followed by an enormous equipment credit. Italy passed legislation to raise its recruitment contingent in June 1913; as did Belgium in August. Austria-Hungary reinforced its army by a law of March 1914, and Russia by the 'Great Programme' approved on the eve of war. Meanwhile, in December 1913 France promised funding to extend the Russian commercial railway network in return for a commitment from its ally to build anti-German strategic lines. By the following spring the Germans were preparing to riposte with a railway programme of their own.

The two coalitions will be analysed in turn, thus corresponding with the action–reaction dynamic: a Central Powers' initiative followed almost instantaneously by a Franco-Russian response. If in the previous phase it was the Russian 1910 reorganization and the Agadir crisis that gave the crucial impetus, now it was the Balkan turmoil and the German law of 1913. In the winter crisis of 1912–13, unlike that of 1908–9, the two blocs competed for short-term readiness. This was followed by a competition for medium-term preparedness, in which the Powers on each side took cognizance of the overall balance as well as of their individual needs. Fortifications, artillery, railways, and aircraft were significant but second-order priorities. Between the four biggest Continental armies the race was pre-eminently for manpower, and for higher strengths in existing units rather than to create new ones. The drive for intensified training and for faster mobilization was of a piece with the evolution from defensive to offensive strategic planning. But it was also a concomitant of the militarization of diplomacy. The spoken or unspoken premiss of the Continental leaders was that Great-Power relations had entered into recurrent and unpredictable 'periods of political tension', to use the EMA's phrase.[295] Heightened preparedness was a deterrent and an insurance premium against the possibility of war, but it was also a precaution against further crises and a tool to facilitate their handling. This element was present in all four cases, but nowhere more explicitly than in Vienna.

* * *

The new Austro-Hungarian armaments programme was approved by the GMR on 3 October 1913, and embodied in an army bill that was passed with little change five months later. Following the Schönaich Pact and the legislation of 1912, this was the final reconditioning of the creaking Habsburg war machine. The two Parliaments were asked for an increase in the annual contingent by 31,300 between 1914 and 1918. The one-off costs would be 108 million crowns, and annual recurrent expenditure would go up by 41 million. 1,500 extra recruits would go to the navy, 16,500 to the common army, 7,300 to the Austrian

---

[295] e.g. War Minister circular on measures in case of political tension, 4 Apr. 1914, SHA 7.N. 134.

Landwehr and 6,000 to the *Honvéd*. The total for the Monarchy's land and naval forces would rise to 251,563 men, corresponding to a peacetime strength on land of 600,000 and a wartime strength of 2 million. Most of the extra soldiers would be incorporated in existing units, 9,600 going to bring 640 frontier infantry companies up to 160 men each, while the interior companies would rise to ninety-three. The machine-gun detachments assigned in wartime to each regiment would rise from two or three to four, and the field and heavy artillery per division would increase as quickly as possible to numbers comparable with those in France, Germany, and Russia.[296] Simultaneously with the army expansion, however, the GMR agreed in principle to 427 million crowns of naval expenditure,[297] and whereas the land bill was expressly directed to the north-eastern and south-eastern frontiers rather than against Italy, the naval programme testified to the continuing dispersion of the Monarchy's efforts. Compared with developments elsewhere in Europe those efforts were still belated and small.

The Austro-Hungarian programme was not immediately a reaction to rearmament by the Monarchy's antagonists. Indeed, there was a lull in Balkan armaments development after the two wars. Bulgaria was defeated and bankrupt, and the cost of victory made Montenegro and Serbia temporarily less dangerous. The Turkish guns captured in Scutari were museum pieces, and during the siege the Montenegrins wore out much of their own heavy artillery. Lack of money and uncertainty over Russian subsidies forced Nikita to suspend plans to boost his infantry battalions from fifty-nine to seventy-five.[298] Similarly, the Serbian military bill that after much delay had been presented to the Skupshina in 1912 was now withdrawn for further revision. A bill to treble the intake of officer cadets was a pointer to Belgrade's ambitions, but until the 250-million franc credit was agreed with Paris there was little possibility of starting reconstruction.[299]

Nor was the programme a response to build-ups in the Monarchy's allies. Conrad still regarded Rome as a potential enemy, but the General Staff accepted that Italy had become less dangerous because of the Libyan involvement and the renewed friction with France. It believed that railway and fortification work opposite the Austrian frontier had all but halted, and that the 1913 Italian army law had increased the effectives by fewer than half the numbers needed to bring units up to adequate strength.[300] More ominous were developments in Romania, the largest and richest of the Balkan States, and the one least damaged by the wars. In December 1912 it ordered twenty field-gun and fifteen mountain-gun batteries from Krupp, and 100 machine guns from the DWMF. In the spring it raised its army budget and introduced a bill for longer service in the reserves. After the Second Balkan War it stepped up its reorganization, the Austro-

[296] Reports on Austro-Hungarian army by *GGS*, 1 Feb. and 15 June 1914, KAM Gstb. 203. Dumaine to Pichon, 6 and 15 Oct. 1913, *DDF* 3rd ser. viii, docs. 275, 324; Ribot to Pichon, 31 Oct. 1913, ibid., doc. 420. Kageneck reports, 9 Oct. and 13 Nov. 1913, PAAA R.8625.

[297] Haus to Bilinski, 12 Jan. 1914, FAW GFM 1914 #21.

[298] Hubka to War Ministry, 21 and 31 Oct. 1913, KAW KM Präs (1913) 47–16.

[299] Gellinek to War Ministry, 13, 19, 20 Apr., 29 Sept. 1913, ibid. 47–7.

[300] Evidenzbureau annual report on Italy, Dec. 1913, KAW Gstb Operationsbureau 820.

Hungarian attaché reporting that Bucharest's entente with Belgrade was becoming a defensive alliance.[301] On the eve of the 30 October GMR Conrad told Franz Joseph that both Romania and Serbia were 'dangerous opponents',[302] and the incipient peril in Transylvania may help explain the support the Hungarians gave to the new Habsburg law. The genesis of the measure, none the less, was unconnected with Romanian developments.

The precipitant was the heightening of military readiness during the winter crisis. The army had been dissatisfied with the law of 1912 even on acquiring it, and the new emergency gave it the pretext to seek more. Early in 1913 Conrad got Franz Joseph's provisional support for an amendment that would allow the Monarchy to make permanent its reinforcements in Bosnia-Herzegovina and Galicia.[303] Berchtold believed he had been handicapped by having to raise frontier strengths with each worsening of the external position, which had caused public alarm and damaged business confidence, and made the Monarchy seem the aggressor. He asked Krobatin whether the north-eastern and south-eastern frontiers could not be garrisoned at a level adequate to defend them and to protect mobilization, suggesting that in present circumstances the two governments could be won over easily. Krobatin welcomed such a step, and Conrad urged that the army should profit from the Foreign Minister's willingness to press the issue. On 15 February he wrote to Moltke that he hoped the eight army corps that had been strengthened would remain at the new levels.[304]

At this point the Continental arms race impinged on the Vienna debate. Moltke welcomed the intended reinforcement,[305] but there is no evidence that the Austro-Hungarian Government was swayed by representations from its ally. None the less, whereas in February Conrad had envisaged an increase in the contingent by only 900 men, by March he wanted 34,500. In the light of the plans announced by other Powers, and the likely subsequent projects of the Balkan States, Austria-Hungary must follow suit at least as far as necessary to retain a chance of victory in a Continental war. France, Germany, Russia, and Italy were all increasing their trained manpower and raising their preparedness, and the Monarchy must ensure that it recruited all its able-bodied men. The CGS asked Franz Joseph for a higher contingent and for the strengths of the frontier infantry companies to be set at 120, and found the Emperor willing to agree.[306]

While the Evidenzbureau prepared an appraisal of the European military balance after the prospective increases had been implemented, Krobatin approached

---

[301] Hranilović to War Ministry, 31 Dec. 1912, 15 Mar., 7 Apr., 9 May, 28 Oct., 12 Nov. 1913, KAW KM Präs (1913) 47–8. F. Käs, 'Versuch einer Zusammenfassten Darstellung der Tätigkeit des Österreichisch-Ungarischen Generalstabes in der Zeit von 1906 bis 1914', Ph.D. thesis (Vienna, 1962), 168.

[302] Conrad, *Dienstzeit*, iii. 456.

[303] Kageneck report, 14 Jan. 1913, *GP* xxiv/1, doc. 12684. Conrad, *Dienstzeit*, iii. 85.

[304] Berchtold to Krobatin, 31 Jan., Conrad to Krobatin, 17 Feb., Krobatin to Berchtold, 21 Feb. 1913, KAW KM Präs (1913) 26–7. Conrad, *Dienstzeit*, iii. 151.

[305] Ibid. 328.

[306] Conrad to Krobatin, 15 Mar. 1913, KAW KM Präs (1913) 26–7; also KAW Gstb (1913) 52–2. Conrad, *Dienstzeit*, iii. 170.

the Austrian and Hungarian Premiers.[307] He shared Berchtold's awareness of the difficulty of crisis management if it was necessary to call up additional armed forces at every rise in tension. Recent events had shown up the particular weakness of the artillery, and underlined the urgency of catching up with other armies. Like Conrad he looked to a bigger contingent and higher peacetime strengths, and he wanted the 1912 law implemented in full by 1915, beyond which his priorities would be bigger frontier garrisons and more guns. He was increasing frontier strengths already in anticipation.[308] But it took the whole of the summer of 1913 to negotiate the bill through the Monarchy's cumbersome liaison procedures, and to win approval for it in principle from a grudging Franz Ferdinand and the two governments.[309] By the time this was accomplished, the military had introduced a second, and more ambitious, demand.

The programme had acquired two separate rationales: eliminating provocative frontier reinforcements in time of crisis, and keeping pace with the other Great-Power increases as well as those expected in the Balkans. It was dwarfed by what was planned elsewhere, and although Conrad and Krobatin appeared to resemble Ludendorff and the radicals of the DWV in their willingness to harness all available resources, they were actually closer to the conservatives of the Prussian War Ministry. They believed a maximum of 36 per cent of each age cohort was suitable to serve—much less than in France or Germany. Bolfras, the head of Franz Joseph's Military Chancellery, felt that a higher proportion should be conscripted, the length of service being cut if it was necessary to economize, but this solution was rejected by Conrad and Krobatin. To shorten the term of duty would damage training and set a dangerous precedent, and Conrad was mindful that the army was the Monarchy's principal internal bulwark.[310] Their resistance, however, was to going too fast too soon, and they developed a more gradual alternative approach. On 25 March Conrad set out before Franz Joseph the likely balance of forces in an Eastern European war. 114 divisions would be available to Russia, Serbia, and Montenegro (possibly joined by sixteen and a half from Romania), against forty-eight to Austria-Hungary, and to Germany, initially, fourteen. He wanted to narrow the gap by creating a 'reserve army' of some twenty divisions, composed of reservists aged between 25 and 32 who would be organized into independent units and trained and equipped to fight alongside active troops. The Balkan Wars, he considered, showed that such forces could operate effectively, and he estimated that over ten years a force of 450,000 men could be built up for the same cost as three battleships. The War

[307] Conrad, *Dienstzeit*, 224–7, 527–8.

[308] Krobatin to Premiers, 19 Mar., Krobatin circular, 27 Apr. 1913, KAW Gstb (1913) 52–2. Krobatin to Franz Joseph, 14 July 1913, KM Präs (1913) 26–7. Krobatin to Zaleski, 10 Sept. 1913, FAW FA 75.732/II-1913.

[309] Conrad, *Dienstzeit*, iii. 322. Note by Bardolff, 1 June 1913, KAW Gstb (1913) 52–2. Krobatin letter, (?)26 Sept. 1913, KAW KM Präs (1913) 26–7.

[310] Bolfras to Krobatin, 4 Apr. 1913, with War Ministry comments, ibid. and Gstb (1913) 52–2. Conrad to Krobatin, 28 July 1913, KAW Gstb Operationsbureau 710.

Ministry agreed that by 1919–20 such a 'second line' could be organized to replace the perfunctorily trained levies of the *Ersatz* reserve.[311]

The fate of these proposals was decided at the 30 October GMR.[312] Berchtold pleaded that the 'armaments fever' in the rest of Europe and the continuing Balkan uncertainty required Austria-Hungary to expand its military strength up to the limits of its economic capacity. The Hungarians were lukewarm, Tisza fearing that the Monarchy faced financial calamity. He wished to cut the programme to what he deemed the indispensable minimum: enough to augment the artillery and technical troops without preying on the infantry, and to raise frontier strengths. He saw no need for higher numbers in the interior or for moving new units to the Serbian border. He resisted War Ministry proposals for extra measures opposite Italy.[313] Berchtold conceded that there was no reason for relations with Rome to deteriorate, and therefore no need to do more in the southwest. The upshot was that Tisza reduced the proposed contingent increase by 4,000 men, and although there were to be additions to the interior and southwestern infantry companies, these supplements would be kept small.

Franz Joseph had doubted whether Tisza would be so petty, as he put it, as to shave off five men per company, but he turned out to be mistaken, and the consequence would be 40,000 fewer in the reserves in a decade's time. None the less, in the German attaché's estimate, Conrad and Krobatin had got 95 per cent of what they wanted: not only men, but also a promise to finance the programme if it was spread over five years. This judgement, however, overlooked the failure of the reserve army plan. The Monarchy still held back from flat-out participation in the arms race, because of Hungarian financial fears and Conrad's and Krobatin's hesitation about the call-up ratios, as well as anxiety that intensified conscription would exacerbate labour shortages in agriculture.[314] Moreover, the Italian subplot testified to a continuing confusion about strategic priorities, with the result that even such resources as were available were not used to greatest effect.

The problem may be illustrated by the questions of the Bosnia-Herzegovina railways and the Adriatic Fleet. In June 1913 the War Ministry pleaded with Franz Joseph that Serbia was spending 60 million francs on new lines and building up to the frontier, while on the Monarchy's side another year was likely to be squandered. When the GMR re-examined the issue Conrad noted that it took three weeks to get the forces in the annexed provinces up to fighting strength, whereas Montenegro required much less time. According to Berchtold, the previous winter had shown 'to what extraordinary military preparations the lack of adequate transport routes to our south-eastern frontier obliges us with every worsening of the situation'. He feared that opinion in the annexed provinces would be antagonized unless work started soon. Bilínski, as common Finance

---

[311] Conrad, *Dienstzeit*, iii. 187–8. Conrad to Krobatin, 24 Dec. 1913, KAW Gstb (1913) 52–2.

[312] GMR, 3 Oct. 1913, HHStA, PA XL 311.

[313] Map with Krobatin to Franz Joseph, 14 July 1913, KAW KM Präs (1913) 26–7.

[314] Conrad, *Dienstzeit*, iii. 457, 466. Kageneck report, 9 Oct. 1913, *GP* xxxvi/1, doc. 14159.

Minister the man responsible for administering Bosnia-Herzegovina, had passed a bill through the local assembly and was ready to place contracts once the Austrian and Hungarian Parliaments had voted the necessary finance. But the former was unwilling to vote its share unless a mass of local railways was simultaneously approved in Austria itself, which the Government could not afford. Bilínski was authorized to go ahead as soon as the Hungarians had passed their bill, but in July 1914 construction had still not begun.[315]

Not only did the civilian authorities continue to dawdle over the south-eastern railways, but at the same time as agreeing to the army's contingent increase the 30 October GMR approved in full a much more expensive naval programme submitted by Montecuccoli's successor, Admiral Haus. The origins of this decision were less diplomatic than industrial. In April 1913 the same three firms that had forced the pace in 1909 (Skoda, Wittkowitz, and the Stabilmento tecnico) approached the navy with backing from the Creditanstalt. As the three first-generation dreadnoughts of the Viribus Unitis class would be completed before Parliament had decided on the second generation, the companies faced a hiatus of idleness, losses, and departures by skilled men for the Italian yards. They proposed that they should start work at their own risk on a new battleship designed to navy specifications. Although Haus insisted that he had not primed the industrialists, he commended their proposals with remarkable dispatch, and found the Austrian Government sympathetic. The Hungarian leaders, in contrast, condemned the proposal as unconstitutional, as a battleship built to Admiralty requirements could not safely be sold abroad and in effect the legislature was being pre-empted.[316] When the GMR first considered the issue, moreover, Haus made a poor case. Now that the Triple Alliance was renewed, he said, 'all of Italy' was willing to co-operate with them against France. Berchtold, when pressed on whether war with Italy was in prospect, waffled. The Hungarians stood their ground, and put financial stability and the Delegations' constitutional rights over lay-offs in what were, after all, Austrian firms.[317]

On 3 October, however, Haus returned to the charge with proposals not for one but four new battleships, as well as for three cruisers and six destroyers. This time the Hungarians, without explaining their change of front, proposed authorizing 427 million crowns at once, so that the work could be completed in 1914–18. The go-ahead contrasted strangely with Tisza's and Berchtold's reluctance to affront the Italians on land, unless the ships were really meant as a guarantee of co-operation with Rome, which is doubtful. Conrad suggested that Budapest had been sweetened by industrial concessions, as two of the four battleships were to be built by Danubius, but he had reason to feel aggrieved at the passage of the navy's full programme almost without debate, whereas even the

[315] War Ministry to Franz Joseph, (?)June 1913, KAW Gstb Operationsbureau 710. GMR, 3 Oct., 10 Nov., 14 Dec., HHStA PA XL 311. Williamson, *Austria-Hungary*, 66.

[316] Bilinski to Zaleski, 23 Apr., Teleszky to Bilinski, 25 Apr. 1913, FAW FM 1913 #1029, 1030. Zaleski to Bilinski, 4 May 1913, FAW GFM 1913 #257.

[317] GMR, 14 May 1913, HHStA PA XL 311.

army's immediate demands had been cut back. As for the stalled reserve army plan, he lamented, it would have cost less than the new naval schedule, and yet the Monarchy's fate would be decided on land.[318] This set-back did not mean, however, that the army was stagnating. Its budget had increased since 1912 and the extra men resulting from the contingent increase were starting to become available. The GGS was impressed by the progress made in artillery and aircraft.[319] In addition, most of what was being done on land was now clearly directed against Russia and the Balkan States rather than Italy. But the Monarchy continued to spend less per capita and to call up a smaller percentage of each age cohort than did the other Powers. Although it participated in the inter-bloc arms race, it still diverted resources to the Adriatic. Yet more than in any other capital there was a hardening determination in Vienna that the new capacity was not simply a precaution or a threat: it was meant for action.

* * *

When the Balkan storm clouds opened the Germans too had just passed an army law, and one that the Prussian army, unlike the Habsburg one, accepted as sufficient. In the autumn of 1912 the military balance seemed to be edging back in the Central Powers' favour, the new legislation and better relations with Italy offsetting the Russian military reorganization and the French *réveil*. At Hubertusstock on 13 October Wilhelm, Bethmann, and Kiderlen conferred with Heeringen and Moltke. The Emperor suggested taking new steps, but found the army chiefs hostile to accelerating the implementation of the 1912 law, which made the army equal to 'all political eventualities'. To ask for another so quickly, felt Heeringen, would be to admit a misjudgement; Moltke did not dissent, and Wilhelm did not insist. The same meeting, however, saw little likelihood of Russia being involved in a Balkan War and showed little concern about her trial mobilization. Once this appraisal changed the Germans acted much more urgently than the Austrians, and accepted a far greater commitment.[320]

At the moment when the arrival of the Krobatin/Conrad team narrowed the gap between the War Ministry and the General Staff in Vienna, the same gap widened in Berlin. The replacement of General von Stein (a Heeringen supporter) as First Quarter-Master General in the GGS by General Georg von Waldersee gave a freer hand to the head of the Second (*Aufmarsch*) Division, Colonel Ludendorff, and allowed him greater access to Moltke. Ludendorff felt himself an outsider. Of relatively humble origins, austere, a fanatical worker, he believed that preparation for victory in war took precedence over social exclusiveness. His responsibilities for planning against the French sensitized him to the precariousness of the army's advantage, and to the indispensability of truly universal service to supply the three and ultimately six more army corps that he

[318] Ibid., 3 Oct. 1913. Conrad, *Dienstzeit*, iii. 461, 466. Conrad report to Franz Joseph, 15 Oct. 1913, KAW Gstb Operationsbureau 739.
[319] Moltke to Krafft, 14 Jan. 1914 (GGS annual report), KAM Gstb 576. Conrad to Krobatin, 27 Dec. 1913, KAW Gstb (1913) 45–1.
[320] Reichsarchiv, *Weltkrieg*, i. 152–6. H. Herzfeld, *Die deutsche Rüstungspolitik vor dem Weltkriege* (Bonn, 1923), 48–9. Heeringen to Bethmann, 13 Mar. 1913, BA Rklei R43F 1252/1.

believed were necessary to implement the Schlieffen Plan. He had made contact with Keim, and it is likely that liaison between the GGS and the DWV continued during the agitation for the 1913 law.[321]

It was Ludendorff who drafted a memorandum, sent from Moltke to Heeringen on the day after Hubertusstock, that signalled the emergence of the GGS into the political arena. It spoke of the need 'decisively to strengthen' the army, and urged that increases in men and horses should take priority over improved organization and *matériel*.[322] In the next two weeks the seismic shifts began. Turkey's defeat meant that Austria-Hungary would have to divert resources from Galicia to Bosnia, and there was alarm at French and Russian preparations. A memorandum from Field Marshal von der Goltz, a veteran soldier and national hero from 1870 who had led the German military mission to Turkey, expressed the new mood. It was addressed to Heeringen and Moltke, but its arguments were conveyed to Wilhelm and Bethmann. Goltz set out a worst-case hypothesis, in which Romania and Bulgaria supported the Balkan League against Austria-Hungary, while Turkey had negligible value as a counterweight. In 'the coming world war' Germany would have to face France, Russia (and probably Britain) effectively alone. It could prevail on condition that it trained all available manpower, provided against seaborne blockade, and took the initiative in opening hostilities at a favourable moment. In discussion with Goltz, Bethmann (as the Field Marshal recollected) endorsed the analysis, but commented that if the Government complied with every military demand 'we must have the definite intention of striking out', and that Bismarck himself had had doubts about preventive war.[323]

Despite Bethmann's hesitation about the extent of the military programme, during the second half of November he, Heeringen, and Moltke were perceptibly changing their views. On 19 November he asked the War Minister if a further strengthening of the army was still unnecessary. He was told that 'the development of German military potential on land could absolutely not be extensive enough': in recent years it had been far too small, and the 1905 and 1911 laws inadequate. Heeringen was disturbed by the altered Balkan balance, but probably at least as much by Russian and French military measures, a meeting of War Ministry and GGS representatives on the same day agreeing to strengthen the guards on the Rhine bridges and eastern railways. Wandel recorded in his diary Moltke's and Heeringen's sudden doubts about Germany's preparedness, as well as the pressure from the Reichstag and the DWV for another bill. At Springe on 23 November, the day after seeing Franz Ferdinand,

---

[321] Herzfeld, *Rüstungspolitik*, 49. R. Parker, *Tormented Warrior: Ludendorff and the Supreme Command* (London, 1978), 13–21; E. Ludendorff, *Mein militärischer Werdegang* (Munich, 1933), 148–50; Förster, *Militarismus*, 249–50. R. Chickering, 'Der "Deutsche Wehrverein" und die Reform der deutschen Armee, 1912–1914', *Militärgeschichtliche Mitteilungen*, 25 (1979), 21–3.

[322] Reichsarchiv, *Weltkrieg*, i. 257.

[323] Goltz memorandum, 17 Nov. 1912, BA-MA von Mudra MSS 80/1, cf. G. Granier, 'Deutsche Rüstungspolitik vor dem Ersten Weltkrieg', *Militärgeschichtliche Mitteilungen*, 38 (1985), 128. B. F. Schulte, *Die deutsche Armee, 1900–1914: Zwischen Beharren und Verändern* (Düsseldorf, 1977), xxv.

Moltke told a meeting with Wilhelm, Bethmann, and Tirpitz that he regarded the situation as extremely serious, and the Chancellor agreed to introduce a bill in the spring, to the disappointment of Müller, who wanted immediate war.[324]

Two days later, in a letter again drafted by Ludendorff, Moltke expounded the GGS case. Russia had dangerously strengthened its frontier regiments, and only now had the Germans learned that it had not released its reservists. In addition, there was the new possibility of a French surprise attack before mobilization. Even if there were warning, the civilians in Berlin might resist precautionary measures while they perceived a chance of keeping peace. Hence the fortresses in East and West must be put on higher alert. The frontier corps must be reinforced and the new machine-gun detachments scheduled for 1913 must be created now. In 'the next war', Moltke like Goltz believed that Germany must be strong enough to win single-handed, and this meant reverting to the historic principle of the *Volk im Waffen*—the people in arms. The GGS was concerned with preparedness against surprise attack as well as Goltz's theme of the European repercussions of the Balkan power shift. But Moltke stressed the latter when he clarified to Heeringen that, although at present the army could still cope with 'all eventualities', in two to three years Russia would be more formidable, France would have pacified Morocco, and the Austro-Italian antagonism might have revived. Then Germany would have to trust to its own strength, and it could not begin preparations soon enough.[325]

This brings us to the impact of the 8 December 'War Council'. The first point to make is that before it met the German leadership was already effectively committed to a new army bill. The GGS was emphatic, and Bethmann favourable in principle. Heeringen dragged his feet for a while longer, telling Moltke that he had read his exposé 'with interest', and replying noncommittally. None the less, the War Minister wrote to the Chancellor on 2 December that expenditure was urgent to keep pace with developments in aviation, as well as on the eastern fortresses because of Russia's acquisition of modern siege artillery. These two factors formed the strongest elements of technological determinism in the origins of the measure. Heeringen wanted to maintain Germany's lead in airships and catch up with France in aircraft by 1914. In addition, he shared the anxiety about surprise attacks, especially if they came when the senior conscript class had been discharged and only one trained cohort remained with the colours. Germany, he said, must never again face war with only forty-seven men per company. Moreover, the army was prospectively inferior in numbers even to France alone, and it must make organizational changes to accelerate mobilization. On the other hand, the War Minister wished to delay a reinforcement until the autumn of 1913, as he lacked accommodation and instructors, the training grounds were full, and he feared that the armaments industry would be

[324] Reichsarchiv, *Weltkrieg*, i. 157–65. Granier, 'Rüstungspolitik', 141. Heeringen to Bethmann, 13 Mar. 1913, BA Rklei R43F 1252/1. B. F. Schulte, *Europäische Krise und Erste Weltkrieg: Beiträge zur Militärpolitik des Kaiserreiches, 1871–1914* (Frankfurt am Main, 1983), 19.

[325] Moltke to Heeringen, 25 Nov. 1912, Reichsarchiv, *Weltkrieg*, i, Anlagen, doc. 48.

overstretched. He was contemplating much lower expenditure than was eventually approved, and was hesitant about legislating as early as the spring. This notwithstanding, on 2 December he authorized the start of outline planning, and in conversations with him and Bethmann on 4 and 5 December the Emperor approved the War Ministry's preparations for the bill. This diminishes the significance of Wilhelm's statement at the War Council that he would order the (absent) Heeringen to prepare a big measure, and the greater novelty of the meeting was the Emperor's statement that he would ask Tirpitz for a bill as well. The meeting confirmed, however, that Germany would intensify the arms race, despite Moltke's fears that by doing so rather than striking at once it would lose yet further ground.[326]

It is true that the 8 December meeting infused the Emperor with an extra sense of urgency. He told the Bavarian Minister that the army and navy must be strengthened against the possibility of war on three fronts. Bethmann was unlikely to resist, and would risk incurring his master's displeasure if he did. On the day after the War Council met Heeringen was required to accelerate his preparations, and on 11 December Wilhelm ordered Tirpitz to ask for more warship construction. He informed the two men via General Plessen that they must profit from the current willingness of the public to approve 'all and everything'. Yet the War Council did not end the Ministers' reservations, which eventually dampened Wilhelm's own ardour. Heeringen wrote to Moltke on 9 December that he agreed to the principle of a bill, but warned that it might be limited by cost and the need to keep the units small enough for training, as well as by shortages of officers and NCOs.[327] When he met Bethmann and Tirpitz on 14 December none of the three protagonists were eager for big increases. Wilhelm had told Tirpitz that Britain was building ten capital ships a year and Germany must lay down at least five, but the London naval attaché had just reported that in 1905–12 Britain's average had been 4.5 and Germany's 3.4.[328] Capelle advised the Navy Secretary that if the army made large claims the navy could 'demand something to fill gaps, and bring forward cruisers, but in no circumstances more'.[329] At the 14 December meeting Tirpitz duly announced that he had been resisting Wilhelm's pressure for a new navy bill, but in the light of Heeringen's new position he must ask for one. Even so, it would be modest, mainly for aviation and for accelerating armoured cruiser construction, while leaving the statutory size of the fleet unchanged. This sequel to the War Council suggests that Tirpitz's plea there for one or two years' delay was a stalling tactic rather than a genuine bid for last-minute preparation time. As for Heeringen, he had moved some distance since

[326] Reichsarchiv, *Weltkrieg*, i. 166–8; ibid., Anlagen, docs. 51–3; Wenninger report, 21 Nov. 1912, KAM MKr. 5587 (aviation); Heeringen to Bethmann, 13 Mar. 1913, BA Rklei R.43F 1252/1. Röhl (ed.), 'Schwelle', docs. 4, 17, 20, 22.

[327] Ibid., docs. 17, 20. Diary of Admiral Hopman, 9–14 Dec. 1912, BA-MA Hopman MSS N326/9. Heeringen to Moltke, 9 Dec. 1912, Reichsarchiv, *Weltkrieg*, i, Anlagen, doc. 53.

[328] Hopman diary, 14 Dec. 1912, BA-MA Hopman MSS N326/9. Müller report, 8 Dec. 1912, *GP* xxxix, doc. 15557.

[329] Hopman diary, 14 Dec. 1912, BA-MA Hopman MSS N326/9.

his letter of 2 December, and accepted that an army bill must be introduced in the spring of 1913. Germany had the manpower available to be much stronger, and if it could not raise taxes it should borrow to meet the cost. It would be unfair if older men were called upon to fight while younger but untrained ones stayed behind, and this prospect was causing public resentment as well as anxiety about military unpreparedness that the Pan-Germans and the DWV were exploiting. Even so, according to Tirpitz, Heeringen still envisaged spending only 300.5 million marks. And for all the modesty of the army and navy proposals Bethmann's reaction was that they were 'completely unrealizable' not merely because of the expense but also because of the danger that the enemy would attack before they were implemented. Preparation in the two departments could continue, but as yet he could take no decision.[330]

Thus the genesis of the German army bill. Despite Wilhelm's early stirrings and Ludendorff's restless activity, it would not have originated when it did had it not been for the challenge to Germany's short-term readiness from Russia's and France's military measures, and to its medium-term preparedness from the Balkan power shift. Moltke said he wanted war now, but if there was to be armed peace instead the GGS planners desired as large and rapid an increase as possible. Wilhelm's position was changeable, as usual, but after the War Council he supported naval as well as land expansion. Conversely, the addition of a navy to the army bill may have made Bethmann hesitate. Heeringen was the slowest to move, but the mid-November alert and the War Council brought him round first to the principle of an army bill and then to the spring 1913 date. He agreed with the GGS on the priority of increasing unit strengths and trained manpower, but differed from them greatly over the scale and scope of the measure.

Attention is needed to the challenges to the War Ministry from the navy and the General Staff before reassessing the Bethmann–Heeringen line that won the Emperor's backing and prevailed over its critics. The pressure for a new navy bill came from Wilhelm, infuriated by the British warnings, rather than from Tirpitz. The struggles of 1912 had left their mark, and the Navy Office had no stomach for a fight. According to a memorandum by Rear-Admiral Dähnhardt there was very little public support for a naval, as opposed to an army increase, and Heeringen's demands put Tirpitz in a quandary. The Navy Secretary regretted the three battlecruisers lost in 1912, but had no wish to reclaim them now. Informed by Müller on 4 January 1913 that Wilhelm wanted a renewed three-ship tempo, Tirpitz commented that any departure from the existing schedule would require new legislation, which would not be worth the legislative struggle if it meant fewer than three ships. None the less, Capelle began to draft a bill for three extra battlecruisers by 1917, as well as additional torpedo boats, aircraft, and submarines.[331]

---

[330] Ibid.; Bethmann memorandum, 14 Dec. 1912, Röhl (ed.), 'Schwelle', doc. 17. Tirpitz, *Aufbau*, 361.

[331] Müller to Tirpitz, 4 Jan. 1913; Tirpitz note, 5 Jan. 1913; Dähnhardt memorandum, (?)Jan. 1913, Capelle draft bill, BA-MA Tirpitz MSS N253/28. Schulte, *Europäische Krise*, 30 n. Tirpitz, *Aufbau*, 368–9.

The navy faced continuing opposition from the Chancellor and could not trust the Emperor. Bethmann stalled over Tirpitz's demands. He objected to the navy working on the press or lobbying Wilhelm without his being consulted.[332] While the Ambassadors' Conference was in progress, he wanted rearmament plans kept secret, to discourage the hawks in London from starting a preventive war. Only when the crisis was over could the navy start canvassing. In any case, he believed that the 1912 *Novelle* had led to Britain building more and strengthening its ties with France, and that a new law would render the entente unbreakable.[333] But it may be that Wilhelm too, after his rage against the British died down, persisted with the naval bill only for the sake of appearances.[334] On 5 January Bethmann formally notified him of his intention to bring in a 'very large' army law worth 300–400 million marks, while for reasons of cost and of relations with Britain he wanted to stay with the existing naval construction schedule. He asked to postpone consideration of the three-ship tempo for another year, and Wilhelm concurred. Within three days of requesting the Navy Office to prepare a bill, the Emperor had killed the idea.[335]

Tirpitz's restraint was facilitated by what Churchill called 'an independent coincidence of opinion between Britain and Germany' over warship ratios.[336] On 6 February the Navy Secretary told the Reichstag Budget Commission that a 16:10 ratio would be 'acceptable'. He was responding to a 16:10 suggestion by Churchill, and on 10 February an Admiralty spokesman told the Commons that Britain was close to a 60 per cent superiority in completed dreadnoughts.[337] In other words, Tirpitz was willing to respect the *status quo*, and although he still warned Wilhelm against an explicit agreement, he could abide a tacit one. Such a ratio (which he wanted to apply to battleship squadrons in home waters, not to individual ships) would leave him free to build cruisers as he wished, and to add to his strength outside the North Sea, while peacefully consolidating the Navy Law.[338] To an extent, his position reconciled him with the Foreign Ministry, where Kiderlen's successor as State Secretary, Gottlieb von Jagow, believed that London was on the verge of accepting Germany's naval strength as 'an unalterable fact', and that it was best to 'let sleeping dogs lie'. The navy's information, however, was that Jagow's priority was strengthening the army against Russia and getting a neutrality pact with Britain. Capelle took this as another reason for doing as the English did (as he put it): speaking of peace and of defensive purposes while arming as fast as possible. For the next five years Germany should concentrate on implementing the existing legislation. He con-

[332] Bethmann memorandum, 14 Dec. 1912, Röhl (ed.), 'Schwelle', doc. 17.

[333] Bethmann to Wilhelm and Eisendecher, 18 and 20 Dec. 1912, ibid., docs. 31, 36.

[334] Bethmann note, 20 Dec. 1912, *GP* xxxix, doc. 15561.

[335] Müller to Tirpitz, 6 Jan. 1913, BA-MA Tirpitz MSS N253/28, cf. Tirpitz, *Aufbau*, 371. Lerchenfeld dispatch, 29 Jan. 1913, GSM Bayerische Gesandtschaft Berlin 1085.

[336] Müller report, 29 Mar. 1913, *GP* xxxix, doc. 15569.

[337] Lichnowsky to Bethmann, 8 and 11 Feb. 1913, ibid., docs. 15563, 15565.

[338] Tirpitz, *Aufbau*, 380–1. 'Referat über Budgetkommission', (?)22 Feb. 1913, BA-MA Tirpitz MSS N253/28.

soled himself with the belief that the Royal Navy, too, was running up against its limits: financially (because of other claims on the British public purse), politically (because of divisions in the Cabinet), and technically (because of shortages of recruits and the obstacles to developing a 15″ gun). Much of this prognosis was wishful thinking, but for the time being it helped to calm the Navy Office.[339]

Of the constraints on army expansion that had operated under Einem, that of naval competition was relaxed at the same time as external developments made action imperative. Public opinion had altered too. Keim called on 29 November for a new army bill, as did the National Liberal leader three days later. In Württemberg between December 1912 and March 1913 the DWV's individual membership doubled; nationally it had 30,000 individual and 100,000 corporate members by June 1913.[340] In the opinion of the French attaché the German public, in contrast to its leaders, cared little about the Slav peril and was fired primarily by anger against France, whipped up by the centenary celebrations of the War of Liberation against Napoleon.[341] The DWV, sharing this priority, had agitated for a new law since the summer of 1912, and specifically for a 25 per cent increase in the contingent, and it had numerous Reichstag sympathizers. It was able to exploit the authorities' divisions by bringing the dispute between the War Ministry and the GGS out into the open.[342] Bethmann noted in March 1913 that 'I am making the bill as the military demand, without reductions. Otherwise fellows [*Kerle*] will come back next year and Keim . . . continue to agitate.' After the passage of the bill, he hoped, the talk of 'war . . . and of perpetual armaments' would cease. Heeringen was nettled by the DWV's criticism, which he thought undermined public confidence in Germany's military security, and which he feared would spread into the army. He met Keim in December and asked him to suspend his campaign while the Ambassadors' Conference met, but the appeal cut no ice.[343] Both Heeringen and Bethmann hoped the bill would take the wind out of the extremists' sails: Wilhelm and Moltke cited public opinion as a reason to legislate. The alliance between the GGS and the militarists in the country strengthened the pressure for an expanded bill and helped secure its passage, but both the growth in the DWV's appeal and the General Staff's assertiveness may be traced back to the external stimulus provided by the Balkan upheaval.

It remained to be seen how far the War Ministry's retreat from conservatism would go. On 21 December Moltke set out a detailed GGS programme in the so-called 'Ludendorff memorandum'. Its premiss was that a military clash between any of the Great Powers would lead to a European war in which the balance had moved against the Triple Alliance. Germany could expect little help

[339] Jagow to Tirpitz, 6 Feb. 1913; Capelle note, 7 Apr. 1913, and undated memo. on British Fleet, (?)May–June 1913, ibid.
[340] Coetzee, 'Wehrverein', 437–9. Chickering, 'Wehrverein', 10.
[341] Serret to War Ministry, 15 Mar. 1913, SHA 7.N. 1112.
[342] Chickering, 'Wehrverein', 20–4.
[343] Bethmann memorandum, 14 Dec. 1912, Röhl (ed.), 'Schwelle', doc. 17. Keim, *Erlebtes*, 181. Förster, *Militarismus*, 263.

from Austria-Hungary and Italy, and would have to defeat France in the open field while holding off the Russians. Yet against Britain, France, and Belgium, its inferiority in infantry battalions would be 192, whereas in 1870 it had had a large infantry superiority and no enemy in the East. It had the edge in light field howitzers and heavy artillery, as well as hand weapons. But France had the money to catch up in equipment, and Russia grew stronger each year. The call-up rate must go up from the present 52–4 per cent to something closer to France's 82, implying an increase in the annual contingent of 150,000 and one in the peacetime establishment of twice that figure. All infantry, cavalry, and artillery units must be brought up at least to the current greatest strengths, and frontier strengths should be higher. New infantry and technical units must be formed from the younger age cohorts with extra officers and weapons, and there should be at least three new army corps, one on the Lower Rhine, one in Silesia, and one in the interior.[344]

There was common ground between the GGS and Heeringen, but the Staff envisaged more than double the 60,000 contingent increase that he recommended, and wanted many more new creations. Both wanted to upgrade the eastern strong points of Posen and Graudenz, but whereas the War Ministry wanted other fortifications to come second to the equipment of the field army, the GGS wanted high priority for both.[345] A conference between the two sides' representatives on 9 January highlighted the differences. Wandel, who was principally responsible for the War Ministry draft, believed the Staff requirements went far beyond what was necessary and were unrealizable because of the officer shortage: he feared that in the event of mobilization they would overstrain the railways.[346] Heeringen insisted that he could not defend before the Reichstag a bill whose provisions could not be implemented, and he did not believe that the three corps could be created before 1916. He did not necessarily oppose the GGS demands as such, but they could not be implemented so quickly.[347]

At one level this was a technical argument between mobilization and strategic-planning specialists and experts in manpower and finance. Experience after August 1914 seemed to vindicate the former. But underlying the discussion was a difference in world-view. Moltke and Ludendorff saw the Schlieffen Plan and the external balances. From 1 April 1913 contingency planning for a principal offensive on the eastern frontier ceased, and everything depended on superiority in the West.[348] Heeringen and Wandel, in contrast, also saw the domestic implications. The War Minister believed it would be politically and 'socially' undesirable to call up so high a percentage of each age cohort. Germany's numerical disadvantage relative to France was offset by a qualitative advantage. Not only would the three extra corps be seen abroad as provocative, but 'with-

[344] Moltke to Bethmann and Heeringen, 21 Dec. 1912, Reichsarchiv, *Weltkrieg*, i, Anlagen, doc. 54.

[345] Reichsarchiv, *Weltkrieg*, i. 171.

[346] Ibid. 177–9. Herzfeld, *Rüstungspolitik*, 60. Granier, 'Rüstungspolitik', 142–3.

[347] Heeringen to Moltke, 20 Jan. 1913, Reichsarchiv, *Weltkrieg*, i, Anlagen, doc. 56.

[348] Trumpener, 'War Premeditated', 76.

out reaching into circles that are little suitable for constituting the officer corps . . . and without a relaxation of requirements we shall be unable to cover the extraordinarily increased demand in the two classes'. Moreover, the extra expense would delay beyond 'the foreseeable future' the re-equipment of the established formations.[349] Heeringen was still loyal to his predecessor's agenda of upholding 'quality', and he had to judge, as Moltke and Ludendorff did not, what it was feasible to ask for. Both administratively and politically he was probably too timid. But in Wandel's views the Minister was only 'half-heartedly' behind the bill anyway, and not convinced that circumstances had changed so radically as to warrant it.[350] Although he paid lip-service to Goltz's arguments, he was moved more by pressure from others, less from the General Staff and the DWV than from Wilhelm and Bethmann.

Intervention by these latter resolved the dispute. Wilhelm understood that it would be difficult for Heeringen to defend a bill that greatly contrasted with that of 1912, but he did not want to make a gesture to the Reichstag by replacing the Minister.[351] Bethmann let the argument run on during January, but then asked Heeringen to prepare the bill as quickly as possible on the basis of the War Ministry draft. Heeringen went to Wilhelm, not (or so he wrote to Moltke) to seek a decision, but the Emperor took one anyway. Its prudence further weakens the thesis that the 'War Council' had witnessed a decision to fight in eighteen months' time. The measures in the 1912 law scheduled for 1914–15 were all to be implemented from 1 October 1913. The three extra corps might be an ultimate objective, but should not yet be declared as such. The claims already made for extra NCOs, officers, and men were enough. Moltke did get satisfaction over lower-level creations: more cavalry brigade staffs and regiments, fortress artillery, and communications troops, and bigger strength increases for the infantry and field-artillery than Heeringen had wanted. Having initially opposed the GGS's infantry and field artillery increases on grounds of cost Bethmann let the former through, while curtailing the latter because of a shortage of horses. Moltke, who had consistently been more emollient in negotiation than were Ludendorff's memoranda, talked of resignation but backed off when Wilhelm appealed to him to stay on. Ludendorff himself was packed off to a line command in Düsseldorf. The basic compromise had now been settled, although further detailed work was needed before 1 March when the contents of the bill were finally published.[352]

In addition to the central discussion over manpower there was a subsidiary one over *matériel*. Once it was clear that the Reich leaders were willing to push through new taxes, Heeringen returned to his tussle with the Finance Ministry, demanding big supplementary credits for fortifications and aircraft. He began

[349] Heeringen to Moltke, 20 Jan. 1913, cf. n. 347.
[350] Granier, 'Rüstungspolitik', 143.   [351] Wenninger report, 6 Feb. 1913, KAM MKr. 1136.
[352] Reichsarchiv, *Weltkrieg*, i. 187–9; Anlagen, docs. 58–60. Heeringen to Bethmann, 23 Jan. and 13 Mar. 1913, BA Rklei R.43F 1252/1. Heeringen to Bavarian War Minister, 25 Jan. 1913, KAM MKr. 1136.

placing orders in advance, in the justified confidence that the Reichstag would approve them retrospectively. He asked Bethmann not only for the costs of the military bill but also for broader measures to improve the army's training, mobilization, and combat-readiness. There would be larger stocks in the border fortresses, additional field howitzers, and a major increase in spending on fortification.[353] It was agreed that Graudenz and Posen should be made ready for Germany to fight a defensive war in the East by 1916, and for the rest of the year efforts were concentrated on the Vistula barrier. In the West, in contrast, the bill secretly provided 'very considerable sums' for 42 cm mortars to assault the Belgian defences.[354]

By the time the bill was presented to the Reichstag, however, the Germans were obliged to reconsider their position in the light of the armaments explosion that their own actions had detonated. Unlike Conrad in Vienna, they stuck to their existing course. In January they had been confident that the bill would give them an advantage over France that the latter could not match, because of its deficient manpower, although this was an advantage less in war strength than in the percentage of each unit kept permanently under arms, and therefore in speed of mobilization.[355] When it became clear that France would respond, and probably Russia as well, there was public outrage, as the bill was threatened with being trumped as soon as it reached the statute-book.[356] Moltke warned that France would bring back three-year service, raising its peacetime strength by 200,000 men, and that Russia would create three or four new corps. As a minimum he wanted Ludendorff's December memorandum implemented in full. Heeringen objected that reworking the bill would mean another two months' delay, and prevent any changes from being implemented on 1 October. In any case the present increase was the maximum possible. Bethmann agreed, and hoped that it would be definitive.[357]

Thus Moltke's fear of being drawn into an arms race that would leave Germany worse off than when it started was halfway to being vindicated. In February 1913 the GGS appears still to have favoured the alternative of an early war, before the French could catch up in artillery,[358] but it was isolated within the leadership, and Moltke went along with the cautions to Vienna. Wilhelm, reaffirming that the three extra army corps should be legislated for in 1916, seems not to have been looking to an early showdown.[359] Bethmann, according to the Emperor, no longer opposed a European war in all circumstances, but he did not want one now.[360] The Chancellor was impressed by a warning from

[353] Wenninger reports, 2, 9, and 10 Jan.; Heeringen to Bethmann, 10 Feb. 1913, KAM MKr. 5588.

[354] Förster, *Militarismus*, 271. Report on German fortification since 1870, KAM MKr. 4605/2. Wenninger report, 14 Feb. 1913, KAM MKr. 1136.

[355] Lerchenfeld report, 28 Jan. 1913, GSM Bayerische Gesandtschaft Berlin 1085.

[356] Serret to French War Ministry, 15 Mar. 1913, SHA 7.N. 1112.

[357] Moltke to Bethmann, 1 and 5 Mar. 1913, Heeringen note, Mar. 1913, Reichsarchiv, *Weltkrieg*, i, Anlagen docs. 62–4. Herzfeld, *Rüstungspolitik*, 75–6.

[358] Conrad, *Dienstzeit*, iii. 153.   [359] Granier, 'Rüstungspolitik', 144.

[360] Röhl (ed.), 'Schwelle', 87. Hantsch, *Berchtold*, i. 387.

Moltke that if nothing were done after the developments in the Balkans he could not continue as CGS.[361] For the moment, although he worried about what was politically and financially feasible, the army bill suited him tactically as a way of undercutting the DWV agitation and heading off Wilhelm's navalist enthusiasm without further damaging relations with Britain. He may also have seen it as a means of defusing the time bomb of the Basserman-Erzberger financial law and of breaking resistance to taxation reform.[362] Hence initially he supported the GGS against Heeringen in favouring a big increase, but in January he went along with Wilhelm's compromise and refused to reconsider it in March. For all the bill's unprecedented size it failed to meet the GGS's operational needs.

All the same, the previous hindrances to military expansion were diminishing. The navy had been blocked completely, and the War Ministry conservatives had made many concessions. Control by the Finance Ministry, like that of its counterparts elsewhere in Europe, was slipping. The draft legislation presented to the Reichstag was in the form of another *Novelle*, or amending law to those of 1911 and 1912. It would be fully implemented by 1916, for a one-off cost of 895 million marks and higher annual recurrent costs of 184 millions.[363] These increases were two or three times what Heeringen and Bethmann had originally envisaged, much of the difference being accounted for by a major investment in construction and equipment: 230 million would go on accommodation for the extra troops, but 210 million on fortifications, 79 million on aviation, and 71 million on artillery. Almost half the fortification work and weapons acquisition, however, would be left over until 1914–15. In contrast to the Einem years, manpower and organization came first. The bill would fully implement that of 1912 by 1 October 1913, but it would also do much more. The recruitment contingent would rise by 63,000, and peacetime strength by some 136,000 to 890,000 officers and men, over 80 per cent of the increase coming in the first year. There would be modest creations of new units, as Wilhelm had stipulated in January, but the main aim would be to reinforce existing ones, as Moltke had demanded all along. The previous three battalion strengths of the German infantry were reduced to two: a lower one of 641 officers and men (the previous maximum) and a higher one of 721. This was a compromise between the War Ministry's preference for 601 and 721, and Moltke's for 641 and 800.

Once the bill had emerged from the administration its passage through the legislature was straightforward, and it became law with little amendment.[364] The debates are revealing mainly for the light they shed on the thinking behind the measure and the arguments used to defend it. Thus Bethmann told the state governments on 10 March that he had not wished to start an arms race (*Wettrüsten*), and that Germany could not win numerical superiority over Russia and France.

[361] Lerchenfeld dispatch, 29 Jan. 1913, GSM Bayerische Gesandtschaft Berlin 1085.
[362] Förster, *Militarismus*, 256.
[363] Text of the bill in KAM MKr. 1136, cf. Reichsarchiv, *Weltkrieg*, i. 195–6.
[364] Serret to War Ministry, 16 July 1913, SHA 7.N. 1112.

He knew that the bill had increased international tension, but he had had to chose between evils and could not leave so many able-bodied men untrained. War was not inevitable and Germany did not seek it, but the Balkan States might start one and Germany's obligations to Austria-Hungary might draw it in.[365] In the Reichstag he set out a similar case, interlarded with Slav versus Teuton rhetoric. Although the German authorities tried at first to to pass off the bill as an answer to the French three-year law (which Heeringen insisted would have been introduced anyway), Bethmann admitted that it had been under discussion since November and was a response to the Balkan events. He stressed its deterrent and defensive aspects. The French and Russian Governments did not want war, but elements in both countries did. 'We propose to you this bill, not because we want war but because we want peace, and because if war comes we want to be the victors.'[366]

In secret hearings of the Reichstag Budget Commission on 24 and 25 April the German leaders sharpened up their case with remarkable, if melodramatic, overstatement. The burden of their testimony was that there was little prospect of a diplomatic solution to Germany's encirclement, and that already now, let alone in the future, the army was uncertain of success. Bethmann said that although he was doing all he could to avoid a war he could not guarantee that none would occur, and if one did it would be a 'struggle for existence' against France and Russia and possibly Britain. According to Wilhelm Groener, the head of the GGS railway section, the French army's new self-confidence rested in part on the justified belief that it had overtaken Germany in speed of mobilization and deployment. Not only did France lack natural disadvantages, such as the bottleneck constituted by the Rhine bridges, it had turned a German lead of 9:4 in strategic lines in 1870 into a French one of 15–16:13. Heeringen believed the French had knocked a day off mobilization since 1912 and that Russia would be ready in two years. Thanks to a sealed frontier and press censorship Russia had got up to war strength in the winter crisis without Germany being aware of it. He had considered calling up reservists in response, but had felt that he would have to do so against France as well and might thereby take the first step to war. The Russians had planned a surprise attack, and such a situation must never be allowed again, while in the Western theatre Germany's strength was insufficient for an offensive, and the gap was widening between its own numbers and those of its potential enemies.[367]

The Socialists justifiably suspected Heeringen of exaggeration, and the authorities hardly needed to go so far. The DWV supported the army bill as a necessary minimum, as did the pan-Germans, who had overcome their navalist prejudices. The Conservatives feared its fiscal implications, but as a 'national' party they could not oppose it. The National Liberals were closer to the posi-

---

[365] MS note on Bethmann's statements, 13 Mar. 1913, BA-Rklei R.43F 1252/1.

[366] Förster, *Militarismus*, 281–2.

[367] Wenninger to Bavarian War Ministry, 24 and 25 Apr. 1913, KAM Militärbevollmächtiger I. Graevenitz to Weizsäcker, 24 and 25 Apr. 1913, HSMA M10/41.

tion of the DWV and GGS, wanting urgent and rapid reinforcement not only to protect national security but also to support colonial and trade expansion. The Catholic Centre accepted the security argument for the bill; only the Progressives, among the middle-class parties, were unconvinced that diplomatic solutions to the international tension were exhausted, and seemed likely to join the Socialists in opposition. In the end they rallied to the measure, and it is on the Progressives as well as the Catholic moderates, such as Erzberger, that the Government disclosures probably had the greatest effect. The only item to cause serious difficulty was the proposed six-regiment increase in the Prussian cavalry, which the Reichstag Commission reporting on the bill wished to halve, although it did not insist.[368] Essentially the Socialists and their alternative conception of a one-year service militia were left isolated. Heeringen insisted that such a system was impossible when the other Powers had trained armies, and that they must be able to defeat the French in a rapid offensive. It was of a piece with this that he should reject the alternative of *détente* with Paris. Political agreements were evanescent, and as the responsible authority he could not rely on them: 'The bill has an eminently peaceful purpose. The army should be strengthened, in order to guarantee peace.'[369]

There remained the question of how the legislation would be paid for. The post-1909 boom was tapering off, but credit was still tight and Bethmann ruled out borrowing. He needed once again to raise revenue without antagonizing one or other element of his political support. A property tax was due for introduction anyway to cover the recurrent costs of the 1912 law, but discussion on it was deadlocked. An inheritance tax would be acceptable to the state governments, but not to the Conservatives and Centre in the Reichstag, and Bethmann wished to avoid dependence on a left-wing majority. He agreed with the state governments that the one-off costs of the 1913 law should be covered by a special *Wehrbeitrag* (defence levy), and the recurrent costs partly by increases in Reich taxes (such as stamp duties) and partly out of the states' matricular contributions. Only if the latter were insufficient would a capital gains tax be introduced.[370] Not a single Reichstag party, however, was satisfied with this formula. In further negotiations it was agreed that the defence levy should be a progressive impost on capital and on professional incomes, and it was expected that this would be adequate to pay for one-off expenditure. But the Budget Commission insisted on a federal capital gains tax to contribute towards the additional recurrent costs. In contrast to the majority for the army bill itself, that for the supporting financial legislation comprised the Socialists, the Progressives, the National Liberals, and most of the Centre: the Catholic Right abstained, and the Conservatives voted against.[371]

[368] Förster, *Militarismus*, 274 ff.

[369] Reichstag Budget Commission, 28 Apr. 1913, KAM MKr. 1136.

[370] Bundesrat discussion of financing of the bill, 10 and 11 Mar. 1913, BA-Rklei R.43F 1252/1. P.-C. Witt, *Die Finanzpolitik des deutschen Reiches von 1903 bis 1913* (Lübeck, 1970), 358–65.

[371] Ibid. 366–74. Reports by French Embassy in Berlin, 30 May, 7, 18, 24 June 1913, MFF F30 258/II.

The defence levy, coupled with a loan to increase the war chest and the Reichsbank's accumulation of gold, was an indicator of the militarization of German finances—notwithstanding which, Kühn forecast a deficit of a million marks in 1914.[372] Like its counterpart in Vienna, the Government was nearing its borrowing limits, but by trying to raise taxes it was breaking up its parliamentary base and forfeiting the Conservative support coveted by both Chancellor and Emperor.[373] The Socialists, whose leaders defended themselves by arguing that the new taxes were progressive and would show the middle classes the cost of militarism, were not a reliable substitute.[374] The constraints on armaments expansion had only temporarily been lifted, and in December 1913 the Bavarian Prime Minister called publicly on financial grounds for a moratorium on further increases.[375] Germany faced the danger of being outspent, not because of a lack of money in the country, but because of an inability to create political coalitions that could tap it. The 1913 law was passed with what outside observers thought an impressive display of unity, but it was already matched by France and Russia and had elements of a last throw.

The possibility was emerging, however, that despite Moltke's fears of Germany losing in the arms race it would be given one more chance. This was because of the speed of implementation of its own bill and its opponents' delays. In August the Bavarian attaché reported that both the French and the German armies would be thrown into chaos if they had to mobilize that autumn,[376] but by November Heeringen's successor, Falkenhayn, was testifying confidently to the Bundesrat. The call-up of reservists had gone well and the training of the new cadres was proceeding smoothly; there was some 'dilution' in the quality of manpower, but nothing to cause concern; the accommodation problem was being solved and fortification was under way. The army had carried through a compensating 'explosion' for its constrained development in earlier years, and although there would now be consolidation, there would be no return to 'standstill', whatever the cost.[377] The greatest increase in the army's peacetime history, a front-end-loaded measure that was mostly to be implemented in the first year, was going rapidly ahead. Financial and political obstacles were likely to impede any comparable further move. But in the meantime a window of opportunity was opening after all for Germany in 1914.

* * *

[372] Kühn to Tirpitz, 25 Aug. 1913, V. R. Berghahn and W. Deist (eds.), *Rüstung im Zeichen der Wilhelminischen Weltpolitik: Grundlegende Dokumente, 1890–1914* (Düsseldorf, 1988), doc. VIII/19.

[373] D. Groh, ' "Je eher, desto besser!" Innenpolitische Faktoren für die Präventivkriegsbereitschaft des deutschen Reiches, 1913/14', *Politische Vierteljahresschrift*, 13 (1972), 501–21. N. Ferguson, 'Public Finance and National Security: The Domestic Origins of the First World War Revisited', *Past and Present*, 142 (1994), 155–8, 164–8.

[374] Witt, *Finanzpolitik*, 374–5.

[375] Allizé to Pichon, 4 Dec. 1913, *DDF* 3rd ser. viii, doc. 587. Wenninger to Bavarian War Ministry, 8 Dec. 1913, KAM Militärbevollmächtiger I.

[376] Wenninger to Bavarian War Ministry, 12 Aug. 1913, KAM MKr. 41.

[377] Wenninger to Bavarian War Ministry, 21 Nov. 1913, KAM MKr. 5589.

In order to understand this development we must turn to the Central Powers' prospective enemies, and examine not only France and Russia but also Belgium's *Loi sur la Milice* (Militia Law) of 30 August 1913. It substituted general and personal service for the system of one son per family, although the fifteen-month term remained unchanged. The proportion of the age cohort recruited was to rise from 27 to 49 per cent, the contingent (15,000 in 1910) to 33,000 annually, and the army's peacetime strength from 42,000 to 57,000 by 1915–16. The war strength would rise from 180,000 to 340,000 men by 1920, about half of whom would serve in the field army.[378] Independently of the bill the army was reorganized in October 1913, a six-division replacing a four-division framework and a redeployment of the standing forces giving better protection to Liège and Namur.[379] Regular annual manœuvres were introduced, an aviation company was created, work on the Antwerp fortifications was intensified, and at Liège there was a several-day siege exercise.[380]

The origins of this upsurge of activity dated back to Agadir. The Moroccan crisis had forced the Government to contemplate the possibility of invasion.[381] *Le Soir* began a press campaign with an editorial entitled 'Are we ready?', although as yet the impact was limited.[382] In the aftermath of the crisis, the Foreign Ministry detected multiplying warning signs. King Albert, who had succeeded Leopold in 1909, was impressed by a message from King Carol of Romania in December 1911 that Belgium could not expect a repeat of the 'miracle' of 1870, and must look to its defences. The British attaché, Bridges, told General Jungbluth, the Chief of Staff, that the British army might have landed during the crisis without Belgian consent. Although Bridges spoke without authorization, the Foreign Ministry considered the episode one 'of an exceptional gravity' and a sign that Britain was no longer a reliable guarantor. Further encouragement to rearm came from Poincaré and from Greindl, the veteran Ambassador in Berlin. German railway development in the Eifel and Germany's 1912 law caused mounting anxiety. According to an analysis prepared for the Premier, Charles de Broqueville, the latter meant German frontier companies of 150 men facing Belgian ones of twenty, and 'the certainty for us of a surprise invasion', before German reservists joined up.[383]

From here on de Broqueville was an essential actor. Although Premier since 1911 he was reluctant to raise taxes until after the elections of June 1912, when he departed on holiday with a dossier on the security question from the Foreign Ministry and returned convinced that something must be done. A Flemish Lloyd

[378] GGS, 9. Abt., annual report, 1 Dec. 1913, KAM Gstb 576. Davignon to de Lalaing, 19 Sept. 1912, MAEB NIDMB 11.

[379] Notebook 'Préliminaires II', AGRB Lesaffre MSS 10.

[380] GGS 9. Abt., report cited in n. 378. *BDFA*, IF v. 389–91.

[381] Discussion in Foreign Ministry, 16 Sept. 1911, MAEB NIDMB 9.

[382] C. Terlinden *et al.*, *Histoire militaire des belges* (Liège, 1931), 31.

[383] L. de Lichtervelde, *Avant l'orage (1911–1914)* (Brussels, 1938), 36–52. De Gaiffier to Davignon, 12 Dec. 1911; notes by Van der Elst and de Gaiffier, 23 and 24 Apr. 1912; Greindl to Davignon, 10 May 1912, MAEB NIDMB 10; Guillaume to Davignon, 6 June 1912, ibid. 11; notes on German railways and military law in AGRB Broqueville MSS #304.

George, he was an intelligent, opportunist representative of a younger generation of Catholic politicians who had not supported the 1909 law but had now
changed his mind. The King persuaded him, however, that the time was not yet
ripe, and only in November 1912 did de Broqueville take over the War Ministry
personally from General Michel and announce his intention to legislate.[384]

Army reform was therefore coming anyway, but in the view of the German
Legation the Balkan crisis helped generate the support needed to get the bill
through.[385] Belgium did less this time than during Agadir, but at the end of
December Liège was reinforced and all measures were taken short of mobilization.[386] The Foreign Ministry considered the situation 'very sombre' and perhaps the gravest yet.[387] Although the winter crisis gave de Broqueville the
opportunity he needed to overcome the reservations among the clericals, however, his bill was intended to raise Belgium's medium-term rather than its short-
term preparedness. His public justification was that rearmament by other Powers
since 1909 had made the earlier law inadequate. Belgium could no longer be sure
that its neutrality would be respected, and its inadequate defences might court
attack—whereas reinforcement would allow it to hold the balance between the
blocs. As the Political Direction of the Foreign Ministry put it, 'The more considerable our military power, the more it will become unlikely that we have to
employ it'.[388]

The Belgian leaders emphasized their continuing neutrality, and the military
reorganization, which left units facing in all three directions, lent their statements credence. To begin with, British and French observers interpreted the bill
as the handiwork of a government and people that were unsympathetic to the
Triple Entente.[389] The Belgian authorities indeed believed that France was
increasing its capacity for rapid intervention, and after the Bridges indiscretions
Michel cited the British danger as justification for an army increase.[390] Michel,
however, was disliked in the army, and was an eccentric figure outside the ambi-
ence of Jungbluth, de Broqueville, and Albert, who were the main authors of the
measure.[391] Although the Belgian leaders took their decision independently, they
knew that the French and British Governments would welcome it, and Poincaré
soon confirmed this expectation.[392] It was in the East that the Premier saw the
greatest danger, and his testimony to a secret parliamentary session in February
1913 singled out the law of 1912 and Germany's border camps and railways,
as well as the warnings about Berlin's intentions.[393] Albert was similarly pes-

[384] Lichtervelde, *Avant l'orage*, 47–57.

[385] Flotow to Bethmann, 6 Dec. 1912, PAAA R.4401. [386] *BDFA*, IF v. 362–3.

[387] Foreign Ministry note for Davignon, 15 Oct. 1912, MAEB NIDMB 11.

[388] Klobukowski to Pichon, 6 Dec., Génie to Millerand, 7 Dec. 1912, Génie to Lebrun, 17 Jan.
1913, *DDF* 3rd ser. vi, docs. 11, 19, 231. Draft by de Gaiffier, Oct. 1912, MAEB NIDMB 11.

[389] *BDFA*, IF v. 361. Génie note, 27 Nov. 1912, *DDF* 3rd ser. iv, doc. 584.

[390] Davignon to Guillaume, 1 Oct. 1912, MAEB NIDMB 11; Michel to de Broqueville, 25 June
1912, AGRB Broqueville MSS #157.

[391] Génie to Millerand, 29 Oct. 1912, *DDF* 3rd ser. iv, doc. 278.

[392] Davignon circular, 17 Dec. 1912; Guillaume to Davignon, 13 Nov. 1912, MAEB NIDMB 11.

[393] Lichtervelde, *Avant l'orage*, 58. 'Huis clos' (14 Feb. 1913), AGRB Broqueville MSS #304.

simistic, warning Wilhelm in 1912 that Belgium would defend itself against all comers.[394] The report on the bill by the Chamber's Central Committee quoted twelve articles by foreign commentators, only one of which referred to a possible French invasion, and eleven to a German one.[395]

As the British Government did not intend to take the initiative in violating Belgian neutrality, and the Poincaré ministry had made the same decision, it was Germany that Belgian plans most affected. As the bill progressed, press comment in the Reich dwelt more persistently on its anti-German aspects, and Bethmann, Heeringen, and Wilhelm all cited it as a reason for their own bill. The Ludendorff memorandum included the Belgian army in the tally of the potential opponents in the West. In the Reichstag debates in early 1913 the Socialists quizzed Heeringen and Jagow on whether Belgium would be respected, and received ambiguous replies.[396] In fact Jagow was secretly querying the intention to go through Belgium, but made no headway.[397] In 1911 Moltke had modified the Schlieffen Plan so as not to pass through the South Limburg province of the Netherlands, which he wished to keep as a neutral windpipe through which Germany could continue trading in the event of a British blockade. But this made the Belgian railway network more vital to German planning than ever, and meant that Liège must be seized in the first days of a campaign.[398] The Belgian bill, however, intended as an answer to the German Law of 1912, was not expanded in response to that of 1913. While imperilling the Schlieffen Plan in the medium term, it prolonged Belgium's short-term exposure. Because of the continuing fifteen-month term of service Belgian front-line troops would remain inferior to German ones, and on the outbreak of war thirteen classes of reservists would fight alongside just one class of serving men. Nor did the bill address the army's weaknesses in *matériel*. Little work was done at Liège and Namur, and in 1914 Belgium went to war with 120 machine guns and no heavy artillery, de Broqueville lamenting, 'That I should have worked so hard and arrive too late.'[399] Almost nothing had been done to reduce his country's vulnerability to surprise attack or to close off Germany's temptation to strike.

* * *

In these months two shock waves passed through the European armaments system. The first was the collapse of Turkey-in-Europe and the ensuing Austro-Russian confrontation. It led to the German and Belgian army bills and launched discussion in Vienna. The Austro-Hungarian programme, however, was enlarged as a consequence of the second shock: the publication of the French and German army bills at the beginning of March 1913. Despite the simultaneity, the French bill was an answer to the German one, as was the Russian planning that

[394] J. Willequet, *Albert Ier: Roi des belges: Un portrait politique et humain* (Brussels, 1979), 76, 82.

[395] Flotow to Bethmann, 21 Jan. 1913, PAAA R.4402.

[396] Graevenitz to Weizsäcker, 29 Apr. 1913, HSMA M10/41.

[397] 'Der Durchmarsch durch Belgien', PAAA Jagow MSS 8.

[398] Kennedy (ed.), *War Plans*, 212.

[399] Notebook, 'Préliminaires No. 1', AGRB Lesaffre MSS 10; Moltke to Krafft, 14 Jan. 1914 (annual report), KAM Gstb 576 (Liège); Lichtervelde, *Avant l'orage*, 169.

culminated in the Great Programme. By reacting to the Balkan power shift and to the growth in French and Russian preparedness, Germany elicited a Franco-Russian counter-reaction; and its reaction to the counter-reaction, it can be argued, was to risk and launch a Continental war. This is not to reduce the diplomacy of these years to window-dressing for competitive armaments, but as the action–reaction sequence became tighter each side armed more in response to the perceived behaviour of its potential antagonists than because of internal imperatives. Yet the German bill was more than a defensive response to the emergency created by the Ottoman defeat and Russia's extraordinary measures: it was intended to keep the Schlieffen Plan viable in the face of Russia's reorganization and the French *réveil*. Similarly, although France and Russia exploited the pretext of the German bill, the content, as opposed to the timing, of their programmes was determined by their strategic planning, and particularly by the new French Plan XVII and the Russian Plan 20. In 1910 only Germany had an offensive war plan and France and Russia had defensive–offensive ones; by 1914 all three Powers intended to take the initiative by attacking at once, and Moltke's modifications had made the Schlieffen Plan more of a hair-trigger operation than ever.[400] The emphasis here, however, will be on the features of the Franco-Russian response that made for continuing short-term vulnerability. The discussion will begin with the separate national programmes adopted in Paris and St Petersburg, and in particular with the Three-Year Law.

The *Loi de trois ans* was passed on 7 August 1913. The bill presented to the Chamber of Deputies on 6 March proposed an extension of service in the active army from two years to three, offset by a reduction from eleven years to ten in the reserves.[401] Unlike the German bill, it was substantially modified in passage. The Reinach-Montebello amendment set maximum unit strengths (for example, 200 for frontier infantry companies), and required the extra conscript class to be retained only in so far as was necessary to maintain them. The Germans estimated that this meant that 160–170,000 of the 200–210,000 men in a class would actually need to be kept on for longer than two years.[402] The Escudier amendment provided for recruits to be called up in their twentieth rather than their twenty-first year, thus permitting them to leave and start a career or family at the age of 23 instead of 24. But it also permitted the Government to call up two new conscript classes in the autumn and to stand down the oldest (that of 1910), which it had previously been intended to retain under arms. The Chamber voted that only to the younger of the two classes called up in 1913 would three-year service first apply, with the result that only from 1916 would the standing army comprise two fully trained classes and one newly recruited one. In the autumn

---

[400] J. Snyder, *The Ideology of the Offensive* (Ithaca, NY, 1984) and 'Civil–Military Relations and the Cult of the Offensive, 1914 and 1984', *International Security*, 9 (1984), 108–46.

[401] Text of the bill in SHA 1.N. 11; AN C7419.

[402] G. Krumeich, *Armaments and Politics in France on the Eve of the First World War: The Introduction of Three-Year Conscription, 1913–1914* (Leamington Spa, 1984), 81, 112–14. I am much indebted to Krumeich's work. Moltke to Wenninger, 12 Aug. 1913 (analysis of Three-Year Law), KAM MKr. 992.

of 1913, in contrast, it would have one class that had served a year and two of raw recruits. It would be bigger but less cohesive.

Numerically, none the less, the effects were impressive. The Germans estimated that the French army called up 440,000 conscripts in the autumn of 1913, compared with some 250,000 in previous years. Its peacetime strength rose from 545,000 to 690,000 by the spring of 1914 (plus 45,000 doing auxiliary service), and by 1916 was expected to be 730,000. The extra class would also add to France's war strength, and help it to keep pace with Germany's for some years, although eventually it would fall behind. The extra manpower, as elsewhere, was used partly to create new units but mainly to raise strengths in existing ones, thereby improving training and hastening mobilization.[403] Such units as were created were specified in a new cadres law, passed in April 1914, whose main implications were for the artillery, as the infantry and cavalry had been reorganized by the laws of December 1912 and March 1913.[404] The Three-Year Law, the new cadres law, and an extraordinary credit of 1,143 million francs for the War Ministry approved in a law of 15 July 1914 were the main French legislative responses to the German bill.[405] Unlike in Germany, *matériel* was treated separately from manpower and provided later. Moreover, whereas the German law had much of its impact from 1 October 1913, the French one, like the Belgian, would take full effect after a delay, which in Russia would be longer still. In what follows, the manpower and equipment issues will therefore be kept separate. But the first point to establish is the catalytic function of the German measure.

The most thoroughly researched analysis of the Three-Year Law has concluded that it would not have passed without the German bill. The GGS admitted as much at the time.[406] The French response to the 1912 German law had been continued piecemeal reinforcement rather than sweeping new reorganization.[407] At the end of 1912 the War Ministry reviewed the question of equipment, and it presented a large new bill to the Chamber in February 1913.[408] But in manpower policy, despite the Balkan crisis, it envisaged no large change, and in June 1912 Millerand had rejected a return to three-year service. Several major dailies began to press for it, at least in the mounted arms,[409] but the twenty-seven-month service proposal mooted by the EMA's 3rd Bureau in November was much more modest. A portion of each conscript class would be encouraged to stay on until December, in return for extra harvest leave, thus alleviating agricultural labour shortages and giving extra security during the autumn turnover

[403] Moltke to Wenninger, 12 Aug. 1913 and 18 Feb. 1914 (report on implementation of Three-Year Law), ibid.

[404] Text of the law (15 Apr. 1914) in AN C7419.

[405] Text of the credit law in *Bulletin des lois de la République française, 1914*, vi, 7325.

[406] Krumeich, *Armaments*, 17. Moltke to Wenninger, 12 Aug. 1913, KAM MKr. 992.

[407] See discussion in Ch. 4, sect. 2, above.

[408] Etienne to Klotz, 24 Feb. 1913, SHA 7.N. 134.

[409] G. Michon, *La Préparation à la guerre: La Loi de trois ans (1910–1914)* (Paris, 1935), 98–9, 104.

at no additional cost.[410] Plans were also under discussion to encourage long-term volunteering, make more use of reservist formations, and increase the numbers of experienced cavalrymen.[411] But as late as 30 January 1913 the German attaché correctly reported that the incoming Briand Government was cautious in its statements about three-year service and seemed wedded to lesser expedients.[412] What made the difference was the news from Berlin.

The first press rumour of German intentions came on 8 January. Jules Cambon and the Berlin attaché, Lt.-Col. Serret, quickly confirmed that a bill was coming, though they underestimated its size. The Ambassador saw it as the consequence of the Balkan crisis and the weakening of Austria-Hungary; Serret as the unfolding of a programme whose origins went back to Agadir and whose objective was less war than to enhance Germany's leverage in the next diplomatic trial of strength. There was a race for quality, in which France must keep the lead.[413] On 20 February the semi-official *Le Temps* opened the public debate by calling in response for the re-establishment of three-year service in all arms. It clashed with the Socialist daily, *L'Humanité*, but otherwise won general support, and observers were impressed by the depth and unanimity of feeling on the issue.[414]

The decisions taken in Paris in late February and early March fell to a weaker ministry than that of the previous year. Millerand had resigned over the du Paty de Clam affair and Poincaré had been elected President of the Republic in January, with the intention of using the considerable powers theoretically vested in his office in order to safeguard the continuity of foreign and defence policy.[415] His successor as Premier was Aristide Briand, whose War Minister was Eugène Etienne. Briand, Etienne, and Klotz, the Finance Minister, conferred with Joffre in the first half of February, anxiety about the frontier defences being a major theme. On 15 February Etienne spoke to Poincaré about 'the necessity of increasing the length of military service, to have higher numbers of effectives and a stronger *couverture*. The measures taken in Germany have convinced the War Ministry of the urgency of parallel dispositions.' Etienne wanted three-year service, but the rest of the Cabinet were uncertain. The public debate suggested that French opinion would wish to maintain the principle of equal liability, but Poincaré and Joffre were not immediately convinced that a three-year term was necessary, and Klotz opposed it. Intermediate periods were suggested, such as the twenty-seven months favoured by the President of the Chamber Army Commission. By the time of a critical meeting of the CSG on 4 March, however, the Government was hardening behind Etienne.[416]

[410] EMA 1st Bureau to Millerand, 15 Nov. 1912, SHA 7.N. 110.

[411] Ibid.; and EMA 1st Bureau note on the reserves, Dec. 1912, 5 and 6 Jan. 1913, ibid., J. J.-C. Joffre, *Mémoires du Maréchal Joffre* (Paris, 1932), i. 86.

[412] Winterfeldt report, 6 Jan. 1913, PAAA R.6755.

[413] Krumeich, *Armaments*, 44. Serret to War Ministry, 20, 31 Jan., 15 Feb., 1 Mar. 1913; Jules Cambon to Jonnart, 24 Jan., 12 Feb. 1913, *DDF* 3rd ser. iv, docs. 239, 302, 404, 494; 253, 380.

[414] Poincaré, Notes journalières, 17, 18, 20 Feb. 1913, BN Poincaré MSS n.a.fr. 16024.

[415] J. F. V. Keiger, *France and the Origins of the First World War* (London, 1983), 117–18.

[416] Krumeich, *Armaments*, 46–9. Joffre, *Mémoires*, 87–92. Poincaré, Notes journalières, 15, 17, 27 Feb. 1913, BN Poincaré MSS n.a.fr. 16024.

The CSG worked to an agenda agreed beforehand by the Council of Ministers,[417] apparently giving technical answers to technical questions. Yet it was constitutionally a gathering of corps commanders rather than a vehicle for civil–military liaison, Klotz, for example, being unable to attend and air his views. None the less, the decisions of the 4 March meeting were accepted by the Council of Ministers and incorporated in the bill presented to the Chamber. In addition to the military chiefs, Briand and Etienne were present, and Poincaré took the chair. According to Joffre, with whose analysis the other generals concurred, the German army's mobilization was already faster than France's and the new law would speed it up further. The field army would be able to go over to a war footing simply by requisitioning horses, without calling up reservists. It might be able to break the French *couverture* and interrupt the concentration as the troops detrained. The *couverture* must be increased to eleven divisions, composed of units permanently at war strength or able to be raised to it in a day. In the interior, company strengths of at least 150 were required, so that when the reservists joined they would not exceed 100 out of 250. The estimates discussed at the meeting suggested that three-year service would provide more men than Joffre needed, but twenty-seven-month and thirty-month compromises were rejected and the meeting unanimously approved the full term. Anything less would not give the cavalry the experienced men that were necessary, and would perpetuate the army's weaknesses in training and preparedness. As Poincaré concluded, unit strengths had fallen not only because of the declining birth rate but also because the law of 1909 had expanded the artillery at the other arms' expense, as had railway building and maintenance and the formation of aviation, wireless, and machine-gun units. The *couverture* could not withstand surprise attack, incoming recruits could not be properly trained, and on mobilization the serving men would be too few in relation to the reservists. Only three-year service could remedy these deficiencies, and close the autumn 'gap' while the new recruits were training. For reasons of equity and to raise the numbers, there could be no exemptions.

There was a potential divide between the preoccupations of the military and the politicians' need for arguments to command a wider debate. Joffre's concerns were less defensive than they might seem. He wanted a strong *couverture* to protect the concentration, but this concentration would be the prelude to an offensive, and, as he put it, if 'better trained and more cohesive, our units will evidently possess a greater offensive power'.[418] The papers prepared for the meeting by the EMA's 1st Bureau elaborated on these points. As Heeringen rebuffed the SPD, so the EMA rejected Jaurès's proposals to suppress the active army and rely on a militia doing six-months' service. These, they argued, would allow only a passive defence, leave enemy territory inviolate, and were accompanied by misguided professions of faith in the Hague Conference system. A three-year term, in contrast, would 'enhance the offensive value of our mobilized

---

[417] Ibid., 3 and 4 Mar. 1913. Minutes of the 4 Mar. session in SHA 1.N. 11.   [418] Ibid.

active formations'. New creations of mobile heavy artillery and mounted batteries would reduce disparities with other armies and add to the attacking potential.[419] The Reinach-Montebello amendment, by specifying higher company strengths, conformed with EMA thinking, even though by allowing some 60,000 of the extra class to be discharged it conflicted with the equal service principle. In preparing recommendations on the amendment the 1st Bureau intended that the *couverture* units should be raisable to war strength 'immediately and in one single stage', and that in the interior units the proportion of reservists added on mobilization should be reduced 'to a figure low enough to maintain their offensive value and cohesion'.[420]

Although the timing of the Three-Year Law was decided by the news from Germany, and without the consequent alarm it would not have passed, the French response reflected the EMA's grievances against two-year service and its conversion to the strategic offensive as much as it did fears of a standing-start attack. The law was less connected with the neeeds of military and diplomatic crisis management than in Austria-Hungary, Germany, and Belgium, and the winter crisis alone would not have made it politically feasible. In the spring of 1913 the preparations for Plan XVII were reaching a point of decision, the CSG on 18 April debating the EMA 3rd Bureau's 'Bases du Plan', and Etienne on 2 May approving a framework document that set the lines for the remaining detailed work before the plan could take effect.[421] One consequence of the Balkan Wars was to lend the preparations new vigour, Joffre writing to Millerand on 24 October 1912 that a revision was urgent and that he needed the infantry cadres law voted through. Although he considered the strategic balance generally was evolving favourably, there was growing evidence from German railway building that the enemy was likely to envelop Belgium, and Variant No. 2 to Plan XVI, adopted in April 1913, moved the centre of gravity of the French concentration yet further north and closer to the border.[422]

Like the Three-Year Law, Plan XVII was directed towards the offensive, and in this it can be seen as another reaction against Jaurès, as well as expressing the confidence of the High Command. It is true that Joffre had reservations about the notorious enthusiasm of Colonel de Grandmaison and the 'Young Turks' of the General Staff for the tactical offensive, although de Grandmaison, as head of the 3rd Bureau, was responsible for new infantry regulations, adopted in October 1913.[423] As regards the strategic offensive, Plan XVII was a concentration plan, but did not prescribe the course of operations beyond that point. No such plan of operations was developed, and Joffre regarded the matter as his personal concern. Even the concentration arrangements were notable for their sup-

---

[419] EMA 1st Bureau note for CSG, 3 Mar. 1913; and 'Exposé des motifs', n.d., SHA 1.N. 11.

[420] CSG session of 24 Apr. 1913; EMA 1st Bureau report to CSG, 23 Apr. 1913, ibid. Poincaré, Notes journalières, 24 and 25 Apr. 1913, BN Poincaré MSS n.a.fr. 16024.

[421] Minute of CSG, 14 Apr. 1913, with supporting documentation; EMA report to Etienne, 2 May 1913, SHA 1.N. 11.

[422] Joffre, *Mémoires*, i. 162–6.

[423] D. Porch, *The March to the Marne* (Cambridge, 1981), ch. 5.

pleness. The deployment zone could be moved forwards, backwards, and sideways after concentration began, and there was discretion to decide where each army would detrain. Joffre's guiding principle, none the less, as he expected the war to be decided in the first engagements, was to commit his reserves at once, in order to keep the initiative, to adhere to the convention with Russia, and to protect France from invasion. For all his stress on flexibility, this was no longer a defensive–offensive conception, and it necessitated a complete reworking of Plan XVI.[424]

The 3rd Bureau's 'Bases du Plan' justified the reappraisal with an analysis of the European situation that resembled that of Moltke and Ludendorff in its assumption that Germany could no longer depend on Austro-Hungarian or Italian support.[425] On the other hand, it feared that with the new army law even Germany's *couverture* units would be strong enough to achieve a 'rupture', which youthful, cohesive, and well-trained troops from the interior could follow through. This was to project on to the potential enemy the capability sought by the EMA for France itself. Against this challenge the French must rely largely on their own resources, but Russia was increasingly able to act effectively in the East and assistance from the Royal Navy was thought certain, even if the EMA planned on the assumption of no BEF assistance. Since Plan XVI had been adopted France had passed the infantry cadres law and knocked a day or two off concentration by improving its railways. It had also become clearer that reserve divisions could be used in the front line, if not for offensive operations. But without three-year service the other changes made would be inadequate for the new strategic requirements, and for the 3rd Bureau the Three-Year Law and Plan XVII were inextricably interconnected. The CSG acknowledged the link when it approved most of the planning documentation without change.[426] Three-year service, and a further law in December 1913 creating a new 21st Corps at Epinal, set the legislative foundations for Plan XVII. In his February 1914 'Instructions on the Concentration' to the army commanders, Joffre affirmed that he would take the offensive when his forces were assembled, while leaving his strategic options open for decision at the time,[427] and on 1 April Plan XVII took effect.

So much for the military rationale. The EMA's projects would never have been realized, however, without support from the French civilian leadership, which had to carry a public that was little concerned with Joffre's offensive schemes. As Izvolsky summarized French press comment, it acknowledged that the Germans had to counter the diversion of Austro-Hungarian forces, and that an attack was not imminent. None the less, France had to stop its neighbour from gaining a big enough advantage to be able to pierce the *couverture*.[428] This was a defensive preoccupation, which to an extent French statesmen shared. Poincaré was infuriated by suggestions that Germany was retaliating against

[424] Joffre, *Mémoires*, i. chs. 9–10.
[425] EMA 3rd Bureau, 'Plan XVII: Bases du Plan' (n.d. but Apr. 1913?), SHA 1.N. 11.
[426] CSG minute, 18 Apr. 1913, ibid.   [427] Joffre, *Mémoires*, i. 189.
[428] Izvolsky to Sazonov, 27 Feb. and 13 Mar. 1913, Stieve (ed.), *Isvolski*, iii, docs. 748, 763.

French preparations. He noted France's abstention from using article 33 of the 1905 law to keep an extra class under arms during the Moroccan crisis. He was equally outraged by a characteristically maladroit Order of the Day issued by Wilhelm on 10 March, proclaiming that if Germany had to defend its honour and interests it would fight 'with a joyful heart'. On the same day the *Kölnische Zeitung* accused France of seeking revenge for 1870 and of being the principal *Störenfried*, the disturber of the peace. '*France* the threat', the President exploded in his diary,

What an audacious lie! . . . It is Germany that menaced us without provocation in 1875, in 1887, in 1905, in 1908, in 1911 . . . The young Frenchmen of today have drawn the conclusion: that their fathers' resignation has not disarmed the conqueror. For us the question is no longer a question of revenge, it is a question of a threat. And it is against this threat that they desire our peaceloving country to be militarily armed.[429]

Poincaré's position was more complex than this might suggest. At the 4 March CSG he had understood and endorsed the army's arguments that three-year service was needed to pursue an offensive strategy, and he regarded the German increase as 'beneficial' in so far as it would refute the arguments of French pacifists and demonstrate the need for military reorganization.[430] To an extent the tension that developed with Germany in the spring of 1913 was useful to French governments, although they wished to keep it under control. This ambivalence was evident under both Briand and Louis Barthou, who took over as Premier in March, Etienne continuing as War Minister. Briand recommended his successor to Poincaré as a man who could pass the three-year bill, and Barthou placed it at the head of his ministry's objectives.[431]

Jules Cambon had warned of the febrile irritation of German court and military circles, quite unlike the mood of 1908 or even 1911. Serret dwelt on the dangerous exaltation roused by the 1813 centenary.[432] Hence French diplomacy was concerned to reassure. The inexperienced Jonnart, Briand's Foreign Minister, told the German Ambassador that the French did not see Germany's bill as a 'provocative gesture', and that its own measures were not a direct response but the outcome of months of consideration. Not only was this a damaging admission, but it was, at best, a half-truth. Poincaré told the Germans that their measures were 'understandable', but it was equally understandable that France should strive not to be militarily inferior. Subsequently, Jonnart admitted that the Three-Year Law was a response to the German one, but suggested that it might be cut to thirty months if there were no more articles like the *Störenfried* one. The attitude of the French press was 'most deplorable', and the Government was trying to restrain it. When Pichon took over, he emphasized

[429] Poincaré, Notes journalières, 4, 11, Mar. 1913, BN Poincaré MSS n.a.fr. 16204.

[430] Isvolsky to Sazonov, 27 Feb. 1913, Stieve (ed.), *Isvolski*, iii, doc. 747.

[431] Poincaré, Notes journalières, 25 Mar. 1913, BN Poincaré MSS n.a.fr. 16024. R. J. Young, *Power and Pleasure: Louis Barthou and the Third French Republic* (Montreal, 1991).

[432] Jules Cambon to Jonnart and Paléologue, 17 Mar. 1913, Serret to War Ministry, 15 Mar. 1913, *DDF* 3rd ser. vi, docs. 12(i), 13.

his wish for peace and *rapprochement*.[433] To some extent these overtures were reciprocated, Jagow telling Jules Cambon that the *Störenfried* article was not officially inspired, and the *Norddeutsche Allgemeine Zeitung* declaring, unconvincingly, that Germany's bill was directed against no Power in particular.[434] None the less, in March and April there was a succession of frontier incidents. There were scuffles between the local inhabitants and Germans who had crossed the border for a night out at Nancy; German boy scouts crossed over as a joke; and a German aircraft and a Zeppelin landed on French territory, though both were allowed to return. Trivial in themselves, the incidents occurred when the military bills were being negotiated through both legislatures, but the French authorities' handling of them showed their resolve to keep the situation in hand.[435]

The other side of the policy was the public justification developed for the Three-Year Law. At the 4 March CSG Poincaré and Briand had been anxious about how to justify the measure to Parliament. If it was to stay in place after the current anxiety subsided, felt the Premier, they would need 'serious arguments, convincing arguments, not technical ones that perhaps will not be understood'.[436] Accordingly, a communiqué issued after the meeting said that the army must be strengthened because the *couverture* could not resist a surprise attack.[437] In a speech at Rennes Etienne suggested that the Germans were approaching double France's peacetime strength, and demanded of his audience whether they wished to be vassals and satellites. According to the German Ambassador in June, both inside and outside Parliament German superiority and the danger of surprise attack was the essential consideration being cited.[438] Three-year service was sold as a response to an emergency, not the concomitant of an offensive strategy.

This emphasis is evident in the Government's fullest statement of its case, the confidential briefing of the Chamber Army Commission in March 1913 by Etienne and Joffre. Their statements may be compared with those of Heeringen and Groener to the Reichstag Budget Commission, in their combination of apparent frankness with a forensic drive to impress. Thus, little was said about the army's strategic planning, although Joffre and his sous-chef, General Legrand, emphasized that the *couverture* must be in place and the reservists absorbed as fast as possible. 'For us the essential is to get the upper hand in the first engagements.' Etienne, in contrast, shared some of Berchtold's concern with military–diplomatic liaison. When it was pointed out that under the 1905 law the authorities could already retain and recall conscript classes, he replied that they could do so only for twelve months, and 'each year you will be making this spectacular demonstration in the eyes of Europe that you are putting yourself on a

[433] Schoen to Foreign Ministry, 19 and 22 Feb., 13 and 27 Mar. 1913, *GP* xxxix, docs. 15626, 15627, 15633, 15636.
[434] Jules Cambon to Jonnart, 11 and 12 Mar. 1913, *DDF* 3rd ser. v, docs. 563, 569.
[435] Poincaré, *Service*, iii, ch. 8.
[436] CSG minutes, 4 Mar. 1913, SHA 1.N. 11. [437] Krumeich, *Armaments*, 51.
[438] Schoen to Bethmann, 17 June 1913, *GP* xxxix, doc. 15647.

war footing'. France must be strong enough 'to provide against the future, to speak with authority abroad, to make her rights and dignity respected'. But his primary concern was deterrence. He did not believe that Germany meant at present to 'fall on' France, but circumstances might arise in which it felt obliged to fight even though not wanting to. It would show restraint if it found a French peacetime strength of over 600,000 and a well-prepared north-eastern frontier, and as France would not start a war French might was the best guarantee of peace. At present both sides had approximately equal covering forces, but Germany's new bill would give it the advantage on the frontiers, and 'once the *couverture* has been breached, I think it would all be over'.[439]

None the less, in its final form the Three-Year Law was so amended as to render the army in certain ways less able either to implement Plan XVII or to deter a German attack, at least until the end of the transition period. The problem was not merely one of numbers. To extend by a year the service of the senior class currently under arms would be the quickest way to increase the proportion of trained manpower in the army and to bridge the gap to the future in which one class with two years of service would be the norm. But the men would resent it, and it would make the bill harder to get through. It was already clear that the Socialists would oppose the measure, which Jaurès condemned as reactionary. On 1 March they issued a joint manifesto with the SPD.[440] The Right and Centre would support it, although they feared that it would be used to justify the introduction of a progressive personal income tax, and wanted to finance it through borrowing. This meant that the Radicals held the balance. At first they warily supported the measure, although they insisted that the principle of equal liability to service must be maintained, and they wanted an income tax to pay for it.[441]

The greatest challenge to the Government came after 4 May, when Barthou announced that he had decided to keep on the senior conscript class for another year.[442] The EMA considered that the authorities were in their rights in invoking their powers under the law of 1905: there would be a 'grave peril' from 1 October if a reinforced German army faced a French one with only one trained cohort.[443] But the reaction endangered both the ministry and the bill itself.[444] The Radicals wanted Barthou toppled, and joined the Left in backing the Paul-Boncour/Messimy counter-proposal—a compromise based on a thirty-month term. On 15 May the Government endured a very difficult debate,[445] and in the next week a wave of protests and demonstrations spread among the troops, including those in Paris and on the Eastern frontier. The Interior Ministry judged that the soldiers' revolts were 'a co-ordinated movement', and on 25–6 May the police raided over 600 Socialist and syndicalist offices nationwide. But

[439] Chamber Army Commission, 11 and 18 Mar. 1913, AN C7421.
[440] Copy in AN F7 13335.   [441] Krumeich, *Armaments*, ch. 3.
[442] Ibid. 88.   [443] EMA 1st Bureau, note of 13 May 1913, SHA 7.N. 134.
[444] Lancken report, 16 May 1913, PAAA R.6755.
[445] Winterfeldt report, 16 May 1913, ibid. Krumeich, *Armaments*, 91.

no evidence was found for CGT subversion. The men tried were mostly soldiers, and civilian agitators had little role. The CGT was becoming more moderate anyway, and co-operated with the Socialists' parliamentary campaign against the bill, although the disturbances made the Radicals less willing to align themselves with the SFIO.[446]

The outcome of the May crisis was that the Socialists rather than Barthou became isolated, although partly because Ministers made concessions on two fronts. Initially they had proposed a million-franc loan to pay for three-year service and re-equipment, with higher excise duties to cover interest and amortization. When the Radical majority in the Chamber Budget Committee threw the idea out, the Government recommended instead a progressive income tax, rather than a German-style capital levy.[447] The second concession was to release the 1910 class. Wilhelm II had been jubilant at the news of the soldiers' revolts and Poincaré profoundly depressed, fearing mass desertions. The police urged the Government to set a date for the men's discharge.[448] Poincaré encouraged Barthou to accept the Escudier amendment, which lowered the age of incorporation from 21 to 20 and facilitated the early release of the 1910 class by enabling two younger ones (1912 and 1913) to be called up as an alternative.[449] At the price, as Jaurès pointed out, of contradicting its own logic, the Government was able to defeat the Paul-Boncour/Messimy counter-proposal and on 19 July to split the Radicals and to carry three-year service by 358 : 204. The Chamber voted that the 1913 class would be the first to serve three years, thus postponing the full benefit of the measure until 1915–16. Until the end, the debate was dominated by discussion of the German build-up and the danger of surprise attack. In answer to that danger there would be created in the autumn an army that was numerically larger but two-thirds composed of raw recruits.[450]

The implications were not lost on German observers. According to Winterfeldt the Three-Year Law had been diluted for reasons of political expediency. It would increase French military power, but have less effect than Germany's bill. Although the French officer corps were pleased with it, they knew the transition would be arduous. It would be hard to train both new classes properly, and desertion, indiscipline, and anti-militarism were likely to increase. Only later would the benefits to confidence, training, and preparedness accrue.[451] The GGS analysis was similar,[452] Wilhelm telling the Austro-Hungarian attaché that in contrast to the situation in Germany the French autumn changeover had begun in confusion. Too little accommodation was available, and recruits had had to be

[446] Ibid. 94–9. See Ministry of Interior circulars in AN F7 13736; the quotation is from Pujalet to Administrator of Belfort, 22 May 1913.

[447] Krumeich, *Armaments*, 100–1. Poincaré, Notes journalières, 17 May 1913, BN Poincaré MSS n.a.fr. 16024.

[448] Porch, *March*, 188–9.

[449] Poincaré, Notes journalières, 1–2 July 1913, BN Poincaré MSS n.a.fr. 16024.

[450] Krumeich, *Armaments*, ch. 5.

[451] Winterfeldt report, 20 Aug. 1913, *GP* xxxix, doc. 15653.

[452] Moltke to Wenninger, 12 Aug. 1913, 18 Feb. 1914, KAM MKr. 992.

sent home.[453] The EMA, however, foresaw the strain on its NCOs, and planned to train the 1912 class intensely before the bad weather, the 1913 class following a gentler schedule.[454] By December there was official optimism. The entire *couverture* had been raised to reinforced strength, and extra infantry and artillery units were being created. The manpower shortages that had blocked progress hitherto were completely removed. The minimum strength levels in the interior set by the law were exceeded in all units, and the additional younger men would rejuvenate the active formations, improve training, and facilitate mobilization.[455] By the spring of 1914 the GGS, too, was more impressed, noting that the 1913 call-up had yielded many more men than predicted. It expected that by the succeeding winter France's unit strengths in trained manpower would exceed Germany's in every arm except the cavalry. Although the French might relax their current level of effort, it appeared that the moment of German opportunity before the reorganization began to bite would be brief.[456]

French disadvantage would last longer, though not indefinitely, in *matériel*. Whereas Germany's bill included large expenditure on equipment, the Three-Year Law was a manpower measure. Both sides acknowledged that the French had greatly improved their railways; that they had spent heavily on their eastern fortresses; and that they were in the lead in aircraft. But they were behind in infantry equipment (rifles, wireless, field kitchens) and in howitzers and heavy guns. This Moltke perceived as the second element in his Western opportunity. It can be explained partly at the budgetary level and partly at the procurement one.

Poincaré and Millerand had already lost precious time by curtailing Messimy's equipment programme. In November 1912, however, against the background of the Balkan crisis, the Chamber Budget Commission asked if Millerand wanted more, and he drew up an expenditure schedule. A conference on 14 February of War and Finance Ministry representatives and of parliamentarians was willing, in view of the reports from Germany, for part of the programme to be implemented in secret. But at this point disclosure of the story to *Le Temps* obliged the legislature to insist on authorization, and a bill was presented for 420 million francs of expenditure on artillery, fortifications, and railways over five years. Joffre felt that this was too little, and decided to profit from the Chambers' generous mood. In April he came forward with new demands, and 504.5 million francs was added to the 420, Etienne justifying the additions on the grounds that Germany's bill meant France must do more. Of the 504.5 million 364 was to go on artillery and only 27.9 million on fortifications: an index of the contrast between French and German priorities. German rearmament transformed the War Ministry's and the EMA's assessment of what was politically feasible

[453] Bienerth to Krobatin, 22 Dec. 1913, KAW KM Präs (1914) 47–4.
[454] EMA 1st Bureau to War Minister, 2 Sept. 1913; circular of 22 Oct. 1913, SHA 7.N. 112.
[455] EMA 1st Bureau notes in reply to parliamentary questions, 13 and 17 Dec. 1913, ibid.
[456] Moltke to Wenninger, 18 Feb. 1914, KAM MKr. 992.

as well as of its urgency, as most of the extra spending was targeted for 1913–14.[457]

From here on, however, they got bogged down. The Finance Minister said he could not demand such sums, and wanted to reduce the 504.5 to 30 million: Etienne singled out 253.7 million in immediate needs. After unsatisfactory experiences in the September manœuvres, the EMA presented yet further claims. A single consolidated bill was drawn up to pay for three-year service, the new cadres law, the creation of the 21st Corps, and the equipment schedule.[458] More changes of ministry and a general election delayed its passage until 15 July 1914. Designed to equip France for 'the next war', it was—in the end—a formidable measure. 389 million francs over four years (in addition to an interim 234.5 million voted in 1913) would pay for three-year service and the cadres law; 754.5 million over seven years would go on *matériel* (28.2 on railways, 21.4 on aviation, 231.3 million on construction and fortification, and 404.3 million on artillery); 211 million of the total was earmarked for 1914.[459] By comparison with an estimated equipment expenditure of 269.6 million in 1908–13, this was huge.[460] It was also too late, and the saga of the armaments credit was a case history in the weaknesses of the French political process.

There was a genuine financial obstacle. The Three-Year Law alone, leaving aside re-equipment, approached the cost of the German bill.[461] The Finance Ministry was trapped between the services' demands and a parliamentary deadlock over income tax. The Paris capital market was far larger than that of Berlin or Vienna, but the Government had to balance its own needs against Russian and Serbian flotations. In any case the Radicals opposed a loan, and their October 1913 Pau Congress supported paying for military spending by means of income tax and a capital levy. This notwithstanding, Barthou's draft 1914 budget envisaged only minor tax increases and heavy borrowing, with tax exemption on the loan interest. The resulting uproar brought his ministry down, and its Radical-dominated successor, under Gaston Doumergue, introduced a bill for a new tax on capital, which was defeated in the more conservative Senate. It was only on the eve of war that the impasse was resolved, Parliament agreeing in June 1914 to a massive loan, 600 million francs of which was for rearmament, but the Senate voting on 2 July for a progressive income tax.[462] As in Britain and Germany defence expenditure was a battering ram that broke up political alignments and forced fiscal change, though the greater scope for borrowing cushioned the impact. But the financial problem brought down the Government that

[457] Joffre, *Mémoires*, i. 53–6. Poincaré, Notes journalières, 18 Mar. 1913, BN Poincaré MSS, n.a.fr. 16024. War Minister to Finance Minister, 24 Feb. and 24 Apr. 1913, SHA 7.N. 134.

[458] Etienne to Joffre, 8 Oct. 1913, ibid. Joffre, *Mémoires*, i. 56–9. On the Sept. manœuvres, Moltke to Wenninger, 10 Dec. 1913, KAM MKr. 992.

[459] For text of the law, cf. n. 405 above.

[460] F. Crouzet, 'Recherches sur la production d'armements en France (1815–1913)', *Revue historique*, 509 (1974), 84.

[461] Moltke to Wenninger, 12 Aug. 1913, KAM MKr. 992.

[462] Krumeich, *Armaments*, 100–1, 131–43, 157–60, 212. Financial law of 20 June 1914 in *Bulletin des lois de la République française*, 1914, vi/7199.

had introduced three-year service and drove the Radicals back into opposition to the measure. The effect of ministerial instability and the military leadership's chopping and changing was to decouple manpower from weaponry and delay the passage of the military credit until two weeks after the Sarajevo assassinations.

Budgetary stringency helped to postpone procurement decisions. Joffre acknowledged that the Lebel rifle was not as good as Germany's, but it was good enough, and the 465 million francs needed to replace it would be better spent elsewhere. It was over his protests, however, that the Chamber Budget Commission decided in March 1913 to save 80 million francs by rejecting the development of a light field howitzer and adopting the *plaquette Malandrin*, a device to be fitted to the 75 mm field gun to allow it to fire along a curved trajectory. This solution was cheap, but not the ballistic equivalent of the German weapon. Munitions provision for the 75 mm guns had reached 1,390 rounds each by 1914, but this fell well below the 3,000 that it was estimated (as it proved, extremely conservatively) might be needed after the experience of the Balkan Wars. In February 1914, moreover, again over Joffre's objections, it was decided not to renew the contingency agreements with private industry for expanding munitions production in the event of hostilities.[463] For a decade after the turn of the century the French artillery had rested its confidence on the superiority of the 75 mm. Now that it realized Germany's advantages in other respects, its countermoves were tragically slow.

The problem was not just the hold-up in approving the armaments credit. There were additional difficulties over manpower, organization, and production. By 1912 the extra officer posts specified in the 1909 artillery law had been created, but additional manpower depended on a struggle with the navy. Fifty batteries and 270,000 men were immobilized in defence of the littoral, and Joffre wanted to transfer at least some of them to the north-east. In the CSG in November 1912 Poincaré objected that Britain might stay neutral and the Channel be left exposed. The navy eventually agreed to take over the seafront guns of its principal bases, but not until April 1914 were men released from the coastal batteries, at a time when three-year service was making more personnel available anyway.[464] Coupled with the legislative authorization given in the new cadres law it was now possible, none the less, to establish five regiments of heavy field artillery, although the task was not completed when war broke out, and in part it was a pirating operation.[465] Of the fifty-eight batteries making up the regiments in peacetime, twenty-one already existed, twenty-two were transferred from the coast, and only fifteen were new creations. On mobilization they would double to 116 batteries, with 504 guns. Although still a provisional arrangement, the reorganization was considered by the War Minister to be 'of the first urgency', and it was 'indispensable' that it should take effect with Plan XVII.

[463] Joffre, *Mémoires*, i. 48, 69–70, 77–8.
[464] CSG minutes, 23 Nov. 1912, 3 May 1913, SHA 1.N. 10. CSDN minutes, 17 May 1913, 26 Feb., 7 Mar., 3 July 1914, SHA 2.N. 1.
[465] Joffre, *Mémoires*, i. 70–1.

The EMA expected it to give the High Command 'much more powerful means of action than in the past': it would double the number of heavy howitzers and entail the introduction of a quite new heavy cannon.[466]

Most of this new material had yet to become available in April 1914, however, and the heavy field artillery went to war with outdated arms. Apart from 104 of the 155 mm Rimailhos, themselves of indifferent performance, their weapons comprised siege and fortress guns, seconded until new and mobile quick-firing pieces became available. Joffre blamed the perfectionism and incompetence of the War Ministry and its rivalry with private industry, although there was a more fundamental failure to agree on a heavy artillery doctrine. In April 1913 the army took the unprecedented step of ordering 220 Schneider heavy cannon, only to cut the number to thirty-six. Similarly, a Schneider 105 mm howitzer was rejected in favour of the *plaquette Malindrin*. In 1914 France still lacked a light field howitzer, the long-range heavy cannon were only just becoming available, and the heavy howitzers were mostly adapted older models. Its siege artillery was similarly outdated, eighteen 280 mm mortars being ordered from Schneider in November 1913, but for delivery in two years' time.[467] The GGS was fully aware of the limitations of current provision and the prospective improvement from 1915.[468] Thereafter the French army would not only be at higher strength but also better trained and integrated, the artillery reorganization would have bedded down and new siege and heavy field guns would be coming into use. But in the interim the opportunity was there—and still more so if account is taken of the Russian dimension of the Franco-Russian alliance. Hence, in part, the paradox that the measure christened by Poincaré 'the indispensable ransom of peace' became a harbinger of war.[469]

* * *

In Russia the winter crisis had a greater impact than in France on immediate military readiness, but the Great Programme of army development was triggered by the German bill. As for the other main development of this period, the Franco-Russian railway agreement, a further mini-crisis with Germany—the Liman von Sanders incident, which will be discussed in the next chapter—was necessary to end tsarist prevarication. None the less, internal pressures for expansion were probably more important and external shock waves less so in Russia than elsewhere. Major military innovation was coming anyway, although the Balkan Wars helped to break down resistance. The combination of financial buoyancy with negligible internal opposition gave the autocracy an unparalleled

[466] EMA 1st Bureau report to War Minister, 12 Dec. 1913, SHA 7.N. 112. EMA 1st Bureau note for Director of Artillery, 7 Nov. 1913, SHA 7.N. 134. EMA 3rd Bureau note on heavy field artillery, Jan. 1914, SHA 7.N. 50.

[467] Joffre, *Mémoires*, i. 66–73. Porch, *March*, ch. 12. Note on armament and organization of the artillery for CSG session of 15 Oct. 1913, SHA 1.N. 11. Etienne to Humbert, 22 Aug. 1913, SHA 7.N. 134.

[468] Moltke to Wenninger, 18 Feb. 1914, KAM MKr. 992.

[469] Schoen to Bethmann, 9 June 1913, PAAA R.6755.

opportunity to develop its armed strength, and it would have been untrue to itself had it not seized the moment.

The GGS, reviewing 'Russia's War Preparedness' in February 1914, already considered it unprecedented.[470] During the winter crisis the Russians had tested out the 1910 reorganization and ordered extra equipment. They had three special advantages over their neighbours. The first was frequent trial mobilizations. The sums allocated to them more than doubled in 1910–13; they took place in twelve military districts in April 1913 and eight in September.[471] The second was the 'Period Preparatory to War', the regulations for which were adopted in February 1913.[472] Modelled on Germany's own state of 'Threatening Danger of War', it required authorization from the Council of Ministers. Although supposedly consisting of measures to protect mobilization and concentration, it was not easily distinguished from mobilization itself, and the GGS was worried that the frontier army corps could secretly be readied before the call-up placards were posted. The third advantage was the retention of the senior conscript class. Although the class kept on in October 1912 was released in March 1913, the measure was repeated for the same length of time in the following winter. At the same time a bill described by Moltke as 'a very significant raising of Russian war preparedness' was introduced to extend service until April as a permanent feature. It was justified as being 'in line with the measures adopted by the Western European Powers to reinforce their armies', but it originated with the satisfaction felt by the Russian authorities with their measures in the crisis winter, which were felt 'very appreciably' to have raised preparedness for little cost.[473] The lessons learned in 1912–13 intensified what, to German eyes, were Russian military organization's most disturbing features.

In addition, the Russians embarked on a major enhancement of their medium-term preparedness. In part they were responding to clarion calls from Paris. According to *Le Temps*, on 26 February 1913, 'the new German projects impose on Russia as on France the duty of an effort for which both are ready . . . Our allies, happy to see that we shall not hesitate before this effort, will on their side do everything they judge necessary.' *Novoe Vremya* replied that France must increase its effectiveness and be strong enough to hold off an enemy surprise attack until Russia could mobilize and concentrate: 'if France does its direct duty in peacetime, war will become impossible for the simple reason that the Central European Powers will not decide on an affair which, even in the event of surprise, would promise them no success.'[474] Each Power made the other's enhancement of its deterrent strength a test of the alliance, and for each the alliance was a principal reason for responding to the German bill with measures of their own.

[470] GGS 1. Abt., 'Die Kriegsbereitschaft Russlands', Feb. 1914, KAM Gstb 925.

[471] GGS 1. Abt., 'Ergänzungen', 15 June and 1 Oct. 1913, KAM Gstb 209.

[472] See Ch. 5, sect. 1, above. Sukhomlinov, *Erinnerungen*, 343. A. M. Zaionchovsky, *Podgotovka Rossii k imperialisticheskoi voine (Plany voiny)* (Moscow, 1926), 120. Frantz, *Eintritt*, 22–3.

[473] Moltke to Auswärtiges Amt, 24 Oct. 1913, PAAA R.10432, also *GP* xxxix, doc. 15655. Wehrlin to War Ministry, 24 Oct. 1913, SHA 7.N. 1112.

[474] *Le Temps*, 26 Feb. 1913, AMAE NS Russie 42. *Novoe Vremya*, 1 Mar. 1913, SHA 7.N. 1478.

In the 1911 and 1912 staff talks France and Russia had committed themselves to early and simultaneous offensives against Germany, and it was towards enhancing France's offensive capacity that the Three-Year Law was directed. In addition, the measure was a bargaining weapon in St Petersburg. At the same time as the Briand Government turned its attention to military service, it was planning to replace Georges Louis as ambassador with Delcassé, a much more heavyweight figure than would normally occupy such a post but a man whose judgement in 1905 appeared to have been vindicated, and who enjoyed the backing of the President.[475] On his departure in March Poincaré and Jonnart gave him a letter reminding Nicholas of the 'great military effort the French Government proposed to make in order to uphold the balance of European forces'. The aim, wrote Poincaré to the Tsar, was to 'draw [the alliance] tighter'—France's sacrifices making it more urgent to construct the railways he had discussed in Russia in 1912.[476] On his arrival Delcassé found Nicholas full of admiration for the Three-Year Law and Sazonov concerned to see it go through: a message from Pichon confirmed France's resolve to keep its forces up to strength.[477] When Delcassé reported the bad effect created by the French soldiers' disturbances Pichon reassured him that they were a limited outbreak engineered by a conspiratorial group and that the Government was prosecuting the ringleaders.[478] Finally in July and August a delegation under Joffre arrived for a new round of staff talks, which confirmed the previous understanding. Joffre expected to attack Germany with at least 1.3 million men on day 11; Zhilinski with 0.7–0.8 million on day 15, although he hoped to knock two days off his concentration time by the end of 1914.[479]

From February 1913 onwards, the tsarist Government was subjected to continuous French pressure. This developed into a sustained and eventually successful attempt to tie an increase in Russian peacetime strength and strategic railway building to the granting of a major loan. But the Russians had been making up their minds even before Delcassé reached St Petersburg. On 24 February Buchanan reported that Nicholas had secretly ordered the formation of two new army corps in reply to the German bill.[480] A week later Sukhomlinov told Colonel Wehrlin of the French Embassy that the term of service would be extended to cover the winter gap, and the recruitment contingent enlarged.[481] A secret defence council on 19 March, chaired by Nicholas, considered in detail the response to Germany's armaments.[482] On Delcassé's arrival it was confirmed

---

[475] Poincaré, Notes journalières, 20 Feb. 1913, BN Poincaré MSS n.a.fr. 16024.

[476] Poincaré, *Service*, iii. 156. Poincaré to Nicholas II, 20 Mar. 1913, *DDF* 3rd ser. vi, doc. 39.

[477] Delcassé to Foreign Ministry, 21 and 24 Mar. 1913, Pichon to Delcassé, 27 Mar. 1913, ibid., docs. 44, 59, 72. Nicholas II to Poincaré, 30 Mar. 1913, Stieve (ed.), *Iswolski*, iii, doc. 800.

[478] Delcassé to Pichon, 24 May, Pichon to Delcassé, 25 May 1913, *DDF* 3rd ser. vi, docs. 603, 609.

[479] Minutes of August staff conversations, ibid. viii, doc. 79. War Minister to Foreign Minister, 2 Oct. 1913, AMAE NS Russie 42.

[480] Buchanan to Grey, 24 Feb. 1913, *BD* ix(ii), doc. 653.

[481] Wehrlin to War Ministry, 1 Mar. 1913, SHA 7.N. 1478.

[482] Doulcet to Jonnart, 20 Mar. 1913, *DDF* 3rd ser. vi, doc. 29.

that there would be extra corps and a big increase in the budget and the contingent, and that work would go ahead on the railways discussed with Poincaré.[483] By 1 April de Laguiche was able to report in detail on Russian thinking, which although still secret had now been approved by the Council of Ministers. One new corps would be created in the Warsaw military district and one in the Caucasus, as well as a new brigade in Finland and twenty-six cavalry regiments, mostly in Europe. As the suppression of permanent fortress garrisons in the 1910 reorganization had complicated mobilization, they would be re-established in the four main Polish strong points and in Vladivostok. The field artillery provision of each army corps would be raised to German levels and the heavy artillery doubled. To achieve all this the peacetime strength would rise by some 208,000, about half the extra men going to new units and half to raising existing company strengths. More railways would be needed to the western frontier, for which the General Staff had made 'vast' proposals, although they would not be accepted as they stood.[484]

Such was the embryo of the Great Programme. Although the Russian plans included reinforcements in Siberia and in Central Asia they appear to have originated as an answer to the German bill, encouraged by French lobbying. Sazonov, Kokovtsov, and Sukhomlinov all said that Russia was replying to Germany's measures, as did Nicholas, who told Buchanan that Russia must be ready to meet the danger of war and he was determined to maintain a 16:10 ratio between the Russian and German armies, analogous to that between the Royal Navy and the High Seas Fleet.[485] The Russian leaders claimed to understand that Germany had had to act to counterbalance the weakening of Austria-Hungary, but they maintained that they must take countermeasures.[486] Sukhomlinov's memoirs, however, portray his work thus far as the creation of a framework for expansion when funds became available, and implicitly downgrade the contribution of the German bill. The General Staff had been working on a development plan since 1912, and a draft was ready by the end of February. This was what was approved at the special conference on 19 March, and it resembled what was reported to de Laguiche. How much it was modified to take account of Germany's plans is unclear.[487] The Russians gave less importance than the other Powers to increasing strengths rather than forming new units, perhaps because the *couverture* was less vital to them, given their 1910 decision to mobilize in the rear and their acceptance that they could afford to lose Poland. As in France, however, work on reorganization and re-equipment went ahead in parallel with work on a new strategic plan (20), preparations for which began in May 1912 after the adoption of Plan 19 altered. More detailed study began early in 1913 and the plan was approved in October, originally to take effect in March

[483] Delcassé to Foreign Ministry, 21 and 24 Mar. 1913, ibid., docs. 44, 59.

[484] De Laguiche to War Ministry, 1 Apr. 1913, SHA 7.N. 1535, cf. summary of report to Joffre by Russian attaché, 18 Mar. 1913, ibid.

[485] Buchanan to Grey, 14 Apr. 1913, *BD* ix(ii), doc. 849.

[486] Wehrlin to War Ministry, 1 Mar. 1913, SHA 7.N. 1478.

[487] Sukhomlinov, *Erinnerungen*, 342. Shatsillo, *Rossia*, 96–7, 110 n.

1914 but subsequently postponed to December.[488] There are grounds for thinking, then, that Germany's bill gave the occasion for something that was intended already.

Unlike in France, moreover, the German bogey may not have been essential to overcome domestic opposition. The Duma was weaker than Western legislatures, and friendlier to army than naval expansion, the *rapporteur* of the War Ministry budget promising 'the most sympathetic reception' for proposals to reinforce *matériel* and effectives.[489] Sukhomlinov told de Laguiche that getting the programme through would be 'a simple formality', and that many deputies would want even more energetic measures. There would be some difficulty in accommodating extra troops, but it could be coped with, and in contrast to the officer shortage when Sukhomlinov took over there was now an excess.[490] Above all, there was money, even on top of the sums voted for the navy's Baltic programme in 1912: Kokovtsov's influence had been weakened in the winter crisis, and in any case in the spring of 1913 he had a budget surplus.[491] Except over strategic railways, he did not resist Sukhomlinov's demands. Nicholas told Buchanan that Germany could find the soldiers for its military law but might not long be able to bear the extra tax burden, whereas Russia had unlimited men and money.[492] The GGS reported in February 1914 that Russia had had another good harvest in the previous year and state revenues had continued to grow; the extraordinary measures during the Balkan crisis had been paid for without extra loans or taxes, and yet the contingency reserve was larger than ever. The economic boom continued, and despite unprecedented military spending there was no need for extra taxation or borrowing.[493] According to the French commercial attaché, the Government had not had to borrow since 1907, and the surplus on the ordinary account was more than enough to cover the deficit on the extraordinary one. The EMA agreed that the military programme could easily be afforded.[494] Kokovtsov's and the Russian economy's very success had destroyed the Finance Ministry's political leverage, and whereas Germany embarked on the Continental arms race in a mood of mounting desperation the Russian response reflected St Petersburg's growing confidence.

None the less, in the summer and autumn of 1913, the impetus given in the spring appeared to have been lost. It is true that there was a declaration of intent. Zhilinski told the Duma on 24 June that the Balkan Wars had made all the Powers re-examine their preparedness, and that because of the decisions taken in Western Europe in the spring Russia must raise strengths and reorganize the field artillery, which would mean a larger contingent and financial

[488] Zaionchovsky, *Podgotovka*, 302, 320.

[489] Press cutting from *Le Temps*, ?Mar. 1913, SHA 7.N. 1535.

[490] De Laguiche to War Ministry, 7 May 1913, ibid.

[491] Kokovtsov, *Out of my Past*, 362–4.

[492] G. Buchanan, *My Mission to Russia and Other Diplomatic Memories* (London, 1923), i. 182.

[493] Moltke to Wenninger, 26 Feb. 1914 (report on Russian army in 1913), KAM MKr. 992.

[494] Commercial attaché report on 1914 Russian budget, MFF B.31252. EMA, 'Note sur les projets d'augmentation de l'armée russe', July 1913, SHA 7.N. 1535.

sacrifice.[495] There seems to have been an argument in the War Ministry about tactics, a separate bill being prepared for a 'small programme' in artillery and aviation and some preliminary legislation being passed in 1913.[496] Action was taken by decree to raise the contingent and begin creating new formations, but even the French were confused about exactly what the Russians were doing.[497] A decree of April 1913 set the contingent at 455,000, as against 436,000 in 1912, the extra men going mainly to the Warsaw military district.[498] Only on 4 November did Nicholas approve the detailed General Staff project for the Great Programme, minuting that it was to be implemented with the highest urgency. The Council of Ministers acquiesced, and in the spring the project went to the Duma. In a secret session on 7 May 1914 a big majority, comprised of the Right and Centre, voted for a contingent of 580,000 from 1 January 1915, and with this precondition met the Great Programme itself was voted with little opposition on 7 July, the prolongation of service from October to April being approved in the same month.[499]

In contrast to Germany and France, Russia, like Austria-Hungary, delayed for over a year. Even once the detail was finalized the Russian leaders showed little haste until early in 1914, Zhilinski telling de Laguiche in February that he hoped the programme would be accepted by May.[500] The timing may have been connected with Plan 20, but more relevant was probably the worsening of relations with Germany and the intensification of Russian military and diplomatic effort that followed the Liman von Sanders affair. In February, moreover, the Stavka was informed by its Berlin attaché that the GGS was studying yet another bill to raise the German contingent, and the Great Programme may have been voted against the possibility of a further round of expansion.[501] Perhaps for this reason, when asked if the programme was their final demand, the military authorities replied that it 'follows one defined task—that is, the creation of new and the strengthening of existing army units in correspondence with those other army increases that are now being implemented in all Western European States after the Balkan War'. In the near future they expected to bring forward significant extra demands, as Germany was outstripping Russia in the pace of preparation and in their judgement war was not far away.[502]

[495] Zhilinski in Duma, 24 June 1913, ibid.

[496] Frantz, *Eintritt*, 25. Shatsillo, *Rossia*, 97, says the 'small programme' became law in 1913; E. Barsukov, *Russkaya artilleriya v mirovaya voiny* (Moscow, 1938), i. 17, says the artillery bill was introduced in June 1913. The sources do not concur.

[497] e.g. EMA 2nd Bureau study, 4 Apr. 1914; de Laguiche to Langlois, 28 Mar. 1914, SHA 7.N. 1535.

[498] EMA 2nd Bureau study of increase in Russian effectives, 5 May 1913, ibid.

[499] Shatsillo, *Rossia*, 97–100. EMA 2nd Bureau note for Joffre, 26 May 1914, SHA 7.N. 1535.

[500] De Laguiche to War Ministry, 22 Feb. 1914, ibid.; and 26 Feb. 1914, SHA 7.N. 1478.

[501] De Laguiche to War Ministry, 21 Feb. 1914, ibid. E. Adamov, 'K voprosi o podgotovke mirovoi voiny (iz dokumentov russkoi voenno-politicheskoi razvedki 1913–1914 gg)', *Krasnyi Arkhiv*, 64 (1934), reports by Bazarov to General Staff, 28 Feb. and 10 Mar. 1914. On Liman von Sanders, see Ch. 6, sect. 1.

[502] Shatsillo, *Rossia*, 99.

From the standpoint of Vienna and Berlin, none the less, the Russian plans were extremely menacing, and made more so by their reworking in 1913–14. Once again the connection with strategic planning must be borne in mind. Like Plan 19 altered, the Russian Plan 20 envisaged rapid offensives against both Central Powers, though with even shorter concentration times. The main blow would still fall on Austria-Hungary, but Germany received more emphasis than previously and the Russians expected numerical superiority over both their enemies. From favouring caution against Germany in 1910 Danilov now wanted an early attack, though less because of faith in tsarist strength than a sense that war with Germany was unavoidable and the best chance of winning lay in a co-ordinated Franco-Russian assault.[503] Overtures for such co-ordination were made to Paris in the run-up to the Scutari crisis, when what purported to be a captured German document suggested that the Germans were convinced that if they attacked first in the East they could not gain a decision before the French threatened Cologne. Although probably bogus, the disclosure pushed the Russians in the right direction, for the Germans had indeed abandoned contingency planning for an eastern offensive. Further evidence was provided by the Germans' new attention to their eastern fortifications, which de Laguiche interpreted as signalling their intention to fight a holding action on the Vistula.[504] By the time the August staff conversations reiterated the intention of a simultaneous offensive, the Russians seem finally to have been convinced that they would not have to withstand the principal German attack.

If the Russians were to open hostilities with a dual offensive, however, they would require, like the other Continental armies, an early mobilization with enough trained men, reinforced unit strengths, and support from field and heavy artillery. In its final form the Great Programme, once implemented, would meet these needs. The contingent increase would be some 136,000 rather than the 115,000 initially envisaged; by 1917 the increase in the peacetime officer corps would be 11,772 (28.2 per cent) and in men 468,000 (39.2 per cent). Combined with the prolongation of service, the programme would raise winter peacetime strength by 800,000, for a one-off cost of 433 million roubles and added recurrent costs of 140 million.[505] In contrast with the 1910 reorganization, moreover, its focus was on Europe. In the spring of 1913, it is true, the EMA considered that developments in Asia necessitated a reinforcement as much as did European politics. Chinese nationalism was growing after the 1911 revolution, there was a dispute in Mongolia, and the Ottomans were reinforcing their frontiers. But subsequently an agreement over Mongolia improved relations with Beijing, and despite the Liman von Sanders incident the Russians decided to create their second new army corps not in the Caucasus but in the Kiev district.[506] The Polish

[503] Zaionchovsky, *Podgotovka*, 302–20. Snyder, *Ideology*, 183–8.

[504] Wehrlin to War Ministry, 8 Apr. 1913; de Laguiche to War Ministry, 25 Apr. 1913, SHA 7.N. 1478.

[505] Frantz, *Eintritt*, 24–8. Zaionchovsky, *Podgotovka*, 92–4.

[506] EMA 2nd Bureau note on Russian strength increases, 2 Apr. 1913, SHA 7.N. 1535. De Laguiche to War Ministry, 3 Dec. 1913, SHA 7.N. 1478; Wehrlin to Vignal, 8 Nov. 1913, ibid.

fortresses of Kovno, Grodno, Brest-Litovsk, and Novogeorgievsk would each receive one infantry brigade, and twenty-three of the twenty-six new cavalry regiments—which were pre-eminently attack formations—would be European-based.[507]

In its revised form, moreover, the Great Programme gave greater emphasis to raising unit strengths. The French estimated that of the additional peacetime effectives some 172,000 would be used for new unit creations, but 153,600 to raise infantry strengths, 86,790 to reinforce the artillery, and 55,610 to raise strengths in the other arms.[508] The Russian staff accepted that the outcome of a war would be decided in the first battles. Casualties would be heavy and quality of troops and speed of mobilization decisive—hence the priority was to expand the active army rather than to plan for large second-line forces. They wished to reduce the proportion of reservists in mobilized units, while adding to the numbers of active men who could be transferred on mobilization to form a cadre for reservist formations. Thus the French calculated that mobilized infantry companies would in future typically comprise 60 rather than 48 per cent serving men.[509] A final feature of the programme was its emphasis on the artillery, the field artillery being completely reorganized in six-gun rather than eight-gun batteries. Each infantry division would receive more field guns and howitzers, and each army corps more heavy weapons, narrowing, though not quite closing, the gap with Germany. The total number of batteries would rise by 558 (87.3 per cent) and of guns by 1,430 (20.7 per cent), and the artillery would be supported by the assignment of one aviation detachment to each army corps. Russia, according to its director of military aviation, did not intend to let Germany beat it into second place behind the French.[510]

The Great Programme would therefore be a formidable addition to the accumulating threats to Germany and Austria-Hungary in the next three years. Yet it was less heavily front-end-loaded than the German bill, and not only tardy in its introduction but also leisurely in its implementation. Although some of it appears to have been carried out in advance of Duma approval, French observers reported that there would be no significant budgetary or contingent increases in 1914, and that the bulk of the proposed new units would be created after that year.[511] Zhilinski explained that the programme would take longer than Germany's to implement, in part because of its greater emphasis, even in its revised form, on creating new units as opposed to reinforcing existing ones. The schedule would be carried out progressively as peacetime strength expanded, the bulk of the task being completed by the spring of 1917. The new army corps in

[507] EMA 2nd Bureau note for Joffre, 2 May 1914; and note on reinforcement of the Russian army, 6 July 1914, SHA 7.N. 1535.

[508] Ibid. Zhilinski expected this to accelerate mobilization. Note on Zhilinski–Joffre conversations, Aug. 1913, ibid.

[509] Zaionchovsky, *Podgotovka*, 92–3. EMA note of 6 July 1914 cited in n. 507 above.

[510] Shatsillo, *Rossia*, 98–9. Zaionchovsky, *Podgotovka*, 94. Frantz, *Eintritt*, 26. Wehrlin to War Ministry, 31 Jan. 1913 (aviation), SHA 7.N. 1478.

[511] Frantz, *Eintritt*, 25. Wehrlin to War Ministry, 24 Oct. 1913, SHA 7.N. 1535.

the Warsaw military district would be created on 1 April 1915; the second, in the Kiev district, a year later. Of the twenty-six cavalry regiments, eighteen would wait until 1916–17. When war broke out the Finnish rifle brigade was the only new unit already created, and none of the projected increases in infantry and artillery strengths had gone through. The significance of the passage of the Great Programme was for what it foreshadowed.[512]

* * *

The same can be said of the Franco-Russian railway agreement. It followed on a programme of strategic building (mainly doubling and quadrupling of sectors of track in Poland) that had been approved by the two General Staffs in September 1912.[513] Delcassé was instructed to press for the implementation of the 1912 agreement and was authorized to offer loans, with the result, according to Sukhomlinov, that after the new ambassador spoke to Nicholas, orders were given to carry the work out.[514] Whatever the contribution of French pressure, by August Delcassé could report that most of the 1912 projects had been completed or were in progress, and he felt that no time had been wasted.[515]

The 1912 agreement, however, concerned 900 kilometres of track; that of December 1913 followed up a Joffre/Zhilinski understanding at their August meeting that concerned 5,330.[516] The new accord arose from the conjunction of French intercession and of the Liman von Sanders incident with an internal debate. As the tsarist economy pulled out of recession the railway network was growing fast and there was strong demand for new concessions, but only a quarter even of the European lines were double-tracked. A commission under General Petrov, appointed by the Duma, had reported on future development, and its proposals were under study in the bureaucracy.[517] A separate General Staff study of strategic lines was considered by Zhilinski to take too little account of commercial viability and was therefore unlikely to be accepted. He told Joffre in August 1913 that the Stavka's ideas still awaited approval.[518]

This was the background to the arrival in St Petersburg in June of de Verneuil, an official of the Paris Bourse. Supposedly he was an envoy of the Bardac group (which sought a concession to build a parallel railway to the Trans-Siberian) and the Crédit mobilier investment bank.[519] Before leaving, however, he spoke to Barthou, to Pichon, and to the Finance Minister, Charles Dumont.

---

[512] De Laguiche to War Ministry, 22 Feb. 1914; EMA 2nd Bureau study of Russian army reinforcement, 4 Apr. 1914; and note on same subject, 9 July 1914, ibid.

[513] Delcassé to Pichon, 2 Aug. 1913, *DDF* 3rd ser. vii, doc. 521.

[514] Izvolsky to Sazonov, 13 Mar. 1913, Stieve (ed.), *Iswolski*, doc. 762. Delcassé to Pichon, 24 and 26 Mar. 1913, *DDF* 3rd ser. vi, docs. 59, 68.

[515] Delcassé to Pichon, 1 and 2 Aug. 1913, ibid. vii, docs. 513, 521.

[516] D. W. Spring, 'Russia and the Franco-Russian Alliance 1905–1914', *Slavonic and East European Review*, 66 (1988), 579–80. Delcassé to Doumergue, 31 Dec. 1913, *DDF* 3rd ser. viii, doc. 698.

[517] Wehrlin to War Ministry, 17 June 1913, SHA 7.N. 1478.

[518] De Laguiche to War Ministry, 7 May 1913; unsigned report on Zhilinski statements to Joffre, Aug. 1913, SHA 7.N. 1535.

[519] R. Girault, *Emprunts russes et investissements français en Russie, 1887–1914* (Paris, 1973), 564.

Although Pichon denied having given the financier a 'mission', de Verneuil seems to have had a more definite brief than ministers were ready to admit. Pichon knew beforehand what he would propose, and hoped it would be accepted. De Verneuil understood that he could tell Kokovtsov that the French Government would allow Russia to borrow 400–500 million francs annually on the Paris capital market to finance its railway construction. The conditions were that the strategic lines 'foreseen' (*prévues*) on the western frontier should be started at once and the Russian army's peacetime strength 'notably augmented'. According to de Verneuil, Kokovtsov accepted these terms, and that order should be brought to the Russian bond market in Paris. Competitive flotations by the railway companies were causing confusion, and there was a danger of Russian state credit being undermined, as well as of foreign concessionaries obtaining French finance. Future Russian railway issues would therefore be grouped in blocks of one or two per year, all under government guarantee.[520]

Thus far all had proceeded with remarkable dispatch, and on 2 July Izvolsky asked for French official confirmation. Dumont approved the idea of consolidating railway issues. De Verneuil pointed out that railway building was a top priority for the Russian Government and that for years ahead it could raise the funding only in Paris. Annual approval by the French authorities of bond flotations would provide the leverage needed to ensure that St Petersburg kept its promises. According to Poincaré, the French Government's main thought was that in a war Russia's main effort should be against Germany rather than Austria-Hungary, and that it should be able to concentrate the greatest possible forces in the shortest possible time. No doubt swayed by these considerations, on 8 August the Council of Ministers approved the de Verneuil/Kokovtsov accord.[521]

It was now that the trouble started. What exactly were the strategic railways to which Kokovtsov had agreed? The Premier understood the centrality of railways to Russian economic development, but was reluctant to commit state resources to them, preferring to reserve the budget surplus for the Great Programme. The French were charging too high interest, but otherwise their offer was acceptable. He supposed, however, that French wishes would be fully met by existing Russian proposals for new building and double-tracking.[522] Yet at this point the only EMA demands known to the Russians were those of 1912, whereas in the August staff conversations Joffre and Zhilinski discussed a schedule six times the size. The military priority was no longer improvements within Poland but better connections to the interior, given that the 1910 reorganization necessitated the transport of entire mobilized corps from the Moscow, Kazan, and Caucasus military districts to the frontiers. The staffs agreed that the

---

[520] De Verneuil to Pichon, 16 June; Pichon to Delcassé, 20 June; de Verneuil to Pichon, 7 July; Pichon note, 21 July 1913, *DDF* 3rd ser. viii, docs. 134, 163, 309, 437.

[521] Dumont to Pichon, 5 July and 2 Aug. 1913; de Verneuil to Pichon, 7 July 1913, Doulcet to Pichon, 30 Aug. 1913, ibid. vii, docs. 291, 523, 309; viii, doc. 104. Poincaré, *Service*, iii. 322.

[522] Kokovtsov to Nicholas II, 2 Dec. 1913, Stieve (ed.), *Iswolski*, iii, doc. 1169. Kokovtsov, *Out of my Past*, 244–5.

Batraki–Smolensk, Rovno–Baranovitchi, and Lozovaia–Kovel lines should be double-tracked, and that a new line should run from Riazan and Tula to Warsaw. The gauges west of the Vistula should be widened, and the river crossings improved. Throughput should be increased by investments in extra rolling stock and more powerful locomotives.[523] Parts of this programme were more compatible with the attack from the head of the Polish salient towards Thorn and Berlin desired by the EMA than with the advance into East Prussia envisaged by the Stavka.[524] None the less, the Tsar approved the Riazan–Warsaw line on 1 August, and the rest of the proposals, according to Kokovtsov, were agreed to by Sukhomlinov at the end of the month, and later by Nicholas, apparently without the Premier being informed.[525] Negotiations proceeded at cross purposes because of lack of co-ordination in St Petersburg.

With the sovereign's support, Kokovtsov proceeded warily. He gave the impression of being in no hurry about the bond flotations, and according to the French Embassy the Russians were hesitating. The texts Kokovtsov offered were unacceptable, as they neither specified the lines to be built nor set dates for their completion. The Premier may have been deliberately vague because of his ignorance of the details of the staff agreement, but his behaviour cast doubt on Russian good faith.[526] Wehrlin warned that the Transport Ministry had little time for strategic railways and that its projected building was almost exclusively in Asia. France would get the lines it wanted only by 'imposing' them as the condition of the loan. De Laguiche agreed that Russia was increasingly self-confident and resentful of foreign control, with defence priorities against Austria-Hungary and in Asia as well as against Germany. French financial leverage, now available for the first time since 1907, was a wasting asset.[527] Pichon agreed to a suggestion from Delcassé that each year when the Russians applied for approval of the railway flotations the French Government should tie specified strategic projects to the proposed commercial lines. All the requirements agreed between the General Staffs in August should be inserted into a single agreement for accomplishment over three or up to five years.[528]

By the time Kokovtsov visited Paris in November, however, he was isolated within the Russian Government. Nicholas and Sazonov as well as Sukhomlinov had agreed in principle to the August proposals. The Premier resisted a sharp distinction between commercial and strategic lines and still hoped for something noncommittal, but the French were determined to pin him down. He needed railway development finance and only they could supply it; but there were

[523] War Minister to Foreign Minister, 2 Oct. 1913, AMAE NS Russie 42. Joffre–Zhilinski minutes, Aug. 1913, *DDF* viii, doc. 79.

[524] EMA 2nd Bureau, Study of Russo-German theatre, May 1914, SHA 7.N. 1535. Danilov, *Russie*, 116–18. Snyder, *Ideology*, 183 ff.

[525] Kokovtsov, *Out of my Past*, 382. Delcassé to Pichon, 5 Nov. 1913, *DDF* 3rd ser. viii, doc. 442. Kokovtsov to Neratov, 4 Oct. 1913, Stieve (ed.), *Iswolski*, iii, doc. 1074.

[526] Doulcet to Pichon, 27 Sept. 1913, *DDF* 3rd ser. viii, doc. 204.

[527] Wehrlin to War Ministry, 6 and 8 Nov. 1913, de Laguiche to War Ministry, 3 Dec. 1913, SHA 7.N. 1478.

[528] Delcassé to Pichon, 5 Nov. 1913, *DDF* 3rd ser. viii, doc. 442.

competing demands on their capital market, including their own armaments programme. The outcome of the negotiations was much closer to the Pichon/Delcassé position than to Kokovtsov's earlier proposals. He estimated the cost of the commercial lines he wanted at 1,500 million francs and that of the strategic ones at 1,000 millions. The Russian Government was authorized to raise up to 500 million francs a year in Paris for five consecutive years, either through state loans or through issues of state-guaranteed bonds, thus setting as a maximum the 2,500 millions that Kokovtsov thought was needed. Russia would have priority over all but the French Government's own requirements and the 250-million franc Serbian loan. The August 1913 Joffre/Zhilinski programme would be started as soon as possible and completed over the four years 1914–18, either at the Russian Government's expense or from the proceeds of the bonds. Yearly construction targets would not be specified, but each year St Petersburg would make known the size of the obligations to be issued and request their admission to the Paris Bourse.[529]

It appears that it was only in Paris that Kokovtsov realized the scope of the General Staff agreement. Sobered by the cost, on his return he made one last effort to wriggle out. But notes exchanged on 30 December confirmed the arrangement, the Russians indeed requesting that the first tranche should be upped to 600 million francs to allow them to go faster and give provincial French banks a role in the lending consortium.[530] The issue went ahead in February with signal success. Just as the von Sanders incident may have galvanized the Russians over the Great Programme, so they forged ahead with their railways also in its wake.[531]

* * *

There were still doubts. A July 1913 briefing warned Joffre that in an international crisis Russia might suffer worse disturbances than in 1905–6 and mobilization be delayed by a week. In May 1914 the GGS pointed to the tension between the Government and the Duma and the threat of working-class unrest. Kokovtsov's replacement as Premier by Goremykin in February 1914 was seen as weakening Sazonov and possibly moving Russia in a more reactionary and pro-German direction. De Laguiche doubted whether France could expect a vigorous offensive from the Russians, though they might tie down five German army corps.[532] None the less, the Delcassé mission had won commitment to the 1912 railway programme, and the de Verneuil mission, possibly beginning as a piece of opportunism, had won commitment to the much more significant programme of 1913. The 1910 reorganization had accelerated mobilization, and the new railways would accelerate the western concentration too, even beyond the strides that were already being made. At the end of March Wehrlin reported a

[529] Kokovtsov to Nicholas II, 2 Dec. 1913, Stieve (ed.), *Iswolski*, iii, doc. 1169. Girault, *Emprunts*, 566–7. Pichon to Delcassé, 16 Nov. 1913, *DDF* 3rd ser. viii, doc. 485.

[530] Russian Embassy note, 13 Dec.; Delcassé to Doumergue, 31 Dec. 1913, ibid., docs. 622, 698.

[531] Krumeich, *Armaments*, 171.

[532] 'La Concentration russe: couverture' (Note for Joffre, July 1913); de Laguiche to Dupont, 4 May, 12 Feb. 1914, SHA 7.N. 1535; de Laguiche to War Ministry, 10 Dec. 1913, SHA 7.N. 1478.

dramatic increase in new construction and double-tracking on 1913 (although little of it was in Europe) and that the successful issue in February had allowed the private companies to double their building plans. The strategic railway programme would create seven double-tracked lines from the interior to eastern Poland, and four running through to the Vistula: three or four lines of continuous double track would link the Volga and the Caucasus to the western border, and several of the new commercial lines would have strategic value. Together with the rise in effectives the extra capacity would greatly increase Russia's European striking power.[533]

The view from Berlin was similar. As ever, the Russians suffered from inadequate training and an incompetent officer corps. They still had little modern siege and heavy field artillery and fewer field guns per division than did Germany. In contrast to the French, however, all their European army corps had Krupp-model light field howitzers, and enough Schneider and Putilov heavy howitzers and cannon were being delivered for the heavy field artillery to be completely re-equipped. There were 250 usable aircraft, and energetic fortification work was proceeding in Poland.[534] Neither the Germans nor the Austrians had detailed advanced knowledge of the Great Programme, but they predicted that it would further accelerate Russian mobilization, and were aware of the contingent increase. Moltke expected the Russians to start mobilization before announcing it, and by so doing to hasten by up to five days their arrival in the concentration zone.[535] During the Scutari crisis he reportedly advised that if Russia mobilized, irrespective of the political circumstances, Germany could not wait: as soon as there was a 90 per cent chance of war it must warn France and act forthwith.[536] As for the railway loan, a preliminary study in November 1913 estimated that at present by the evening of day 15 twenty-three and a half full corps and eight separate divisions might be assembled in the concentration zone; on completion of the programme the number of corps might rise to twenty-nine. An update in July 1914 thought it might reach thirty: though it supposed that the completion date for the programme was to be 1922 rather than 1918.[537] Had the Germans known that the programme was scheduled for completion almost immediately after the army reinforcement they would have had even greater grounds for concern.

The French and Germans could at least agree in their common appreciation of the growth of Russian power. For the French, it threatened their leadership of the alliance; for the Germans, it was another menace to the Schlieffen Plan.

---

[533] Wehrlin to War Ministry, 2 Jan. 1914, AMAE NS Russie 42; and 28 Mar. 1914, SHA 7.N. 1478.

[534] Moltke to Wenninger, 26 Feb. 1914, KAM MKr. 992. GGS report on Russian tactics, 14 June 1913, ibid. 998.

[535] Hohenlohe to Austro-Hungarian War Ministry, 14 and 31 Mar. 1914, KAM KM Präs (1914) 47–2. GGS 1. Abt., 4 July 1914, 'Die wachsende Macht Russlands', PAAA R.996. Moltke to Bethmann, 15 Dec. 1913 (memorandum on Russian railways), PAAA R.11011.

[536] Jules Cambon to Pichon, 6 May 1913, *DDF* 3rd ser. vi, doc. 509.

[537] Moltke to Bethmann, 15 Dec. 1913, 11 July 1914, PAAA R.11011. Wehrlin to Vignal, 8 Nov. 1913, SHA 7.N. 1478.

Germany's 1913 law was primarily anti-French, at least in its military rationale, because of the plan's requirement for a western attack. But the law's emphasis on eastern fortification was designed to keep the Russians at bay, and to do so would grow harder with every year that passed. Meanwhile Italy would contribute little, if it helped at all, while Austria-Hungary would be preoccupied in the Balkans. No sooner had Germany adopted the law in order to compensate for the weakening of its allies than Franco-Russian, not to mention Belgian, retaliation, shifted the balance back. By the spring of 1914 the Three-Year Law was bedding down faster than expected, and the Great Programme, the railway loan, and the French equipment credit would soon take effect. Germany had the possibility of recruiting yet more men, but to do so would dilute the composition of the army and the officer corps and perhaps necessitate progressive taxes and dependence on a Centre–Left coalition, if one could be formed. The financial and demographic advantage seemed to lie with the Franco-Russian combination, and its disadvantages, especially in artillery, were being remedied. None the less, in the spring of 1914 there seemed to be an opportunity, perhaps a final opportunity, for Germany to fight on favourable terms because of the lagging implementation of its opponents' response. The even greater lag in Austria-Hungary's rearmament mattered less, for only Germany could unleash a Continental conflict. But there were arguments in Vienna too for seeing 1914 as the best chance to strike before the balance moved irreversibly in favour of the Monarchy's enemies. The militarization of Habsburg policy and the curtailment of Germany's options pointed down the same ominous path.

6

Vials of Wrath, 1913–1914

1. On the Eve

This book began with two questions: what caused the pre-war arms race, and did the arms race cause the war? The analysis thus far has concentrated on the former. By 1913 the transformation of European armaments competition was complete, and it was dominated by the confrontation between the two alliance blocs, the rivalry between the Habsburg Monarchy and its Balkan neighbours supplying an additional incendiary ingredient. There remains the interconnection between this evolution and the outbreak of war. The first half of this chapter will take stock of the position in early 1914. It will readdress the underlying pressures for armaments expansion, the balance between the central and the peripheral arms races, and examine the stage that the central race had reached. The second half will turn to military preparedness in the July crisis.

* * *

To what extent did developments in technology and in civil–military relations cause the resurgence of the inter-bloc arms race? It was still at sea rather than on land that the pace of innovation was greatest. The dreadnought revolution introduced a decade of growth in the size, power, sophistication, and expense of capital ships. Whereas HMS *Dreadnought* had 12″ guns, the Queen Elizabeth-class battleships adopted by the Admiralty in 1912 had 15″ ones, were significantly faster, and were driven by oil rather than coal. The battleships of the 1913–14 programme cost some 60 per cent more than did their predecessors of 1909–10.[1] New optical and electrical systems were introduced for rangefinding and fire control, while aircraft and wireless linked destroyers with the battlefleet.[2] Yet whereas in 1905 or 1909 European armies were being starved of funds because of the greater dynamism of the naval race, in the North Sea by 1913–14 higher building and maintenance costs helped to bridle new construction, given the priorities elsewhere. A primarily technological interpretation of armaments expansion cannot accommodate the passage from sea to land of the storm centre.

By 1910 re-equipping with quick-firing field artillery was virtually complete in the front-line forces of the Powers, bar Italy. Of the next wave of innovations

---

[1] J. T. Sumida, *In Defence of Naval Supremacy* (Boston, 1989), 193.

[2] K. Lautenschläger, 'Technology and the Evolution of Naval Warfare', *International Security*, 8 (1983), 18–20.

the most dramatic was heavier-than-air flight, which European armies began to take seriously from about 1909. Italy, the first Power to use aircraft operationally, in the Libyan War, had twenty-five in military service in 1912 but planned to increase them tenfold.[3] Russia ordered its first eleven, from France, in 1910; by the end of 1913 it had taken delivery of 400 and ordered another 326, and had over 170 qualified pilots.[4] Britain was slower, and fell behind France and Germany, whose rivalry was central to the aviation race.[5] In March 1914 the GGS computed that France had increased its qualified military pilots from seventy-three to 300 in two years, and its machines from 208 to about 600. French success in breaking performance records and in establishing the leading European aero-engine and airframe industries swelled national pride and the mood of *réveil*.[6] Germany, by concentrating on dirigibles, seemed to have backed the wrong horse. Yet by 1914 German aviators had matched French feats of speed, height, and endurance, and by some estimates Germany went to war with more numerous serviceable machines. The French advance was losing momentum, German airframes were beginning to capture export markets, and French volunteers for the highly dangerous work of piloting were diminishing.[7]

The potential of aviation was widely perceived. The Russians feared that German airships would rain bombs upon their cities; Russian aircraft were reportedly being acquired as a defence, and Russian airships to present a countervailing menace.[8] In 1913 there was panic about London's vulnerability to air attack.[9] Yet despite the speed with which aircraft needed replacement they made a minor addition to armaments spending. In 1913 the French War Ministry budget was 983 million francs, of which 34 million were for capital spending on aviation.[10] Of 335.4 million marks of non-recurrent spending in the Prussian army estimates, 23 million were for aircraft, airships, and ground infrastructure. In relation to the totality of expansion, the claim on manpower (the Germans in 1913 planned for another 147 personnel) was even smaller.[11]

Aviation was not, of course, the sole dimension of technological change. More mundane was the introduction of field kitchens, an expensive innovation to which Conrad and Schönaich, for example, attached much urgency during the Bosnian crisis. Alongside them came telephones, wireless, and the internal combustion engine—for lorries, staff cars, and tractors to pull heavy artillery,

---

[3] GGS 9. Abt., report on Italian army for 1913; and report on Italian aviation, 15 Mar. 1913, KAM Gstb. 196.

[4] Moltke to Wenninger, 5 May 1914 (Russian military aviation), KAM MKr. 997.

[5] A. M. Gollin, *The Impact of Air Power on the British People and their Government, 1909–1914* (Basingstoke, 1989), 307.

[6] GGS reports on French military aviation, Apr. 1912, KAM Gstb 165; and Mar. 1914, KAM Gstb 167.

[7] Ibid. and Gollin, *Air Power*, 307. Serret to War Ministry, 10 Apr. 1914, SHA 7.N. 1112. German War Ministry to Foreign Ministry, 5 July 1913, PAAA R.927.

[8] De Laguiche to War Ministry, 2 May 1914, SHA 7.N. 1478.

[9] Gollin, *Air Power*, 238–43.

[10] GGS, 3. Abt., Report on French army budget, Oct. 1913, KAM Gstb 166.

[11] Heeringen to Bethmann (for Kühn), 10 Feb. 1913, KAM MKr. 5588.

although draught animals remained far more important. Germany and France planned to requisition civilian lorries on mobilization, and those available in France rose from eighty-eight in 1910 to 1,058 two years later.[12] But the biggest demands on money and men came from developments in artillery, especially howitzers and heavy guns. The Skoda 30.5 cm mortar and the Krupp *M-Gerät* were devastating contributions to the Central Powers' siege park, even if their numbers were few. In heavy field artillery the other Continental armies tried to narrow Germany's lead, although none caught up. Guns and fortification drew the big money in capital expenditure before 1914, but less to develop and re-equip with new weapons systems than to add to the numbers of existing ones. Similarly, the need for extra men to fire the guns—as well as to drive the lorries and operate the wireless sets—intensified manpower constraints, but the increases in peacetime strength in 1912–14 went far beyond what was needed to remedy this weakness. Innovation helped to quicken the pace of armaments expansion, without being adequate to explain it.

* * *

What of the military-industrial complexes? Within the Anglo-Franco-German triangle, despite the boom in private warship building, the public/private-sector balance in land armaments was much the same in 1914 as at the century's beginning. Schneider broke into the French army's supply of heavy artillery under Millerand, but the War Ministry remained suspicious. Skoda, similarly, became more important as a Habsburg army contractor, but was still kept at arm's length. As part of the naval construction industry, it is true, it could advance its interests at the army's expense, although it needed support from Admiral Haus and the Austrian and Hungarian Governments. Wilhelm II remained in close contact with Krupp von Bohlen und Halbach, telling him early in the July crisis, for example, that if Russia mobilized Germany would go to war.[13] None the less, the Essen firm's reputation suffered from the scandal of 1913, and the ensuing Reichstag inquiry. It benefited from the upsurge in army spending, but not sufficiently to compensate for the loss of naval orders, and its overall profitability suffered.

The arms firms were bound into a supranational nexus that transcended military and diplomatic alignments. Although the nickel-steel consortium had lapsed by 1914 the Anglo-German dynamite trust survived and negotiations were beginning for a shipbuilding cartel. Yet the same firms were backed by their respective governments in ferocious rivalry for weapons and warship orders and for infrastructure contracts, in which the Triple Entente was gaining the upper hand. In the Balkans French enterprises were winning a decisive advantage over their German competitors, although even in Serbia their ascendancy was not unchallenged. In Belgium Krupp was implicated in another scandal in 1913, accused of using illicit influence to win a coastal artillery contract on which it

[12] GGS report on French army in 1912, Feb. 1913, KAM Gstb 166.
[13] W. Manchester, *The Arms of Krupp, 1587–1968* (London, 1968), 302. BA Hugenberg MSS 74. F. Fischer, *War of Illusions: German Policies from 1911 to 1914* (London, 1975), 478.

had then failed to deliver.[14] Like the Italian affair of 1907, this one gave French firms new opportunities in a previously German-dominated market, although the Quai d'Orsay felt that Schneider was slow to exploit them.[15]

The biggest story of the pre-war years, however, was the rise of Russia, which overshadowed the industrial scene as it did the military balance. Little of the expenditure on the tsarist naval programmes was translated into orders abroad, and the labour force in the modernized Admiralty plants and yards doubled from 11,874 in 1908–11 to 21,837 in 1914. But that in the private yards sextupled from 5,400 to 30,400, signalling a transformation comparable to that in Western Europe twenty years before. Even re-equipped, the state sector could not turn out enough turrets and armour; nor could it manufacture the most modern explosives, or electrical, optical, and wireless gear.[16] To compensate, a largely new-founded private construction industry grew up after 1911, nurtured by foreign assistance.

Directly owned foreign subsidiaries were rare. In 1912 the Ziese subsidiary of Schichau at Elbing agreed to build a yard at Riga in exchange for a destroyer order.[17] The Admiralty yard at St Petersburg was leased to a Franco-Russian consortium, Nicholas approving the company statutes in June 1914.[18] But more typical were agreements for technical aid. Of the two main private firms at Nicolaiev, Russud was advised by John Brown and the Franco-Belgian Naval' by Vickers: when they merged in 1912 the French interests in Naval' were ousted, but Vickers continued in its consultative role.[19] By the eve of war the merged concern had ultra-modern equipment and was working on six warships.[20] In the Baltic the main developments were in St Petersburg and round the first-class forward naval base being established at Reval. Two firms there, the Société Becker and the Société Franco-baltique, had agreements with the Méditerranée company and with Schneider, while the new consortium in the St Petersburg Admiralty yard negotiated with Saint-Chamond for a move into turret construction.[21] Alignments in the emerging sector were not necessarily determined by politics. German and Austrian firms were present in the Russian defence

---

[14] Krupp to Jagow, 12 Jan. 1914, PAAA R.4403.

[15] Génie to War Ministry, 8 Jan. 1914, SHA 7.N. 1159. Fontarce to Doumergue, AMAE NS Belgique 11.

[16] K. F. Shatsillo, *Russkii imperializm i razvitie flota nakanune pervoi mirovoi voiny* (Moscow, 1968), 223, 225, 240. Once again P. W. Gatrell, *Government, Industry, and Rearmament in Russia, 1900–1914: The Last Argument of Tsarism* (Cambridge, 1994) is fundamental for what follows.

[17] K. F. Shatsillo, 'Inostrannyi kapital i voenno-morskie programmy Rossii nakanune pervoi mirovoi voiny', *Istorichiskie Zapiski*, 69 (1961), 81. Gallaud to French Marine Ministry, 20 Dec. 1912, SHM BB7 122.

[18] Shatsillo, 'Inostrannyi kapital', 180.

[19] G. G. Jones and R. C. B. Trebilcock, 'Russian Industry and British Business, 1910–1930: Oil and Armaments', *Journal of European Economic History*, 11 (1982), 74. Vickers/Nicolaiev agreement, VA #735. R. Girault, *Emprunts russes et investissements français en Russie, 1887–1914* (Paris, 1973), 541.

[20] R. C. B. Trebilcock, 'British Armaments and European Industrialization, 1890–1914', *Economic History Review*, NS 26 (1973), 264.

[21] Gallaud to Marine Ministry, 16 Oct. and 7 and 12 Nov. 1913, SHM BB7 122.

industries, and the French were divided into three groupings round Schneider, Châtillon-Commentry, and Saint-Chamond that sometimes co-operated and sometimes did not.[22] They felt as much under British as under German pressure, and in 1914 twelve Russian armaments firms had technical agreements with British ones (mainly Vickers) and only four with French.[23]

None the less, in 1913–14 the Russian armaments regrouping became prominent in European diplomacy, and Germany was again the main loser. A complex of issues concerned heavy guns. The only Russian plant that could produce them was Obukhov, smaller pieces being manufactured in the state arsenal at Perm. The Baltic naval programme greatly increased demand, and Obukhov was unable to cope.[24] Negotiations with Schneider to re-equip Perm foundered on bureaucratic objections to privatization and on nationalist opposition to foreign influence.[25] Instead it was decided to establish a great new private plant, a choice between tenders being made in April 1913. Schneider's bid, to reconstruct Putilov, was cheaper and supported by the French Embassy, but the Council of Ministers favoured a location in the interior and opted for a Vickers proposal to build a brand new plant at Tsaritsyn.[26] The Russian Artillery Works Company was established in September, with technical assistance and a quarter of its 13 million roubles capital coming from Vickers and the remainder from a consortium of domestic bankers, whose leader described the enterprise as a 'Russian Krupp'. Construction went ahead with great speed, but when war broke out the plant was still unfinished, destined to join the other cathedrals in the desert that were scattered across the south of the country.[27] Within months of this defeat for Schneider an interministerial commission recommended that Perm should be modernized by Armstrong, although the French firm had again bid more cheaply and Kokovtsov had apparently promised it the contract in exchange for French agreement in January 1914 to increase the first tranche of the Russian railway loan. This time the French Embassy lobbied hard and successfully, and the Council of Ministers decided to award Schneider the business.[28]

The Tsaritsyn and Perm affairs exhibited strains within the Triple Entente: Anglo-French industrial rivalry and Russian hostility to foreign encroachment. By contrast, the Putilov affair squared off the two alliance blocs.[29] The firm's output had risen by two-thirds in 1910–13 and its capitalization had doubled, but it was poorly managed and heavily indebted. It had links with most of the

[22] Girault, *Emprunts russes*, 557.   [23] Jones and Trebilcock, 'Russian Industry', 75.

[24] Gallaud to Marine Ministry, 15 Feb. 1913, SHM BB7 122; and 22 Feb. 1914, SHM SS Em 157.

[25] Gallaud to Marine Ministry, 24 Oct. 1912, SHM BB7 121.

[26] Gallaud to Marine Ministry, 24 Apr. 1913, SHM BB7 122.

[27] Trebilcock, 'European Industrialization', 265. E. R. Goldstein, 'Vickers Limited and the Tsarist Regime', *Slavonic and East European Review*, 58 (1980), 566–8. See also VA #1219.

[28] Paléologue to Doumergue, 16, 17, 18, 25 Feb., 3, 6, 12 Mar. 1914, *DDF* 3rd ser. ix, docs. 310, 319, 325, 357, 390, 404, 445. Gallaud to Marine Ministry, 25 Feb. and 18 Apr. 1914, SHM SS Em 157.

[29] R. Girault, 'Finances internationales et relations internationales (là propos des usines Poutiloff', *Revue d'histoire moderne et contemporaine*, 13 (1966), 217–36, gives the best account of this episode.

major Continental arms firms, and tried to play them off in order to preserve its independence. In 1912 it acquired the Neva shipyard in St Petersburg, with French financial support and promises of technical advice from Schneider and Skoda; in the same year, to Schneider's irritation, it began work on a second St Petersburg yard with help from the Hamburg shipbuilders, Blohm and Voss. Schneider and the other French interests represented in the company were tired of being responsible for its debts without controlling its management, and Alexei Putilov tried to act pre-emptively before a reorganization curtailed him. In January 1914 he hinted that Krupp wanted to take over and he might have to do a deal. Krupp and German banking representatives had indeed offered an increase in capital, although it is doubtful if the Berlin market could have absorbed a Putilov issue large enough to marginalize French interests.[30] Probably Putilov hoped by dealing with the Germans to scare the French. He succeeded to the extent that Schneider organized a counter-offer, roped in the Quai d'Orsay, and tipped off the press, the *Echo de Paris* on 30 January starting a month-long journalistic campaign. After being approached by the French Embassy Kokovtsov vetoed a German deal, and in February agreement was reached. The French bought half the Neva yard, and Putilov's capital was raised from 25 to 40 million roubles. But as a condition of the necessary share and bond issue being admitted to the Paris Bourse Skoda's advisory role was restricted, and at least three of the eight directors were to be French from then on.[31]

Much of the growth in Russian armaments capacity was projected rather than completed in July 1914. But the struggle for shares in it was one with high stakes. Although the French were losing ground to Vickers, they fought back over Perm and Putilov. The German and Austrian presence, on the other hand, was being reduced to isolated footholds. The backdrop to all these incidents was one of anti-foreign agitation. Domestic capital raised by a larger and more sophisticated banking sector was increasingly significant. The ten-year contract granted to Vickers at Tsaritsyn was symptomatic of a wish to utilize foreign assistance as a stepping-stone to later independence. Industrial diplomacy, as well as the negotiations over strategic railways, showed Russia's new self-assurance in dealings with its allies. It would be misleading, none the less, to attribute the spectacular growth of defence expenditure to the formation of an industrial lobby, and particularly so on land.[32] The truth was rather that changes in official perceptions caused the creation of the new private sector.

* * *

[30] Pourtalès to Bethmann, 31 Jan. 1914, PAAA R.10433. De Laguiche to Dupont, 12 Feb. 1914, SHA 7.N. 1478.

[31] Doumergue to Delcassé, 27 and 29 Jan., Russian Embassy Note, 31 Jan., Gallaud to Gauthier, 9 Feb., Doulcet to Doumergue, 10 and 11 Feb. 1914, *DDF* 3rd ser. ix, docs. 168, 186, 198, 251, 262–3. President of Banque de l'union parisienne to French Finance Ministry, 3 Mar. 1914, MFF B.31267.

[32] Gatrell, *Last Argument*, chs. 5 and 6, for the growth of a private armaments complex and the limits to its influence.

The military component of the European military-industrial complexes was constituted by the upper echelons of the War Ministry bureaucracies and of the officer corps. Here too there had been measured rather than radical changes since the turn of the century, probably the most significant being Russia's approximation to the European norm. Since 1906 a Russian General Staff had existed separately from the War Ministry, at first independently responsible to the sovereign on the German model, but since 1909 subordinate to the War Minister as elsewhere in the Triple Entente. The Duma, despite its restricted powers and skewed franchise, exercised some financial surveillance and was required to approve extraordinary credit and manpower bills. In France, the 1911–12 reforms had strengthened the High Command relative to the Minister, and the remodelled CSDN extended scope for military influence. In Britain the creation of the CID and General Staff similarly gave the professionals new opportunities to express their views. In Austria-Hungary, on the other hand, Conrad, despite a formal extension of his powers in 1913,[33] was never respected by Franz Joseph as Beck had been, and by 1914 he was losing Franz Ferdinand's confidence as well. Moltke, if less overbearing, was probably more respected by his sovereign and his civilian opposite numbers, although he far from inevitably won in bureaucratic disputes. Institutions counted for less than did personality and circumstance.

Relations between War Ministries and General Staffs showed a trend to greater European homogeneity. So did military service, which in 1905–13 outside Russia was gravitating towards a two-year norm. Whereas strategic planning was everywhere outside legislative control, however, the size and effectiveness of peacetime armies depended heavily on the vagaries of quasi-democratic politics. For a time, domestic factors encouraged contraction; after 1909 and still more after 1912 their influence moved decisively the other way. Part of the reason was recovery from the 1907–9 recession in Western Europe and from revolution, slump, and harvest failure in Russia, followed in 1910–13 by a sustained boom. Buoyant revenues and easier borrowing freed up armaments policy in the pacemaker states of Russia and Germany. But by 1913 credit was tight and budgets reverting to deficit, while the economic conjuncture faltered. Had peace continued, the arms race might have lost momentum because of an economic downturn.

Such an approach neglects the competing claims on government revenues. Kokovtsov and Wermuth wanted money for debt repayment; Tirpitz and Grigorovich for navies; Lloyd George for social reform. Superimposed on the economic cycle was a political one. The years round 1905 witnessed a movement to the Left in most European capitals; those after 1909 a trend towards realignment and paralysis.[34] Popular and parliamentary opposition to military

---

[33] F. Käs, 'Versuch einer Zusammenfassten Darstellung der Tätigkeit des Österreichisch-Ungarischen Generalstabes in der Zeit von 1906 bis 1914', Ph.D. thesis (Vienna, 1962), 25.

[34] Cf. N. Stone, *Europe Transformed, 1878—1919* (London, 1983), 107-53. On the economic cycle, W. A. Rostow, *The World Economy: History and Prospect* (London, 1978), table on p. 325.

expansion disintegrated, and until the Socialist successes in the 1914 French elections the advocates of rearmament had things their own way. German army bills passed with little amendment, and the Duma was willing to vote for more than the Russian army asked for. Only in France and Austria-Hungary was there a real fight, but neither the SFIO nor the Magyar nationalists were able to prevail. The French nationalist revival was partly responsible for eroding anti-militarism, and it had counterparts elsewhere. But both the change in public mood, and the political realignment, can be retraced to the darkening diplomatic horizon and the recurrent international crises. Within the military establishment expansionists gained ground over conservatives, and won support outside from Foreign Ministers and heads of government, leaving Treasuries isolated. In one capital after another the military (more truly than a 'military-industrial complex') staged its breakthrough, and action-reaction repercussions were set in train.

* * *

From the underlying determinants we may now return to medium-term preparedness, and the pace and trajectory of armaments competition in the six months before Sarajevo. The first question to consider is whether the contestants in the peripheral races were discovering a second wind. Another attempt at Anglo-German naval negotiations proved abortive, and Britain's 1914–15 naval estimates showed the biggest jump since 1909. Yet there was greater convergence than there seemed, and the naval race was not about to siphon off fresh funds from army budgets, as both armaments diplomacy and construction policies demonstrate.

Diplomacy centred on Churchill's proposals for a one-year naval holiday, set out most fully in a speech at Manchester on 18 October 1913. Under existing plans Britain was to lay down four capital ships in 1914 against Germany's two, and three more battleships would be built in British yards at Canada's expense. Churchill offered to drop the four British ships (and, privately, to postpone the Canadian ones) if Germany would drop its two, although all the other Powers must also honour the freeze.[35] The German press condemned the speech, which was neither officially forwarded to Berlin nor given an official reply.[36] But in the Reichstag Budget Commission on 4 February Tirpitz probed its ambiguities. To cancel Germany's two scheduled ships would violate the Navy Law, which he would have all-party support in resisting. If Churchill meant postponement, a one-year pause would damage Germany, with its excess building capacity, much more than Britain, whose industry was overburdened and could more easily find compensating export orders.[37] Moreover, neither France nor Russia wanted a standstill, the French being committed to their law of 1912 and the Russians to their Baltic programme. The Germans had an opportunity to divide Britain

---

[35] J. H. Maurer, 'Churchill's Naval Holiday: Arms Control and the Anglo-German Naval Race, 1912–1914', *Journal of Strategic Studies*, 15 (1992), 106–7.

[36] Goschen to Grey, 22 Oct. 1913, *BD* x(ii), doc. 485.

[37] Tirpitz in Budget Committee, 6 Feb. 1914, ibid., doc. 502(i). British Embassy *aide-mémoire*, 6 Feb. 1914, *GP* xxxix, doc. 15589 n.

against its entente partners, but they were too suspicious of Churchill, and too wedded to their own construction schedule, to attempt to do so.

The risks to the ententes bulked large in the Foreign Office, where Churchill was thought to have gone out on a limb. Crowe feared that negotiations would be very dangerous, and in a speech on 3 February Grey said it was no good making proposals that other countries would be unwilling to receive.[38] Tirpitz commented that no serious proposals had reached him, though if they did they would be considered with goodwill. This put the British in a dilemma, Grey observing that they had made no definite proposals precisely because of warnings from Berlin that these would be unwelcome, and that they must clarify whether Tirpitz really wanted to negotiate.[39] The response to the ensuing sounding confirmed that Jagow and Bethmann shared Tirpitz's objections to a freeze, as did Wilhelm himself. Even after this rebuff Churchill still hoped to discuss the idea in a face-to-face meeting with the Navy Secretary, but Grey counselled him against it and the meeting never took place.[40]

The holiday idea was rejected in Berlin and distrusted in London. All the same, Churchill had had good reasons for suggesting it. One was 'to conciliate the Radical wing of the [Liberal] party and to show them that every effort was being made to moderate naval armaments' when the estimates battle was about to begin.[41] Second, 'the simultaneous building by so many Powers great and small of capital ships, and their general naval expansion, are sources of deep anxiety to us', he wrote to Grey. Russia, in particular, from being a 'counterpoise' might become a 'makeweight'. Its loyalty could not be guaranteed, and, even if Germany fell behind, diplomatic realignments might suddenly create elsewhere 'a great preponderance of loose Dreadnoughts' for Britain to face. Since 1912 the Germans had seen Russia as a complicating factor in negotiations, and now the British did too. Significantly, Jagow set as a condition for negotiations that other Powers must 'not continue with excessive armaments'.[42]

Yet if Germany opposed a freeze, Tirpitz told the Budget Commission of his continued willingness to accept an 8:5 ratio in battleship squadrons, which would imply a two-ship tempo for Germany and a three-ship one for Britain. Although the British did not take him up, Churchill maintained that he sought a 60 per cent superiority and was gearing his construction to what Tirpitz was doing. The Germans aimed for an absolute level of strength; the British for a specified margin above it. The elements of a tacit understanding existed, and both sides acknowledged that much heat had gone out of Anglo-German relations in general and naval relations in particular. The Kaiser expressed pleasure at having

[38] Ibid., and Maurer, 'Naval Holiday', 108.

[39] Grey to Goschen, 28 Oct. 1913, 5 Feb. 1914, *BD* x(ii), docs. 488, 498.

[40] Bethmann to Wilhelm, 8 Feb., Wilhelm to Bethmann, 9 Feb., Jagow to Goschen, 10 Feb. 1914, *GP* xxxix, docs. 15590–92. Memoranda by Churchill and Grey, 20, 25, 26 May 1914, *BD* x(ii), docs. 511–13.

[41] Maurer, 'Naval Holiday', 116.

[42] Churchill to Grey, 24 Oct. 1913, *BD* x(ii), doc. 487. Jagow to Goschen, 10 Feb. 1914, *GP* xxxix, doc. 15592.

achieved *détente* without a freeze, and the Foreign Office supposed relations had improved in part precisely because armaments were no longer being discussed.[43] Such portents of a new equilibrium must be reconciled, however, with the evidence that expenditure was again rising.

Churchill's Radical critics inveighed against his 1914–15 estimates as necessitating tax increases in the run-up to an election, and as needless and provocative now that relations with Germany had eased. If it was not possible to economize now, asked Asquith's wife, when would it be?[44] Many colleagues regarded Churchill as exasperating and disloyal, and half a dozen members of the Cabinet tried to use the issue to unseat him. They signally failed, and the estimates passed much as he had wanted them, although he had to sacrifice three light cruisers. From £46.3 million in 1913–14 (raised by a supplementary credit to £48.8 million) they rose to £51.85 million, though Churchill agreed in principle to a reduction in 1915–16 without specifying by how much.[45] The four new capital ships envisaged were fewer than the five of 1913–14, but he held they would suffice, if barely, to uphold the 60 per cent ratio. The navalist press wanted six and the Cabinet Radicals two. Lloyd George was willing for a time to hunt with the pack, but on the promise of future cuts he grudgingly came round. Churchill and the Board of Admiralty were willing to resign rather than go below four, and they enjoyed the 'solid, silent support' of the Prime Minister, who threatened to call a premature election if the Cabinet split.[46] Behind the scenes, they also had the backing of Grey.

As on the Continent, the Premier and Foreign Minister could tip the balance between the Treasury and the service departments. Churchill feared for maritime security in the face of worldwide naval expansion, but he also invoked political considerations.[47] Britain's credibility would suffer if it unilaterally took a semi-holiday after Germany had rebuffed the idea. If it redefined the acceptable security margin it would undercut the Canadian Prime Minister in his struggle for legislative approval for the three dreadnoughts. Nor was it acceptable indefinitely for British interests in the Mediterranean to depend on French naval support. More generally, at a time of unprecedented military expansion on the Continent the establishment of the regular army had fallen by 6,500 in 1913. The navy was an indispensable support for British diplomacy; and if diplomacy failed

---

[43] Lerchenfeld dispatch, 8 Jan. 1914, GSM Bayerische Gesandtschaft Berlin 1086. R. T. B. Langhorne, 'The Naval Question in Anglo-German Relations, 1912–1914', *Historical Journal*, 14 (1971), 301.

[44] B. K. Murray, 'Lloyd George, the Navy Estimates, and the Inclusion of Rating Relief in the 1914 Budget', *Welsh Historical Review*, 15 (1990), 58–78. F. W. Wiemann, 'Lloyd George and the Struggle for the Navy Estimates of 1914', in A. J. P. Taylor (ed.), *Lloyd George: Twelve Essays* (London, 1971), 71–91.

[45] A. J. Marder, *From the Dreadnought to Scapa Flow: The Royal Navy in the Fisher Era, 1904–1914* (London, 1961), i. 325–6.

[46] W. S. Churchill, *The World Crisis, 1911–1914* (London, 1923), 173–4, 178. Wiemann, 'Navy Estimates', 82–3.

[47] Churchill to Grey, 24 Oct. 1913, *BD* x(ii), doc. 487.

they must be ready for another such alert as had followed the Mansion House speech.[48]

The question, however, was not simply one of warship numbers. Churchill told the Cabinet that there were four main reasons why expenditure had risen during his tenure. More ships had been built and more kept in commission, in response to the 1912 *Novelle*. The size, speed, and armament of warships had increased worldwide. New technology had contributed, especially oil burning, aviation, and wireless. Finally, there had been inflation in wages and prices, including those of fuel and construction materials. The First Lord's critics complained that he had worsened matters by ordering the 'Fast Division' of Queen Elizabeth-class battleships. As with the *Dreadnought*, the Admiralty had forced the pace rather than being a passive accessory to technological change. But only a small proportion of the jump in the estimates was attributable to the adoption of 15″ gun capital ships, and the main cause of the increase was higher maintenance costs. Thirty-three dreadnoughts were now in service, against a maximum under McKenna of sixteen. Contrary to German expectations, the British could crew them without difficulty, Churchill advising that recruiting was going well and shortfalls had been made good.[49] Lloyd George had hoped to avoid tax increases in his 1914 budget, but resigned himself to them after Churchill's Cabinet victory, although it has been argued that if the strain had gone on for much longer Britain would have been forced into borrowing.[50] None the less, if both sides stuck to the programmes announced in 1912 the Admiralty projected that after a tight passage in 1914–15 Britain would maintain its 60 per cent edge with increasing ease for the rest of the decade.[51]

It was Germany that was feeling the pinch, and there was despondency in the Navy Office. Tirpitz was restrained in his public comments on the British estimates, saying that they were unnecessarily large but might be directed against countries other than Germany.[52] Privately he lamented his department's fall from grace and its lack of imperial support. Reversion to a two-ship tempo had let Britain widen its lead, and while Bethmann remained Chancellor there was no chance of catching up.[53] Capelle, previously confident that Britain was reaching its limits, now saw 'the risk principle and with it the foundations of our naval policy endangered'. He wanted an even higher proportion of the fleet kept in commission, in readiness for a 'lightning-fast offensive' with all Germany's strength.[54] Tirpitz did not yet endorse this strategy, but of a 50-million mark increase in the estimates that he envisaged for 1915, most would be for larger

[48] Churchill, *World Crisis*, 175–7. Churchill to Asquith and Grey, 18 and 25 Dec. 1913, in R. S. Churchill, *Winston S. Churchill*, companion vol. part 3, *1911–1914* (London, 1969), 1834–6.

[49] Churchill memorandum, 5 Dec. 1913, ibid. 1818–23.

[50] Sumida, *Defence*, 195–6.

[51] Churchill memorandum, 13 Dec. 1913, R. S. Churchill, *Winston S. Churchill*, companion vol., 1825–7.

[52] Capt. Henderson to Goschen, 21 Mar. 1914, *BD* x(ii), doc. 503(i).

[53] Tirpitz to Müller, 30 Apr. 1914, Tirpitz, *Aufbau*, 421–2.

[54] Capelle note, 17 May 1914, BA-MA Tirpitz MSS N.253/29.

ships and guns, more costly maintenance, oil-fuelling, and extra personnel.[55] He had no thought of a new *Novelle*, and an inspired press article in July 1914 admitted that none was contemplated.[56] When the Emperor pressed for new legislation to provide for extra Mediterranean cruisers, Tirpitz fended him off.[57] The increasing cost of capital ships was forcing the Navy Secretary to consider reducing the numbers stated in the Navy Law, and it was essential to concentrate resources in the North Sea. He was reluctant even to claim the third capital ship allowed to him in 1915 under the 1912 *Novelle*, agreeing with Bethmann that Churchill would exploit it to start a scare.[58] His priorities, like his rival's, were larger guns and more money and men. But in February Bethmann ruled that new tax laws were completely out of the question. He acknowledged the strength of Tirpitz's arguments for an increase, but refused to commit himself in view of the 'extraordinarily difficult' financial position. Kühn objected still more strongly, and refused to find even a 3-million mark supplementary credit for 1914.[59] On the eve of war Tirpitz had little prospect of accomplishing what Churchill had managed earlier in the year, and he faced the prospect of another uphill struggle in which the army had a formidable counterclaim.

* * *

Similar conclusions may be drawn about armaments rivalry in the Adriatic. Austro-Italian diplomatic relations deteriorated in 1914, because of friction over the Italian-speakers under Habsburg rule and competition for influence in Albania, but with little impact on defence policy. The new Austro-Hungarian army law was directed primarily against Russia and Serbia; Haus's dreadnought programme, approved by the Delegations in May 1914, was driven in good measure by the need to keep the shipyards busy and to replace obsolescent vessels, and was justified as a contribution to the Triple Alliance. Churchill worked on the premiss of Austro-Italian co-operation, implausible as his critics found it, and the two Powers' naval reinforcements were one reason for his Manchester speech.[60]

Italy was starting to renew its efforts on land and at sea. Four new battleships were laid down in 1913–14, to be armed with 15″ guns. If they were completed on schedule in 1917–18 the Italian navy would have ten dreadnoughts in service, and a decisive numerical edge. It was highly questionable whether they would be, and they were widely criticized for being too thinly armoured and too slow.[61] For the army, the Government requested an extraordinary credit in April, which

[55] Tirpitz to Bethmann, 22 May 1914, BA Rklei R.43F/954.

[56] Tirpitz, *Memoirs*, i. 234. *Kölnische Zeitung*, 10 July 1914, PAAA R.2284.

[57] Tirpitz, *Memoirs*, i. 234. Bethmann minutes, 5 and 6 Feb.; Müller to Bethmann, 18 Feb. 1914, BA Rklei R.43F/954.

[58] Tirpitz to Müller, 30 Apr. 1914, A. von Tirpitz, *Politische Dokumente: Der Aufbau der deutschen Weltmacht* (Stuttgart, 1924), 423.

[59] Bethmann minute, 6 Feb.; Bethmann to Tirpitz, 2 June; Kühn to Bethmann, 13 June 1914, BA Rklei R.43F/954.

[60] Marder, *Dreadnought*, i. 314.

[61] D'Huart to Marine Ministry, 10 and 20 Jan., 10 and 20 Mar., 28 Apr., 20 June 1914, SHM SS Ea(1) 139.

was passed by the Chambers in June. 21 million lire were authorized for small arms and machine guns, 55 million for artillery, 36 million for fortifications, 8 million for aviation, and 30 million for barracks. At the same time the authorities committed themselves to raising the regulation peacetime strength the following year from 250,000 to 275,000 men.[62] Given that the *de facto* strength in January 1914 was 285,000 (225,000 in metropolitan Italy), this had little significance,[63] and the armaments credit, totalling 144 million lire to be spent between 1914–15 and 1918–19, should be compared with War Ministry estimates for 1914–15 of 375 million ordinary and 87 million extraordinary spending.[64] Italy's new energies might usefully strengthen its forces in the next quinquennium, but they were small in relation to developments north of the Alps.

Nor were there real indications of an Italian departure from the Triple Alliance. Diplomacy and military policy were notoriously poorly co-ordinated, but San Giuliano wanted to improve relations with the Central Powers, and staff conversations were in line with his objectives. There resulted the Italo-Austro-German naval convention of 1913, and in the following spring the revival of plans to transport Italian troops through Habsburg territory in order to fight alongside Germany.[65] Pollio's sincerity impressed the German and Austro-Hungarian chiefs, and Moltke believed that he was loyal.[66] Even Conrad, in his 1913 annual report, thought the Italians likely to join their allies in a European war, and conducted his calculations accordingly.[67] He still saw Italy as a future enemy, and his attaché in Rome warned that in another ten years it would be a first-rate Power that would threaten the Monarchy in the Balkans and its Italian-speaking territories.[68] None the less, although contingency planning against Italy continued, it was supposed that for the moment the units concerned could be redeployed.

Italy's allies knew that the 1914 extraordinary credit was less than the army had wanted.[69] The slow pace of recovery from the Libyan War caused a miniature civil–military crisis in the spring of 1914. Pollio and Spingardi had been pressing fruitlessly for over a year for more resources when the resignation of the Giolitti Government in March 1914 ended Spingardi's tenure of office. A new, more conservative, administration under Antonio Salandra turned to General Porrò as a successor. Faced with a growing floating debt and fearing that it was reaching its borowing limits, the ministry rejected Porrò's demands.[70] Behind the general, however, stood the unanimous wishes of the military chiefs,

---

[62] De Gondrecourt to War Ministry, 8 Apr. and 17 June 1914, SHA 7.N. 1370.

[63] De Gondrecourt to War Ministry, 7 Jan. 1914, ibid.

[64] Evidenzbureau report on Italian military developments, 14 Feb. 1914, KAW Gstb Operationsbureau 820.

[65] Cf. Ch. 4 above.

[66] F. Conrad von Hötzendorf, *Aus meiner Dienstzeit 1906–1918* (Vienna, 1921–5), ii. 670–1.

[67] Ibid. 787–8.   [68] Ibid. 489.

[69] Evidenzbureau report on Italian military developments, 1 May 1914, KAW Gstb Operationsbureau 820.

[70] Ibid. and de Gondrecourt to French War Ministry, 29 Nov. 1913, 7 Jan. and 8 Apr. 1914, SHA 7.N. 1370.

including Pollio, who apparently threatened to resign unless money were found at least for the most urgent artillery needs.[71] He wanted between 198 and 551 million lire of extraordinary expenditure, ten additional first-line divisions, and a peacetime strength of 345,000 men. His programme, he told Salandra, was essential simply to get the army back to pre-Libya levels of effectiveness, let alone to compensate for reinforcements abroad.[72] Even so, in the compromise accepted by the new War Minister, Grandi, Salandra and his Finance Minister cut the army's proposals across the board by about two-thirds, the Prime Minister's inaugural address underlining the contribution to national defence of a balanced budget.[73]

Part of Pollio's problem may have been the lack of a persuasive strategic rationale with which to challenge the retrenchment imperative. He presented a stark picture of his service's deficiencies. The Spingardi programme had run its course, and the army lacked direction. But Pollio failed to designate a potential enemy; or, rather, made clear indirectly that it was Paris. His fortification priorities were the north-western frontier and the Tyrrhenian Sea. He wanted higher unit strengths to improve training and frontier protection, and modern siege artillery for the attack.[74] As he had only defensive plans against the Habsburgs, his armaments priorities made sense if he intended to hold the French in the Alps while attacking them on the Rhine. In March 1914 he noted the growth of French 'antipathy' towards Italy and discussed the possibility of war.[75] On the eve of the July crisis he may have been changing his perception of the threat, telling Grandi that Austria-Hungary's military strength endangered Italy and that it had almost as many troops facing her as facing Russia. San Giuliano was reappraising the value of the alliance at the same time.[76] But in the last year before the war Italy's military efforts seem to have been principally anti-French, and neither Pollio's nor Conrad's policy in 1914 displays much evidence that the Adriatic contest was reviving.

* * *

The third possible diversion of resources from the inter-bloc race was towards the Black Sea. In the winter of 1913/14 there was another confrontation between the two alliances. Whereas the Moroccan and Balkan crises had pitted France against Germany and Russia against Austria-Hungary, according to the pattern established in the 1870s and 1880s, the conflict over the military mission to Turkey led by General Liman von Sanders cast Germany and Russia as principals. It was shorter and simpler than its predecessors, and a relatively low-level

[71] De Gondrecourt to War Ministry, 29 Mar. 1914, ibid. Szeptycki to Austrian War Ministry, 5 Apr. 1914, KAW KM Präs (1914) 47–5.

[72] J. Gooch, *Army, State, and Society in Italy* (Basingstoke, 1989), 153. Pollio to Salandra, 30 Mar. 1914, in A. Salandra, *La neutralità italiana (1914): Ricordi e pensieri* (Milan, 1928), 301 ff.

[73] G. Rochat, 'L'esercito italiano nell'estate 1914', *Nuova rivista storica*, 45 (1961), 314–16. De Gondrecourt to War Ministry, 19 June 1914, SHA 7.N. 1370. Salandra, *Neutralità*, 298.

[74] Ibid. 303, 313.

[75] Pollio to Brusati, 4 Mar. 1914, ACS Carte Brusati Scatola 11, VII. 1. 45.

[76] Pollio to Brusati, 25 May 1914, ibid. Gooch, *Italy*, 155. C. J. Lowe and F. Marzari, *Italian Foreign Policy, 1870–1940* (London, 1975), doc. 26.

affair. But if negotiation had failed this time, the alternative envisaged was not just a call-out of reservists but the forcible seizure of territory. The burden of decision on whether to escalate lay primarily in St Petersburg, where attention here must concentrate. But the Russians were responding to a German initiative.

The mission originated with a Turkish request in May 1913.[77] According to the Germans it was the Turks' idea: perhaps the German Ambassador, Wangenheim, put it into their heads. The Turkish army, largely German-equipped and trained, had been thoroughly defeated by forces using, in Serbia's case at least, French weaponry. The new Young-Turk-dominated Government formed after the *coup* of January 1913 made military recovery a high priority and might, if Germany refused more aid, turn to Vienna or Paris. In addition to the loss of their special relationship with the Turkish military, the Germans feared the disintegration and partition of Turkey-in-Asia, following that of Turkey-in-Europe. Arms sales, the military mission, and the Berlin–Baghdad railway had given the Ottoman connection a high political profile over the previous generation, and Wilhelm himself had a long-standing interest in it. Jagow insisted that Germany must not be frozen out, as from Morocco after Agadir, while Bethmann told the Russians that to have rebuffed the Turks would have reversed previous policy.[78]

The Liman von Sanders mission, however, intensified Germany's commitment. The military presence was to be enlarged to over forty officers, and Liman to assume a command as well as advisory role. According to Wilhelm the Turks themselves wanted the general to command their First Army Corps, based at Constantinople, and extra powers were needed for the reforms to stick. Liman's authority did not extend to the city itself, nor to the Straits defences.[79] He was directed not to interfere in Turkish internal politics, and the Germans protested that the mission was not anti-Russian and they could not understand why St Petersburg should object to it.[80] None the less, he would be able to carry out inspections all over the Ottoman Empire, foreign officers could not be engaged without his approval, all military education and training would come within his purview, and he could influence officer promotions, including those of generals.[81] Wilhelm knew that the Russians would fear an increase in Ottoman military power that might be used against them, and Wangenheim and Jagow admitted that St Petersburg had reason for preoccupation.[82] According to the Ambassador, 'in Turkey the Power that controls the army will always be the strongest. If we control the army no anti-German Government will be able to

---

[77] See the account by R. J. Kerner, 'The Mission of Liman von Sanders', *Slavonic Review*, 6 (1927), 12–27, 344–63, 543–60, and 7 (1928), 90–112.

[78] Wangenheim to Jagow, 22 May, Zimmermann to Lucius, 8 Nov., Bethmann memorandum, 18 Nov. 1913, *GP* xxxviii, docs. 15440, 15446, 15450. Kerner, 'Mission', 14–18.

[79] Bethmann memorandum, 19 Nov. 1913, *GP* xxxviii, doc. 15451. Maucorps to Etienne, 29 Nov. and 18 Dec.; Bompard to Doumergue, 15 Dec. 1913, *DDF* 3rd ser. viii, docs. 552, 647, 628.

[80] Bienerth to Austrian War Ministry, 22 Dec. 1913, KAW KM Präs (1914) 47–4.

[81] Jagow to Wilhelm, 20 Sept. 1913, *GP* xxxviii, doc. 15443.

[82] Jagow to Wilhelm, 23 Nov.; Wangenheim to Jagow, 17 Dec. 1913, ibid., docs. 15452, 15493.

stay at the helm.' He had visions of acquiring a position comparable to Britain's in Egypt.[83]

It was not the diplomats who conducted the negotiations with Constantinople, but the Emperor's Military Cabinet, and it did so with extreme secrecy.[84] The purpose, presumably, was to achieve a *fait accompli*, but contracts had not yet been ratified when Sazonov's deputy spoke to the German chargé in St Petersburg on 7 November, warning that rumours had reached the Russians and that they would see a German-commanded unit in the vicinity of the Straits as highly sensitive. But at first they tried to settle the matter amicably. Visiting Berlin ten days later, Kokovtsov asked for a reduction in the powers of the command or that it should be transferred to the corps stationed at Adrianople: he appears to have been too easily reassured by his soothing reception, while Bethmann and Jagow concluded that they could safely go ahead. They told the Russians that matters were too far advanced for the terms of reference to be modified, and Liman's appointment was announced on 4 December. It was up to the Tsar and his advisers to decide what, if anything, to do next.[85]

Russian interests were deeply engaged at the Straits, but Sazonov had few means of leverage. The Chief of the Naval Staff had reported in November 1912 that, from a strategic viewpoint, control of the Straits was 'a convenience and not a vital interest', but for economic reasons secure maritime communication through them was 'a question of absolutely primary importance for the free development of our empire and it will become so in the future to an immeasurably greater degree'. In fact Russia's economic interest was so substantial as to be difficult to distinguish from a strategic one. Between one-third and a half of the country's exports passed through the Bosphorus and the Dardanelles—principally wheat—and machinery for its fastest developing industrial region came in the reverse direction. When the Turks closed the waterway in April–May 1912 for fear of Italian attacks Russian exports were disrupted, and interest rates and unemployment rose. In November 1913 Sazonov wrote that if another Power controlled the Straits, it would mean 'the complete subservience of the economic development of all the south of Russia to that State'.[86] Nicholas himself had long been anxious about the impact on the European balance of Turkish action on Germany's behalf in the Caucasus. Sazonov, however, professed to be unworried about the military aspects of the mission or the use that Germany might make of the Ottoman army, concentrating instead on the political influence it would gain over the Sultan's government.[87] But against so indirect a challenge

[83] Wangenheim to Bethmann, 26 Apr. 1913, ibid., doc. 15439. Kerner, 'Mission', i. 16.

[84] Ibid. 14. Bethmann memorandum, 18 Nov. 1913, *GP* xxxviii, doc. 15450.

[85] Lucius to Auswärtiges Amt, 7 Nov.; Bethmann memoranda, 18 and 19 Dec.; Bethmann to Pourtalès, 26 Nov. 1913, ibid., docs. 15445, 15450–1, 15454.

[86] D. W. Spring, 'Russian Foreign Policy, Economic Interests, and the Straits Question, 1905–14', in R. B. McKean (ed.), *New Perspectives on Modern Russian History* (Basingstoke, 1992), 208–13. A. Bodger, 'Russia and the End of the Ottoman Empire', in M. Kent (ed.), *The Great Powers and the End of the Ottoman Empire* (London, 1984), 82–3.

[87] Doulcet to Doumergue, 26 Dec. 1913, *DDF* 3rd ser. viii, doc. 675. O'Beirne to Grey, 9 Dec. 1913, *BD* x(i), doc. 412.

it would be hard for him to win the co-operation from his entente partners that was essential if diplomatic, economic, or military pressure were to be effective.

Sazonov's first move was to seek a tripartite *démarche*, but even though this was to be in Constantinople rather than Berlin he failed to win the solidarity he wanted. On 13 December the three Entente Ambassadors made a mild (and not even collective) enquiry as to whether the contract respected Ottoman sovereignty and the status of the Dardanelles: the Turks refused to discuss the issue. Sazonov was 'furious' with the British, who had been embarrassed to discover that the head of their naval mission at Constantinople, Admiral Limpus, had similar command powers to Liman. They doubted whether the affair was as important as Sazonov said it was, and as in 1912 they questioned his judgement and steadiness. Their caution blocked further progress along the diplomatic road.[88]

Yet economic sanctions too were problematic. Russia accounted for only 6 per cent of Ottoman foreign trade, and supplied nothing the Turks really needed. Its investments were small, and it held little of the Ottoman public debt.[89] The most effective step would be to close the Paris market to Turkish borrowers. But the French Government had just approved the flotation of a Turkish loan in return for advantages for French missionary activity and trade, and for port and railway concessions. Whereas Sazonov insisted that a financial boycott would work, the French maintained that it would not, and that the Turks would merely turn to Germany. They refused to go along with one.[90]

There remained the possibility of more drastic measures. On 7 December Sazonov suggested to the British that, if economic and financial pressures failed, the entente should consider seizing Turkish ports in the Mediterranean and Black Seas. This, he suggested, Germany would not consider an unfriendly act— a notion that caused derision in the Foreign Office.[91] Twelve days later he unveiled a graduated programme of, first, financial pressure, then the appointment of French and Russian inspectors to oversee the Turkish administration of Armenia, and finally Russian occupation of Bayazid and Erzerum. 'Nothing was so likely to bring about war', he remarked, 'as to appear to be afraid of it, and the impression had unfortunately gained ground that Russia would not fight. This was a great danger for peace.'[92] Although negotiations with the Germans now made more headway and the outlines of a settlement were coming into view, Sazonov was under domestic pressure to obtain a prestige victory. Early in January there was renewed tension, Buchanan warning that if the affair dragged on much longer it would become very serious.[93] On the 5 January Sazonov asked

[88] Buchanan to Grey, 23 Dec.; Nicolson to O'Beirne, 2 Dec.; Mallet to Grey, 5 Dec.; Grey to O'Beirne, 9, 11, 16 Dec. 1913, ibid., docs. 446, 393, 405, 411, 417, 434.

[89] Bodger, 'Russia', 84.

[90] Poincaré, *Service*, iv. 10–11, 24. Buchanan and Bertie to Grey, 8 and 11 Jan. 1914, *BD* x(i), docs. 465–6.

[91] O'Beirne to Grey, 7 and 9 Dec., ibid., docs. 406, 412.

[92] Buchanan to Grey, 19 Dec. 1913, ibid., doc. 440.

[93] Buchanan to Grey, 7 Jan. 1914, ibid., doc. 463.

Nicholas for a special conference in view of the continuing deadlock and the possibility that Germany would refuse concessions. Simply to acquiesce in Liman's appointment would be 'a great political defeat and might have very disastrous consequences'; it would leave Russia exposed to further challenges, and Britain and France might look elsewhere. Sazonov was also mindful of a message from his chargé in London, whom Crowe had asked three questions that the Russians should have asked themselves. What exactly did they want? What means of pressure did they envisage applying to the Ottomans? And would they push the issue to the point of armed conflict with Berlin?[94] Thus far the Russians had taken no special military measures. Their Ambassador in Constantinople had warned that the Turks would not submit to mere threats and unless it was intended to use force he opposed concentrating troops on the frontier.[95] It was time to decide how far Russia would go.

The answer, to judge from the special conference when it was held on 13 January, was not very far. In his briefing Sazonov again envisaged occupying Trebizond or Bayazid until Russia's demands were met, but only after a preparatory phase of financial boycott, ultimatum, and redeployments in the Caucasus. There must be French and British commitment to see the action through, and with such caution and a united front, he believed, there would be no European war. All present at the conference (Sazonov, Kokovtsov, Grigorovich, Sukhomlinov, and Zhilinski) opposed a war with Germany. Sukhomlinov and Zhilinski said Russia was prepared for one-to-one hostilities with Berlin or Vienna, but given the certainty of Triple Alliance involvement this meant little. Kokovtsov insisted that even Sazonov's graduated escalation would lead to war with the Central Powers, and was more sceptical about the existence of a middle way. He would go along only with a financial boycott, and the conference agreed that anything beyond that would depend on Britain and France (which meant principally Britain). According to Sazonov, Germany did not fear France and Russia, but if the Royal Navy were involved the Reich might face social catastrophe within six weeks.[96]

Sazonov admitted to the conference, however, that he still lacked the requisite British commitment. There were signs that the French were more adventurous. Maurice Paléologue, the Political Director at the Quai d'Orsay, suggested unofficially that the Russians should send a warship and remove it only when the Turks yielded. Delcassé told Sazonov that French support would be unlimited.[97] Yet even he came to fear that a seizure of 'strategic points' (as Sazonov called them) would cause a clash with Germany over an issue that had little bear-

[94] Kerner, 'Mission', iv. 95–7. *BD* x(i), doc. 452. De Etter to Sazonov, 29 Dec. 1913, G. A. Schreiner (ed.), *Entente Diplomacy and the World: Matrix of the History of Europe, 1909–1914* (London, 1921), doc. 818.

[95] Giers to Sazonov, 14 Dec. 1913, ibid., doc. 804.

[96] Kerner, 'Mission', iv. 96–102. M. Pokrowski (ed.), *Drei Konferenzen (zur Vorgeschichte des Weltkrieges)* (1920), 32 ff.

[97] V. I. Bovykin, *Iz istorii vozniknoveniya pervoi mirovoi voiny: Otnosheniya Rossii i Frantsii v 1912–1914 gg* (Moscow, 1961), 174.

ing on French interests. Pichon, once again Foreign Minister, sympathized at first with demands for compensation but then backed off, perhaps because of warnings from his Berlin Embassy. Before going beyond *démarches* in Constantinople the French believed that there must be consultation—in other words, Britain's attitude was crucial for them too.[98] But before the special conference Buchanan told Sazonov that occupying Turkish territory was likely to cause German intervention and it was improbable that Britain would support it. Sazonov warned that if London refused co-operation the entente would be at an end and that whereas collective action could achieve the objective peacefully, unilateral Russian measures would lead to a war into which Britain would be dragged anyway. None the less, Grey and Crowe were agreed that the von Sanders affair was not worth fighting over and they advised Buchanan that the Liberal Government was unlikely to take serious measures, though it could not object to St Petersburg doing so. In any case Kokovtsov insisted at the conference that, even before imposing a financial boycott, Russia must continue negotiating until all hope of compromise was lost.[99]

The Triple Entente was too disunited to be able to force a resolution. All the same, the Turks were worried. Major Eggeling reported from St Petersburg that the Turkish War Ministry was interrogating its attaché there about Russian concentration times in Armenia. The Erzerum garrison was poorly trained and equipped, and the attaché believed that Russia could occupy the city without mobilizing. Although Eggeling doubted that the Russians would take action, in Vienna there were similar rumours.[100] Turkish fears of Russian attack may have helped bring on a settlement, as well as British and French reluctance to confront the Central Powers. So too, however, did Germany's willingness to sidestep. Perhaps because the Military Cabinet had made the running, German diplomats were less committed to the von Sanders enterprise, and Wangenheim saw a means of feinting Sazonov. Really, he supposed, the Russians objected to the mission *per se*, but they had focused on the Constantinople command. Germany could concede this while leaving intact the General's more important training and inspection roles. Jagow agreed that Germany's interests did not merit making the affair a 'European prestige question', and the ambassador sounded out his Russian opposite number, though explaining that a compromise must seem the outcome of a Turkish change of heart rather than a German climb-down.[101]

The Russian special conference was willing to accept a general inspection right for Liman, on the condition that it was not linked to a territorial command, and

[98] Delcassé to Doumergue, 7 Jan. 1914, *DDF* 3rd ser. ix, doc. 31; Pichon to Paul Cambon, 22 Nov.; Pichon note, 9 Dec., Jules Cambon to Pichon, 30 Nov. 1913, ibid. viii, docs. 516, 598, 556.

[99] Buchanan to Grey, 6 Jan. 1914; Crowe and Grey minutes, 29 Dec. 1913; Nicolson to Buchanan, 14 Jan. 1914, ibid., docs. 463, 452, 467.

[100] Eggeling to War Ministry, 3 Jan. 1914, PAAA R.10433. Kageneck report, 8 Jan. 1914, PAAA R.8625.

[101] Wangenheim to Jagow, 17 Dec. 1913; Jagow to Mutius and Pourtalès, 3 and 6 Jan. 1914, *GP* xxxviii, docs. 15493, 15509–10. Schreiner (ed.), *Entente Diplomacy*, doc. 814.

in mid-January an accommodation was reached. Liman was promoted to the rank of a German cavalry general and a Turkish marshal, thus becoming too senior to command a corps, although he retained his other functions. The conflict was thus liquidated before attaining the intensity of the Balkan and Moroccan crises. Except for Russia, none of the Powers felt their vital interests were committed, and Russia would not resort to force without a British green light. All the same, the special conference showed that Kokovtsov was becoming isolated as a steadying influence even before Goremykin replaced him in February. Sazonov, like Berchtold, was increasingly willing to support his diplomacy by military threats and acts, and the army and navy chiefs were increasingly willing to go along with him.

The von Sanders affair exacerbated Russo-Turkish rivalry, but without significantly distracting resources from the central inter-bloc confrontation. On the contrary, it heightened Continental military tension. The Russians had responded to Turkey's dreadnought orders with their 1911 naval programme, and a land confrontation was developing in the Caucasus. But investigations during an alert in April 1913 suggested that they could transport a mere 700 men to the Bosphorus,[102] and when contemplating pressure on the Ottomans Sazonov had to confine his options to the eastern shores of the Black Sea. In a memorandum of 6 December he argued that Turkey was likely to collapse in the near future and that Russia could not allow another Power to control the Straits. Another special conference was required to consider the feasibility of seizing them and Constantinople. A follow-up paper by the naval staff, however, argued that Turkey's warship purchases ruled out offensive action and hoped that there would be no war between 1914 and 1916. 'What Russia desires in the next few years is a postponement of the final settlement of the Eastern Question and the strict maintenance of the political status quo.'[103]

This gloomy prognosis set the tone for the second special conference on 21 February 1914, whose conclusions the Tsar 'entirely' approved.[104] Although Captain Nemitz, the chief of operations in the Naval Staff, wanted a landing at the outbreak of hostilities, the navy admitted to a woeful shortage of transport. Moreover, the two Turkish dreadnoughts would arrive in the autumn, and the first two Russian ones (armed with smaller guns) would not be ready before June and September 1915. Sazonov and Zhilinski agreed that an operation to seize Constantinople was inconceivable outside the context of a general European war (which the previous conference had opposed), and in such a war Zhilinski and Danilov would insist on the Western front taking priority. None the less, the conference decided on a series of steps to increase preparedness, including raising troop strengths in the units designated for the assault, expanding the Black Sea shipping fleet, and improving the Caucasus railways. In March the Duma

---

[102] Spring, 'Straits Question', 207.

[103] Kerner, 'Mission', iv. 93–4. I. V. Bestuzhev, 'Russian Foreign Policy, February–June 1914', *Journal of Contemporary History*, 1/3 (1966), 96.

[104] Kerner, 'Mission', 104–6; Pokrowski (ed.), *Drei Konferenzen*, 46 ff.

secretly voted funds to speed up progress on the 1911 dreadnoughts, the French naval attaché reporting that because of the von Sanders affair the labour force in the Black Sea yards had doubled in a year and work was proceeding night and day.[105] Russian diplomacy moved up a gear, reaching an understanding with Romania jointly to resist any closure of the Straits to the commerce of the Black Sea Powers.[106] Finally, the special conference approved Grigorovich's plans for a second generation of Black Sea capital ships. The Duma was asked to approve an emergency programme of over 100 million roubles for one more battleship to be laid down in 1914–15, together with two cruisers, eight destroyers, and six submarines, and early in July it did so.[107]

* * *

Simultaneously with the Black Sea credit, however, the Duma voted for the Great Programme. Although the programme had an anti-Turkish component, its emphasis was on Europe, and the additional army corps originally intended for the Caucasus was relocated to Kiev.[108] Russia could afford both Black Sea battleships and extra divisions in the West, and the von Sanders affair intensified tsarist preparations against Austria-Hungary and Germany as well as against the Ottomans, rather than moderating the central arms race by stimulating a peripheral one. On the contrary, in the spring of 1914 the Central Powers had reason to fear that the Triple Entente was tightening its encirclement.

The compromise over the military mission had left neither side satisfied. Pourtalès reported that Sazonov and Nicholas were pointedly avoiding thanking Germany and that the Russian press was hostile.[109] Sazonov followed up the affair with a diplomatic offensive not only in the Balkans and the Black Sea but also on the Great-Power plane. As he put it, perhaps tongue-in-cheek, he regarded the successful result as being in considerable measure due to tripartite co-operation, and he wished to turn the entente into an alliance.[110] Nicholas shared this view, Paléologue (who had now replaced Delcassé) reporting that the Russians hoped that a British alliance would deter Constantinople from counting on German support in a future Straits crisis.[111] Buchanan warned that the tsarist empire was growing so powerful that Britain must keep its friendship at almost any cost, and that a Russian deal with Berlin was on the cards if London seemed unreliable. Doumergue, similarly, feared German attempts to detach

[105] Czernin telegram, 16 Mar. 1914, HHStA PA XL Russland, 1914. Gallaud to Marine Ministry, 7 Apr. 1914, SHM SS Em 157.

[106] Kerner, 'Mission', iv. 106.

[107] Austrian chargé in St Petersburg, 30 May 1914, HHStA PA XL Russland 1914. Gallaud to Marine Ministry, 7 Apr. 1914, SHM SS Em 157, and 22 May 1914, SHM SS (Ea) 160. Paléologue to Doumergue, 13 Apr. 1914, *DDF* 3rd ser. x, doc. 100. The French reports refer to three battleships, but the Austrians and Shatsillo, *Russkii imperializm*, 158, say one.

[108] See Ch. 5, sect. 2, above.

[109] Szyögény to Berchtold, 23 Jan. 1914, HHStA PA X Kartone 139. Pourtalès to Bethmann, 31 Jan. 1914, *GP* xxxviii, doc. 15525.

[110] Poincaré, Notes journalières, 22 Jan. 1914, BN Poincaré MSS n.a.fr. 16026.

[111] Paléologue to Doumergue, 17 Feb. 1914, *DDF* 3rd ser. ix, doc. 322; and 18 Apr. 1914, ibid. x, doc. 123.

St Petersburg.[112] Hence the French acted as intermediaries, explaining to Grey when he visited Paris with George V in April 1914 that an arrangement was needed not primarily on strategic grounds but in order to safeguard Russia's friendship.[113]

The gesture selected was to offer conversations on the basis of the November 1912 Grey–Cambon letters. Britain and Russia would seek technical understandings that would be taken into account in the event of war without being binding. The BEF was dedicated to Western Europe, and even at sea there was limited scope for co-operation, given the interposition between the two navies of the High Seas Fleet. The Russians hoped, none the less, for a British undertaking to draw the Germans into the North Sea, perhaps making possible a landing in Pomerania; for assistance in protecting the Black Sea; and for access to Britain's Eastern Mediterranean bases. In June 1914 discussions began between the Admiralty and the Russian attaché in London, who soon discovered that his hosts were in no haste.[114] The naval conversations fell far short of Sazonov's vision.

All the same, the manner of the Foreign Secretary's handling of the issue turned out to be as important as the substance. The news of the conversations was leaked from the Russian Embassy in London to the German Government, which arranged for allegations in the *Berliner Tageblatt* of a Russo-British understanding. Quizzed in the Commons on 11 June, Grey said that there existed no agreements that would restrict Britain's political freedom in case of war (which was technically correct) and that no negotiations were in progress that would make this less true (which was also correct, but misleading). Jagow told the British Ambassador that he had 'so much confidence in your [Grey's] loyalty and straightforwardness that his mind was now completely at rest', but he warned that a naval agreement would destroy the present Anglo-German cordiality and encourage a new armaments agitation.[115] Grey had been caught out as disingenuous, and the Power with which Germany enjoyed the best relations within the Triple Entente seemed more closely linked than ever with the most menacing.

At the same time as Sazonov sought to consolidate the entente diplomatically, inter-bloc tension was rising over Russian armaments. The most visible evidence was a press war, sparked off by a commentary on 'Russia and Germany' in the *Kölnische Zeitung* on 2 March. According to the newspaper's St Petersburg correspondent there was no immediate danger of war, but once the Russians were militarily prepared, in three or four years' time, it would be quite a different matter. The article caused great concern in Russia, where it triggered a fall on the Bourse; it was followed by a similar analysis in *Germania*, although other newspapers were less alarmist. According to Pourtalès the article was inept and

---

[112] Buchanan to Nicolson, 16 Apr.; Grey to Bertie, 1 May 1914, *BD* x(ii), docs. 538, 541.

[113] Grey, *Twenty-Five Years*, i. 283–5.

[114] Sazonov to Benckendorff, 28 May 1914; Volkoff to Chief of Naval Staff, 28 June 1914, Schreiner (ed.), *Entente Diplomacy*, docs. 850–1. Churchill to Grey, 7 July 1914, *BD* x(ii), doc. 559.

[115] E. Grey, *Twenty-Five Years* (London, 1925), i. 289–96. Goschen to Grey, 23 May and 16 June 1914, *BD* ix(ii), 544, 550.

inaccurate, and had been cleared beforehand with neither his embassy nor with the German Foreign Ministry. Pourtalès and Jagow pledged that it had not been officially inspired, Sazonov replying that no one in Russia thought seriously of attacking Germany, and that 'Russian armaments are nothing other than a symptom of the sickness prevailing in all Europe of Armaments Fever'.[116]

Unfortunately this was not the end of the affair. Sazonov was not convinced, and told Buchanan that he believed the article was planted. The agitation spread, and there was a notable delay before the German Government tried to stop it. Only on 11 March, after more than a week, did the *Frankfurter Zeitung* deny that Russo-German relations had deteriorated, and a semi-official communiqué to the same effect appeared in the *Norddeutsche Allgemeine Zeitung*. Jagow told the British Ambassador that he was intervening because the campaign had gone too far and lasted too long, but the British and French Embassies suspected that he did not disapprove of it in principle, and Sazonov warned that if the aim was to intimidate Russia it would have the opposite effect. The Empire could readily afford another two or three army corps, and any new German measures could be easily matched.[117] The Tsar drew a similar conclusion.[118] Once Sazonov had been assured that the German press had orders to end the campaign he inspired a conciliatory statement in *Rossiya* on 13 March, but the effect was neutralized by a commentary in the *Birshevaia Viedemosti* that 'Russia desires peace but is prepared for war'. This latter was placed by Sukhomlinov, but approved by Nicholas himself, who was determined to show that he would not be bullied. A response in the *Norddeutsche Allgemeine Zeitung* criticized both the *Birshevaia Viedemosti* and the *Kölnische Zeitung*, and hoped for continuing Russo-German friendship.[119]

The press war was no superficial phenomenon. It had echoes in Vienna, centred on reports that Russia intended a series of trial mobilizations. In April a new campaign in Germany focused on the Baltic Fleet. There were accompanying diplomatic incidents between Russia and its Western neighbours.[120] Sazonov told Pourtalès that relations had not fundamentally changed, but he was almost certainly right to see the episode as a warning shot, perhaps started unofficially but officially tolerated. His Ambassador in Berlin reported that there was anxiety about tsarist military strength, especially in siege artillery, and confirmed the intimidatory intent, as did the military attaché. But the size of the Duma

[116] Pourtalès to Jagow, 6 Mar. 1914, *GP* xxxix, doc. 15843. Goschen to Grey, 6 Mar. 1914, *BD* x(ii), doc. 518. De Manneville to Doumergue, 5 Mar. 1914, *DDF* 3rd ser. ix, doc. 402.

[117] Ibid. and Buchanan to Grey, 8 Mar.; Goschen to Grey, 10, 11, and 13 Mar. 1914, *BD* x(ii), docs. 520, 523–5. Doulcet to Doumergue, 12 Mar. 1914, *DDF* 3rd ser. ix, doc. 441.

[118] Buchanan to Grey, 15 Mar. 1914, *BD* x(ii), doc. 527.

[119] Buchanan to Grey and Nicolson, 15 and 18 Mar. 1914, *BD* x(ii), docs. 527–9. Jagow to Pourtalès, 12 Mar.; Pourtalès to Jagow and Bethmann, 12 and 16 Mar. 1914, *GP* xxxix, docs. 15845, 15841, 15851. Doulcet and J. Cambon to Doumergue, 13 and 14 Mar. 1914, *DDF* 3rd ser. ix, docs. 450, 457.

[120] De Bunsen to Grey, 6 and 13 Mar. 1914, *BD* x(ii), docs. 519, 526. Faramond to Gauthier, 11 Apr. 1914, *DDF* 3rd ser. ix, doc. 99. Szyögyény to Austrian Foreign Ministry, 15 and 22 Apr., 29 May, 15 July 1914, HHStA, PA III Kartone 171.

majorities for military and naval increases bears out the British Ambassador's conclusion that the effect was to harden Russian resolve.[121]

* * *

So far from the inter-bloc arms race losing impetus in the spring of 1914, it continued at the forefront of public consciousness. Britain's expenditure increase did not revive the North Sea race, nor Italy's that in the Adriatic, if only because of the absence of German and Austro-Hungarian retaliation. Russia's resources permitted it to sustain a Black Sea and a European race simultaneously. If the French and German army bills had dominated armaments developments a year earlier, the delayed Russian response now overshadowed the scene, and the Central Powers' response to that response must next be traced. Informed by an avalanche of evidence about Russian capabilities, the debate in Vienna and Berlin turned on the interpretation of Russian intentions, and on whether the reaction should be a new round of military and diplomatic countermeasures or a preventive war.

The Austro-Hungarian leaders had to balance the easing of the threats from Italy, Serbia, and Montenegro against the rising perils from Russia and Romania. *Vis-à-vis* the latter, 1913–14 marked a watershed comparable to the Italian war scare of 1904. Romania's alliance with the Central Powers was a secret to all but King Carol and his senior ministers, and vulnerable once public opinion turned against the Habsburgs. After accounts had been settled with Bulgaria, the three million Romanian-speakers under Magyar rule in Transylvania loomed larger than the one million under Russian control in Bessarabia. Negotiations between the Hungarians and the leaders of the Romanians within the Dual Monarchy broke down.[122] Berchtold sent Count Ottokar Czernin, a senior diplomat and confidant of Franz Ferdinand, to cajole Carol into a public commitment, but Czernin's efforts were fruitless and the Bratianu Government, formed in January 1914, moved towards the Franco-Russian camp. In June Nicholas II visited Carol at Constantza, and Sazonov drove with his Romanian hosts across the unfortified Hungarian border. Meanwhile the German and Austro-Hungarian Foreign Ministries failed to co-ordinate their efforts either in maintaining Romania's allegiance or in bidding for Bulgaria.[123]

The implications were grave. Conrad estimated that Romania could field sixteen and a half divisions, compared with Serbia's eleven, Montenegro's four, and the Monarchy's forty-eight. Its defection would deprive him of an ally against

[121] Pourtalès to Jagow, 28 Apr. 1914, *GP* xxxix, doc. 15859. Sverbeyev to Sazonov, 12 Mar. 1913, Schreiner (ed.), *Entente Diplomacy*, doc. 838. Bazarov to Stavka, 28 Feb. 1914, E. Adamov, 'K voprosi podgotovke mirovoi voiny', *Krasnyi Arkhiv*, 64 (1934), 119. Buchanan to Nicolson, 18 Mar. 1914, *BD* x(ii), doc. 529.

[122] B. Jelavich, 'Romania in the First World War: The Pre-War Crisis, 1912–1914', *International History Review*, 14 (1992), 441–51. K. Hitchins, 'The Nationality Problem in Hungary: István Tisza and the Rumanian National Party, 1910–1914', *Journal of Modern History*, 53 (1981), 619–51.

[123] L. Albertini, *The Origins of the War of 1914* (London, 1952–7), i, ch. 9. S. R. Williamson, *Austria-Hungary and the Origins of the First World War* (Basingstoke, 1991), 160 ff. F. R. Bridge, 'The Habsburg Monarchy and the Ottoman Empire, 1900–1918', in Kent (ed.), *Ottoman Empire*, esp. 42–5.

Russia and double the odds against him in the south-east.[124] Moreover, the Romanians aimed to have ten reserve divisions well enough organized and equipped to fight alongside the front-line troops by 1916. Having ordered 200,000 rifles from Steyr in 1912–13, they now intended to increase their field guns from 740 to 1,264, double their heavy field artillery, and multiply their mountain-gun batteries from four to thirty, with the manifest objective of a Carpathian campaign. In June 1914 their War Ministry was assigned 107 million francs to begin purchases, and mobilization and concentration against Austria-Hungary were reportedly under study.[125]

Already in November 1913 Conrad had decided to place Romania under intelligence surveillance, and soon afterwards he authorized his chief of operations to start work on a concentration plan. In February he asked for reconnaissance prior to fortification of the border, and began discussion of railway needs.[126] He told the German attaché that he thought he could count on Italy but assumed a Russian–Serb–Montenegrin–Romanian combination against him. Against such a combination he could not, even with German help, foresee a reasonable prospect of success.[127] Before beginning preparation on the ground, however, he needed political confirmation that his assumption of Romanian hostility was justified. On 4 June the Emperor reluctantly gave it by agreeing that, if war broke out with Russia, troops must be left in Transylvania.[128] Except for Germany and (for the moment) Italy, the Monarchy faced a continuous front of hostility.

Yet whatever the medium-term danger from the South Slav States, their present exhaustion might give Conrad one more opportunity before the ring was closed. There was a disturbing prospect of Serb–Montenegrin unification, which by giving Belgrade access to the sea would nullify the damage limitation accomplished during the First Balkan War. Negotiations for a customs union had begun in 1913, and in January 1914 the Montenegrin Government announced that it would pursue foreign-policy harmonization and common military organization and training. The two War Ministers discussed standard rifle and artillery calibres and tactical doctrine.[129] Nicholas II and Sazonov encouraged the process, while urging that it should proceed gradually in order to deny the Austrians a pretext for stopping it.[130] In fact the piecemeal nature of the challenge persuaded Berchtold that it would be difficult to do so, especially as Germany was disinclined to help him. Conrad's and Krobatin's pleas that Austria-Hungary should intervene (or at least demand the Montenegrin coast in compensation) failed to win his support.[131]

[124] Conrad, *Dienstzeit*, iii. 760.

[125] Hranilović to War Ministry, 11 and 24 Feb., 10 and 22 Mar., 6 June 1914, KAW KM Präs (1914) 47–8. Conrad, *Dienstzeit*, iii. 557.

[126] Ibid. 492, 494, 554.

[127] Kageneck report, 8 Jan. 1914, PAAA R.8625. Conrad, *Dienstzeit*, iii. 561.   [128] Ibid. 647, 700.

[129] Hubka to War Ministry, 6 Feb. 1914, KAW KM Präs (1914) 47–16. Delaroche-Vernet to Doumergue, 26 May 1914, *DDF* 3rd ser. x, doc. 286.

[130] Paléologue to Doumergue, 22 Apr. 1914, ibid., doc. 141. Albertini, *Origins*, i. 509 ff.

[131] Conrad, *Dienstzeit*, iii. 616, 661. Berchtold diary, 10 Nov. 1913 and 17 Feb. 1914, HHStA Berchtold MSS 2.

A second danger came from South Slav military plans. The army budget presented to the Montenegrin Skupshina in 1914 was sixteen times bigger than in 1912. Henceforth there was to be a standing force of 5,000 men, which in wartime could be raised to 65,000.[132] Similar projects in Belgrade, however, became caught up in a vicious civil–military struggle. In January the War Minister asked for a budget of 90 million dinars, an extraordinary credit, and a peacetime strength of 95,000. When the Government offered barely half of what he asked, he resigned, other officers refusing to serve until the young and previously obscure Colonel Stefanović took the post.[133] A major confrontation followed in the early summer, ostensibly over whether civilians or military should have ceremonial precedence in the newly conquered territories, but fuelled by the unsatisfied military demands. Culminating in King Peter's abdication and Crown Prince Alexander's becoming regent, the conflict delayed two bills intended to prolong military service and grant 123 million dinars for re-equipment. Although the War Ministry announced in May that the army would grow from six to twelve divisions over the next ten years, the practicalities had still not been worked out.[134]

Serbia and Montenegro laboured under major disadvantages. The Serbian army remained at exceptional strength throughout the first half of 1914, stationing 75–85,000 men in the new territories, which had so far yielded only 12–13,000 recruits of dubious quality. Montenegro, too, was at reinforced strength, and occupation costs exacerbated the two governments' financial difficulties.[135] Montenegro could contemplate military increases only because of prospective Russian subsidies,[136] and in August 1913 Nikita had pleaded with the French that he was near insolvency. A loan by a Franco-Italian consortium was approved, though the King was warned against further 'intrigues'. But by May 1914 no money had come through, and the officers were not receiving their salaries.[137] Serbia was little better off. The 123-million dinar credit was to be financed by Treasury bills, as the Government could borrow no more abroad. It could remain solvent only because of the 250-million franc French loan, which in January was finally admitted to the Paris Bourse. Yet after payment of commissions and clearance of previous debts, the operation would yield only 59 million francs of 'new' money against predicted budget deficits of 30 and 50 millions for 1913 and 1914.[138]

[132] Hubka to War Ministry, 25 Feb. 1914, KAW KM Präs (1914) 47–16. Annual report on Montenegro, 1913, KAW KM Präs (1914) 56–6.

[133] Gellinek to War Ministry, 6, 17, 22 Jan. 1914, KAW KM Präs (1914) 47–7.

[134] Gellinek to War Ministry, 16 Feb., 10, 25, 27 May, 21 June 1914, ibid. Giesl to Berchtold, 20 and 29 May 1914, ibid. 51–7.

[135] Gellinek to War Ministry, 9 May and 16 June 1914, ibid. 47–7. Hubka to War Ministry, 16 and 17 Feb. 1914, ibid. 47–16.

[136] Hubka to War Ministry, 6 May, ibid.

[137] Delaroche-Vernet to Pichon, 26 Aug.; Barthou to Delaroche-Vernet, 8 Oct. 1913, *DDF* 3rd ser. viii, docs. 82, 284; Russian Embassy note, 23 Feb. 1914, ibid. ix, doc. 345; Tailhand to Doumergue, 20 Mar.; Russian Embassy note, 25 May 1914, ibid. x, docs. 43, 283.

[138] Gellinek to War Ministry, 29 May 1914, KAW KM Präs (1914) 47–7. Giesl to Berchtold, 20 May 1914, ibid. 51–7. Note on Serb loan, 22 Oct. 1913, Pichon to Delcassé, 18 Nov. 1913, *DDF* 3rd ser. viii, docs. 370, 494. Clément-Simon to Doumergue, 9 Dec. 1913, AMAE NS Serbie 9.

The French were able to drive a hard bargain, and they insisted on the loan being tied to purchases from their manufacturers. 400,000 rifles (worth 33.6 million francs) were to be ordered from Châtellerault; 22 millions worth of field and mountain guns were to come from Schneider and other firms. Belgrade agreed reluctantly, and the deal at once began to fall apart.[139] In March it was reported that fifteen batteries of mountain guns were to be ordered from Krupp. Schneider appealed for 'energetic intervention' by the Quai d'Orsay, and Serbia found itself caught in a trial of strength between the two enterprises, each supported by their diplomats.[140] As for the rifles, the Serbs had only 150,000 modern weapons, which had deteriorated in the recent fighting. They preferred a French supplier, but for Châtellerault to deliver all 400,000 would take five and a half years. Belgrade agreed to purchase all it could deliver in three, but by June 1914 the contract was still not signed.[141] The Serbs alleged they could get better terms elsewhere, and although the Quai d'Orsay was enthusiastic for the contract the French War Ministry begrudged committing itself to a large and unprofitable production run and objected that France's own needs would suffer. Discussions with French private companies made no headway, and in July the Serbs ordered 208,000 weapons from Vickers. It was much too late.[142]

The Serbian army was overstretched and Serbian finances were precarious. When war seemed possible between Greece and Turkey Pašić warned his ally that he was in no condition to fight.[143] Both Serbia's and Montenegro's weak spots were accurately reported to the Vienna General Staff, where the unavailing quest for rifles was closely monitored. According to the Belgrade attaché, Gellinek, the Serbian army was weaker than before the Balkan Wars and would need four years to recover, but the officer corps' hostility to Austria-Hungary was undiminished.[144] On the other hand, Potiorek reported that he needed more railways and fortifications in the annexed provinces and at least another 20,000 mobile troops. His position had improved since 1911 but so had that of the potential adversary.[145] By 1916–17 new Bosnian railways might be ready and the reforms of 1912–14 would have yielded extra equipment and men. But by then Serbia and Montenegro would have recuperated, the Romanian build-up would have progressed, and Italy would be freed from the Libyan incubus and probably hostile once more. Bad as Austria-Hungary's position was now, if it waited its rearmament would be outmatched by its enemies.

Developments in the Balkans were dwarfed by those unfolding to the

[139] Paléologue to Doumergue, 19 Dec. 1913; Doumergue to Clément-Simon, 7 Jan.; Clément-Simon to Doumergue, 13 Jan. 1914, ibid.

[140] e.g. Fourmier to Foreign Ministry, 7 Mar.; Foreign Ministry to Descos, 12 Mar.; Schneider to Foreign Ministry, 20 June 1914, ibid.

[141] War Ministry to Foreign Ministry, 22 Oct. 1913; Descos to Doumergue, 11 Feb.; Clément-Simon to Doumergue, 13 Jan. 1914, ibid.

[142] Bouniols to War Ministry, 29 May; Viviani to Messimy, 28 June 1914, ibid. Bouniols to Finance Ministry, 22 July 1914, MFF B.31269.

[143] Artamov to Stavka, 3 June 1914, Adamov, 'Podgotovke', 127.

[144] Berchtold diary, 3 Dec. 1913, 23 Jan. 1914, HHStA Berchtold MSS 2.

[145] Potiorek to Conrad, 9 Mar. 1914, KAW Gstb Operationsbureau 615.

north-east. Franz Joseph was briefed by Conrad on Russian military preparations, and discussed with Berchtold the political consequences.[146] The Austrians took a calmer view of the immediate danger than of the longer-term prospects. There had even developed something of a *détente* between them and St Petersburg as Russo-German relations deteriorated, Sazonov sending a reassurance that military increases safeguarded the peace.[147] The War Ministry attempted to assuage anxieties about another tsarist trial mobilization, Krobatin advising Berchtold that Russia was trying to force them to waste millions and they should not call out a single reservist in response. In May the press reported that Russia planned to call up three conscript classes in the autumn, in an unprecedented exercise that would raise its standing army to over 2 million. But Conrad shared Krobatin's reluctance to retain the senior Austro-Hungarian class in retaliation, because of the expense and the unsettlement of civilian morale.[148]

The longer-term prospect was more daunting. Conrad in retrospect described Russia's preparations as his most serious preoccupation at this time, and that about which he knew least. The General Staff estimated that the Russians could run 260 trains a day into the concentration zone, against the Monarchy's 153; they disposed of nine lines against Austria-Hungary's seven (five of which were single-tracked). Early in 1914 Conrad modified his Galician deployment in order to position his men further back, and he expected the balance to continue to worsen.[149] Czernin warned that although St Petersburg inclined to peace at present, when it was militarily prepared in 1917 a more forceful policy could be expected, and Berchtold and Franz Joseph knew of the disquiet in Berlin.[150] The Emperor told the German Ambassador that Russia's preparations were 'very hazardous', and he was 'very apprehensive' about the tendencies of its policy, fearing that the Tsar, who did not want war, would be carried away by other forces: 'with the Russians there is nothing more to be done.'[151]

The upshot was that the General Staff was increasingly willing to envisage not only a Balkan but a European war, and preventive action against Russia as well as Serbia. In January Conrad still considered a localized war the preferable option if Russia could be kept inactive; a general conflict would be a 'break-the-bank game'. But in the following month he told his chief of operations that war with France and Russia was inevitable and he asked why it should not be launched now before they were ready and the Balkan States grew stronger. On 12 March he told Berchtold that France and Russia would 'start it' (*losgehen*) when it suited them. He conceded that the Habsburg artillery would have improved in three years' time, but the overall position would not. At present

[146] Conrad reports to Franz Joseph, 24 Feb. and 10 Mar. 1914, KAW Gstb Operationsbureau 739. Berchtold diary, 16 Feb., 14 Mar. 1914, HHStA Berchtold MSS 2.

[147] Ibid. 13 Mar. 1914; Hohenlohe to War Ministry, 22 Feb. 1914, KAW KM Präs (1914) 47–2.

[148] Kageneck report, 4 Mar. 1914, PAAA R.10433; and 30 May 1914, ibid. R.10434.

[149] Conrad, *Dienstzeit*, iii. 582. Kageneck report, 11 Feb. 1914, PAAA R.10453. Käs, 'Generalstab', 181–7, 256. R. Ropponen, *Die Kraft Russlands* (Helsinki, 1968), 255.

[150] Berchtold diary, 20 Mar. and 16 Feb. 1914, HHStA Berchtold MSS 2.

[151] Tschirschky to Bethmann, 13 Feb. 1914, PAAA R.10433.

Italy seemed to be on their side, Britain was vacillating, and Serbia had not recovered from the Balkan Wars. To the German Ambassador he remarked that they would risk war with Russia if they could be sure of Romania. When he met Moltke at Karlsbad on 12 May he had become more guarded about Italy, but he still felt that time was against the Monarchy, as its South Slav and Romanian troops were becoming disloyal.[152]

No one was better aware than Conrad of Austria-Hungary's unpreparedness, but he preferred to act while its enemies were weak rather than await the completion of its rearmament, and he urged his views on his superiors and his ally. A preventive Continental war, however, had not become accepted policy before Sarajevo. Berchtold was less inclined to a worst-case scenario, and Habsburg rearmament aimed at readiness in a matter of years rather than months. At the same time as advocating preventive war, Conrad himself was still pushing the reserve army scheme, for which War Ministry planning began in January. Krobatin warned, however, that his own priorities were railways and artillery, and that funds were unlikely to become available before 1916–17.[153] There may have been doubts about whether a war would be short—Conrad was thinking of developing munitions capacity, and the Ministry was discussing economic mobilization, including food and labour supply.[154] In June 1914 both railway building and the reserve army project were marking time, which may have increased the temptation to act now rather than continue with an arms race that the Monarchy would lose. On the other hand, Moltke at Karlsbad warned that Austria-Hungary would have to bear the brunt of the fighting against Russia for at least six weeks, and this, coupled with the doubts about Italy, may have dampened Conrad's ardour.[155] Now as ever, whether Austria-Hungary took the plunge would depend on its ally.

* * *

As Conrad perceived an opportunity in the south-east, so did Moltke in the west. The Belgian army completed its divisional reorganization in January, but its re-equipping and reinforcement had hardly started. Over Britain there was a debate in Berlin early in 1914, Lichnowsky maintaining that it would not permit France to be diminished, but his superiors were less convinced. Wilhelm von Stumm, director of the Political Division in the Foreign Ministry, expected the British to hesitate, though they would intervene to prevent Germany from reaping the full fruits of victory. Jagow believed that the High Seas Fleet might now be strong enough to deter them from coming in. According to the Bavarian Minister in Berlin, the prevailing view was that Britain was unlikely to stay neutral, although it would not necessarily intervene straightaway.[156] In any case, in early

---

[152] Conrad, *Dienstzeit*, iii. 596, 604–6, 615–16, 597, 671–2.

[153] Conrad to Krobatin, 19 Jan. 1914, KAW KM Präs (1914) 37–2. Conrad, *Dienstzeit*, iii. 617, 622, 627, 697. Krobatin to Stürgkh, 19 Mar. 1914, FAW FM GFM Pr. 29.290/II-1914.

[154] Conrad, *Dienstzeit*, iii. 769. Minutes of inter-departmental meeting on economic mobilization, 23 Feb. 1914, FAW Z.L. 320, 433/FM ex. 1914.

[155] Conrad, *Dienstzeit*, iii. 673.

[156] Lichnowsky to Bethmann, 19 Feb. 1914, *GP* xxxix, doc. 15622. Jagow to Lichnowsky, 26 Feb.

1913 Moltke told Jagow that he was still confident he could deal with the BEF, and did not even mention the Royal Navy. His attaché in London advised him of the shortfalls in recruiting for the territorials and of a hint by Asquith in March 1914 that it was very unlikely that all the regulars would leave the country at the outset of war.[157] The discouragement in the Reich Navy Office was little reason for the German army to reconsider its plans.

The French army remained by far the leading Western antagonist. Yet it appeared to have overinvested in untrained manpower at the price of neglecting its equipment and of straining French finances and domestic solidarity. In November 1913 Bethmann observed that the nationalist revival was subsiding and the French were feeling the budgetary pinch. Wilhelm agreed that the combination of Russian and Balkan loans with their own requirements had overstretched them. If they increased taxes on the rich more money would fly the country; if on the poor there would be disorder.[158] The Foreign Ministry believed that France lacked the manpower to implement the Three-Year Law, and that its revision was already contemplated.[159] The GGS considered that 'great anxiety' awaited the country financially, and agreed that the present effort might slacken.[160] This might seem to make a case for waiting, but Moltke was more impressed by the arguments for striking without delay. He expected that increased reliance on African troops would release men for Europe, and that the French would catch up in heavy artillery 'in the not distant future'. But following on the simultaneous induction of two conscript classes they were at present in 'a very unfavourable military position'. He told Conrad at Karlsbad that 'I will do what I can. We are not superior to the French', yet also that he hoped to deal with them in six weeks, at least sufficiently to move troops eastwards.[161] Waldersee, too, in a memorandum on 18 May, was confident that a rapid offensive could be successful. The French army was in turmoil, and the crisis over Irish Home Rule meant that Britain did not want war.[162]

Two events in the summer of 1914 emphasized French fragility. The first was the swing to the Left in the May and June legislative elections, benefiting the Socialists and Radicals. A prolonged ministerial crisis followed. Poincaré wanted a government that was loyal to three-year service, but it was questionable whether one could command a stable majority. The Cabinet that emerged in mid-June was headed by René Viviani, who had voted against the law. He agreed to implement it for the present, but envisaged amending it in the autumn, and

1914, *GP* xxxvii, doc. 14697. Lerchenfeld dispatch, 12 Apr. 1914, GSM Gesandtschaft in Berlin 1086.

[157] Jagow memorandum, 'Der Durchmarsch durch Belgien', PAAA Jagow MSS 8. Reports by Renner, 6 Dec. 1913 and 2 Mar. 1914, PAAA R.5508.

[158] Conversation with Bethmann (unsigned), 24 Nov. 1913, GSM MA.I. 962. Bienerth to Austrian War Ministry, 21 Mar. 1914, KAW KM Präs (1914) 47–4.

[159] Wenninger report, 6 Mar. 1914, KAM MKr. 41.

[160] GGS report on French army budget, Oct. 1913, KAM Gstb 166; and report on implementation of Three-Year Law, 18 Feb. 1914, KAM MKr. 992.

[161] Moltke to Bethmann, 9 Mar. 1914, BA Rklei R.43F/107. Conrad, *Dienstzeit*, iii. 611, 669, 673.

[162] Cited in paper by Professor John Röhl to conference at Leeds Univ., 29 July 1994.

Messimy, who had returned as War Minister, began planning to reduce the term.[163] Meanwhile the Duma was about to vote unprecedented sums for defence. On 13 June the *Birshevaia Viedemosti* carried another piece inspired by Sukhomlinov: 'Russia is ready, France must be also.' It insisted on three-year service being preserved, as the higher was France's peacetime strength the faster it would be able to attack. Sazonov went out of his way to welcome Viviani's declarations to the Chamber on the need to safeguard French military power, but the French Embassy reported that there was great distrust in Russian military circles, which Germanophiles were trying to exploit.[164] Although the challenge to the Three-Year Law was beaten off for now, Poincaré went into the July crisis knowing that it would soon be renewed.[165] The Germans, conversely, saw that the measure had survived its first test.[166]

The other development was the speech to the Senate on 13 July by Charles Humbert. Although it caused an outcry it said little that the GGS did not know: France's heavy field artillery was out of date, and its siege and fortress guns were inferior to Germany's.[167] On the following day, the German attaché, Major von Klüber, met Colonel Dupont, the head of the 2nd Bureau, who was irritated by 'disclosures' about matters that the EMA itself had long protested against, and spoke more freely than was wise. Germany, he admitted, had an enormous advantage in heavy field artillery; the Rimailho was unusable and everything else was either scrap iron or not yet in service. Neither the 75 mm nor the Lebel rifle equalled their German counterparts. The eastern fortresses lacked undisturbed radio communications, and munitions and other stocks were low. Disarmingly, he assumed that Klüber knew all this already, but he hinted that the French army was none the less committed to a strategic offensive, which until now the GGS had doubted. Such an offensive would play into Moltke's hands, and the intelligence arrived at an exceptional moment.[168]

The question remained, if the German army was to be launched against the West, of security in its rear. No more than the Austrians did the Germans see a danger of imminent Russian attack. True, at the end of January Moltke enquired about mysterious Russian military preparations, but these Pourtalès discounted. In the light of similar rumours that the CGS again asked to be checked (but that enquiries showed to be groundless), Zimmermann concluded that Russia was not preparing 'an early strike' and its army was 'generally . . . not ready' for war.[169] The military authorities and the Foreign Ministry were

[163] R. N. L. Poincaré, *Au service de la France* (Paris, 1926–33), iv. 144–68. A.-M. Messimy, *Mes souvenirs* (Paris, 1937), 124–5.

[164] Doulcet to Bourgeois, 13 and 18 June, Paléologue to Viviani, 27 June 1914, *DDF* 3rd ser. x, docs. 369, 404, 449.

[165] G. Krumeich, *Armaments and Politics in France on the Eve of the First World War* (Leamington Spa, 1984), 215.

[166] Serret to War Ministry, 21 June 1914, SHA 7.N. 1112.

[167] Moltke memorandum, 31 July 1914, HSMA M 1/4, Bd. 794.

[168] Klüber to War Ministry, 16 July 1914, PAAA R.6756.

[169] Foreign Ministry to Embassy and Consulates in Russia, 28 Jan.; Pourtalès reply, 29 Jan., PAAA R.10450. Lerchenfeld report, 18 Feb. 1914, GSM Gesandtschaft in Berlin 1086.

unperturbed by the creation on the Western frontier in February of a new army corps, and in May Zimmermann considered a call-up of Russian reservists to be without political significance.[170] These judgements were echoed higher up. In November 1913 Bethmann believed that Russia would be obliged to keep the peace 'for years hence'.[171] Wilhelm described Russian sabre-rattling as bluff, and told Berchtold that St Petersburg would not 'for a long time yet' be able to wage war against Austria-Hungary and Germany; nor did its present measures on the frontier signal aggressive intentions.[172] Moltke wrote to Conrad that 'none of our information from Russia points to an intentionally aggressive attitude at present', and 'in the near future' Russia would not seek or cause an occasion for war.[173] The Germans had neither lost their sense of proportion nor their ability to distinguish the extraordinary from the routine.

Their future projections were another matter. Waldersee's memorandum of 18 May conceded that the present was not a good moment for the entente to attack. The Russian army was getting stronger but its reorganization and railway building would take time, and it could still be held off if Austria-Hungary took the offensive, although Germany's ally was growing weaker.[174] Falkenhayn similarly acknowledged the Habsburg Monarchy's limitations and its belated entry into the arms race.[175] On the other hand, GGS appraisals tabulated the growth in Russian numbers, firepower, and speed of mobilization to be expected by 1917. This theme became something of a litany. In October 1913 Wilhelm told Berchtold that although there was nothing to fear for six years, Russia desired the 'downfall' of the Central Powers.[176] In January 1914 Major Eggeling reported that in the previous summer Nicholas II had set a five-year period during which major conflict must be avoided. Wilhelm supposed that five years was the time envisaged as necessary to complete the French-financed strategic railways. 'From which it must be concluded that Russia is thinking very seriously of a war against us, and therefore it has become necessary to secure the German eastern frontier with a strong belt of fortresses.'[177] When Pourtalès commented that he did not believe that Russia was preparing to launch a war in three to four years' time, the Emperor exploded. 'But that is true! Quite unconditionally! . . . As a military man, on the basis of all my information I harbour not the minutest doubt that Russia is systematically preparing war against us, and I conduct my policy accordingly.'[178]

[170] Szögyény to Austrian Foreign Ministry, 25 Feb. 1914, HHStA PA III 171. Lerchenfeld report, 28 May 1914, GSM Gesandtschaft in Berlin 1086.

[171] Conversation with Bethmann (unsigned), 24 Nov. 1913, GSM MA.I 962.

[172] Bienerth to War Ministry, 21 Mar. 1914, KAW KM Präs (1914) 47–4. Berchtold diary, 23 Mar. 1914, HHStA Berchtold MSS 2.

[173] Conrad, *Dienstzeit*, iii. 610.   [174] Cf. n. 162 above.

[175] Wenninger to Bavarian War Ministry, 21 Nov. 1913, KAM MKr. 5589.

[176] Cf. Ch. 5, sect. 2, above.

[177] Berchtold diary, 26 Oct. 1913, HHStA Berchtold MSS 2. Eggeling to War Ministry, 3 Jan. 1914, PAAA R.10433. Lerchenfeld report, 8 Jan. 1914, GSM Gesandtschaft in Berlin 1086.

[178] Pourtalès to Bethmann, 11 Mar. 1914, *GP* xxxix, doc. 15844.

The Austrians looked to greater Russian assertiveness in three or four years' time; the Germans, possibly, to a Russian invasion. If war was indeed inevitable when the entente had rearmed it would be logical to begin it now, but if the enemy's purpose was defensive a further round of counter-armaments would be more prudent, not to say humane. In Berlin as in Vienna the debate was not foreclosed and both options were under consideration, it being widely forecast that Germany intended yet another military law. Bazarov thought the press war might be intended to ready the public; Serret disagreed, but reported on the repeated rumours of a bill and the official denials. Both attachés supposed that the defence levy had yielded more than was needed for the 1913 law, and that there was money to spare; Bazarov noted that Britain's interest was for the army to benefit more than the navy, and France's and Russia's the reverse.[179] Meanwhile, the DWV continued its agitation, with the primary objective that all able-bodied men should be trained.[180] Falkenhayn told the Reichstag Budget Commission that no new bill was planned at present, but he refused assurances for the future. By next winter, thought Serret, things might look different, and Jules Cambon expected the lobbying for another bill and for a larger peacetime strength to succeed.[181]

These suspicions were not without foundation. Falkenhayn thought another 36,000 able-bodied men a year might be available, and did not exclude an increase. Waldersee called for one in his memorandum of 18 May, and in the same month Moltke urged on Bethmann an increase from 1914–15. Wilhelm agreed, and was willing to raise taxes to pay for it.[182] But in a letter to Moltke on 8 July, Falkenhayn reverted to gradualism. The army needed calm, and a further expansion after that of 1913 would mean dilution and deterioration. He was willing to set the training of all able-bodied men as an objective, but progress towards it could not begin before October 1916 and must be spread over ten years. Ten days later Moltke appealed to Bethmann that what was possible in France and Russia must also be possible in Germany; but time had now run out.[183]

In fact, manpower was not the focus of official thinking. Falkenhayn's new estimates envisaged further big increases in expenditure on heavy artillery, aviation, and fortification.[184] Moltke, like Conrad, may have doubted whether a war would really be short, and inter-departmental discussions on economic mobilization continued. Legislation on food stockpiling was held up by a dispute between the imperial and state authorities over the cost, in this resembling the

---

[179] Bazarov to Stavka, 28 Feb. and 10 Mar. 1914, Adamov, 'Podgotovke', 117, 126. Serret to War Ministry, 15 Mar. and 3 May 1914, SHA 7.N. 1112.

[180] Documentation on DWV campaign in HSMA M1/4, Bd. 503.

[181] Serret to War Ministry, 3 May 1914, SHA 7.N. 1112. J. Cambon to Doumergue, 3 May 1914, *DDF* 3rd ser. x, doc. 194.

[182] Serret to War Ministry, 3 May 1914, loc. cit. For Waldersee, see n. 162 above; for Moltke, see Fischer, *Illusions*, 399. For Wilhelm, *GP* xxxix. 587 n.

[183] H. Herzfeld, *Die deutsche Rüstungspolitik vor dem Weltkriege* (Bonn, 1923), 160–1.

[184] Falkenhayn to Bethmann, 30 July 1913, KAM MKr. 5589.

major new initiative in 1914, which concerned the railways.[185] Heeringen and Moltke had already protested about the inadequacy of the railway system in 1909–10, and in the spring of 1913 the GGS had stepped up the pressure. Germany remained inferior to the French, who in 1914 had fifteen concentration lines against the Reich's twelve. Moltke estimated, though probably for purposes of advocacy, that France could complete its concentration on day 11 against Germany's day 16. In East Prussia there were only two through lines, one running parallel to the Russian border. Hence the GGS demanded, first and foremost, twenty Rhine bridges between Wesel and Strasbourg, as well as twenty double-tracked lines from the river to the Western concentration zone and a third railway into East Prussia, all to be completed by 1917–20.[186] The French loan to Russia made the task more pressing, and Moltke urged that there would be 'a decisive turning point to Germany's disadvantage' if its eastern and Western enemies achieved greater simultaneity. A railway programme would be the 'crowning' of the 1913 law and would get the faster mobilized formations more quickly to the frontier: 'the conduct of war in the present and future has railways as its guiding star!'[187]

The obstacle, predictably, was funding. Prussia and the other States had traditionally resisted expenditure on strategic railways, two-thirds of which had come out of the Reich budget. An inter-departmental meeting on 15 January estimated the cost of the military programme at 500 million marks, and the Finance Ministry said it could not afford even the interest and amortization on a loan. Hence they must look to the States, although most of the expenditure would not yield a commercial return. Ruling out a general meeting of heads of government as too conspicuous, Bethmann toured the State capitals. He found the Prussians willing to start work quickly, though not to bear all the cost.[188] The Bavarian Prime Minister was more sceptical, and said Munich's finances were too strained for it to contribute appreciably.[189] By May Bethmann was retreating, and agreed the Empire must bear part of the expense, but Kühn warned that it could not do so before 1916. Until then only preparatory work was possible, and although in June and July Moltke and Falkenhayn continued pressing for an early start, the financial deadlock persisted.[190] Bethmann had already ruled out big increases on extra-European naval expenditure because new taxes were out of the question, and the defence levy, so far from yielding a sur-

[185] I owe the suggestion about Moltke to Professor Stig Förster, based on newly released documentation in Potsdam. On economic planning, BA Rklei R.43F/1268, and Burchardt, *Friedenswirtschaft*, *passim*.

[186] Moltke to Bethmann, 9 Mar. 1914, BA Rklei R.43F/107. See undated memorandum on the correspondence in BA-MA Groener MSS 46/77.

[187] Moltke to Bethmann, 1 Jan. 1914, BA Rklei R.43F/1268.

[188] President of Imperial Railway Office to Bethmann, 6 Mar.; Minister of Public Works to Bethmann, 31 Mar. 1914, ibid.

[189] Hertling to Lerchenfeld, 15 Apr. 1914, E. Deuerlein (ed.), *Briefwechsel Hertling–Lerchenfeld, 1912–1917* (2 vols., Boppard, 1973), i. doc. 94.

[190] Note by Bavarian War Ministry, 10 June 1914, KAM MKr. 9739. Lentze to Bethmann, 28 May 1914, BA Rklei R.43F/1268.

plus, seemed likely to raise less than had been foreseen.[191] Not only in the naval race but also on land Germany seemed near the limits of its ability to keep pace.

Dieter Groh and Niall Ferguson have argued that with the *Wehrbeitrag* the German political system made the maximum effort of which it was capable.[192] Apparently it was not enough. The French Minister in Munich reported that the tax increase had caused great pessimism, and people were growing accustomed to the idea of war as a way out of the present tension. In the words of the Munich press: 'Where we are going, the Gods alone know. It is really astonishing that more and more people do not prefer a resolution at the price of catastrophe to a catastrophe without resolution, to which the people are continually exposed.' According to Serret, increasing numbers of conservatives saw war as a distraction from Germany's internal problems, and the press campaign in March won broader favour for a preventive strike.[193]

Within the leadership, too, advocates of preventive war were gaining a hearing. As the Austrians, with their dreadnought-building and the reserve army plan, were looking several years ahead, so too were the Germans, with Falkenhayn's recruitment scheme, the railway programme, and the corps creations scheduled for the 1916 *Quinquennat*. For both Powers before Sarajevo, preventive war was considered only as one possible option. But that it was considered is not in doubt. When King Albert of Belgium visited Potsdam in November 1913, Wilhelm and Moltke attempted to intimidate him by warning that France's provocative behaviour made war inevitable and close.[194] The Foreign Ministry informed the Bavarian attaché that the aim of the strategic railway programme would be to improve the chances of a rapid victory over France in a two-front conflict. Kageneck told Conrad in January that Moltke inclined to war although his superiors were decisively for peace,[195] and Moltke himself told Conrad at Karlsbad that 'every delay signified a reduction in our chances; one cannot undertake a competition in numbers with Russia'. Yet, the German leaders were still awaiting a non-intervention pledge that he believed Britain would never give. Moltke wrote to Bethmann that by 1917 Russia would have a fully modernized army able to cross the frontier at a moment's notice, and that because of Romania's defection Austria-Hungary would be tied down in the Balkans and unable to take the offensive against the Tsar. None the less, like Waldersee he recommended reinforcing the army rather than attacking.[196] But in a conversation with Jagow on 20 May or 3 June he was less circumspect. In two to three

---

[191] Cf. n. 59 above.

[192] Groh, ' "Je eher, desto besser!" ', *Politische Vierteljahresschrift*, 13 (1972), 502 ff. N. Ferguson, 'Public Finance and National Security', *Past and Present*, 142 (1994), 164.

[193] Allizé to Viviani, 14 July 1914, *DDF* 3rd ser. x, doc. 510. Serret to War Ministry, 15 Feb. and 15 Mar. 1914, SHA 7.N. 1112.

[194] Keiger, *France*, 132. J. Cambon to Pichon, 22 Nov. 1913, *DDF* 3rd ser. viii, doc. 517. Cf. J. Stengers, 'Guillaume II et le Roi Albert à Potsdam en novembre 1913', *Académie royale de la Belgique. Bulletin de la classe des lettres et des sciences morales et politiques*, 6th ser. 4 (1993), 227–53.

[195] Wenninger to Bavarian War Ministry, 6 Mar. 1914, KAM MKr. 41. Conrad, *Dienstzeit*, iii. 596.

[196] Conrad, *Dienstzeit*, iii. 670. Fischer, *Illusions*, 399. For Waldersee, n. 162 above.

years' time Russia's armaments would be completed, and would have a superiority over Germany's that he did not know how to counter, whereas 'at present we would be to some degree a match for them. In his opinion there remained nothing left but to wage a preventive war, in order to strike the enemy while we still had a fair chance of winning the battle.' Policy should be directed to bringing about an early showdown. Jagow did not object in principle, but felt that the best chance had passed. Germany's economic strength would grow and the international situation might become more favourable, especially if Britain could be detached. None the less, Jagow took Moltke's words seriously, especially as a year previously the General had been inclined against war, and in July 1914 they gave him confidence that if war resulted Germany was likely to triumph.[197]

On 3 June the Bavarian Minister had a gloomy conversation with Bethmann. The Chancellor believed that neither France nor Britain wanted armed conflict. Russia was a different matter, and Pan-Slav enthusiasm might lead it into 'stupidities'. Many military men were calling for preventive war, and there were circles who believed it could benefit conservatism. But he did not believe that a war would be over as quickly as in 1870; he questioned how the population would be fed; and believed that war would generally strengthen the Socialists and might even 'topple a few thrones'.[198] None the less, he was on the defensive. Wilhelm was infuriated by the 13 June *Birschevaia Viedemosti* article, minuting that France and Russia were obviously preparing intensively for early hostilities.[199] Bethmann wrote to Lichnowsky that no inspired article had revealed more clearly the bellicosity of the Russian military party. Previously only extreme pan-Germans and militarists had accused Russia of planning an early attack, but now this conviction was spreading, and there would be pressure for the army to be immediately and substantially strengthened. Wilhelm himself had thoroughly accepted this reasoning. Bethmann had not, although he believed Russia was the readiest of all the Powers to risk a conflict, and with its new armaments it would behave more forcefully in the next Balkan crisis. Germany would not add to the existing navy law, but it could not renounce the right to expand its army commensurately with its population. There was an important difference, however, between introducing such measures gradually and in a mood of panic. He looked to Anglo-German co-operation to contain a Russo-Austrian conflict, and warned that British naval co-operation with Russia would hearten the chauvinists in Paris and St Petersburg and start another outbreak in Germany of 'armaments fever'.[200]

This long and careful communication caught the subtleties in the Chancellor's position. Bethmann still envisaged armaments expansion rather than preventive war, and was not convinced that hostilities were inevitable. Russia was dangerously unpredictable, and the moderates in St Petersburg might lose control. But

---

[197] Jagow, 'Gespräch mit General von Moltke im Frühjahr 1914', PAAA Jagow MSS 8.
[198] Lerchenfeld to Hertling, 4 June 1914, Deuerlein (ed.), *Hertling–Lerchenfeld*, i. doc. 97.
[199] Pourtalès to Bethmann, 13 June 1914 (Wilhelm minute), *GP* xxxix, doc. 15861.
[200] Bethmann to Lichnowsky, 16 June 1914, ibid., doc. 15883.

if Russia was not preparing an attack, calm nerves and vigilance might see Germany through. None the less, a point seemed to lie ahead at which the Central Powers would be manifestly inferior. Even if they were not invaded, they would lose their independence and their Great-Power status, and they would suffer constant insecurity. How far France and Russia might exploit such a position would depend considerably on Britain, of whom Moltke and Wilhelm took a more jaundiced view than did Bethmann. Britain's *rapprochement* with Russia, however, and the political and financial obstacles to defence increases, were reducing the Chancellor's room for manœuvre. Like Jagow and Berchtold he resisted the military's worst-case scenario, but Franz Joseph and Wilhelm were more susceptible to Conrad's and Moltke's logic than were their civilian ministers. Germany's laws of 1912 and 1913 were largely implemented; Austria-Hungary's of 1912 and 1914 were not, but Conrad saw no advantage in waiting. Italy seemed securely in the Triple Alliance, and Britain's significance in a Continental campaign would be limited. France and Russia were in no condition to fight now—on the contrary, they were vulnerable. The argument for going to war made sense, if it was assumed that war could solve the Central Powers' problems.

* * *

Unofficial voices in the entente countries also called for war. But there is no surviving evidence (unless in Russia) that their governments were looking to a war of aggression. All the same, French diplomacy was taking the initiative, through Balkan arms deals, the Russian loan, and the Anglo-Russian naval conversations. And although the Russians had been the challenged party in the von Sanders incident, they had achieved a partial success in it, following on that of their armed diplomacy in 1912. They were determined not to be intimidated by press attacks, and believed they had the financial and demographic strength to continue their expansion. The army had hinted at further plans beyond the Great Programme and Grigorovich envisaged a parallel programme at sea for eight battlecruisers and twenty battleships by 1930, to be started in 1915. This he disclosed in February, saying that in three to five years neither the Russian state nor the private yards would need foreign advisers.[201] Despite the fragilities of the Russian Empire and the Franco-Russian alliance, in the Continental arms race the entente was winning, and the February 1914 special conference testified to the Russians' intention to use military power to get their way. At the end of January Nicholas II told Delcassé he would be firm in another clash with Germany, and the public would support him. He said to Paléologue that he did not believe Wilhelm II wanted war, but if France and Russia wanted peace they must be strong enough to make themselves respected 'manu militari'.[202] Rather than allow Germany to dominate Constantinople and shut up Russia in the Black

---

[201] Gallaud note, 14 Feb. 1914, SHM SS Em 157; monthly reports on Russia, 1 Nov. 1913, Mar./Apr. 1914, SHM SS (Ea) 160.

[202] Delcassé and Paléologue to Doumergue, 29 Jan. and 17 Feb. 1914, *DDF* 3rd ser. x, docs. 189, 322.

Sea, he informed Buchanan, he would fight. As the British Ambassador put it, 'in this race for armaments she can always outdistance Germany. Russia is conscious of her latent strength and determined to use it. She is and will, I believe, remain thoroughly pacific, but she has had enough of the weakness and vacillation which marked her policy during last year's crisis.' Unless Germany made greater financial sacrifices, its days of European hegemony were numbered. Russia had more staying power in the arms race, and in the next few years Germany might be tempted to precipitate a conflict.[203] Russia did not intend to start a war, but it knew that the balance was moving in its favour and both in official circles and in public opinion there was an unprecedentedly anti-German mood, Sazonov and others warning that signs of Russian weakness would be exploited.[204] On the other hand, before June 1914 neither Germany nor Austria-Hungary was committed to launch a war, but the option had clearly been presented, the civilian and monarchical leadership was increasingly receptive to military arguments, and the apparent moment of opportunity was drawing to a close. Bethmann and the Tsar alike looked ahead to the next Balkan crisis, and a crisis the Balkans were now to provide.

2. From Arms Race to War

Thus far it has been argued that heightened international tension led to greater military preparedness. Diplomatic crises helped tip the balance in favour of larger armies and hair-trigger organizational readiness. But there was also a reciprocal effect. By 1914 the British and German navies both feared surprise attack. In the Balkans both power blocs could underpin their policies with military measures. Armaments themselves were feeding tension, as the press war showed. A lobby for preventive war had implanted itself in Berlin and Vienna, while in the opposing camp there was growing confidence, and an undercurrent of enthusiasm at the prospect of hostilities. Greater Austro-German willingness to provoke a clash was matched by greater Franco-Russian willingness to accept one, as the two sides moved towards equivalence.

Armaments developments made it likely that a new confrontation in the Balkans or the Mediterranean would be handled differently from its predecessors. In addition, the coalitions were more cohesive. Britain, France, and Russia had updated their co-operation agreements; Italy's reconciliation with its partners encouraged Conrad and Moltke to see the military option as still feasible. Since the winter of 1913/14 Germany had been more reluctant to pursue *détente* with London at the risk of Habsburg goodwill, and the Liman von Sanders affair had left Grey and Poincaré more beholden to Sazonov. The same alliance cohesiveness, however, was undermining the Germans' faith in diplomatic solutions

---

[203] Buchanan to Grey, 3 Apr.; Buchanan to Nicolson and Grey, 18 Mar. 1914, *BD* x(ii), docs. 537, 529, 528.
[204] Buchanan to Grey, 18 Mar. 1914, ibid. and Doulcet to Doumergue, 14 Mar. 1914, *DDF* 3rd ser. ix, doc. 458.

to their Continental encirclement, as it was Berchtold's in diplomatic solutions to his Balkan dilemmas. For both Austria-Hungary and Germany the prospect loomed in three years' time of near-certain defeat in the event of war, and the forfeiture of their independence even if their territory remained inviolate.

These considerations are essential to an understanding of why the Sarajevo murders had such cataclysmic effects. On 28 June 1914 the Archduke Franz Ferdinand and his wife were assassinated by Bosnian Serb nationalists. On 5–6 July Germany secretly promised Austria-Hungary to support whatever steps it took in consequence. On 23 July a Habsburg ultimatum accused Belgrade of sheltering terrorist organizations with designs on the Monarchy's South Slav lands, and alleged that Serbian officials had supplied the assassins with their weapons and helped them cross the frontier. Such organizations, and all anti-Austrian propaganda, must be suppressed, and the officials punished. Serbia accepted almost all the Austro-Hungarian demands, but objected on two points, in particular that for Habsburg representatives to participate in a judicial inquiry into those implicated in the conspiracy would violate the Serbian constitution and criminal law. This was enough for the Austrians to break off diplomatic relations and on 28 July to declare war, bombarding Belgrade on the following day. Russia warned that it would retaliate by a partial mobilization against the Monarchy, but instead on 31 July it ordered a general mobilization against both Central Powers. German ultimata at once required Russia to cease mobilizing within twelve hours, and gave France eighteen hours to pledge neutrality in a Russo-German conflict. Neither demand was conceded, and the Reich declared war on its Eastern and Western neighbours on 1 and 3 August respectively. As German troops invaded Belgium, in violation of warnings from London to respect the country's neutrality, on 4 August Britain too entered the war.

The real issue in the Balkans was not Belgrade's partial rejection of the ultimatum but Austria-Hungary's determination to use the assassinations as a pretext to crush its enemy. At first the Central Powers hoped to stage a localized punitive operation and to fend off Triple Entente intervention. Rather than acquiesce, the Russian leaders retaliated with military measures that they knew would risk, and even precipitate, a Continental war, but by the time they took their final decisions they had convinced themselves that such a war was inevitable anyway. Rather than permit the Russian measures to continue, the German Government resolved to mobilize and to implement the Schlieffen–Moltke Plan—from which the Belgian, French, and British involvement in hostilities followed. Military measures, and Russian and German measures especially, became so prominent as to obscure the initial conflict over whether Austria-Hungary should be permitted to overwhelm the Serbs. Once a threshold of preparedness had been crossed, war might seem to have resulted as the unintended outcome of a loss of control over military machines. It has been persuasively argued, however, that such an interpretation is misleading.[205] To appraise it, we must

---

[205] M. Trachtenberg, 'The Coming of the First World War: A Reassessment', ch. 2 of his *History and Strategy* (Princeton, 1991).

consider the influence of the military in each capital and the underlying evolution of the arms race, as well as the interaction between more immediate military and diplomatic exigencies in each Power's decision-making. What follows is not a comprehensive account of the July crisis but an analysis of the part played in it by military preparedness. From this perspective, there is a dramatic distinction between the surface calm before the delivery of the Austro-Hungarian ultimatum and the subsequent onrush of events.

* * *

Before 23 July the militarization of diplomacy was scarcely perceptible: on the Central Powers' side this was deliberate, while their entente counterparts still scarcely realized what lay in store. In Bosnia-Herzegovina Potiorek, whose lax security bore some responsibility for the assassinations, recalled the troops from manœuvres and alerted the frontier *Grenzjäger* and gendarmerie. He called for 'energetic action'. Conrad wanted immediate mobilization against Serbia followed by war, although he acknowledged that the Monarchy must assure itself of German support beforehand. Berchtold agreed that it was time to solve the Serbian question, and told Tisza that he meant to settle accounts. He was swayed both by Conrad and Krobatin and by the hawkishness of his Foreign Ministry officials. But he wanted a pretext, and to prepare public opinion. He preferred to await the outcome of the inquiry into the events at Sarajevo, as did Stürgkh and Franz Joseph. With Franz Ferdinand himself removed from the scene, however, Tisza was now unique among the Monarchy's leaders in advising that war against Serbia would be a 'fateful error'. He expected Russia to intervene, and feared German abandonment. The rest of the élite agreed with him at least in seeing Germany's attitude as crucial, Franz Joseph telling Conrad that if Berlin gave its backing there would be war. The balance of opinion was reflected in the *démarche* undertaken to sound the Germans out. Count Hoyos, Berchtold's *chef du cabinet* in the Foreign Ministry, took a letter from Franz Joseph to Wilhelm and a memorandum from Berchtold, both of which strongly hinted at using force without explicitly advocating it. But Hoyos himself wanted military action, and he was to brief the Germans on the Foreign Ministry's pro-war views.[206]

The granting of the Potsdam 'blank cheque' on 5–6 July was the origin of the militarization of the crisis. Hoyos returned from Germany with unconditional backing, and the meeting of the GMR on 7 July showed the effects. Berchtold called unambiguously for war against the Serbs, arguing that it was better to strike now than to wait. The Monarchy's diplomatic situation and its control over its Romanians and South Slavs might so deteriorate that action became impossible, and the Continental balance would move further against Germany and in favour of Russia. Krobatin shared the latter fear, and Stürgkh cited Germany's emphatic support as being itself a reason for going forward, as it might not be offered again.

[206] Conrad, *Dienstzeit*, iv. 33–6. F. Fellner, 'Die "Mission Hoyos" ', in W. Alff (ed.), *Deutschlands Sonderung von Europa, 1862–1945* (Frankfurt am Main, 1984), 283–316. Williamson, *Austria-Hungary*, 190–5. Albertini, *Origins*, ii. 120–36. Bridge, *Sadowa*, 368 ff. J. Leslie, 'The Antecedents of Austria-Hungary's War Aims', *Wiener Beiträge zur Geschichte der Neuzeit*, 20 (1993), *passim*.

Once more Tisza was alone in preferring a diplomatic victory to an expedition that he expected to result in the 'terrible calamity' of a European war. He was more optimistic that the Balkan and the Continental balances could be peacefully modified to the Central Powers' advantage, and questioned the benefit of incorporating more South Slavs. The meeting agreed with him that mobilization against Serbia (which Krobatin had wanted to be immediate and secret) should follow 'concrete demands' and an ultimatum, but all others present believed that 'a purely diplomatic success . . . would be worthless and that therefore such stringent demands must be addressed to Serbia as will make a refusal almost certain, so that the road to a radical solution by means of a military action shall be opened'.[207]

Conrad's advice to the Ministers took it as axiomatic that Italy and Romania must not join the Monarchy's enemies. War against Serbia, Montenegro, and Russia he was willing to support, although the prospects were not 'brilliant', and privately he still considered it a 'break-the-bank game'. But the alternative was a Great-Power balance moving further 'to our disfavour'; the entente build-up would continue while the Habsburg forces would be starved of funds, and separatist agitation would undermine the troops' loyalty. With Germany's backing (and assuming, as Moltke had told him, that Germany could beat France), he wished to move now.[208] The GMR gave remarkably little attention to the strains that a Russian war would impose on the Dual Monarchy, although it seems that almost all the Vienna leaders considered intervention by St Petersburg to be likely or almost inevitable.[209] According to the German attaché the military set the probability at 50 per cent; Gustav Hubka, a well-connected staff officer who was attaché in Montenegro, believed that Conrad thought it unavoidable. In retrospect Krobatin admitted to the same opinion, Hoyos said at the time that intervention was 'virtually certain', and Berchtold told the GMR (in a comment that was deleted from the minutes) that it was 'very probable'.[210] The Emperor, when approving the ultimatum, is reported to have said that Russia could not let it pass and that the outcome would be a European war. Tisza again raised the question of world war in a memorandum of 8 July that Franz Joseph ordered to be filed. Yet by 14 July the Hungarian Prime Minister had come round to the consensus view, probably less because of Germany's attitude than because of evidence that Romania's neutrality was assured.[211]

---

[207] GMR Protocol, 7 July 1914, I. Geiss (ed.), *July 1914: The Outbreak of the First World War: Selected Documents* (New York, 1967), doc. 9. I have cited the English language edn. of this collection rather than the German *Julikrise und Kriegsausbruch, 1914* (2 vols., Hanover, 1963–4), unless documents appear only in the latter.

[208] Conrad, *Dienstzeit*, iv. 53–7, 72.

[209] W. Jannen, Jr., 'The Austrian Decision for War in July 1914', in S. R. Williamson and P. Pastor (eds.), *Essays on World War I: Origins and Prisoners of War* (New York, 1983), 55 ff.

[210] Kageneck (to Waldersee?), 13 July 1914, PAAA R.8627. Hubka correspondence, 1957, in KAW B/61 No. 32. N. Stone, 'Die Mobilmachung der Österreichisch-Ungarischen Armee, 1914', *Militärgeschichtliche Mitteilungen*, 16/2 (1974), 84. G. A. Ritter, *The Sword and the Scepter* (Coral Gables, Fla., 1970), ii. 385. Minutes of 7 July *GMR* in HHStA PA XL 312.

[211] R. A. Kann, *Kaiser Franz Joseph und der Ausbruch des Weltkrieges* (Vienna, 1971), 12. G. Vermes, *István Tisza: The Liberal Vision and Conservative Statecraft of a Magyar Nationalist* (New York, 1985), 222–31. Leslie, 'Antecedents', 343.

If the Austrians thought Russian intervention likely, their military preparations rested on the assumption that it could be avoided. The hypothetical permutations of warfare on a multiplicity of fronts had tried the ingenuity of Conrad's planners. The mobilized Habsburg armies would comprise three groups, of which the smallest, *Minimalgruppe Balkan*, would concentrate on the south-eastern frontier, and the largest, *A-Staffel*, would detrain in Galicia. The third, *B-Staffel*, would go south for 'Case B'—a localized Balkan offensive—and north if Russia came in, necessitating a defensive posture against the South Slavs. But Conrad expected even mobilization for Case B to take sixteen days, which augured poorly for a *fait accompli*.[212] None the less, he recommended to the GMR such a partial mobilization against Serbia and Montenegro, while doing nothing against Russia. He wanted an ultimatum with a short time limit, rejection to be followed immediately by mobilization. If Russia 'threatened', and specifically if it mobilized against the Monarchy, the latter should exploit its faster call-up times by at once going to war, *B-Staffel* being concentrated with *A-Staffel* and the three Galician army corps for an offensive into Poland. But to be able to redirect *B-Staffel* after embarking on a Case B mobilization, Conrad would need to know Russian intentions not later than day 5, eleven days before he could begin operations in the south-east.[213]

This consideration would already make it difficult to synchronize the military and diplomatic timetables. Others further lessened the chances of pulling off a Balkan blitzkrieg. Berchtold wished to postpone the *démarche* not only until after the inquiry into the murders but also until Poincaré and Viviani had concluded their visit to St Petersburg scheduled for 20–3 July, as the 'champagne mood' while they were in the Russian capital might encourage a vigorous response.[214] Up to a point, delay suited Conrad because of his dilemma over harvest leave— an exemption he had tried to suppress, and because of which the army was below strength. All the Continental Powers granted it, and Krobatin believed it made the Russians more vulnerable than Austria-Hungary, but it made sense to wait until the grain was garnered in and carts and animals became available, especially as an early recall would give the game away.[215] Leave was due to continue into early August,[216] but on 12 July Berchtold told Conrad that the ultimatum was set for 23 July and mobilization for 28 July, and the CGS fell into line with this schedule.[217]

In the meantime, both diplomatic and military exigencies counselled restraint. Conrad would need to move rapidly if enemy forces moved up to guard the river

---

[212] E. Glaise-Horstenau, *Österreich-Ungarns Letzter Krieg, 1914–1918*, i. (Vienna, 1930), 6–7. Stone, 'Mobilmachung', 68 ff.

[213] Conrad, *Dienstzeit*, iv. 78, 40, 62, 53–4.

[214] Tschirschky to Bethmann, 14 July 1914, *Die deutschen Dokumente zum Kriegsausbruch, 1914*, ed. M. Montgelas and W. Schücking (3rd edn., Berlin, 1926) (henceforth *DDK*), doc. 50.

[215] Conrad, *Dienstzeit*, iv. 61, 72. Krobatin in GMR, 7 July 1914, HHStA PA XL (312). Williamson, *Austria-Hungary*, 199–200.

[216] According to Kageneck to Moltke, 10 July 1914, BA Bauer MSS 14; Williamson, *Austria-Hungary*, 200, says 25 July.

[217] Conrad, *Dienstzeit*, iv. 72.

passages on Serbia's northern frontier, but subject to this he fell in with Berchtold's wish that military preparations should be inconspicuous.[218] On 10 July the German attaché reported that the General Staff was keeping the press quiet and that Conrad and Krobatin were departing on vacation.[219] The CGS refrained from visiting Moltke, even though the latter was holidaying within the Monarchy's frontiers at Karlsbad. Although the two Prime Ministers were circulated on precautions against attacks on military and railway installations, and Conrad asked for intensified border surveillance of Serbia and Montenegro, police and gendarmerie were to be employed for the purpose rather than soldiers. Potiorek acted accordingly, making no change to his military dispositions. Only on 19 July was it decided to suspend exercises in the annexed provinces forthwith,[220] while in Galicia, secured by the reinforcement of 1912–13, no action was taken.[221]

The contrast between 1914 and the graduated escalations of previous crises will be evident: minimal precautions, undertaken as unobtrusively as possible, but then mobilization and war. Because the priority was to avoid suspicion, little could be done before 23 July to hasten mobilization after that date, making a successful surgical strike even less probable. Admittedly, a second GMR on 19 July was more sympathetic to a peaceful resolution, if Serbia ceded after mobilization. Berchtold even contemplated that the Serbs might swallow the ultimatum, after having deliberately framed it so as to make it almost impossible for them to do so. He was well aware, he wrote to his Ambassador in Rome, of 'my grave responsibility', given Italy's unreliability, Romania's hostility, and the Slavophile influence on the Tsar; but to continue 'letting things drift until the waves meet over our heads' would be worse still.[222] With whatever doubts, the Monarchy had set its course not towards coercive diplomacy but towards war. Most of its leaders had reached this point reluctantly and as the outcome of a cumulative process. Alternative solutions to the Serbian problem appeared discredited, and although the present moment was hardly favourable for military operations it seemed a feasible one and possibly the final such. This perception was an essential precondition for the Austro-Hungarian decision, if hardly the entire explanation for it. But given the probability that the war would spread, it was crucial that the Monarchy's leaders should have faith in German military prowess, and that they could count on German assistance. The key influence on their decision-making was less a measured assessment of the Balkan and the Continental balances than the impetus given from Berlin.

* * *

[218] Ibid. 72, 78.

[219] Kageneck to Moltke, 10 July 1914, BA Bauer MSS 14; Conrad, *Dienstzeit*, iv. 42.

[220] Krobatin to Premiers, 10 July; Conrad to Krobatin, 13 July; Potiorek to Conrad, 20 and 24 July, KAW Gstb 1914 (615). Conrad, *Dienstzeit*, iv. 91.

[221] Kageneck to Waldersee, 15 July 1914, PAAA R.8627.

[222] GMR, 19 July 1914, HHStA PA XL 312. Berchtold to Mérey, 21 July 1914, Bridge, *Sadowa*, doc. 38.

How then did the arms race influence the giving of Germany's blank cheque, and what military measures were associated with it? The answer to the question is complicated by a lack of evidence. There was no formal and collective discussion of the issues and the options in the way that was atttempted, however imperfectly, in Vienna. Afterwards Bethmann and others denied that there had been a 'Crown Council'.[223] Instead there were *ad hoc* exchanges between Wilhelm II and his military and civilian chiefs. As Jagow, Moltke, and Tirpitz, among others, were away, this procedure left the Emperor's impulsiveness unusually wide scope.

Hoyos's first meeting on the morning of 5 July was with Zimmermann, who was deputizing for Jagow at the Foreign Ministry. According to Hoyos, Zimmermann said there was a 90 per cent chance of European war if Austria-Hungary acted against Serbia, but that none the less Germany expected it to do so. The German army was well placed because of the 1913 law, and even if Austria-Hungary could send few troops against Russia Germany was strong enough to fight on two fronts.[224] At lunch, a first reading of Hoyos's missives persuaded Wilhelm that 'a serious European complication [was] possible' and he must consult Bethmann, but in fact he did not wait to do so before urging that the Monarchy should take 'warlike action' and 'march into' Serbia. If war with Russia resulted 'Germany, our old faithful ally, would stand at our side'. However, the present moment was 'all in our favour', as Russia was 'in no way prepared for war, and would think twice before it appealed to arms'. The Emperor, like Zimmermann, was aware of armaments developments, but he saw them as reducing the likelihood of a European conflagration.[225] On the following afternoon Bethmann amplified with an official statement that 'with regard to our relations towards Serbia the German Government is of opinion that we must judge what is to be done to clear the course; whatever way we decide, we may always be certain that we will find Germany at our side, a faithful ally and friend', but 'immediate action . . . against Serbia' was recommended. According to Hoyos's recollection, the Chancellor was thinking of an Austro-Serb rather than a Continental conflict, though he thought that if the latter was inevitable the circumstances were more favourable than they would be later.[226] The German leaders shared their Austrian counterparts' fear that the military situation would further deteriorate. As to whether they supposed that they were backing a Balkan or a Continental war, however, the evidence suggests the former, and Zimmermann's prediction of a 90 per cent probability of escalation was not shared by his superiors. This is said with the dual proviso that much of the documentation has not survived (and was probably deliberately purged), and that the *possibility* of escalation was explicitly foreseen and accepted.

This interpretation of the blank cheque—as a 'calculated risk' or two-way bet—might seem supported by the account of the Chancellor's ruminations after

[223] Bethmann Hollweg, *Betrachtungen*, i. 133.   [224] Fellner, 'Mission Hoyos', 311.
[225] Szyögyény to Berchtold, 5 July 1914, Geiss (ed.), *July 1914*, doc. 6.
[226] Szyögyény to Berchtold, 8 July 1914, ibid., doc. 8. Fellner, 'Mission Hoyos', 11.

the event by his private secretary, Kurt Riezler. They convey Bethmann's over-bearing sense of Russia's rising power and his apprehension that the Anglo-Russian naval conversations had undermined his diplomatic counter to it. An Austro-Serb war, if it was successfully limited, might break up the entente; if not, there would be a Continental war that the military thought Germany could still win. Either was preferable to the *status quo*, although it seemed that the Chancellor preferred the former. It is clear, however, that Riezler later rewrote this section of his diaries, and it is anyway difficult to disengage his own from Bethmann's views.[227] His testimony must be supplemented from elsewhere. In June, as has been seen, the Chancellor had been critical of preventive action. But by the time Wilhelm consulted him on 5 July the Emperor had already encouraged the Austrians to use force. Wilhelm said that Austria-Hungary was endangered by Pan-Serb propaganda and that its preservation was a German vital interest: it was not for Germany to tell it what to do, but Franz Joseph must know that he could count on them.[228] Whereas on other occasions Bethmann was willing enough to resist his sovereign, on this one he did not. His temperamental fatalism may have come into play, for the blank cheque set up a challenge that would test St Petersburg's intentions, and he agreed with Wilhelm that if Russia mobilized Germany must do also. Although unapprized of the details of the Schlieffen–Moltke Plan, and particularly of the 1913 modification requiring Liège to be seized on day 3, he knew enough to realize that German mobilization would set all Europe ablaze. Undeterred, he steered into the storm.[229]

There was uncertainty in Germany about whether the Austrians meant business. This lent an air of unreality to the discussions, especially as there would be a delay before matters came to a head, which may have facilitated brinkmanship. Falkenhayn, who was impressed by the 'hurriedness of the proceedings', wrote to Moltke that he and Bethmann doubted if Vienna was 'really in earnest'. As 'in no circumstances will the coming weeks bring any decision', the CGS could remain on vacation.[230] The Emperor told Captain Zenker, of the Naval Staff, that he did not expect Russia to support Serbia, which was tarnished by the assassinations, and France was scarcely likely to permit a war when it lacked heavy field artillery. War with France and Russia was 'not probable', though the possibility must be envisaged. The navy could begin on schedule its trip to Norway planned for mid-July, and the Chief of the Admiralty Staff, like Moltke, could continue his holiday.[231] He informed General von Bertrab, the most senior GGS officer available, that he did not expect 'serious repercussions' and that no military preparations were needed; the latter so briefed Waldersee, who

---

[227] K.-D. Erdmann (ed.), *Kurt Riezler: Tagebücher-Aufsätze-Dokumente* (Göttingen, 1972), 189. K. H. Jarausch, 'The Illusion of Limited War: Chancellor Bethmann Hollweg's Calculated Risk in July 1914', *Central European History*, 2 (1969), 57–9. Discussion of the diaries by B. Sösemann and K.-D. Erdmann in *Historische Zeitschrift*, 236 (1983), 327–402.

[228] Bethmann Hollweg, *Betrachtungen*, 135–6.

[229] Kennedy (ed.), *War Plans*, 213. Ritter, *Sword*, ii. 266.

[230] Falkenhayn to Moltke, 5 July 1914, Geiss (ed.), *July 1914*, doc. 7.   [231] *DDK* i. xviii.

resurfaced on 8 July before going off again, as did the chief of the mobilization section.[232] Finally, although supporting low-key naval precautions, Wilhelm told Capelle, too, on 6 July that Russia and France were unlikely to support Serbia against an Austro-Hungarian invasion, because militarily and financially they were unprepared.[233]

In the first instance Germany's decision was made by Wilhelm, endorsed by Bethmann, and unchallenged by the army, navy, and diplomatic leaderships. The explanations of the blank cheque given by the Foreign Ministry in the next few days tallied with Wilhelm's statements at the time, though in view of Zimmermann's remarks to Hoyos it is questionable how far he, at least, believed what he was saying. After the Emperor departed for his cruise on 6 July the Ministry took the lead in conducting events, and its official line was that an Austro-Serb war should stay localized. Zimmermann so informed the naval authorities, adding that he did not expect a European conflict.[234] He said the same to the Bavarian representative in Berlin, and Jagow, on his return, differed little. On 12 July the Austro-Hungarian Ambassador, Szögyény, reported that for Germany 'general political considerations . . . form the conclusive argument'. Russia intended a war with the Central Powers in the future, but it was 'anything but certain' that it would fight for Serbia now. A week later Zimmermann and Jagow told the Bavarian Minister that they expected Paris and London to counsel restraint and believed that if Vienna confined itself to a punishment expedition and did not take territory the conflict could be contained. To Lichnowsky the Foreign Minister wrote that, the more determined Austria-Hungary and Germany showed themselves, the less likely was the Tsar to intervene. In a few years' time Russia would have its strategic railways and its Baltic Fleet, and would have enhanced its numerical superiority, while Austria-Hungary would have grown weaker. Then St Petersburg would be willing to fight. But no Entente Power wanted war at present, and 'even today' he hoped and believed that the conflict could be localized.[235]

For Germany, Jagow continued, 'Russian hegemony in the Balkans' would be intolerable. 'The maintenance of Austria, and in fact of the most powerful Austria possible, is a necessity for us for both internal and external reasons.' As Bethmann put it retrospectively, Austria-Hungary's collapse would turn the clock back to the time of Nicholas I, when Prussia, as Russia's vassal, might drop out of the circle of Great Powers whenever St Petersburg wanted.[236] Such anxieties gained extra potency from the armaments rivalry, which was even more

[232] *DDK* i. xvi–xvii.

[233] Hopman to Tirpitz, 6 July 1914, V. R. Berghahn and W. Deist (eds.), 'Kaiserliche Marine und Kriegsausbruch 1914: Neue Dokumente zur Juli-Krise', *Militärgeschichtliche Mitteilungen* (1970), doc. 1.

[234] Hopman to Tirpitz, 9 July 1914, ibid., doc. 4. Hopman diary, 8 and 13 July 1914, BA-MA Hopman MSS N.326/11.

[235] Soden and Schoen to Hertling, 9 and 18 July 1914, Deuerlein (ed.), *Hertling-Lerchenfeld*, i, docs. 103–4. Szögyény to Berchtold, 12 July; Jagow to Lichnowsky, 18 July, Geiss (ed.), *July 1914*, docs. 18, 30.

[236] Ibid. Bethmann Hollweg, *Betrachtungen*, i. 133.

central to German than to Austrian thinking. Wilhelm was moved at Potsdam by outrage at the assassination of a comrade and by a reflex of monarchical solidarity, but he had already promised in the previous autumn to back military action against Serbia, and he was well aware of Austria-Hungary's strategic significance. Both he and his Foreign Ministry officials had been thoroughly briefed by Moltke in preceding months. They understood the scale and scheduling of Russian preparations and the Franco-Russian alliance's temporary weakness. They supposed that the latter would assist them in containing a punitive operation in the Balkans, but if European war resulted both Zimmermann and Jagow believed Germany's chances to be favourable. That if Russia mobilized Germany and France would do so and European war would follow, was for them, as for Bethmann and Wilhelm, perfectly clear.[237]

Although the Central Powers were unquestionably the aggressors in the July crisis, the Germans as well as the Austrians were slow to implement exceptional measures. On 5 July Wilhelm asked Falkenhayn whether the army was ready for all eventualities and was told that it was—when Falkenhayn asked whether he should make any preparations the Emperor said no. The War Ministry considered doing some fortification work, but in fact gave no special orders. Nor did the General Staff, where Waldersee considered nothing need be done. 'The regular work on the mobilization plan had been completed on 31 March 1914. The army was, as ever, ready.'[238] The intelligence section, whose chief was also on holiday, began closer surveillance of Russia only on 16 July, even then not committing all of its resources. On the following day Waldersee again told Jagow that no more was necessary at present.[239] The reluctance to make preparations, however, was not simply because of the army's confidence. It was an essential accompaniment to German diplomacy, and testifies to the German leaders' preference for confining the conflict to the Balkans, even if they jeopardized their readiness should confinement fail. On 6 July Wilhelm authorized preparatory measures only if they were unobtrusive and entailed no special costs. The Navy Office decided to speed up repairs and finishing work, to make up fuel stocks, and to retain four U-boats that Krupp was building for Greece, but these steps fell within the guidelines, and Jagow confirmed that he approved them.[240] Not only did the Foreign Ministry oppose German mobilization, but it asked that Conrad should not mobilize in Galicia, and the latter confirmed to Kageneck that he had no intention of doing so.[241]

---

[237] Schoen to Hertling, 18 July 1914, Deuerlein (ed.), *Hertling–Lerchenfeld*, i, doc. 104.

[238] Reichsarchiv, *Weltkrieg*, i. 25. Hopman to Tirpitz, 7 July 1914, Berghahn and Deist (eds.), 'Kaiserliche Marine', doc. 3. *DDK* i, xvii.

[239] Trumpener, 'War Premeditated?', 63–4. Waldersee to Jagow, 17 July, *DDK* i, doc. 74.

[240] Hopman to Tirpitz, 6, 7, 13 July, Behncke note, 20 July 1914, Berghahn and Deist (eds.), 'Kaiserliche Marine', docs. 1, 3, 6, 10. Hopman diary, 6, 7, 13 July, BA-MA Hopman MSS N.326/11.

[241] Schoen to Hertling, 18 July 1914, Deuerlein (ed.), *Hertling–Lerchenfeld*, doc. 104. Waldersee to Jagow, 17 July 1914, *DDK* i, doc. 74. However, Dr Hartmut Pogge von Strandmann has discovered evidence of more extensive German measures during the first phase of the crisis, including steps taken by Krupp.

As the ultimatum date approached, none the less, German as well as Austrian nerves became strained. On 20 July Rear Admiral Behncke of the Naval Staff found Jagow worried and unwilling to rule out a European war. On 21 July von Lyncker, the Chief of the Military Cabinet, telegraphed to Moltke from the Emperor's yacht to warn of an imminent growth in Austro-Serb tension and a war into which Germany might be drawn. It was time to protect the railways in the concentration zones.[242] At this point there was a revealing conflict over the High Seas Fleet, which had put to sea as Wilhelm had directed for a visit to Scandinavia, during which it would temporarily disperse among the Norwegian ports. The Berlin Bourse was reassured by its departure on schedule, but on 19 July Wilhelm telegraphed that the fleet should stay together until 25 July, so that it could speedily return to its home stations. The order infuriated Jagow, and Bethmann feared that it would thwart his localization efforts. He recognized the danger of the ships being wrongly positioned, but he feared the impression that would be created if conspicuous naval movements immediately followed the ultimatum's rejection.[243]

The problem was the more delicate because the Royal Navy was fortuitously at its highest readiness since Agadir. Churchill had decided in the previous autumn on a trial mobilization of the Third Fleet and the whole of the Royal Fleet Reserve. From 15 July onwards more than 20,000 men presented themselves at the depots, and the Third Fleet was coaled and concentrated at Spithead for a week of exercises.[244] Yet on 22 July the German Foreign Ministry decided that the High Seas Fleet could safely visit Norway, ignoring not only Wilhelm but also the Naval Staff, which opposed dispersal unless Bethmann could promise there would be no war with Britain in the next six days, as they expected one to begin with a surprise attack. Jagow thought both such an attack and so rapid a culmination unlikely, and that to recall the fleet prematurely would discourage the British demobilization due on 27 July. Bethmann agreed that early recall would be 'a grave error'. The Foreign Ministry advised Wilhelm to expect a period of diplomacy before matters came to a head, and the fleet was dispatched to the fiords, though it was ordered to take on coal, restrict shore leave, and be ready for a speedy return. Naval as well as land preparedness remained subordinate to civilian direction and to the localization imperative.[245]

* * *

If the objective was to create a false sense of security, it had considerable success, for the other Powers did little before the ultimatum. Italy was an excep-

[242] Hopman to Tirpitz, 21 July 1914, Berghahn and Deist (eds.), 'Kaiserliche Marine', i. 54. Lyncker to Moltke, 21 July 1914, BA-MA MSg 101/154.

[243] Hopman to Tirpitz, 16, 20, 21, 22, 24, 25 July 1914, Berghahn and Deist (eds.), 'Kaiserliche Marine', 51–6. Hopman diary, BA-MA Hopman MSS N.326/11. CAS to Jagow, Bethmann to Auswärtiges Amt., 20, 21 July 1914, *DDK* i, docs. 82, 101.

[244] Churchill, *World Crisis*, 189–90, 193.

[245] Behncke to Jagow, Jagow to Bethmann, Bethmann to Jagow, 22 July, Bethmann to Wedel, 23 July 1914, *DDK* i, docs. 111, 115–16, 125. Berghahn and Deist (eds.), 'Kaiserliche Marine', 56–8. Hopman diary, BA-MA Hopman MSS N.326/11.

tion. A decree on 11 July called up the 1891 conscript class, which would raise the peacetime strength to 273,000 men, and by late August to 298,000. Officially the reason was internal unrest. The 'Red Week' disturbances in June had been sparked off by the execution of a soldier who had murdered his officer in Libya. In the province of Emilia army discipline had broken down, leading to a quasi-revolutionary situation. According to the Austrian attaché, however, the purposes of the reinforcement were also to remedy the damage caused to training by low troop strengths and to be prepared for intervention in the civil war that had broken out in Albania. The French attaché, who believed that the shortage of effectives had plunged the army into 'crisis', took a similar view.[246] And although Austria-Hungary decided not to tell the Italians about the ultimatum, Germany notified them after the blank cheque, and cables from the Rome Foreign Ministry to its diplomats in St Petersburg and Belgrade possibly allowed Russia and Serbia to get wind.[247] Although ostensibly the reinforcement was unrelated to the Austro-Serb crisis, appearances may have been deceptive.

In Belgrade Pašić foresaw that Austria-Hungary would make demands, but appears to have been expecting them to be reasonable.[248] Gellinek reminded his superiors in Vienna that for Serbia it was a highly unfavourable time for war. Most of the standing army was in the new territories, leaving the capital exposed. Albania and Bulgaria were hostile, and the infantry short of rifles. On 17 July he communicated that the danger was not being taken seriously: reservists were being released, and as yet there had been no extraordinary measures.[249] There was evidence for limited reinforcement of the northern frontier, which at the 19 July GMR Conrad made use of in an unsuccessful attempt to urge speedy retaliation.[250] But on the following day Potiorek confirmed that there had still been no large reservist call-ups or movements of Serb troops towards the border, and no special measures in Montenegro, which confined itself to transporting searchlights and barbed wire up to Mount Lovcen.[251]

The softly, softly approach seemed also to have lulled the Triple Entente. Grey forwarded to the Russians a warning from Lichnowsky that there might be an Austrian *démarche*, and by 18 July Sazonov felt 'great uneasiness', telling Buchanan that if there were an ultimatum Russia 'might be forced to take some precautionary military measures'.[252] However, when Poincaré and Viviani reached St Petersburg they agreed with their hosts on trying to forestall Austria-Hungary by diplomatic action, Sazonov (according to Poincaré) saying nothing

[246] De Gondrecourt to French War Ministry, 19 July 1914, SHA 7.N. 1370. Szepticki to Austrian War Ministry, 13 and 27 July 1914, KAW KM Präs (1914) 47–5.

[247] Williamson, *Austria-Hungary*, 201.

[248] Paper by Dr Mark Cornwall to conference at Leeds University, 28 July 1994.

[249] Gellinek to Austrian War Ministry, 6, 14, 17 July 1914, KAW KM Präs (1914) 47–7.

[250] Consular reports for July 1914 in KAW KM Präs (1914) 51–7. GMR, 19 July 1914, HHStA PA XL 312.

[251] Potiorek to Conrad, 20 July 1914, KAW Gstb (1914) 615. Hubka to Austrian War Ministry, 13, 14, 17 July 1914, KM Präs (1914) 47–16.

[252] Grey to Rumbold and Buchanan, 6 and 8 July; Buchanan to Grey, 18 July 1914, *BD* xi, docs. 32, 39, 60.

about military steps and apparently taking none.[253] From Berlin on 20 July Jules Cambon reported (misleadingly) that Italy was concentrating troops on the Adriatic, Austria-Hungary had cancelled harvest leave, and Germany was apparently to call up its recruits *en bloc* for autumn manœuvres, thus giving the Triple Alliance an exceptional numerical superiority that was probably intended to support an anti-Serb initiative. Two days later he passed on unconfirmed information that Germany was distributing the preliminary notifications of possible mobilization. This message, however, though reaching the Quai d'Orsay on 23 July, was not forwarded to the French War Ministry for five days.[254] Before the ultimatum there was little increase in military readiness either between the Powers or even in the Balkans.

* * *

The Austro-Hungarian note impressed every Foreign Ministry in Europe by its forty-eight-hour time limit and its drastic demands. It was accompanied by a German warning to the Triple Entente that Austria-Hungary's Great-Power status was at issue and the Monarchy would be justified in taking strong, perhaps military, measures. In view of the European alliance obligations, intervention by other governments might have 'inestimable consequences'. The Germans urged the Austrians to resist mediation, declare war, and start operations as fast as possible, as every delay would make it harder to carry off a *fait accompli*. Although Jagow forwarded to Vienna a British proposal for an Anglo-Franco–German–Italian conference, he advised that he was doing so purely to humour London and that the proposal should be disregarded.[255] German policy remained set in favour of an Austro-Serb war.

Austria-Hungary too, in contrast to previous crises, was taking the initiative according to a pre-arranged schedule rather than reacting against the Serbs. On the evening of 25 July, after Belgrade's unsatisfactory reply, Franz Joseph signed the order for partial mobilization to begin on 28 July, preceded by an 'alarm day' of preparatory measures. Barracks and depots were placed under guard, and the frontiers and the railways secured. Partial mobilization meant that of *B-Staffel* and the *Minimalgruppe Balkan*, with additional troops to make good casualties and guard the Italian border—in total, eight army corps or two-fifths of the land forces, as well as the whole of the navy and the Danube flotilla. The Galician units were ordered to stay in their quarters, those opposite Romania and Italy to do nothing that might disturb their neighbours, and even those opposite Montenegro to show 'the greatest restraint'. The aim, therefore, was still to limit operations.[256] Against Serbia itself Conrad wanted enough men for a rapid and

[253] De Margerie note (*c*.11 July 1914), *DDF* 3rd ser. x, doc. 502. Buchanan to Grey, 24 July 1914, Geiss (ed.), *July 1914*, doc. 68. Poincaré, Notes journalières, 23 July 1914, BN Poincaré MSS, n.a.fr. 16027. Poincaré, *Service*, iv. 291.

[254] J. Cambon to Bienvenu-Martin, 20 and 22 July 1914, *DDF* 3rd ser. x, docs. 538 and 551. Messimy, *Mes souvenirs*, 130.

[255] Bethmann circular, 21 July; Szögyény to Berchtold, 25 July and 27 July 1914, Geiss (ed.), *July 1914*, docs. 39, 71, 95.

[256] Glaise-Horstenau, *Letzter Krieg*, 17–18. Stone, 'Mobilmachung', 78. Conrad, *Dienstzeit*, iv. 122–3. De Bunsen to Grey, 25 July 1914, *BD* xi, doc. 124.

overwhelming victory yet was in no hurry to declare war, as operations could not begin until approximately 12 August and he feared to commit himself before knowing Russia's attitude. Berchtold, with the Germans behind him, pressed for an early rupture with Belgrade in order to fend off mediation, and an exchange of fire at Temes Kubin on 26 July may have encouraged him to go ahead.[257] But from this point on, tsarist preparations cast a lengthening shadow over the localization strategy and confronted all the Powers with the menace of imminent Continental hostilities.

In Belgrade the ultimatum caused surprise and consternation. At first the Serbs lacked definite assurance of solidarity either from Russia or from their Balkan allies. But they were resolved to fight rather than submit to the most imperious demands. Preparations began on the day the document arrived, and Serbia accompanied its reply by ordering general mobilization. Instead of meeting Conrad on the river line, the Serbs' troop transports indicated that they would concentrate in the centre of the country. Archives, gold, munitions, and men were moved out of the capital, and the border region evacuated. The Serbs may have responded to advice from Sazonov on 25 July that if they could not resist they should withdraw their army southwards and appeal to the Powers, although a later telegram on the same morning suggested that Russia might mobilize. After an anxious two days it became clear to Pašić that he would not be left isolated, and on 28 July Montenegro mobilized in support.[258]

Whether Serbia would be abandoned and Germany and Austria-Hungary would be permitted to localize hostilities depended primarily on Russia, where Sazonov was pivotal in the choice between diplomatic and military options. Tsarist decision-making went through two key phases, on 24–5 and 28–30 July, of which the first can be seen as a commitment to armed diplomacy on the lines of 1912, albeit in a bolder form; the second as for practical purposes an acceptance of war.

To begin with, Russia's course was set at a meeting of the Council of Ministers on the afternoon of 24 July and a Crown Council at Tsarkoe Selo on the following morning. The Council of Ministers endorsed Sazonov's proposals to seek an extension of the time limit and to advise Serbia not to resist if invaded, but also agreed to ask the Tsar to mobilize the Kiev, Odessa, Moscow, and Kazan military districts and the Black Sea Fleet if called for, to speed up the stockpiling of war materials, and to withdraw short-term financial deposits from Berlin and Vienna. At the Crown Council Nicholas approved all these steps, including the partial mobilization if circumstances dictated. In addition, at the Ministers' request he agreed to institute at once the Period Preparatory to War, which was ordered throughout European Russia in the small hours of 26 July.

---

[257] Conrad, *Dienstzeit*, iv. 110, 130–2, 145–6. On Temes Kubin, see letters by Hubka in KAW B/61 No. 32.

[258] Paper by Mark Cornwall, cited in n. 43 above. Gellinek to Austrian War Ministry, 24, 25 July 1914, KAW KM Präs (1914) 47–7. Potiorek to Conrad, 20 July 1914, KAW Gstb (1914) 615. GGS intelligence summaries, 27 and 28 July 1914, HSMA M 1/2, Bd. 109.

The Empire thus moved to a degree of militarization unprecedented in previous crises, and prepared to go further still.[259]

The idea of partial mobilization seems to have originated with Sazonov.[260] Although he had resisted it in 1912 he had, like Berchtold, become more of a convert to armed diplomacy, and even before the ultimatum he was contemplating military precautions. It was presumably at his behest that on the morning of 24 July Janushkevich, the newly appointed CGS, asked Dobrorolsky, the head of his mobilization division, for the documentation on a mobilization against Austria-Hungary alone. Dobrorolsky replied with one memorandum opposing the idea and another recommending pre-mobilization measures. Partial mobilization he considered pointless, as Germany was bound to support its ally. No railway schedules had been prepared for it, and it would divert troops who were targeted against the main enemy. Moreover, the Warsaw military district in the Polish salient adjoined both Central Powers. If it were mobilized Austrian Galicia could be enveloped by a pincer offensive, but a partial call-up, not extending north of Kiev, would leave Russian Poland open to invasion.[261]

Dobrorolsky's reservations were general among the military chiefs, except for the inexperienced Janushkevich. None the less, on 24–5 July Sazonov won over his colleagues. To acquiesce in Austria-Hungary's demands, he told the Council of Ministers, would reduce Serbia to a *de facto* protectorate and Russia to a second-rank Power. Past concessions to Germany had encouraged further aggression, and to yield now would neither secure the peace nor stop future challenges. Despite the uncertainty over Britain's attitude, it was time to take a stand. Krivoshein, the Minister of Agriculture and the most authoritative member of the Cabinet, admitted that the armaments programmes were incomplete, but felt that there had been such progress in political stabilization and in building up the country's strength that public opinion would insist on Russia's vital interests being defended. War was not desirable, but firmness was the best way to avert it. Privately he acknowledged the 'serious risks', and believed in taking all necessary precautions to withstand an attack. Sukhomlinov and Grigorovich agreed that great advances had been made, but the work was not finished and Russian superiority could not be assured: none the less, they too favoured a resolute line, as did the Finance Minister, Bark. Goremykin concluded that 'it was the Imperial Government's duty to decide definitely in favour of Serbia', that firmness was more likely than conciliation to keep the peace, and that if it failed 'Russia should be ready to make the sacrifices required of her'.[262]

In contrast to Kokovtsov's style of leadership, Goremykin left the field to the

---

[259] Council of Ministers, 24 July and Crown Council, 25 July 1914, *Die Internationalen Beziehungen im Zeitalter des Imperialismus: Dokumente aus den Archiven der Zarischen und der Provisorischen Regierung* (series 1, vol. v), ed. O. Hoetzsch (Berlin, 1934) (henceforth *IB*), docs. 19, 42.

[260] Albertini, *Origins*, ii. 294.

[261] S. Dobrorolsky, 'La Mobilisation de l'armée russe en 1914', *Revue d'histoire de la Guerre mondiale*, 1 (1923), 64–9. Frantz, *Russland*, 35–9.

[262] D. C. B. Lieven, *Russia and the Origins of the First World War* (Basingstoke, 1983), 141–4.

Foreign Minister and Krivoshein. The Agriculture Minister wanted Russia's defences secured; Sazonov to strengthen his diplomatic signalling. Once they set the line, the service ministers followed.[263] At the Crown Council Sazonov again led off, claiming that partial mobilization was required to call Vienna to order. But a peaceful settlement was still thought possible, and Nicholas supposed that a partial call-up would be less hazardous than a general one. The 'severe warning' deemed necessary would be balanced by continued efforts to talk. Sukhomlinov suppressed his misgivings and yielded to the prevailing view. He wrote later that as a technician he felt he could not comment on a political question, or plead that the army was unready, given that he had indeed raised its efficiency and given Sazonov's assurances that Russia would not be isolated.[264] Yet he had warned the Foreign Ministry that Russia could not match Germany's 1913 law until 1917–18.[265] The Stavka wanted 1914 to be a year of calm, in which to bring in the Great Programme and Plan 20 and to raise the Tsaritsyn plant to full capacity. Grigorovich was even more conscious of the navy's weakness, pleading that he could not protect St Petersburg from bombardment.[266] The army leaders knew of the EMA's optimism, and some of the younger staff officers relished the prospect of operations, but it was not felt that Russia alone had military superiority, and much depended on the messages from its partners.[267]

Sazonov had reason to expect full backing from the French. He had no such assurance from London, and went ahead despite his apprehension that without it he was less likely to deter the Germans and more likely to end up in armed conflict. When he met the two ambassadors on the morning of 24 July, Paléologue pledged 'that France would not only give Russia strong diplomatic support but would, if necessary, fulfil all the obligations imposed on her by the alliance', but Buchanan resisted involvement in a joint warning to the Central Powers. This notwithstanding, Sazonov 'personally thought that Russia would at any rate have to mobilize'. In reporting to Paris Paléologue toned down his words, but the damage was done, and the Ambassador compounded it by telling Sazonov that he believed Germany would not support Austria-Hungary, and that the Triple Entente's situation had never been better.[268] So far from moderating Franco-Russian conduct, Berchtold's delaying of the ultimatum until after Poincaré left St Petersburg probably did the opposite. Between 23 and 29 July the President and Viviani were returning by sea and in very imperfect radio contact. French diplomacy was left to the inexperienced deputy premier, Bienvenu-Martin, and the Assistant Political Director at the Quai d'Orsay, Philippe Berthelot, who were kept poorly informed by Paléologue and failed to control

[263] Cf. D. Spring, 'Russia and the Coming of War', in R. J. W. Evans and H. Pogge von Strandmann (eds.), *The Coming of the First World War* (Oxford, 1988), 65–74.
[264] V. A. Sukhomlinov, *Erinnerungen* (Berlin, 1924), 357–60.
[265] Snyder, *Offensive*, 185.   [266] Dobrorolsky, 'Mobilisation', 62–3, 147.
[267] Sukhomlinov, *Erinnerungen*, 373.
[268] Buchanan to Grey, 24 July 1914, Geiss (ed.), *July 1914*, doc. 68. Paléologue to Bienvenu-Martin, 24 July 1914, *DDF* 3rd ser. xi, doc. 19. Russian Foreign Ministry logbook, 24 July 1914, *IB* i, v, doc. 25.

him. The Ambassador was a self-dramatizing and unstable romantic, but he was well-versed in military matters and believed that the French and Russian armies were at a peak of strength.[269] Before departing on his mission he had been reminded that French survival in an emergency might depend on how quickly Russia was pushed into war.[270] He now applied his influence accordingly.

Both Nicholas and his Ministers accepted that firmness might lead to hostilities. Despite the violent general strike in progress in St Petersburg, the Interior Ministry advised that there was no danger of internal disturbances and that the whole nation would be behind the Government. Indeed, Sazonov claimed to fear a blow to the tsarist regime's domestic prestige if nothing was done.[271] On the other hand, the external challenge—that Serbia might be reduced to an Austrian 'Bokhara'—was much more drastic than in 1909 or 1912, and it was taken for granted that Germany stood behind the Habsburgs. After the Crown Council Sazonov again met the Ambassadors, Paléologue reiterating that 'France placed herself unreservedly on Russia's side'. Buchanan, by contrast, warned that if Russia mobilized Germany would probably immediately declare war. The Foreign Minister acknowledged that if Berlin failed to restrain Vienna the situation would be desperate, but he maintained that 'Russia cannot allow Austria to crush Serbia and become the predominant Power in the Balkans, and, secure in the support of France, she will face all the risks of war'.[272]

This being said, Sazonov still hoped to avert a conflict, the military apparently sharing in his judgement that the best way to do so was by showing resolve. This judgement rested on the delusion that Russia could have its cake and eat it, preventing an Austro-Serb war without fighting a Continental one. Given the Central Powers' determination to crush Belgrade, the only way for Russia to avoid a Continental war was to give them free rein, but to do so, even if buying time for rearmament, might spell calamity for the Empire's international prestige and domestic stability. None the less, both Janushkevich and the Tsar shared Sazonov's wish to reassure Berlin, and they were encouraged by Jagow's statement on 27 July (which he later retracted) that Germany would mobilize only if Russian troops mobilized on its border or they attacked its ally.[273] As against this, Russian policy, as Janushkevich briefed the General Staff, was to carry out partial mobilization opposite Austria-Hungary if Habsburg forces entered Serbia, which did not necessarily mean taking the offensive.[274] If the Central Powers persisted, a collision was highly probable, but Sazonov's goal was to persuade them to swerve.

[269] M. B. Hayne, *The French Foreign Office and the Origins of the First World War, 1898–1914* (Oxford, 1993), 277–9, 284–301.

[270] Kennedy (ed.), *War Plans*, 259.

[271] Buchanan to Grey, 28 July 1914, *BD* xi, doc. 247. H. Rogger, 'Russia in 1914', *Journal of Contemporary History*, 1/4 (1966), 109.

[272] Buchanan to Grey, 25 July 1914, *BD* xi, doc. 125.

[273] J. Cambon to Bienvenu-Martin, Goschen to Grey, 27 July 1914, Geiss (ed.), *July 1914*, docs. 103, 110. Bronewski to Sazonov, 27 July 1914, *IB* i, v, doc. 135.

[274] General Staff logbook, 25 July 1914, ibid., doc. 79.

In the absence of British solidarity the Russians were anyway unlikely to achieve this objective, but they compounded their difficulties by communicating their intentions poorly and by imperfectly matching ends and means. Sukhomlinov told the German attaché on the night of 26 July that if Austria-Hungary crossed the Serbian frontier the four military districts would be mobilized, but when asked why he merely shrugged his shoulders and referred to 'the diplomats'. Sazonov was similarly vague in speaking to Pourtalès, and it seems that it was not until the evening of 28 July that the Austrians fully understood the position.[275] In addition, the Russians embarked on their localization strategy less confident than the Germans both in the chances of success and in their own strength, and were more inclined to overinsure. The partial mobilization they envisaged—1.1 million men in thirteen army corps—was considerably larger than Austria-Hungary's for 'Case B', and Nicholas II decided to mobilize the Baltic as well as the Black Sea Fleet, thus threatening Germany directly.[276] Above all, the implementation of the Period Preparatory to War was inimical to containing the conflict.

The Preparatory Period seems to have emanated from the General Staff rather than the Foreign Minister. According to Sukhomlinov the latter understood little of military technicalities,[277] and although Sazonov approved the measure as a precondition for a rapid mobilization he may not have realized its full significance. Janushkevich told the Stavka on the evening of 25 July that Austria-Hungary and Italy were making preparations and that it was time to implement energetically everything in the 1913 regulation and even go beyond it.[278] Yet there was no evidence so far that Germany had taken extraordinary measures.[279] None the less, mobilization and concentration arrangements were now to be checked, baggage trains inspected, and horses, fodder, and food to be purchased, while their export was banned. Special security would be imposed in the arsenals, railways were to be placed under military protection and frontier lines cleared of rolling stock, and under the guise of manœuvres extra forces would be stationed in the frontier districts. Mines could be laid off naval harbours, infantry and artillery munitions would be distributed, fortress garrisons would be strengthened, officers would be briefed on the opposing armies and their families moved into the interior. Reservist training would be accelerated. Not only would all of this speed up a later mobilization, to some extent it *was* mobilization, in that reservists and draught animals were being added to the standing army, even if the former were supposedly being called up for exercises and the latter purchased rather than requisitioned.[280] On the basis of these flimsy distinctions Sukhomlinov told Eggeling that Russia was engaged in military preparations, not mobilization; although he warned that if Germany took measures

[275] Pourtalès to Auswärtiges Amt, 26 and 27 July 1914, *DDK* i, docs. 230, 247.
[276] Buchanan to Grey, 25 July 1914, *BD* xi, doc. 125. For the Baltic Fleet, *IB* i, v, doc. 25.
[277] Sukhomlinov, *Erinnerungen*, 375.   [278] General Staff logbook, 25 July 1914, *IB* i, v, doc. 79.
[279] Berens to Russin, and Sazonov circular, 26 July 1914, ibid., docs. 99, 83.
[280] Frantz, *Russland*, 55–63.

opposite Russia or France mobilization would be authorized. This was characteristic of the Russian army's coyness, Janushkevich even telling Eggeling as late
as 29 July that so far not a single preparation had been undertaken against
Germany.[281] In fact the GGS quickly recognized that the Preparatory Period
regulations were being implemented. But the French attaché, who was told of
'secret preparatory measures' in the northern military districts of Warsaw, Vilna,
and St Petersburg, was kept little better informed.[282]

On 26 and 27 July the tension briefly relaxed, Sazonov in his usual fashion
becoming excessively optimistic before relapsing into pessimism. But it was
during this period that support for the middle course of partial mobilization
crumbled. The process began with Danilov's return to the capital. He agreed
with Dobrorolsky's criticisms and believed that thirteen army corps would be too
few even against Austria-Hungary alone. Janushkevich himself was now being
won round, and he and Sazonov appear to have been Nicholas's closest advisers
during the final phase.[283] The Foreign Minister was steeled by the evidence that
Germany was backing Austria-Hungary and that France would support Russian
retaliation. Viviani instructed Paléologue on 27 July that he was ready 'fully to
support, in the interests of peace, the action of the Imperial [Russian]
Government', and although this meant diplomatic action Paléologue told the
Russians that he was authorized to convey 'the full readiness of France to fulfil
its alliance obligations if necessary'.[284] On the same day Messimy asked de
Laguiche to remind the Stavka of its commitment to an early invasion of East
Prussia—an operation that partial mobilization would impede. Meanwhile,
according to the Russian attaché in Paris, Messimy and Joffre had assured him
of their 'full and spirited readiness . . . loyally to fulfil their alliance obligations'.[285]

This was the context for the news on 28 July that Austria-Hungary had
declared war, while Sazonov was still seeking to negotiate. He had earlier
planned to mobilize only when Austria-Hungary crossed the Serbian frontier,
but now he felt the need to prevent Vienna from getting ahead, telling Pourtalès
that the mobilization of eight Habsburg army corps 'must be seen as in part
directed against Russia'. Nicholas telegraphed to Wilhelm that unless the
Austrians could be restrained the enormous indignation in Russia would push
the Empire into extreme measures that would lead to European war: which suggests that he had little doubt about the consequences of mobilizing. According
to Dobrorolsky, Sazonov now accepted that general war was inevitable, told

[281] Paléologue to Bienvenu-Martin, 27 July 1914, *DDF* 3rd ser. xi, doc. 124. Buchanan to Grey,
29 July, *BD* xi, doc. 271.

[282] Paléologue to Bienvenu-Martin, 26 July 1914, *DDF* 3rd ser. xi, doc. 89.

[283] Letter from Danilov, 31 July 1923, *Revue d'histoire de la Guerre mondiale*, 1 (1923), 259–66.
Szápary to Berchtold, 29 July 1914, Geiss (ed.), *July 1914*, doc. 123. Sukhomlinov, *Erinnerungen*,
365–7.

[284] Viviani to Paléologue, 27 July 1914, *DDF* 3rd ser. xi, doc. 138. Russian Foreign Ministry logbook, 28 July 1914, *IB* i, v, doc. 172.

[285] Joffre, *Mémoires*, i. 211. Ignatiev to General Staff, 28 July, *IB* i, v, doc. 180.

Janushkevich that mobilization must be delayed no further, and expressed surprise that it had not begun already begun. But orders were prepared that evening for both partial and general mobilization, and all hope of peace was not yet jettisoned.[286] The Foreign Minister told Buchanan that it was because of Jagow's earlier suggestion that Germany could tolerate a partial mobilization that 'it had been decided not to order the general mobilization which [the] military authorities had strongly recommended'. Although he telegraphed to Berlin that partial mobilization of the four military districts would begin the following day, Sazonov stressed that Russia did not intend to attack Germany, that for the tsarist army mobilization was not synonymous with war, and that the troops could remain under arms for weeks without crossing the border. Pourtalès warned, none the less, that the General Staffs of other Powers could be expected to press for countermeasures so that Russia did not get a head start.[287]

It was on 29 July that Sazonov gave up hope of a peaceful settlement, the crucial development being the warning delivered by Pourtalès at 3 p.m. that continued Russian military preparations, even without mobilization, would force Germany immediately to take the offensive. If anything the Ambassador sharpened up Bethmann's message that 'further continuation of Russian mobilization measures would force us to mobilize, and in that case a European war could scarcely be prevented'. Although Sazonov apparently understood the warning to be directed against partial mobilization, the implication was that even a continuation of the Preparatory Period would lead to war. He and his advisers had concluded that morning that Germany was either not trying to restrain Austria-Hungary or was incapable of doing so: now he telegraphed to Izvolsky that as Russia could not comply with Germany's wishes it had no alternative but to hasten its own preparations and to assume 'that war is probably inevitable'. Soon afterwards the news of the bombardment of Belgrade caused the Foreign Minister to break off, in great agitation, a conversation with the Austro-Hungarian Ambassador in which he was still insisting that partial mobilization was a defensive precaution. Sazonov, Sukhomlinov, and Janushkevich decided that 'in view of the small probability of avoiding a war with Germany it was indispensable to prepare for it in every way in good time, and that therefore the risk could not be accepted of delaying a general mobilization later by effecting a partial mobilization now'.[288] Nicholas accepted their recommendation and agreed to a general mobilization while announcing a partial one, in order to gain a little more time. When the French Ambassador asked if Russia could stay temporarily with a partial call-up he was told at the Foreign Ministry that this would leave Russia defenceless if Germany came to Austria-Hungary's aid. The

---

[286] Nicholas II to Wilhelm II, 29 July 1914, Geiss (ed.), *July 1914*, doc. 116. Dobrorolsky, 'Mobilisation', 145. Pourtalès to Jagow, 29 July 1914, Geiss (ed.), *July 1914*, doc. 124a.

[287] Buchanan to Grey, 29 July 1914, *BD* xi, doc. 276. Sazonov to Bronevski, 28 July; Pourtalès to Jagow, 29 July 1914, Geiss (ed.), *July 1914*, docs. 118, 124a.

[288] Bethmann to Pourtalès, 29 July; Russian Foreign Ministry logbook, 29 July, Sazonov to Izvolsky, 29 July 1914, Geiss (ed.), *July 1914*, docs. 128, 137, 136. Sazonov, *Fateful Years*, 193–6.

Russian diplomats seemed convinced by the military reasoning and were over the brink.[289]

The remaining obstacle to general mobilization was Nicholas himself, who changed his mind and substituted partial mobilization at 11 p.m. He was swayed by a warning telegram from Wilhelm, which reinforced the moderating efforts of Goremykin and some of the military household.[290] On the following morning he rejected telephone appeals to reconsider from Sukhomlinov and Janushkevich, although he agreed to meet Sazonov in the afternoon. Before the fateful audience that resulted, Janushkevich reiterated that war was inevitable and Russia in danger of losing it before it had unsheathed its sword. The General Staff had evidence that German mobilization was much further advanced than previously believed, including a report passed on by Ignatiev in Paris that the Reich was secretly calling up six conscript classes in its eastern provinces.[291] Moreover, Jagow had retracted his previous assurance about partial mobilization, and confessed to the Russian Ambassador that 'he personally could see no further possibility of averting a European war'. Further, it was reported that, according to the Berlin press, Germany had proclaimed general mobilization, and Jagow's denial of the story arrived after the Russians took their final decision. None the less, down to the afternoon of 30 July, mobilization measures were confined to the four designated districts, and the Tsar's wishes were respected.[292] The essential figure remained the Foreign Minister, who was able to win over Nicholas where Sukhomlinov and Janushkevich had failed.

Sazonov's argument on the afternoon of 30 July echoed the conclusions of the previous evening:

war was becoming inevitable, as it was clear to everybody that Germany had decided to bring about a collision, as otherwise she would not have rejected all the pacification proposals that had been made . . . it was better to put away any fears that our warlike preparations would bring about a war, and to continue these preparations carefully rather than by reason of such fears to be taken unawares.

Because Germany would send personal notices to reservists rather than posting up placards, its mobilization was probably already well advanced. It was demanding a capitulation that Russia would never forgive. Yet general mobilization, pleaded Nicholas, would mean sending hundreds of thousands of men to their deaths, and Sazonov agreed that it meant unspeakable efforts and sacrifices. But it would not be their fault, for they had been placed in an impossible position. Finally the Tsar agreed that they must get ready for what appeared to be an

[289] M. Paléologue, *La Russie des Tsars pendant la Grande Guerre* (Paris, 1921), 35–6.

[290] Wilhelm II to Nicholas II, 29 July 1914, Geiss (ed.), *July 1914*, doc. 131.

[291] Foreign Ministry logbook, 30 July 1914, ibid., doc. 147. Sazonov, *Fateful Years*, 197–205. Ignatiev to General Staff, 30 July, *IB* v, i. doc. 294.

[292] Sverbeyev to Sazonov, 29 July 1914, Geiss (ed.), *July 1914*, doc. 138. Danilov letter, *Revue d'histoire de la Guerre mondiale* (cf. n. 283), 263–6.

inevitable conflict, and approved the order.[293] Even now the Germans were assured that this did not mean war, although it was 'technically impossible' to suspend the measure. Indeed, Sazonov had hoped at first to keep the decision secret, but this proved impossible and early on 31 July the red mobilization placards went up.[294]

At no point had the Russian military taken control. They did not want war in 1914, although they were concerned that Russia should be ready for it and after Janushkevich had been brought round they consistently opposed partial mobilization. None the less, they deferred to Sazonov on 24 and 25 July, and to Nicholas on 29 and 30 July. As for the Ministers, their basic decision for firmness also reflected no desire for war, but a sense that Russia had made progress since 1909 and 1912, and could accept war if the alternatives were deemed intolerable. French diplomatic backing and military confidence contributed to this sense, although the General Staff remained uncertain about French effectiveness, and the Humbert disclosures reinforced its doubts. Whereas in Germany and Austria-Hungary the arms race was critical in official deliberations and encouraged the decision to fight, in Russia its role was more permissive. Conditions were not as favourable as they would be three years hence, but they did not make war inconceivable, and this was enough.

Russia's leaders still felt vulnerable, and unable to delay military precautions as could Germany in the hope of containing the crisis. In any case, it was not in their interest to localize it on their opponents' terms. Hence the introduction of the Preparatory Period, and the substituting of general for partial mobilization. Although even the Preparatory Period brought Berlin and St Petersburg close to breaking point, neither it nor partial mobilization were seen as being tantamount to hostilities. General mobilization, in contrast, was so seen, and was ordered on the assumption that war with Germany was inevitable and that the Central Powers were gaining an advantage over Russia's more ponderous forces. These assumptions about military exigencies, however, rested on a prior political assumption that Germany had wilfully used the crisis to force a confrontation. Until 28–9 July Sazonov and Nicholas were not convinced that war was certain, and they threatened or implemented military measures as complements to their diplomacy as well as to ensure their military preparedness. On 29–30 July they changed their minds. It is therefore difficult to see Russian general mobilization as a miscalculated diplomatic gesture.[295] Its authors knew the likely consequence was a blood bath, yet when they said war was 'inevitable' they meant not that there was no choice but that the alternative was an abdication far worse than in 1909 that might rock the foundations of the tsarist regime.

* * *

[293] Foreign Ministry logbook, 30 July 1914, Geiss (ed.), *July 1914*, doc. 147. Sazonov, *Fateful Years*, 200–5. Paléologue, *Russia*, 38-9. D. C. B. Lieven, *Nicholas II: Emperor of All the Russias* (London, 1993), 202.
[294] Nicholas II to Wilhelm II, 31 July; Pourtalès to Auswärtiges Amt, 31 July and 1 Aug. 1914, *DDK* iii. docs. 487, 535-6. Russian Foreign Ministry logbook, 31 July 1914, *IB* i, v, doc. 349.
[295] Trachtenberg, *History and Strategy*, 78-80.

By giving the blank cheque Germany had resolved to risk a Continental war. The decision not just to risk such a war but to launch one came at the end of July and in the first instance because of Russian general mobilization. An influx of reports on military preparations in Western Europe also contributed, those from France coming foremost. Like the Russians, the French were eventually driven by Germany into accepting war or scarcely precedented humiliation, but before St Petersburg embarked on military measures they had more freedom of manœuvre and might, had it not been for Poincaré's and Viviani's inaccessibility, have exerted themselves more forcefully. Instead French influence was largely felt through Paléologue's misleading assurances. By contrast, in the second period of Russian decision-making, on 29–30 July, Paris did enjoin caution, but its admonitions came too late.

Little evidence has survived of French military appreciations during the July crisis, but since 1911 the EMA had become more sanguine about the balance between the blocs, and while preparing Plan XVII it had become still more so. Although the French would feel before the Russians the main weight of German attack, they were more hopeful that they could withstand it. Between 28 and 30 July the Russian Embassy in Paris reported of Joffre and Messimy that 'the mood is calm and firm', 'the mood of military circles and the High Command is very elated', and even that there was 'unconcealed joy at exploiting the . . . favourable strategic situation'.[296] If there were no war, on the other hand, the prospect ahead was of pressure on the Three-Year Law, but also of continuing improvements in the army's readiness and in Russia's value as an ally. There was little reason to fight rather than to wait, and no pro-war lobby at the highest level. By the end of the crisis the EMA wanted preparatory measures as urgently as did its counterparts in St Petersburg and Berlin, but it was much more constrained by political considerations.

In the first days after the ultimatum a pattern established itself of hesitant French responses to real or imagined enemy measures. The EMA complained that because of a German news blackout it had to rely for its information on agents' reports, with a twelve- to forty-eight-hour delay, whereas the GGS could get what it needed from the French press. In fact a lot of information came in from the border intelligence services, and the 2nd Bureau tended to exaggerate what the Germans were doing. The burden of responding fell on Joffre and Messimy, whose decisions, according to the latter, were purely reactive.[297] On the evening of 24 July he told Joffre that the Government was worried by the Austrian ultimatum and thought there might be war. 'Very well, *Monsieur le Ministre*', came the reply, 'We shall wage war if we must.' On the following day Messimy ordered commanders and generals on leave to return to their posts, without consulting the CGS, who then showed him the EMA's newly revised schedule of 'measures that may be prescribed in cases of political tension'. It con-

[296] Ignatiev to General Staff, 28 and 30 July, Izvolsky to Sazonov, 29 July 1914, *IB* i, v, docs. 180, 296, 234.
[297] EMA, 28 July 1914, *DDF* 3rd ser. xi, doc. 211. Messimy, *Souvenirs*, 130, 134.

tained blocks of measures to be taken in sequence or independently, divided into those of precaution, surveillance, and protection; and those needed to prepare for mobilization and operations. From now on Messimy followed its provisions, and did nothing without consulting Joffre, although not agreeing to everything that the general wanted.[298]

During the first week French precautions did not amount to much. Messimy felt he could do nothing that might disturb the public without consulting his Cabinet colleagues, and although he was willing to take the initiative in security precautions he would not authorize mobilization preparations unless he was sure that Germany was doing the same. The Council of Ministers quickly agreed to suspend movements of units, to cancel any new leave, and to recall officers, but not, as Joffre wanted, both officers and men. 100,000 soldiers were away on harvest leave, and it would cause too much 'emotion' if France summoned them back before Germany did. Similarly, Messimy ordered regiments to return to their garrisons only if they could do so without using rail transport, as the latter might suggest the beginnings of mobilization. He held to his line when Joffre presented him with a so-called 'Ludendorff document' that had fallen into the EMA's hands and which, if genuine, demonstrated that Germany had plans for secret mobilization and concentration prior to a surprise attack. On 27 July, however, the incoming evidence became more threatening, and Messimy agreed to recall both officers and men after Germany was said to be doing so. The frontier was to be made ready, railways guarded, and the youngest class of reservists put on notice, while the authorities in North Africa were to prepare to send all available men. On the following day the Germans were reported to be setting up frontier surveillance, moving railway trucks into the interior, and preparing the Lorraine fortresses and disembarkation platforms. The EMA believed that they were applying their prescribed measures for political tension; and Jules Cambon's dispatch of 21 July, forwarded belatedly by the Quai d'Orsay, suggested that the Germans might be a week in the lead. After seeing the dispatch Joffre wanted at once to establish the full *couverture* of five frontier corps at full strength, but Messimy would agree only to certain units being relocated and to stronger frontier surveillance, without calling up territorials to implement it.[299]

Poincaré's and Viviani's return, amid tumultuous scenes, on 29 July made little immediate difference. The President found the Cabinet 'closely united in the resolution to do the impossible to avoid war and also in that of neglecting no preparation for defence',[300] but it was the former that continued to be emphasized. This was the day of Germany's warning to Russia, and the 2nd Bureau reported, in fact prematurely, that German troops were detraining on the frontier and setting up their own *couverture*. Joffre now considered war inevitable and

[298] Joffre, *Mémoires*, i. 207–9. *Les Armées françaises dans la Grande Guerre* (Paris, 1936), i. 94–5. Text of the memento in SHA 7.N. 134.

[299] Messimy, *Souvenirs*, 130–9. Joffre, *Mémoires*, i. 207–13. *Armées françaises*, 95–101. *DDF* 3rd ser. xi, docs. 49, 76, 79, 87, 93, 106, 113, 118, 129, 185, 201, 207, 211, 240, 265.

[300] Poincaré, *Service*, iv. 371.

that the politicians were irresponsibly temporizing. But the Council of Ministers rejected his appeals and would agree only to a full guard on fortified works, without calling up reservists, and to wirelaying and other precautions in the fortresses in so far as was possible without attracting attention.[301]

At this point France's own restraint was nullified by its failure to restrain Russia. Inadequate information was partly to blame. The Russians were slow to brief Paléologue, whom they considered indiscreet, and he sent his cables by a circuitous Scandinavian route for fear that if he transmitted them via Germany they would be deciphered. In fairness, he had reported on 25 and 26 July the Russian decision in principle for partial mobilization and that preparations were beginning at once, including opposite Germany. But he telegraphed the news of the decision to mobilize against Austria-Hungary only at 11.45 p.m. on 29 July, twenty-four hours after Sazonov had notified his Berlin Embassy.[302] After receiving Pourtalès's warning earlier in the day, the Russian Foreign Minister signalled to Paris that Russia could only hasten its armaments, counting on French support, and envisage a probably inevitable war. Angry and bewildered, the French leaders were tumbled from their beds in the small hours of 30 July, with an urgent request from Izvolsky and Ignatiev to know their attitude to Russian partial mobilization.[303]

In effect France was being presented with a *fait accompli*, and Messimy asked with justice whether Russia's action was compatible with the alliance. Viviani considered Sazonov's interpretation of French support to be excessive: the message of 27 July had been sent before mobilization had been envisaged (or, at least, before he and Poincaré had been informed of it). Hence a new telegram went out at 7 a.m. on 30 July, confirming that France would honour its obligations but asking that Russia's precautionary measures should give Germany no pretext for total or partial mobilization. When Ignatiev and Izvolsky enquired what this meant, they were told it meant no mobilization or mass troop transports. As Messimy had recognized the sensitivity of railway movements in France, so it was the strategic concentration, rather than the preceding call-up, that caused Viviani most anxiety. Yet the attitude of the French was ambiguous. They wished not only to buy time for diplomacy but also to forestall a military deployment that would disadvantage them, the War Minister approaching Ignatiev in order to prevent a primary concentration against the Habsburg Monarchy. To Izvolsky he insisted once again on operations against East Prussia as being in the joint interest.[304] As Poincaré put it later,

---

[301] *Armées françaises*, 301. Joffre, *Mémoires*, i. 213–4. Messimy, *Souvenirs*, 138–9.

[302] J. Stengers, '1914: The Safety of Cyphers and the Outbreak of the First World War', in C. M. Andrew and J. Noakes (eds.), *Intelligence and International Relations, 1900–1945* (Exeter, 1987), 34–7. Paléologue to Bienvenu-Martin, 25 and 26 July 1914, *DDF* 3rd ser. xi, docs. 50, 89. Hayne, *French Foreign Office*, 299.

[303] Viviani to Poincaré, 30 July 1914, *BD* xi, doc. 294. Messimy, *Souvenirs*, 181–5.

[304] Ibid. 183–7. Viviani to Paléologue, 30 July 1914, Geiss (ed.), *July 1914*, doc. 148. Poincaré, *Service*, iv. 383–7.

On us rested two duties, difficult to reconcile but equally sacred: to do our utmost to prevent a conflict, to do our utmost in order that, should it burst forth in spite of us, we should be prepared. But there were still two other duties, which also at times ran the risk of being mutually contradictory: not to break up an alliance on which French policy had been based for a quarter of a century and the break-up of which could leave us in isolation and at the mercy of our rivals; and nevertheless to do what lay in our power to induce our ally to exercise moderation in matters in which we were much less directly concerned than herself.[305]

The telegram of 30 July arrived too late to prevent the decision for general mobilization, and henceforth the French authorities' options narrowed to a choice between repudiating the alliance or accepting war. Yet they still hesitated to give military readiness absolute priority. They were uncertain about their public opinion, and still more uncertain about Britain. On the evening of 30 July Jules Cambon advised that Germany was probably trying to make France mobilize first, and should be resisted out of consideration for the British attitude. The 2nd Bureau drew up a synopsis, which was forwarded to London, of French and German preparations, purporting to show that Germany had been the first to implement each category of measure. On delivering it, the French Ambassador invoked the consultation provision of the November 1912 exchange of letters, and asked what Britain would do if Germany attacked, but Grey gave him nothing definite.[306] Because the Council of Ministers feared appearing as the aggressor, it refused to install the *couverture*, and agreed instead to a compromise. Those *couverture* troops that could be transported without railways would move into place; horses would be purchased but not requisitioned; no reservists would be called up; and French forces would stay an average of 10 kilometres behind the frontier. Orders went out at 5 p.m. on 30 July, and although Joffre disliked the arrangement he again acquiesced.[307]

It was only over the next two days that the French threw themselves into a race for immediate readiness. By 31 July German patrols were reported to have crossed the frontiers, but the crucial developments were the ultimatum to Russia and Berlin's proclamation of the *Kriegsgefahrzustand*, the condition of danger of war. Joffre wanted an immediate call-up or at least full installation of the *couverture*, on the ground that Germany was widening its lead. Further piecemeal measures would damage France's own mobilization and concentration, and every twenty-four hour delay would mean losing 15–20 kilometres of territory. The Council of Ministers opted for the less extreme alternative of the *couverture*, and threw out a proposal from Messimy to arrest the political activists listed in the so-called 'Carnet B', who were suspected of being dangerous to the war effort. That evening, however, there arrived the expected ultimatum from the German

---

[305] Ibid. iv. 412.
[306] Ibid. 420. Jules Cambon to Viviani; EMA memorandum, 30 July 1914, *DDF* 3rd ser. xi, docs. 339, 361. Grey to Bertie, 30 July 1914, *BD* xi, doc. 319.
[307] Poincaré, *Service*, iv. 422–4. Messimy, *Souvenirs*, 140–2. Messimy circular, 30 July, *DDF* 3rd ser. xi, doc. 333.

Ambassador, demanding to know whether France would stay neutral in a Russo-German war, to which Viviani replied tersely that it would look to its interests. On 1 August Joffre returned to the fray, urging that Germany was following the Ludendorff memorandum plan for a surprise attack and might have completed a disguised mobilization within three days. France's general mobilization decree eventually went out at 3.55 p.m., shortly before Germany's, and although the 10-kilometre limit was maintained, this was out of consideration for Britain rather than because any hope remained of preserving peace. Poincaré reassured Izvolsky that the Government was united in its commitment to fulfil its undertakings, but to ensure parliamentary unanimity and avoid seeming provocative in London it preferred the Germans to be the first to declare war. Two days later they duly complied.[308]

In France there was more united ministerial resistance than in Russia to military pressure. Joffre established his right to be consulted, but he achieved neither the *couverture* nor mobilization as quickly as he wished. The French understood that their actions might be misinterpreted, as is demonstrated by their delay in authorizing railway movements and their belated attempt to make Russia refrain from doing so. Despite their more exposed position, they went neither so far nor so fast as their ally while a chance of peace remained. But the more important constraints were public opinion and anxiety about Britain. As against such concerns the EMA, the more nervous because of the paucity of good intelligence, was mesmerized by Germany's supposed capacity for creeping mobilization, to which France, according to Joffre, had nothing comparable.[309] Politicians, especially Poincaré, shared the fear of surprise, and eventually the French mobilized just before Germany did. Until then they resisted the temptation to pre-empt. It was their failure to make Russia do likewise, given their overriding commitment to the alliance, that sealed their destiny. All the same, in contrast with their warning to St Petersburg in February 1909, they were willing to accept hostilities, not only because of the provocation by the Central Powers but also because of the much more opportune military balance. As Moltke had communicated his appraisal to Jagow and the German Emperor, so had Joffre to Messimy and Poincaré; and the military appreciation also weighed with Paléologue. For France as for Russia, the favourable evolution of the arms race was a *sine qua non*, and a necessary, if not sufficient, explanation of Paris's willingness to fight.

* * *

In London, similarly, the influence of the naval balance was permissive, in not impeding decisions that were taken for other reasons. In contrast to 1911 the CID was not convened and the Cabinet sought no formal naval and military opinions. Grey was aware, however, of Admiralty plans to inflict great damage

---

[308] Poincaré, Notes journalières, 30 July 1914, BN n.a.fr. 16027. Messimy, *Souvenirs*, 142–55. Joffre, *Mémoires*, i. 221–31. Izvolsky to Sazonov, 1 Aug. 1914, Geiss (ed.), *July 1914*, doc. 176.
[309] Joffre, *Mémoires*, i. 225. EMA, 1 Aug. 1914, *DDF* 3rd ser. xi, doc. 537.

on Germany through a distant (rather than inshore) blockade,[310] and Churchill believed the fleet had become more combat-ready under his leadership, despite the narrowness of the margin of dreadnought superiority. During the crisis he once again forced the pace, deciding on 28 July after the test mobilization to leave the First Fleet concentrated at Portland and to station the ships of the Second in their home ports and in close proximity to their balance crews. Naval commanders had already been advised that war was possible, and Asquith agreed to magazines and oil tanks being placed under guard. On 29 July, the day that the Admiralty issued its 'warning telegram', Churchill decreed the Preparatory Period: harbours were cleared, bridges watched, steamers boarded and searched, and observers placed along the coast. Repairs were speeded up, and the German naval attaché reported that the fleet was mobilizing on the quiet. Churchill now wanted to move it to its war station in the Orkneys, for which, fearing that the Cabinet might object, he got authority from the Prime Minister. It departed secretly on 29 July. On 1 August he reported that the German fleet was mobilizing and that he wanted to call up the reserves. This concerned only the oldest ships and mattered less than the steps already accomplished. But when his colleagues resisted Churchill summoned the men anyway, without legal authority, but with Grey's and Asquith's endorsement.[311]

Unlike the French army, the British navy kept ahead of its antagonist, for security reasons but also as a warning. The Admiralty knew the identities of the German agents in Britain and was opening their mail, but it allowed them to continue reporting, as it wanted Tirpitz to know that it was taking precautions. Grey hoped that the announcement of the non-dispersal of the fleet would sober the Central Powers, telling the Russian Ambassador that it should dispel misapprehensions that Britain would in all circumstances stand aside.[312] The measure also suited him as a means of countering pressure from Sazonov, and can be seen as part of a strategy of simultaneously restraining Vienna and St Petersburg. Zimmermann indeed regarded the dispersal or non-dispersal of the fleet as a litmus of British intentions, and Wilhelm interpreted non-dispersal as a signal that Britain was ready for war and a reason to recall his own ships from Norway. But it failed to make the Germans reconsider their support for Austria-Hungary until it was followed by a declaration from Grey on 29 July that early British intervention was likely. As a political gesture it was of questionable effectiveness, and increasingly the objective of British naval preparations was to avoid being taken by surprise, given that a clash of arms might come even earlier at sea than on land. Thus Grey told Lichnowsky of the fleet's departure for Scotland only after the movement was already well under way, though underlining that it did not

[310] Callwell (ed.), *Wilson*, 153. A. Offer, *The First World War: An Agrarian Interpretation* (Oxford, 1989), 309–10.

[311] Churchill, *World Crisis*, 204–17.

[312] Ibid. 211. Grey to Buchanan, 27 July 1914, *BD* xi, doc. 177.

mean mobilization and that neither Britain nor France would mobilize unless Germany did so.[313]

Towards the army the Liberal Cabinet, perhaps reflecting its traditional distrust, was much more wary. A private memorandum from the General Staff to Churchill and Lloyd George took Wilson's usual line: Russia counted for little and Germany would try to beat France quickly. A prompt dispatch of the BEF would exert an influence disproportionate to its numbers on French and Belgian morale.[314] None the less, on 1 August, the Cabinet decided not to send the Expeditionary Force in any event. Although ordering the Preparatory Period on 28 July and two days later calling up 25,000 Special Reservists to guard the railways leading to the ports, Asquith rejected Wilson's appeals to prepare for an eventual mobilization by recalling to their home garrisons units that were away for training. Nor, despite the DMO's liaison with the Unionist Opposition, did he change his mind until Sunday 2 August, the day on which the Cabinet resolved to assist France against an attack by the German fleet and to protect Belgium against a 'substantial violation' of its territory. Mobilization of the army was ordered on the morning of 4 August, two and a half days behind the French although pre-war planning had envisaged a simultaneous start, and it was only after war had been declared that a subcommittee of ministers decided after all that the BEF should go.[315] Grey, Asquith, Churchill, and, more reluctantly, Lloyd George, accepted that Britain could not let France be overwhelmed, but few British ministers were familiar with the intricacies of Continental armaments. They expected Britain's contribution to be primarily economic and naval, and Asquith's concern in the crisis was to get intervention accepted with minimum damage to Cabinet unity. Delaying the dispatch of the Expeditionary Force was a small price to pay.[316]

* * *

For Moltke London's actions probably mattered less than those of Brussels, and the wide sweep of his forces through the centre of Belgium provided exactly the 'substantial violation' that the Liberal Cabinet had agreed would be a *casus belli*. The pre-war arms race, among whose products were the 1913 reinforcement of the German army and the 42 cm mortars that destroyed the Liège forts, made the sweep both possible and necessary, and in this sense contributed to Britain's decision for war.[317] But it also mattered that the Belgians resisted and appealed

---

[313] Hopman to Tirpitz, 25 July 1914, Berghahn and Deist (eds.), 'Kaiserliche Marine', 58. Wilhelm II to Auswärtiges Amt, 26 July, Lichnowsky to Auswärtiges Amt, 30 July 1914, *DDK* i. doc. 231, ii, doc. 438.

[314] C. Hazelhurst, *Politicians at War, July 1914 to May 1915: A Prologue to the Triumph of Lloyd George* (London, 1971), 321–6.

[315] Callwell (ed.), *Wilson*, 152–6. Paul Cambon to Viviani, 30 July 1914, *DDF* 3rd ser. doc. 306.

[316] For general accounts of British policy in the crisis see C. Hazelhurst, *Politicians at War, July 1914 to May 1915* (London, 1971); Z. S. Steiner, *Britain and the Origins of the First World War* (London, 1977), ch. 9; K. M. Wilson, *The Policy of the Entente: Essays on the Determinants of British Policy, 1904–1914* (Cambridge, 1985), ch. 8; and M. Brock, 'Britain Enters the War', in Evans and Strandmann (eds.), *Coming*, ch. 7.

[317] Ibid. 169–70.

for aid, rejecting an ultimatum sent on 2 August that they should allow German troops to pass unmolested. They did so even though the 1913 reinforcement had not had time to take effect, their new mobilization plan was completed only on 25 July, and the concentration had to be improvised. For Belgium, even more than France and Russia, 1914 was an unfavourable year in which to fight.[318]

Given their special vulnerability to a lightning attack, King Albert and his advisers were in a dilemma. To prepare too early might provoke their neighbours, but to wait might leave Belgium defenceless. In fact their handling of the situation resembled France's more than Russia's: initial hesitation, but then they acted quickly.[319] By 25 July the frontier surveillance was in operation, opposite France as well as Germany. Two days later the Cabinet decided to confine itself at present to halting cavalry manœuvres and recalling troops on leave, but de Broqueville submitted to pressure from Albert's military cabinet to start mobilization preparations. On 29 July the new CGS, de Selliers de Moranville, got the crucial authorization to call up three conscript classes from the following day, raising the army's strength to 100,000. The garrisons at Liège and elsewhere were to be reinforced, and transport requisitioned. Although the units remained in their peacetime locations, these dispositions were equivalent to the French *couverture* and meant that there would be no promenade through Belgian territory. The Government still claimed to be defending itself against all comers, but it was obvious that Germany would be the Power most affected. On the evening of 31 July, after news arrived of the *Kriegsgefahrzustand* and closure of the cross-border railways, Albert prevailed on the Cabinet to order general mobilization from 1 August, officially to allow Belgium to meet its defence obligations and because the Dutch were doing the same. The concentration zone was shifted westwards in order to keep the appearance of even-handedness, and out of respect for 'German susceptibilities' the commander at Liège was restrained from organizing his perimeter defences and denied balloons and aircraft.[320] Up until the end, their neutral tradition and their anxiety to avoid provocation made the Belgians pause. They did enough to put up a fight, although less than they could have done if they had been more single-minded. None the less, with their measures of 29 July they set a clock ticking under the Schlieffen Plan.

* * *

It is now necessary to turn to the Triple Alliance, and to the choices that inaugurated Armageddon. Italy, in contrast to its partners, offers the most striking instance in the crisis of civilian disregard for the military. One reason may have been Pollio's death on 1 July and his replacement three weeks later by Luigi Cadorna, a prickly and francophobe Piedmontese. After calling up an extra class before the ultimatum, and bringing the 11th Corps at Bari almost to full

---

[318] AGRB Lesaffre MSS 10, 11.

[319] Ibid. 10. Génie to French War Ministry, 27, 29, 30 July 1914, SHA 7.N. 1159. Lichtervelde, *Avant l'orage*, ch. 7; and correspondence in MAEB INDMB 14, for this section.

[320] Note by de Selliers de Moranville, 31 July 1914, MAEB INDMB 14.

strength, until the end of July Italy took only precautionary measures.[321] None the less, on 29 July Cadorna assured Moltke that it would stand by its agreements, and Grandi agreed to nearly all the CGS's requests for reinforcement of the north-western frontier and for preparations to send troops northwards. On 31 July Grandi sought authority from the King to transfer to the Rhine all forces not absolutely needed in Italy and Libya, Victor Emmanuel approving the War Minister's 'basic assumptions' on 2 August. On the very next day, however, Italian neutrality was proclaimed.[322]

It was not the General Staff that made Italian foreign policy but San Giuliano, with Salandra's backing and Victor Emmanuel's acquiescence. Whereas the military had been tightening their agreements with the Central Powers, the Foreign Minister had become increasingly estranged from Vienna. He was not treaty-bound to assist Austria-Hungary if the latter was the aggressor, especially as the Austrians had violated their alliance obligation to offer compensation if they embarked on Balkan expansion. Even so, he suggested that Italy might participate if Austria-Hungary ceded the Italian-speaking territory of the Trentino. But the Austrians hedged, and the growing likelihood of British belligerency confirmed the neutrality decision. The Chief of the Naval Staff warned that against the Royal Navy he could neither assure communications with the colonies nor protect the coastal cities, which would be blockaded and shelled.[323] Grandi reported that the army was unready because of Libya and equipment shortages, and San Giuliano feared internal unrest.[324] It was thought to be too dangerous to intervene until the outcome was clearer, especially as Italy could not stand a long war. Such a course, felt the Foreign Minister, even if unheroic was patriotic and wise. Salandra opposed mobilization because it might appear to contradict the neutrality declaration and suggest that Italy would come in after all. He agreed to call up two more conscript classes and to requisition horses and transport, Cadorna protesting unavailingly that only mobilization would do.[325] All of this confirmed the impression given since 1911 that Italy had dropped out of the arms race and was willing neither to pursue its claims against Austria-Hungary nor its *rapprochement* with the Central Powers to the point of going to war. Arguably the Government in Rome assessed the situation more shrewdly than did any other: the balance was too even to permit a quick decision, and it was better not to fight. The military were allowed to pursue their intervention projects until the time came for decision, and then were abruptly disabused.

* * *

In the later stages of the crisis the Austrians were drawn behind Germany's chariot wheels into a war with Russia that they had expected but regarded with foreboding. For five days after the partial mobilization order on 25 July their preparations were directed primarily against Belgrade, but a serpent rapidly appeared in Conrad's paradise in the shape of Russia's military measures. On 25

[321] Barrère to Viviani, 31 July 1914, *DDF* 3rd ser. xi, doc. 410.
[322] Gooch, *Italy*, 156–9. Rochat, 'L'esercito italiano', 324–5.   [323] Bosworth, *Italy*, 124.
[324] Gooch, *Italy*, 157.   [325] Rochat, 'L'esercito italiano', 236–37.

and 26 July rumours reached Vienna that the tsarist army had started mobilizing. Despite the General Staff's paucity of funds for espionage, the embassy and consulates in Russia supplied considerable, if inaccurate, information.[326] It included reports of mobilization preparations and reservist call-ups on the border, although Sukhomlinov gave his word that there would be no mobilization unless Serbia were invaded. On 26 July Conrad told Berchtold that he wished the Monarchy to keep pace with the Russians. On 28 July he said that he must know where he stood by 1 August, and he proposed a *démarche* by Germany, which would have the incidental benefit of verifying Berlin's continued support. On the same evening Berchtold duly reported to the Germans Sukhomlinov's warning that as soon as Austro-Hungarian troops entered Serbia the Kiev, Odessa, Moscow, and Kazan military districts would be mobilized. Conrad needed to know whether to send his forces north or south; and if the Russians were already mobilizing in the four districts Austria-Hungary and Germany must take 'comprehensive counter-measures'. The Foreign Minister requested a 'friendly' German reminder to St Petersburg that partial mobilization against Austria-Hungary would elicit both Austrian and German retaliation. By the time that his request arrived, however, the Germans had already delivered the far from friendly warning by Pourtalès, which instead of relieving the tension gravely exacerbated it.[327]

Before taking this initiative, Conrad and Berchtold had agreed that they would not let Russian partial mobilization distract them from their Balkan venture. In consequence, when at 1 a.m. on 30 July Berchtold further telegraphed to Berlin that the corps commanders in Galicia had confirmed that Russian partial mobilization was going ahead, he added that unless it were immediately suspended Austria-Hungary would order general mobilization. He wanted joint warnings in St Petersburg and Paris—to which Jagow replied that Germany had already given warnings independently.[328] Russia had now capped Austria-Hungary's localized threat to Serbia with a localized threat to the Monarchy, and both sides were willing to widen the conflict rather than give way.

As the initial strategy teetered on the edge of breakdown its authors were getting cold feet. Berchtold asked whether Austria-Hungary could sustain a war against Russia at the same time as fighting a Serb army of 400,000 men. He agonized with Stürgkh about the likely financial, though not human, sacrifice. Although Conrad said it was too late for such doubts, he calculated that even if he mobilized promptly he would be taking the offensive with twenty-seven and a half divisions against Russia's thirty-three. He wrote to his mistress that it would be a hopeless struggle but the Monarchy must not perish ingloriously.

[326] Szápáry, Hein, Széchenyi, *et al.* to Berchtold, 25, 26, 27 July 1914, KAW KM Präs (1914) 51–2. Czernin to Berchtold, 26 July 1914, ibid. 51–8. Hubka memorandum, 'Der kritische Monat, Juli 1914', KAW, lent by Herr Broucek.

[327] Conrad, *Dienstzeit*, iii. 130–8. Austrian Embassy note, Bethmann to Pourtalès and Tschirschky, 29 July 1914, *DDK* i, docs. 352, 380, 385.

[328] Conrad, *Dienstzeit*, iii. 142. Berchtold to Szögyény, 30 July 1914, Geiss (ed.), *July 1914*, doc. 124. Austrian Embassy note, and Jagow to Berchtold, 30 July 1914, *DDK* ii, docs. 427, 429.

Franz Joseph agreed that 'if the Monarchy goes to ruin, at least it should do so decently'.[329] At this point Germany, too, wavered, and belatedly attempted to stop Austria-Hungary in its tracks by committing it to halt after taking Belgrade and to accept British mediation.

There was no mood to yield, however, over war against Serbia. On the afternoon of 30 July, after the arrival of a memorandum from Bethmann urging the halt in Belgrade, Conrad conferred with Berchtold and the Emperor. He claimed that the 'mood of the army' made it impossible to suspend operations. Berchtold foresaw that a call-up in Galicia would lead to war against Russia, but it was resolved to reject the German proposal and order general mobilization. On the following day the GMR agreed that British mediation could be accepted only if operations in the Balkans continued and Russia ceased its mobilization. Berchtold insisted that there must be no repeat of the London Conference experience. A mere occupation of Belgrade was valueless, and if the Serbian army were left intact it would attack the Monarchy in more favourable circumstances two or three years hence.[330] It is true that, also on 30 July, Moltke warned that Russian partial mobilization was not a sufficient pretext for Germany, and that Austria-Hungary should await Russia's attack rather than declare war. Although Conrad at once promised to comply, thereby placing his army in great danger, he still pressed on against Serbia. General mobilization was ordered on 31 July, but the first day of mobilization against Russia was postponed to 4 August. This contrasted with the urgency felt by Moltke, who on the morning of 31 July contradicted both his and Bethmann's communications of the previous day by appealing for mobilization against Russia at once and for mediation to be rejected. Succeeding messages from the Chancellor and Wilhelm confirmed that the Germans, now reunited, wanted the bulk of the Habsburg forces to go north.[331] Only at this point did Conrad agreed to change *B-Staffel*'s destination, although still directing it towards the Balkan theatre before rerouting it to Galicia. The resulting delay, added to the March 1914 decision to move the concentration zone back from the frontier, deprived the Austrians of the chance to strike while they enjoyed the advantages of faster mobilization, and contributed to the débâcle that followed.[332]

The consistent thread in Austrian policy after 23 July was the refusal to abandon the invasion of Serbia, despite Russian threats, British intercession, and German vacillation. The Vienna leaders doubted their chances in a contest with Russia, even with German backing, and attempted to avert one, but the device of a warning via Berlin misfired. Habsburg preparations were targeted on a localized rather than a Continental war, but only sustained and insistent German pressure might have caused them to be suspended, and such pressure was not

---

[329] Conrad, *Dienstzeit*, iv. 136, 148, 150, 162. G. E. Rothenberg, *The Army of Francis Joseph* (West Lafayette, 1976), 177.

[330] Ibid. 150–1. GMR, 31 July 1914, Geiss (ed.), *July 1914*, doc. 154.

[331] Conrad, *Dienstzeit*, iii. 151–6. Bethmann to Tschirschky, 31 July 1914, *DDK* ii, doc. 479.

[332] Stone, 'Mobilmachung', 87–91.

applied. Disappointed by Italy's neutrality, although reassured by Romania's, the Austro-Hungarian leaders anticipated the consequences of their actions, but went ahead.

* * *

Austria-Hungary switched to preparing for a Continental rather than a local war because of pressure from Berlin; and after 31 July German policy became highly dynamic. The ultimata to St Petersburg and Paris heralded the unrolling of the Schlieffen Plan. Whereas France, Russia, and Belgium took preparatory measures, and even mobilized, without declaring war or opening fire, it was Germany that cast the die. Before 31 July, in contrast, despite having taken the initiative with the blank cheque, Germany was more reluctant to move to higher readiness than were its potential enemies. Russia and Britain were quicker to back diplomacy with military gestures, and Belgium to strengthen its standing forces. Instead of following a graduated course of armed diplomacy, Berlin swung suddenly and savagely between extremes. Yet the Emperor and his civilian ministers continued to dominate decision-making, the professional military becoming more influential but only once taking matters into their own hands. Although preparatory measures, principally Russian, eventually impelled the Germans into action, they had accepted from the start that tsarist mobilization must be answered by their own. From the granting of the blank cheque onwards their policy was consistent, until Wilhelm and Bethmann belatedly attempted between 28 and 30 July to engineer a compromise. After 31 July, they reverted to their previous course, while the army leadership displayed great optimism, and even exultation, at the prospect of war.

Immediately after the ultimatum localization remained the watchword to which military and naval preparations were subordinated, although the Emperor remained a wild card. On 25 July he ordered the fleet to return from Norway to its home ports, overriding objections from Bethmann that the British were taking no extraordinary measures. Wilhelm insisted that they had already mobilized, but his most pressing fear was a surprise attack by the Russian Baltic Fleet. At first he wanted the entire battlefleet to go into the Baltic, but he was persuaded to send only the Second and Third Squadrons of battleships to Kiel, stationing the First Squadron and the battlecruisers at Wilhelmshaven.[333] On 27 July he incensed Tirpitz and the naval chiefs by ordering the securing (*Sicherung*) of the approaches to the Kiel Bight, but was persuaded to commute this into observation (*Beobachtung*). To this extent, although the Emperor's advisers moderated his interventions, Germany was already anticipating Russian initiatives.[334]

But it was the land theatre that really mattered, and here the policy of minimal precautions continued. Some steps were taken behind the scenes. Falkenhayn instructed his commanders on conduct in a state of siege; the

---

[333] Bethmann to Wilhelm II, 25 and 26 July, Wilhelm II to Auswärtiges Amt, 26 July, *DDK* i, docs. 182, 197, 221, 231. A. von Tirpitz, *Deutsche Ohnmachtpolitik im Weltkriege* (Hamburg, 1926), 1–2.

[334] Hopman diary, 27–8 July, BA-MA Hopman MSS N.326/11.

Interior Ministry authorized grain stockpiling in the Ruhr. On 23 July the intelligence section of the General Staff ordered its agents to cross the French and Russian frontiers to check on war preparations, but not all available manpower was yet to be committed, as the danger might last for some time and then subside. On 26 July the section still reckoned with a 'lengthy period of tension', which its head, Colonel Nicolai, thought could last 'for weeks'.[335]

At first the evidence from Western Europe was reassuring. The British were reported to have started to demobilize, and George V to have said that they would stay neutral.[336] According to the daily appreciation prepared by the GGS for 27 July, the situation in France was quiet, except for leave being cancelled for the frontier troops.[337] Returning to Berlin on the previous day Moltke wrote to his wife that 'the further development of affairs depends purely on Russia's attitude: if it undertakes no hostile act against Austria the war will remain localized', and on the same day Bethmann wrote to Wilhelm that 'so long as Russia undertakes no hostile act, I believe that our attitude, directed towards localization, must remain calm', adding that the CGS shared his view.[338]

But the information coming from Russia was disturbing, Pourtalès reporting that the attaché was sure that mobilization had already been ordered in at least two military districts, and Bethmann being informed at lunchtime on 26 July that the Empire was to call up several classes of reservists.[339] The Foreign Ministry considered the situation 'really serious' and 'thoroughly critical', though it still hoped that London and Paris would restrain St Petersburg. In the evening the Chancellor informed Pourtalès that 'Russian preparatory military measures that were in any way directed against us would compel us to take countermeasures, which must comprise the mobilization of the army. But mobilization would mean war, and moreover would have to be directed simultaneously against Russia and France, as France's obligations to Russia are well known.' The implication was that even pre-mobilization measures must force a showdown.[340] Admittedly, assurances from Sazonov and Sukhomlinov that Russia had not mobilized made the Foreign Ministry more optimistic on 27 July. Russia seemed to understand the danger of a preparedness race against Germany, and the most acute phase was now expected to come with the invasion of Serbia, which was still some distance away. The evidence reaching the General Staff,

---

[335] Falkenhayn circular, 25 July 1914, HSMA M.1/4, Bd. 1524. Minister of Interior to Bethmann, 24 July 1914, BA Rklei R.43F/1268. Trumpener, 'War Premeditated?', 64–8. Instructions from Nicolai, 25, 26, and 27 July 1914, HSMA M 1/2, Bd. 53.

[336] Chief of the Admiralty Staff to Jagow, 27 July 1914, PAAA R.5594. London attaché to Navy Office, 26 July, *DDK* i, doc. 207.

[337] GGS intelligence summary, 27 July 1914, HSMA M 1/2, Bd. 109. Reports from Belfort, 26, 27 July 1914, ibid., Bd. 53; and from Strasbourg, 27 July 1914, PAAA R.6756. Reports forwarded from Admiralty Staff, 27, 28 July in PAAA R.5594.

[338] H. von Moltke, *Erinnerungen-Briefe-Dokumente, 1877–1916*, ed. E. von Moltke (Stuttgart, 1922), 381. Bethmann to Wilhelm, 26 July 1914, *DDK* i, doc. 197.

[339] Pourtalès to Auswärtiges Amt, Bethmann to Lichnowsky, 26 July 1914, ibid., docs. 216, 199.

[340] Graevenitz to Württemberg War Ministry, 26 July 1914, HSMA M 1/2, Bd. 54. Lerchenfeld report, 26 July 1914, GSM Bayerische Gesandtschaft Berlin 1087. Bethmann to Pourtalès, 26 July 1914, *DDK* i, doc. 219.

however, was that the Russians were implementing the Period Preparatory to War. Waldersee was particularly exercised by a report from Königsberg that they were strengthening their security screen on Germany's border and preparing large troop movements, and he forwarded it urgently to Jagow.[341] On the same day the Germans began stepping up their own precautions, although these were still very preliminary. The Interior Ministry ordered the Prussian officials in the eastern fortress towns to buy in grain; Falkenhayn and Moltke asked Bethmann to place the railways under military control. The Chancellor agreed to greater civilian protection for the frontier lines and for some installations in the interior, while Tirpitz returned to the Navy Office and discussed preparatory steps. According to the Württemberg representative, no other special measures were yet taken.[342]

After 28 July, however, the drive to militarization became much more powerful. The GGS's intelligence detected greatly heightened activity in France and a range of frontier preparations, although it discerned no trace of mobilization and little desire to fight.[343] The naval authorities supposed that Britain was clandestinely mobilizing, but they were concerned less about this than about developments in the Baltic, as in crises the Admiralty had always taken extensive precautions.[344] But the GGS considered that the Russian measures on the border were preparatory to war. Although rumours of horse purchases and reservist call-ups in the Warsaw military district had yet to be verified, the frontier garrisons were being reinforced, rolling stock was being made ready, and units were on the move.[345]

For the time being, none the less, Bethmann resisted pressure on him either to raise the stakes or to retreat. On the one hand, on the evening of 27 July Berchtold first reported to Tschirschky Conrad's view that if Russia mobilized in its south-western military districts both Central Powers should retaliate. The Chancellor replied that the reports from Russia were still unconfirmed; he held, and said that Moltke held with him, that a categorical declaration would be premature. On the other, on returning from the Baltic on the morning of 28 July the Kaiser backtracked, declaring that now that he had read Serbia's reply to Austria-Hungary he regarded it as a capitulation that removed all need for war. He proposed that the Austrians should confine themselves to occupying Belgrade until Serb pledges had been carried out, and said that he had Moltke's full support. Rather than be pitchforked into such a drastic change of course, however, Bethmann waited for most of the day before sending a telegram to Vienna whose

---

[341] Schoen to Hertling, 27 July 1914, Deuerlein (ed.), *Hertling-Lerchenfeld*, doc. 107. GGS intelligence summary, 27 July 1914, HSMA M 1/2, Bd. 109. Waldersee to Jagow, 27 July 1914, PAAA R.10450.

[342] Interior Minister and Falkenhayn to Bethmann, 27 July 1914, BA Rklei R.43F/1268. Graevenitz to Weizsäcker, 28 July 1914, HS E. 74 #164.

[343] Ibid. and GGS intelligence summaries, 28 July, HSMA M 1/2, Bd. 109; 29 July, ibid., Bd. 54.

[344] Hopman diary, 28 July 1914, BA-MA Hopman MSS N.326/11.

[345] GGS intelligence summaries, 28 and 29 July 1914, cf. n. 343 above.

convolutions undermined his sovereign's purpose and testified to his own embarrassment. He wanted, he said, to avoid giving the impression that Germany wished to hold Austria-Hungary back: the aim was to destroy the Pan-Serb agitation without bringing on a world war, and if one were unavoidable to wage it in the best possible conditions, particularly by demonstrating to German and to European public opinion that Russia was to blame.[346] This latter twist betrayed the prominence on the Chancellor's agenda of maintaining national consensus. He was in contact with the German Socialist leaders, and knew the importance that they attached to the circumstances in which hostilities broke out. The 'tendency' of German policy as summed up by Admiral Müller, was to keep calm and put Russia in the wrong, though if war proved necessary not to shrink from it.[347]

At this point the GGS abandoned its passivity. The big new development on 29 July was the reinforcement of the Belgian army, although Colonel Dupont in Paris was said to be astonished that Germany had done so little, and the Russians were reported to be installing their *couverture*. It was, however, the *absence* of tsarist mobilization that Moltke took as his starting-point in an 'Appreciation of the Political Situation' that he submitted to Bethmann. Its gravamen was that St Petersburg was being very cunning in preparing mobilization opposite the Central Powers without announcing it. Vienna would be obliged to protect its rear, and if the Austrians ordered general mobilization Germany must do likewise. Russia would then be able to mobilize while labelling Berlin the aggressor, and could do so all the faster because of its preliminary steps. The situation was worsening daily, and Germany must force its enemies to declare their hand. Whereas a waiting game suited Bethmann, the CGS could no longer accept its risks.[348]

This was not military insubordination, but it was certainly military intervention in policy-making, and the Chancellor deferred to it. At 12.50 p.m. two warnings went out. The French were told that if they continued their preparations Germany would proclaim the *Kriegsgefahrzustand*. Bethmann said that this condition was not a mobilization, though he knew that it was not much distinct from one. The second warning was the blunt message to Sazonov that started off the second round of decision-making in St Petersburg and culminated in Russian general mobilization. Simultaneously, there was a crisis within a crisis in Berlin.

The conflict within German policy-making centred on relations with Vienna and on Germany's own military readiness. Having sabotaged Wilhelm's efforts to restrain the Austrians on 28 July, Bethmann now attempted to restrain them

---

[346] Tschirschky to Auswärtiges Amt, 27 July, Bethmann to Tschirschky, 28 July 1914, *DDK* ii, docs. 281, 299. Wilhelm II to Jagow, Bethmann to Tschirschky, 28 July 1914, Geiss (ed.), *July 1914*, docs. 112, 115.

[347] D. Groh, 'The "Unpatriotic Socialists" and the State', *Journal of Contemporary History*, 1/4 (1966), 173–4. W. Görlitz (ed.), *Regierte der Kaiser?* (Berlin, 1959), 36.

[348] GGS intelligence summary, 29 July 1914, *DDK* ii, doc. 372. Moltke to Bethmann, Bethmann to Schoen and Pourtalès, 29 July 1914, Geiss (ed.), *July 1914*, docs. 125–7.

himself. His tone was direct, urgent, and sincere, and his purpose apparently to prevent war altogether rather than to start it in favourable circumstances. The news of Russia's intended partial mobilization has been cited to explain this turnabout, but Bethmann responded to it calmly, and the reason given by the Chancellor himself was Grey's statement to the German Ambassador in London (linked to an appeal for four-Power mediation once Austria-Hungary had occupied Belgrade) that if war spread to Western Europe the British Government would be forced to intervene and intervene quickly.[349] Three days previously there had been confidence in the German Foreign Ministry that Britain would stay out, perhaps encouraged by Grey's reluctance to commit himself. Bethmann shared in the complacency to the extent of launching earlier on 29 July a crass bid for British neutrality, in exchange for a pledge to respect Belgian and French integrity in Europe (though not the French colonies). In contrast, on receiving Grey's warning he immediately forwarded it to Vienna and urged that mediation should be accepted. His telegram No. 200 on 30 July pleaded that if Austria-Hungary refused British intercession it would be impossible to blame the war on Russia, and the German Government would be placed in an untenable position *vis-à-vis* its own people. Yet later that same evening he called off his *démarche*, partly because of a renewed British halt-in-Belgrade proposal, but also because of notification by the GGS that Russian preparations were 'driving us to a speedy decision, if we do not wish to be exposed to surprises'.[350]

The confrontation over Germany's military readiness had begun on 28 July. Falkenhayn wanted all units to return to their garrisons, but the Chancellor resisted until the same measure was reported in France, and he continued to oppose recalling all officers and men from harvest leave. Falkenhayn brought back the troops from exercises and summoned the most important officers in the General Staff, but nothing done thus far fell even into the 'political tension' category that was the second of the German army's stages of alert, intermediate between winter troop increases and the two levels of the *Kriegsgefahrzustand*.[351] By the afternoon of 29 July Falkenhayn wanted to declare a state of 'threatening danger of war', but neither Wilhelm nor Moltke wanted to go so far, and Bethmann again held the War Minister at bay. That evening, however, apparently before the news of Grey's warning, there was a fraught discussion of Russia's intended partial mobilization. Bethmann opposed responding, for the sake of public opinion in Germany and in Britain, which he still hoped could be detached from St Petersburg. He resisted measures that might cause similar

[349] Lichnowsky to Jagow, 29 July 1914, Bethmann to Tschirschky, 30 July 1914, Geiss (ed.), *July 1914*, docs. 130, 133–4. See the discussion by J. S. Levy, T. J. Christensen, and M. Trachtenberg, 'Mobilization and Inadvertence in the July Crisis', *International Security*, 16 (1991), 189–203.

[350] F. Fischer, *Germany's Aims in the First World War* (London, 1967), 78. Goschen to Grey, 29 July, Bethmann to Tschirschky, 30 July 1914, Geiss (ed.), *July 1914*, docs. 139, 143. Bethmann draft, 30 July 1914, *DDK* ii, doc. 451.

[351] Wenninger to Bavarian War Minister, 29 July 1914, KAM Militärbevollmächtiger Bd. 1. Prussian to Württemberg War Ministry, 28 July 1914, HSMA M 1/4, Bd. 1524. Bucholz, *War Planning*, 298–300.

steps elsewhere and 'set the stone rolling'. The evidence about Moltke's attitude is conflicting, and he may have withdrawn his previous support for the Chancellor. According to the Bavarian Minister, the French and Russian military measures had made the situation very tense, and the GGS was pressing for a response in kind. The Saxon attaché understood that Moltke wanted war and believed that Germany would never again have so promising an opportunity. His Bavarian counterpart believed that there was a struggle in progress between the War Ministry and the General Staff on the one hand and the Chancellor and the Foreign Ministry on the other. The War Ministry wanted additional preparations, and Moltke wanted to strike now while France and Russia were in difficulties, given that the season was favourable, the harvest was mostly in, and the 1913 recruits were trained. And yet, according to Falkenhayn and Tirpitz, at the meeting on 29 July Moltke was surprisingly moderate, perhaps because he recognized that war needed domestic and diplomatic preparation, and perhaps because he sensed that he could wait a little longer. Falkenhayn, isolated and disgruntled, judged that in view of Germany's faster mobilization it was not yet vital to clarify matters. Although an order went out to recall Prussian troops on leave, Bethmann was able to exploit his opponents' divisions in order to secure a stand-off, and there was no immediate reply to Russia's announcement.[352]

A classic civil–military struggle seemed in the making, but Bethmann accepted much of his critics' argumentation and was increasingly beleaguered. During 30 July he pleaded for holding off until the Austrians had replied to his *démarche*, but he sensed that he was reaching the end of the road and the need to pin the blame on Germany's enemies was becoming uppermost. He telegraphed to Lichnowsky that Russian partial mobilization and France's military measures had upset his hopes of mediating on the basis of Grey's proposal: the position was 'extremely critical'. He told the Prussian Council of Ministers that St Petersburg's actions had sabotaged his and Britain's efforts to prevent a European war. He would agree to naval precautionary measures, a military guard on the railways, and a ban on grain exports to the East. But he would resist declaring a 'threatening danger of war', as this would signify mobilization, and he still awaited a reply from Vienna. All the Powers, even Russia, wanted peace, 'but things have got out of control, and the stone has begun to roll'.[353] There was a self-serving element in the Chancellor's fatalism, and a tendency to blame every government but his own for a war that he said nobody wanted. But he briefed the representatives of the German States in similar terms, warning that if Germany were not to lag behind the opposing alliance a resolution could not be long postponed.[354]

[352] Wenninger to Bavarian War Ministry, 29 July 1914, KAM Militärbevollmächtiger, Bd. 1. Lerchenfeld dispatch, 30 July 1914, GSM Bayerische Gesandtschaft Berlin 1087. Geiss (ed.), *Julikrise*, docs. 674, 676, 704–5.
[353] Bethmann to Lichnowsky, 30 July 1914, *DDK* ii, doc. 409; Prussian Council of Ministers, 30 July 1914, ibid., doc. 456.
[354] Varnbüler to Weizsäcker, 30 July 1914, HS E.74 #164. Lerchenfeld to Hertling, 30 July 1914, Deuerlein (ed.), *Hertling–Lerchenfeld*, doc. 111.

On 30 July, while the uncertainty continued, the main precaution taken was the navy's implementation of the *Sicherung*. Cruisers, torpedo boats, and submarines were moved into position to guard the German Bight, and the capital ships in Wilhelmshaven took on extra munitions and stokers. Bethmann agreed to this after a conversation with Tirpitz, in which he admitted to having misjudged Britain's attitude.[355] On land, meanwhile, according to a new GGS appreciation, Russia had mobilized four military districts, the French were busy on the frontier, and the Belgians had called up reservists and were placing the Liège garrison in readiness. Wilhelm was alarmed by a telegram from Nicholas from which he mistakenly construed that Russia had been mobilizing behind his back for five days. These circumstances perhaps explain why Moltke now took a decisively harder line. In his one step outside his constitutional prerogatives (for which he may have had Wilhelm's authorization) he cabled to the Austrians that they should mobilize against Russia and that Germany would do the same.[356] At the same time as thus undercutting the Chancellor, he joined Falkenhayn in renewing the pressure for the *Kriegsgefahrzustand*, and was promised a decision by noon on 31 July. Indeed, Bethmann seems to have decided to send an ultimatum to the Russians to cease their preparations irrespective of what happened to the halt-in-Belgrade initiative. Unanimity had thus been re-established when the news of Russian general mobilization arrived on the morning of 31 July and German agents brought a sample placard from across the frontier. This settled the issue even before Franz Joseph formally rejected Bethmann's appeals.[357]

The immediate consequences included the ultimata to Paris and St Petersburg and the proclamation of the *Kriegsgefahrzustand*. The navy moved the Second and Third Squadrons to the North Sea, and mobilized torpedo boats and minelayers. A state of siege was introduced throughout the country, the frontier guard was reinforced, and mass call-ups of up to 104,000 reservists took place even before mobilization itself was ordered on 1 August, to begin the following day.[358] According to the Bavarian attaché there were 'beaming faces' at the War Ministry; the Bavarian Minister said the Prussian military were 'in the best of spirits', Moltke having commented months previously that the situation was more favourable than it would be again in the foreseeable future. France and Russia had no howitzers, Germany possessed a superior rifle, and the French troops were inadequately trained because two new classes had been called up in 1913. The Belgian Minister understood that the Foreign Ministry had wanted

[355] A. von Tirpitz, *Deutsche Ohnmachtpolitik im Weltkriege* (Hamburg, 1926), 5. H. Rahne, *Mobilmachung: Militärische Mobilmachungsplanung und -technik in Preussen und im deutschen Reich von Mitte des 19. Jahrhunderts bis zum Zweiten Weltkrieg* (East Berlin, 1983), 148. Hopman diary, 30 July 1914, BA-MA Hopman MSS N.326/11.

[356] GGS intelligence summary, 30 July 1914, HSMA M 1/2 Bd. 109. Trumpener, 'War Premeditated?', 79–80. Conrad, *Dienstzeit*, iv. 152. L. C. F. Turner, 'The Role of the General Staffs in July 1914', *Australian Journal of Politics and History*, 11 (1965), 315–16.

[357] Albertini, *Origins*, iii. 7–11, 24. Trumpener, 'War Premeditated?', 82.

[358] Tirpitz, *Ohnmachtpolitik*, 5. Rahne, *Mobilmachung*, 142, 148–9. Bucholz, *War Planning*, 299.

to wait another twenty-four hours, but the army had said no.[359] Bethmann told Tirpitz that he had had no choice but to send the ultimata or Germany would have fallen too far behind. Russia's general mobilization, he wrote afterwards, showed its 'will to war'.[360] In his statement to the Bundesrat on 1 August he described the tsarist action as a 'provocation' that threatened Germany's honour and security. It could not be accepted, 'if we do not wish to abdicate as a Great Power'. Berlin had shown patience at the risk of losing the advantage of its faster mobilization, and could wait no longer. It had delayed enough, however, to make Russia seem the aggressor, Müller commenting on how well the authorities had succeeded in making Germany seem to be attacked.[361] As Bethmann explained in retrospect, once Russia had begun general mobilization there was no other course but to strike in the West as soon as possible. He was aware of the injustice to Belgium, but as a civilian he could not take responsibility for challenging military strategy.[362] Thus the Chancellor: yet he had known the fundamental features of the Schlieffen Plan all along. If he was trapped by 31 July, it was in a logic of his own making.

During the crisis the German Government alerted the shipping lines and there was some liaison with Krupp, whose Managing Director and later ally of Hitler, Alfred Hugenberg, welcomed the rejection of Grey's 'cowardly mediation'.[363] But there is no evidence of the German armaments industry lobbying for war, or of such lobbying elsewhere. The French War Ministry believed it had enough artillery shells to hand, and need not resort to private firms; the Director of the Creditanstalt, the cornerstone of the Habsburg armaments industry, called on 1 August for a peaceful solution.[364] As for the military half of the military-industrial complex, Moltke's one act of insubordination on 30 July came when Russian general mobilization was already being decided. In other respects it is the restraint of the German military that stands out almost until the end of the critical period. Moltke's advice was influential, for example in leading to the warning that so crucially affected Sazonov, and on 29–30 July there were two days of civil–military tension, but there was no question of the military compelling unwilling civilians into war. The point was underlined on 1 August, when a report from Lichnowsky suggested that Britain might stay neutral after all, and even keep France out. It quickly showed itself to rest on a misunderstanding,

[359] Wenninger diary, 31 July, B. F. Schulte, 'Neue Dokumente zum Kriegsausbruch und Kriegsverlauf, 1914', *Militärgeschichtliche Mitteilungen*, 25 (1979), 123–85, doc. 139. Lerchenfeld dispatch, 31 July 1914, GSM Bayerische Gesandtschaft Berlin 1087. Beyens to Davignon, 1 Aug. 1914, MAEB INDMB 14.

[360] Tirpitz, *Ohnmachtpolitik*, 10. Bethmann comment on Tirpitz's memoirs in BA Kl. Erw. Nachlass Bethmann Hollweg 342–3.

[361] Minutes of 1 August session, GSM Bayerische Gesandtschaft Berlin 1087. Röhl, 'Müller', 670.

[362] Bethmann comment on Tirpitz's memoirs, BA Kl. Erw Nachlass Bethmann Hollweg 342–3. Bethmann, *Betrachtungen*, i. 167.

[363] Wedel to Auswärtiges Amt, 19 July 1914, *DDK* i, doc. 80. Hugenberg to Klaassen, 29 July 1914, BA Hugenberg MSS 73.

[364] Messimy note, 22 Aug. 1915, AN Messimy MSS 7. B. Michel, *Banques et Banquiers en Autriche au début du 20e siècle* (Paris, 1976), 367.

but in the interim Wilhelm and Bethmann suspended the march to the West and delayed the occupation of Luxemburg even after German troops had crossed the frontier. It was Moltke, pleading that this would mean disaster for his operations, who gave way, retreating to sob in his study with frustration.[365] Bethmann regretted the failure of localization, but committed no intellectual abdication in ceding to the GGS analysis. With Wilhelm as an unpredictable quantity, oscillating between hawkishness and conciliation, it is true that the Chancellor was never fully in control of policy. But neither were Moltke and Falkenhayn.

The earlier assumptions about the armaments balance continued to be evident. Moltke and the GGS deemed the strategic prospects encouraging. Tirpitz denied in retrospect that he had thought so, but on 30 July he wanted to do battle with the Royal Navy as early as possible. Bethmann, on the same day, was impressed by Russia's and France's unpreparedness and unwillingness for armed conflict, which he took as evidence that they might back down, though also as a reason for accepting war if they did not.[366] There was perceived to be a moment of opportunity.

That this was so weakens the contention that the imperatives of short-term readiness drew Germany inadvertently into conflict. Bethmann, in another of his fatalistic metaphors, spoke of the rolling of the 'iron dice',[367] but he, like Berchtold and Sazonov, knew what he was doing. One of the striking features of the crisis is how belated were Berlin's extraordinary measures, following the pattern set in 1905–6, in 1908–9, in 1911, and in 1912. Coercive diplomacy and military precautions were more a feature of Russian and Austrian, and even of British and French, crisis management than of German. The Chancellor's options were restricted, as on previous occasions, by Germany's all-or-nothing posture, the *Kriegsgefahrzustand* leading ineluctably, in his judgement, to general mobilization (there was no provision for partial mobilization) and a Continental war. But he acknowledged the danger of an unintended reciprocal escalation, and subordinated military readiness to his localization strategy, to his diplomacy in London, and to his need to carry domestic opinion. Believing that their faster call-up allowed them to run military risks, the German leaders did so until 31 July, and then hurtled to the opposite pole. Bethmann's defence of the apparent change of tack was that tsarist general mobilization showed that St Petersburg wanted war and it was coming anyway, although Sazonov had made clear that his forces could remain on the frontiers for weeks. But Russia was not prepared to let Austria-Hungary invade Serbia, and Germany was not prepared to let Russia gain a further advantage. The events of 1912 had underlined the interconnection between the Balkan balance and the wider European one, and neither side was willing to allow the other to dictate a solution in the peninsula, as Austria-Hungary could if Russia did nothing, and Russia could if Germany stayed aloof.

[365] Trachtenberg, *History and Strategy*, 58–9. H. F. Young, 'The Misunderstanding of August 1, 1914', *Journal of Modern History*, 48 (1976), 644–65.

[366] Tirpitz, *Memoirs*, i. 240. Varnbüler to Weizsäcker, 30 July 1914, HS E. 74 #164.

[367] Bundesrat, 1 Aug. 1914, GSM Bayerische Gesandtschaft Berlin 1087.

To submit, according to the leaders of all three Eastern monarchies, would be to lose their status as Great Powers. The military measures of 1914 grew from deeply rooted conceptions of how such Powers should act and of the limits to what they could tolerate. All were ready to fight if those conceptions were challenged, and the element of miscalculation was secondary. European war was not the desired outcome of the heads of state and their civilian advisers, but it was willingly accepted over alternatives that seemed worse.[368] Thus, across the Continent in that brilliant August the peasant soldiers trekked back from harvest leave, all too many of them for the last time. A different harvest now stood ready to be reaped.

[368] Cf. J. S. Levy, 'Preferences, Constraints, and Choices in July 1914', *International Security*, 15 (1990/1), 151–86.

Conclusion

Courage was mine, and I had mystery;
Wisdom was mine, and I had mastery,
To miss the march of this retreating world
Into vain citadels that are not walled.
(Wilfred Owen, 'Strange Meeting')

It was the shells that men most feared. Novices to the Western Front soon learned the language of the guns that pounded them—their sound, their range, their trajectory—and their hideous effects. One field gun per ten yards of front, and a heavy every twenty, was the soundest all-purpose distribution. In the opening phase at Verdun the Germans gathered 1,220 artillery pieces along an assault line of 8 miles.[1] Shrapnel and high explosive pierced men's skulls, tore off their limbs, pulverized their flesh, deafened, stupefied, and maddened them, and buried them alive. The crushing impact of mortars, cannon, and howitzers, the detonations of grenades, the rattle of machine guns, and the crack of snipers' rifles forced soldiers to endure a troglodyte existence beneath a shattered landscape from whose surface all living humanity had been expelled. When they raised themselves above the parapets, to brave the full destructive force of modern firepower, perhaps their most palpable sensation was nakedness.

We have witnessed the construction of a killing machine. Perhaps the fury was creative, the progenitor of the accelerated, restless sensibility of the later twentieth century that separates us off so sharply from the moral and customary certitudes of the generation before 1914. But it is the impression of an immense enterprise of demolition that still, in retrospect, dominates. The First World War was something new, not only in the terrible experiences that it visited on the combatants, but in being the first general war, involving all the Powers of the day, to be fought out in the modern industrialized world. Its impact seemed so total as to rupture all lines of continuity with what came before. To some of the most reflective minds in Europe, none the less, the edifice of pre-war stability appeared with hindsight to be fraudulent, masking a condition not of true peace but of latent hostilities, a civilization monstrously flawed.[2]

[1] D. Winter, *Death's Men: Soldiers of the Great War* (Harmondsworth, 1978), 115–16. M. Eksteins, *Rites of Spring: The Great War and the Birth of the Modern Age* (London, 1989). I am much indebted to these two works. I have been influenced in other ways by S. Faulks, *Birdsong* (London, 1993), and by Faulks's article in the *Guardian*, 15 Sept. 1993.

[2] D. Pick, *War Machine: The Rationalisation of Slaughter in the Modern Age* (New Haven, 1993), 190–2.

The search for causes began at once, and has grown into one of the largest bodies of investigation into any historical theme. Sovereign states, industrial capitalism, and masculine aggression have all been blamed for the catastrophe. Such approaches fail to accommodate the rarity of war in Europe for many decades in the nineteenth century, in contrast to what happened after that time. More directed analysis is needed to address the origins, not of wars in general, but of this war in particular and of the breakdown of the long preceding peace. Those writing in the immediate aftermath understandably focused on human agency and on individual and collective responsibility. Probably they would have done so even without the assertion of German war guilt in Article 231 of the Treaty of Versailles. But the war-guilt controversy added an incentive for historians to address the issue, and generated the necessary raw material. The Government of Weimar Germany followed that of Bolshevik Russia in publishing multi-volume selections of Foreign Ministry correspondence, prompting the Allies to follow suit. Unprecedented quantities of confidential information about the origins of the war became available unprecedentedly soon after the event. Because of this, as well as the conventions of the historical craft, the leading studies in the 1920s and the 1930s were narratives of diplomatic history, neglecting what Paul Kennedy has christened, perhaps misleadingly, the underlying 'realities'.[3] In the embittered atmosphere of the Great Depression, in contrast, attention shifted to the structural characteristics of the international system. Strategy, economics, and public opinion were scrutinized, as well as armaments. In Britain and America public inquiries probed the contribution of the 'merchants of death' as stringpullers in the origins of the war.[4] But most historians still emphasized not the domestic roots of national foreign policies but the 'primacy' in shaping them of the external environment: the *Primat der Aussenpolitik*, in the German phrase. So too did Luigi Albertini, whose monumental study of *The Origins of the War of 1914* was a summation of what was possible on the basis of the inter-war evidence revolution, and remains indispensable in a way that previous studies are not. Yet Albertini's work marked the culmination of an earlier research phase rather than the opening of a new one, and may have closed off, rather than stimulated, debate. The very magnitude of its achievement discouraged emulation, and its thesis—which stressed miscalculation as well as Berlin's responsibility—was no longer, outside Germany, provocative. Dwelling principally, and exhaustively, on diplomacy and high policy, it devoted only a few perfunctory pages to the arms race.[5]

---

[3] P. M. Kennedy, *The Realities behind Diplomacy: Background Influences on British External Policy, 1865–1980* (London, 1981). J. W. Langdon, *July 1914: The Long Debate, 1918–1980* (Providence, RI, 1991) is a good survey of the historiography.

[4] On Britain, see D. G. Anderson, 'British Rearmament and the "Merchants of Death": The 1935–36 Royal Commission on the Manufacture and Trade in Armaments', *Journal of Contemporary History*, 29 (1994), 5–37.

[5] L. Albertini, *The Origins of the War of 1914* (London, 1952–7), i. 550–5. The surveys by L. C. F. Turner, *Origins of the First World War* (London, 1970) and J. Joll, *The Origins of the First World War* (London, 1984) give more attention to armaments.

The work of Fritz Fischer in the 1960s reignited controversy over war guilt. Rather than a single 'Fischer thesis', however, there was a progressive radicalization. According to his first book, 'As Germany willed and coveted the Austro-Serbian war, and, in her confidence in her military superiority, deliberately faced the risk of a conflict with Russia and France, her leaders must bear a substantial share of the historical responsibility for the outbreak of general war in 1914.' According to his second, 'the plan decided on . . . to use the favourable opportunity of the murder at Sarajevo for the start of the Continental war which Germany regarded as necessary was carried out successfully'.[6] The earlier position—that the German Government willed an Austro-Serbian war and knowingly courted a Continental one—resembles Albertini's and has found wide acceptance in Germany and outside. The later—that it intended from the start of the July crisis to wage a war for European hegemony (and may have been planning for this moment since 1912)—has won much less support. None the less, Fischer accomplished a Copernican revolution in historical study, made possible by a second evidence explosion associated with the opening of the Western European archives. The inter-war publications of Foreign Ministry documents naturally concentrated attention on the reporting and negotiation that form the stuff of diplomatic business. Access to the archives enabled comparisons between the edited correspondence and the unpublished files, and opened the records of the economic and service ministries as well as those of such co-ordinating bodies as the Austro-Hungarian GMR and the British CID. Non-governmental material, from pressure groups, businesses, or political parties, became available, as did policy-makers' private papers. The vastly enriched evidence could help resolve more searching questions about the mainsprings of diplomacy, and integrate diplomatic with other forms of history. As well as riding the crest of the archive wave, moreover, Fischer and his disciples reorientated interpretation. They concentrated on a single national foreign policy rather than the international system, and launched hypotheses about that policy's domestic roots and about continuity in German history, rather than about the interaction between German policies and those of the entente. It is true that Fischer urged the need for complementary analyses of the other Powers, and such analyses appeared in the 1970s and early 1980s. They tested the applicability elsewhere of his assumption of the primacy of domestic policy, and tended to be sceptical. Other research questioned its applicability to Germany itself.[7]

As a result of the opening of the archives and the worldwide attention given to the Fischer controversy, as well as the expansion of the historical profession, more titles on the origins of the First World War appeared after 1961 than even in the inter-war years. By the same token, and given the new emphasis on

---

[6] F. Fischer, *Germany's Aims in the First World War* (London, 1967), 88, and *War of Illusions: German Policies from 1911 to 1914* (London, 1975), 515.

[7] Cf. the volumes by Z. S. Steiner (Britain), J. F. V. Keiger (France), D. C. B. Lieven (Russia), and R. J. B. Bosworth (Italy), in the MacMillan 'Making of the Twentieth Century' series. On Germany, see e.g. E. Oncken, *Panthersprung nach Agadir: Die deutsche Politik während der zweiten Marokkokrise 1911* (Düsseldorf, 1981).

individual Powers, it grew ever harder to achieve a synthesis. But from the 1970s onwards there was reviving interest in systemic analysis of international politics. Once again, contemporary concerns energized inquiry, the issue being no longer war guilt and reparations but the search for lessons and precedents at a time of resurgent superpower conflict. Professor Marc Trachtenberg's 'The Coming of the First World War: A Reassessment' exemplifies the new school.[8] It rejects the notion that German pre-planning was responsible for the war, but criticizes Albertini for over-emphasizing inadvertence and civilian loss of control over the military. We are driven back to a middle-road interpretation of the outbreak as a consequence of decisions to run calculated, or miscalculated risks, and, when armed diplomacy failed, to go forward rather than back down.

This book has tried to break new ground and to reformulate the terms of the debate by interweaving diplomacy with defence policy, international with domestic developments, and narrative with conceptual insights from strategic studies. Geographically, in contrast with recent attention to the global setting of European diplomacy,[9] it has focused on the Continental marchlands: on Bosnia and Galicia, on the Low Countries and Lorraine. Its sources have included both the published Foreign Ministry documents and the archival files. Armaments history is located in the terrain where internal and external influences on national policy interact. It touches on the economic, financial, and technological, as well as diplomatic and strategic branches of the discipline, and lends itself to an eclectic approach. The emphasis here, however, has been on the political rather than the technical history of the pre-war build-up, and on two interrelated dynamics: the drift towards militarized diplomacy, and the rise of inter-bloc armaments competition. The emergence of a self-reinforcing cycle of heightened military preparedness and more acute political conflict has been inadequately stressed by previous writers, but it was an essential element in the conjuncture that led to disaster.

* * *

There seems little basis for a primarily technological explanation of the intensified competition between about 1910 and the outbreak of war. Quick-firing artillery, machine guns, and aircraft accounted for part of the growth in military budgets, but on land, unlike at sea, there was little prospect of a technical breakthrough giving a decisive advantage, and no substitute for superior resources in money, equipment, and men. The pre-war land arms race was essentially for extra soldiers and for more of the existing weapons, although it extended to organization and strategic planning. Nor, on the other hand, did internal political calculations enjoy 'primacy' in shaping armaments policy, or in so far as they did they were a restraining element. There is little evidence of defence spending being employed as a counter-revolutionary or counter-cyclical device for capitalist stabilization. Navies needed to maintain skilled workforces and keep highly

---

[8] Ch. 2 of his *History and Strategy*. An earlier version of the essay appeared in *International Security*, 15 (Winter 1990/1), 120–50.

[9] Cf. A. Offer, *The First World War: An Agrarian Interpretation* (Oxford, 1989), parts 2 and 3.

capitalized shipyards in being: but in relation to armies the military-industrial complex was less potent. Although Lloyd George and Tirpitz may have seen the utility of armaments spending for economic management, in general high defence expenditure was considered an impediment to fiscal soundness. In Germany, Britain, and France, it put conservative politicians in a dilemma, and played into the Left's hands. Nor did the professional military unrelentingly urge expansion. In all the Continental Powers there was ambivalence in the officer corps about larger standing armies and a higher take-up of conscripts. Given the dissensions in the military establishment, opposition from Parliaments and Finance Ministries to intensified recruiting and higher taxes stalemated demands from General Staffs until the darkening of the external scene. It was Russia, even after 1906 the country with the weakest representative checks on defence policy, that can be said most accurately to have begun the land arms race, and it raised its striking power in 1910 with fewer standing troops and no extra funds. Even after Agadir the domestic constraints on army expansion were only provisionally relaxed, and remained stronger in Germany and Austria-Hungary than in their potential enemies. This, rather than fear of revolution, strengthened the temptation for the Central Powers to strike at once rather than succumb to an unsustainable financial burden or be reduced to impotence.[10]

Internal political influences would not have triggered the land arms race without a deteriorating international environment. New foreign dangers reordered the agendas of monarchs, diplomats, and premiers, and allowed the expansionists in the military to gain the upper hand. This is not to say, at least on present evidence, that any state built up its army with the prior intention of launching European war. There were unashamed advocates of doing so in both Germany and Austria-Hungary, but in neither country prior to 1914 did their opinions become government policy. The Potsdam 'War Council' of December 1912 did not decide to start hostilities in eighteen months time. What became the 1913 army law had been agreed in principle before the Council met, and afterwards Wilhelm still rejected Moltke's demands for extra recruits and for three additional corps. After the Second Balkan War almost all the Vienna leaders believed a showdown with Serbia was inevitable, but battleships remained their biggest spending priority. In both countries, none the less, the civilian as well as military chiefs were increasingly prepared to contemplate the option of using force, and armaments spending helped to keep that option open. It cannot be said before 1914, as perhaps it can of such a decade as the 1960s, that weapons were stockpiled in the expectation that they would never be used in anger.

None the less, armaments were viewed more generally as a defensive insurance premium, a deterrent, and an instrument of diplomatic leverage than as the means of military aggression. In persuading governments that more was needed for these purposes, the diplomatic crises played a central role. An isolated confrontation, such as that of 1905–6, might temporarily spur activity in Western

[10] Cf. N. Ferguson, 'Public Finance and National Security: The Domestic Origins of the First World War Revisited', *Past and Present*, 142 (1994), 141–68.

Europe but could be shrugged off. A succession of ever more serious crises at ever shorter intervals presaged a more turbulent and threatening world. It is true that in their absence there would still have been a smouldering Franco-German rivalry, centred on artillery and fortresses. After the Japanese war the Russian Government was determined to regain and to exceed its previous military effectiveness, and would have increased its expenditure even without the Bosnian affair. But so rapid and general a breakdown of the land equilibrium is difficult to envisage if not for the annexation crisis, and more particularly if not for Agadir and the Balkan Wars. Germany switched priorities from sea to land as a consequence of the reappraisal forced by the second Moroccan conflict, although the fears aroused by the Russian reorganization were already pointing the way. The onset of the Balkan Wars broke the Hungarian parliamentary deadlock and permitted the Habsburg army law of 1912; the ensuing winter crisis led on to the law of 1914. Together with the collapse of Turkey, the winter crisis also precipitated Germany's 1913 bill, to which the Three-Year Law, the Russian railway loan, and the Great Programme were the reply. The sense of a heightened risk of war, and the concern to prevent or at least to win it, were the principal stimuli to the inter-bloc arms race.

The typical response to the new external situation was to enhance war-fighting capacity, for defence or for attack. Even if no European government before 1914 intended to start a war, all had contingency plans to fight one, and from 1910 the plans were increasingly offensive, designed to protect the homeland and seize the initiative by carrying the campaigning into enemy territory.[11] The German Laws of 1912 and 1913 complemented the Schlieffen–Moltke Plan, as did Bethmann's 1914 railway scheme. The Three-Year Law and the railway loan to St Petersburg were bound up with Plan XVII and the Franco-Russian staff agreements, as probably was the Great Programme with Plan 20. Because such technical considerations could not readily be acknowledged, however, the more usual public justification was deterrence. The language of Vegetius—if you desire peace, prepare for war—underpinned French and German legislative debate, as it did Britain's justification for maritime supremacy and Russia's for the Great Programme. Deterrence arguments were taken seriously and not deployed merely for public consumption. French military and civilian leaders feared a standing-start attack that would pierce their frontier cover; their Austro-Hungarian opposite numbers feared Montenegrin, Serb, or Russian invasion. The rising tide of insecurity turned all eyes to the dykes.

In addition to deterrence and defence, armed forces were needed for political leverage; and it is here that medium-term preparedness and short-term crisis readiness, the militarization of society and the militarization of diplomacy, become inextricable. Military preparedness, in the categorization of strategic analysis, may be used not only to discourage invasion but also for coercion and compellence—to impose one's views upon another Power or at least to prevent

---

[11] Cf. J. Snyder, *The Ideology of the Offensive* (Ithaca, NY, 1984).

that Power from imposing its views upon you. Armaments mean *influence*.[12] An extended exposition of precisely such a view was penned by Bethmann's private secretary, Kurt Riezler, whose *Grundzüge der Weltpolitik der Gegenwart* (Characteristics of Contemporary World Politics), written under a pseudonym, enjoyed a publishing success in the spring of 1914. For Riezler, decisions for war were based on estimates of the prospective gains against the prospective losses, and of the likelihood of victory. In the modern world national destinies had grown more closely intertwined, binding states into an integrated economic system and balance of power; but embroiling them in unceasing competition and conflicts of interest. In this environment self-assertion was essential, but the costs of war, especially between coalitions, had become extreme and incalculable, while the benefits of annexing rebarbative, nationally awakened subject peoples were much smaller than in earlier epochs. Armaments—'perhaps the most controversial, urgent, and difficult problem of the present time'—had become a kind of substitute for fighting, and the outcome of a crisis depended partly on each side's estimate of the other's military power. But it depended still more on the ability to bluff: on determination, patience, and nerves. The greatest danger of war Riezler saw in 'overbluffing', when governments locked themselves into positions from which their own ambitions and their fears of nationalist outcry made it impossible, even when their vital interests were not engaged, to retreat.[13]

Riezler stressed the limitations of armaments as an implement of diplomacy, but also their indispensability. The influence of such views in motivating armaments expansion was all-pervasive. It is evident in Aehrenthal's support for Adriatic dreadnoughts and Grey's and Churchill's for North Sea ones, in Berchtold's endorsement of the Austro-Hungarian extraordinary credit of 1912 and the army law of 1914, in Izvolsky's support for Russian naval and in Sukhomlinov's for army expansion. It can be found in Kiderlen-Wächter's advocacy of Germany's 1913 bill and in Etienne's of the Three-Year Law. Because of such considerations, as well as concern for deterrence, in one capital after another Foreign Ministers and heads of government lent the military the support that was needed in order to overcome Finance Ministry opposition. The prevailing conceptions of the nature of the international system and of the role of armed diplomacy within it illuminate the origins of the military build-up with a precision that an elementary action–reaction model cannot give.

The use of military measures in inter-state bargaining was nothing new. The British had long used naval redeployments to show that they meant business. In 1904, after the Russian Baltic Fleet shelled Hull trawlers on the Dogger Bank, the Gibraltar squadron shadowed it until St Petersburg agreed to arbitration.[14]

[12] T. C. Schelling, *Arms and Influence* (New Haven, 1966) is the classic analysis.

[13] J. J. Ruedorffer [K. Riezler], *Grundzüge der Weltpolitik in der Gegenwart*; I have used a later edn. (Stuttgart, 1916), 183 ff., esp. 221–2. See the discussion in J. A. Moses, *The Politics of Illusion: The Fischer Controversy in German Historiography* (London, 1975), 27 ff.

[14] R. Bobroff, 'Diplomacy Enhanced: British Diplomacy and Military Measures after the Dogger Bank Incident, October–November 1904', M.Sc. thesis (LSE, 1994).

But in the 1905–6 Moroccan crisis first France and then Germany accepted diplomatic defeat rather than raise the stakes by increasing military readiness. In the run-up to the Algeciras conference the Entente Powers took precautions against attack, but Berlin omitted to do likewise. Over Bosnia, in contrast, Aehrenthal used military preparations to browbeat Serbia into submission, and Russia was unable credibly to answer him. In the Agadir crisis, Britain, France, and to a lesser extent Germany all safeguarded themselves against surprise attack, although after Kiderlen-Wächter's initial error of sending the *Panther* his purpose of extricating himself peacefully was best served by refraining from extraordinary measures. Indeed, German circumspection is one of the most arresting features of the story, if less surprising than it might seem. In 1909 Berlin did not need military gestures to get its way; in 1906 and 1911 it resolved to cut its losses.

It was in 1912 and after that diplomacy became most militarized, and the Eastern Empires played with fire. Russia's military recovery permitted it to enter the game of armed diplomacy, which it did in earnest by retaining the senior conscript class, in glaring contrast to France and Germany in 1911. Under Sazonov tsarist diplomacy became accustomed to seeking reinforcement from the military arm. Austria-Hungary (and Berchtold in particular) travelled down a similar road, and concluded that peaceful solutions to its Balkan quandaries were exhausted. As near-permanent crisis came to seem the norm, the machinery of foreign relations was adjusted accordingly. In 1912 the Habsburg Government was determined to maintain its prerogative to call up reservists in an emergency, and the laws of 1905 and 1913 assured French governments similar powers. Germany and Austria-Hungary overhauled their intelligence-gathering; Russia enlarged its standing army during the winter changeover and introduced the regulations for the Period Preparatory to War; France updated its precautionary schedule. Against this backdrop, the Sarajevo crisis may appear the climax of a cumulative process. Yet there is ample evidence that statesmen acknowledged the danger discerned by Riezler of being enmeshed in conflict over non-essential interests, and that they tried to define their ground carefully. They sensed that emergency precautions might set the 'stone' or 'wheel' rolling towards war. Bülow was influenced by this perception before Algeciras, as were Caillaux and Kiderlen in 1911, Sazonov and Berchtold in 1912, and Bethmann Hollweg in 1914. That this was so—and among German statesmen the perception was almost a commonplace—lends depth and strength to Trachtenberg's arguments and weakens the case for seeing the July crisis as an unintentional slide into the abyss. As he neared the decision to pre-empt, Bethmann portrayed events as a juggernaut hurtling loose from his direction, but he did so with little justification and presumably to obscure his own agency. German military quiescence in the earlier crises, and during the opening stages in July itself, underlines the contrast between 1914 and what preceded it, but supplies no exoneration of Berlin's policy. As the nineteenth century had unfolded, liberal optimism that technological progress would make war obsolete was tinged by contrary apprehensions that humanity was building a voracious engine of destruction.[15] In the eyes of many, the July crisis vindicated these fears. This notwithstanding, it is not true that in 1914 the guns went off by themselves.

* * *

The interconnection between military preparedness and diplomacy is central to the larger question of whether armaments competition caused the war. Certainly, diplomacy failed to regulate the arms race. Britain and Germany were unable to reach a naval agreement, and only during the Haldane mission did they come close to substantive negotiation. All the Powers shared responsibility for the charade that passed for discussion of arms limitation at the Second Hague Conference. On land there was no comparable yardstick to dreadnoughts, verification was more difficult than in the shipyards, and two coalitions rather than two single states were at odds. Russia and Germany broached the army build-up at Baltic Port, as did both countries and France in the exchanges of 1913–14, but the right of governments to determine their level of preparedness remained unchallenged. It may be argued that this did not matter and that in itself arms racing did not undermine the peace, being merely an outward manifestation of an underlying disorder. When Britain and Germany abandoned their attempts at naval limitation the atmosphere between them superficially improved. But the pre-1914 evidence supports the view of competitive armaments as a cause as well as a consequence of international tension. It is true that growing friction between the Powers, and the chain of diplomatic crises, helped revive land armaments rivalry. But once in motion the spiral intensified public anxiety and instilled both resignation and enthusiasm in the face of impending conflict. Spy scares, press campaigns, and monitory speeches bore witness to this development, as they had at the peak of the Anglo–German naval race.

The same example of the Anglo–German rivalry, however, should remind us that armaments competition does not invariably lead to war, and that the 1914 crisis, as well as being the sequel to its predecessors, profoundly differed from them. By violently destroying Serbia's independence, Austria-Hungary would challenge much more radically than in 1908–9 and 1912 a Russia that was less disposed to shrink from challenge. But Vienna and St Petersburg would not have acted as they did without support from Berlin and Paris, who were charier than were their partners of armed diplomacy. It is here that the evolution of the arms race contributed most decisively to the outbreak of war, by modifying both sides' perception of the military balance, and persuading both that they could win.

French encouragement of Russia in 1914 arose partly from administrative confusion, and Poincaré and Viviani would rather have postponed the tsarist mobilization. But if called upon to repudiate the alliance they preferred to fight, and Paléologue's assurances were motivated by the strategic considerations that the EMA was simultaneously pressing on the Stavka. Germany's encouragement of Austria-Hungary was more deliberate, and the role played in it by military

---

[15] Pick, *War Machine*, ch. 12.

calculation more explicit. In 1908–9 both Germany and Russia knew that war would spell disaster for the latter, and both France and Russia lacked confidence in their alliance. But after Agadir French military appraisals became more positive, and Paris and St Petersburg formed a more cohesive bloc. In 1914 neither Power was as strong individually as it expected to be by 1917, but neither felt that as a combination they were obliged to give way. Conversely, Moltke's self-assurance during the annexation crisis had receded as the implications of Russian reorganization and the French nationalist revival dawned. Perhaps German superiority, even in 1905–9 less overwhelming than it appeared, was already lost. But French disorganization after the Three-Year Law, coupled with the implementation of Germany's own army bill, promised one last opportunity before all chance of victory faded. The encircling alignment appeared to be consolidating rather than disintegrating, and delay would leave Germany outspent and outclassed. The outlook for its ally was even worse. The ascending curve of Franco-Russian power and the descending Austro-German one intersected: the one alliance could contemplate war with greater confidence than previously, and the other might lose the option altogether if it failed to exercise it now.

This is not to ignore the question of perceptions. Military effectiveness rests on an amalgam of tangibles and intangibles that are difficult enough to estimate for one state, let alone a combination. There were many examples before 1914 of mistaken assessments, sometimes made for self-serving reasons. In 1908 the British Admiralty exaggerated German warship construction; in 1913 the German military overstated the speed of the French concentration, although privately confident that they still had the edge. None the less, British, French, and German evidence all supports the view that observers on both sides felt that the blocs were approaching equality. This sense was vindicated when it was put to the test and neither alliance could knock the other out. The implication is that peace grew more precarious as the blocs converged, which contradicts the thesis that a balance of strength, in which neither side can expect an easy triumph, will deter war. But the pre-1914 balance was unstable, a temporary equivalence between rising and declining elements. Such a balance may offer both sides a chance of victory and encourage both to attack. It proved a weaker guarantor of peace than the imbalance of 1905–6, in which the stronger Austro-German combination foresaw no early danger and felt no need to strike, while the weaker Franco-Russian one was less satisfied with the *status quo* but saw no prospect of successfully using force to change it. In 1914 there was balance but no equilibrium; previously there was equilibrium without balance. Armaments convergence made it easier for war to start, and more likely that once having started it would be devastating and prolonged.

* * *

To regard the origins of the First World War through the prism of armaments history is to perceive much, but still with a restricted view. Analysis of defence policy can deepen our understanding of the diplomacy of these years, and offer an alternative map of the past, in which the 1910 Russian reorganization and the

1911–12 German *Rüstungswende* bulk as large as the political framework of inter-state antagonisms and ententes. But it cannot replace more conventional accounts, and the two must be taken in conjunction. The great alliances were fundamental in shaping armaments policy, as were the clashes of interest in the Balkans, the Rhine valley, and the Adriatic. So too were the Austro–German phobia of encirclement and the Entente Powers' dread of German hegemony and of satellite status. It was the very failure, as it seemed, of diplomatic solutions that drove Berchtold and Bethmann towards military ones. Armaments policy must also be seen against the backdrop of what James Joll, in a celebrated phrase, christened the 'unspoken assumptions' of the European statesmen.[16] To con-ceptualize decisions for war, as Riezler did, as products of rational calculation takes us only so far. It leaves unexplained why rulers believed that violence could solve their difficulties (a belief that few examined rigorously in 1914), and why they valued certain policy objectives so highly that rather than surrender them they would send men to die.

Modris Eksteins has illuminated the English sense of defending a moral and social order that Germany had flouted; and the Germans' sense, for all their con-servatism at home, of leading a liberating revolt against a decaying and hypo-critical bourgeois regime.[17] Two sets of assumptions are particularly significant. The first, copiously invoked during the July crisis, was that leaders of Great Powers were custodians of a code of honour. The ability to threaten and to use force was central to their identity. To forfeit Great-Power status would strike at the heart of the legitimacy of the governing order, both at home and abroad. Such views were not confined to clanking Eastern European autocrats, Sir Eyre Crowe minuting in the Foreign Office on 31 July that 'the theory that England cannot engage in a big war means her abdication as an independent State', and Grey telling the Commons that if Britain pledged itself to non-intervention in any circumstances 'we should, I believe, sacrifice our respect and good name and reputation before the world'.[18] The second set of assumptions revolved around the vision of what hostilities would be like: the notorious 'short-war illusion'.[19] In fact, in the last years of peace even the German and Austrian military were coming to doubt whether the fighting would really end in six months, and begin-ning to hedge their bets. On the Left, predictions of a long and ruinous slaugh-ter were common, and statesmen such as Grey and Bethmann sometimes echoed them. Indeed, the German Chancellor seems to have shared the foreboding of Nicholas II and Franz Joseph that something terrible was impending. Even so, the memories of 1866 and 1870, the contingency planning for swift and decisive

---

[16] J. Joll, '1914: The Unspoken Assumptions' in H. W. Koch (ed.), *The Origins of the First World War: Great Power Rivalry and German War Aims* (London, 1972), 307–28.

[17] Eksteins, *Rites of Spring*, chs. 2 and 3.

[18] Crowe memorandum, 31 July 1914, I. Geiss (ed.), *July 1914* (New York, 1967), doc. 164. Grey speech, 3 Aug. 1914, K. Bourne, *The Foreign Policy of Victorian England, 1830–1902* (Oxford, 1970), 504.

[19] L. L. Farrar, *The Short-War Illusion: German Policy, Strategy, and Domestic Affairs, August–December 1914* (Santa Barbara, Calif., 1973).

offensives, and both sides' calculations that the auspices were favourable, made it easier to take the plunge. Like other such dismaying human situations, Europe's descent from relative tranquillity before the Bosnian crisis into the subsequent morass resulted not from a single decision but from incremental steps, each bringing fresh repercussions in its wake. In 1914 the German Government resolved to risk war, and accepted it when it came, and in this sense its actions were not inadvertent. It failed remotely to foresee the consequences.

If the conclusions drawn here about pre-1914 armaments rivalry must be grounded in the early twentieth-century context, can they be extended to other arms races and other wars? Certain insights may have a wider application. A quantitative approach exposes general trends, but is insensitive and may be misleading. The 1910 Russian reorganization, for example, registered barely a blip in the budgetary statistics. Further violence may be done to the historical reality by concentrating on weapons and equipment to the exclusion of a broader definition of the armaments phenomenon. That competition in 'armaments', so understood as to embrace all aspects of military preparation, may be both cause and consequence of international political tension may seem banal. More provocative is the evidence that diplomatic confrontations can dynamize latent arms races, and that situations of stagnating or declining military effort can rapidly be reversed. The openness of the choices as late as 1907, and the speed of the subsequent destabilization, both stand out. 'Central' arms races, between the leading political groupings of the day, are evidently more dangerous than tangential or peripheral ones. They become more dangerous still when one side, to avoid internal upheaval or financial collapse, must choose between withdrawing and resorting to force. Above all there is menace when both sides see a chance of victory and the advantage appears about to change hands. There may have been similar crossover points before 1870, when French rearmament began eroding Prussia's superiority, and in 1939, when that of the Western Powers began to lessen Hitler's lead. In the Anglo-German naval race, by contrast, a crossover seemed possible from the vantage point of 1909, but turned out never to have been near.

All of this is said about conditions in which governments, contrary to Riezler's prognosis, still saw war as an extreme, but sometimes effective and legitimate, instrument of policy. In a world of thermonuclear weapons, such conditions may no longer apply. Yet it was at the climaxes of post-1945 superpower confrontation that strategic analysts were most fascinated by the Sarajevo precedent, and that historians of mentalities and of common experience revisited the Golgotha of the combatants and the home front. Since the middle of the 1980s the central superpower arms race has moved into reverse, and a kaleidoscope of local rivalries threatens to arise in its stead—mostly in conventional armaments, but a number with the potential to go nuclear. Whether this world will be safer than its predecessor remains to be seen. At a time when the virtues of the nation-state as a basis for European organization are being reinvoked, it is well to remember how such a system may operate. The emerging international order is one in which the use of force between substantial Powers has become more conceivable than during the long stability that followed 1945, and in which arms races may develop more quickly and with much more sophisticated weaponry than ever before. Sometime, somewhere, a crossover point may be reached. As between the Soviet Union and the United States in the 1950s and the early 1960s, it is the transition from conventional to nuclear forces, particularly before both sides acquire secure second-strike capabilities, that is likely to be the testing time.

These are sombre thoughts: and we must hope that the hecatomb of 1914–18 will not again return to haunt us. The past does not precisely reproduce itself, and the forty years of Soviet–American competition have turned out more closely to resemble the turn-of-the-century naval rivalry than the contest that followed. We return to where we started, with Sir Edward Grey and the warning to be handed on to those who come after us. The armaments race that mattered before the First World War was the land arms race between the blocs that took off after 1910. It was a necessary precondition for the outbreak of hostilities. Yet armaments were the wheels and pistons of the locomotive of history, not the steam, and if considered in isolation they offer neither a sufficient nor an all-embracing explanation of the destruction of the peace. For such an explanation we must go back further and dig down deeper into the world from which the weapons emanated. The militarization of diplomacy and of society were made possible by the militarization of men's minds. The dreadful destiny that befell it may make pre-1914 Europe seem remote to us, but it is not unrecognizably so. To explore the universe of our grandfathers and great-grandfathers is to light, more often than we might care to, upon the troubled image of ourselves.

Bibliography

This bibliography is not intended to provide a comprehensive survey of the immense literature on the origins of the First World War. Its purpose is to list the principal sources consulted, and to help the reader to identify the works cited in the references. It is divided into six sections: (1) archival sources; (2) published primary material; (3) memoirs and contemporary accounts; (4) secondary works: books; (5) secondary works: articles; (6) theses and other unpublished writings.

I. ARCHIVAL SOURCES

Austria

Haus-, Hof-, und Staatsarchiv, Vienna: Minutes of the Joint Council of Ministers; Austro-Hungarian Foreign Ministry papers (Politisches Archiv); Aehrenthal and Berchtold MSS.

Kriegsarchiv, Vienna: War Ministry (KM Präs), General Staff (Gstb), General Staff Operationsbureau, and Military Chancellery of Franz Ferdinand (MKFF) papers; reports of military attachés; Marine Ministry annual reports.

Finanzarchiv, Vienna: Common and Austrian Finance Ministry papers (series FM Präs and GFM).

Belgium

Archives générales du Royaume, Brussels: De Broqueville and Lesaffre MSS.

Archives du Ministère des Affaires étrangères, Brussels: Foreign Ministry papers in the series Neutralité, Indépendance, Défense militaire de la Belgique.

Britain

Public Record Office, Kew: Cabinet, Foreign Office, War Office, and Committee of Imperial Defence papers; Grey MSS.

Churchill College Archive Centre, Cambridge: Fisher and McKenna MSS.

University Library, Cambridge: Vickers Archive.

National Library of Scotland, Edinburgh: Haldane MSS.

Bodleian Library, Oxford: Asquith MSS.

Imperial War Museum: Wilson MSS.

France

Service historique de l'armée de terre, Château de Vincennes: Series 1N, 2N, 5N, 7N; minutes of Conseil supérieur de la guerre, and Conseil supérieur de la défense nationale; État major de l'armée and War Ministry papers; reports of military attachés.

Service historique de la marine, Château de Vincennes: Ministry of Marine papers; reports of naval attachés.

Archives du Ministère des Affaires étrangères, Paris: Foreign Ministry papers, Nouvelle série, 1898–1914; Doulcet, Paléologue MSS.

Archives nationales, Paris: Archives of Chambre des députés, especially Chamber Commissions; Messimy and Millerand MSS; Ministry of Interior papers.

Archives du Ministère des Finances, Paris: Finance Ministry papers.

Bibliothèque nationale, Paris: Poincarè MSS.

Germany

Bayerisches Hauptstaatsarchiv, Munich: Geheime Staatsarchiv, reports from Bavarian Mission in Berlin, and series MA.I.

Bayerisches Hauptstaatsarchiv-Kriegsarchiv, Munich: Bavarian War Ministry (MKr) and General Staff (Gstb) papers. Reports of Militärbevollmächtiger.

Bundesarchiv, Koblenz: Akten der Reichskanzlei (series R.43F); Bauer, Bethmann Hollweg, Bülow, Hugenberg MSS.

Bundesarchiv-Militärarchiv, Freiburg-im-Breisgau: Einem, Groener, Hopman, Ludendorff, Moltke, Mudra, Tirpitz, Winterfeldt MSS.

Politisches Archiv des Auswärtigen Amtes, Bonn: German Foreign Ministry papers; Jagow, Pourtalès MSS.

Historisches Archiv Krupp, Essen: Krupp company records, series FAH and WA.

Hauptstaatsarchiv, Stuttgart: Reports from Württemberg Mission in Berlin; Württemberg Staatsministerium papers.

Hauptstaatsarchiv Stuttgart, Abteilung Militärarchiv: Württemberg War Ministry papers Series M 1/2, 1/3, 1/4, 1/6.

Italy

Archivio di Stato Centrale, Rome: Brusati and Giolitti MSS.

2. PUBLISHED PRIMARY MATERIAL

Annuaire statistique (Paris, 1913–14).

BERGHAHN, V. R., and DEIST, W. (eds.), *Rüstung im Zeichen der Wilhelminischen Weltpolitik: Grundlegende Dokumente, 1890–1914* (Düsseldorf, 1988).

BOELCKE, W. (ed.), *Krupp und die Hohenzollern: Aus der Korrespondenz der Familie Krupp, 1850–1916* (Berlin, 1956).

British Documents on Foreign Affairs: Reports and Papers from the Foreign Office Confidential Print, ed. K. Bourne and D. Cameron Watt: series IA. *Russia, 1859–1914* ed. D. C. B. Lieven (6 vols., Frederick, Md., 1983), and IF. *Europe, 1848–1914* (eds.), J. F. V. Keiger and D. Stevenson. (35 vols., Frederick, Md., 1987–91).

British Documents on the Origins of the War, 1898–1914 ed., G. P. Gooch and H. V. Temperley (11 vols., London, 1926–38).

Bulletin des lois de la République française (Paris, annual).

Commission de publication des documents relatifs aux origines de la guerre de 1914, *Documents diplomatiques français, 1871–1914* (41 vols., Paris, 1929–59).

CHURCHILL, R. S. (ed.), *Winston S. Churchill.* companion vol., part 3, *1911–1914* (London, 1969).

DEUERLEIN, E. (ed.), *Briefwechsel Hertling-Lerchenfeld, 1912–1917* (2 vols., Boppard, 1973).

Die deutschen Dokumente zum Kriegsausbruch, 1914, ed., M. Montgelas and W. Schücking (3rd edn., 3 vols., Berlin, 1926).

ERDMANN, K.-D. (ed.), *Kurt Riezler: Tagebücher-Aufsätze-Dokumente* (Göttingen, 1972).

FISHER, JOHN ARBUTHNOT, *Fear God and Dread Nought: The Correspondence of Admiral of the Fleet Lord Fisher of Kilverstone*, ii. *Years of Power, 1904–1914*, ed. A. J. Marder (London, 1956).

GEISS, I. (ed.), *Julikrise und Kriegsausbruch, 1914* (2 vols., Hanover, 1963–4).

—— (ed.), *July 1914. The Outbreak of the First World War: Selected Documents* (New York, 1967).

Die Grosse Politik der Europäischen Kabinette, 1871–1914, ed., J. Lepsius *et al.* (40 vols., Berlin, 1922–7).

Die Grossindustrie Österreichs (Vienna, 1898).

Die Internationalen Beziehungen im Zeitalter des Imperialismus: Dokumente aus den Archiven der Zarischen und der Provisorischen Regierung, 1878–1917, ed., O. Hoetzsch (Series I, vol. v, German edn., Berlin, 1934).

Österreich-Ungarns Aussenpolitik von der Bosnischen Krise 1908 bis zum Kriegsausbruch 1914, ed. L. Bittner and H. Übersberger (9 vols., Vienna, 1930).

POKROWSKI, M., *Drei Konferenzen (zur Vorgeschichte des Weltkrieges)* (1920).

SCHREINER, G. A. (ed.), *Entente Diplomacy and the World: Matrix of the History of Europe, 1909–1914* (London, 1921).

SCOTT, J. B., *The Hague Peace Conferences of 1899 and 1907.* (2 vols., Baltimore, 1909).

SIEBERT, B. von (ed.), *Diplomatische Aktenstücke zur Geschichte der Ententepolitik der Vorkriegsjahre* (Berlin, 1921).

Situation des marines étrangères au 1er janvier 1914 (Ministère de la Marine, Paris, 1914).

STIEVE, F. (ed.), *Der diplomatische Schriftwechsel Iswolskis, 1911–1914* (4 vols., Berlin, 1924).

3. MEMOIRS AND CONTEMPORARY ACCOUNTS

ANDRÉ, L., *Cinq ans de ministère* (Paris, 1907).

AUFFENBERG-KOMARÓW, M., *Aus Österreichs Höhe und Niedergang: Eine Lebensschilderung* (Munich, 1921).

BERNHARDI, F. VON, *Deutschland und der Nächste Krieg* (Stuttgart, 1912).

BETHMANN HOLLWEG, T. VON, *Betrachtungen zum Weltkriege*, i (Berlin, 1919).

BRONSART VON SCHELLENDORF, W., *The Duties of the General Staff* (4th edn., London, 1905).

BUCHANAN, G., *My Mission to Russia and Other Diplomatic Memories* (2 vols., London, 1923).

BÜLOW, B. VON, *Memoirs* (3 vols., London, 1931).

CAILLAUX, J. M. A., *Mes mémoires* (3 vols., Paris, 1943).

CARTON DE WIART, E., *Léopold II: Souvenirs des dernières années, 1901–1909* (Brussels, 1944).

CHURCHILL, W. S., *The World Crisis, 1911–1914* (London, 1923).

CONRAD VON HÖTZENDORF, F., *Aus meiner Dienstzeit, 1906–1918* (5 vols., Vienna, 1921–5).

DANILOV, Y., *La Russie dans la Guerre mondiale (1914–1917)* (Paris, 1927).

EHRHARDT, H., *Erinnerungen eines 89-jährigen Mannes und Erfinders* (Zelle-Mehlis, 1928).

EINEM, K. VON, *Erinnerungen eines Soldaten, 1853–1933* (Leipzig, 1933).

GIOLITTI, G., *Memoirs of My Life* (London, 1923).

GREY, E., *Twenty-Five Years, 1892–1916* (2 vols., London, 1925).

HALDANE, R. B., *Before the War* (London, 1920).

—— *An Autobiography* (London, 1929).

JAURÈS, J., *L'Armée nouvelle* (Paris, 1911).

JOFFRE, J. J.-C., *Mémoires du Maréchal Joffre, 1910–1917* (2 vols., Paris, 1932).

KEIM, A., *Erlebtes und Erstrebenes: Lebenserinnerungen von Generalleutnant Keim* (Hanover, 1925).

KOKOVTSOV, V. N., *Out of my Past* (Stanford, Calif.,1935).

LICHTERVELDE, L. DE, *Avant l'orage (1911–1914)* (Brussels, 1938).

LLOYD GEORGE, D., *War Memoirs* (6 vols., London. 1933–6).

LUDENDORFF, E., *Mein militärischer Werdegang* (Munich, 1933).

MESSIMY, A.-M., *Mes souvenirs* (Paris, 1937).

MOLTKE, H. VON, *Erinnerungen, Briefe, Dokumente, 1877–1916*, ed. E. von Moltke (Stuttgart, 1922).

Notes sur les établissements de MM. Schneider et Cie (Nevers, 1900).

PALÉOLOGUE, M., *La Russie des Tsars pendant la Grande Guerre* (Paris, 1921).

—— *Un grand tournant de la politique mondiale (1904–1906)* (Paris, 1934).

POINCARÉ, R. N. L., *Au service de la France. Neuf années de souvenirs* (10 vols., Paris, 1926–33).

SALANDRA, A., *La neutralità italiana (1914): Ricordi e pensieri* (Milan, 1928).

SAZONOV, S., *Fateful Years, 1909–1916* (London, 1928).

SEYMOUR, C. M. (ed.), *The Intimate Papers of Colonel House* (4 vols., London, 1926–8).

SUKHOMLINOV, V. A., *Erinnerungen* (Berlin, 1924).

TAUBE, M. DE, *La Politique russe d'avant-guerre et la fin de l'empire des tsars (1904–1917)* (Paris, 1928).

TIRPITZ, A. von, *Politische Dokumente: Der Aufbau der deutschen Weltmacht* (Stuttgart, 1924).

—— *Deutsche Ohnmachtpolitik im Weltkriege* (Hamburg, 1926).

—— *My Memoirs* (2 vols., London, n.d.).

WERMUTH, A., *Ein Beamtenleben: Erinnerungen* (Berlin, 1922).

WIDENMANN, W., *Marine-Attaché an der Kaiserlich-Deutschen Botschaft in London, 1907–1912* (Göttingen, 1952).

4. SECONDARY WORKS: BOOKS

ADAMS, R. J. Q., and POIRIER, P. P., *The Conscription Controversy in Great Britain, 1900–1918* (Basingstoke, 1987).

ALBERTINI, L., *The Origins of the War of 1914* (Eng. edn., 3 vols., London, 1952–7).

ALFF, W. (ed.), *Deutschlands Sonderung von Europa, 1862–1945* (Frankfurt am Main, 1984).

ALLAIN, J.-C., *Agadir, 1911: Une crise impérialiste en Europe pour la conquête du Maroc* (Paris, 1976).

ANDERSON, E. N., *The First Moroccan Crisis, 1904–1906* (Chicago, 1930).

ANDREW, C. M., *Théophile Delcassé and the Making of the Entente Cordiale: A Reappraisal of French Foreign Policy, 1898–1905* (London, 1968).

—— and NOAKES, J. (eds.), *Intelligence and International Relations, 1900–1945* (Exeter, 1987).

Les Armées françaises dans la Grande Guerre, i (Paris, 1936).

ART, R. J. and WALTZ, K. N. (eds.), *The Use of Force: International Politics and Foreign Policy* (Lanham, Md., 1983).

BARNETT, C., *Britain and her Army, 1509–1970: A Military, Political, and Social Survey* (Harmondsworth, 1979).

BARRACLOUGH, G., *From Agadir to Armageddon: Anatomy of a Crisis* (London, 1982).

BARSUKOV, E., *Russkaya artilleriya v mirovaya voiny*, i (Moscow, 1938).

BECKER, J.-J., *1914: Comment les Français sont entrés dans la Guerre* (Paris, 1977).

BEHNEN, M., *Rüstung-Bündnis-Sicherheit: Dreibund und informeller Imperialismus, 1900–1908* (Tübingen, 1985).

BERGHAHN, V. R., *Der Tirpitz-Plan: Genesis und Verfall einer innenpolitischen Krisenstrategie unter Wilhelm II* (Düsseldorf, 1971).

—— *Germany and the Approach of War in 1914* (London, 1973).

—— *Rüstung und Machtpolitik: Zur Anatomie des 'Kalten Krieges' vor 1914* (Düsseldorf, 1973).

—— *Militarism: The History of an International Debate, 1861–1979* (Cambridge, 1981).

BOND, B., *War and Society in Europe, 1870–1970* (London, 1984).

BOSWORTH, R. J. B., *Italy, the Least of the Great Powers: Italian Foreign Policy before the First World War* (Cambridge, 1979).

—— *Italy and the Approach of the First World War* (London, 1983).

BOVYKIN, V. I., *Iz istorii vozniknoveniya pervoi mirovoi voiny: Otnosheniya Rossii i Frantsii v 1912–1914 gg* (Moscow, 1961).

BRIDGE, F. R., *Great Britain and Austria-Hungary, 1906–1914: A Diplomatic History* (London, 1972).

—— *From Sadowa to Sarajevo: The Foreign Policy of Austria-Hungary, 1866–1914* (London, 1972).

—— *The Habsburg Monarchy among the Great Powers, 1815–1918* (Leamington Spa, 1990).

BUCHOLZ, A., *Moltke, Schlieffen, and Prussian War Planning* (New York, 1991).

BULL, H., *The Control of the Arms Race: Disarmament and Arms Control in the Missile Age* (London, 1961).

BURCHARDT, L., *Friedenswirtschaft und Kriegsvorsorge. Deutschlands Wirtschaftliche Rüstungsbestrebungen vor 1914* (Boppard, 1968).

BUZAN, B., *An Introduction to Strategic Studies: Military Technology and International Relations* (Basingstoke, 1987).

CALLWELL, C. E., *Field Marshal Sir Henry Wilson: His Life and Diaries* (2 vols., London, 1967).

CAYRE, Y., *Histoire de la manufacture d'armes de Tulle, de 1690 à 1970* (1970).

CHALLENER, R. D., *The French Theory of the Nation in Arms, 1866–1939* (New York, 1955).

CHICKERING, R., *Imperial Germany and a World without War: The Peace Movement and German Society, 1892–1914* (Princeton, 1975).

CHURCHILL, R. S., *Winston S. Churchill*, ii. *Young Statesman, 1901–1914* (London, 1967).

COOLING, B. F. (ed.), *War, Business, and World Military-Industrial Complexes* (Port Washington, NY, 1987).

CRAIG, G. A., *The Politics of the Prussian Army, 1640–1945* (London, 1964).

CRAMPTON, R. J., *The Hollow Détente: Anglo-German Relations in the Balkans, 1911–1914* (London, 1979).

DAVIS, C. D., *The United States and the First Hague Peace Conference* (Ithaca, NY, 1962).

—— *The United States and the Second Hague Peace Conference: American Diplomacy and International Organization, 1899–1914* (Durham, NC, 1975).

DEAK, I., *Beyond Nationalism: A Social and Political History of the Habsburg Officer Corps, 1848–1918* (New York, 1990).

DEDIJER, V., *The Road to Sarajevo* (New York, 1966).

DEMETER, K., *The German Officer Corps in Society and State, 1640–1945* (London, 1965).

DE VOS, L., *Het Effectief van de Belgische Krijgsmacht en de Militiewetgeving, 1830–1914* (Brussels, 1985).

DOISE, J., and VAÏSSE, M., *Diplomatie et outil militaire* (Paris, 1987).

D'OMBRAIN, N., *War Machinery and High Policy: Defence Administration in Peacetime Britain, 1902–1914* (Oxford, 1973).

DOPPLER, H., *75 Jahre Steyr-Werke* (Vienna, 1939).

DUKES, J. R., and REMAK, J. (eds.), *Another Germany: A Reconsideration of the Imperial Era* (Boulder, Colo., 1988).

DÜLFFER, J., *Regeln gegen den Krieg? Die Haager Friedenskonferenzen von 1899 und 1907 in der internationalen Politik* (Frankfurt, 1981).

EKSTEINS, M., *Rites of Spring: The Great War and the Birth of the Modern Age* (London, 1989).

ELEY, G., *Reshaping the Right: Radical Nationalism and Political Change after Bismarck* (New Haven, 1980).

ELLIS, J., *The Social History of the Machine Gun* (London, 1975).

Encyclopaedia Britannica (11th edn., 29 vols., London, 1910–11).

ENGELBRECHT, H. C., and HANIGHEN, F. C., *Merchants of Death: A Study of the International Armament Industry* (3rd impr., London, 1935).

EPKENHANS, M., *Die Wilhelminische Flottenrüstung, 1908–1914: Weltmachtstreben, industrieller Fortschritt, soziale Integration* (Munich, 1991).

EVANS, R. J. (ed.), *Society and Politics in Imperial Germany* (London, 1978).

EVANS, R. J. W., and POGGE VON STRANDMANN, H. (eds.), *The Coming of the First World War* (Oxford, 1988).

FARRAR, L. L., *The Short-War Illusion: German Policy, Strategy, and Domestic Affairs, August–December 1914* (Santa Barbara, Calif., 1973).

FEIS, H., *Europe—the World's Banker, 1870–1914* (repr., New York, 1964).

FISCHER, F., *Germany's Aims in the First World War* (Eng. edn., London, 1967).

—— *War of Illusions: German Policies from 1911 to 1914* (Eng. edn., London, 1975).

FLORA, P., *State, Economy, and Society in Western Europe: The Growth of Industrial Societies and Capitalist Economies*, ii (London, 1987).

FÖRSTER, S., *Der doppelte Militarismus: Die deutsche Heeresrüstung zwischen Status-Quo-Sicherung und Aggression, 1890–1913* (Stuttgart, 1985).

FRANTZ, G. (ed.), *Russlands Eintritt in den Weltkrieg: Der Ausbau der russischen Weltmacht und ihr Einsatz beim Kriegsausbruch* (Berlin, 1924).

FRENCH, D., *British Economic and Strategic Planning, 1905–1915* (London, 1982).

FRY, M. G., *Lloyd George and Foreign Policy*, i *The Education of a Statesman, 1890–1916* (Montreal, 1977).

FULLER, W. C., *Civil–Military Conflict in Imperial Russia, 1881–1914* (Princeton, 1985).

—— *Strategy and Power in Russia, 1600–1914* (New York, 1992).

50 Jahre Schiffbau, 1857–1907: Stabilmento Tecnico Triestino (Vienna, 1907).

GATRELL, P. W., *Government, Industry, and Rearmament in Russia, 1900–1914: The Last Argument of Tsarism* (Cambridge, 1994).

GEORGE, A. L. (ed.), *Avoiding War: Problems of Crisis Management* (Boulder, Colo., 1991).

Geschichte und Ergebnisse der Zentralen Amtlichen Statistik in Österreich 1829–1979: Beiträge zur Österreichischen Statistik, Heft 550 (Vienna, 1979).

GEYER, D., *Russian Imperialism: The Interaction of Domestic and Foreign Policy, 1860–1914* (Leamington Spa, 1987).

GEYER, M., *Deutsche Rüstungspolitik, 1866–1980* (Frankfurt am Main, 1984).

GILLIS, J. R. (ed.), *The Militarization of the Western World* (London, 1989).

GIRARDET, R., *La Société militaire dans la France contemporaine (1875–1939)* (Paris, 1953).

GIRAULT, R., *Emprunts russes et investissements français en Russie, 1887–1914* (Paris, 1973).

GLAISE-HORSTENAU, E., *Österreich-Ungarns Letzter Krieg, 1914–1918*, i (Vienna, 1930).

GODFREY, J. F., *Capitalism at War: Industrial Policy and Bureaucracy in France, 1914–1918* (Leamington Spa, 1987).

GOLLIN, A. M., *The Impact of Air Power on the British People and their Government, 1909–1914* (Basingstoke, 1989).

GOOCH, J., *The Plans of War: The General Staff and British Military Strategy, 1900–1916* (London, 1974).

—— *Armies in Europe* (London, 1980).

—— *Army, State, and Society in Italy, 1870–1915* (Basingstoke, 1989).

GÖRLITZ, W., *The German General Staff: Its History and Structure, 1657–1945* (Eng. edn., London, 1953).

—— *Regierte der Kaiser?* (Berlin, 1959).

—— *Der Kaiser . . . Aufzeichnungen des Chefs des Marinekabinetts Admiral Georg von Müller über die Ära Wilhelms II* (Göttingen, 1965).

GRANT, A., *Steel and Ships: The History of John Brown's* (London, 1956).

GREGORY, P. R., *Russian National Income, 1885–1913* (Cambridge, 1982).

GUILLEN, P., *L'Allemagne et le Maroc de 1870 à 1905* (Paris, 1967).

HALLGARTEN, G. W. F., *Das Wettrüsten: Seine Geschichte bis zur Gegenwart* (Frankfurt am Main, 1967).

HALPERN, P. G., *The Mediterranean Naval Situation, 1908–1914* (Cambridge, Mass., 1971).

HAMER, W. S., *The British Army: Civil–Military Relations, 1885–1905* (Oxford, 1970).

HANTSCH, H., *Leopold Graf Berchtold: Grandseigneur und Staatsmann* (2 vols., Graz, 1963).

HAYCOCK, R., and NEILSON, K. (eds.), *Men, Machines, and War* (Waterloo, Ontario, 1988).

HAYNE, M. B., *The French Foreign Office and the Origins of the First World War, 1898–1914* (Oxford, 1993).

HAZLEHURST, C., *Politicians at War, July 1914 to May 1915: A Prologue to the Triumph of Lloyd George* (London, 1971).

HELMREICH, E. C., *The Diplomacy of the Balkan Wars, 1912–1913* (repr. New York, 1969).

HERWIG, H. H., *The German Naval Officer Corps: A Social and Political History, 1890–1918* (Oxford, 1973).

HERZFELD, H., *Die deutsche Rüstungspolitik vor dem Weltkriege* (Bonn, 1923).

HINSLEY, F. H. (ed.), *British Foreign Policy under Sir Edward Grey* (Cambridge, 1977).

HÖBELT, L., 'Die Marine', in A. Wandruszka and P. Urbanitsch (eds.), *Die Habsburgermonarchie, 1848–1914*, v (Vienna, 1985).

HOBSBAWM, E. J., *The Age of Empire, 1875–1914* (London, 1987).

HOGG, I. V., *A History of Artillery* (London, 1974).

HOGG, O. F. G., *The Royal Arsenal: Its Background, Origin, and Subsequent History* (2 vols., London, 1963).

HOLSTI, O. R., *Crisis–Escalation–War* (London, 1972).

HOWARD, M. E., *The Franco-Prussian War: The German Invasion of France, 1870–1871* (London, 1961).

—— *The Continental Commitment: The Dilemma of British Defence Policy in the Era of Two World Wars* (Harmondsworth, 1974).

HUGHES, Q., *Military Architecture* (London, 1974).

HULL, I. V., *The Entourage of Kaiser Wilhelm II, 1888–1918* (Cambridge, 1982).

100 Jahre Eisenwerke Witkowitz, 1828–1928 (1928).

JOLL, J., *The Origins of the First World War* (London, 1984).

KANN, R. A., *Kaiser Franz Joseph und der Ausbruch des Weltkrieges* (Vienna, 1971).

KEEP, J. C. H., *Soldiers of the Tsar: Army and Society in Russia, 1462–1874* (Oxford, 1985).

KEHR, E., *Schlachtflottenbau und Parteipolitik, 1894–1901: Versuch eines Querschnitts durch die innenpolitischen, sozialen, und ideologischen Voraussetzungen des deutschen Imperialismus* (Berlin, 1930).

KEIGER, J. F. V., *France and the Origins of the First World War* (London, 1983).

KENNEDY, P. M., *The Rise of the Anglo-German Antagonism, 1860–1914* (London, 1980).

—— *Strategy and Diplomacy, 1870–1945* (London, 1984).

—— *The Rise and Fall of the Great Powers: Economic Change and Military Conflict from 1500 to 2000* (paperback edn., London, 1989).

—— (ed.), *The War Plans of the Great Powers, 1880–1914* (London, 1979).

KENT, M. (ed.), *The Great Powers and the End of the Ottoman Empire* (London, 1984).

KHROMOV, P. A., *Ekonomicheskoe razvitie Rossii v XIX i XX vekakh (1800–1917)* (Moscow, 1950).

KIRÁLY, B. K., and DJORDJEVIC, D. (eds.), *East Central European Society and the Balkan Wars* (New York, 1987).

KITCHEN, M., *The German Officer Corps, 1890–1914* (Oxford, 1968).

—— *A Military History of Germany: From the Eighteenth Century to the Present Day* (Bloomington, Ind., 1975).

KLEIN, F., and OTMAR VON ARETIN, K. (eds.), *Europa um 1900* (Berlin, 1989).

KOCH, H. W. (ed.), *The Origins of the First World War: Great Power Rivalry and German War Aims* (London, 1972).

KOSSMAN, E. H., *The Low Countries, 1780–1940* (Oxford, 1978).

KROBOTH, R., *Die Finanzpolitik des deutschen Reiches während der Reichkanzlerschaft Bethmann Hollwegs und die Geld- und Kapitalmarktverhältnisse (1909–1913/14)* (Frankfurt, 1986).

KRUMEICH, G., *Armaments and Politics in France on the Eve of the First World War: The Introduction of Three-Year Conscription, 1913–1914* (Leamington Spa, 1984).

LAMBI, I. N., *The Navy and German Power Politics, 1862–1914* (Boston, 1984).

LANGDON, J. W., *July 1914: The Long Debate* (Providence, RI, 1991).

LEBOW, R. N., *Between Peace and War: The Nature of International Crisis* (Baltimore, 1981).

LIEVEN, D. C. B., *Russia and the Origins of the First World War* (Basingstoke, 1983).

—— *Nicholas II: Emperor of All the Russias* (London, 1993).

LOWE, C. J., and MARZARI, F., *Italian Foreign Policy, 1870–1940* (London, 1975).

MACKAY, R. F., *Fisher of Kilverstone* (Oxford, 1973).

MCKEAN, R. B. (ed.), *New Perspectives on Modern Russian History* (Basingstoke, 1992).

MCKERCHER, B. J. C. (ed.), *Arms Limitation and Disarmament: Restraints on War, 1899–1939* (Westport, Conn., 1992).

MCNEILL, W. H., *The Pursuit of Power: Technology, Armed Force, and Society since A.D. 1000* (Oxford, 1983).

MALGERI, F., *La guerra libica (1911–1912)* (Rome, 1970).

MANCHESTER, W., *The Arms of Krupp, 1587–1968* (London, 1968).

MARDER, A. J., *From the Dreadnought to Scapa Flow: The Royal Navy in the Fisher Era, 1904–1914* (London, 1961).

—— *The Anatomy of British Sea Power: A History of British Naval Policy in the Pre-Dreadnought Era, 1880–1905* (repr., London, 1964).

MAY, E. R. (ed.), *Knowing one's Enemies: Intelligence before the Two World Wars* (Princeton, 1984).

MAYER, A. J., *The Persistence of the Old Regime: Europe to the Great War* (London, 1981).

MAZZETTI, M., *L'esercito italiano nella triplice alleanza: Aspetti della politica estera, 1870–1914* (Naples, 1974).

MEIER-WELCKE, H., and GROOTE, H. VON (eds.), *Handbuch der deutschen Militärgeschichte, 1648–1939*, v (Frankfurt, 1968).

MEISNER, H. O., *Der Kriegsminister, 1814–1914: Ein Beitrag zur militärischen Verfassungsgeschichte* (Berlin, 1940).

MENNE, B., *Krupp: Or the Lords of Essen* (London, 1937).

MICHEL, B., *Banques et banquiers en Autriche au début du 20e siècle* (Paris, 1976).

MICHON, G., *La Préparation à la guerre: La Loi de trois ans (1910–1914)* (Paris, 1935).

MITCHELL, B. R., *International Historical Statistics: Europe, 1750–1988* (Basingstoke, 1992).

—— and DEANE, P., *Abstract of British Historical Statistics* (Cambridge, 1962).

MONGER, G., *The End of Isolation: British Foreign Policy, 1900–1907* (London, 1963).

MORITZ, A., *Das Problem des Präventivkrieges in der deutschen Politik während der Ersten Marokkokrise* (Frankfurt, 1974).

MORRIS, A. J. A., *Radicalism against War, 1906–1914: The Advocacy of Peace and Retrenchment* (Totowa, NJ, 1972).

—— *The Scaremongers: The Advocacy of War and Rearmament, 1896–1914* (London, 1984).

MOSES, J. A., *The Politics of Illusion: The Fischer Controversy in German Historiography* (London, 1975).

MURRAY, B. K., *The People's Budget, 1909/10: Lloyd George and Liberal Politics* (Oxford, 1980).

90 Jahre Rheinmetall, 1889–1979 (Düsseldorf, 1979).

NOEL-BAKER, P., *The Private Manufacture of Armaments* (2 vols., London, 1936).

OFFER, A., *The First World War: An Agrarian Interpretation* (Oxford, 1989).

ONCKEN, E., *Panthersprung nach Agadir: Die deutsche Politik während der zweiten Marokkokrise 1911* (Düsseldorf, 1981).

PANTENIUS, H. J., *Der Angriffsgedanke gegen Italien bei Conrad von Hötzendorf* (2 vols., Vienna, 1984).

PARKER, R., *Tormented Warrior: Ludendorff and the Supreme Command* (London, 1978).

PERPILLOU, M. A., *L'Industrie des constructions navales* (Paris, n.d.).

PICK, D., *War Machine: The Rationalisation of Slaughter in the Modern Age* (New Haven, 1993).

POIDEVIN, R., *Les Relations économiques et financières entre la France et l'Allemagne de 1898 à 1914* (Paris, 1969).

POLLARD, S., and ROBERTSON, P., *The British Shipbuilding Industry, 1870–1914* (Cambridge, Mass., 1979).

PORCH, D., *The March to the Marne: The French Army, 1871–1914* (Cambridge, 1981).

PRATT, E. A., *The Rise of Rail Power in War and Conquest, 1833–1914* (London, 1915).

RAHNE, H., *Mobilmachung: Militärische Mobilmachungsplanung und -technik in Preussen und im deutschen Reich von Mitte des 19. Jahrhunderts bis zum Zweiten Weltkrieg* (East Berlin, 1983).

RALSTON, D. B., *The Army of the Republic: The Place of the Army in the Political Evolution of France, 1871–1914* (Cambridge, Mass., 1967).

RAULFF, H., *Zwischen Machtpolitik und Imperialismus: Die deutsche Frankreichpolitik, 1904/06* (Düsseldorf, 1976).

READER, W. J., *Imperial Chemical Industries: A History*, i (London, 1970).

REICHSARCHIV, *Der Weltkrieg, 1914–1918. Kriegsrüstung und Kriegswirtschaft* (2 vols., Berlin, 1930).

RICHARDSON, L. F., *Arms and Insecurity: A Mathematical Study of the Causes and Origins of War* (London, 1960).

RITTER, G. A., *The Schlieffen Plan: Critique of a Myth* (London, 1958).

—— *The Sword and the Scepter: The Problem of Militarism in Germany* (Eng. tr., vol. ii, Coral Gables, Fla., 1970).

ROCHAT, G., and MASSOBRIO, G., *Breve storia dell'esercito italiano dal 1861 al 1943* (Turin, 1978).

ROGGER, H., *Russia in the Age of Modernization and Revolution, 1881–1917* (London, 1983).

RÖHL, J. C. G. (ed.), *Der Ort Kaiser Wilhelms II in der deutschen Geschichte* (Munich, 1991).

ROPPONEN, R., *Die Kraft Russlands: Wie Beurteilte die politische und die militärische Führung der Europäischen Grossmächte in der Zeit von 1905 bis 1914 die Kraft Russlands?* (Helsinki, 1968).

ROTHENBERG, G. E., *The Army of Francis Joseph* (West Lafayette, 1976).

ROY, J.-A., *Histoire de la famille Schneider et du Creusot* (Paris, 1962).

RUEDORFFER, J. J. [RIEZLER, K.], *Grundzüge der Weltpolitik in der Gegenwart* (Stuttgart, 1916).

SCHELLING, T. C., *Arms and Influence* (New Haven, 1966).

SCHMITT, B. E., *The Annexation of Bosnia, 1908–1909* (Cambridge, 1937).

SCHOTTELIUS, H., and DEIST, W. (eds.), *Marine und Marinepolitik im Kaiserlichen Deutschland, 1871–1914* (Düsseldorf, 1972).

SCHULTE, B. F., *Die deutsche Armee, 1900–1914: Zwischen Beharren und Verändern* (Düsseldorf, 1977).

—— *Europäische Krise und Erster Weltkrieg: Beiträge zur Militärpolitik des Kaiserreichs, 1871–1914* (Frankfurt am Main, 1983).

SCOTT, J. D., *Vickers: A History* (London, 1962).

SERMAN, W., *Les Officiers français dans la nation (1848–1914)* (Paris, 1982).

SHATSILLO, K. F., *Russkii imperializm i razvitie flota nakanune pervoi mirovoi voiny (1906–1914 gg)* (Moscow, 1968).

—— *Rossia pered pervoi mirovoi voiny (vooruzhennye sily tsarizma v 1905–1914 gg)* (Moscow, 1974).

SIDOROV, A. L., *Finansovoe polozhenie Rossii v gody pervoi mirovoi voiny (1914–1917)* (Moscow, 1960).

SNYDER, J., *The Ideology of the Offensive: Military Decision Making and the Disasters of 1914* (Ithaca, NY, 1984).

SPIERS, E. M., *Haldane: An Army Reformer* (Edinburgh, 1980).

—— *The Army and Society, 1815–1914* (London, 1980).

STATO MAGGIORE DELL'ESERCITO (Ufficio Storico), *L'esercito italiano dall'Unità alla Grande Guerra (1861–1918)* (Rome, 1980).

STEGMAN, B., WENDT, B.-J., and WITT, P.-C. (eds.), *Industrielle Gesellschaft und Politisches System: Beiträge zur politischen Sozialgeschichte: Festschrift für Fritz Fischer* (Bonn, 1978).

STEINBERG, J., *Yesterday's Deterrent: Tirpitz and the Birth of the German Battle Fleet* (New York, 1965).

STEINER, Z. S., *Britain and the Origins of the First World War* (London, 1977).

STONE, N., *The Eastern Front, 1914–1917* (London, 1975).

—— *Europe Transformed, 1878–1919* (London, 1983).

STRACHAN, H. F. A., *European Armies and the Conduct of War* (London, 1983).

STÜRMER, M. (ed.), *Das Kaiserliche Deutschland: Politik und Gesellschaft, 1870–1918* (Düsseldorf, 1970).

SUGAR, P. F., *The Industrialization of Bosnia-Hercegovina, 1878–1918* (Seattle, 1963).

SUMIDA, J. T., *In Defence of Naval Supremacy: Finance, Technology, and British Naval Policy, 1889–1914* (Boston, 1989).

TATE, M., *The Disarmament Illusion: The Movement for a Limitation of Armaments to 1907* (New York, 1942).

TAYLOR, A. J. P., *The Struggle for Mastery in Europe, 1848–1918* (Oxford, 1954).

—— *War by Timetable: How the First World War Began* (London, 1969).

—— (ed.), *Lloyd George: Twelve Essays* London, 1971).

TERLINDEN, C., *et al.*, *Histoire militaire des belges* (Liège, 1931).

THADEN, E. C., *Russia and the Balkan Alliance of 1912* (Philadelphia, 1965).

THEE, M. (ed.), *Arms and Disarmament: SIPRI Findings* (Oxford, 1986).

TRACHTENBERG, M., *History and Strategy* (Princeton, 1991).

TRAVERS, T., *The Killing Ground: The British Army, the Western Front, and the Emergence of Modern Warfare, 1900–1918* (London, 1987).

TREBILCOCK, R. C., *The Vickers Brothers: Armaments and Enterprise, 1854–1914* (London, 1977).

TURNER, L. C. F., *Origins of the First World War* (London, 1970).

VAGTS, A., *A History of Militarism: Romance and Realities of a Profession* (New York, 1937).

—— *Defense and Diplomacy: The Soldier and the Conduct of Foreign Relations* (New York, 1956).

VERMES, G., *István Tisza: The Liberal Vision and Conservative Statecraft of a Magyar Nationalist* (New York, 1985).

VUCINICH, W. S., *Serbia between East and West: The Events of 1903–1908* (Stanford, Calif., 1954).

WAGNER, W., 'Die K. und K. Armee', in A. Wandruszka and P. Urbanitsch (eds.), *Die Habsburgermonarchie, 1848–1914*, v (Vienna, 1987).

WANDRUSZKA, A., and URBANITSCH, P. (eds.), *Die Habsburgermonarchie, 1848–1914*, i (Vienna, 1973), v (Vienna, 1987).

WARD, D. M., *The Other Battle* (York, 1946).

WARREN, K., *Armstrongs of Elswick: Growth in Engineering and Armaments to the Merger with Vickers* (Basingstoke, 1989).

WEBER, E., *The Nationalist Revival in France, 1905–1914* (Berkeley, 1959).

WEBSTER, R. A., *Industrial Imperialism in Italy, 1908–1915* (Berkeley, 1975).

Eine Werksgeschichte: Fünfzig Jahre Mauser, 1896–1946 (Cologne, 1946).

WESTWOOD, J. N., *Railways at War* (London, 1980).

WHITTAM, J., *The Politics of the Italian Army* (London, 1977).

WILDMAN, A. K., *The End of the Russian Imperial Army: The Old Army and the Soldiers' Revolt* (Princeton, 1980).

WILLEQUET, J., *Albert Ier: Roi des belges: Un portrait politique et humain* (Brussels, 1979).

WILLIAMS, P., *Crisis Management: Confrontation and Diplomacy in the Nuclear Age* (London, 1972).

WILLIAMS, R., *Defending the Empire: The Conservative Party and British Defence Policy, 1899–1915* (New Haven, 1991).

WILLIAMSON, S. R., *The Politics of Grand Strategy: Britain and France Prepare for War, 1904–1914* (Cambridge, Mass., 1969).

—— *Austria-Hungary and the Origins of the First World War* (Basingstoke, 1991).

—— and PASTOR, P. (eds.), *Essays on World War I: Origins and Prisoners of War* (New York, 1983).

WILSON, A. W., *The Story of the Gun* (Woolwich, 1985 edn.).

WILSON, K. M., *The Policy of the Entente: Essays on the Determinants of British Foreign Policy, 1904–1914* (Cambridge, 1985).

WINZEN, P., *Bülows Weltmachtkonzept: Untersuchungen zur Frühphase seiner Aussenpolitik, 1897–1901* (Boppard, 1977).

WITT, P.-C., *Die Finanzpolitik des deutschen Reiches von 1903 bis 1913* (Lübeck, 1970).

YOUNG, R. J., *Power and Pleasure: Louis Barthou and the Third French Republic* (Montreal, 1991).

ZAIONCHOVSKY, A. M., *Podgotovka Rossii k imperialisticheskoi voine (Plany voiny)* (Moscow, 1926).

ZECHLIN, E., *Krieg und Kriegsrisiko: Zur Deutschen Politik im Ersten Weltkrieg* (Düsseldorf, 1979).

5. SECONDARY WORKS: ARTICLES

ADAMOV, E., 'K voprosi o podgotovke mirovoi voiny (iz dokumentov russkoi voenno-politicheskoi razvedki 1913–1914 gg)', *Krasnyi Arkhiv*, 64 (1934), 85–129.

AMES, E., and ROSENBERG, N., 'The Enfield Arsenal in Theory and Practice', *Economic Journal*, 78 (1968).

ANDIC, S. and VEVERKA, J., 'The Growth of Government Expenditure in Germany since the Unification', *Finanz Archiv*, 23/2 (1963–4), 169–278.

ANDREW, C. M., and KANYA-FORSTNER, A. S., 'The French "Colonial Party": Its Composition, Aims, and Influence, 1885–1914', *Historical Journal*, 14 (1971), 99–128.

ASHWORTH, W., 'Economic Aspects of Late Victorian Naval Administration', *Economic History Review*, NS 22 (1969), 491–505.

BERGHAHN, V. R., and DEIST, W. (eds.), 'Kaiserliche Marine und Kriegsausbruch, 1914: Neue Dokumente zur Juli-Krise', *Militärgeschichtliche Mitteilungen* (1970), 37–58.

BESKROVNY, L. S., 'Proizvodstvo vooruzheniia i boepripasov dlia armii v Rossii v period imperializma (1898–1917 gg)', *Istorichiskie Zapiski*, 99 (1977), 88–139.

BESTUZHEV, I. V., 'Russian Foreign Policy, February–June 1914', *Journal of Contemporary History*, 1/3 (1966), 91–112.

BRIDGE, F. R., 'Izvolsky, Aehrenthal, and the End of the Austro-Russian Entente, 1906–1908', *Mitteilungen des Österreichischen Staatsarchivs*, 29 (1976), 315–62.

BUSHNELL, J., 'Peasants in Uniform: The Tsarist Army as a Peasant Society', *Journal of Social History*, 13 (1980), 565–76.

—— 'The Tsarist Officer Corps, 1881–1914: Customs, Duties, Inefficiency', *American Historical Review*, 86 (1981), 753–80.

CHICKERING, R., 'Der "Deutsche Wehrverein" und die Reform der deutschen Armee, 1912–1914', *Militärgeschichtliche Mitteilungen*, 25 (1979), 7–34.

—— 'Patriotic Societies and German Foreign Policy, 1890–1914', *International History Review*, 4 (1979), 470–89.

COETZEE, M. S., 'The Mobilization of the Right? The *Deutscher Wehrverein* and Political Activism in Württemberg, 1912–14', *European History Quarterly*, 15 (1985), 431–52.

COOGAN, J. W., and P. F., 'The British Cabinet and the Anglo-French Staff Talks, 1905–1914: Who Knew What and When did he Know it?', *Journal of British Studies*, 24 (1985), 110–31.

CROUZET, F., 'Recherches sur la production d'armements en France (1815–1913)', *Revue historique*, 509 (1974), 45–84.

—— 'Remarques sur l'industrie des armements en France (du milieu du XIXe siècle à 1914)', *Revue historique*, 251 (1974), 409–27.

DOBROROLSKY, S., 'La Mobilisation de l'armée russe en 1914', *Revue d'histoire de la Guerre mondiale*, 1 (1923), 64–9.

EDWARDS, E. W., 'The Franco-German Agreement on Morocco, 1909', *English Historical Review*, 78 (1963), 483–513.

ELEY, G., 'Reshaping the German Right: Radical Nationalism and the German Navy League, 1898–1908', *Historical Journal*, 21 (1978), 327–54.

EPKENHANS, M., 'Grossindustrie und Schlachtflottenbau, 1897–1914', *Militärgeschichtliche Mitteilungen*, 43/1 (1988), 65–140.

FAIRBANKS, C. H., 'The Origins of the Dreadnought Revolution: A Historiographical Essay', *International History Review*, 13 (1991), 246–72.

FARRAR, M. M., 'Politics versus Patriotism: Alexandre Millerand as French Minister of War', *French Historical Studies*, 11 (1980), 577–609.

FERGUSON, N., 'Germany and the Origins of the First World War: New Perspectives', *Historical Journal*, 35 (1992), 725–52.

—— 'Public Finance and National Security: The Domestic Origins of the First World War Revisited', *Past and Present*, 142 (1994), 141–68.

FONTVIELLE, L., 'Evolution et croissance de l'État français de 1815 à 1969', *Economies et sociétés*, 13 (1976), 1657–2144.

GATRELL, P. W., 'Industrial Expansion in Tsarist Russia, 1908–1914', *Economic History Review*, NS 35 (1982), 99–110.

—— 'After Tsushima: Economic and Administrative Aspects of Russian Naval Rearmament, 1905–1913', *Economic History Review*, NS 43 (1990), 255–70.

GEORGE, A. L., 'Crisis Management: The Interaction of Political and Military Considerations', *Survival*, 26 (1984), 223–34.

GILBERT, B. B., 'Pacifist to Interventionist: David Lloyd George in 1911 and 1914. Was Belgium an Issue?', *Historical Journal*, 28 (1985), 866–79.

GIRAULT, R., 'Finances internationales et relations internationales (à propos des usines Poutiloff)', *Revue d'histoire moderne et contemporaine*, 13 (1966), 217–36.

—— 'Les Balkans dans les relations franco-russes en 1912', *Revue historique*, 513 (1975), 155–84.

GOLDSTEIN, E. R., 'Vickers Limited and the Tsarist Regime', *Slavonic and East European Review*, 58 (1980), 561–71.

GRANIER, G., 'Deutsche Rüstungspolitik vor dem Ersten Weltkrieg: General Franz Wandels Tagebuchaufzeichnungen aus dem preussischen Kriegsministerium', *Militärgeschichtliche Mitteilungen*, 38 (1985), 123–62.

GRAY, C. S., 'The Arms Race Phenomenon', *World Politics*, 24 (1971), 39–79.

GROH, D., 'The "Unpatriotic Socialists" and the State', *Journal of Contemporary History*, 1/4 (1966), 151–77.

—— ' "Je eher, desto besser!" Innenpolitische Faktoren für die Präventivkriegsbereitschaft des deutschen Reiches, 1913/14', *Politische Vierteljahresschrift*, 13 (1972), 501–21.

HEAD, J. A., 'Public Opinion and Middle Eastern Railway Negotiations: The Russo-German Negotiations of 1910–1911', *International History Review*, 6 (1984), 28–47.

HELMREICH, E. C., 'An Unpublished Report on Austro-German Military Conversations of November 1912', *Journal of Modern History*, 5 (1933), 197–207.

HERRMAN, D. G., 'The Paralysis of Italian Strategy in the Italian–Turkish War, 1911–1912', *English Historical Review*, 104 (1989), 332–56.

HERWIG, H. H., 'The German Reaction to the Dreadnought Revolution', *International History Review*, 13 (1991), 272–83.

HITCHINS, K., 'The Nationality Problem in Hungary: István Tisza and the Rumanian National Party, 1910–1914', *Journal of Modern History*, 53 (1981), 619–51.

HOAG, M. W., 'On Stability in Deterrent Races', *World Politics*, 13 (1961), 505–27.

HOBSON, J. M., 'The Military-Extraction Gap and the Wary Titan: The Fiscal Sociology of British Defence Policy, 1870–1913', *Journal of European Economic History*, 22 (1993), 461–506.

HOWARD, M., 'Men against Fire: Expectations of War in 1914', *International Security*, 9 (1984), 41–57.

HUBATSCH, W., 'Der Kulminationspunkt der Deutschen Marinepolitik im Jahre 1912', *Historische Zeitschrift*, 176 (1953), 291–322.

JARAUSCH, K. H., 'The Illusion of Limited War: Chancellor Bethmann Hollweg's Calculated Risk in July 1914', *Central European History*, 2 (1969), 48–76.

JAUFFRET, J.-C., 'La Défense des frontières françaises et l'organisation des forces de couverture (1874–1895)', *Revue historique*, 279 (1988), 359–79.

JELAVICH, B., 'Romania in the First World War: The Pre-War Crisis, 1912–1914', *International History Review*, 14 (1992), 441–51.

JERVIS, R., 'Co-operation under the Security Dilemma', *World Politics*, 30 (1978), 167–214.

JONES, G. G., and TREBILCOCK, R. C. B., 'Russian Industry and British Business, 1910–1930: Oil and Armaments', *Journal of European Economic History*, 11 (1982), 61–103.

KENEZ, P., 'A Profile of the Prerevolutionary Officer Corps', *California Slavic Studies*, 7 (1973), 121–58.

KENNEDY, P. M., 'The First World War and the International Power System', *International Security*, 9 (1984), 7–40.

KERNER, R. J., 'The Mission of Liman von Sanders', *Slavonic Review*, 6 (1927), 12–27, 344–63, 543–60; 7 (1928), 90–112.

KISZLING, R., 'Russlands Kriegsvorbereitungen im Herbst 1912 und ihre Rückwirkungen auf Österreich-Ungarn', *Berliner Monatshefte*, 13 (1935), 181–92.

—— 'Die Österreichisch-Ungarische Armee in den letzten Decennien vor 1914', *Österreichische militärische Zeitschrift*, 2 (1964), 29–34.

LACHMANN, M., 'Probleme der Bewaffnung des Kaiserlichen Deutschen Heeres', *Zeitschrift für Militärgeschichte*, 6 (1967), 23–37.

LANGHORNE, R. T. B., 'The Naval Question in Anglo-German Relations, 1912–1914', *Historical Journal*, 14 (1971), 359–70.

LAUTENSCHLÄGER, K., 'Technology and the Evolution of Naval Warfare', *International Security*, 8 (1983), 3–51.

LESLIE, J., 'The Antecedents of Austria-Hungary's War Aims: Policies and Policy-Makers in Vienna and Budapest before and during 1914', *Wiener Beiträge zur Geschichte der Neuzeit*, 20 (1993), 307–94.

LEVY, J. S., 'Preferences, Constraints, and Choices in July 1914', *International Security*, 15 (1990/1), 151–86.

—— CHRISTENSEN, T. J., and TRACHTENBERG, M., 'Mobilization and Inadvertence in the July Crisis', *International Security*, 16 (1991), 189–203.

MACKINTOSH, J. P., 'The Role of the Committee of Imperial Defence before 1914', *English Historical Review*, 77 (1962), 490–503.

MARDER, A. J., 'The English Armament Industry and Navalism in the Nineties', *Pacific Historical Review*, 3 (1938), 241–53.

MAURER, J. H., 'Churchill's Naval Holiday: Arms Control and the Anglo-German Naval Race, 1912–1914', *Journal of Strategic Studies*, 15 (1992), 102–27.

MAYZEL, M., 'The Formation of the Russian General Staff, 1880–1917: A Social Study', *Cahiers du monde russe et soviétique*, 16 (1975), 297–321.

MITCHELL, A., ' "A Situation of Inferiority": French Military Reorganization after the Defeat of 1870', *American Historical Review*, 86 (1981), 49–62.

—— 'The Freycinet Reforms and the French Army, 1888–1893', *Journal of Strategic Studies*, 4 (1981), 19–28.

MORRIS, A. J. A., 'The English Radicals' Campaign for Disarmament and the Hague Conference of 1907', *Journal of Modern History*, 43 (1971), 367–93.

MORTIMER, J. S., 'Commercial Interests and German Diplomacy in the Agadir Crisis', *Historical Journal*, 10 (1967), 440–56.

MURRAY, B. K., 'Lloyd George, the Navy Estimates, and the Inclusion of Rating Relief in the 1914 Budget', *Welsh Historical Review*, 15 (1990), 58–78.

NEILSON, K., 'Watching the "Steamroller": British Observers and the Russian Army before 1914', *Journal of Strategic Studies*, 8 (1975), 199–217.

PALUMBO, M., 'German–Italian Military Relations on the Eve of World War I', *Central European History*, 12 (1979), 343–71.

PEDRONCINI, G., 'Stratégie et relations internationales: La Séance du 9 janvier 1912 du Conseil supérieur de la défense nationale', *Revue d'histoire diplomatique*, 91 (1977), 143–58.

PINTNER, W. M., 'The Burden of Defence in Imperial Russia, 1725–1914', *Russian Review*, 43 (1984), 231–59.

POIDEVIN, R, 'Les Intérêts financiers français et allemands en Serbie de 1895 à 1914', *Revue historique*, 182 (1964), 49–66.

—— 'Fabricants d'armes et relations internationales au début du XXe siècle', *Relations internationales*, 1 (1974), 39–56.

POLLARD, S., '*Laissez-faire* and Shipbuilding', *Economic History Review*, NS 5 (1952), 98–115.

PRETE, R. A., 'The Preparation of the French Army Prior to World War I: An Historiographical Reappraisal', *Canadian Journal of History*, 26 (1991), 241–66.

ROCHAT, G., 'L'esercito italiano nell'estate 1914', *Nuova rivista storica*, 45 (1961), 295–348.

ROGGER, H., 'Russia in 1914', *Journal of Contemporary History*, 1/4 (1966), 95–119.

RÖHL, J. C. G., 'Admiral von Müller and the Approach of War, 1911–1914', *Historical Journal*, 12 (1969), 651–73.

—— (ed.), 'An der Schwelle zum Weltkrieg: Eine Dokumentation über den "Kriegsrat" vom 8. Dezember 1912', *Militärgeschichtliche Mitteilungen* (1977), 77–134.

SCHELLING, T. C., 'War Without Pain, and Other Models', *World Politics*, 15 (1963), 465–87.

SCHULTE, B. F., 'Neue Dokumente zum Kriegsausbruch und Kriegsverlauf, 1914', *Militärgeschichtliche Mitteilungen*, 25 (1979), 123–85.

—— 'Zu der Krisenkonferenz vom 8. Dezember 1912 in Berlin', *Historisches Jahrbuch*, 102 (1982), 183–97.

SEGRETO, L., 'More Trouble than Profit: Vickers' Investment in Italy, 1906–39', *Business History*, 27 (1985), 316–37.

SHATSILLO, K. F., 'Inostrannyi kapital i voenno-morskie programmy Rossii nakanune pervoi mirovoi voiny', *Istorichiskie Zapiski*, 69 (1961), 73–100.

—— 'O disproportsii v razvitii vooruzhennykh sil Rossii nakanune pervoi mirovoi voiny, 1906–1914', *Istorichiskie Zapiski*, 83 (1969), 123–36.

SIDOROV, A. L., 'Iz istorii podgotovki tsarizma k pervoi mirovoi voine', *Istorichiskii Arkhiv* (1962), 2, 120–55.

SKED, A., 'A Patriot for Whom? Colonel Redl and a Question of Identity', *History Today*, 36 (July 1986), 9–14.

SKODA, K., 'Emil Ritter von Skoda', *Neue Österreichische Biographie*, iv (Vienna, 1927), 165.

SNYDER, J., 'Civil–Military Relations and the Cult of the Offensive, 1914 and 1984', *International Security*, 9 (1984), 108–46.

SOKOL, A. E., 'Der Flottenbau der k.u.k. Kriegsmarine, 1895 bis 1914', *Marine-Gestern, Heute*, 8 (1981), 8–13.

SPRING, D. W., 'Russia and the Franco-Russian Alliance, 1905–1914: Dependence or Interdependence?', *Slavonic and East European Review*, 66 (1988), 565–92.

STEINBERG, J., 'The Copenhagen Complex', *Journal of Contemporary History*, 1/3 (1966), 23–46.

—— 'Germany and the Russo-Japanese War', *American Historical Review*, 75 (1970), 1965–86.

—— 'The *Novelle* of 1908: Necessities and Choices in the Anglo-German Naval Arms Race', *Transactions of the Royal Historical Society*, 21 (1971), 25–43.

STENGERS, J., 'Guillaume II et le Roi Albert à Potsdam en novembre 1913', *Académie royale de la Belgique. Bulletin de la classe des lettres et des sciences morales et politiques*, 6th ser. 4 (1993), 227–53.

STONE, N., 'Army and Society in the Habsburg Monarchy, 1900–1914', *Past and Present*, 33 (1966), 95–111.

—— 'Moltke–Conrad: Relations between the Austro-Hungarian and German General Staffs, 1909–1914', *Historical Journal*, 9 (1966), 201–28.

—— 'Constitutional Crisis in Hungary, 1903–1906', *Slavonic and East European Review*, 45 (1967), 163–82.

—— 'Die Mobilmachung der Österreichisch-Ungarischen Armee 1914', *Militärgeschichtliche Mitteilungen*, 16/2 (1974), 67–95.

STRACHAN, H. F. A., 'Germany in the First World War: The Problem of Strategy', *German History*, 12 (1994), 237–49.

SUMLER, D. E., 'Domestic Influences on the Nationalist Revival in France, 1909–1914', *French Historical Studies*, 6 (1970), 517–37.

TRAVERS, T., 'The Hidden Army: Structural Problems in the British Officer Corps, 1900–1918', *Journal of Contemporary History*, 17 (1992), 523–44.

TREBILCOCK, R. C. B., 'A "Special Relationship": Government, Rearmament, and the Cordite Firms', *Economic History Review*, NS 19 (1966), 364–79.

—— 'Legends of the British Armaments Industry, 1890–1914: A Revision', *Journal of Contemporary History*, 5/4 (1970), 3–19.

—— 'British Armaments and European Industrialization, 1890–1914', *Economic History Review*, NS 26 (1973), 254–72.

TRUMPENER, U., 'War Premeditated? German Intelligence Operations in July 1914', *Central European History*, 9 (1976), 58–85.

—— 'Junkers and Others: The Rise of Commoners in the Prussian Army, 1871–1914', *Canadian Journal of History*, 14 (1979), 29–47.

TURNER, L. C. F., 'The Role of the General Staffs in July 1914', *Australian Journal of Politics and History*, 11 (1965), 305–23.

VAN EVERA, S., 'The Cult of the Offensive and the Origins of the First World War', *International Security*, 9 (1984), 58–107.

VEGO, M., 'Zur Beginn des Rüstungswettlaufes zur See zwischen Ö-U und Italien, 1904–05', *Marine-Gestern, Heute*, 9 (1982), 54–9.

WATSON, D. R., 'The Making of French Foreign Policy during the First Clemenceau Ministry, 1906–1909', *English Historical Review*, 86 (1971), 774–82.

WEINROTH, H., 'Left-Wing Opposition to Naval Armaments in Britain before 1914', *Journal of Contemporary History*, 6 (1971), 93–120.

WILLIAMSON, S. R., 'Influence, Power, and the Policy Process: The Case of Franz Ferdinand, 1906–1914', *Historical Journal*, 17 (1974), 417–34.

WILSON, K. M., 'The Agadir Crisis, the Mansion House Speech, and the Double-Edgedness of Agreements', *Historical Journal*, 15 (1972), 513–32.

WOHLFORTH, W. C., 'The Perception of Power: Russia in the Pre-1914 Balance', *World Politics*, 39 (1987), 353–81.

YOUNG, H. F., 'The Misunderstanding of August 1, 1914', *Journal of Modern History*, 48 (1976), 644–65.

6. THESES AND OTHER UNPUBLISHED WRITINGS

BEAUD, C., 'Les Schneider "marchands de canons"', European University Institute Colloquium Paper 304/91 Col. 16 (Florence, 1991).

BOBROFF, R., 'Diplomacy Enhanced: British Diplomacy and Military Measures after the Dogger Bank Incident, October–November 1904', M.Sc. thesis (LSE, 1994).

DEUTSCHMAN, W., 'Die militärischen Massnahmen in Österreich-Ungarn während der Balkankriege, 1912/13', Ph.D. thesis (Vienna, 1965).

EPKENHANS, M., 'The German Armament Industry and Economic Development, 1870–1914', European University Institute Colloquium Paper 303/91 Col. 15 (Florence, 1991).

HETZER, W., 'Franz von Schönaich: Reichskriegsminister von 1906–1911', Ph.D. thesis (Vienna, 1968).

KÁS, F., 'Versuch einer Zusammenfassten Darstellung der Tätigkeit der Österreichisch-Ungarischen Generalstabes in der Zeit von 1906 bis 1914: Unter Besonderer Berücksichtigung der Aufmarschplänen und Mobilmachungen', Ph.D. thesis (Vienna, 1962).

KESSLITZ, R., 'Die Lasten der Militärischen Rüstungen Österreich-Ungarns im neuesten Zeit (1868–1912)', KAW MS Allg. Nr. 54 II 45. 163.

MANN, J., 'FML Blasius Schemua: Chef des Generalstabes am Vorabend des Weltkrieges, 1911–1912', Ph.D. thesis (Vienna, 1978).

PRUCHA, V., 'Development of the Skoda Works and its Role in Czechoslovak Industry up to the Year 1938', European University Institute Colloquium Paper 309/91 Col. 21 (Florence, 1991).

SEGRETO, L., 'Armament Industry and Italian Economic Development (1880s–1939)', European University Institute Colloquium Paper 306/91 Col. 18 (Florence, 1991).

SIDOROWICZ, A. T., 'The Liberal Government and the Second Hague Peace Conference', 'Social Reform, Free Trade, and the Quest for Peace, 1907–1914', unpubl. TSS, LSE, 1991.

ULLREICH, J., 'Moritz von Auffenberg-Komarów: Leben und Wirken, 1911–1918', Ph.D. thesis (Vienna, 1961).

Index

Notes: 1. Sub-entries are generally in chronological order; 2. When there are several page references for an entry, the most important pages are in bold figures e.g. Russia, development of armaments 15, 19, 28, **34-7**, 38; 3. Throughout the index *Germany* as a qualifier usually includes *Prussia*